Oracle Database Programming with Java

Databases have become an integral part of modern life. Today's society is an information-driven society, and database technology has a direct impact on all aspects of daily life. Decisions are routinely made by organizations based on the information collected and stored in databases. Database management systems such as Oracle are crucial to apply data in industrial or commercial systems. Equally crucial is a graphical user interface (GUI) to enable users to access and manipulate data in databases. The Apache NetBeans IDE with Java is an ideal candidate for developing a GUI with programming functionality.

Oracle Database Programming with Java: Ideas, Designs, and Implementations is written for college students and software programmers who want to develop practical and commercial database programming with Java and relational databases such as Oracle Database XE 18c. This book details practical considerations and applications of database programming with Java and is filled with authentic examples as well as detailed explanations. Advanced topics in Java Web like Java Web Applications and Java Web Services are covered in real project examples to show how to handle the database programming issues in the Apache NetBeans IDE environment.

This book features:

- A real sample database, **CSE _ DEPT**, which is built with Oracle SQL Developer, provided and used throughout the book
- Step by step, detailed illustrations and descriptions of how to design and build a practical relational database
- Fundamental and advanced Java database programming techniques practical to both beginning students and experienced programmers
- Updated Java desktop and Web database programming techniques, such as Java Enterprise Edition 7, JavaServer Pages, JavaServer Faces, Enterprise Java Beans, Web applications and Web services, including GlassFish and Tomcat Web servers
- More than 30 real database programming projects with detailed illustrations
- Actual JDBC APIs and JDBC drivers, along with code explanations
- Homework and selected solutions for each chapter to strengthen and improve students' learning and understanding of the topics they have studied

Oracle Database Programming with Java

Ideas, Designs, and Implementations

Ying Bai
Department of Computer Science and Engineering
Johnson C. Smith University
Charlotte, North Carolina

CRC Press
Taylor & Francis Group
Boca Raton London

CRC Press is an imprint of the
Taylor & Francis Group, an informa business
AN AUERBACH BOOK

First edition published 2023
by CRC Press
6000 Broken Sound Parkway NW, Suite 300, Boca Raton, FL 33487–2742

and by CRC Press
4 Park Square, Milton Park, Abingdon, Oxon, OX14 4RN

CRC Press is an imprint of Taylor & Francis Group, LLC

ISBN: 978-1-032-30229-4 (hbk)
ISBN: 978-1-032-20197-9 (pbk)
ISBN: 978-1-003-30402-9 (ebk)

DOI: 10.1201/9781003304029

Typeset in Times
by Apex CoVantage, LLC

This book is dedicated to my lovely wife, Yan Wang,
and my beautiful daughter, Xue (Susan) Bai.

Contents

Preface....xix
Acknowledgments....xxi
About the Author....xxiii
Copyrights and Trademarks....xxv

Chapter 1 Introduction....1

1.1 Outstanding Features of This Book....2
1.2 Whom This Book Is For....2
1.3 What This Book Covers....2
1.4 How This Book Is Organized and How to Use This Book....4
1.5 How to Use the Source Code and the Sample Database....5
1.5.1 Instructor Materials and Customer Support....5

Chapter 2 Introduction to Databases....9

2.1 What Are Databases and Database Programs?....9
2.1.1 File Processing System....10
2.1.2 Integrated Databases....10
2.2 Developing a Database....11
2.3 A Sample Database....12
2.3.1 Relational Data Model....15
2.3.2 Entity-Relationship (ER) Model....16
2.4 Identifying Keys....16
2.4.1 Primary Key and Entity Integrity....16
2.4.2 Candidate Key....17
2.4.3 Foreign Keys and Referential Integrity....17
2.5 Define Relationships....18
2.5.1 Connectivity....18
2.6 ER Notation....21
2.7 Data Normalization....21
2.7.1 First Normal Form (1NF)....22
2.7.2 Second Normal Form (2NF)....22
2.7.3 Third Normal Form (3NF)....23
2.8 Database Components in Some Popular Databases....25
2.8.1 Microsoft Access Databases....25
2.8.1.1 Database File....25
2.8.1.2 Tables....26
2.8.1.3 Queries....26
2.8.2 SQL Server Databases....26
2.8.2.1 Data Files....27
2.8.2.2 Tables....27
2.8.2.3 Views....27
2.8.2.4 Stored Procedures....27
2.8.2.5 Keys and Relationships....27
2.8.2.6 Indexes....28
2.8.2.7 Transaction Log Files....28

2.8.3 Oracle Databases 28
2.8.3.1 Data Files 29
2.8.3.2 Tables 29
2.8.3.3 Views 29
2.8.3.4 Stored Procedures 29
2.8.3.5 Initialization Parameter Files 30
2.8.3.6 Control Files 30
2.8.3.7 Redo Log Files 31
2.8.3.8 Password Files 31
2.9 Create a New Oracle XE 18c Sample Database 31
2.9.1 Connect to Default Oracle Database from the Oracle SQL Developer 31
2.9.2 Create an Oracle User Account for the User Schema 32
2.9.3 Create LogIn Table 36
2.9.4 Create Faculty Table 37
2.9.5 Create Other Tables 40
2.9.6 Create Relationships among Tables 43
2.9.6.1 Create Relationship between LogIn and Faculty Tables 43
2.9.6.2 Create Relationship between LogIn and Student Tables 45
2.9.6.3 Create Relationship between Faculty and Course Tables 48
2.9.6.4 Create Relationship between Student and StudentCourse Tables 48
2.9.6.5 Create Relationship between Course and StudentCourse Tables 49
2.9.7 Store Images in the Oracle 18c Express Edition Database 52
2.9.7.1 Store Images in the FACULTY Table 53
2.9.7.2 Store Images in the STUDENT Table 60
2.10 A ShortCut: How to Use the Sample Database without Building It 63
2.11 Chapter Summary 63
Homework 64

Chapter 3 JDBC API and JDBC Drivers 67

3.1 What Are JDBC and JDBC API? 67
3.2 JDBC Components and Architecture 67
3.3 How Does JDBC Work? 69
3.3.1 Establish a Connection 69
3.3.1.1 Using DriverManager to Establish a Connection 69
3.3.1.2 Using DataSource Object to Establish a Connection 70
3.3.2 Build and Execute Oracle Statements 71
3.3.3 Process Results 71
3.3.3.1 Using a ResultSet Object 71
3.3.3.2 Using a RowSet Object 72
3.4 JDBC Driver and Driver Types 72
3.4.1 Type I: JDBC-ODBC Bridge Driver 72
3.4.2 Type II: Native-API-Partly-Java Driver 73
3.4.3 Type III: JDBC-Net-All-Java Driver 74
3.4.4 Type IV: Native-Protocol-All-Java Driver 75
3.5 JDBC Standard Extension API 75
3.5.1 JDBC DataSource 75
3.5.1.1 Java Naming and Directory Interface 76
3.5.1.2 Deploy and Use a Basic Implementation of DataSource 76

3.5.2 JDBC Driver-Based Connection Pooling ... 77
3.5.3 Distributed Transactions ... 79
3.5.3.1 Distributed Transaction Components and Scenarios ... 80
3.5.3.2 The Distributed Transaction Process ... 80
3.5.4 JDBC RowSet ... 81
3.5.4.1 Introduction to Java RowSet Object ... 82
3.5.4.2 Implementation Process of a RowSet Object ... 82
3.6 Chapter Summary ... 83
Homework ... 84

Chapter 4 JDBC Applications and Design Considerations ... 87

4.1 JDBC Application Models ... 87
4.1.1 Two-Tier Client-Server Model ... 87
4.1.2 Three-Tier Client-Server Model ... 88
4.2 JDBC Application Fundamentals ... 89
4.2.1 Loading and Registering Drivers ... 89
4.2.2 Getting Connected ... 91
4.2.2.1 The DriverManager and Driver Classes ... 91
4.2.2.2 Using the DriverManager.getConnection() Method ... 91
4.2.2.3 Using the Driver.connect() Method ... 92
4.2.2.4 The JDBC Connection URL ... 93
4.2.2.5 Establish a Database Connection ... 93
4.2.3 Executing Statements ... 95
4.2.3.1 Overview of Statement Objects and Their Execution Methods ... 95
4.2.3.2 Using the Statement Object ... 99
4.2.3.2.1 Creating the Statement Object ... 99
4.2.3.2.2 Executing the Statement Object ... 99
4.2.3.3 Using the PreparedStatement Object ... 99
4.2.3.3.1 Creating the PreparedStatement Object ... 100
4.2.3.3.2 Setting the Input Parameters ... 100
4.2.3.3.3 Set Primitive Data Type and Object IN Values ... 101
4.2.3.3.4 Executing the PreparedStatement Object ... 102
4.2.3.4 Using the CallableStatement Object ... 103
4.2.3.4.1 Building a CallableStatement Query String .. 103
4.2.3.4.2 Creating the CallableStatement Object ... 104
4.2.3.4.3 Setting the Input Parameters ... 105
4.2.3.4.4 Registering the Output Parameters ... 105
4.2.3.4.5 Executing the CallableStatement Object ... 106
4.2.3.5 More about the Execution Methods ... 106
4.2.3.6 Creating and Executing Oracle Statements ... 108
4.2.3.6.1 Creating and Executing DDL Statements ... 108
4.2.3.6.2 Creating and Executing DML Statements ... 109
4.2.3.6.3 JDBC Escape Syntax ... 109
4.2.4 Retrieving Results ... 110
4.2.4.1 The ResultSet Interface ... 112
4.2.4.2 Getting and Processing the ResultSet Object ... 113
4.2.4.2.1 Fetching by Row ... 113
4.2.4.2.2 Fetching by Column ... 114
4.2.5 Using JDBC MetaData Interfaces ... 115

4.2.5.1 Using the ResultSetMetaData Interface ... 115
4.2.5.2 Using the DatabaseMetaData Interface ... 117
4.2.5.3 Using the ParameterMetaData Interface ... 118
4.2.6 Closing the Connection and Statements ... 119
4.3 Chapter Summary ... 119
Homework ... 120

Chapter 5 Introduction to Apache NetBeans IDE ... 123

5.1 Overview of Apache NetBeans 12 ... 123
5.1.1 The Apache NetBeans Platform ... 125
5.1.2 The Apache NetBeans Open-Source IDE ... 126
5.2 Installing and Confirming the Apache NetBeans IDE ... 128
5.3 Exploring the Apache NetBeans IDE 12 ... 129
5.3.1 An Overview of the Apache NetBeans IDE 12 GUI ... 129
5.3.2 Build a New Java with Ant Project ... 131
5.3.2.1 Build a Java Application Project ... 132
5.3.2.1.1 Add a Graphical User Interface ... 134
5.3.2.1.2 Add Other GUI-Related Components ... 136
5.3.2.1.3 Develop the Code for Three Buttons ... 137
5.3.2.1.3.1 Code for the Display Button ... 138
5.3.2.1.3.2 Code for the Clear Button ... 138
5.3.2.1.3.3 Code for the Exit Button ... 139
5.3.2.1.4 Run the Project ... 140
5.3.2.2 Build a Java Class Library ... 140
5.3.2.2.1 Create a Java Class Library Project ... 141
5.3.2.2.2 Create a Java Application Project ... 142
5.3.2.2.3 ConFigure the Compilation Classpath ... 143
5.3.2.2.4 Add Code to the Main.java Tab in the Java Application Project ... 144
5.3.2.2.5 Run the Application Project to Call the Java Library ... 145
5.3.2.2.6 Build and Deploy the Application ... 146
5.3.2.2.7 Distribute the Application to Other Users ... 147
5.3.2.3 Build a Java Project with Existing Sources ... 148
5.3.2.4 Build a Free-Form Java Project ... 148
5.3.3 Build a Java Web Application Project ... 149
5.4 Set up the Environment for the Apache NetBeans IDE 12 to Build Our Customer Projects ... 149
5.5 Chapter Summary ... 149
Homework ... 150

PART I Building Two-Tier Client-Server Applications

Chapter 6 Querying Data from Databases ... 155

6.1 Introduction to Runtime Object Method ... 155
6.2 Connect to the Oracle Database 18c Express Edition CSE_DEPT ... 155
6.3 Create a Java Application Project to Access the Oracle Database ... 158
6.3.1 Create Graphic User Interfaces ... 159

6.3.2 Create a Message Box with JDialog Form Class 163
6.3.3 Add Oracle JDBC Driver to the Project 166
6.3.3.1 Load and Register the Oracle JDBC Driver 167
6.3.3.2 JDBC Uniform Resource Locators (URLs) 168
6.3.3.3 Create and Manage the Statement and PreparedStatement Objects 169
6.3.3.4 Use ResultSet Object 170
6.3.3.4.1 Fetching by Row: 171
6.3.3.4.2 Fetching by Column: 171
6.3.4 Develop Code for the LogIn Table to Connect to Our Sample Database 172
6.3.5 Use the PreparedStatement Object to Perform Dynamic Query for the LogIn Table 173
6.3.6 Develop the Code for the SelectionFrame Form 175
6.3.7 Perform a Data Query for the Faculty Table 178
6.3.7.1 Add Java Package and Code for the Constructor 179
6.3.7.2 Introduction to Some Popular JDBC MetaData Interfaces 180
6.3.7.2.1 The DatabaseMetaData Interface 180
6.3.7.2.2 The ResultSetMetaData Interface 181
6.3.7.2.3 The ParameterMetaData Interface 181
6.3.7.3 Use Java executeQuery() with the DatabaseMetaData Interface to Query the Faculty Table 181
6.3.7.4 Use the Java execute() Method to Query the Faculty Table 183
6.3.7.5 Use the Java CallableStatement Method to Query the Faculty Table 184
6.3.7.5.1 Build and Formulate the CallableStatement Query String 185
6.3.7.5.2 Create a CallableStatement Object 186
6.3.7.5.3 Set the Input Parameters 186
6.3.7.5.4 Register the Output Parameters 188
6.3.7.5.5 Execute CallableStatement 189
6.3.7.5.6 Retrieve the Run Results 189
6.3.7.5.7 The Syntax of Creating Stored Procedures in the Oracle Database 190
6.3.7.5.8 The Syntax of Creating Packages in the Oracle Database 190
6.3.7.5.9 Create an Oracle Package FacultyInfo 192
6.3.7.5.10 Develop the Code to Perform the CallableStatement Query 194
6.3.7.6 Display an Image for the Selected Faculty Member in Canvas 197
6.3.7.6.1 Operational Sequence to Display an Image in Java 197
6.3.7.6.2 Create a User-Defined Method to Select and Display Desired Faculty Image 198
6.3.7.6.3 Develop Additional Code to Coordinate theImage Display 200
6.3.7.7 Develop the Code for the Back Button Click Event Handler 201

6.3.7.8 Build and Run the Project to Test Functions of the FacultyFrame Form 201
6.3.8 Perform the Data Query for the Course Table 202
6.3.8.1 Import Java Packages and Code for the CourseFrame Constructor 203
6.3.8.2 Create an Oracle Package, FacultyCourse 203
6.3.8.3 Develop the Code to Perform the CallableStatement Query 206
6.3.9 Query Data from the Student Table Using the Java RowSet Object 211
6.3.9.1 Introduction to Java RowSet Object 211
6.3.9.2 The Operational Procedure of Using the JDBC RowSet Object 212
6.3.9.3 Coding for the Constructor of the StudentFrame Class 213
6.3.9.4 Coding for the Select Button Event Handler to Query Data Using the CachedRowSet 214
6.3.9.5 Display a Student Picture for the Selected Student 217
6.4 Chapter Summary 219
Homework 219

Chapter 7 Insert, Update and Delete Data from Databases 223

7.1 Perform Data Manipulations to Oracle Database Using the Java Runtime Object 223
7.2 Perform Data Insertion to Oracle Database Using the Java Runtime Object Method 223
7.2.1 Develop the Code for the Insert Button Event Handler 225
7.2.2 Develop a Method for Data Checking Prior to Data Insertion 226
7.2.3 Develop a Method for Selecting a Valid Faculty Image 226
7.2.4 Find a Way to Enable the Insert Button to Begin a New Data Insertion 228
7.2.5 Develop a Method for Clearing Original Faculty Information 228
7.2.6 Develop the Code for the Validation of the Data Insertion 229
7.2.7 Build and Run the Project to Test the Data Insertion 229
7.3 Perform Data Update to Oracle Database Using the Java Runtime Object Method 231
7.3.1 Modify the Code Inside the FacultyFrame Constructor 231
7.3.2 Develop the Code for the Update Button Event Handler 233
7.3.3 Build and Run the Project to Test the Data Update 234
7.4 Perform Data Delete to Oracle Database Using the Java Runtime Object 235
7.4.1 Develop the Code for the Delete Button Event Handler 236
7.4.2 Build and Run the Project to Test the Data Deletion 237
7.5 Perform Data Manipulation Using UpdaTable ResultSet 239
7.5.1 Introduction to ResultSet Enhanced Functionalities and Categories 239
7.5.2 Perform Data Manipulation Using the UpdaTable ResultSet Object 241
7.5.2.1 Insert a New Row Using the UpdaTable ResultSet 241
7.5.2.2 Update a Data Row Using the UpdaTable ResultSet 246
7.5.2.3 Delete a Data Row Using the UpdaTable ResultSet 250
7.6 Perform Data Manipulation Using Callable Statements 252
7.6.1 Insert Data to the Course Table Using Callable Statements 252

7.6.1.1 Develop the Oracle Stored Procedure InsertNewCourse() 252
7.6.1.2 Develop the Code for the Insert Button Click Event Handler 255
7.6.2 Update Data to the Course Table Using Callable Statements 258
7.6.2.1 Develop the Oracle Stored Procedure UpdateCourse() 259
7.6.2.2 Develop the Code for the Update Button Click Event Handler 262
7.6.3 Delete Data from the Course Table Using Callable Statements 264
7.6.3.1 Develop the Stored Procedure DeleteCourse() 265
7.6.3.2 Develop the Code for the Delete Button Click Event Handler 266
7.7 Chapter Summary 268
Homework 268

PART II Building Three-Tier Client-Server Applications

Chapter 8 Develop Java Web Applications to Access Databases 275

8.1 A Historical Review about Java Web Application Development 275
8.1.1 Using Servlet and HTML Web Pages for Java Web Applications 275
8.1.2 Using JavaServer Pages Technology for Java Web Applications 278
8.1.3 Using Java Help Class Files for Java Web Applications 281
8.1.4 Using the JSP Implicit Object Session for Java Web Applications 286
8.1.4.1 Modify the FacultyPage JSP File to Use the Session Object 287
8.1.4.2 Build the Transaction JSP File, FacultyQuery.jsp 288
8.1.4.3 Build the Help Class FacultyBean 289
8.1.5 Using Java Beans Technology for Java Web Applications 292
8.1.5.1 Modify the Help Class FacultyBean to Make It a Java Bean Class 294
8.1.5.2 Build a New Starting Web Page, FacultyBeanPage 296
8.1.6 Using JavaServer Faces Technology for Java Web Applications 297
8.1.6.1 The Application Configuration Resource File, faces-config.xml 299
8.1.6.2 Sample JavaServer Face Page Files 300
8.1.6.3 The Java Bean Class File 302
8.1.6.4 The Web Deployment Descriptor File, web.xml 302
8.1.6.5 A Complete Run Procedure of JSF Web Applications 303
8.1.6.5.1 The Java Bean–JSF Page Relationship and Page Navigation 304
8.1.6.5.2 The Detailed Code for the Java Bean Class 308
8.2 Java EE Web Application Model 309
8.2.1 Java EE Web Applications with and without EJB 309
8.3 The Architecture and Components of Java Web Applications 311
8.3.1 Java EE Containers 312
8.3.2 Java EE 8 APIs 312
8.3.2.1 Enterprise Java Beans API Technology 313
8.3.2.2 Java Servlet API Technology 313

9.7.1 Create a Web-Based Client Project, WebClientFaculty_Select 428
9.7.2 Create a Java Managed Bean Class, FacultyMBean 429
9.7.3 Modify Three Files to Make Them Work for Our Web Client Project 429
9.7.4 Add a Web Service Reference to Our Web-Based Client Project 431
9.7.5 Build and Run Our Client Project to Query Faculty Data via Web Service 433
9.8 Build Java Web Services to Insert Data into the Oracle Database 433
9.8.1 Add a New Operation InsertFaculty() into Our Web Service Project 434
9.8.2 Deploy the Web Service Project 436
9.9 Build a Window-Based Client Project to Consume the Web Service 437
9.9.1 Refresh the Web Service Reference for Our Window-Based Client Project 438
9.9.2 Develop the Code to Call Our Web Service Project 438
9.9.3 Build and Run Our Client Project to Insert Faculty Data via Web Service 440
9.10 Build a Web-Based Client Project to Consume the Web Service 442
9.10.1 Refresh the Web Service Reference for Our Web-Based Client Project 442
9.10.2 Develop the Code to Call Our Web Service Project 443
9.10.3 Build and Run Our Client Project to Insert Faculty Data via Web Service 446
9.11 Build Java Web Service to Update and Delete Data from the Oracle Database 448
9.11.1 Add a New Operation, UpdateFaculty(), to Perform Faculty Data Update 449
9.11.2 Add a New Operation, DeleteFaculty(), to Perform Faculty Data Delete 451
9.11.3 Deploy and Test the Web Service Project 453
9.12 Build a Window-Based Client Project to Consume the Web Service 455
9.12.1 Refresh the Web Service Reference for Our Window-Based Client Project 456
9.12.2 Build the Code to Call the UpdateFaculty() Operation 456
9.12.3 Build the Code to Call the DeleteFaculty() Operation 458
9.12.4 Build and Run Our Client Project to Update and Delete Faculty Record via Web Service 459
9.13 Build a Web-Based Client Project to Consume the Web Service 462
9.13.1 Refresh the Web Service Reference for Our Web-Based Client Project 462
9.13.2 Develop the Code to Call Our Web Service Operation, UpdateFaculty() 463
9.13.3 Develop the Code to Call Our Web Service Operation DeleteFaculty() 464
9.13.4 Add Necessary Code to the FacultyProcess.jsp Page to Do Data Updating and Deleting 465
9.13.5 Build and Run Our Client Project to Update and Delete Faculty Record via Web Service 467
9.14 Build Java Web Service Project to Access Course Table in Our Sample Database 470
9.14.1 Create a New Java Web Application Project, WebAppCourse 470

9.14.2 Create a New Java SOAP-Based Web Service Project, WebServiceCourse ... 470
9.14.3 The Organization of Web Service Operations ... 471
9.14.4 Create and Build Web Service Operations ... 471
9.14.4.1 Create and Build the Web Operation QueryCourseID() .. 472
9.14.4.2 Build and Run the Web Service to Test the CourseID Query Function ... 475
9.14.4.3 Create and Build the Web Operation QueryCourse() ... 476
9.14.4.4 Create and Build the Web Operation InsertCourse() ... 478
9.14.4.5 Create and Build the Web Operation UpdateCourse() ... 481
9.14.4.6 Create and Build the Web Operation DeleteCourse() ... 483
9.15 Build Windows-Based Project to Consume the Web Service Project ... 485
9.15.1 Update the Web Service Reference for Our Window-Based Client Project ... 486
9.15.2 Develop the Code to Query Course Information from our Web Service ... 487
9.15.3 Build Code for the Select Button Event Handler to Query CourseIDs ... 487
9.15.4 Build Code for the CourseListValueChanged() Method to Get Course Details ... 488
9.15.5 Build Code for the Insert Button Event Handler to Insert a New Course ... 491
9.15.6 Build Code for the Update Button Method to Update Course Records ... 495
9.15.7 Build Code for the Delete Button Method to Delete Course Records ... 498
9.16 Build a Web-Based Client Project to Consume our Web Service Project ... 499
9.16.1 Create a Web-Based Client Project, WebClientCourse_Select ... 500
9.16.2 Add a Web Service Reference to Our Web-Based Project and Change the Ports ... 501
9.16.3 Modify the Java Bean CourseQuery.java and the Control File CourseProcess.jsp ... 502
9.16.4 Build and Run Our Client Project to Query Course Record via Our Web Service ... 505
9.16.5 Build a Web Client Project to Insert New Course Records via Our Web Service ... 506
9.16.6 Build Our Client Project to Update Course Records via Our Web Service ... 510
9.16.7 Build Our Client Project to Delete Course Records via Our Web Service ... 516
9.17 Chapter Summary ... 518
Homework ... 520

Appendix A: Download and Install Oracle Database XE 18c ... 525

Appendix B: Download and Install Apache NetBeans 12.0 ... 531

Appendix C: Download and Install Oracle SQL Developer ... 535

Appendix D: Download and Install DevExpress WinForms ... 537

Appendix E: How to Use the Sample Database ... 539

Appendix F: How to Export the Sample Database ... 543

establish a valid database connection, build a query statement and process the query results are introduced in detail with example code. Some useful tools, such as Java RowSet, Java CallableStatement, Oracle stored procedures and Oracle packages, are also discussed and analyzed with example code.

6) Homework and selected solutions are provided for each chapter to strengthen and improve students' learning and understanding of the topics they have studied.
7) PowerPoint teaching slides are also provided on the Routledge website (www.routledge.com/9781032302294) to help instructors prepare their teaching materials and organize their classes easily and effectively.
8) A collection of Appendices, A–N, are provided with detailed download and installation instructions for the most popular Java database development tools and components, such as Oracle Database XE 18c, Apache NetBeans IDE 12, Oracle SQL Developer, Java JDBC Driver, Tomcat Web server and JDK 8. By using these appendices, readers can quickly and efficiently dive into the actual Java database programming development processes with the help of these tools and components.
9) It is a good textbook for college students and a good reference book for programmers, software engineers and academic researchers.

I sincerely hope that this book can provide useful and practical guidance and assistance to all readers or users, and I will be more than happy to know that you will be able to develop and build professional and practical database applications with the help of this book.

About the Author

Dr. Ying Bai is a professor in the Department of Computer Science and Engineering at Johnson C. Smith University. His special interests include artificial intelligence, softcomputing, mixed-language programming, fuzzy logic and deep learning, robotic controls, robot calibration and database programming.

His industry experience includes positions as a software and senior software engineer at companies such as Motorola MMS, Schlumberger ATE Technology, Immix TeleCom and Lam Research.

Since 2003, Dr. Bai has published 18 books with publishers such as Prentice Hall, CRC Press LLC, Springer, Cambridge University Press and Wiley IEEE Press. The Russian translation of his first book, titled *Applications Interface Programming Using Multiple Languages*, was published by Prentice Hall in 2005. The Chinese translation of his eighth book, titled *Practical Database Programming with Visual C#.NET*, was published by Tsinghua University Press in China in 2011. Most of his books are about artificial intelligence and softcomputing, software interfacing and serial port programming, database programming, fuzzy logic controls and microcontroller programming as well as classical and modern control technologies.

Recently, Dr. Bai has also published more than 65 academic research papers in IEEE *Transactions*. journals and international conferences.

Acknowledgments

First and most special thank to my wife, Yan Wang; I could not have finished this book without her sincere encouragement and support.

Special thanks to Dr. Satish Bhalla, who made great contributions to Chapter 2. Dr. Bhalla is a specialist in database programming and management, especially in SQL Server, Oracle and DB2. Dr. Bhalla spent a lot of time preparing materials for the first part of Chapter 2, and he is deserving of this thanks.

Many thanks should be given to the acquisition editor, Mr. John Wyzalek, who made this book available to the public. You could not find this book in the current book market without John's deep perspective and hard work. The same thanks are extended to the editorial team of this book. Without this team's contributions, it would be impossible for this book to be published.

Last but not least, thanks should be given to all the people who supported me to finish this book.

Copyrights and Trademarks

- Apache®, Apache NetBeans, NetBeans and the NetBeans logo are either registered trademarks or trademarks of the Apache Software Foundation in the United States and/or other countries. No endorsement by the Apache Software Foundation is implied by the use of these marks.
- Microsoft Visual Studio® is a registered trademark of Microsoft Corporation in the United States and/or other countries.
- Microsoft Visual Basic® is a registered trademark of Microsoft Corporation in the United States and/or other countries.
- Devart® is a trade mark of Devart Ltd.
- DevExpress® is a trademark or registered trademark of Developer Express Inc.
- Oracle and Java are registered trademarks of Oracle and/or its affiliates. Other names may be trademarks of their respective owners.
- Java JDK and JDBC are copyrighted by Oracle and its affiliates. Used with permission.

1.1 OUTSTANDING FEATURES OF THIS BOOK

1) This book covers both fundamental and advanced Java database programming techniques to help both beginning and experienced students as well as programmers.
2) A sample database, **CSE _ DEPT**, which represents an example computer science department and is built with Oracle 18c Express Edition (XE), is used for all program examples developed in the book.
3) Different types of database projects, including the standard Java desktop applications, Java with Ant, Java class library, Java EE7 applications, Java Web applications and Java Web services, are discussed, analyzed and implemented in 35 actual projects with line-by-line explanations.
4) Updated Java database programming tools, such as Java Enterprise Edition 7, JavaServer Pages, Java Beans, Enterprise Java Beans, GlassFish and Tomcat Web servers, are discussed and analyzed with real projects to give readers a clear picture and an easy-to-learn path for Java database applications.
5) A detailed introduction to and discussion of the Apache NetBeans IDE 12.4 are provided in Chapter 5. Starting from a simple Java application, all the different project types built in the Apache NetBeans IDE are discussed and presented to give readers a detailed, global picture of the working structure and operational principles of the NetBeans IDE.
6) Thirty-five real sample database programming projects are covered in the book, with detailed illustrations and explanations to help students to understand key techniques and programming technologies with Java and Oracle databases.
7) Homework and selected solutions are provided for each chapter to strengthen and improve students' learning and understanding abilities for topics they have studied.
8) PowerPoint teaching (PPT) slides are also provided to help instructors with teaching and organizing their classes.
9) It is a good textbook for college students and a good reference book for programmers, software engineers and academic researchers.

1.2 WHOM THIS BOOK IS FOR

This book is designed for college students and software programmers who want to develop practical and commercial database programming with Java and relational databases such as Oracle 18c XE. Fundamental knowledge and understanding of the Java language and Java programming techniques are required.

1.3 WHAT THIS BOOK COVERS

Nine chapters are included in this book. The contents of each chapter can be summarized as follows.

- Chapter 1 provides an introduction to and summary of the entire book.
- Chapter 2 provides detailed discussions and analyses of the structures and components of relational databases. Some key technologies in developing and designing databases are also given and discussed in this chapter. The procedure and components used to develop a practical relational database with Oracle 18c XE are analyzed in detail with some real data Tables in our sample database **CSE _ DEPT**.
- Chapter 3 provides discussions of JDBC APIs and drivers. A detailed introduction to the components and architecture of JDBC is given with step-by-step illustrations. Four popular types of JDBC drivers are discussed and analyzed with both their advantages and disadvantages emphasized in actual database applications. The working structure and operational principles of using JDBC drivers to establish a valid database connection, build a query statement and process the query results are also discussed and presented in

detail. One of the most useful tools, JDBC RowSet, is also discussed and analyzed with some example code.

- Chapter 4 provides a detailed discussion and analysis of JDBC design and actual application considerations. The fundamentals of using JDBC to access and manipulate data against databases are discussed and introduced with example code. Different JDBC interfaces, including the ResultSet, ResultSetMetaData, DatabaseMetaData and ParameterMetaData, are introduced and discussed with example code.
- Chapter 5 provides a detailed description of the Apache NetBeans IDE 12.4, including the components and architecture. This topic is necessary for college students who have no knowledge of the Apache NetBeans IDE. Starting from an introduction to installing the Apache NetBeans IDE 12.4, this chapter goes through each aspect of the NetBeans IDE 12.4, including the NetBeans Platform, NetBeans Open Source and all plug-in tools. Different projects built with the Apache NetBeans IDE 12.4 are also discussed and presented in detail, with one example project.
- Starting from Chapter 6, real database programming techniques with Java and query data from a database are provided and discussed. This chapter covers the so-called runtime object method to develop and build professional data-driven applications. Detailed discussions and descriptions of how to build professional and practical database applications using this runtime object method are provided, with three real projects. In addition to basic query techniques, advanced query methods such as PreparedStatement, CallableStatement and Oracle stored procedures are also discussed and implemented in this chapter, with some real sample projects.
- Chapter 7 provides detailed discussions and analyses of how to insert, update and delete data from an Oracle database—Oracle 18c XE. This chapter covers some techniques to manipulate data in our sample database using the runtime object method. Nine real projects are used to illustrate how to perform data manipulations against our sample database, **CSE _ DEPT**, which is built with Oracle SQL Developer. Professional and practical data validation methods are also discussed in this chapter to confirm data manipulations. Some advanced data manipulation techniques and methods, such as UpdaTable ResultSet and Callable Statements, are also introduced and discussed in this chapter, with real projects.
- Chapter 8 provides introductions to and discussions of the developments and implementations of three-tier Java Web applications in the NetBeans IDE 12.4 environment. At the beginning of this chapter, a detailed and complete historical review of Java Web application development is provided, and this part is especially important and useful to college students or programmers who do not have any background knowledge of Java Web application development and implementation. Following the introduction section, different techniques used to build Java Web applications are introduced and discussed in detail. The target database, **CSE _ DEPT**, which is built with Oracle SQL Developer, is utilized as the objective database for these development and building processes. JavaServer Pages and Java Beans techniques are also discussed and used in four real Web application projects.
- Chapter 9 provides introductions to and discussions of the developments and implementations of Java Web Services in the NetBeans IDE 12.0 environment. A detailed discussion and analysis of the structure and components of the Java Web services is provided at the beginning of this chapter. Each Web service contains different operations that can be used to access different databases and perform the desired data actions, such as Select, Insert, Update and Delete via the Internet. To consume those Web services, different Web service client projects are also developed in this chapter. Both Windows-based and Web-based client projects are discussed and built for each kind of Web service listed previously. In all, 17 projects, including 3 Web service projects and 14 associated Web service client projects, are developed in this chapter. All projects have been debugged and tested and can be run in most Windows-compatible operating systems such as Windows 10.

1.4 HOW THIS BOOK IS ORGANIZED AND HOW TO USE THIS BOOK

This book is designed for both college students who are new to database programming with Java and professional database programmers who have some experience on this topic.

Chapters 2 and 3 provide the fundamentals on database structures and components, the JDBC API and related components. Chapter 4 covers an introduction to JDBC design and application considerations. Chapter 5 provides a detailed introduction to the Apache NetBeans IDE 12 and its working environment, with some actual project examples. Starting from Chapters 6 and 7, the runtime object method is introduced, with detailed code development for real projects to perform different data actions against our sample Oracle database, such as data query, data insertion and data updating and deleting. All projects discussed in these two chapters are Java Ant Applications or Java Desktop database applications.

Chapters 8 and 9 give a full discussion and analysis of the developments and implementations of Java Web applications and Web services. These technologies are necessary to students and programmers who want to develop and build Web applications and Web services to access and manipulate data via the Internet.

Based on the organization of this book as described, the book can be used according to two categories, Level I and Level II, which are shown in Figure 1.1, in the following ways.

- For undergraduate college students or beginning software programmers, it is highly recommended they that learn and understand the contents of Chapters 2~7, since those include fundamental knowledge and techniques used in database programming with Java. Chapters 8 and 9 are optional to instructors and depend on time and the schedule.
- For experienced college students or software programmers who have already learned some knowledge and techniques in database programming and Java, it is highly recommended that they learn and understand the contents of Chapters 4~9, since the run-time data objects method and some sophisticated Web database programming techniques, such as Java RowSet object, Callable Statements, stored procedures, Java Beans, JSP and EJB, are discussed and illustrated with real examples.

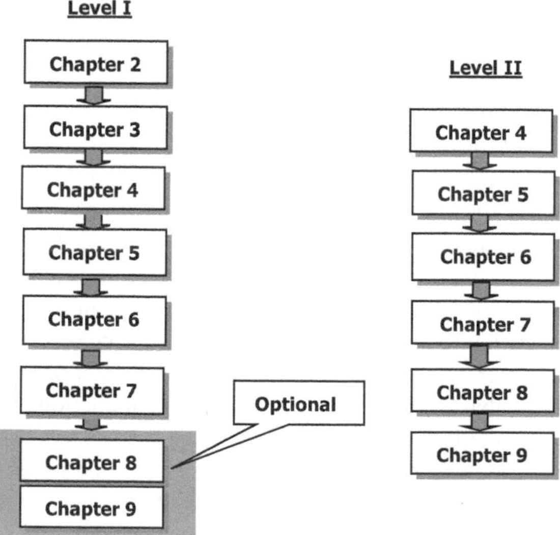

FIGURE 1.1 Two possible teaching levels applied in this book.

1.5 HOW TO USE THE SOURCE CODE AND THE SAMPLE DATABASE

All source code for each real class project developed in this book is available. All projects are categorized into the associated chapters that are located in the folder **`Class DB Projects`** that is located in the **`Students`** folder on the CRC Press site, www.routledge.com/9781032302294. You can copy those projects onto your computer and run each of them as you like. To successfully run these projects on your computer, the following conditions must be met:

- Apache NetBeans IDE 12, JDK 8 and JDBC 18.3 must be installed in your computer for all projects in Chapters 2~9.
- An Oracle database development and management system, Oracle SQL Developer, must be installed on your computer. It is used to build our sample database, **`CSE _ DEPT`**, and to check and confirm all our database actions in our all class projects.
- A sample Oracle 18c XE database, **`CSE _ DEPT`**, must be installed on your computer in the appropriate folder. Refer to Appendix E for more details about how to duplicate this sample database if you do not want to build it.
- To run the projects developed in Chapters 8 and 9, in addition to the conditions listed previously, two Web servers, GlassFish v5.1.0 and Tomcat v8.0.27, must be installed on your computer.

The following appendices are available to all readers to help them to install database management systems and develop actual database application projects:

Appendix A: Download and Install Oracle Database XE 18c
Appendix B: Download and Install Apache NetBeans IDE 12.0
Appendix C: Download and Install Oracle SQL Developer
Appendix D: Download and Install DevExpress WinForms
Appendix E: How to Use Sample Database
Appendix F: How to Export Sample Database
Appendix G: Download and Install dotConnect Express
Appendix H: Download JDBC Driver for Oracle XE 18c
Appendix I: Download and Install Java Tomcat Server 8.0.27
Appendix J: Download and Install Java JDK 8
Appendix K: Troubleshooting for WS00041 Service Exception
Appendix L: Download and Install Apache NetBeans12.4
Appendix M: Configure Apache NetBeans 12.0 for Initial Running
Appendix N: Download and Install Java JDK 14

All of these appendices can be found in the folder **`Appendix`** that is located in the **`Students`** folder on the CRC Press website, www.routledge.com/9781032302294.

A sample database file, **`CSE _ DEPT`**, is located in the folder **`Sample Database`** in the **`Students`** folder on the CRC Press site, www.routledge.com/9781032302294. To use this database for your applications or sample projects, refer to Appendix E.

Details on these teaching and learning materials located on the CRC Press site are shown in Figure 1.2.

1.5.1 Instructor Materials and Customer Support

All teaching materials for all chapters have been extracted and are represented by a sequence of Microsoft PowerPoint slide files, one file for one chapter. Interested instructors can find those teaching materials in the **`Teaching PPT`** folder located in the **`Instructors`** folder on the CRC Press site, www.routledge.com/9781032302294. These teaching materials are password protected and are available to instructors who adopt this book as their textbook. All of these materials can be requested from the book's listing on the CRC Press site, www.routledge.com/9781032302294.

The Book-Related Materials on the Web Site

FOR INSTRUCTORS:

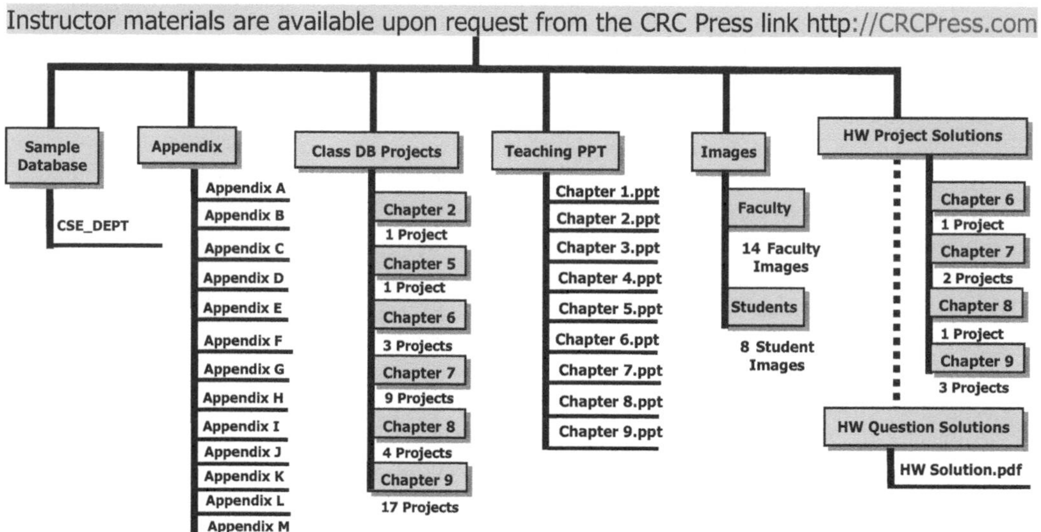

FOR STUDENTS:

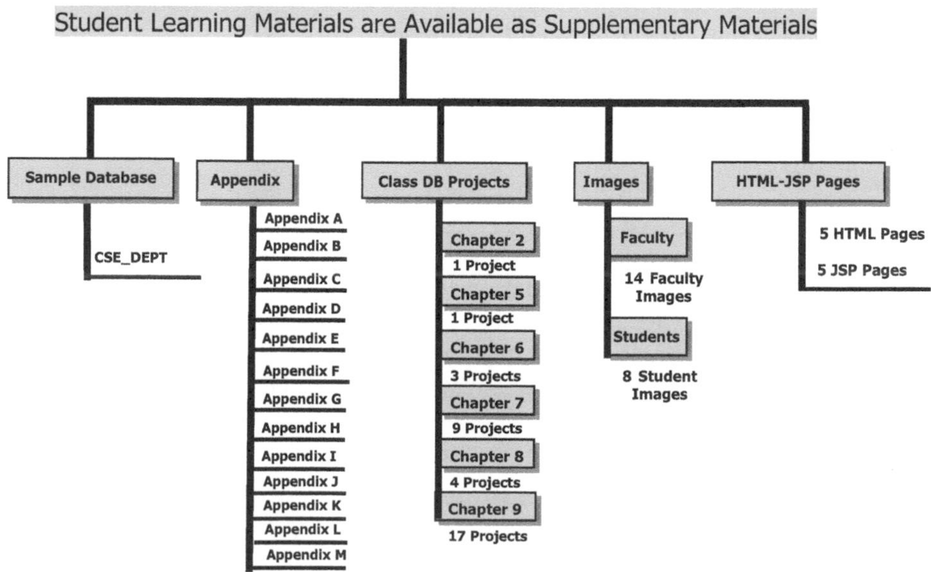

FIGURE 1.2 Book-related materials on the website.

The homework solutions are provided, and they are divided into two parts: project solutions and question solutions. At the end of each chapter, the homework is assigned with two parts: the question part and the project development part. Therefore, the solutions are also divided into two parts. Solutions to the question part are located in the **`HW Questions Solutions`** folder, and solutions to the project part are located in the **`HW DB Projects Solutions`** folder. Both folders are in the **`Instructors`** folder located at the CRC Press ftp site. The selected homework solutions belong to the teaching materials and are available upon request from the book's listing on the CRC Press site, www.routledge.com/9781032302294.

E-mail support is available to all readers of this book. When you send e-mail to us, please provide the following information:

- A detailed description of your problem, including the error message and debug message as well as the error or debug number, if it is provided.
- Your name, job title and company name.

Please send all questions to the e-mail address: ybai@jcsu.edu.

2 Introduction to Databases

Ying Bai and Satish Bhalla

Databases have become an integral part of our modern day life. Today we are an information-driven society. Large amounts of data are generated, analyzed and converted into different information every moment. A recent example of biological data generation is the Human Genome project that was jointly sponsored by the Department of Energy (DOE) and the National Institutes of Health (NIH). Many countries participated in this venture for more than ten years. The project was a tremendous success. It was completed in 2003 and resulted in generation of a huge amount of genome data, currently stored in databases around the world. The scientists will be analyzing this data in years to come.

Database technology has a direct impact on our daily lives. Decisions are routinely made by organizations based on the information collected and stored in databases. A record company may decide to market certain albums in selected regions based on the music preference of teenagers. Grocery stores display more popular items at eye level, and reorders are based on inventories taken at regular intervals. Other examples include book orders by libraries, club memberships, auto part orders, winter clothing stocked by department stores and many others.

Database management programs have been in existence since the 1960s. However, it was not until the 70s, when E. F. Codd proposed the then-revolutionary relational data model, that database technology really took off. In the early 80s, it received a further boost with the arrival of personal computers and microcomputer-based data management programs like dBase II (later followed by dBase III and IV). Today we have a plethora of vastly improved programs for PCs and mainframe computers, including Microsoft Access, SQL Server, IBM DB2, Oracle, Sequel Server, MySQL and others.

This chapter covers the basic concepts of database design, followed by implementation of a specific relational database to illustrate the concepts discussed here. The sample database, **CSE _ DEPT**, is used as a running example. The database structure is shown by using Microsoft Access, Microsoft SQL Server and Oracle databases with a real Oracle 18c XE database sample in detail. The topics discussed in this chapter include:

- What are databases and database programs?
  - File processing systems
  - Integrated databases
- Various approaches to developing a database
- Relational data model and entity-relationship (ER) model
- Identifying keys
  - Primary keys, foreign keys and referential integrity
- Defining relationships
- Normalizing the data
- Implementing the relational sample database
  - Create an Oracle 18c XE sample database

2.1 WHAT ARE DATABASES AND DATABASE PROGRAMS?

A modern-day database is a structured collection of data stored in a computer. The term “structured” implies that each record in the database is stored in a certain format. For example, all entries

DOI: 10.1201/9781003304029-2

in a phone book are arranged in a similar fashion. Each entry contains a name, an address and a telephone number of a subscriber. This information can be queried and manipulated by database programs. The data retrieved in answer to queries becomes information that can be used to make decisions. The databases may consist of a single Table or related multiple Tables. The computer programs used to create, manage and query databases are known as database management systems (DBMSs). Just like databases, DBMSs vary in complexity. Depending on the needs of the user, one can use either a simple application or a robust program. Some examples of these programs were given earlier.

2.1.1 File Processing System

The file processing system (FPS) is a precursor of the integrated database approach. The records for a particular application are stored in a file. An application program is needed to retrieve or manipulate data in this file. Thus, various departments in an organization will have their own file processing systems with their own individual programs to store and retrieve data. The data in various files may be duplicated and is not available to other applications. This causes redundancy and may lead to inconsistency, meaning that various files that supposedly contain the same information may actually contain different data values. Thus duplication of data creates problems with data integrity. Moreover, it is difficult to provide access to multiple users with file processing systems without granting them access to the respective application programs, which manipulate the data in those files.

The FPS may be advantageous under certain circumstances. For example, if data is static and a simple application will solve the problem, a more expensive DBMS is not needed. For example, in a small business environment, you want to keep track of the inventory of the office equipment purchased only once or twice a year. The data can be kept in an Excel spreadsheet and manipulated with ease from time to time. This avoids the need to purchase an expensive database program and hire a knowledgeable database administrator. Before DBMSs became popular, data was kept in files, and application programs were developed to delete, insert or modify records in the files since specific application programs were developed by using specific data.

These programs lasted for months or years before modifications were necessitated by business needs.

2.1.2 Integrated Databases

A better alternative to a file processing system is an integrated database approach. In this environment, all data belonging to an organization is stored in a single database. The database is not a mere collection of files; there is a relation between the files. Integration implies a logical relationship, usually provided through a common column in the Tables. The relationships are also stored within the database. A set of sophisticated programs known as a database management system (DBMS) is used to store, access and manipulate the data in the database. Details of data storage and maintenance are hidden from the user. The user interacts with the database through the DBMS. A user may interact either directly with the DBMS or via a program written in a programming language such as Visual C++, Java, Visual Basic or Visual C#. Only the DBMS can access the database. Large organizations employ database administrators (DBAs) to design and maintain large databases.

There are many advantages of using an integrated database approach over that of a file processing approach:

1) `Data sharing:` The data in the database is available to a large numbers of users who can access the data simultaneously, create reports and manipulate the data given proper authorization and rights.

2) **Minimizing data redundancy:** Since all the related data exists in a single database, there is a minimal need for data duplication. Duplication is needed to maintain relationships between various data items.
3) **Data consistency and data integrity:** Reducing data redundancy will lead to data consistency. Since data is stored in a single database, enforcing data integrity becomes much easier. Furthermore, the inherent functions of the DBMS can be used to enforce integrity with minimum programming.
4) **Enforcing standards**: DBAs are charged with enforcing standards in an organization. The DBA takes into account the needs of various departments and balances them against the overall needs of the organization. The DBA defines various rules such as documentation standards, naming conventions, update and recovery procedures and so on. It is relatively easy to enforce these rules in a database system, since it is a single set of programs that is always interacting with the data files.
5) **Improving security:** Security is achieved through various means such as controlling access to the database through passwords, providing various levels of authorization, data encryption, providing access to restricted views of the database and so on.
6) **Data independence:** Providing data independence is a major objective for any database system. Data independence implies that even if the physical structure of a database changes, applications are allowed to access the database the same way as before the changes were implemented. In other words, applications are immune to changes in the physical representation and access techniques.

The downside of using an integrated database approach has mainly to do with the exorbitant costs associated with it. The hardware, software and maintenance are expensive. Providing security, concurrency, integrity and recovery may further add to this cost. Furthermore, since a DBMS consists of a complex set of programs, trained personnel are needed to maintain it.

2.2 DEVELOPING A DATABASE

The database development process may follow a classical systems development life cycle.

1) **Problem Identification**—Interview the user, identify user requirements. Perform preliminary analysis of user needs.
2) **Project Planning**—Identify alternative approaches to solving the problem. Does the project need a database? If so, define the problem. Establish scope of the project.
3) **Problem Analysis**—Identify specifications for the problem. Confirm the feasibility of the project. Specify detailed requirements.
4) **Logical Design**—Delineate detailed functional specifications. Determine screen designs, report layout designs, data models and so on.
5) **Physical Design**—Develop physical data structures.
6) **Implementation**—Select DBMS. Convert data to conform to DBMS requirements. Code programs, perform testing.
7) **Maintenance**—Continue program modification until desired results are achieved.

An alternative approach to developing a database is through a phased process that will include designing a conceptual model of the system that will imitate real-world operation. It should be flexible and change when the information in the database changes. Furthermore, it should not be dependent upon the physical implementation. This process follows the following phases:

1) **Planning and Analysis**—This phase is roughly equivalent to the first three steps mentioned in the systems development life cycle. This includes requirement

specifications, evaluating alternatives and determining input and output and reports to be generated.

2) **Conceptual Design**—Choose a data model and develop a conceptual schema based on the requirement specification that was laid out in the planning and analysis phase. This conceptual design focuses on how the data will be organized without having to worry about the specifics of the Tables, keys and attributes. Identify the entities that will represent Tables in the database, identify attributes that will represent fields in a Table and identify each entity–attribute relationship. Entity-relationship diagrams provide a good representation of the conceptual design.
3) **Logical Design**—Conceptual design is transformed into a logical design by creating a roadmap of how the database will look before actually creating the database. The data model is identified; usually it is the relational model. Define the Tables (entities) and fields (attributes). Identify primary and foreign keys for each Table. Define relationships between the Tables.
4) **Physical Design**—Develop physical data structures; specify file organization, data storage and so on. Take into consideration the availability of various resources, including hardware and software. This phase overlaps with the implementation phase. It involves the programming of the database, taking into account the limitations of the DBMS used.
5) **Implementation**—Choose the DBMS that will fulfill the users' needs. Implement the physical design. Perform testing. Modify if necessary or until the database functions satisfactorily.

2.3 A SAMPLE DATABASE

We will use a sample database, **CSE _ DEPT**, to illustrate some essential database concepts. Tables 2.1~2.5 show sample data Tables stored in this database.

TABLE 2.1
LogIn Table

user_name	pass_word	faculty_id	student_id
abrown	america	B66750	
ajade	tryagain		A97850
awoods	smart		A78835
banderson	birthday	A52990	
bvalley	see		B92996
dangles	tomorrow	A77587	
hsmith	try		H10210
terica	excellent		T77896
jhenry	test	H99118	
jking	goodman	K69880	
dbhalla	india	B86590	
sjohnson	jermany	J33486	
ybai	come	B78880	

TABLE 2.2
Faculty Table

faculty_id	faculty_name	title	office	phone	college	email	fimage
A52990	Black Anderson	Professor	MTC-218	750–378–9987	Virginia Tech	banderson@college.edu	NULL
A77587	Debby Angles	Associate Professor	MTC-320	750–330–2276	University of Chicago	dangles@college.edu	NULL
B66750	Alice Brown	Assistant Professor	MTC-257	750–330–6650	University of Florida	abrown@college.edu	NULL
B78880	Ying Bai	Associate Professor	MTC-211	750–378–1148	Florida Atlantic University	ybai@college.edu	NULL
B86590	DavisBhalla	Associate Professor	MTC-214	750–378–1061	University of Notre Dame	dbhalla@college.edu	NULL
H99118	Jeff Henry	Associate Professor	MTC-336	750–330–8650	Ohio State University	jhenry@college.edu	NULL
J33486	Steve Johnson	Distinguished Professor	MTC-118	750–330–1116	Harvard University	sjohnson@college.edu	NULL
K69880	Jenney King	Professor	MTC-324	750–378–1230	East Florida University	jking@college.edu	NULL

TABLE 2.3
Course Table

course_id	course	credit	classroom	schedule	enrollment	faculty_id
CSC-131A	Computers in Society	3	TC-109	M-W-F: 9:00–9:55 AM	28	A52990
CSC-131B	Computers in Society	3	TC-114	M-W-F: 9:00–9:55 AM	20	B66750
CSC-131C	Computers in Society	3	TC-109	T-H: 11:00–12:25 PM	25	A52990
CSC-131D	Computers in Society	3	TC-109	M-W-F: 9:00–9:55 AM	30	B86590
CSC-131E	Computers in Society	3	TC-301	M-W-F: 1:00–1:55 PM	25	B66750
CSC-131I	Computers in Society	3	TC-109	T-H: 1:00–2:25 PM	32	A52990
CSC-132A	Introduction to Programming	3	TC-303	M-W-F: 9:00–9:55 AM	21	J33486
CSC-132B	Introduction to Programming	3	TC-302	T-H: 1:00–2:25 PM	21	B78880
CSC-230	Algorithms & Structures	3	TC-301	M-W-F: 1:00–1:55 PM	20	A77587
CSC-232A	Programming I	3	TC-305	T-H: 11:00–12:25 PM	28	B66750
CSC-232B	Programming I	3	TC-303	T-H: 11:00–12:25 PM	17	A77587
CSC-233A	Introduction to Algorithms	3	TC-302	M-W-F: 9:00–9:55 AM	18	H99118
CSC-233B	Introduction to Algorithms	3	TC-302	M-W-F: 11:00–11:55 AM	19	K69880
CSC-234A	Data Structure & Algorithms	3	TC-302	M-W-F: 9:00–9:55 AM	25	B78880
CSC-234B	Data Structure & Algorithms	3	TC-114	T-H: 11:00–12:25 PM	15	J33486
CSC-242	Programming II	3	TC-303	T-H: 1:00–2:25 PM	18	A52990
CSC-320	Object Oriented Programming	3	TC-301	T-H: 1:00–2:25 PM	22	B66750
CSC-331	Applications Programming	3	TC-109	T-H: 11:00–12:25 PM	28	H99118
CSC-333A	Computer Arch & Algorithms	3	TC-301	M-W-F: 10:00–10:55 AM	22	A77587
CSC-333B	Comp Arch & Algorithms	3	TC-302	T-H: 11:00–12:25 PM	15	A77587
CSC-335	Internet Programming	3	TC-303	M-W-F: 1:00–1:55PM	25	B66750
CSC-432	Discrete Algorithms	3	TC-206	T-H: 11:00–12:25 PM	20	B86590

(Continued)

TABLE 2.3 (*Continued*)

course_id	course	credit	classroom	schedule	enrollment	faculty_id
CSC-439	Database Systems	3	TC-206	M-W-F: 1:00–1:55 PM	18	B86590
CSE-138A	Introduction to CSE	3	TC-301	T-H: 1:00–2:25 PM	15	A52990
CSE-138B	Introduction to CSE	3	TC-109	T-H: 1:00–2:25 PM	35	J33486
CSE-330	Digital Logic Circuits	3	TC-305	M-W-F: 9:00–9:55 AM	26	K69880
CSE-332	Foundation of Semiconductor	3	TC-305	T-H: 1:00–2:25 PM	24	K69880
CSE-334	Elec. Measurement & Design	3	TC-212	T-H: 11:00–12:25 PM	25	H99118
CSE-430	Bioinformatics in Computer	3	TC-206	Thu: 9:30–11:00 AM	16	B86590
CSE-432	Analog Circuits Design	3	TC-309	M-W-F: 2:00–2:55 PM	18	K69880
CSE-433	Digital Signal Processing	3	TC-206	T-H: 2:00–3:25 PM	18	H99118
CSE-434	Advanced Electronics Systems	3	TC-213	M-W-F: 1:00–1:55 PM	26	B78880
CSE-436	Automatic Control and Design	3	TC-305	M-W-F: 10:00–10:55 AM	29	J33486
CSE-437	Operating Systems	3	TC-303	T-H: 1:00–2:25 PM	17	A77587
CSE-438	Advd Logic & Microprocessor	3	TC-213	M-W-F: 11:00–11:55 AM	35	B78880
CSE-439	Special Topics in CSE	3	TC-206	M-W-F: 10:00–10:55 AM	22	J33486

TABLE 2.4
Student Table

student_id	student_name	gpa	credits	major	schoolYear	email	simage
A78835	Andrew Woods	3.26	108	Computer Science	Senior	awoods@college.edu	NULL
A97850	Ashly Jade	3.57	116	Info System Engineering	Junior	ajade@college.edu	NULL
B92996	Blue Valley	3.52	102	Computer Science	Senior	bvalley@college.edu	NULL
H10210	Holes Smith	3.87	78	Computer Engineering	Sophomore	hsmith@college.edu	NULL
T77896	Tom Erica	3.95	127	Computer Science	Senior	terica@college.edu	NULL

TABLE 2.5
StudentCourse Table

s_course_id	student_id	course_id	credit	major
1000	H10210	CSC-131D	3	CE
1001	B92996	CSC-132A	3	CS/IS
1002	T77896	CSC-335	3	CS/IS
1003	A78835	CSC-331	3	CE
1004	H10210	CSC-234B	3	CE
1005	T77896	CSC-234A	3	CS/IS
1006	B92996	CSC-233A	3	CS/IS
1007	A78835	CSC-132A	3	CE
1008	A78835	CSE-432	3	CE
1009	A78835	CSE-434	3	CE
1010	T77896	CSC-439	3	CS/IS

TABLE 2.5 (*Continued*)

s_course_id	student_id	course_id	credit	major
1011	H10210	CSC-132A	3	CE
1012	H10210	CSC-331	2	CE
1013	A78835	CSC-335	3	CE
1014	A78835	CSE-438	3	CE
1015	T77896	CSC-432	3	CS/IS
1016	A97850	CSC-132B	3	ISE
1017	A97850	CSC-234A	3	ISE
1018	A97850	CSC-331	3	ISE
1019	A97850	CSC-335	3	ISE
1020	T77896	CSE-439	3	CS/IS
1021	B92996	CSC-230	3	CS/IS
1022	A78835	CSE-332	3	CE
1023	B92996	CSE-430	3	CE
1024	T77896	CSC-333A	3	CS/IS
1025	H10210	CSE-433	3	CE
1026	H10210	CSE-334	3	CE
1027	B92996	CSC-131C	3	CS/IS
1028	B92996	CSC-439	3	CS/IS

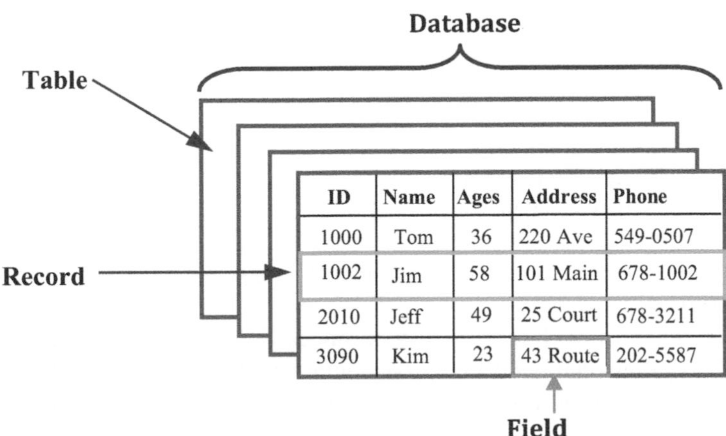

FIGURE 2.1 Records and fields in a Table.

The data in **CSE _ DEPT** database is stored in five Tables—LogIn, Faculty, Course, Student and StudentCourse. A Table consists of rows and columns (Figure 2.1). A row represents a record, and a column represents a field. A row is called a tuple, and a column is called an attribute. For example, the Student Table has eight columns or fields—student_id, student_name, gpa, credits, major, schoolYear, email and simage. It has five records or rows.

2.3.1 Relational Data Model

A data model is like a blueprint for developing a database. It describes the structure of the database and various data relationships and constraints on the data. This information is used in building

Tables and keys and defining relationships. A relational model implies that a user perceives the database as made up of relations, database jargon for Tables. It is imperative that all data elements in the Tables be represented correctly. In order to achieve these goals, designers use various tools. The most commonly used tool is the entity-relationship model. A well-planned model will give consistent results and allow changes if needed later on. The following section further elaborates on the ER model.

2.3.2 Entity-Relationship (ER) Model

The ER model was first proposed and developed by Peter Chen in 1976. Since then, Charles Bachman and James Martin have added some refinements. The model was designed to communicate the database design in the form of a conceptual schema. The ER model is based on the perception that the real world is made up of entities, their attributes and their relationships. The ER model is graphically depicted as entity-relationship diagrams (ERDs). ERDs are a major modeling tool; they graphically describe the logical structure of the database. ER diagrams can be used with ease to construct relational Tables and are a good vehicle for communicating the database design to the end user or a developer. The three major components of ERD are entities, relationships and attributes.

Entities: An entity is a data object, either real or abstract, about which we want to collect information. For example, we may want to collect information about a person, a place or a thing. An entity in an ER diagram translates into a Table. It should preferably be referred to as an entity set. Some common examples are departments, courses and students. A single occurrence of an entity is an instance. There are four entities in the **CSE _ DEPT** database, LogIn, Faculty, Course and Student. Each entity is translated into a Table with the same name. An instance of the Faculty entity is Alice Brown and her attributes.

Relationships: A database is made up of related entities. There is a natural association between the entities; it is referred to as a relationship. For example,

- Students take courses
- Departments offer certain courses
- Employees are assigned to departments

The number of occurrences of one entity associated with single occurrence of a related entity is referred to as **cardinality**.

Attributes: Each entity has properties or values called attributes associated with it. The attributes of an entity map onto fields in a Table. *Database Processing* is one attribute of an entity called *Courses*. The domain of an attribute is a set of all possible values from which an attribute can derive its value.

2.4 IDENTIFYING KEYS

2.4.1 Primary Key and Entity Integrity

An attribute that uniquely identifies one and only one instance of an entity is called a primary key. Sometimes a primary key consists of a combination of attributes. It is referred to as a *composite key*. The *entity integrity rule* states that no attribute that is a member of the primary (composite) key may accept a null value.

A **faculty _ id** may serve as a primary key for the Faculty entity, assuming that all faculty members have been assigned a unique FaultyID. However, caution must be exercised when picking an attribute as a primary key. Last Name may not make a good primary key because a department is likely to have more than one person with the same last name. Primary keys for the **CSE _ DEPT** database are shown in Table 2.6.

TABLE 2.6
Faculty Table

faculty_id	faculty_name	title	office	phone	college	email	fimage
A52990	Black Anderson	Professor	MTC-218	750–378–9987	Virginia Tech	banderson@ college.edu	NULL
A77587	Debby Angles	Associate Professor	MTC-320	750–330–2276	University of Chicago	dangles@college. edu	NULL
B66750	Alice Brown	Assistant Professor	MTC-257	750–330–6650	University of Florida	abrown@college. edu	NULL
B78880	Ying Bai	Associate Professor	MTC-211	750–378–1148	Florida Atlantic University	ybai@college.edu	NULL
B86590	DavisBhalla	Associate Professor	MTC-214	750–378–1061	University of Notre Dame	dbhalla@college .edu	NULL
H99118	Jeff Henry	Associate Professor	MTC-336	750–330–8650	Ohio State University	jhenry@college .edu	NULL
J33486	Steve Johnson	Distinguished Professor	MTC-118	750–330–1116	Harvard University	sjohnson@college .edu	NULL
K69880	Jenney King	Professor	MTC-324	750–378–1230	East Florida University	jking@college .edu	NULL

Primary keys provide a tuple-level addressing mechanism in the relational database. Once you define an attribute as a primary key for an entity, the DBMS will enforce the uniqueness of the primary key. Inserting a duplicate value for primary key field will fail.

2.4.2 Candidate Key

There can be more than one attribute that uniquely identifies an instance of an entity. These are referred to as *candidate keys*. Any one of them can serve as a primary key. For example, ID Number as well as Social Security Number may make a suiTable primary key. Candidate keys that are not used as primary key are called *alternate keys.*

2.4.3 Foreign Keys and Referential Integrity

Foreign keys are used to create relationships between Tables. It is an attribute in one Table whose values are required to match those of primary key in another Table. Foreign keys are created to enforce *referential integrity*, which states that you may not add a record to a Table containing a foreign key unless there is a corresponding record in the related Table to which it is logically linked. Furthermore, the referential integrity rule also implies that every value of a foreign key in a Table must match the primary key of a related Table or be null. MS Access also makes provision for cascade update and cascade delete, which imply that changes made in one of the related Tables will be reflected in the other of the two related Tables.

Consider two Tables Course and Faculty in the sample database, **`CSE _ DEPT`**. The Course Table has a foreign key entitled faculty_id, which is a primary key in the Faculty Table. The two Tables are logically related through the **`faculty _ id`** link. Referential integrity rules imply that we may not add a record to the Course Table with a faculty_id that is not listed in the Faculty Table. In other words, there must be a logical link between the two related Tables. Second, if we change or delete a faculty_id in the Faculty Table, it must be reflected in the Course Table, meaning that all records in the Course Table must be modified using a cascade update or delete (Table 2.7).

TABLE 2.7

Course (Partial Data Shown)

course_id	course	faculty_id
CSC-132A	Introduction to Programming	J33486
CSC-132B	Introduction to Programming	B78880
CSC-230	Algorithms & Structures	A77587
CSC-232A	Programming I	B66750
CSC-232B	Programming I	A77587
CSC-233A	Introduction to Algorithms	H99118
CSC-233B	Introduction to Algorithms	K69880
CSC-234A	Data Structure & Algorithms	B78880

Faculty (Partial Data Shown)

faculty_id	faculty_name	office
A52990	Black Anderson	MTC-218
A77587	Debby Angles	MTC-320
B66750	Alice Brown	MTC-257
B78880	Ying Bai	MTC-211
B86590	Davis Bhalla	MTC-214
H99118	Jeff Henry	MTC-336
J33486	Steve Johnson	MTC-118
K69880	Jenney King	MTC-324

2.5 DEFINE RELATIONSHIPS

2.5.1 Connectivity

Connectivity refers to the types of relationships that entities can have. Basically, the relationship can be *one-to-one, one-to-many* and *many-to-many.* In ER diagrams, these are indicated by placing 1, M or N at one of the two ends of the relationship diagram. Figures 2.2–2.5 illustrate the use of this notation.

- A *one-to-one* (1:1) relationship occurs when one instance of entity A is related to only one instance of entity B, for example, **`user_name`** in the LogIn Table and **`user_name`** in the Student Table (Figure 2.2).
- A *one-to-many* (1:M) relationship occurs when one instance of entity A is associated with zero, one or many instances of entity B. However, entity B is associated with only one instance of entity A. For example, one department can have many faculty members; each faculty member is assigned to only one department. In the **`CSE_DEPT`** database, a one-to-many relationship is represented by **`faculty_id`** in the Faculty Table and **`faculty_id`** in the Course Table, **`student_id`** in the Student Table and **`student_id`** in the StudentCourse Table and **`course_id`** in the Course Table and **`course_id`** in the StudentCourse Table (Figure 2.3).
- A *many-to-many* (M:N) relationship occurs when one instance of entity A is associated with zero, one or many instances of entity B and one instance of entity B is associated with zero, one or many instance of entity A. For example, a student may take many courses, and one course may be taken by more than one student (Figure 2.4).

LogIn

user_name	pass_word
ajade	tryagain
awoods	smart
bvalley	see
hsmith	try
terica	excellent

Student

user_name	gpa	credits	student_id
ajade	3.26	108	A97850
awoods	3.57	116	A78835
bvalley	3.52	102	B92996
hsmith	3.87	78	H10210
terica	3.95	127	T77896

FIGURE 2.2 One-to-one relationship in the LogIn and Student Tables.

Faculty

faculty_id	faculty_name	office
A52990	Black Anderson	MTC-218
A77587	Debby Angles	MTC-320
B66750	Alice Brown	MTC-257
B78880	Ying Bai	MTC-211
B86590	Davis Bhalla	MTC-214
H99118	Jeff Henry	MTC-336
J33486	Steve Johnson	MTC-118
K69880	Jenney King	MTC-324

Course

course_id	course	faculty_id
CSC-132A	Introduction to Programming	J33486
CSC-132B	Introduction to Programming	B78880
CSC-230	Algorithms & Structures	A77587
CSC-232A	Programming I	B66750
CSC-232B	Programming I	A77587
CSC-233A	Introduction to Algorithms	H99118
CSC-233B	Introduction to Algorithms	K69880
CSC-234A	Data Structure & Algorithms	B78880

FIGURE 2.3 One-to-many relationship between the Faculty and Course Tables.

Student

student_id	student_name	gpa	credits
A78835	Andrew Woods	3.26	108
A97850	Ashly Jade	3.57	116
B92996	Blue Valley	3.52	102
H10210	Holes Smith	3.87	78
T77896	Tom Erica	3.95	127

Course

course_id	course	faculty_id
CSC-132A	Introduction to Programming	J33486
CSC-132B	Introduction to Programming	B78880
CSC-230	Algorithms & Structures	A77587
CSC-232A	Programming I	B66750
CSC-232B	Programming I	A77587
CSC-233A	Introduction to Algorithms	H99118

StudentCourse

s_course_id	student_id	course_id	credit	major
1000	H10210	CSC-131D	3	CE
1001	B92996	CSC-132A	3	CS/IS
1002	T77896	CSC-335	3	CS/IS
1003	A78835	CSC-331	3	CE
1004	H10210	CSC-234B	3	CE
1005	T77896	CSC-234A	3	CS/IS
1006	B92996	CSC-233A	3	CS/IS

FIGURE 2.4 Many-to-many relationship between the Student and Course Tables.

In the **CSE _ DEPT** database, a many-to-many relationship can be realized by using the third Table. For example, in this case, the StudentCourse that works as the third Table sets a many-to-many relationship between the Student and Course Tables.

This database design assumes that the course Table only contains courses taught by all faculty members in this department for one semester. Therefore, each course can only be taught by a unique faculty member. If one wants to develop a Course Table that contains courses taught by all faculty in more than one semester, the third Table, say, FacultyCourse Table, should be created to set up a many-to-many relationship between the Faculty and the Course Table, since one course may be taught by different faculty members in different semesters.

The relationships in **CSE _ DEPT** database are summarized in Figure 2.5.

Database name: **CSE _ DEPT**
The five entities are:

- LogIn
- Faculty
- Course

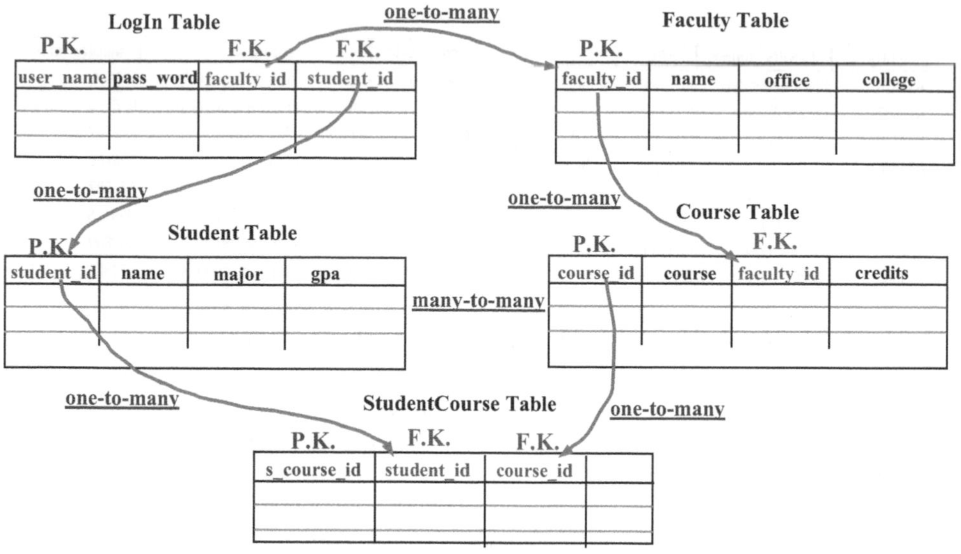

FIGURE 2.5 Relationships in the **CSE _ DEPT** database.

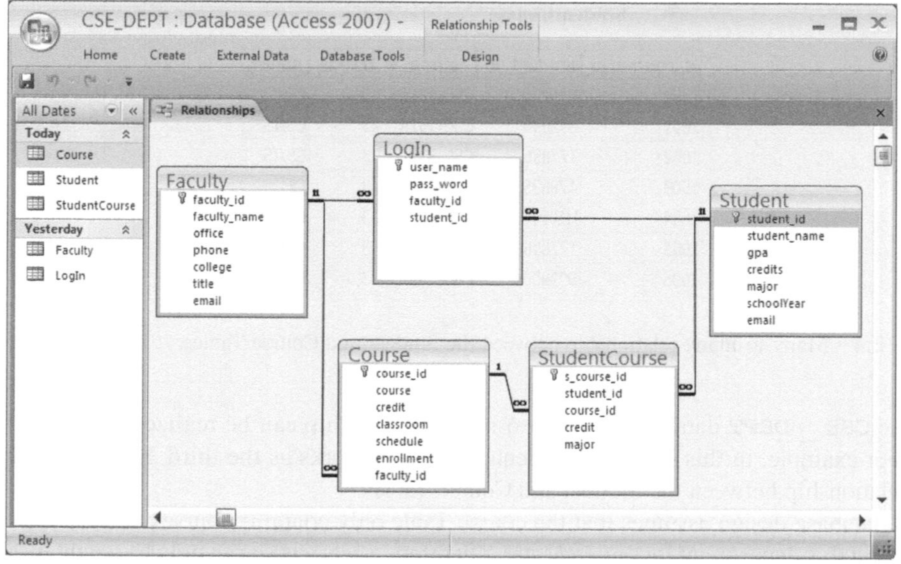

FIGURE 2.6 Relationships are illustrated using MS Access in the **CSE _ DEPT** database.

- Student
- StudentCourse

The relationships between these entities are shown in the following. **P.K.** and **F.K.** represent the primary key and the foreign key, respectively.

Figure 2.6 displays the Microsoft Access relationships diagram among various Tables in the **CSE _ DEPT** database. One-to-many relationships are indicated by placing 1 at one end of the link and ∞ at the other. The many-to-many relationship between the Student and the Course Table was broken down to two one-to-many relationships by creating a new StudentCourse Table.

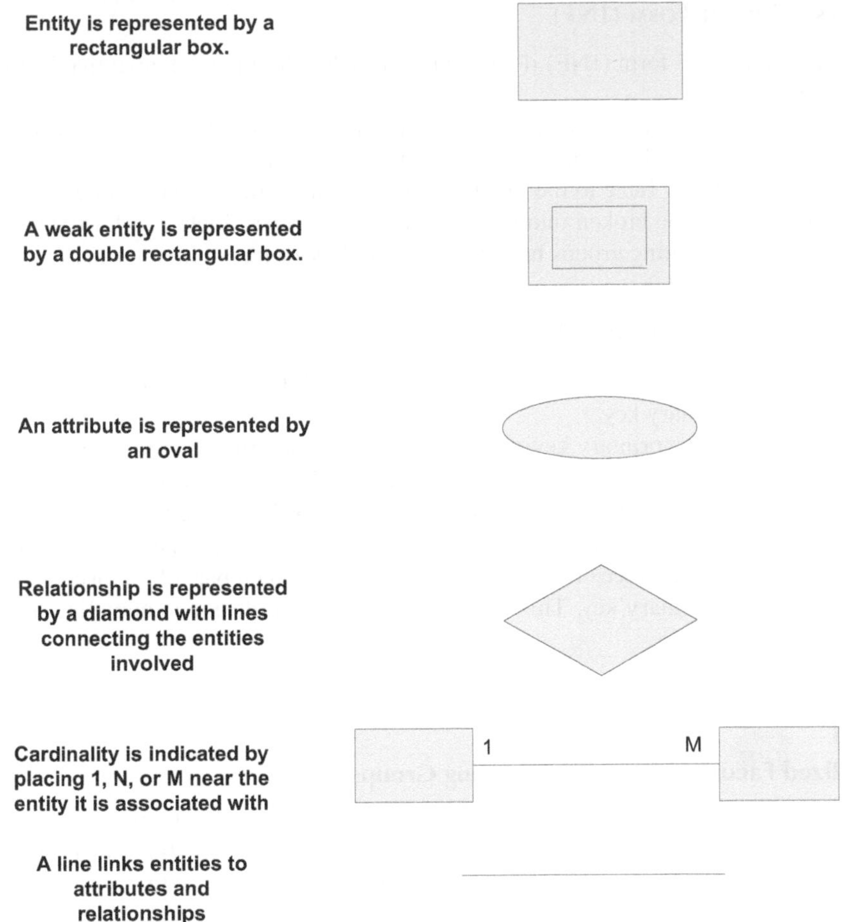

Entity is represented by a rectangular box.
A weak entity is represented by a double rectangular box.
An attribute is represented by an oval
Relationship is represented by a diamond with lines connecting the entities involved
Cardinality is indicated by placing 1, N, or M near the entity it is associated with
1
M
A line links entities to attributes and relationships

FIGURE 2.7 Commonly used symbols for ER notation.

2.6 ER NOTATION

There are a number of ER notations available, including Chen's, Bachman, crow's foot and a few others. There is no consensus on the symbols and the styles used to draw ERDs. A number of drawing tools are available to draw ERDs. These include ER Assistant, Microsoft Visio and Smart Draw, among others. Commonly used notations are shown in Figure 2.7.

2.7 DATA NORMALIZATION

After identifying Tables, attributes and relationships, the next logical step in database design is to make sure that the database structure is optimum. Optimum structure is achieved by eliminating redundancies, various inefficiencies and update and deletion anomalies that usually occur in the unnormalized or partially normalized databases. Data normalization is a progressive process. The steps in the normalization process are called normal forms. Each normal form progressively improves the database and makes it more efficient. In other words, a database that is in second normal form is better than one in first normal form, and one in third normal form is better than one in second normal form. To be in third normal form, a database has to be in first and second normal forms. There are fourth and fifth normal forms, but for most practical purposes, a database meeting the criteria of third normal form is considered to be of good design.

2.7.1 First Normal Form (1NF)

A Table is in first normal form (1NF) if the values in each column arc atomic; that is, there are no repeating groups of data.

The following Faculty Table (Table 2.8) is not normalized. Some faculty members have more than one telephone number listed in the phone column. These are called repeating groups.

In order to convert this Table to the first normal form, the data must be atomic. In other words, the repeating rows must be broken into two or more atomic rows. Table 2.9 illustrates the Faculty Table in 1NF where repeating groups have been removed. Now it is in first normal form.

2.7.2 Second Normal Form (2NF)

A Table is in second normal form (2NF) if it is already in 1NF and every non-key column is fully dependent upon the primary key.

This implies that if the primary key consists of a single column, then the Table in 1NF is automatically in 2NF. The second part of the definition implies that if the key is composite, then none of the non-key columns will depend upon just one of the columns that participate in the composite key.

The Faculty Table in Table 2.9 is in first normal form. However, it has a composite primary key made up of faculty_id and office. The phone number depends on a part of the primary key, office, and not on the whole primary key. This can lead to update and deletion anomalies, as mentioned previously.

TABLE 2.8
Unnormalized Faculty Table with Repeating Groups

faculty_id	faculty_name	office	phone
A52990	Black Anderson	MTC-218, SHB-205	750–378–9987, 555–255–8897
A77587	Debby Angles	MTC-320	750–330–2276
B66750	Alice Brown	MTC-257	750–330–6650
B78880	Ying Bai	MTC-211, SHB-105	750–378–1148, 555–246–4582
B86590	Davis Bhalla	MTC-214	750–378–1061
H99118	Jeff Henry	MTC-336	750–330–8650
J33486	Steve Johnson	MTC-118	750–330–1116
K69880	Jenney King	MTC-324	750–378–1230

TABLE 2.9
Normalized Faculty Table

faculty_id	faculty_name	office	phone
A52990	Black Anderson	MTC-218	750–378–9987
A52990	Black Anderson	SHB-205	555–255–8897
A77587	Debby Angles	MTC-320	750–330–2276
B66750	Alice Brown	MTC-257	750–330–6650
B78880	Ying Bai	MTC-211	750–378–1148
B78880	Ying Bai	SHB-105	555–246–4582
B86590	Davis Bhalla	MTC-214	750–378–1061
H99118	Jeff Henry	MTC-336	750–330–8650
J33486	Steve Johnson	MTC-118	750–330–1116
K69880	Jenney King	MTC-324	750–378–1230

Old Faculty table in 1NF

faculty_id	faculty_name	office	phone
A52990	Black Anderson	MTC-218	750-378-9987
A52990	Black Anderson	SHB-205	555-255-8897
A77587	Debby Angles	MTC-320	750-330-2276
B66750	Alice Brown	MTC-257	750-330-6650
B78880	Ying Bai	MTC-211	750-378-1148
B78880	Ying Bai	SHB-105	555-246-4582
B86590	Davis Bhalla	MTC-214	750-378-1061
H99118	Jeff Henry	MTC-336	750-330-8650
J33486	Steve Johnson	MTC-118	750-330-1116
K69880	Jenney King	MTC-324	750-378-1230

New Faculty table

faculty_id	faculty_name
A52990	Black Anderson
A52990	Black Anderson
A77587	Debby Angles
B66750	Alice Brown
B78880	Ying Bai
B78880	Ying Bai
B86590	Davis Bhalla
H99118	Jeff Henry
J33486	Steve Johnson
K69880	Jenney King

New Office table

office	phone	faculty_id
MTC-218	750-378-9987	A52990
SHB-205	555-255-8897	A52990
MTC-320	750-330-2276	A77587
MTC-257	750-330-6650	B66750
MTC-211	750-378-1148	B78880
SHB-105	555-246-4582	B78880
MTC-214	750-378-1061	B86590
MTC-336	750-330-8650	H99118
MTC-118	750-330-1116	J33486
MTC-324	750-378-1230	K69880

FIGURE 2.8 Converting Faulty Table into 2NF by decomposing the old Table into two, Faculty and Office.

By splitting the old Faculty Table (Figure 2.8) into two new Tables, Faculty and Office, we can remove the dependencies mentioned earlier. Now the faculty Table has a primary key, faculty_id, and the Office Table has a primary key, office. The non-key columns in both Tables now depend only on the primary keys.

2.7.3 Third Normal Form (3NF)

A Table is in third normal form (3NF) if it is already in 2NF and every non-key column is non-transitively dependent upon the primary key. In other words, all non-key columns are mutually independent, but at the same time, they are fully dependent upon the primary key only.

Another way of stating this is that in order to achieve 3NF, no column should depend upon any non-key column. If column B depends on column A, then A is said to functionally determine column B; hence the term determinant. Another definition of 3NF says that the Table should be in 2NF, and the only determinants it contains are candidate keys.

For the Course Table in Table 2.10, all non-key columns depend on the primary key—course_id. In addition, the name and phone columns also depend on faculty_id. This Table is in second normal form, but it suffers from update, addition and deletion anomalies because of transitive dependencies.

TABLE 2.10
The Old Course Table

course_id	course	classroom	faculty_id	faculty_name	phone
CSC-131A	Computers in Society	TC-109	A52990	Black Anderson	750–378–9987
CSC-131B	Computers in Society	TC-114	B66750	Alice Brown	750–330–6650
CSC-131C	Computers in Society	TC-109	A52990	Black Anderson	750–378–9987
CSC-131D	Computers in Society	TC-109	B86590	Davis Bhalla	750–378–1061
CSC-131E	Computers in Society	TC-301	B66750	Alice Brown	750–330–6650
CSC-131I	Computers in Society	TC-109	A52990	Black Anderson	750–378–9987
CSC-132A	Introduction to Programming	TC-303	J33486	Steve Johnson	750–330–1116
CSC-132B	Introduction to Programming	TC-302	B78880	Ying Bai	750–378–1148

TABLE 2.11
The New Course Table

course_id	course	classroom
CSC-131A	Computers in Society	TC-109
CSC-131B	Computers in Society	TC-114
CSC-131C	Computers in Society	TC-109
CSC-131D	Computers in Society	TC-109
CSC-131E	Computers in Society	TC-301
CSC-131I	Computers in Society	TC-109
CSC-132A	Introduction to Programming	TC-303
CSC-132B	Introduction to Programming	TC-302

TABLE 2.12
The New Instructor Table

faculty_id	faculty_name	phone
A52990	Black Anderson	750–378–9987
B66750	Alice Brown	750–330–6650
A52990	Black Anderson	750–378–9987
B86590	Davis Bhalla	750–378–1061
B66750	Alice Brown	750–330–6650
A52990	Black Anderson	750–378–9987
J33486	Steve Johnson	750–330–1116
B78880	Ying Bai	750–378–1148
A77587	Debby Angles	750–330–2276

In order to conform to third normal form, we can split this Table into two Tables, Course and Instructor (Tables 2.11 and 2.12). Now we have eliminated the transitive dependencies that are apparent in the Course Table in Table 2.10.

2.8 DATABASE COMPONENTS IN SOME POPULAR DATABASES

All databases allow for storage, retrieval and management of the data. Simple databases provide basic services to accomplish these tasks. Many database providers, like Microsoft SQL Server and Oracle, provide additional services that necessitate storing many components in the database other than data. These components, such as views, stored procedures and so on, are collectively called database objects. In this section, we will discuss various objects that make up MS Access, SQL Server and Oracle databases.

There are two major types of databases, *file server* and *client server.*

In a file server database, data is stored in a file, and each user of the database retrieves the data, displays the data or modifies the data directly from or to the file. In a client server database, the data is also stored in a file; however, all these operations are mediated through a master program called a server. MS Access is a file server database, whereas Microsoft SQL Server and Oracle are client server databases. Client server databases have several advantages over file server databases. These include minimizing the chance of crashes, provision of features for recovery, enforcement of security, better performance and more efficient use of the network compared to file server databases.

2.8.1 Microsoft Access Databases

The Microsoft Access Database Engine is a collection of information stored in a systematic way that forms the underlying component of a database. Also called Jet (Joint Engine Technology), it allows the manipulation of a relational database. It offers a single interface that other software may use to access Microsoft databases. The supporting software is developed to provide security, integrity, indexing, record locking and so on. By executing the MS Access program, MSACCESS.EXE, you can see the database engine at work and the user interface it provides. Figure 2.9 shows how a Java application accesses the MS Access database via the ACE OLE database provider.

2.8.1.1 Database File

An Access database is made up of a number of components called objects, which are stored in a single file referred to as *database file*. As new objects are created or more data is added to the database, this file gets bigger. This is a complex file that stores objects like Tables, queries, forms, reports, macros and modules. Access files have an. mdb (Microsoft DataBase) extension. Some of these objects help the user work with the database; others are useful for displaying database information in a comprehensible and easy-to-read format.

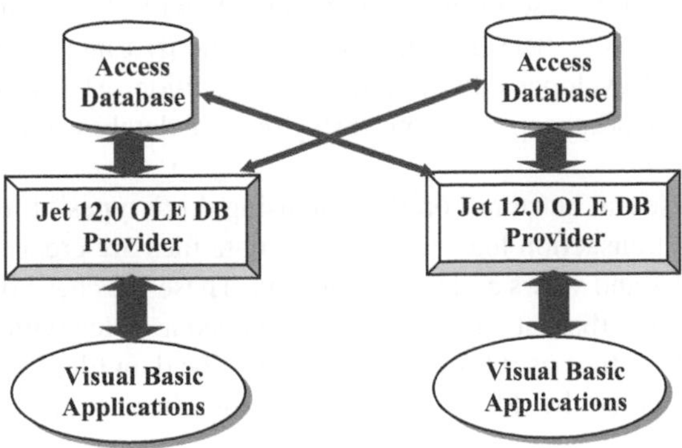

FIGURE 2.9 Microsoft Access database illustration.

2.8.1.2 Tables

Before you can create a Table in Access, you must create a database container and give it a name with the extension. mdb. Database creation is simple process and is explained in detail with an example later in this chapter. Suffice it to say that a Table is made up of columns and rows. Columns are referred to as fields, which are attributes of an entity. Rows are referred to as records, also called tuples.

2.8.1.3 Queries

One of the main purposes of storing data in a database is that the data may be retrieved later as needed without having to write complex programs. This purpose is accomplished in Access and other databases by writing SQL statements. A group of such statements is called a query. It enables you to retrieve, update and display data in the Tables. You may display data from more than one Table by using a Join operation. In addition, you may insert or delete data in the Tables.

Access also provides a visual graphic user interface to create queries. This bypasses writing SQL statements and makes it appealing to beginning and not-so-savvy users, who can use wizards or a GUI interface to create queries. Queries can extract information in a variety of ways. You can make them as simple or as complex as you like. You may specify various criteria to get desired information or perform comparisons, or you may want to perform some calculations and obtain the results. In essence, operators, functions and expressions are the building blocks for Access operation.

2.8.2 SQL Server Databases

The Microsoft SQL Server Database Engine is a service for storing and processing data in either relational (tabular) format or as XML documents. Various tasks performed by the Database Engine include:

- Designing and creating a database to hold relational Tables or XML documents
- Accessing and modifying the data stored in the database
- Implementing Web sites and applications
- Building procedures
- Optimizing the performance of the database

The SQL Server database is a complex entity, made up of multiple components. It is more complex than MS Access database, which can be simply copied and distributed. Certain procedures have to be followed for copying and distributing a SQL server database.

SQL Server is used by a diverse group of professionals with diverse needs and requirements. To satisfy different needs, SQL Server comes in five editions: Enterprise edition, Standard edition, Workgroup edition, Developer edition and Express edition. The most common editions are Enterprise, Standard and Workgroup. It is noteworthy that the database engine is virtually the same in all of these editions.

A SQL Server database can be stored on the disk using three types of files—primary data files, secondary data files and transaction log files. Primary data files are created first and contain user-defined objects like Tables and views and system objects. These files have the extension. mdf. If the database grows too big for a disk, it can be stored as secondary files with the extension. ndf. The SQL Server still treats these files as if they were together. The data file is made up of many objects. The transaction log files carry the. ldf extension. All transactions to the database are recorded in this file.

Figure 2.10 illustrates the structure of the SQL Server Database. Each Java application has to access the server, which in turn accesses the SQL database.

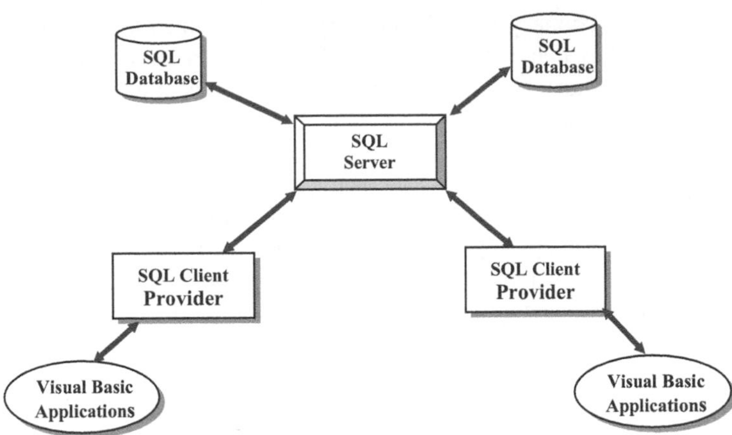

FIGURE 2.10 SQL Server database structure.

2.8.2.1 Data Files

A data file is a conglomeration of objects, which includes Tables, keys, views, stored procedures and others. All these objects are necessary for the efficient operation of the database.

2.8.2.2 Tables

The data in a relational database resides in Tables. These are the building blocks of the database. Each Table consists of columns and rows. Columns represent various attributes or fields in a Table. Each row represents one record. For example, one record in the Faculty Table consists of name, office, phone, college, title and email. Each field has a distinct data type, meaning that it can contain only one type of data, such as numeric or character. Tables are the first objects created in a database.

2.8.2.3 Views

Views are virtual Tables, meaning that they do not contain any data. They are stored as queries in the database, which are executed when needed. A view can contain data from one or more Tables. The views can provide database security. Sensitive information in a database can be excluded by including non-sensitive information in a view and providing user access to the views instead of all Tables in a database. The views can also hide the complexities of a database. A user can be using a view that is made up of multiple Tables, but it appears as a single Table to the user. The user can execute queries against a view just like a Table.

2.8.2.4 Stored Procedures

Users write queries to retrieve, display or manipulate data in the database. These queries can be stored on the client machine or on the server. There are advantages associated with storing SQL queries on the server rather than on the client machine. It has to do with the network performance. Usually users use same queries over and over again, and frequently different users are trying to access the same data. Instead of sending the same queries on the network repeatedly, it improves network performance and executes queries faster if the queries are stored on the server, where they are compiled and saved as stored procedures. The users can simply call the stored procedure with a simple command like *execute stored_procedure* A.

2.8.2.5 Keys and Relationships

A *primary key* is created for each Table in the database to efficiently access records and to ensure *entity integrity*. This implies that each record in a Table is unique in some way. Therefore, no two records can have the same primary key. The primary key is defined as a globally unique identifier. Moreover, a primary key may not have a null value, that is, missing data. SQL Server creates a unique index for each primary key. This ensures fast and efficient access to data. One or more columns can be combined to designate a primary key.

In a relational database, relationships between Tables can be logically defined with the help of *foreign keys*. A foreign key of one record in a Table points specifically to a primary key of a record in another Table. This allows a user to join multiple Tables and retrieve information from more than one Table at a time. Foreign keys also enforce *referential integrity*, a defined relationship between the Tables that does not allow insertion or deletion of records in a Table unless the foreign key of a record in one Table matches a primary key of a record in another Table. In other words, a record in one Table cannot have a foreign key that does not point to a primary key in another Table. Additionally, a primary key may not be deleted if there are foreign keys in another Table pointing to it. The foreign key values associated with a primary key must be deleted first. Referential integrity protects related data stored in different Tables from corruption.

2.8.2.6 Indexes

Indexes are used to find records quickly and efficiently in a Table just like one would use an index in a book. SQL Server uses two types of indexes to retrieve and update data—clustered and non-clustered.

A *clustered index* sorts the data in a Table so that the data can be accessed efficiently. It is akin to a dictionary or a phone book where records are arranged alphabetically, so one can go directly to a specific letter and from there search sequentially for the specific record. A clustered index is like an inverted tree. The index structure is called a B-tree, for binary tree. You start with the root page at the top and find the location of other pages further down at secondary level, following to the tertiary level and so on until you find the desired record. The very bottom pages are the leaf pages and contain the actual data. There can be only one clustered index per Table because clustered indexes physically rearrange the data.

Non-clustered indexes do not physically rearrange the data as do clustered indexes. They also consist of a binary tree with various levels of pages. The major difference, however, is that the leaves do not contain the actual data as in clustered indexes; instead, they contain pointers that point to the corresponding records in the Table. These pointers are called row locators.

Indexes can be unique, where duplicate keys are not allowed, or non-unique, which permits duplicate keys. Any column that can be used to access data can be used to generate an index. Usually the primary and the foreign key columns are used to create indexes.

2.8.2.7 Transaction Log Files

A transaction is a logical group of SQL statements that carry out a unit of work. Client server databases use log files to keep track of transactions that are applied to the database. For example, before an update is applied to a database, the database server creates an entry in the transaction log to generate a before picture of the data in a Table and then applies a transaction and creates another entry to generate an after picture of the data in that Table. This keeps track of all the operations performed on a database. Transaction logs can be used to recover data in case of crashes or disasters. Transaction logs are automatically maintained by SQL Server.

2.8.3 Oracle Databases

Oracle was designed to be platform independent, making it architecturally more complex than the SQL Server database. An Oracle database contains more files than a SQL Server database.

The Oracle DBMS comes in three levels: Enterprise, Standard and Personal. The Enterprise edition is the most powerful and is suiTable for large installations using a large number of transactions in a multi-user environment. The Standard edition is also used by high-level multi-user installations.

It lacks some of the utilities available in the Enterprise edition. The Personal edition is used in a single-user environment for developing database applications. The database engine components are virtually the same for all three editions.

The Oracle architecture is made up of several components, including an Oracle server, Oracle instance and Oracle database. The Oracle server contains several files, processes and memory structures. Some of these are used to improve the performance of the database and ensure database recovery in case of a crash. The Oracle server consists of an Oracle instance and an Oracle database. An Oracle instance consists of background processes and memory structures. Background processes perform input/output and monitor other Oracle processes for better performance and reliability. An Oracle database consists of data files that provide the actual physical storage for the data.

2.8.3.1 Data Files

The main purpose of a database is to store and retrieve data. It consists of a collection of data that is treated as a unit. An Oracle database has a logical and physical structure. The logical layer consists of Table spaces, necessary for the smooth operation of an Oracle installation. Data files make up the physical layer of the database. These consist of three types of files: *data files*, which contain actual data in the database; *redo logfiles*, which contain records of modifications made to the database for future recovery in case of failure; and *control files*, which are used to maintain and verify database integrity. The Oracle server uses other files that are not part of the database. These include a *parameter file* that defines the characteristics of an Oracle instance; a *password file* used for authentication; and *archived redo log* files, which are copies of the redo log files necessary for recovery from failure. A partial list of some of the components follows.

2.8.3.2 Tables

Users can store data in a regular Table, partitioned Table, index-organized Table or clustered Table. A *regular Table* is the default Table, as in other databases. Rows can be stored in any order. A *partitioned Table* has one or more partitions where rows are stored. Partitions are useful for large Tables that can be queried by several processes concurrently. *Index-organized Tables* provide fast key-based access for queries involving exact matches. The Table may have an index on one or more of its columns. Instead of using two storage spaces for the Table and a B-tree index, a single storage space is used to store both the B-tree and other columns. A *clustered Table* or group of Tables share the same block, called a cluster. They are grouped together because they share common columns and are frequently used together. Clusters have a cluster key for identifying the rows that need to be stored together. Cluster keys are independent of the primary key and may be made up of one or more columns. Clusters are created to improve performance.

2.8.3.3 Views

Views are like virtual Tables and are used in a similar fashion as in the SQL Server databases discussed previously.

2.8.3.4 Stored Procedures

In Oracle, functions and procedures may be saved as stored program units. Multiple input arguments (parameters) may be passed as input to functions and procedures; however, functions return only one value as output, whereas procedures may return multiple values as output. The advantages to creating and using stored procedures are the same as mentioned previously for SQL Server. By storing procedures on the server, individual SQL statements do not have to be transmitted over the network, thus reducing network traffic. In addition, commonly used SQL statements are saved as functions or procedures and may be used again and again by various users, thus saving users from rewriting the same code over and over again. Stored procedures should be made flexible so that different users are able to pass input information to the procedure in the form of arguments or parameters and get the desired output.

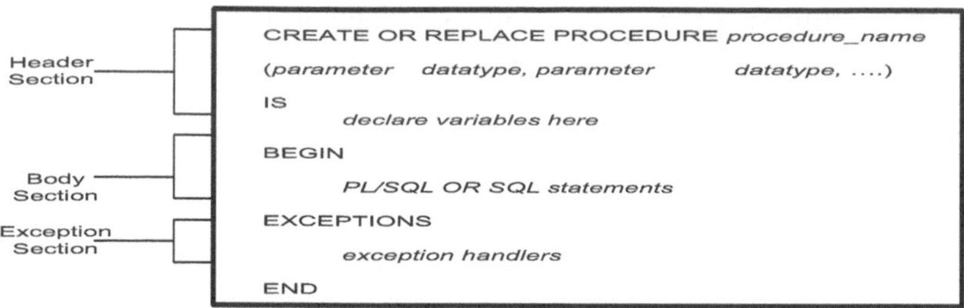

FIGURE 2.11 Syntax for creating a stored procedure in Oracle.

Figure 2.11 shows the syntax to create a stored procedure in Oracle. It has three sections—a header, a body and an exception section. The procedure is defined in the header section. Input and output parameters, along with their data types, are declared here and transmit information to or from the procedure. The body section of the procedure starts with the keyword BEGIN and consists of SQL statements. The exceptions section of the procedure begins with the keyword EXCEPTION and contains exception handlers that are designed to handle the occurrence of some conditions that change the normal flow of execution.

Indexes are created to provide direct access to rows. An index is a tree structure. Indexes can be classified by their logical design or their physical implementation. Logical classification is based on an application perspective, whereas physical classification is based on how the indexes are stored. Indexes can be partitioned or nonpartitioned. Large Tables use partitioned indexes, which spread an index to multiple Table spaces, thus decreasing contention for index look-up and increasing manageability. An index may consist of a single column or multiple columns; it may be unique or non-unique. Some of these indexes are outlined in the following.

Function-based indexes precompute the value of a function or expression of one or more columns and store it in an index. They can be created as a B-tree or as a bitmap. They can improve the performance of queries performed on Tables that rarely change.

Domain indexes are application specific and are created and managed by the user or applications. Single-column indexes can be built on text, spatial, scalar, object or Large Object (LOB) data types.

B-tree indexes store a list of row IDs for each key. The structure of a B-tree index is similar to the ones in SQL Server described previously. The leaf nodes contain indexes that point to rows in a Table. The leaf blocks allow scanning of the index in either ascending or descending order. The Oracle server maintains all indexes when insert, update or delete operations are performed on a Table.

Bitmap indexes are useful when columns have low cardinality and a large number of rows. For example, a column may contain a few distinct values like Y/N for marital status or M/F for gender. A bitmap is organized like a B-tree, where the leaf nodes store a bitmap instead of row IDs. When changes are made to the key columns, the bitmaps must be modified.

2.8.3.5 Initialization Parameter Files

The Oracle server must read the initialization parameter file before starting an Oracle database instance. There are two types of initialization parameter files: static parameter files and persistent parameter files. An initialization parameter file contains a list of instance parameters, the name of the database the instance is associated with, the name and location of control files and information about the undo segments. Multiple initialization parameter files can exist to optimize performance.

2.8.3.6 Control Files

A control file is a small binary file that defines the current state of the database. Before a database can be opened, the control file is read to determine if the database is in a valid state or not. It maintains the integrity of the database. Oracle uses a single control file per database. It is maintained continuously by the server and can be maintained only by the Oracle server. It cannot be edited by a user or database administrator. A control file contains: the database name and identifier, time stamp of database creation, Tablespace name, names and location of data files and redo logfiles, current log file sequence number and archive and backup information.

2.8.3.7 Redo Log Files

Oracle's redo log files provide a way to recover data in the event of a database failure. All transactions are written to a redo log buffer and passed on to the redo log files.

Redo log files record all changes to the data, provide a recovery mechanism and can be organized into groups. A set of identical copies of online redo log files is called a redo log file group. The Oracle server needs a minimum of two online redo logfile groups for normal operations. The initial set of redo log file groups and members are created during database creation. Redo log files are used in a cyclic fashion. Each redo log file group is identified by a log sequence number and is overwritten each time the log is reused. In other words, when a redo log file is full, then the log writer moves to the second redo log file. After the second one is full, the first one is reused.

2.8.3.8 Password Files

Depending upon whether the database is administered locally or remotely, one can choose either operating system or password file authentication to authenticate database administrators. Oracle provides a password utility to create a password file. Administrators use the GRANT command to provide access to the database using the password file.

2.9 CREATE A NEW ORACLE XE 18C SAMPLE DATABASE

After you finish the installation of Oracle 18c Express Edition database (refer to Appendix A), you can begin to use it to connect to the server and build our database.

Now let's start to create a new Oracle 18c XE sample database, **CSE _ DEPT**.

2.9.1 Connect to Default Oracle Database from the Oracle SQL Developer

Open the Oracle SQL Developer (refer to Appendix C to download and install it) by clicking on the icon stored in the taskbar. The opened Developer is shown in Figure 2.12. Perform the following operations to connect to the default Oracle database, **XE**:

1) On the **Database Detected** panel, some default or installed Oracle databases are displayed. One of them is the **XE** database.
2) Click on the **Create a Connection Manually** button to try to connect to it.
3) In the opened New/Select Database Connection wizard, as shown in Figure 2.13, enter all connection parameters into the related fields on this wizard, which are shown in Figure 2.13. The password is **oracle _ 18c**, which is identical to the one we used when we installed this database (refer to Appendix A).
4) Now let's first test this connection by clicking on the **Test** button. A successful connection message should be displayed to indicate that this connection is OK.
5) Then click on the **Connect** button to actually connect to our **XE** database. Immediately, you can see that the default database, **XE**, has been connected and is displayed in the **Connections** panel under the **Oracle Connections** tab on the left.

Next we need to create our customer database, **CSE _ DEPT**, and add our five Tables one by one into this sample database.

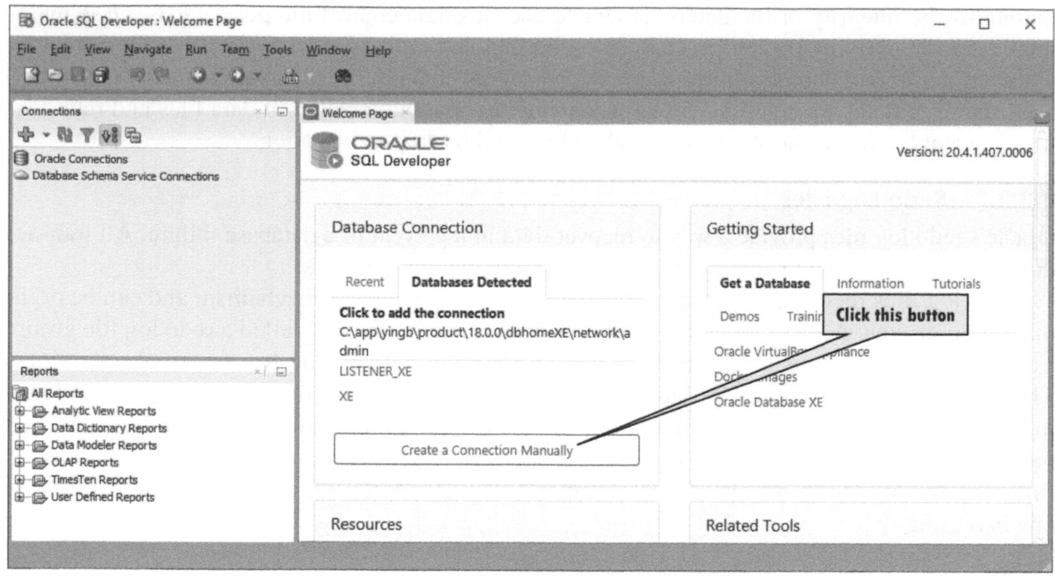

FIGURE 2.12 The opened Oracle SQL Developer (Copyrighted by Oracle and used with permission).

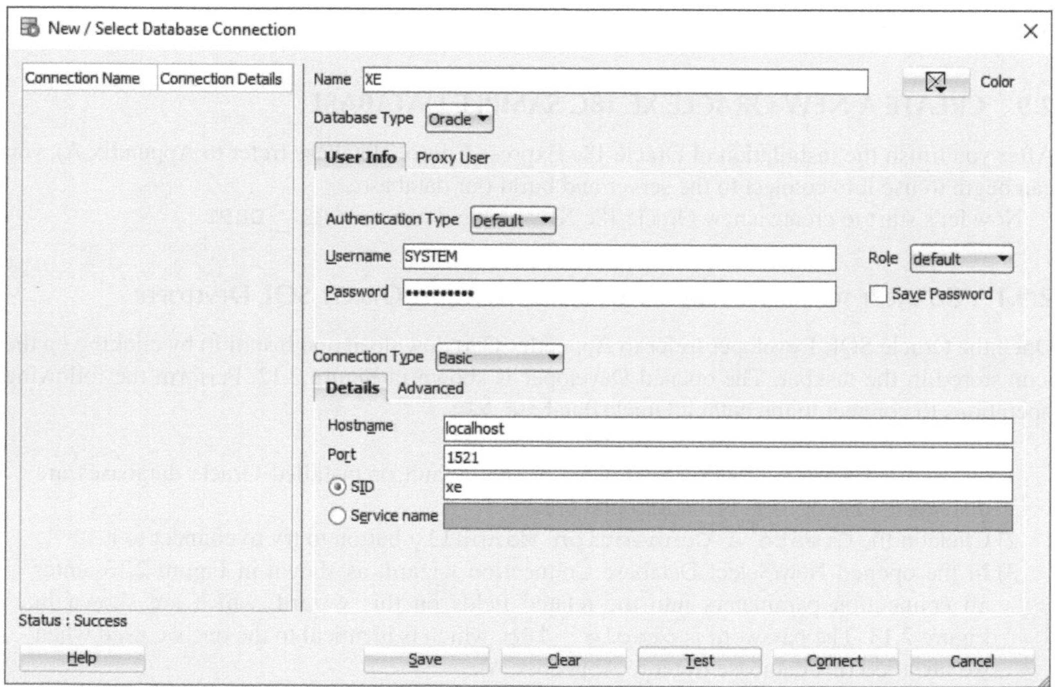

FIGURE 2.13 The opened New/Select Database Connection wizard (Copyrighted by Oracle and used with permission).

2.9.2 Create an Oracle User Account for the User Schema

After the default Oracle 18c XE database is connected, we need to create our customer Oracle database. Creating a customer database in Oracle18c XE is different from creating a customer database in the Microsoft SQL Server database management system (MDBS). In Oracle 18c XE, you need to create a new user or a new user account if you want to create a new customer database. Each user or user account is related to a schema or a database, and the name of each user is equal to the name of the associated schema or the database.

Therefore, you need to perform two steps to create a customer Oracle database:

1) Create a new customer user or user account.
2) Create Oracle database objects, such as Tables, schemas and relations, under that user account.

First, let's create a user account with Oracle SQL Developer now.

Perform the following operations to create a new user account, **`CSE _ DEPT`**, which is identical to our sample database:

1) In the connected XE database in the Oracle SQL Developer, as shown in Figure 2.14, expand the connected XE database folder and scroll down to the last folder named **`Other Users`**. Right-click on this folder and select **`Create User`** from the popup menu to open the Create User wizard, as shown in Figure 2.15.
2) Enter our user's name, **`CSE _ DEPT`**, into the User Name box with your desired password. In our case, it still is **`oracle _ 18c`**. Enter this password in both the **`New Password`** and **`Confirm Password`** boxes, as shown in Figure 2.15. Here we want to create all our components, including Tables, relations and keys, and embed them in our single user account, which can be considered a database.
3) For all options, such as **`Password Expired`**, **`Operating System User`**, **`Account is Locked`** and **`Edition Enabled`**, just keep them unchecked with their default status, since we do not want to apply any limitations for our account.
4) Select **`SYSTEM`** and **`TEMP`** for the **`Default Tablespace`** and **`Temporary Tablespace`** since we need to assign this account Administration privilege (Figure 2.15).

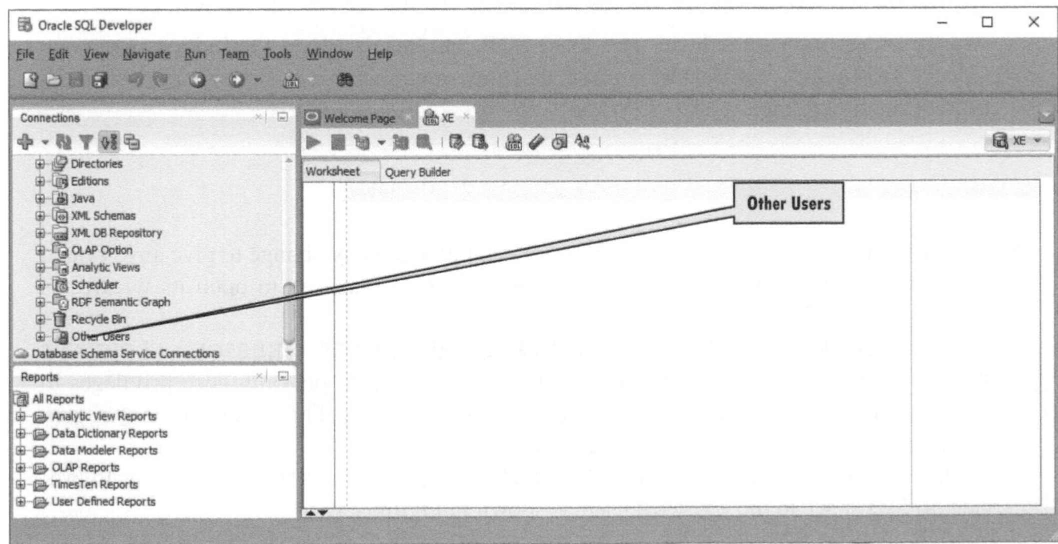

FIGURE 2.14 All data components related to the default database XE (Copyrighted by Oracle and used with permission).

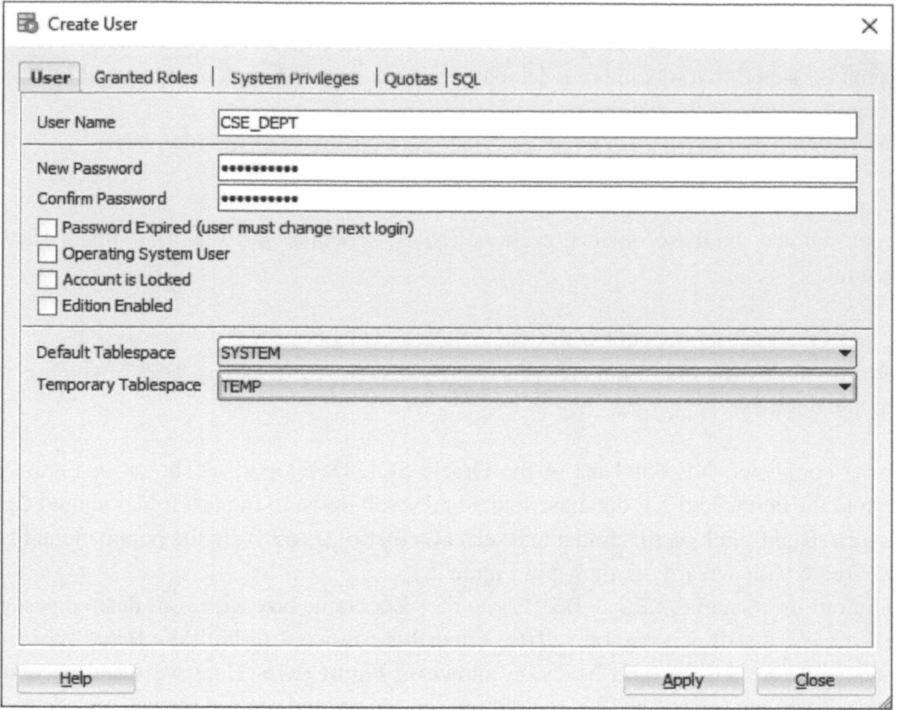

FIGURE 2.15 The opened Create User wizard (Copyrighted by Oracle and used with permission).

In an Oracle database, there are two kinds of users, container database (CBD) users and pluggable database (PDB) users. The former is called a common user, but the latter is a local user. To create a common user for CBD, one needs to use C## or c## as a prefix to the user name. It is the same to create a local user for a PDB.

In order to create a local user for a PDB, one needs to set the hidden parameter **"_ORACLE_SCRIPT"=true**; then one can create a user without a C## in front of the user name.

5) For the **Granted Roles** setups, we do not want to make any change to give any granted access to this user, so click on the **System Privileges** tab to open its wizard, as shown in Figure 2.16.
6) Select the **CREATE PROCEDURE**, **CREATE RULE**, **CREATE SESSION** and **CREATE Table** items by checking them in the list, since we want to provide these privileges to enable the user to create new sessions, procedures and Tables. Then click on the **Quotas** tab to open its wizard, as shown in Figure 2.17.
7) Click on the **SYSTEM** line and enter **50** and **M** to the **Quota** and **Units** columns to provide 50 MB space to the **SYSTEM** user, as shown in Figure 2.17.
8) Finally, open the **SQL** wizard by clicking on the **SQL** tab, as shown in Figure 2.18.

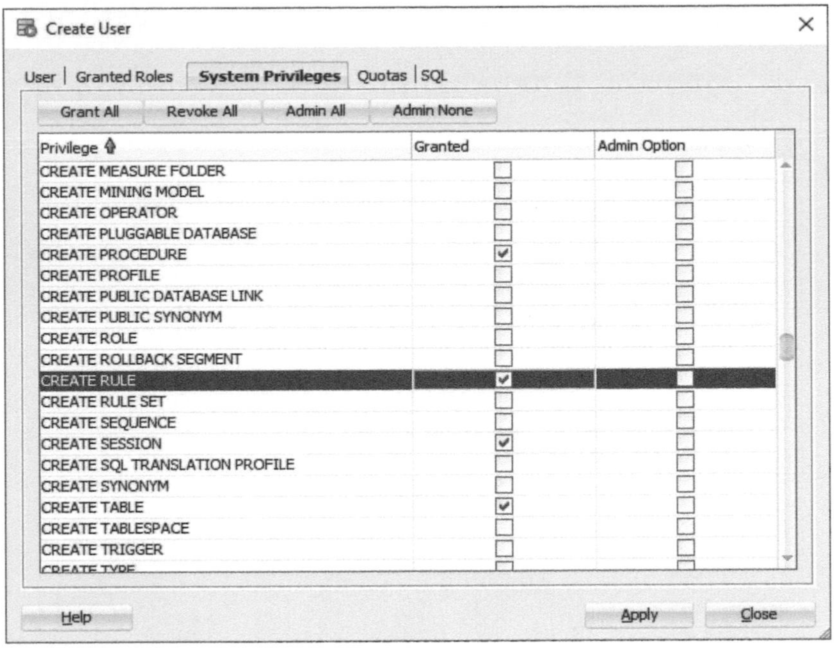

Create User

User | Granted Roles | System Privileges | Quotas | SQL

Grant All | Revoke All | Admin All | Admin None

Privilege	Granted	Admin Option
CREATE MEASURE FOLDER	☐	☐
CREATE MINING MODEL	☐	☐
CREATE OPERATOR	☐	☐
CREATE PLUGGABLE DATABASE	☐	☐
CREATE PROCEDURE	☑	☐
CREATE PROFILE	☐	☐
CREATE PUBLIC DATABASE LINK	☐	☐
CREATE PUBLIC SYNONYM	☐	☐
CREATE ROLE	☐	☐
CREATE ROLLBACK SEGMENT	☐	☐
CREATE RULE	☑	☐
CREATE RULE SET	☐	☐
CREATE SEQUENCE	☐	☐
CREATE SESSION	☑	☐
CREATE SQL TRANSLATION PROFILE	☐	☐
CREATE SYNONYM	☐	☐
CREATE TABLE	☑	☐
CREATE TABLESPACE	☐	☐
CREATE TRIGGER	☐	☐

Help | Apply | Close

FIGURE 2.16 The opened System Privileges wizard (Copyrighted by Oracle and used with permission).

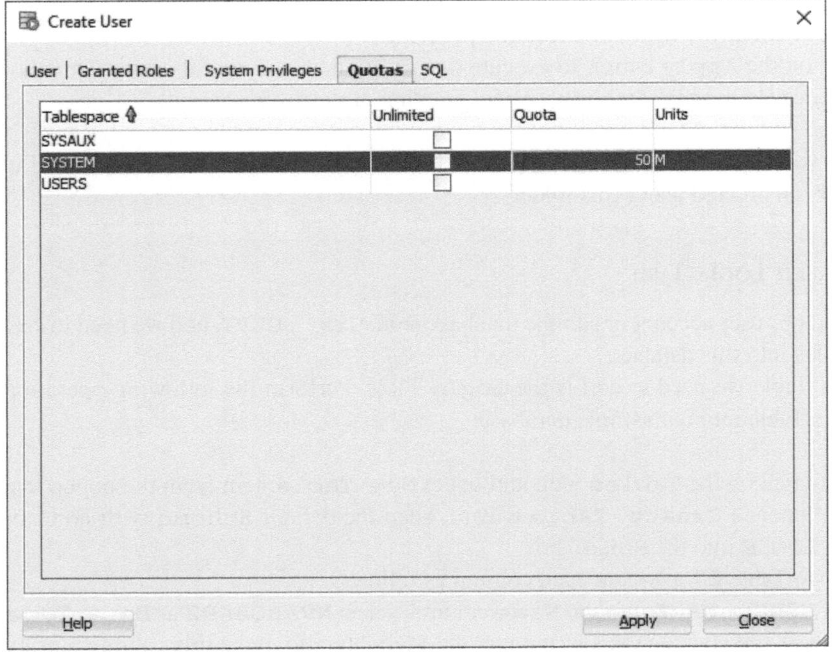

FIGURE 2.17 The opened Quotas wizard (Copyrighted by Oracle and used with permission).

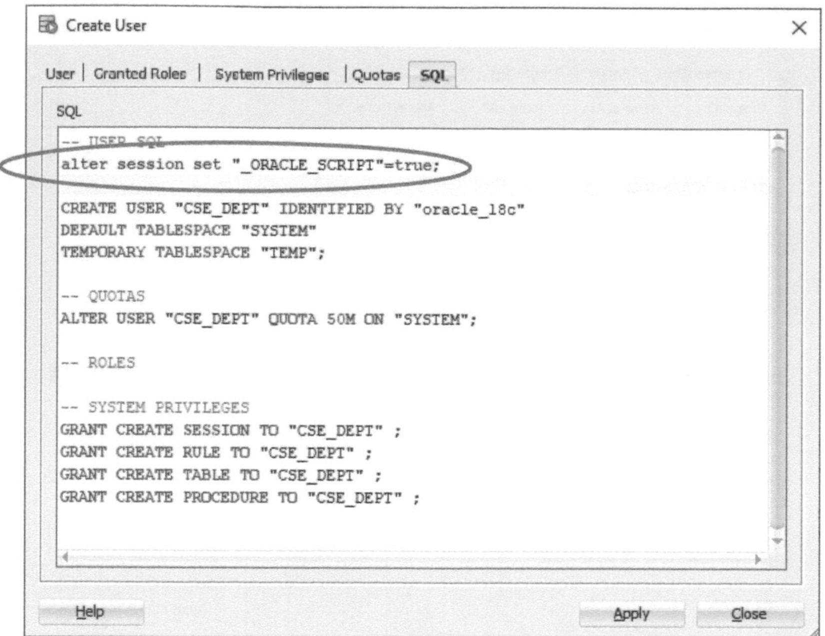

FIGURE 2.18 The opened and completed SQL wizard (Copyrighted by Oracle and used with permission).

9) To use this hidden parameter, enter **alter session set "_ORACLE_SCRIPT"=true;** in the first line of this opened SQL wizard, as shown in Figure 2.18. This is critically important to create this local user account; otherwise, you will encounter an error when you apply this creation process.
10) Click on the **Apply** button to execute this creation. A successful execution message will be displayed to indicate the successful creation of this user account.

Now, if you expand the **Other User** folder, you can find that our new created user, **CSE_DEPT**, has been created under this folder.

2.9.3 Create LogIn Table

Now expand our user account or sample database icon, **CSE_DEPT**, and we need to create and add all five Tables into this database.

The first Table we need to add is the **LogIn** Table. Perform the following operations to create and add this Table into our sample database:

1) Right-click on the **Tables** icon and select **New Table** item from the popup menu.
2) In the opened **Create Table** wizard, keep the default **Schema** with no changes and enter **LOGIN** into the **Name:** box.
3) Refer to Table 2.1 to create each column as follows.
4) Enter **USER_NAME** into the **Name** column, select **NVARCHAR2** as **Data Type** and **50** as **Size**, and click on the space under the **PK** column to make this column a primary key.
5) Click on the + sign on the upper-right corner to add this column into our sample database.
6) In a similar way, complete all other columns, including **PASS_WORD**, **FACULTY_ID** and **STUDENT_ID**, based on the data components in Table 2.1.

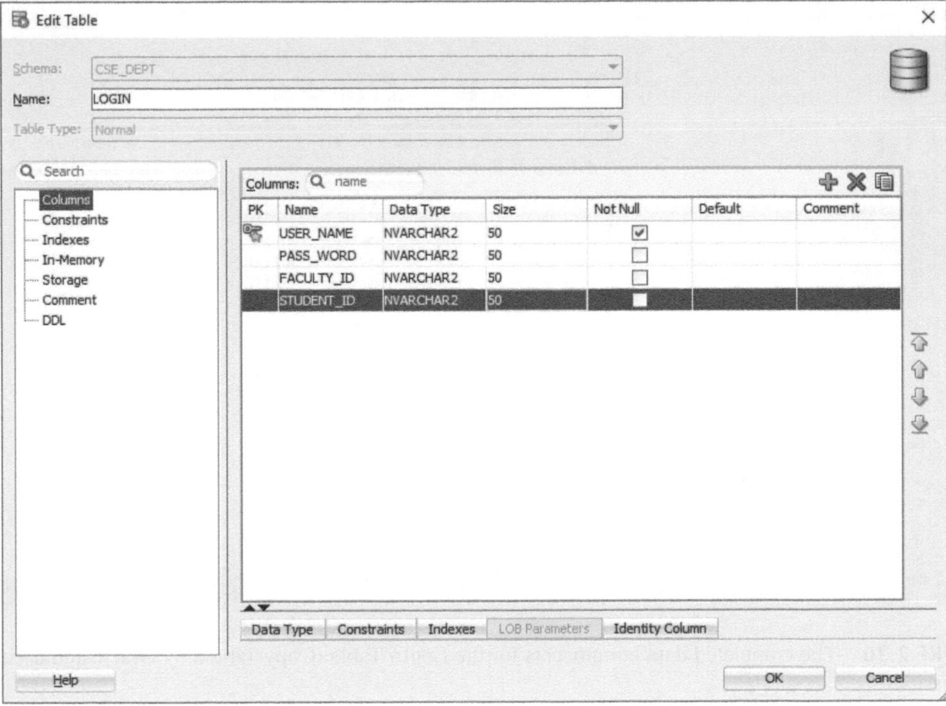

FIGURE 2.19 The completed design view of the LogIn Table (Copyrighted by Oracle and used with permission).

7) You can check the **Advanced** checkbox in the upper-right corner to get a detailed view for this Table when you complete this Table, as shown in Figure 2.19.
8) Click on the **OK** button to create and add this Table into our sample database.

Now expand the **Tables** icon on the left, and you can find our new created Table, **LOGIN**. Let's enter all the data for each column one by one based on Table 2.1.

1) Click on the icon for our new created Table, **LOGIN**, to open the detailed view for this Table.
2) Click on the **Data** tab from the opened **LOGIN** Table.
3) Click on the green + icon (**Insert Row**) on the top to add a new row.
4) Enter the first record into this row based on Table 2.1.
5) In a similar way, add all rows to complete this Table.

Finally, go to the **File|Save All** menu item to save these new added records. A **Commit Successful** message should be displayed in the **Message–Log** window under this Table view if these records are successfully added into this Table.

Your finished data records for this Table should look like those shown in Figure 2.20.

2.9.4 Create Faculty Table

Right-click on the **Tables** folder on the left and select the **NewTable** item to open the design view of a new Table, which is shown in Figure 2.21.

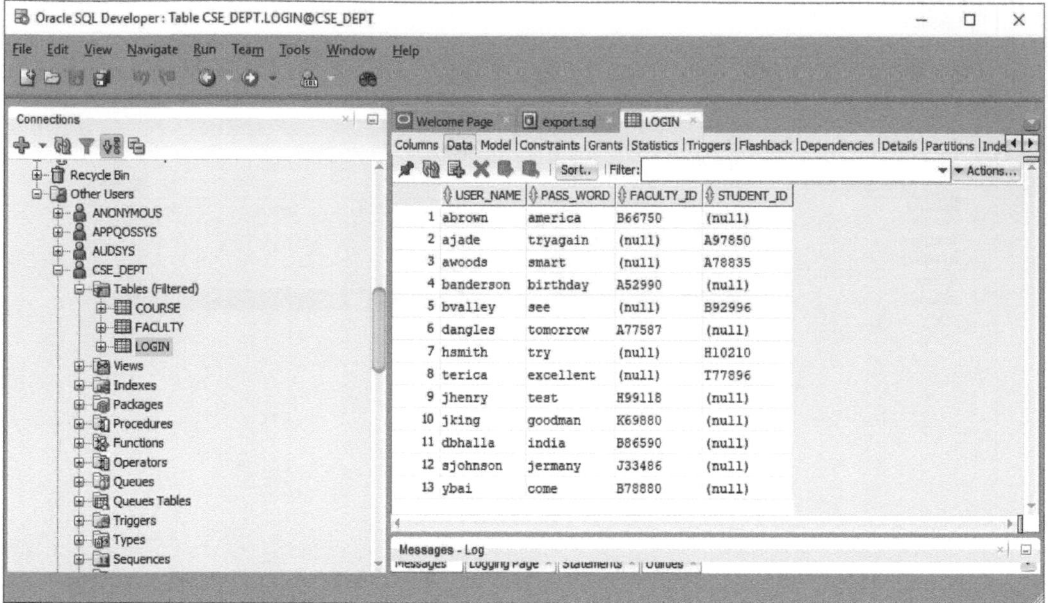

FIGURE 2.20 The completed data components for the LogIn Table (Copyrighted by Oracle and used with permission).

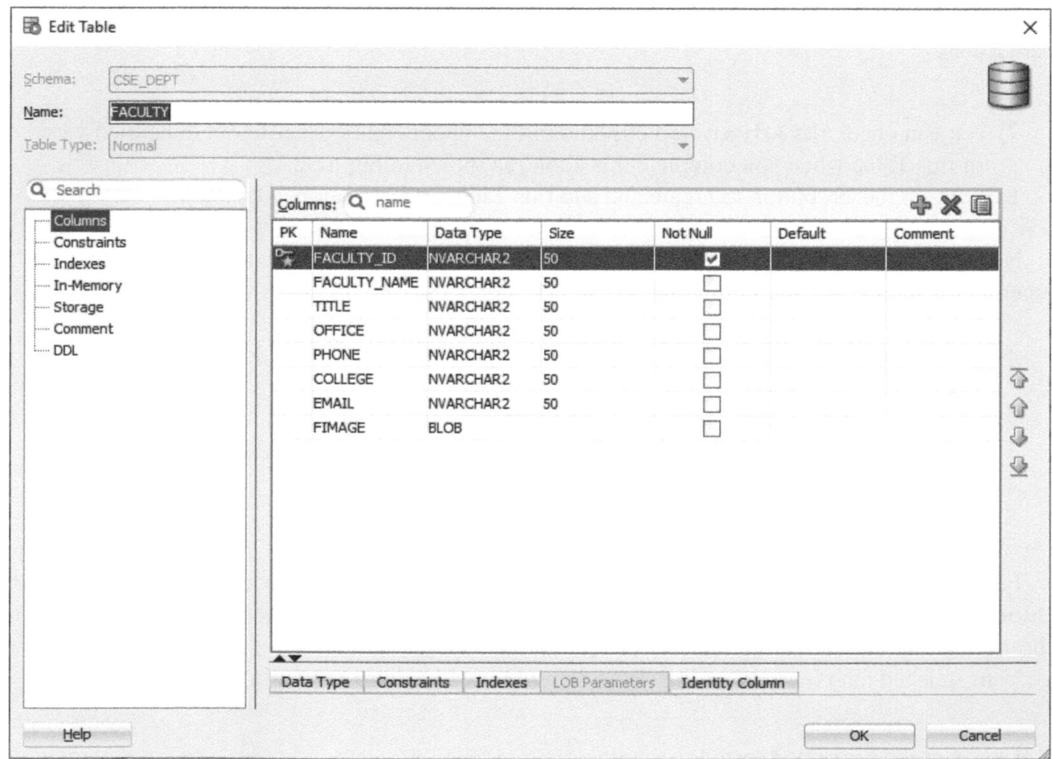

FIGURE 2.21 The design view of the Faculty Table (Copyrighted by Oracle and used with permission).

TABLE 2.13
The Data in the FacultyTable

faculty_id	faculty_name	title	office	phone	college	email	fimage
A52990	Black Anderson	Professor	MTC-218	750–378–9987	Virginia Tech	banderson@ college.edu	NULL
A77587	Debby Angles	Associate Professor	MTC-320	750–330–2276	University of Chicago	dangles@college. edu	NULL
B66750	Alice Brown	Assistant Professor	MTC-257	750–330–6650	University of Florida	abrown@college. edu	NULL
B78880	Ying Bai	Associate Professor	MTC-211	750–378–1148	Florida Atlantic University	ybai@college. edu	NULL
B86590	DavisBhalla	Associate Professor	MTC-214	750–378–1061	University of Notre Dame	dbhalla@college .edu	NULL
H99118	Jeff Henry	Associate Professor	MTC-336	750–330–8650	Ohio State University	jhenry@college. edu	NULL
J33486	Steve Johnson	Distinguished Professor	MTC-118	750–330–1116	Harvard University	sjohnson@ college.edu	NULL
K69880	Jenney King	Professor	MTC-324	750–378–1230	East Florida University	jking@college. edu	NULL

For this Table, we have eight columns: **faculty _ id**, **faculty _ name**, **title**, **office**, **phone**, **college**, **email** and **fimage**. The data types for the columns **faculty _ id** and **faculty _ name** are **nvarchar(50)**, and all other data types, except the **fimage** column, can be either **text** or **nvarchar(50)**, since all of them are string variables. The data type for the **fimage** column is **BLOB**, since all faculty images are stored in this column. The reason we selected **nvarchar(50)** as the data type for **faculty _ id** is that a primary key can work for this data type, but it does not work for **text**.

Do not forget to enter **FACULTY** into the **Name:** box on the top as the name for this Table. The finished design view of the Faculty Table is shown in Figure 2.21. Click on the **OK** button to create this Faculty Table and add it into our sample database.

Now expand the **Tables** icon on the left, and you can see our new created data Table, **FACULTY**. Let's enter all the data for each column one by one based on Table 2.13.

1) Click on the icon for our new created Table, **FACULTY**, to open the detailed view for this Table.
2) Click on the **Data** tab from the opened **FACULTY** Table.
3) Click on the green + icon (**Insert Row**) on the top to add a new row.
4) Enter the first record into this row based on Table 2.13.
5) In a similar way, add all rows to complete this Table.

Your finished **FACULTY** Table should match the one shown in Figure 2.22.

Finally, go to the **File|Save All** menu item to save these new added records. A **Commit Successful** message should be displayed in the **Message–Log** window under this Table view if these records are successfully added into this Table.

For the moment, just keep NULL for the **fimage** column, and we will add actual faculty images later by using Visual Studio.NET and Devexpress controls.

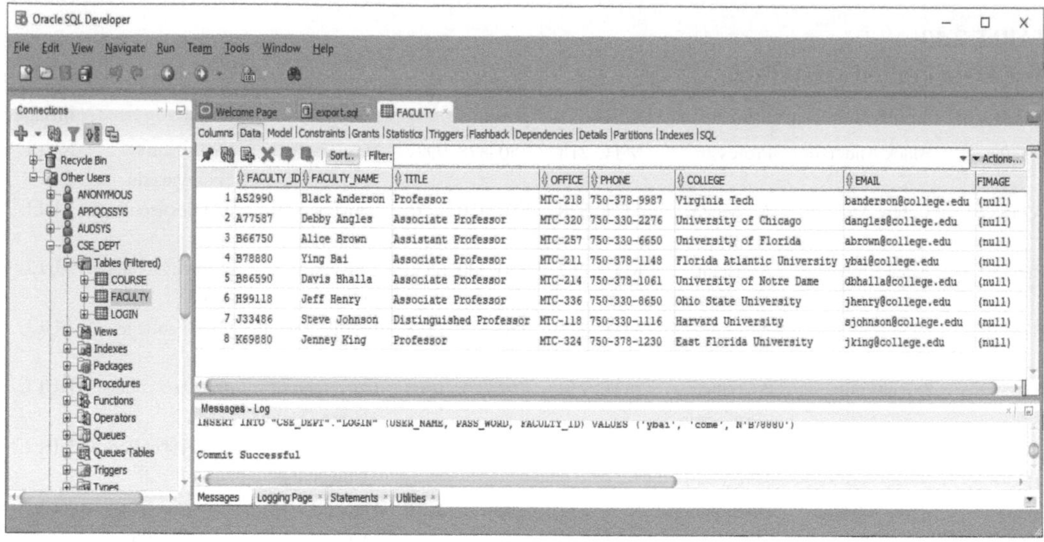

FIGURE 2.22 The completed Faculty Table (Copyrighted by Oracle and used with permission).

2.9.5 Create Other Tables

In a similar way, create the rest of three Tables: **Course**, **Student** and **StudentCourse**. Select **course _ id**, **student _ id** and **s _ course _ id** as the primary keys for these Tables (refer to Tables 2.14, 2.15 and 2.16). For the data type selections, follow the subsequent directions.

The data type selections for the **Course** Table:

- **course _ id**—nvarchar(50) (primary key)
- **credit**—smallint
- **enrollment**—int
- **faculty _ id**—nvarchar(50)
- All other columns—either nvarchar(50) or text

The data type selections for the **Student** Table:

- **student _ id**—nvarchar(50) (primary key)
- **student _ name**—nvarchar(50)
- **gpa**—float
- **credits**—int
- **simage**—BLOB
- All other columns—either nvarchar(50) or text

The data type selections for the **StudentCourse** Table:

- **s _ course _ id**—int (primary key)
- **student _ id**—nvarchar(50)
- **course _ id**—nvarchar(50)
- **credit**—int
- **major**—either nvarchar(50) or text

TABLE 2.14
The Data in the Course Table

course_id	course	credit	classroom	schedule	enrollment	faculty_id
CSC-131A	Computers in Society	3	TC-109	M-W-F: 9:00–9:55 AM	28	A52990
CSC-131B	Computers in Society	3	TC-114	M-W-F: 9:00–9:55 AM	20	B66750
CSC-131C	Computers in Society	3	TC-109	T-H: 11:00–12:25 PM	25	A52990
CSC-131D	Computers in Society	3	TC-108	M-W-F: 9:00–9:55 AM	30	B86590
CSC-131E	Computers in Society	3	TC-301	M-W-F: 1:00–1:55 PM	25	B66750
CSC-131I	Computers in Society	3	TC-109	T-H: 1:00–2:25 PM	32	A52990
CSC-132A	Introduction to Programming	3	TC-303	M-W-F: 9:00–9:55 AM	21	J33486
CSC-132B	Introduction to Programming	3	TC-302	T-H: 1:00–2:25 PM	21	B78880
CSC-230	Algorithms & Structures	3	TC-301	M-W-F: 1:00–1:55 PM	20	A77587
CSC-232A	Programming I	3	TC-305	T-H: 11:00–12:25 PM	28	B66750
CSC-232B	Programming I	3	TC-303	T-H: 11:00–12:25 PM	17	A77587
CSC-233A	Introduction to Algorithms	3	TC-302	M-W-F: 9:00–9:55 AM	18	H99118
CSC-233B	Introduction to Algorithms	3	TC-302	M-W-F: 11:00–11:55 AM	19	K69880
CSC-234A	Data Structure & Algorithms	3	TC-302	M-W-F: 9:00–9:55 AM	25	B78880
CSC-234B	Data Structure & Algorithms	3	TC-114	T-H: 11:00–12:25 PM	15	J33486
CSC-242	Programming II	3	TC-303	T-H: 1:00–2:25 PM	18	A52990
CSC-320	Object Oriented Programming	3	TC-301	T-H: 1:00–2:25 PM	22	B66750
CSC-331	Applications Programming	3	TC-109	T-H: 11:00–12:25 PM	28	H99118
CSC-333A	Computer Arch & Algorithms	3	TC-301	M-W-F: 10:00–10:55 AM	22	A77587
CSC-333B	Computer Arch & Algorithms	3	TC-302	T-H: 11:00–12:25 PM	15	A77587
CSC-335	Internet Programming	3	TC-303	M-W-F: 1:00–1:55 PM	25	B66750
CSC-432	Discrete Algorithms	3	TC-206	T-H: 11:00–12:25 PM	20	B86590
CSC-439	Database Systems	3	TC-206	M-W-F: 1:00–1:55 PM	18	B86590
CSE-138A	Introduction to CSE	3	TC-301	T-H: 1:00–2:25 PM	15	A52990
CSE-138B	Introduction to CSE	3	TC-109	T-H: 1:00–2:25 PM	35	J33486
CSE-330	Digital Logic Circuits	3	TC-305	M-W-F: 9:00–9:55 AM	26	K69880
CSE-332	Foundations of Semiconductors	3	TC-305	T-H: 1:00–2:25 PM	24	K69880
CSE-334	Elec. Measurement & Design	3	TC-212	T-H: 11:00–12:25 PM	25	H99118
CSE-430	Bioinformatics in Computer	3	TC-206	Thu: 9:30–11:00 AM	16	B86590
CSE-432	Analog Circuits Design	3	TC-309	M-W-F: 2:00–2:55 PM	18	K69880
CSE-433	Digital Signal Processing	3	TC-206	T-H: 2:00–3:25 PM	18	H99118
CSE-434	Advanced Electronics Systems	3	TC-213	M-W-F: 1:00–1:55 PM	26	B78880
CSE-436	Automatic Control and Design	3	TC-305	M-W-F: 10:00–10:55 AM	29	J33486
CSE-437	Operating Systems	3	TC-303	T-H: 1:00–2:25 PM	17	A77587
CSE-438	Advd Logic & Microprocessor	3	TC-213	M-W-F: 11:00–11:55 AM	35	B78880
CSE-439	Special Topics in CSE	3	TC-206	M-W-F: 10:00–10:55 AM	22	J33486

TABLE 2.15
The Data in the Student Table

student_id	student_name	gpa	credits	major	schoolYear	email	simage
A78835	Andrew Woods	3.26	108	Computer Science	Senior	awoods@college.edu	NULL
A97850	Ashly Jade	3.57	116	Info System Engineering	Junior	ajade@college.edu	NULL
B92996	Blue Valley	3.52	102	Computer Science	Senior	bvalley@college.edu	NULL
H10210	Holes Smith	3.87	78	Computer Engineering	Sophomore	hsmith@college.edu	NULL
T77896	Tom Erica	3.95	127	Computer Science	Senior	terica@college.edu	NULL

TABLE 2.16
The Data in the StudentCourse Table

s_course_id	student_id	course_id	credit	major
1000	H10210	CSC-131D	3	CE
1001	B92996	CSC-132A	3	CS/IS
1002	T77896	CSC-335	3	CS/IS
1003	A78835	CSC-331	3	CE
1004	H10210	CSC-234B	3	CE
1005	T77896	CSC-234A	3	CS/IS
1006	B92996	CSC-233A	3	CS/IS
1007	A78835	CSC-132A	3	CE
1008	A78835	CSE-432	3	CE
1009	A78835	CSE-434	3	CE
1010	T77896	CSC-439	3	CS/IS
1011	H10210	CSC-132A	3	CE
1012	H10210	CSC-331	3	CE
1013	A78835	CSC-335	3	CE
1014	A78835	CSE-438	3	CE
1015	T77896	CSC-432	3	CS/IS
1016	A97850	CSC-132B	3	ISE
1017	A97850	CSC-234A	3	ISE
1018	A97850	CSC-331	3	ISE
1019	A97850	CSC-335	3	ISE
1020	T77896	CSE-439	3	CS/IS
1021	B92996	CSC-230	3	CS/IS
1022	A78835	CSE-332	3	CE
1023	B92996	CSE-430	3	CE
1024	T77896	CSC-333A	3	CS/IS
1025	H10210	CSE-433	3	CE
1026	H10210	CSE-334	3	CE
1027	B92996	CSC-131C	3	CS/IS
1028	B92996	CSC-439	3	CS/IS

Enter the data shown in Tables 2.14, 2.15 and 2.16 into each associated Table, and save each Table as Course, Student and StudentCourse, respectively.

Similar to the **`Faculty`** Table, for the moment, just keep NULL for the **`SIMAGE`** column in the Student Table, and we will add actual student images later by using Visual Studio.NET and DevExpress Drive controls.

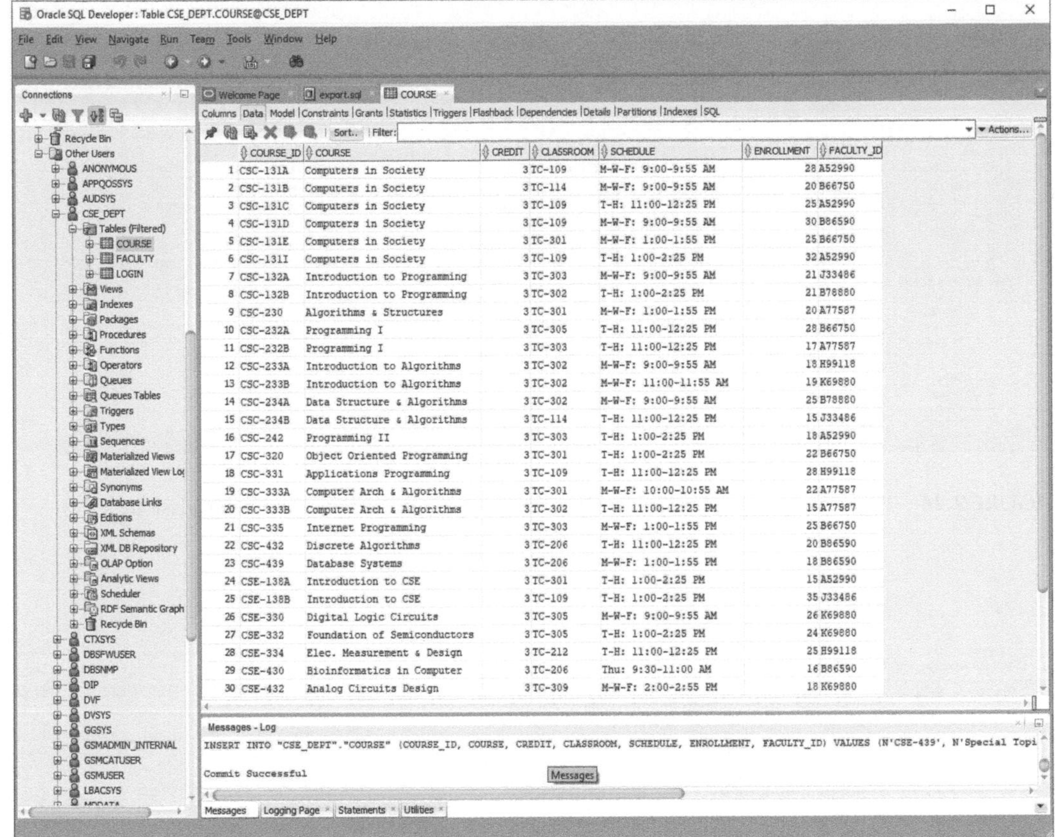

FIGURE 2.23 The completed Course Table (Copyrighted by Oracle and used with permission).

The finished **Course** Table should match the one shown in Figure 2.23. The finished **Student** Table should match the one shown in Figure 2.24. The finished **StudentCourse** Table should match the one shown in Figure 2.25.

2.9.6 Create Relationships among Tables

Next we need to setup relationships among these five Tables using the primary and foreign keys. In the Oracle 18c Express Edition database environment, the relationship between Tables can be set by using the **Property** wizard under each Table. Now let's begin to setup the relationship between the **LogIn** and the **Faculty** Tables by using the Oracle SQL Developer.

2.9.6.1 Create Relationship between LogIn and Faculty Tables

The relationship between the Faculty and the LogIn Tables is one-to-many, which means that the **faculty _ id** is a primary key in the **Faculty** Table, and it can be mapped to many **faculty _ id** values that are foreign keys in the LogIn Table.

To setup this relationship, we can either use the Oracle SQL Developer or an Oracle SQL Developer extension, Developer Modeler, that was included in the Developer when it was installed. To make thing simple and easy, we prefer to setup these relationships directly by using the Oracle SQL Developer.

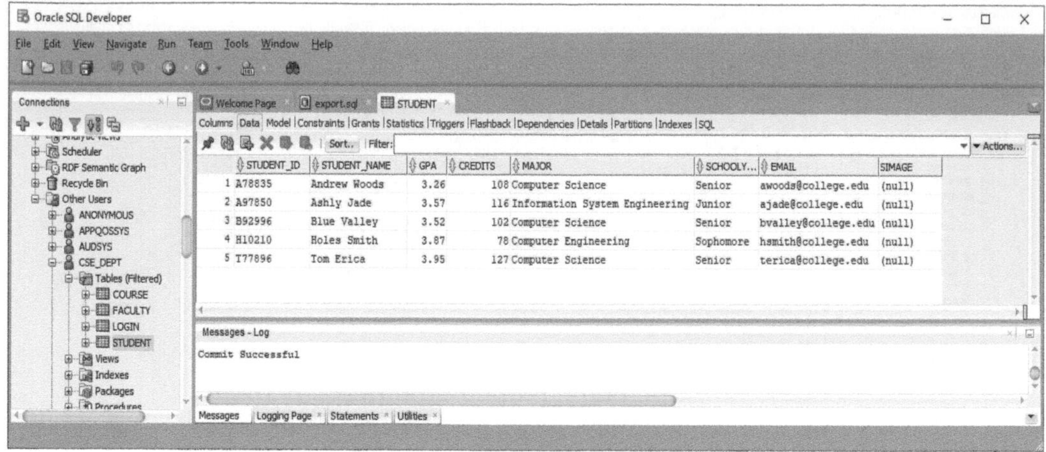

	STUDENT_ID	STUDENT_NAME	GPA	CREDITS	MAJOR	SCHOOLY...	EMAIL	SIMAGE
1	A78835	Andrew Woods	3.26	108	Computer Science	Senior	awoods@college.edu	(null)
2	A97850	Ashly Jade	3.57	116	Information System Engineering	Junior	ajade@college.edu	(null)
3	B92996	Blue Valley	3.52	102	Computer Science	Senior	bvalley@college.edu	(null)
4	H10210	Holes Smith	3.87	78	Computer Engineering	Sophomore	hsmith@college.edu	(null)
5	T77896	Tom Erica	3.95	127	Computer Science	Senior	terica@college.edu	(null)

FIGURE 2.24 The completed Student Table (Copyrighted by Oracle and used with permission).

	S_COURSE_ID	STUDENT_ID	COURSE_ID	CREDIT	MAJOR
+1	1000	H10210	CSC-131D	3	CE
+2	1001	B92996	CSC-132A	3	CS/IS
+3	1002	T77896	CSC-335	3	CS/IS
+4	1003	A78835	CSC-331	3	CE
+5	1004	H10210	CSC-234B	3	CE
+6	1005	T77896	CSC-234A	3	CS/IS
+7	1006	B92996	CSC-233A	3	CS/IS
+8	1007	A78835	CSC-132A	3	CE
+9	1008	A78835	CSE-432	3	CE
+10	1009	A78835	CSE-434	3	CE
+11	1010	T77896	CSC-439	3	CS/IS
+12	1011	H10210	CSC-132A	3	CE
+13	1012	H10210	CSC-331	3	CE
+14	1013	A78835	CSC-335	3	CE
+15	1014	A78835	CSE-438	3	CE
+16	1015	T77896	CSC-432	3	CS/IS
+17	1016	A97850	CSC-132B	3	ISE
+18	1017	A97850	CSC-234A	3	ISE
+19	1018	A97850	CSC-331	3	ISE
+20	1019	A97850	CSC-335	3	ISE
+21	1020	T77896	CSE-439	3	CS/IS
+22	1021	B92996	CSC-230	3	CS/IS
+23	1022	A78835	CSE-332	3	CE
+24	1023	B92996	CSE-430	3	CE
+25	1024	T77896	CSC-333A	3	CS/IS
+26	1025	H10210	CSE-433	3	CE
+27	1026	H10210	CSE-334	3	CE
+28	1027	B92996	CSC-131C	3	CS/IS
+29	1028	B92996	CSC-439	3	CS/IS

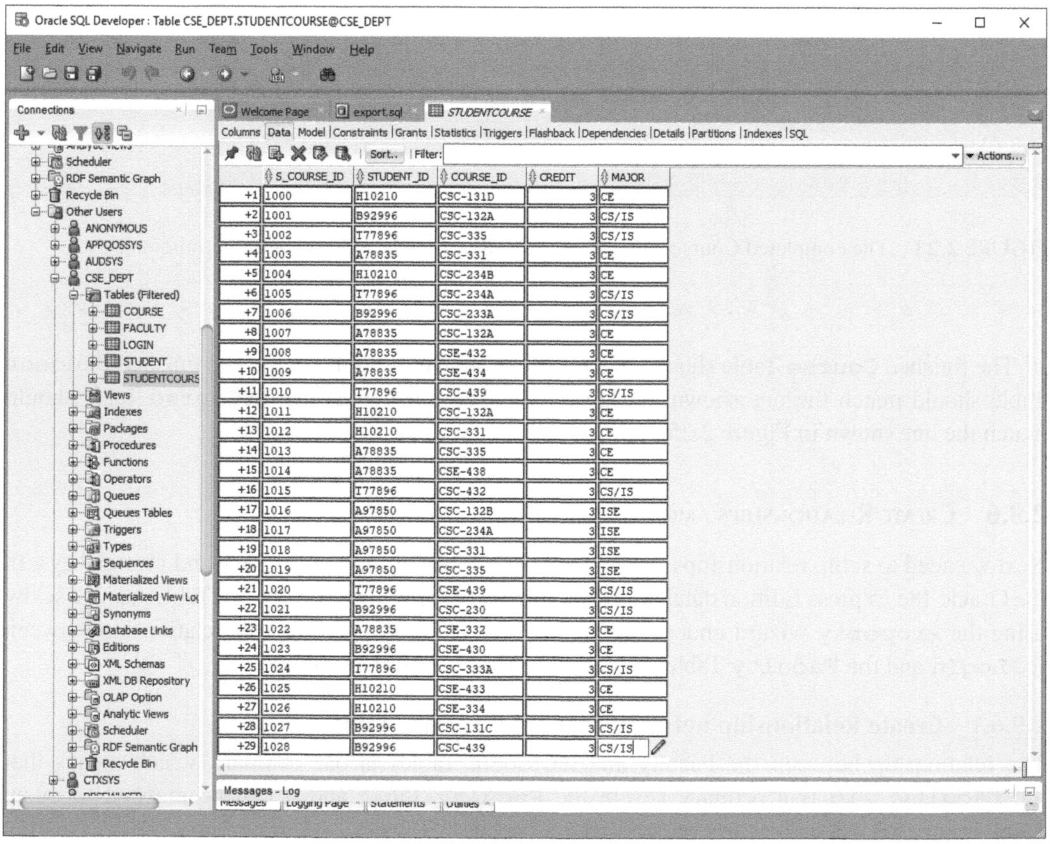

FIGURE 2.25 The completed StudentCourse Table (Copyrighted by Oracle and used with permission).

Perform the following operations to setup this foreign key for the **LOGIN** Table.

1) Click on the **LOGIN** Table under our customer database account, **CSE _ DEPT**, to open this Table.
2) In the open **LOGIN** Table, select the **Constraints** tab on the top and click on the **Edit** icon, as shown in Figure 2.26, to open the **Edit Table** wizard.
3) In the opened **Edit Table** wizard, as shown in Figure 2.27, click on the **Constraints** item on the left pane; click on the green + icon, as shown in Figure 2.27; and select the **New Foreign Key Constraint** item from the popup menu.
4) Change the name of this foreign key, which is located at the second line under the **Name** column in the **Constraints** list, to **LOGIN _ FACULTY _ FK** (Figure 2.28).
5) Select the **FACULTY** Table from the **Table** box, **FACULTY _ PK** from the **Constraints** box and **Cascade** from the **On Delete** box. Your completed wizard is shown in Figure 2.28.
6) Click on the **OK** button to add this foreign key to the **LOGIN** Table.

Now you can find this new added foreign key, **LOGIN _ FACULTY _ FK**, at the top line in the **Constraints** wizard, as shown in Figure 2.29.

The reason to setup a cascading relationship between the primary key (**FACULTY _ ID**) in the parent Table **FACULTY** and the foreign key (**FACULTY _ ID**) in the child Table **LOGIN** is because we want to simplify the data updating and deleting operations between these Tables in our relational database, **CSE _ DEPT**. You will have a better understanding of this cascading relationship later after you learn how to update and delete data against a relational database in Chapter 7.

2.9.6.2 Create Relationship between LogIn and Student Tables

In a similar way, you can create a foreign key for the **LOGIN** Table and setup a one-to-many relationship between the **STUDENT** and **LOGIN** Tables.

Perform the following operations to setup this relationship between the **LOGIN** and **STUDENT** Tables:

1) Click on the **LOGIN** Table under our customer database, **CSE _ DEPT**, to open it.
2) In the open **LOGIN** Table, select the **Constraints** tab on the top and click on the **Edit** icon to open the **Edit Table** wizard.

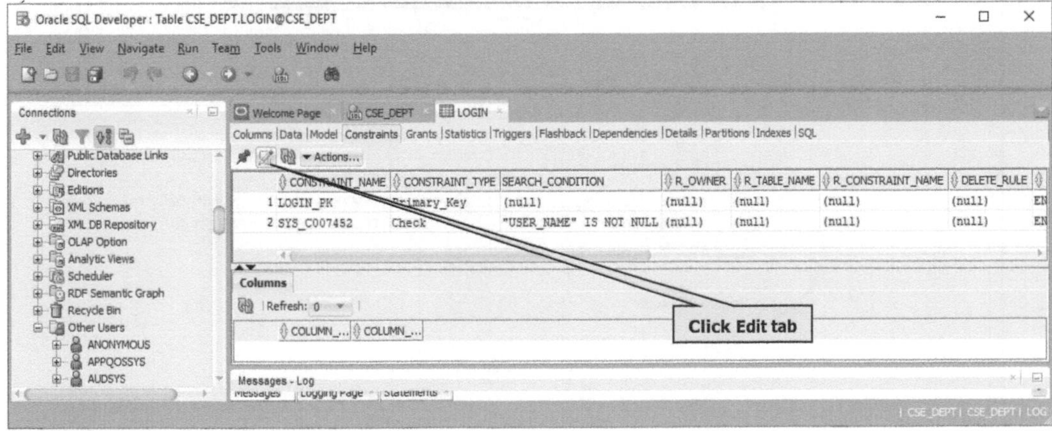

FIGURE 2.26 The opened Model view for the LOGIN Table (Copyrighted by Oracle and used with permission).

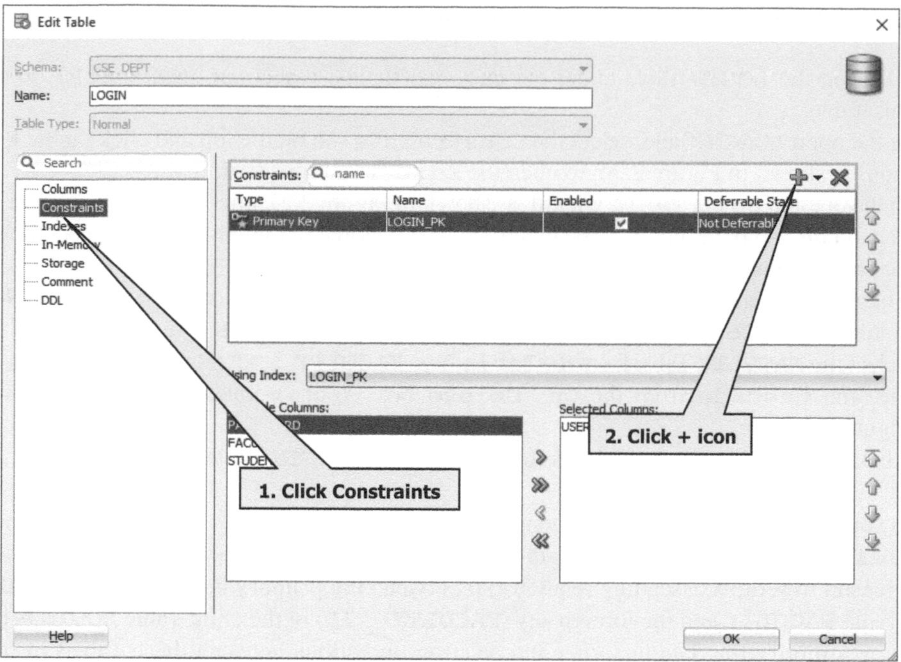

FIGURE 2.27 The opened Edit Table wizard (Copyrighted by Oracle and used with permission).

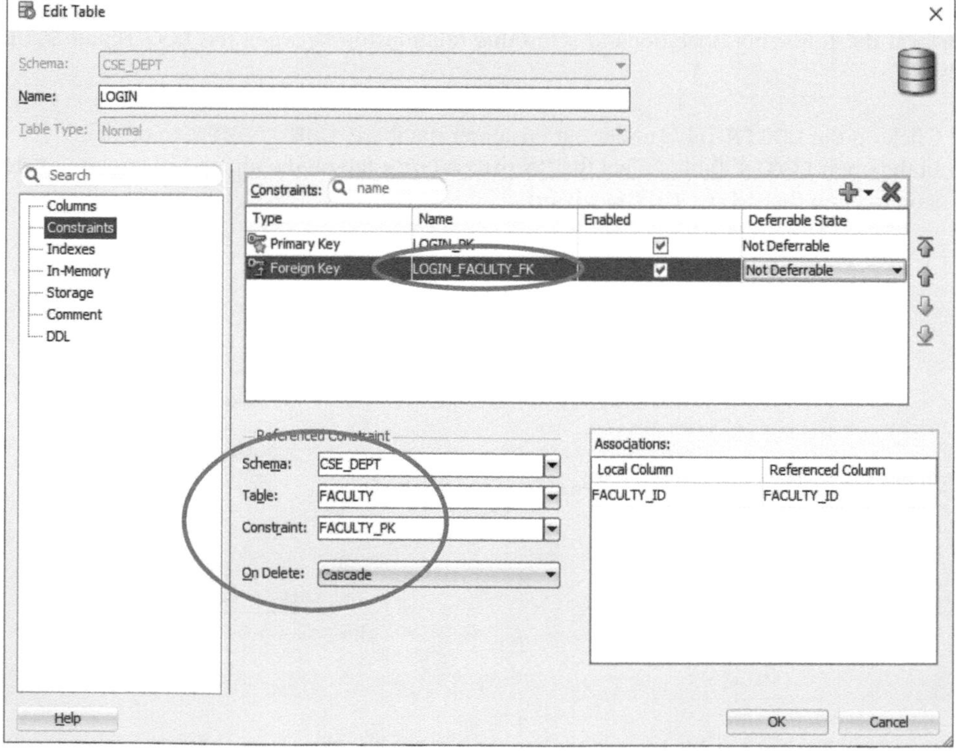

FIGURE 2.28 The finished Edit Table wizard (Copyrighted by Oracle and used with permission).

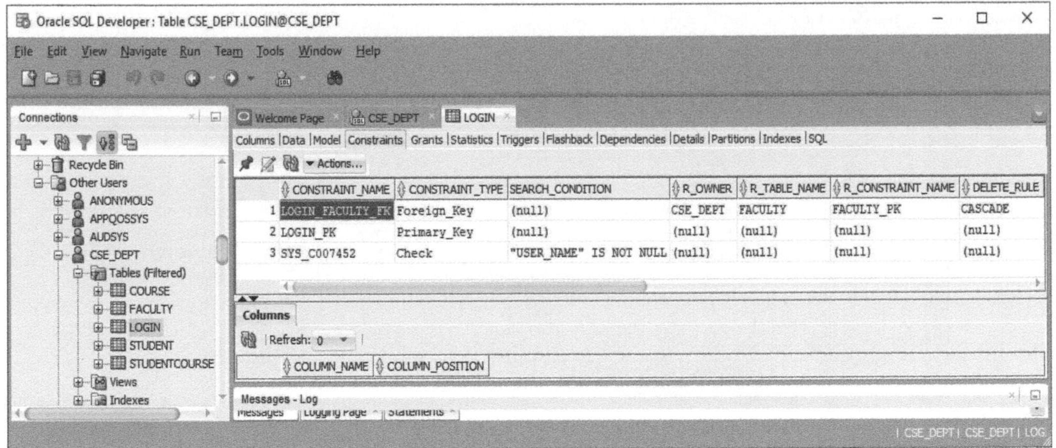

FIGURE 2.29 The added foreign key, LOGIN_FACULTY_FK (Copyrighted by Oracle and used with permission).

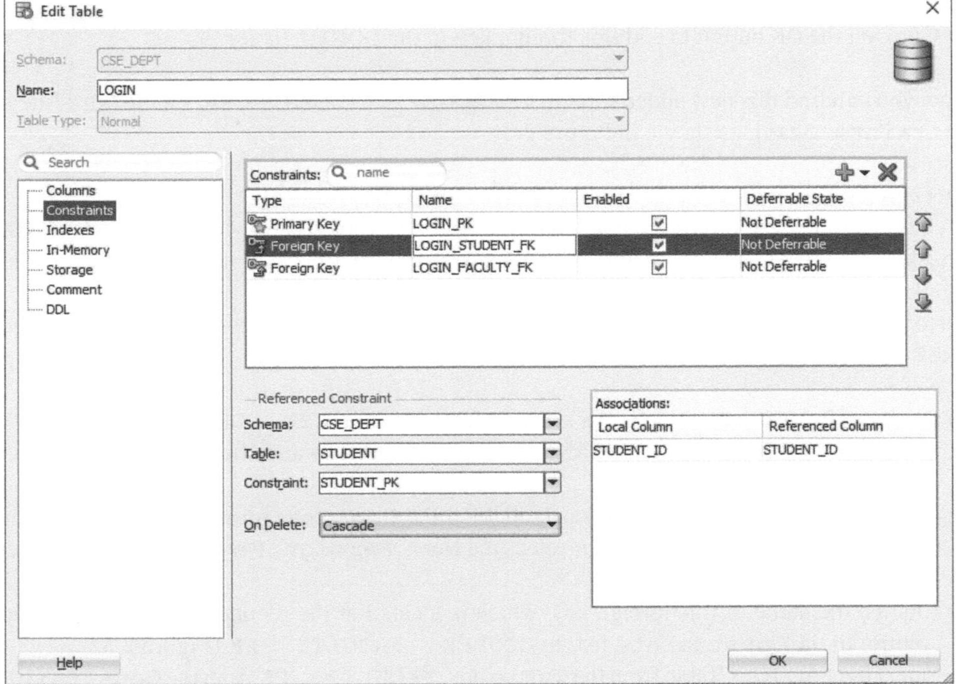

FIGURE 2.30 The created foreign key in the LOGIN and STUDENT Tables (Copyrighted by Oracle and used with permission).

3) In the opened **`Edit Table`** wizard, click on the **`Constraints`** item on the left pane, click on the green + icon and then select the **`New Foreign Key Constraint`** item from the popup menu.
4) Change the name of this foreign key, which is located at the second line under the **`Name`** column in the **`Constraints`** list, to **`LOGIN _ STUDENT _ FK`** (Figure 2.30).
5) Select the **`STUDENT`** Table from the **`Table`** box, **`STUDENT _ PK`** from the **`Constraints`** box and **`Cascade`** from the **`On Delete`** box. Your completed wizard is shown in Figure 2.30.

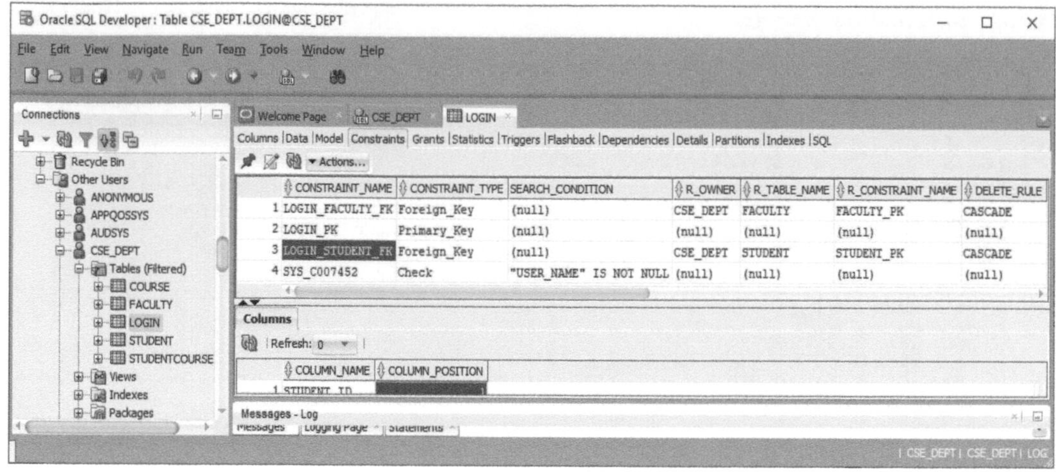

FIGURE 2.31 The added foreign key wizard (Copyrighted by Oracle and used with permission).

6) Click on the **OK** button to add this foreign key to the **LOGIN** Table.

Now you can find this new added foreign key, **LOGIN _ STUDENT _ FK**, on the third line in the **Constraints** wizard, as shown in Figure 2.31.

2.9.6.3 Create Relationship between Faculty and Course Tables

The relationship between the **FACULTY** and the **COURSE** Tables is one-to-many, the **FACULTY _ ID** in the **FACULTY** Table is a primary key and the **FACULTY _ ID** in the **COURSE** Table is a foreign key.

Perform the following operations to setup this relationship between the **FACULTY** and the **COURSE** Tables:

1) Click on the **COURSE** Table under our customer account, **CSE _ DEPT**, to open it.
2) In the open Table, select the **Constraints** tab on the top and click on the **Edit** icon to open the **Edit Table** wizard.
3) In the opened **Edit Table** wizard, click on the **Constraints** item on the left pane, click on the green + icon and then select the **New Foreign Key Constraint** item from the popup menu.
4) Change the name of this foreign key, which is located at the second line under the **Name** column in the **Constraints** list, to **COURSE _ FACULTY _ FK** (Figure 2.32).
5) Select the **FACULTY** Table from the **Table** box, **FACULTY _ PK** from the **Constraints** box and **Cascade** from the **On Delete** box. Your completed wizard is shown in Figure 2.32.
6) Click on the **OK** button to add this foreign key to the **COURSE** Table.

Now you can find this new added foreign key, **COURSE _ FACULTY _ FK**, on the top line in the **Constraints** wizard.

2.9.6.4 Create Relationship between Student and StudentCourse Tables

The relationship between the **STUDENT** and the **STUDENTCOURSE** Tables is one-to-many, the **STUDENT _ ID** in the **STUDENT** Table is a primary key and the **STUDENT _ ID** in the **STUDENTCOURSE** Table is a foreign key.

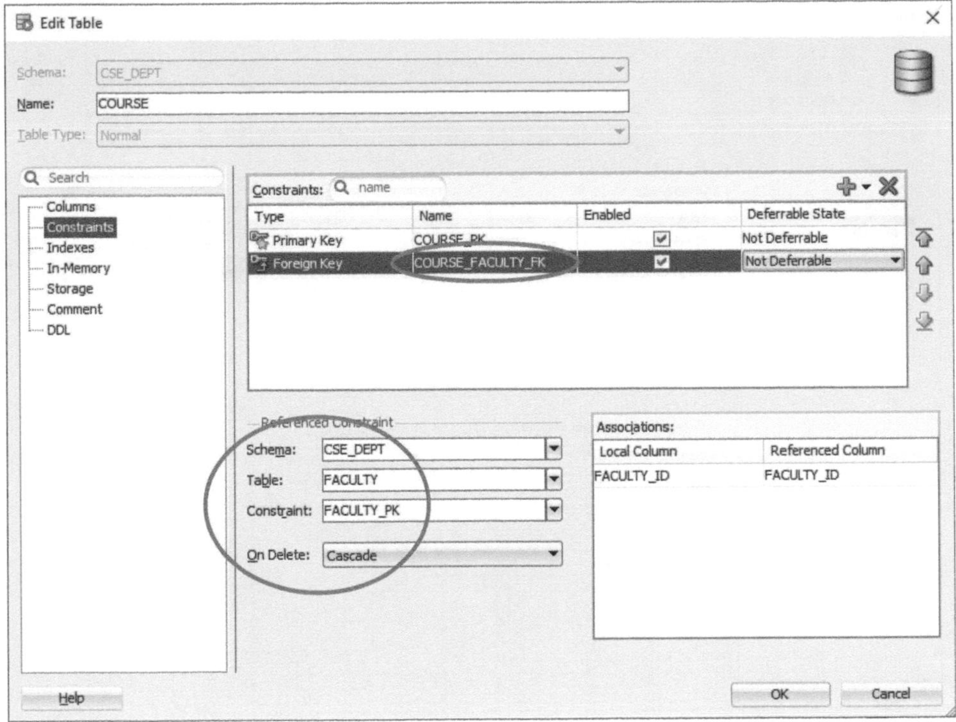

FIGURE 2.32 The finished foreign key for the COURSE Table (Copyrighted by Oracle and used with permission).

Perform the following operations to set up this relationship between the **STUDENT** and the **STUDENTCOURSE** Tables:

1) Click on the **STUDENTCOURSE** Table under our customer account, **CSE _ DEPT**, to open it.
2) In the open Table, select the **Constraints** tab on the top and click on the **Edit** icon to open the **Edit Table** wizard.
3) In the opened **Edit Table** wizard, click on the **Constraints** item on the left pane, click on the green + icon and then select the **New Foreign Key Constraint** item from the popup menu.
4) Change the name of this foreign key, which is located at the second line under the **Name** column in the **Constraints** list, to **STUDENTCOURSE _ STUDENT _ FK**.
5) Select the **STUDENT** Table from the **Table** box, **STUDENT _ PK** from the **Constraints** box and **Cascade** from the **On Delete** box. In this way, these two Tables have a cascading deletion relationship for this column when a delete action is performed later. Your completed wizard is shown in Figure 2.33.
6) Click on the **OK** button to set up this foreign key relationship.

Finally, let's handle the relationship between the **COURSE** and **STUDENTCOURSE** Tables.

2.9.6.5 Create Relationship between Course and StudentCourse Tables

The relationship between the **COURSE** and the **STUDENTCOURSE** Tables is one-to-many, the **COURSE _ ID** in the **COURSE** Table is a primary key and the **COURSE _ ID** in the **STUDENTCOURSE** Table is a foreign key.

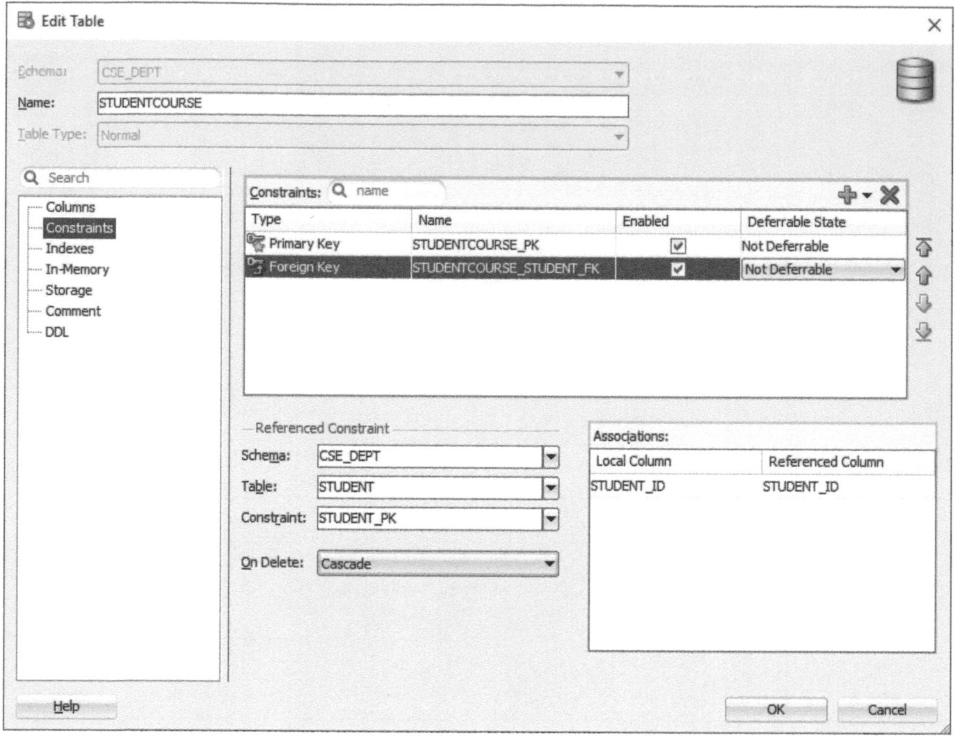

FIGURE 2.33 The finished foreign key for **STUDENTCOURSE** Table (Copyrighted by Oracle and used with permission).

Perform the following operations to set up this relationship between the **COURSE** and the **STUDENTCOURSE** Tables:

1) Click on the **STUDENTCOURSE** Table under our customer database account, **CSE _ DEPT**, to open it.
2) In the open Table, select the **Constraints** tab on the top and click on the **Edit** icon to open the **Edit Table** wizard.
3) In the opened **Edit Table** wizard, click on the **Constraints** item on the left pane, click on the green + icon and then select the **New Foreign Key Constraint** item from the popup menu.
4) Change the name of this foreign key, which is located at the second line under the **Name** column in the **Constraints** list, to **STUDENTCOURSE _ COURSE _ FK**.
5) Select the **COURSE** Table from the **Table** box, **COURSE _ PK** from the **Constraints** box and **Cascade** from the **On Delete** box. In this way, these two Tables have a cascading deletion relationship for this column when a delete action is performed later. Your completed wizard is shown in Figure 2.34.
6) Click on the **OK** button to set up this foreign key relationship.

At this point, we complete setting up the relationships among our five data Tables. Go to the **File|Save All** item to save this foreign key setup. Now, if you open the **Model** tab from the **LOGIN** Table, you can see that two foreign keys, **LOGIN _ FACULTY _ FK** and **LOGIN _ STUDENT _ FK**, have been set up, as shown in Figure 2.35.

Next let's discuss how to store an image in the related column in the Oracle database.

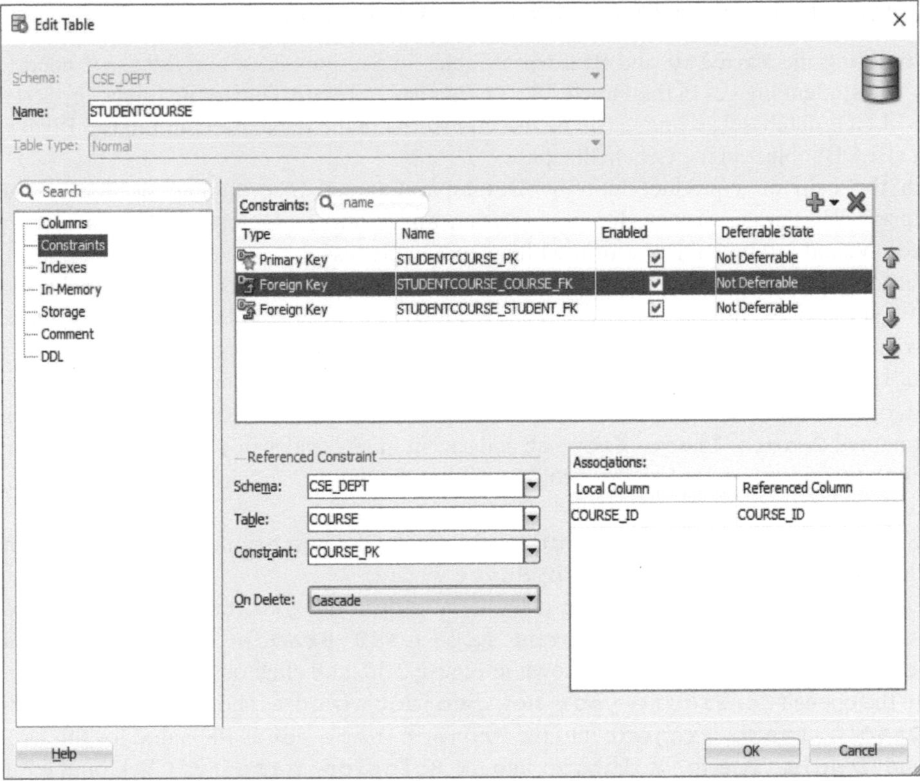

FIGURE 2.34 The finished Tables and Columns dialog (Copyrighted by Oracle and used with permission).

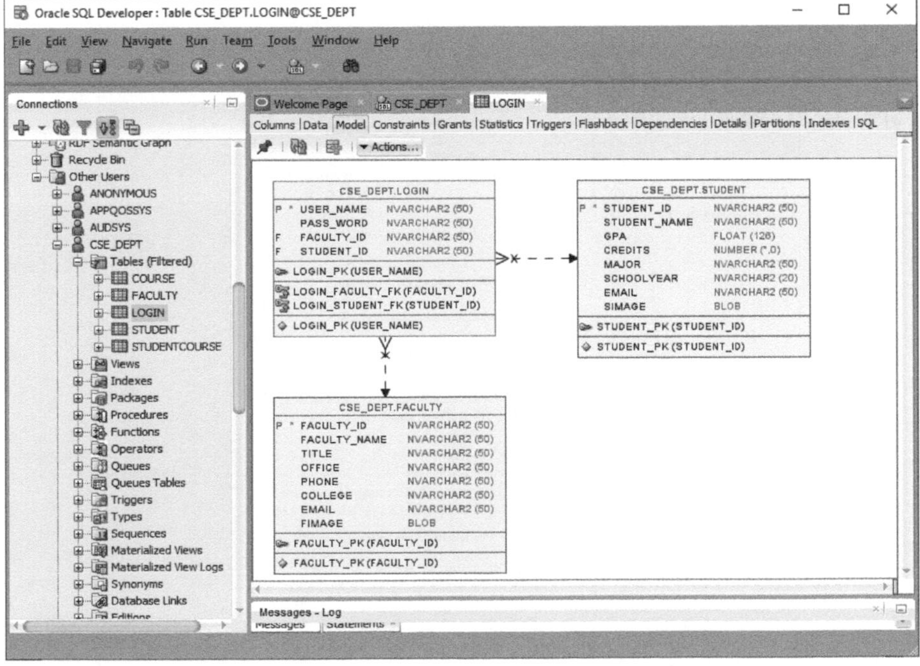

FIGURE 2.35 Relationships among LOGIN, FACULTY and STUDENT Tables (Copyrighted by Oracle and used with permission).

2.9.7 Store Images in the Oracle 18c Express Edition Database

When building the **Faculty** and **Student** Tables in Sections 2.9.4 and 2.9.5, we need to store faculty and student images in the Oracle 18c XE database directly. Due to the image property of the Oracle 18c XE database, an image can be directly stored in the database column as a Binary Large OBject (BLOB) object in the Oracle database.

With the help of a product built by Developer Express Incorporated or a user interface, DevExpress WinForms, we can directly insert an image into an Oracle database column via the Microsoft Visual Studio.NET platform with no coding process.

Refer to Appendix D to download and install DevExpress WinForms from the site DevExpress.com. When it is done, this component should be added into the Visual Basic.NET environment.

Now we will use Visual Studio.NET 2019 as an IDE and DevExpress WinForms as a tool to insert or store images in the related columns in the Oracle 18c XE database.

First, open Visual Studio.NET 2019, create a new **Visual Basic.NET Windows Form App** project named **Oracle Image Project** and save it in any folder in your computer. Perform the following operations to complete this project creation process.

1) Click on the **Continue without code** item at the lower-right corner, which is under the **Get started** tab, to open the **Start** wizard.
2) Go to the **File|New Project** menu item to open the **Create a new project** wizard. Select the **Windows Forms App (.NET Framework)—Visual Basic** template from the right side, as shown in Figure 2.36, and click on the **Next** button.
3) In the opened **ConFigure your new project** wizard, as shown in Figure 2.37, enter **Oracle Image Project** into the **Project name** box as the name for this project and **Oracle Image Solution** into the **Solution name** box. Click on the three-dot (browse) button to find a location; here, **C:\Temp** is used as the location to store this project (Figure 2.37). Then click on the **Create** button to create this project.

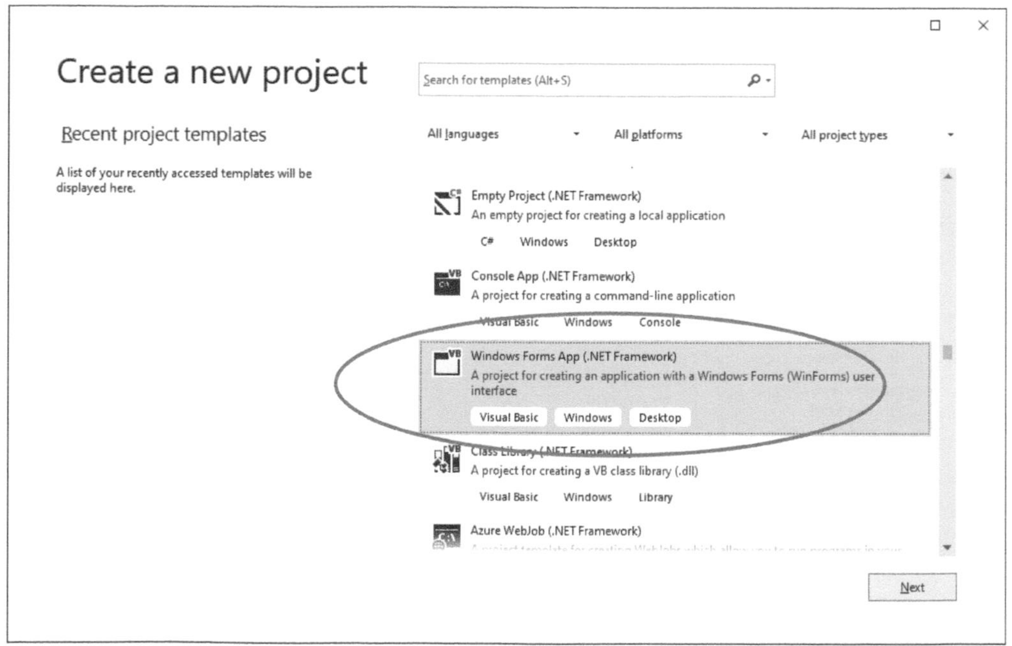

FIGURE 2.36 Create a blank Oracle Image Solution.

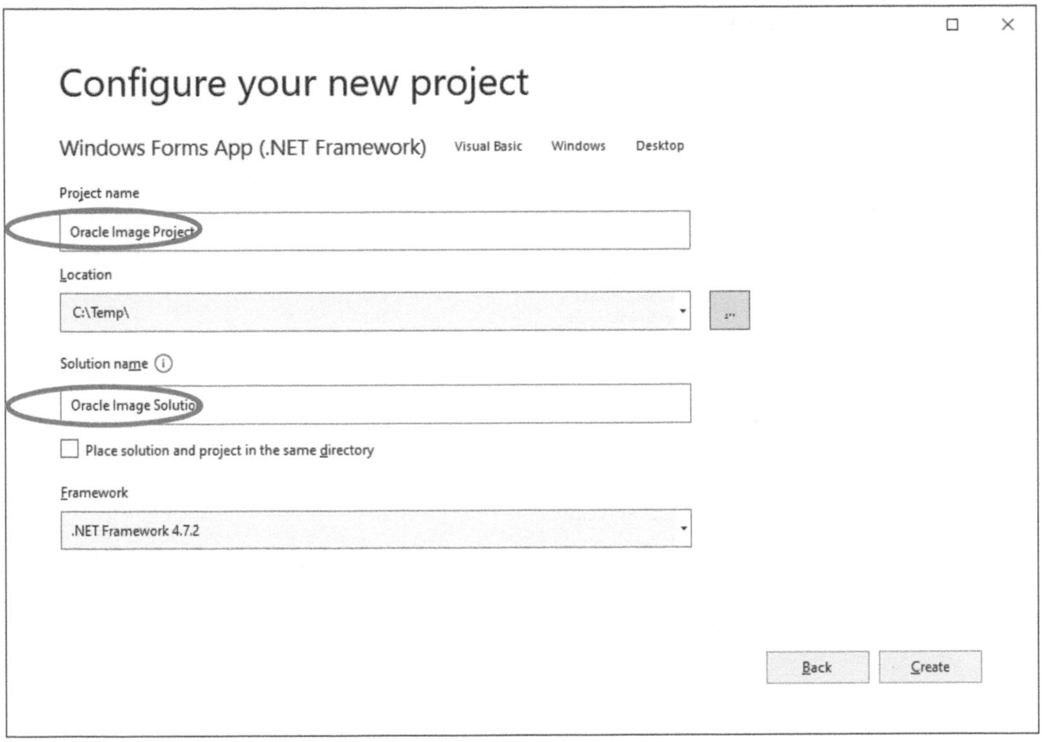

Configure your new project

Windows Forms App (.NET Framework) Visual Basic Windows Desktop

Project name

Oracle Image Project

Location

C:\Temp\

Solution name

Oracle Image Solution

Place solution and project in the same directory

Framework

.NET Framework 4.7.2

Back Create

FIGURE 2.37 Enter the solution name and location.

In the opened project window, go to the Solution Explorer window on the right, click on the windows form object or GUI to select it and then go to the `Properties` window to find the `Name` and `Text` property. Change its name from `Form1` to `Faculty _ Form` and `Text` from `Form1` to `Faculty Form`.

Now we are ready to use DevExpress WinForms as a tool to add each faculty image to the related `fimage` column in the `Faculty` Table in our sample database. However, prior to using that tool, we need to use the Data Source tool in Visual Studio. NET to connect to our Oracle 18c XE database to enable us to access and manipulate any Table in that database. Thus, we need first to add some database drivers into the project to enable us to use it as an adaptor to connect and implement our sample database and add images into our `FACULTY` and `STUDENT` Tables. Let's start with the `FACULTY` Table.

2.9.7.1 Store Images in the FACULTY Table

To access different databases, various data providers that work as adaptors or a data drivers are needed. These adaptors provide various functions, such as connecting to a target data source and accessing, retrieving, inserting, updating and deleting data from the data source.

In this book, we adopt a third-party product, dotConnect, as our driver to use as an adaptor to access and implement our Oracle 18c XE sample database, `CSE _ DEPT`.

Refer to Appendix G to download and install this free driver, dotConnect for Oracle, to your computer. Then we need to add some references related to this driver into our project to enable the compiler to know this driver at project building time. Perform the following operations to add these references:

1) Right-click on our new created project, `Oracle Image Project`, from the Solution Explorer window, and select the `Add|Reference` item from the popup menu to open the Reference Manager wizard.

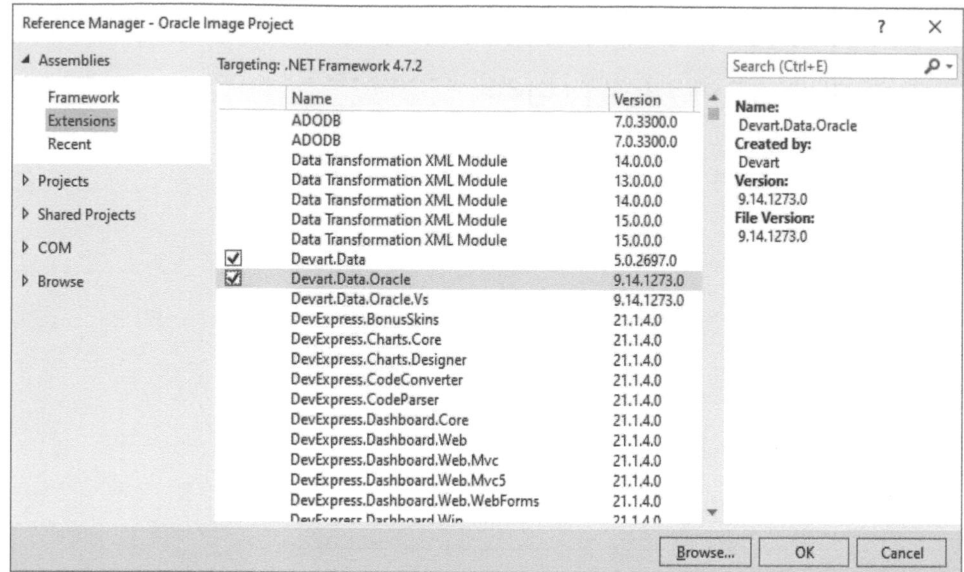

FIGURE 2.38 The opened Reference Manager wizard.

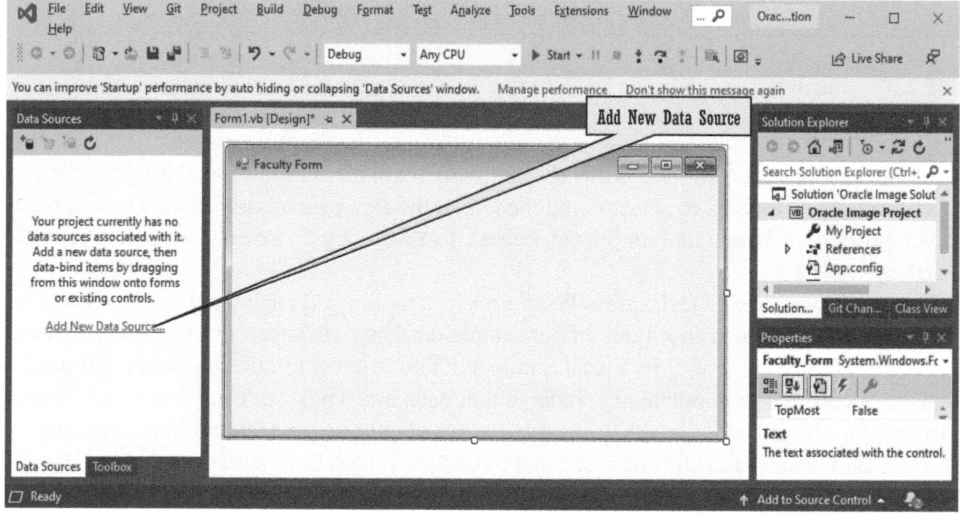

FIGURE 2.39 The Add Data Source link.

2) Click on the **`Extensions`** item on the left and select two items, **`Devart.Data`** and **`Devart.Data.Oracle`**, from the mid-pane by checking both of them, as shown in Figure 2.38. Click on the **`OK`** button to add them into our project.

Now let's use one of the Visual Studio. NET tools, Data Source, to connect to our sample Oracle 18c XE database via the added database drivers.

1) Click on the **`Add New Data Source`** link, as shown in Figure 2.39, in the **`Data Sources`** window located at the lower-left corner to open the **`Data Source Configuration`** wizard to connect to our designed Oracle 18c XE database, **`CSE _ DEPT`**.

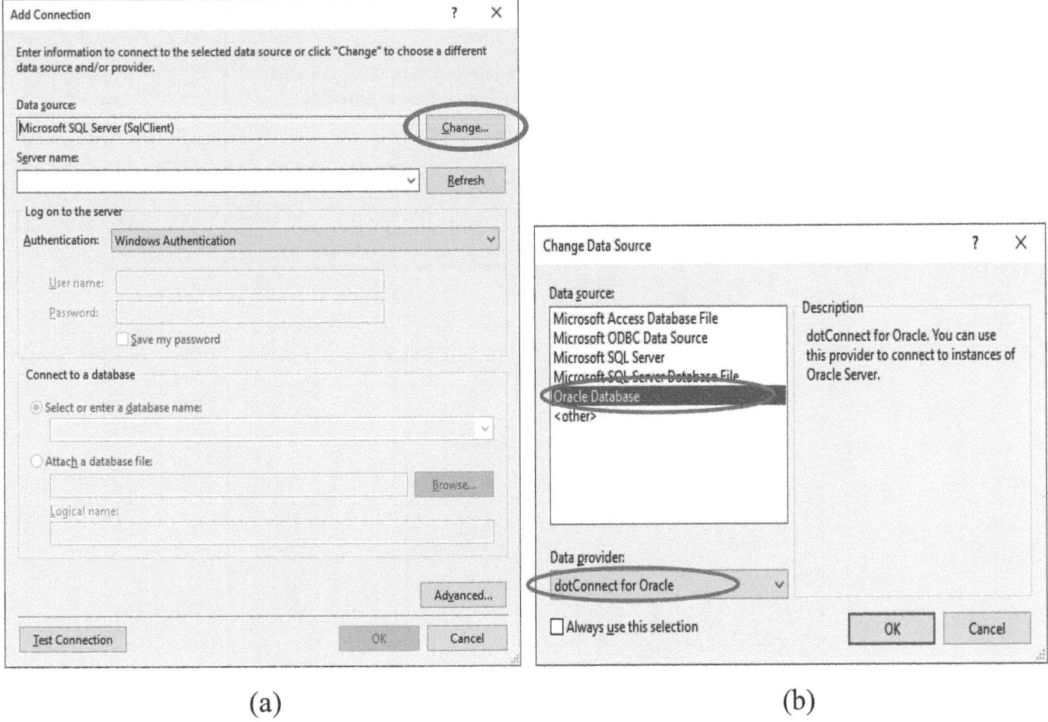

(a) (b)

FIGURE 2.40 The opened Add Connection wizard.

2) In the opened **Choose a Data Source Type** and **Choose a Database Model** wizards, keep the default **Database** and **DataSet** selections, and click on the Next button to come to our database connection wizard, the **Choose Your Data Connection** wizard. Click on the **New Connection** button to open the **Add Connection** wizard, which is shown in Figure 2.40a.
3) On the opened **Choose a Data Source Type** and **Choose a Database Model** wizards, keep the default **Database** and **DataSet** selection and click on the **Next** buttons to come to our database connection wizard, **Choose Your Data Connection** wizard. Click the **New Connection** button to open the **Add Connection** wizard (Figure 2.40a).
4) Click on the **Change** button to open the **Change Data Source** wizard (Figure 2.40b).
5) Select **Oracle Database** from the **Data source** list on the left, and make sure the **dotConnect for Oracle** component is selected in the **Data provider** box, as shown in Figure 2.40b. Click on the **OK** button to return to the Add Connection wizard.
6) In the Add Connection wizard, as shown in Figure 2.41, enter the following in the related box as the connection parameters:

   a. Server: **localhost:1521/XE**
   b. User Id: **CSE _ DEPT**
   c. Password: **oracle _ 18c**

   The server contains the data source; it is formatted as **Host:Listener/Database Server**. The User Id is our user account, **CSE _ DEPT**, and the password is **oracle _ 18c**.
7) Check the **Allow saving password** checkbox, since we want to keep it.
8) You can click on the **Test Connection** button to test this connection. A successful connection message should be displayed if this connection is complete.

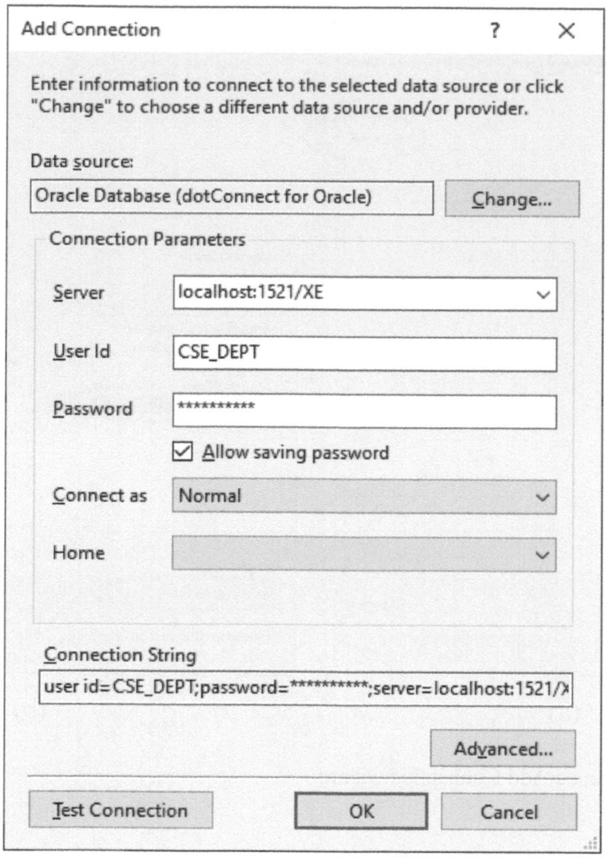

FIGURE 2.41 The parameters used to connect to our sample database.

9) Click on the **OK** button to continue this connection process.
10) In the opened **Data Source Configuration Wizard**, which is shown in Figure 2.42, check the **Yes, include sensitive data in the connection string** radio button, since we want to keep all of these connection parameters to be used in the future in our project. For the same reason, also check the **Show the connection string that you will save in the application** checkbox. Click on the **Next** button to continue.
11) In the next wizard, check the **Yes, save the connection as** checkbox to save our connection string as the default one, which may be used in the future. Click on the **Next** button to go to the next wizard to select our database objects.
12) The **Choose Your Database Objects** wizard is opened, as shown in Figure 2.43. Expand the **Tables** and then **FACULTY** icons, then select the **FACULTY _ ID**, **FACULTY _ NAME** and **FIMAGE** columns by checking each of them (of course, you can select all columns, as we will do later, but right now we only need these columns for demo purposes).
13) In a similar way, select three columns, **STUDENT _ ID**, **STUDENT _ NAME** and **SIMAGE**, from the **STUDENT** Table, since we also need to add the student images to the **simage** column in that Table. Also, change the DataSet name to **OracleImageDataSet** in the **DataSet name** box, as shown in Figure 2.43.
14) Click on the **Finish** button to complete this connection process.

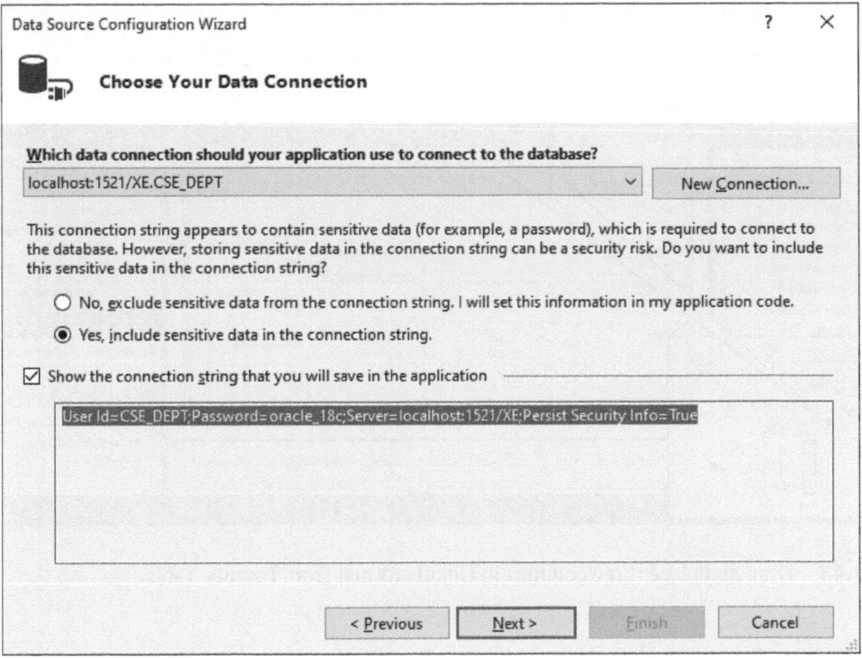

FIGURE 2.42 The opened Data Source Configuration wizard.

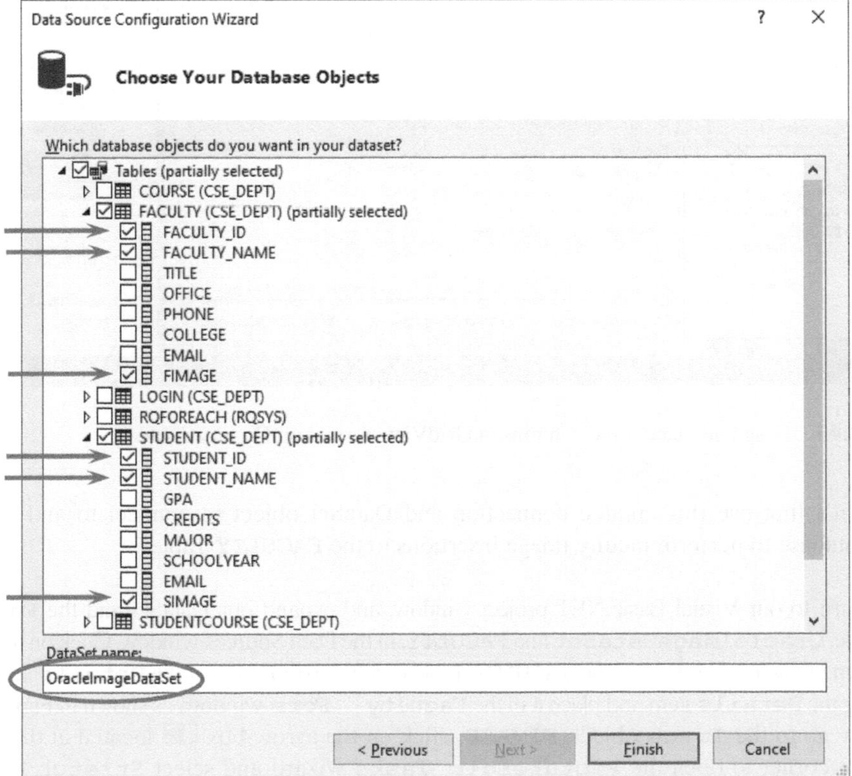

FIGURE 2.43 The connected database and dataset OracleImageDataSet.

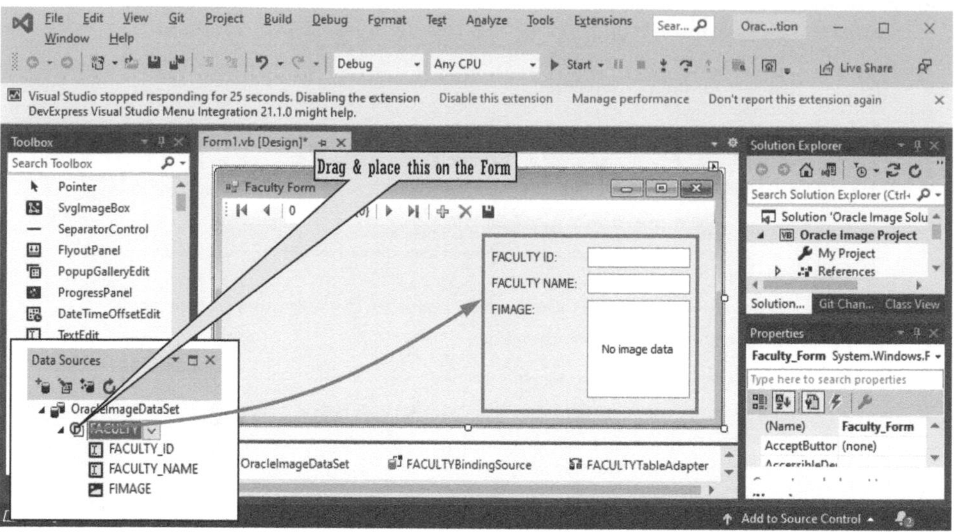

FIGURE 2.44 Drag and place three columns in Details format from Faculty Table.

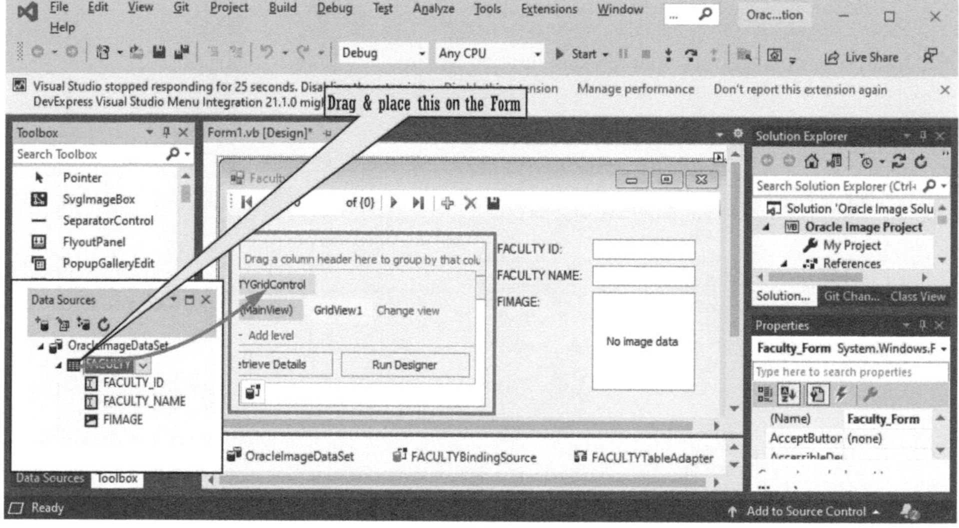

FIGURE 2.45 Drag and place three columns in GridView format on Faculty Table.

Next let's first use this created connection and DataSet object to connect to and access our sample database to perform faculty image insertions to the **FACULTY** Table.

1) Return to our Visual Basic.NET project window, and expand our DataSet and the **Faculty** Table, **OracleImageDataSet** and **FACULTY**, in the Data Sources window. Click on the drop-down arrow on the right of the **FACULTY** Table combo box and select the **Details** item, then drag the **Details** item and place it in the **Faculty _ Form** window, as shown in Figure 2.44.
2) Now go to the **Image** object, **FIMAGE**, click on the arrow box located at the upper-right corner to open the **PictureEdit Tasks** wizard and select **Stretch** from the **Size Mode** combo box. Then click anyplace in the **Faculty _ Form** window to close the **PictureEdit Tasks** wizard.

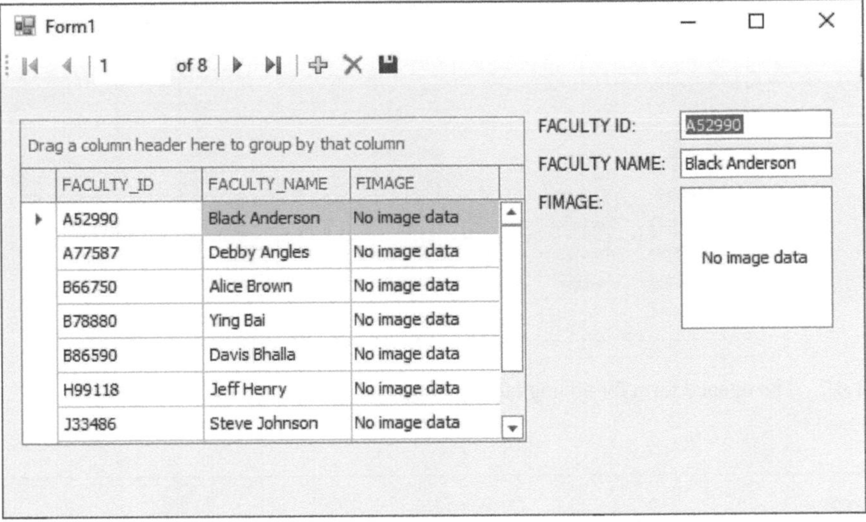

FIGURE 2.46 The opened form for adding faculty images.

3) Then click on the drop-down arrow on the right of the **`Faculty`** Table combo box again, select the **`GridView`** item and then drag the GridView item and place it in the **`Faculty _ Form`** window, as shown in Figure 2.45.
4) Now go to **`File|Save All`** to save all of these additions and modifications.
5) Then click on the **`Start`** button (green arrow on the tool bar) to run this Visual Basic project. As the project runs, the contents of three columns for all faculty members in this **`FACULTY`** Table are displayed in both Details and GridView, except the faculty image **`FIMAGE`**, as shown in Figure 2.46.
6) To add an image to the **`FIMAGE`** box for the selected faculty member, click on the arrow for that faculty member, first click (left-click) on the **`FIMAGE`** column in the GridView and then right-click on the **`FIMAGE`** column again. From the popup menu, select the **`Load`** item to try to load an image for the selected faculty member.
7) In the opened dialog, browse to the related faculty image—in our case, all faculty images are stored in the folder: **`C:/Images/Faculty`**—and select the associated faculty image, such as **`Anderson.jpg`**, for the faculty member **`Black Anderson`**, by clicking on it, and click on the **`Open`** button to add it to the **`OracleImageDataSet`**. One can find all the faculty images in a folder, **`Students\Images\Faculty`**, on the CRC Press ftp site. Copy and paste them into your local folder, such as **`C:\Images\Faculty`**.
8) In a similar way, insert all other faculty images one by one into the **`FIMAGE`** column in the **`FACULTY`** Table.
9) Then click on the **`Save Data`** button located at the upper-right corner on the tool bar to save this image into our sample database, **`CSE _ DEPT`**.

All faculty images are located at the CRC Press ftp site at the folder **`Students/Images/Faculty`**, and you can copy those image files with the folders and save them to your computer (refer to Figure 1.2 in Chapter 1 to get more details about these image files).

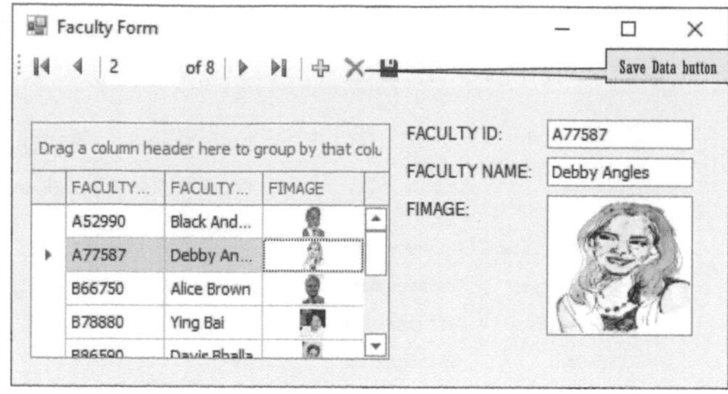

FIGURE 2.47 The opened form for adding faculty images.

TABLE 2.17
The Image Files in the FacultyTable

faculty_id	faculty_name	fimage
A52990	Black Anderson	Anderson.jpg
A77587	Debby Angles	Angles.jpg
B66750	Alice Brown	Brown.jpg
B78880	Ying Bai	Bai.jpg
B86590	DavisBhalla	Davis.jpg
H99118	Jeff Henry	Nenry.jpg
J33486	Steve Johnson	Johnson.jpg
K69880	Jenney King	King.jpg

Your finished Form window is shown in Figure 2.47. The relationships between each faculty member and related image file are shown in Table 2.17.

Now you can test the image insertion operations by clicking each **FACULTY _ ID** in the GridView box. Immediately, the selected faculty, including the **FACULTY _ ID**, **FACULTY _ NAME** and **FIMAGE**, will be displayed in the Details View in this Form window, as shown in Figure 2.47.

Now open the Oracle SQL Developer and click on the default database, **XE**, under the **Recent** tab in the **Database Connection** panel; enter the password **oracle _ 18c** into the Password box; and click on the **OK** button to connect to it. Then expand three folders under the **XE** database, **Other Users > CSE _ DEPT > Tables**, and double-click on our **FACULTY** Table to open it. Then click on the **Data** tab, and you can find that all **NULL** values in the **FIMAGE** column (the last column) have been changed to **BLOB**, as shown in Figure 2.48.

2.9.7.2 Store Images in the STUDENT Table

In a similar way, you can add all the student images into the **STUDENT** Table in our database, **CSE _ DEPT**. All student images can be found at the CRC Press ftp site in the folder **Students/Images/Students**. Refer to Figure 1.2 in Chapter 1 for more details about this folder. You can copy those image files and save them to your local folder, such as **C:\Images\Students**, if you like.

The relationships between each student and related image file are shown in Table 2.18. You are not required to create a new project and can just add a new Windows Form, **Form2.vb**, to the

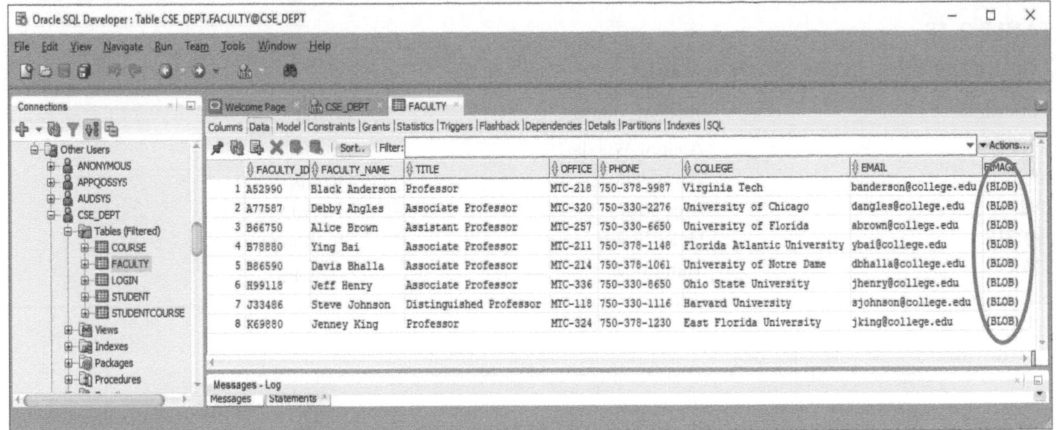

FIGURE 2.48 The modified FIMAGE column (Copyrighted by Oracle and used with permission).

current project to do this image addition. Perform the following operations to add this new Windows Form, **Form2.vb**, into this project and conFigure the Form to enable us to insert all the student images in the **simage** column:

1) Right-click our project, **Oracle Image Project**, in the Solution Explorer window, and select the **Add|Form (Windows Forms)** item to open the Add New Item wizard.
2) In the opened wizard, select the item **Form (Windows Forms)** from the mid-panel. Keep the default name, **Form2.vb**, in the **Name** box (bottom) with no change, and click on the **Add** button to add this form into our project.
3) Click on this new add form and go to the **Name** property in the Properties window. Change its name to **Student _ Form**. Also, change its **Text** to **Student Form**.
4) Open the Data Sources window, click on the drop-down arrow on the right of the **STUDENT** Table combo box and select the **Details** item. Then drag the **Details** item and place it in the **Student _ Form** window, as shown in Figure 2.49.
5) Now go to the **Image** object, **SIMAGE**, click on the arrow box located at the upper-right corner to open the **PictureEdit Tasks** wizard and select **Stretch** from the **Size Mode** combo box. Then click anyplace in the **Student _ Form** window to close the **PictureEdit Tasks** wizard.
6) Then click on the drop-down arrow on the right of the **Student** Table combo box again and select the **GridView** item, then drag this GridView item and place it in the **Student _ Form** window, as shown in Figure 2.50.
7) Go to **File|Save All** menu item to save these operations.

Before we can run the project to insert student images into the **Student** Table, we need to set up the **Student _ Form** as the Startup Form to enable Visual Basic to run that form first as the project runs. Perform the following operations to complete this setup:

1) Go to the **Project|Oracle Image Project Properties** menu item to open the project properties wizard.
2) Make sure that the **Application** item on the left panel is selected.
3) Click on the drop-down arrow in the **Startup form** combo box, and select the **Student _ Form** by clicking on it.

TABLE 2.18
The Image Files in the Student Table

student_id	student_name	simage
A78835	Andrew Woods	Woods.jpg
A97850	Ashly Jade	Jade.jpg
B92996	Blue Valley	Valley.jpg
H10210	Holes Smith	Smith.jpg
T77896	Tom Erica	Erica.jpg

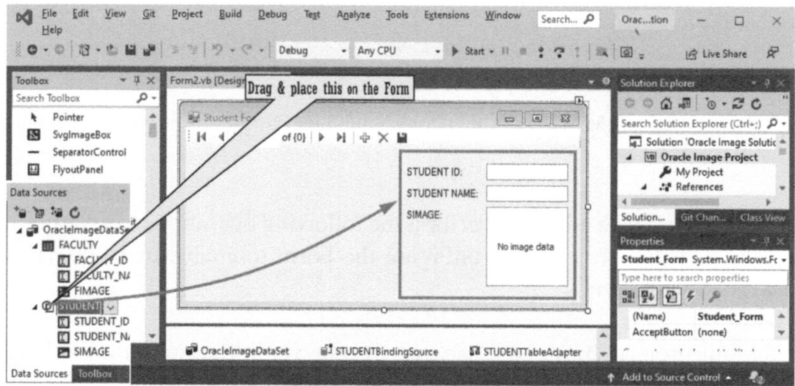

FIGURE 2.49 Drag and place three columns in Details format from the Student Table.

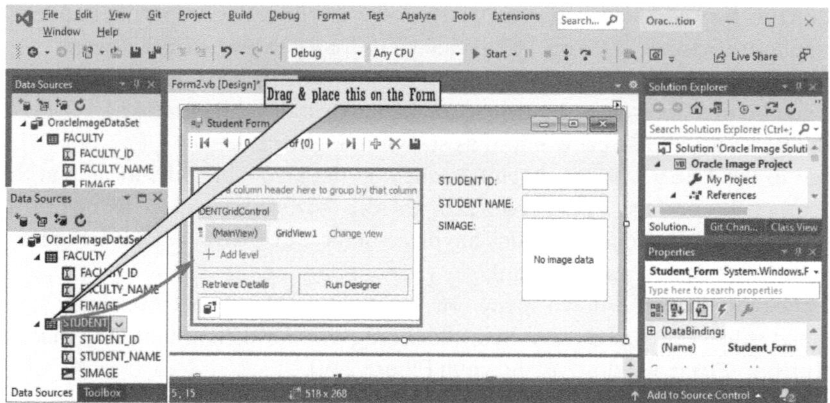

FIGURE 2.50 Drag and place three columns in GridView format on the Student Table.

Now you can run the project to start adding all images for all students. Insert each student's image into the **SIMAGE** column in the **STUDENT** Table by first left-clicking on each **SIMAGE** column and then right-clicking on that **SIMAGE** column again. Click on the **Load** item from the popup menu to browse to the folder where all student images are stored in your local machine, in this case, **C:\Images\Student**, and select the related student image file. Then click on the **Open** button to add each image into that column.

One can find all student images from the folder **Students\Images\Student** at the CRC Press ftp site. Copy and paste them into your local folder, such as **C:\Images\Student**.

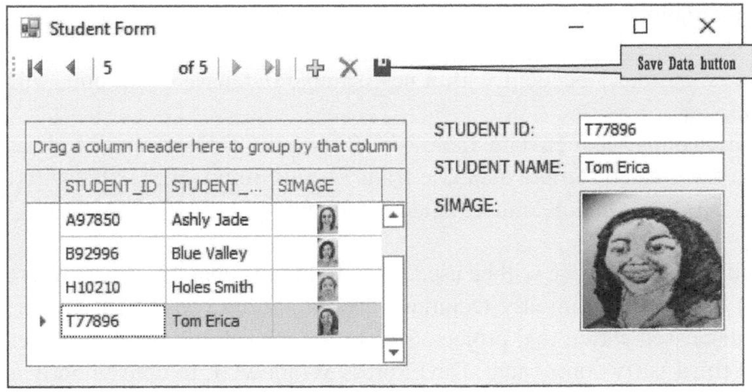

FIGURE 2.51 The completed form for adding all student images.

Do not forget to click on the **Save Data** button on the top to save these images. Your finished Form window should match the one that is shown in Figure 2.51.

Now if you open the **STUDENT** Table in our sample database, **CSE _ DEPT**, by using either Oracle SQL Developer or Server Explorer in the Visual Studio. NET environment, you can find that all data values in the **SIMAGE** columns have been changed to BLOB.

A complete project, **Oracle Image Project**, with its solution can be found in the folder **Class DB Projects\Chapter 2** in the **Students** folder at the CRC Press ftp site.

The only issue with successfully running this project is to check and confirm whether the trial version of the DevExpress WindowUI has expired. If it has, download a new or current version to keep it updated and make the project work.

2.10 A SHORTCUT: HOW TO USE THE SAMPLE DATABASE WITHOUT BUILDING IT

Refer to Appendix E to get more details on how to quickly duplicate the sample database, **CSE _ DEPT**, by using the Oracle SQL Developer if users do not want to build it.

2.11 CHAPTER SUMMARY

A detailed discussion and analysis of the structure and components of popular database systems is provided in this chapter. Some key technologies used to develop and design databases are also given and discussed in this part. The procedure and components used to develop a relational database are analyzed in detail, with some real data Tables in our sample database, **CSE _ DEPT**. The process of developing and building a sample database is discussed in detail, with the following points:

- Defining relationships
- Normalizing the data
- Implementing the relational database

In Section 2.9, a sample Oracle database, **CSE _ DEPT**, is built with Oracle Express Edition 18c, with a popular database development system, Oracle SQL Developer.

Detailed step-by-step illustrations and explanations are provided for those development stages to provide readers a crystal-clear picture of how to create a new Oracle 18c XE database and Tables with the help of Oracle 18c XE and Oracle SQL Developer, which are difficult or rarely to be found in most other books related to Oracle 18c XE development.

The covered technologies include, but are not limited to:

- Create a new customer account with a new sample database or schema with the Oracle SQL Developer.
- Set up relationships between data Tables with Oracle SQL Developer Modeler.
- Connect to the created sample database from Visual Studio. NET 2019 with the help of a third-party product, the dotConnect data component.

The developed sample database will be used in the following chapters throughout the whole book.

At the end of this chapter, an easy technique used to store or insert images in the Oracle 18c XE database is discussed with a real project. Step-by-step illustrations are provided to show readers how to use a third-party component, DevExpress WindowUI, to conveniently and quickly add both faculty and student images to the related columns in the **FACULTY** or **STUDENT** Tables in our sample database.

HOMEWORK

I. True/False Selections

______1. The database development process involves project planning, problem analysis, logical design, physical design, implementation and maintenance.

______2. Duplication of data creates problems with data integrity.

______3. If the primary key consists of a single column, then a Table in 1NF is automatically in 2NF.

______4. A Table is in first normal form if there are no repeating groups of data in any column.

______5. When a user perceives the database as made up of Tables, it is called a network model.

______6. The entity integrity rule states that no attribute that is a member of the primary (composite) key may accept a null value.

______7. When creating data Tables for the Oracle database, a blank field can be kept as a blank without any value in it.

______8. To create data Tables in an Oracle Server database, the data type for an image field can be a binary large object (BLOB).

______9. The name of each data Table in an Oracle Server database must be prefixed by the keyword or a.

______10. Each relational database Table can contain multiple primary keys but only one unique foreign key.

II. Multiple Choice

1. There are many advantages to using an integrated database approach over a file processing approach. These include
   a. Minimizing data redundancy
   b. Improving security
   c. Data independence
   d. All of the above

2. The entity integrity rule implies that no attribute that is a member of the primary key may accept a ____________
   a. Null value
   b. Integer data type
   c. Character data type
   d. Real data type

3. Reducing data redundancy will lead to ___________
   a. Deletion anomalies
   b. Data consistency
   c. Loss of efficiency
   d. None of the above
4. ___________ keys are used to create relationships among various Tables in a database
   a. Primary
   b. Candidate
   c. Foreign
   d. Composite
5. In a small university, the Computer Science Department has six faculty members. However, each faculty member belongs to only the computer science department. This type of relationship is called ___________
   a. One-to-one
   b. One-to-many
   c. Many-to-many
   d. None of the above
6. Client server databases have several advantages over file server databases. These include ___________
   a. Minimizing chances of crashes
   b. Provision of features for recovery
   c. Enforcement of security
   d. Efficient use of the network
   e. All of the above
7. One can create the foreign keys between Tables ___________
   a. Before any Table can be created
   b. When some Tables are created
   c. After all Tables are created
   d. With no limitations
8. To create foreign keys between Tables, first one must select the Table that contains a ___________ key and then select another Table that has a ___________ key
   a. Primary, foreign
   b. Primary, primary
   c. Foreign, primary
   d. Foreign, foreign
9. The data type nvarchar(50) in an Oracle Server database is a string with ___________
   a. Limited length up to 50 letters
   b. Fixed length of 50 bytes
   c. A certain number of letters
   d. Varying length
10. For data Tables in an Oracle Server database, a blank field must be ___________
   a. Indicated by NULL Avoided
   b. Kept as a blank
   c. Indicated either by NULL or a blank
   d. Indicated by NULL

III. Exercises

1. What are the advantages to using an integrated database approach over a file processing approach?
2. Define entity integrity and referential integrity. Describe the reasons for enforcing these rules.
3. Entities can have three types of relationships, one-to-one, one-to-many and many-to-many. Define each type of relationship. Draw ER diagrams to illustrate each type of relationship.
4. List all steps to create foreign keys between data Tables for the Oracle 18c Express Edition database in the Oracle SQL Developer Modeler. Illustrate those steps by using a real example, for instance, how to create foreign keys between the LogIn and the Faculty Table.
5. List all steps to create foreign keys between data Tables for the Oracle 18c Express Edition database in the Oracle SQL Developer Modeler. Illustrate those steps by using a real example, for instance, how to create foreign keys between the StudentCourse and the Course Table.

3 JDBC API and JDBC Drivers

This chapter discusses the fundamentals of JDBC and the JDBC API, which include an overview of the JDBC and the JDBC API, JDBC drivers and related components used in the JDBC API.

3.1 WHAT ARE JDBC AND JDBC API?

JDBC is the standard *Java Database Connectivity*, and the JDBC API is the *Java Database Connectivity Application Programming Interface*. All components and techniques of JDBC are embedded and implemented in the JDBC API. Basically, the JDBC API is composed of a set of classes and interfaces used to interact with databases from Java applications.

Generally, the JDBC API performs the following three functions

1) Establish a connection between your Java application and related databases
2) Build and execute Oracle statements
3) Process the results

Different database vendors provide various JDBC drivers to support their applications to different databases. The most popular JDBC components are located in the following packages:

- **`java.sql`**: contains the standard JDBC components.
- **`javax.sql`**: contains the Standard Extension of JDBC, which provides additional features such as the Java Naming and Directory Interface (JNDI) and Java Transaction Service (JTS).
- **`oracle.jdbc`**: contains the extended functions provided by the java.sql and javax.sql interfaces.
- **`oracle.sql`**: contains classes and interfaces that provide Java mappings to SQL data types.

All of these parts are combined to provide the necessary components and classes to build database applications using Java.

Generally, the JDBC API enables users to access virtually any kind of tabular data source such as spreadsheets or flat files from a Java application. It also provides connectivity to a wide scope of SQL or Oracle databases. One of the most important advantages of using JDBC is that it allows users to access any kind of relational database with similar code, which means that the user can develop one program with similar code to access either a SQL Server database, Oracle database or MySQL database with some modifications.

The JDBC 4.0 and JDBC 4.3 specifications contain additional features, such as extensions to the support to various data types, metadata components and improvements on some interfaces.

3.2 JDBC COMPONENTS AND ARCHITECTURE

The JDBC API is the only part of the entire JDBC product line.

The core of the JDBC API is called a JDBC driver, which implements all JDBC components, including the classes and interfaces, to build a connection and manipulate data between your Java application and the selected database. To be exact, a JDBC driver, which is a class that is composed of a set of methods, builds a connection and accesses databases through those methods.

DOI: 10.1201/9781003304029-3

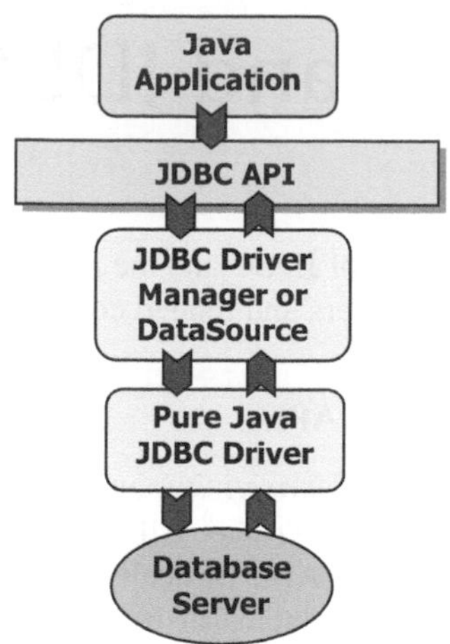

FIGURE 3.1 The components and architecture of the JDBC API.

TABLE 3.1
Classes Defined in the JDBC API

Class	Function
DriverManager	This class handles loading and unloading of drivers and establishes a connection to a database
DriverPropertyInfo	All methods defined in this class are used to set up or retrieve properties of a driver. The properties can then be used by the Connection object to connect to the database
Type	The Type class is only used to define the constants used for identifying Oracle types
Date	This class contains methods to perform conversion of Oracle date formats and Java Date objects
Time	This class is similar to the Date class, and it contains methods to convert between Oracle time and Java Time objects
TimeStamp	This class provides additional precision to the Java Date object by adding a nanosecond field

The JDBC API contains two major sets of interfaces: the first is the JDBC API for application writers (interface to your Java applications), and the second is the lower-level JDBC driver API for driver writers (interface to your database). JDBC technology drivers fit into one of four categories. Applications and applets can access databases via the JDBC API using pure Java JDBC technology-based drivers, as shown in Figure 3.1.

As we mentioned, the JDBC API is composed of a set of classes and interfaces used to interact with databases from Java applications. Table 3.1 lists all classes defined in the JDBC API and their functions, and Table 3.2 shows all interfaces defined in the JDBC API.

It can be seen in Table 3.1 that the most popular classes in the JDBC API are the top three classes: DriverManager, DriverPropertyInfo and Type, and they are widely implemented in Java database programming applications.

All the interfaces listed in Table 3.2 are popular and widely implemented in Java database applications. More detailed discussion and example applications of these interfaces will be provided in Chapter 5, with real project examples.

The core of the JDBC API is the JDBC Driver that can be accessed and called from the DriverManager class method. Depending on the different applications, a JDBC driver can be categorized into four types: Type I, Type II, Type III and Type IV. A more detailed discussion of the JDBC Driver and its types will be given in Section 3.4. An optional way to access the database is to

TABLE 3.2
Interfaces Defined in the JDBC API

Interface	Function
Driver	The primary use of the Driver interface is to create Connection objects. It can also be used for the collection of JDBC driver metadata and JDBC driver status checking
Connection	This interface is used for the maintenance and status monitoring of a database session. It also provides data access control through the use of transaction locking
Statement	Statement methods are used to execute query statements and retrieve data from the ResultSet object
PreparedStatement	This interface is used to execute pre-compile statements. Pre-compile statements allow for faster and more efficient statement execution and, more importantly, allow running dynamic queries with querying parameter variation. This interface can be considered a subclass of Statement
CallableStatement	This interface is mainly used to execute Oracle stored procedures. Both IN and OUT parameters are supported. This interface can be considered a subclass of Statement
ResultSet	The ResultSet object contains the queried result in row and column format. This interface also provides methods to retrieve data returned by an Oracle statement execution. It also contains methods for Oracle data type and JDBC data type conversion
ResultSetMetaData	This interface contains a collection of metadata information or physical descriptions associated with the last ResultSet object
DatabaseMetaData	This interface contains a collection of metadata regarding the database used, including the database version, Table names, columns and supported functions

use the DataSource object, which is a better way to identify and connect to a data source and makes code even more porTable and easier to maintain.

3.3 HOW DOES JDBC WORK?

As we mentioned in the last section, the JDBC API has three functions: 1) set up a connection between your Java application and your database, 2) build and execute query statements and 3) process results. We will discuss these functions in more detail in this section based on the JDBC architecture shown in Figure 3.1.

3.3.1 Establish a Connection

The JDBC Driver class contains six methods, and one of the most important methods is the **connect()** method, which is used to connect to the database. When using this Driver class, a point to be noted is that most methods defined in the Driver class can never be called directly; instead, they should be called via the DriverManager class methods.

3.3.1.1 Using DriverManager to Establish a Connection

The DriverManager class is a set of utility functions that work with the Driver methods and manage multiple JDBC drivers by keeping them as a list of drivers loaded. Although loading a driver and registering a driver are two steps, only one method call is necessary to perform these two operations. The operational sequence of loading and registering a JDBC driver is:

1) Call class methods in the DriverManager class to load the driver into the Java interpreter
2) Register the driver using the **registerDriver()** method

When loaded, the driver will execute the **DriverManager.registerDriver()** method to register itself. These two operations will never be performed until a method in the DriverManager is executed, which means that both operations have been coded in an application; however, the driver cannot be loaded and registered until a method such as **connect()** is first executed.

To load and register a JDBC driver, two popular methods can be used:

1) Use the Class.forName() method:
```
Class.forName("oracle.jdbc.OracleDriver");
```
2) Create a new instance of the Driver class:
```
Driver oraDriver = new oracle.jdbc.OracleDriver;
```

Relatively speaking, the first method is more professional, since the driver is both loaded and registered when a valid method in the DriverManager class is executed. The second method cannot guarantee that the driver has been registered by using the DriverManager.

3.3.1.2 Using DataSource Object to Establish a Connection

Another, better way to establish a connection is to use the DataSource object.

The DataSource interface, introduced in the JDBC 2.0 Standard Extension API, is a better way to connect to a data source to perform data actions. In JDBC, a data source is a class that implements the interface **javax.sql.DataSource** to connect to more than one desired database. The **getConnection()** method is always used to set up this connection.

A DataSource object is normally registered with a Java Naming and Directory Interface naming service. This means that an application can retrieve a DataSource object by name from the naming service independently of the system configuration.

Perform the following three operations to deploy a DataSource object:

1) Create an instance of the DataSource class
2) Set its properties using setter methods
3) Register it with a JNDI naming service

After a valid connection has been set up using the DataSource object, one can use any of the data query methods listed in Tables 3.3 and 3.4 to perform data actions against the desired database.

TABLE 3.3
The Function of Three Query Statement Execution Methods

Method	Function
executeQuery()	This method performs a data query and returns a ResultSet object that contains the queried results
executeUpdate()	This method does not perform a data query; instead, it only performs either a data update, insertor delete action against the database and returns an integer that equals the number of rows that have been successfully updated, inserted or deleted
execute()	This method is a special method, and it can be used either way. All different data actions can be performed by using this method, such as data query, data insertion, data updating and data deleting. The most important difference between the execute() method and the two previous methods is that this method can be used to execute some query statements that are unknown at compile time or return multiple results from stored procedures. Another difference is that the execute() method does not return any results itself, and one needs to use getResultSet() or getUpdateCount() method to pick up the results. Both methods belong to the Statement class

3.3.2 Build and Execute Oracle Statements

Once a valid connection is established and a Connection object is created, the JDBC driver is responsible for ensuring that an application has consistent and uniform access to any database. It is also responsible for ensuring that any requests made by the application are presented to the database in a way that can be recognized by the database.

To build an Oracle statement, one needs to call the method createStatement() that belongs to the Connection class to create a new Statement object. Usually, there are three types of Statement objects widely implemented in the JDBC API: Statement, PreparedStatement and CallableStatement. The relationship among these three classes is: the PreparedStatement and CallableStatement classes are the subclasses of the Statement class.

To execute an Oracle statement, one of the following three methods can be called:

1) **`executeQuery()`**
2) **`executeUpdate()`**
3) **`execute()`**

All of these methods belong to the Statement and PreparedStatement classes and are used to access the database to perform different data actions.

The differences between these three methods are dependent on the different data operations and actions. Table 3.3 lists the function for each method and the situation in which the appropriate method should be utilized. More detailed discussion about these three methods and their implementations can be found in Chapter 5.

3.3.3 Process Results

After a desired Oracle statement is executed, you need to retrieve the execution results. Depending on the different execution methods you called, you need to use different methods to pick up the results.

Table 3.4 lists some necessary methods used to pick up the appropriate results based on the different execution methods utilized.

3.3.3.1 Using a ResultSet Object

A ResultSet object will be created after the **`executeQuery()`** method is executed or a **`getResultSet()`** method is executed. A ResultSet object is a data structure that presents rows and columns returned by a valid query. It maintains a cursor pointing to its current row of data. Initially, the cursor is positioned before the first row. One can use the **`next()`** method to move the cursor to

TABLE 3.4
The Desired Method Used to Pick up the Oracle Execution Results

Execution Method	Pick-up Method
executeQuery()	getResultSet(), getXXX(), where XXX equals the desired data type of the returned result
executeUpdate()	getUpdateCount() This method will return an integer that equals the number of rows that have been successfully updated, inserted or deleted
execute()	getResultSet(), getUpdateCount() This method does not return any result itself, and one needs to use the getResultSet() or getUpdateCount() method to pick up the results. Both methods belong to the Statement class

the next row, and, continuing this moving, one can scan the entire ResultSet. With a loop, one can use the appropriate **getXXX()** method of the ResultSet class to pick up each row in the ResultSet object. The XXX indicates the corresponding Java data type of the selected row. A more detailed discussion about these methods will be provided in Chapter 4.

3.3.3.2 Using a RowSet Object

A RowSet object contains a set of rows from a result set or some other source of tabular data, like a file or spreadsheet. Because a RowSet object follows the JavaBeans model for properties and event notification, it is a JavaBeans component that can be combined with other components in an application. As it is compatible with other Beans, application developers can use a development tool to create a RowSet object and set its properties.

RowSets may have many different implementations to fill different needs. These implementations fall into two broad categories, connected and disconnected:

1) A connected RowSet is equivalent to a ResultSet, and it maintains a connection to a data source as long as the RowSet is in use.
2) A disconnected RowSet works as a DataSet, and it can connect to a data source to perform data updates periodically. Most time, it is disconnected from the data source and uses a mapping memory space as a mapped database.

While a RowSet is disconnected, it does not need a JDBC driver or the full JDBC API, so its footprint is very small. Thus a RowSet is an ideal format for sending data over a network to a thin client.

Because it is not continually connected to its data source, a disconnected RowSet stores its data in memory. It needs to maintain metadata about the columns it contains and information about its internal state. It also needs a facility for making connections, for executing commands and for reading and writing data to and from the data source. A connected RowSet, by contrast, opens a connection and keeps it open for as long as the RowSet is being used. A more detailed discussion about the RowSet object and its implementation will be given in Chapter 5.

Since the JDBC driver is a core for the entire JDBC API, we will have a more detailed discussion about this component in the next section.

3.4 JDBC DRIVER AND DRIVER TYPES

The JDBC driver builds a bridge between your Java applications and your desired database and works as an intermediate-level translator to perform a double-direction conversion: convert your high-level Java code to the low-level native code to interface to the database and convert the low-level native commands from the database to your high-level Java code.

As we discussed in the last section, a JDBC driver class contains six methods, and one of the most important is the **connect()** method, which is used to connect to the database. When using this Driver class, a point to be noted is that most methods defined in the Driver class can never be called directly; instead, they should be called via the DriverManager class methods.

Generally, the JDBC API will not contain any JDBC drivers, and you need to download the desired JDBC driver from the corresponding vendor if you want to use a specified driver. Based on different configurations, JDBC drivers can be categorized into the following four types.

3.4.1 Type I: JDBC-ODBC Bridge Driver

Open Database Connectivity (ODBC) is a Microsoft-based database application programming interface (API), and it aims to be independent of programming languages, database systems and

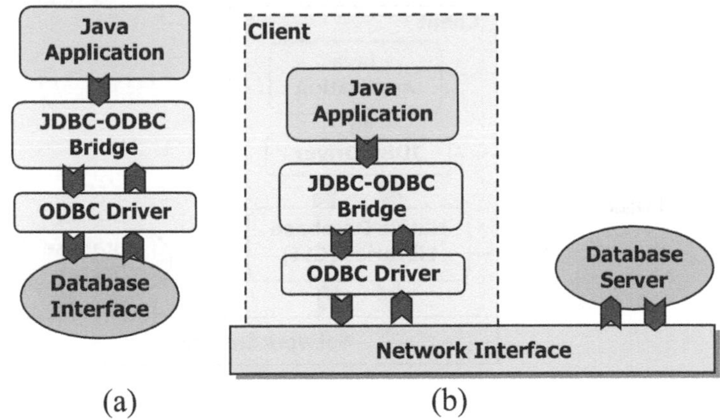

FIGURE 3.2 JDBC-ODBC bridge driver.

operating systems. In other words, the ODBC is a database- and operating system–independent API, and it can access any database in any platform without problems.

Figure 3.2 shows a typical architecture of the JDBC-ODBC Bridge Driver application. Figure 3.2a is for a Java stand-alone application, and 3.2b is a two-tier Java application.

Basically, ODBC is built and based on various call level interface (CLI) specifications from the Oracle Access Group and X/Open techniques. To access ODBC to interface to a desired database, a JDBC-ODBC bridge is needed, and this bridge works just like a translator or a converter, which interprets the JDBC requests to the CLI in ODBC when a request is sent from the JDBC to the ODBC and performs an inverse translation (from CLI in ODBC to JDBC) when a result is returned from the database. The advantage of using a Type I driver is simplicity, since we do not need to know the details inside ODBC and transactions between the ODBC and DBMS. Refer to Figure 3.2a, which is a typical Java stand-alone application that uses the JDBC-ODBC Bridge Driver to access a local database, and it will work fine. However, a problem will be exposed if applying the JDBC-ODBC Bridge Driver in a two-tier application, as shown in Figure 3.2b. The problem is that the network standard security manager will not allow the ODBC that is downloaded as an applet to access any local files when you build a Java Applet application to access a database located in a database server. Therefore, it is impossible to build a Java Applet application with this JDBC-ODBC Bridge Driver configuration.

3.4.2 Type II: Native-API-Partly-Java Driver

The native-API-partly-Java driver makes use of local native libraries to communicate with the database. The driver does this by making calls to the locally installed native call level interface using a native language, either C or C++, to access the database. The CLI libraries are responsible for the actual communications with the database server. When a client application makes a database access request, the driver translates the JDBC request to the native method call and passes the request to the native CLI. After the database processes the request, results will be translated from their native language back to the JDBC and presented to the client application. Figure 3.3 shows a Type II driver configuration.

Compared with a Type I driver, the communications between the driver and the database are performed by using the native CLI without needing any translation between JDBC and the ODBC driver; therefore, the speed and efficiency of Type II drivers are higher than those of Type I drivers. When available, Type II drivers are recommended over Type I drivers.

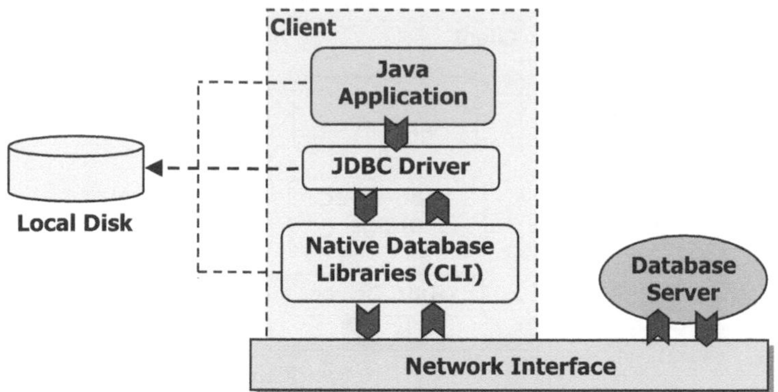

FIGURE 3.3 Type II driver.

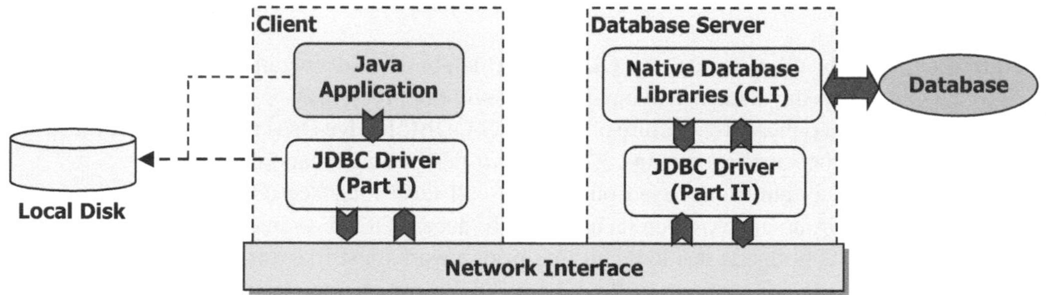

FIGURE 3.4 Type III driver configuration.

3.4.3 Type III: JDBC-Net-All-Java Driver

Basically, Type III drivers are similar to Type II drivers, and the only difference between them is the replacement of the native database access libraries.

For both Type I and Type II drivers, either the ODBC driver or the native CLI libraries must be installed and located on the client machine. All communications between the server processes and the JDBC driver are through the native program interface. However, in a Type III driver configuration, the native CLI libraries are placed on a server, and the driver uses a network protocol to facilitate communications between the application and the driver. The result of this modification is to separate the driver into two parts: 1) a part of the JDBC driver that is an all-Java portion and can be downloaded to the client and 2) a server portion containing both another part of the JDBC driver and native CLI methods. All communications between the application and the database server are 100% Java to Java. However, the communication between the database and the server is still done via a native database CLI. Figure 3.4 shows this configuration.

It can be seen from Figure 3.4 that the client does not need to perform either database-specified protocol translation or a Java-to-CLI translation by using Type III drivers, and this will greatly reduce the workload for the client machine; the client piece of a Type III driver only needs to translate requests into the network protocol to communicate with the database server. Another advantage of using a Type III driver is that the second part of the Type III driver, which is used to communicate with the database native libraries, does not need to be downloaded to the client, and as a result, Type III drivers are not subject to the same security restrictions as Types I and II. Since all database-related code resides on the server side, a large driver that is capable of connecting to many different databases can be built.

3.4.4 Type IV: Native-Protocol-All-Java Driver

Type IV drivers are totally different from any drivers we have discussed so far. These types of drivers are capable of communicating directly with the database without the need for any type of translation, since they are 100% Java without using any CLI native libraries. Figure 3.5 shows a typical Type IV driver configuration.

The key issue in use of a Type IV driver is that the native database protocol will be rewritten to convert the JDBC calls into vendor-specific protocol calls, and the result of this rewriting is that the driver can directly interact with the database without needing any other translations. Therefore, Type IV drivers are the fastest drivers compared with Type I–III drivers. Using a Type IV driver will greatly simplify database access for applets by eliminating the need for native CLI libraries.

3.5 JDBC STANDARD EXTENSION API

Besides the standard JDBC API (or core API), Sun added an extension package called JDBC 2.0 Standard Extension API to support extended database operations. This package contains the following components:

1) JDBC DataSource
2) JDBC driver-based connection pooling
3) JDBC RowSet
4) Distributed transactions

We will take a close look at these components and provide a more detailed discussion about these elements in the following sections.

3.5.1 JDBC DataSource

In Section 3.3.3.2, we had a brief discussion about the DataSource object. Because of its specialty and advantage over JDBC drivers and DriverManagers, we will provide a more detailed discussion about this interface in this part.

As we know, the DataSource interface is introduced in the JDBC 2.0 Standard Extension API, and it is a better way to connect to a data source to perform data actions. In JDBC, a data source is a class that implements the interface `javax.sql.DataSource` to connect to more than one desired database. The `getConnection()` method is always used to set up this connection.

As we discussed in Section 3.3.1, to establish a connection by using a JDBC driver, you need to use the DriverManager to load a desired driver and register that driver to the driver list. You also need to know the exact driver name and the driver URL to complete this connection. In fact, the DataSource can provide an alternative better way to do that connection in a faster and more efficient way.

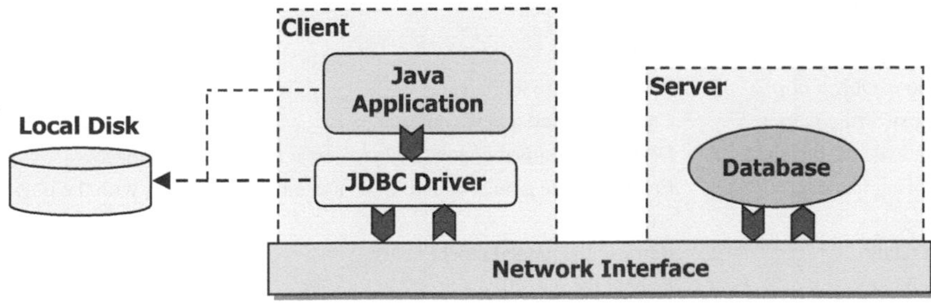

FIGURE 3.5 Type IV driver configuration.

The advantage of using a DataSource to perform this database connection is that a DataSource object is normally registered with a Java Naming and Directory Interface naming service. This means that an application can retrieve a DataSource object by the name of that DataSource only, without needing to know the driver name, database name and driver URLs, even without needing to register any drivers. In other words, this naming service is independent of system configurations and databases.

3.5.1.1 Java Naming and Directory Interface

The Java Naming and Directory Interface provides naming and directory functionality and service to Java applications. It is defined to be independent of any specific directory service implementation so that different directories can be accessed in a common way.

To be exact, the JNDI is analogous to a file directory that allows users to find and work with files by name. In this way, the JNDI is used to find the DataSource using the logical name assigned to it when it is registered with the JNDI.

The association of a name with an object is called a binding process. A DataSource object stores the attributes that tell it how to connect to a database, and those attributes are assigned when you bind the DataSource instance to its JNDI directory. The core JNDI interface that performs looking up, binding, unbinding, renaming objects and creating and destroying subcontexts is the Context interface.

The Context interface represents a naming context, which consists of a set of name-to-object bindings. It contains methods for examining and updating these bindings. Table 3.5 shows some of the most popular methods used by this interface.

In fact, using JNDI can significantly improve the portability of a Java application by removing the need to hardcode a driver name and database name, and it is very similar to a file directory that improves file access by overcoming the need to reference disk cylinders and sectors. To establish a valid database connection using the JNDI, the only information you need is the name of the DataSource—yes, that is all you need, and it is so simple and easy, is it not?

3.5.1.2 Deploy and Use a Basic Implementation of DataSource

In this section, we will use a piece of code to illustrate the implementation of a DataSource object. Perform the following three operations to deploy a DataSource object:

1) Create an instance of the DataSource class.
2) Set its properties using setter methods.
3) Register it with a JNDI naming service.

TABLE 3.5
The Most Popular Methods Used in the Context Interface

Method	Function
bind(String name, Object obj)	Bind a name to an object
createSubcontext(String name)	Create and bind a new context
destroySubcontext(String name)	Destroy the named context and remove it from the namespace
listBindings(String name)	Enumerate the names bound in the named context, along with the objects bound to them
lookup(String name)	Retrieve the named object
unbind(String name)	Unbind the named object
close()	Close this context

```
Vendor_DataSource ds = new Vendor_DataSource();
ds.setServerName("localhost");
ds.setDatabaseName("CSE_DEPT");
ds.setDescription("CSE_DEPT Database");
Context ctx = new InitialContext();
ctx.bind("jdbc/CSE_DEPT", ds);
```

FIGURE 3.6 Example code for the creation of a new DataSource object.

```
Context ctx = new InitialContext();
DataSource ds = (DataSource)ctx.lookup("jdbc/CSE_DEPT");
Connection con = ds.getConnection("myUserName", "myPassWord");
// Execute the query statements to perform data actions via database......
```

FIGURE 3.7 Example codefor execution of the database connection via DataSource.

The first step is to create a DataSource object, set its properties and register it with a JNDI naming service. A DataSource object is usually created, deployed and managed separately from the Java applications that use it. A point to be noted is that a DataSource object for a particular data source is created and deployed by a developer or system administrator, not the user. Figure 3.6 shows a piece of example code to create a new DataSource object with some property setting using setters. The class `Vendor _ DataSource` would most likely be supplied by a driver vendor.

In Figure 3.6, the first codeline is to create a new DataSource object based on the data source provided by the vendor. The following three lines are used to set up different properties using a setter. The last two lines are used to create an InitialContext object and to bind and register the new DataSource object `ds` to the logical name `jdbc/CSE _ DEPT` with a JNDI naming service.

The JNDI namespace consists of an initial naming context and any number of subcontexts under it. It is hierarchical, similar to the directory/file structure in many file systems, with the initial context being analogous to the root of a file system and subcontexts being analogous to subdirectories. The root of the JNDI hierarchy is the initial context, here represented by the variable `ctx`. There may be many subcontexts under the initial context, one of which is JDBC, the JNDI subcontext reserved for JDBC data sources. The logical data source name may be in the subcontext jdbcor in a subcontext under jdbc. The last element in the hierarchy is the object being registered, analogous to a file, which in this case is a logical name for a data source.

The code shown in Figure 3.7 shows how an application uses this to connect to a data source.

To get a connection using a DataSource object, create a JNDI Context instance and use the name of the DataSource object to its `lookup()` method to try to find it from a JNDI subcontext jdbc. The returned DataSource object will call its `getConnection()` method to establish a connection to the database.

As soon as a database connection has been established, you can execute any Oracle statements you want to perform any desired data action against the connected database.

3.5.2 JDBC Driver-Based Connection Pooling

By using a DataSource object, you can easily set up a connection with your database and perform any data operation you want. Sounds good! Yes, this kind of operation is good for two-tier database applications without problems. However, a problem would occur if you applied this operation in a three-tier database application. The main issue is the overhead in transactions between the application server and client. If you are running a three-tier database application, each time you communicate between your application server and your database via a database server to perform a connection or a disconnection, there would be a lot of communication traffic running between your server and your database, and this would introduce multiple opening and closing operations to your database and greatly reduce the efficiency of the database.

To solve this overhead problem, a Connection Pooling API has been provided by the JDBC Standard Extension API. The pooling implementations do not actually close connections when the client calls the close() method but instead return the connections to a pool of available connections for other clients to use. This avoids any overhead of repeatedly opening and closing connections and allows a large number of clients to share a small number of database connections.

The connection pooling API is an extension of the regular connection API. The working principle of using connection pooling is when a resource or connection is no longer needed after a task has been completed, it is not destroyed but is added into a resource pool instead, making it available when required for a subsequent operation. In other words, we can temporarily store all unused connections to a connection pool and reuse them as soon as a new data action is required for the target database. In this way, we can greatly improve database performance by cutting down on the number of new connections that need to be created.

The JDBC API provides a client and a server interface for connection pooling. The client interface is javax.sql.DataSource, which is what application code will typically use to acquire a pooled database connection. The server interface is javax.sql.ConnectionPoolDataSource, which is how most application servers will interface with the PostgreSQL JDBC driver. Both interfaces are defined in the JDBC 2.0 Standard Extension (also known as the JDBC 2.0 Optional Package).

The server interface for connection pooling, the **ConnectionPoolDataSource** object, is a factory for **PooledConnection** objects. All Connection objects that implement this interface are registered with a JNDI naming service.

To implement a DataSource object to create pooled connections, you need to perform the following operations:

1) Create a ConnectionPoolDataSource object.
2) Set its properties to the data source that produces connections.
3) Register the **ConnectionPoolDataSource** object with the JNDI naming service.
4) Create a DataSource object.
5) Set properties to the DataSource object by using setter.

Figure 3.8 shows a piece of example code to illustrate how to use the connection pooling API to create and deploy a DataSource object that an application can use to get pooled connections to the database.

The first codeline is used to create a new **ConnectionPoolDataSource** object, and this object is equivalent to a pool body to hold unused data sources later.

The following four lines are used to set appropriate properties for this created object. Then, in the sixth and seventh lines, the created **ConnectionPoolDataSource** object is registered with the JNDI naming service. The logical name associated with **cpds** has a subcontext pool added under the subcontext **jdbc**, which is similar to adding a subdirectory to another subdirectory in a file system.

Now we need to create our DataSource object implemented to work with it, or, in other words, we can add this DataSource object into our pool, the **ConnectionPoolDataSource** object, when it is temporarily unused in an application. The eighth to tenth code lines are used to create our DataSource object, **ds**, with the **PooledDataSource** class. Note in the tenth codeline, the name of the DataSource is **jdbc/pool/CSE _ DEPT**, which is identical to the logical name of our **ConnectionPoolDataSource** object we created before.

```
ConnectionPoolDataSource  cpds = new  ConnectionPoolDataSource();
cpds.setServerName("localhost");
cpds.setDatabaseName("CSE_DEPT");
cpds.setPortNumber(1251);
cpds.setDescription("CSE_DEPT Database");
Context ctx = new InitialContext();
ctx.bind("jdbc/pool/CSE_DEPT", cpds);
PooledDataSource  ds = new  PooledDataSource();
ds.setDescription("CSE_DEPT database pooled connection source");
ds.setDataSourceName("jdbc/pool/CSE_DEPT");
Context  ctx = new InitialContext();
ctx.bind("jdbc/CSE_DEPT", ds);
```

FIGURE 3.8 Example code for the connection pooling DataSource.

```
Connection con = null;
 try {
     con = ds.getConnection();
     // use connection
    }
catch(Exception e)
   {
     // log error
    }
finally
   {
        if(con != null)
          try {con.close();}catch(Exception e) {}
   }
```

FIGURE 3.9 Example code for retrieving and reusing a connection.

The last two code lines are used to register our DataSource object with the JNDI naming service.

Now you can use this connection pooling for your data source object. The point is that when you finish a task to your current database, you must call the `close()` method from your client to inform the server that this database connection will be temporarily unused, and this will allow the Connection Pooling API to add this unused connection to the `ConnectionPoolDataSource` object. Later on, if you want to reuse this database, you need to use the code shown in Figure 3.9 to get that connection from the pool.

Another situation in which to use a DataSource object is when you need to implement distributed transactions, which means that you need to use multiple databases synchronously in your applications. In that case, use of a DataSource object with built-in distributed transaction capabilities is the best solution.

3.5.3 Distributed Transactions

A distributed transaction, sometimes referred to as a global transaction, is a set of two or more related transactions that must be managed in a coordinated way. The transactions that constitute a distributed transaction might be in the same database but more typically are in different databases and often in different locations. Each individual transaction of a distributed transaction is referred to as a transaction branch.

In the JDBC 2.0 extension API, distributed transaction functionality is built on top of connection pooling functionality, which we discussed in the last section. This distributed transaction functionality is also built upon the open XA standard for distributed transactions. (XA is part of the X/Open standard and is not specific to Java.)

3.5.3.1 Distributed Transaction Components and Scenarios

A typical distributed transaction can be composed of the following components and scenarios:

- A distributed transaction system typically relies on an external transaction manager, such as a software component that implements standard Java Transaction API (JTA) functionality to coordinate the individual transactions. Many vendors will offer XA-compliant JTA modules. This includes Oracle, which is developing a JTA module based on the Oracle implementation of XA.
- XA functionality is usually isolated from a client application, being implemented instead in a middle-tier environment such as an application server. In many scenarios, the application server and transaction manager will be together on the middle tier, possibly together with some of the application code as well.
- The term "resource manager" is often used in discussing distributed transactions. A resource manager is simply an entity that manages data or some other kind of resource. Wherever the term is used in this chapter, it refers to a database.

By definition, XA is a standard protocol that allows coordination, commitment and recovery between transaction managers (e.g. CICS, Tuxedo and even BEA Web Logic Server) and resource managers (e.g. databases, message queuing products such as JMS or Web Sphere MQ, mainframe applications, ERP packages).

As with the connection pooling API, two classes must be used for a distributed transaction:

- An XADataSource that produces XAConnections supporting distributed transactions.
- A DataSource object that is implemented to work with it.

The transaction manager is responsible for making the final decision either to commit or rollback any distributed transaction. A commit decision should lead to a successful transaction; rollback leaves the data in the database unaltered. JTA specifies standard Java interfaces between the transaction manager and the other components in a distributed transaction: the application, the application server and the resource managers.

3.5.3.2 The Distributed Transaction Process

The transaction manager is the primary component of the distributed transaction infrastructure; however, the JDBC driver and application server components should have the following characteristics:

- The driver should implement the JDBC 2.0 API (including the Optional Package interfaces XADataSource and XAConnection) or higher and the JTA interface XAResource.
- The application server should provide a DataSource class that is implemented to interact with the distributed transaction infrastructure and a connection pooling module.

The first step of the distributed transaction process is to send a request to the transaction manager by the application. Although the final commit/rollback decision treats the transaction as a single logical unit, there can be many transaction branches involved. A transaction branch is associated with a request to each resource manager involved in the distributed transaction. Requests to three different RDBMSs, therefore, require three transaction branches. Each transaction branch must be committed or rolled back by the local resource manager. The transaction manager controls the boundaries

```
XATransactionIDS  xads = new  XATransactionIDS ();
xads.setServerName("localhost");
xads.setDatabaseName("CSE_DEPT");
xads.setPortNumber(1521);
xads.setDescription("CSE_DEPT Database");
Context ctx = new InitialContext();
ctx.bind("jdbc/xa/CSE_DEPT", xads);
TransactionIDS  ds  = new  TransactionIDS();
ds.setDescription("CSE_DEPT distributed transaction connection source");
ds.setDataSourceName("jdbc/xa/CSE_DEPT");
Context  ctx = new InitialContext();
ctx.bind("jdbc/CSE_DEPT", ds);
```

FIGURE 3.10 Example code for the distributed transaction implementation.

of the transaction and is responsible for the final decision as to whether the total transaction should commit or rollback. This decision is made in two phases, called the two-phase commit protocol.

In the first phase, the transaction manager polls all of the resource database managers (RDBMSs) involved in the distributed transaction to see if any of them is ready to commit. If a resource manager cannot commit, it responds negatively and rolls back its particular part of the transaction so that data is not altered.

In the second phase, the transaction manager determines if any of the resource managers have responded negatively; if so, it rolls back the whole transaction. If there are no negative responses, the translation manager commits the whole transaction and returns the results to the application.

The DataSource implemented to produce connections for distributed transactions is almost always implemented to produce connections that are pooled as well. The XAConnection interface extends the PooledConnection interface.

To begin a distributed transaction, an XADataSource object should be created first, and this can be done by creating a new instance of the XATransactionIDS and setting its properties.

Figure 3.10 shows example code for a distributed transaction.

The first codeline is used to create a new **XADataSource** object, and it produces XAConnections supporting distributed transactions.

The following four lines are used to set appropriate properties for this created object.

Then, in the sixth and seventh lines, the created **XADataSource** object is registered with the JNDI naming service. The logical name associated with **xads** has a subcontext, **xa**, added under the subcontext **jdbc**, which is similar to adding a subdirectory to another subdirectory in a file system.

Finally, the DataSource object is created to interact with **xads**, and other **XADataSource** objects are deployed.

Now that instances of the **TransactionIDS** and **XATransactionIDS** classes have been created, an application can use the DataSource to get a connection to the **CSE _ DEPT** database, and this connection can then be used in any distributed transactions.

3.5.4 JDBC RowSet

A JDBC RowSet object is one of the JavaBeans components with multiple support from JavaBeans, and it is a new feature in the java.sql package. By using the RowSet object, a database query can be performed automatically with the data source connection and query statement creation. In this section, we will provide a brief introduction to this new feature to reduce the code load and improve the efficiency of the data query with the help of this RowSet object. A more detailed discussion with real project examples will be given in Section 6.4.6 in Chapter 6.

3.5.4.1 Introduction to Java RowSet Object

A RowSet object contains a set of rows from a result set or some other source of tabular data, like a file or spreadsheet. Because a RowSet object follows the JavaBeans model for properties and event notification, it is a JavaBeans component that can be combined with other components in an application. As it is compatible with other Beans, application developers can use a development tool to create a RowSet object and set its properties.

RowSets may have many different implementations to fill different needs. These implementations fall into two broad categories, connected and disconnected:

1) A connected RowSet is equivalent to a ResultSet, and it maintains a connection to a data source as long as the RowSet is in use.
2) A disconnected RowSet works as a DataSet in Visual Studio. NET, and it can connect to a data source to perform data updates periodically. Most of the time, it is disconnected from the data source and uses a mapping memory space as a mapped database.

While a RowSet is disconnected, it does not need a JDBC driver or the full JDBC API, so its footprint is very small. Thus a RowSet is an ideal format for sending data over a network to a thin client.

To make writing an implementation easier, the Java Software division of Sun Microsystems, Inc., plans to provide reference implementations for five different styles of RowSets in the future. Among them, two components are very popular and widely implemented in Java database applications:

1) A CachedRowSet class—a disconnected RowSet that caches its data in memory; it is not suiTable for very large data sets but an ideal way to provide thin Java clients, such as a personal digital assistant (PDA) or network computer (NC), with tabular data
2) A JDBCRowSet class—a connected RowSet that serves mainly as a thin wrapper around a ResultSet object to make a JDBC driver look like a JavaBeans component

To effectively apply RowSet objects to perform data actions against desired databases, the following operational sequence should be used.

3.5.4.2 Implementation Process of a RowSet Object

Generally, the operational procedure of using a RowSet object to query data can be divided into the following four steps:

1) Set up and conFigure a RowSet object.
2) Register the RowSet Listeners.
3) Set input and output parameters for the query command.
4) Traverse through the result rows from the ResultSet.

The first step is used to set up and conFigure the static or dynamic properties of a RowSet object, such as the connection URL, username, password and run command, to allow the RowSet object to connect to the data source, pass user parameters into the data source and perform the data query.

The second step allows users to register different Listeners for the RowSet object with different event sources. The RowSet feature supports multiple listeners being registered with the RowSet object. Listeners can be registered using the **`addRowSetListener()`** method and unregistered through the **`removeRowSetListener()`** method. A listener should implement the **`javax.sql.`**

RowSetListener interface to register itself as the RowSet listener. Three types of events are supported by the RowSet interface:

1) cursorMoved event: Generated whenever there is a cursor movement, which occurs when the **next()** or **previous()** methods are called.
2) rowChanged event: Generated when a new row is inserted, updated or deleted from the row set.
3) rowsetChanged event: Generated when the whole row set is created or changed.

In this book, the Apache NetBeans IDE 12.4 is used, and the event-listener model has been set up by the NetBeans IDE, so we can skip this step and do not need to take care of this issue during our coding process in the following chapters.

Step 3 allows users to set up all static or dynamic parameters for the query statement of the RowSet object. Depending on the data type of the parameters used in the query statement, the suiTable **setXXX()** method should used to perform this parameter setup process.

The fourth step is used to retrieve each row from the ResultSet object.

3.6 CHAPTER SUMMARY

This chapter discusses the fundamentals of JDBC and the JDBC API, which include an overview of the JDBC and the JDBC API, JDBC drivers and related components used in the JDBC API.

The JDBC components and architecture are discussed and analyzed in detail in the first part of this chapter. All classes and interfaces defined in the JDBC API are discussed and presented with sequence Tables. With some basic idea of JDBC and its components, the function and operational procedures of using the JDBC API to perform data actions are described by three key steps:

1) Establish a connection between your Java application and related databases.
2) Build and execute Oracle statements.
3) Process the results.

To set up a valid database connection, two popular connection methods are introduced: using the DriverManager class method and using the DataSource object. Relatively speaking, the second method is simple and easy to use in real applications since no detailed data source information is needed for this database connection.

To build and execute a typical Oracle statement, the **Statement**, **PreparedStatement** and **CallableStatement** components are introduced and discussed. Both the PreparedStatement and CallableStatement classes are subclasses of the Statement class; however, both of them have more flexibility compared to the Statement component.

To process a returned query result, different objects, such as ResultSet and RowSet, are introduced and discussed to provide users a clear picture of those objects and their functionalities.

Following the JDBC API and JDBC driver discussion, a detailed discussion about the types of JDBC drivers is provided. Four popular types of drivers are analyzed and compared with architectures and their implementations.

Finally, four important components defined in the JDBC Standard Extension API, DataSource, Connection Pooling, Distributed Transactions and RowSet, are introduced and discussed with example code.

The topics discussed in this chapter are a prerequisite for the next chapter, and some components will be discussed and analyzed in more detail to give users a deeper understanding and better picture of their roles in real Java database applications.

HOMEWORK

I. True/False Selections

_______1. JDBC is standard Java Database Connectivity, and the JDBC API can be considered the Java Database Connectivity Application Programming Interface.

_______2. The JDBC API is not the only component included in a JDBC.

_______3. The JDBC API is composed of a set of classes and interfaces used to interact with databases from Java applications.

_______4. JDBC drivers are implementation dependent, which means that different applications need different drivers.

_______5. The core of the JDBC 4.0 API provides standard JDBC components that are located in the `java.sql` package, and some additional components such as JNDI and JTS are defined in the JDBC 4.0 Standard Extension that is located in the `javax.sql` package.

_______6. One can establish a database connection by directly calling the Driver class method **`connect()`**.

_______7. To load and register a JDBC driver, two popular methods can be used: either using the Class.forName() method or creating a new instance of the Driver class.

_______8. Three components can be used to build an Oracle statement: Statement, Prepared-Statement and CallableStatement.

_______9. To pick up the execution results, one can use the executeQuery() and executeUpdate() methods. The former returns an integer, and the latter returns a ResultSet.

______10. There are four types of JDBC drivers, and a Type IV driver is a pure Java driver with fast running speed and high efficiency in data actions.

II. Multiple Choice

1. Generally, the JDBC API perform the following three functions ____________
   a. Connect to database, load JDBC driver, perform the query
   b. Perform the query, connect to database, load JDBC driver
   c. Get result from ResultSet, connect to database, load JDBC driver
   d. Establish a connection to database, execute query statements and get run results

2. To establish a connection with a DataSource object, you need to ____________
   a. Create a DataSource object, set properties and use this object
   b. Set properties, set up a connection and perform queries
   c. Create a DataSource object, set properties and register it with a JNDI naming service
   d. Register a DataSource object, set properties and create a DataSource object

3. To build and run an Oracle statement, the following components can be utilized ____________
   a. Statement
   b. Statement, PreparedStatement
   c. Statement, PreparedStatement, CallableStatement
   d. None of them

4. To execute an Oracle statement to get a query result, the ____________ method(s) should be used.
   a. executeQuery()
   b. executeUpdate()
   c. execute() and executeUpdate()
   d. executeQuery() and execute()

5. To perform an insert, update or delete operation, the __________ method(s) should be used.
   a. executeUpdate()
   b. executeQuery()
   c. executeQuery() and execute()
   d. executeQuery() and executeUpdate()

6. The __________ method can be used to either pick up a query result or update a datum.
   a. executeUpdate()
   b. execute()
   c. executeQuery()
   d. None of them

7. A distributed transaction is defined as accessing __________ data source(s) at __________ location(s).
   a. Single, single
   b. Multiple, same
   c. Multiple, different
   d. Single, multiple

8. The execute() method can __________
   a. Not return any results
   b. Return some results
   c. Be used either to return a result or not return any result
   d. None of these

9. A CachedRowSet class is a __________ that caches its data in __________
   a. Connected RowSet, database
   b. Disconnected RowSet, database
   c. Connected RowSet, memory
   d. Disconnected RowSet, memory

10. The ResultSet object can be created by either executing the __________ or __________ method, which means that the ResultSet instance cannot be created or used without executing a query operation first.
    a. executeQuery(), getResultSet()
    b. getResultSet(), execute()
    c. createResultSet(), getResultSet()
    d. buildResultSet(), executeQuery()

III. Exercises

1. Provide a detailed description of the JDBC API, which includes:
   a. The definition of the JDBC and JDBC API
   b. The components defined in the JDBC API, including all classes and interfaces
   c. The architecture of the JDBC API
   d. The regular functions the JDBC API performs
   e. The packages the JDBC API is involved in

2. Provide a brief discussion of database connection using the JDBC API, which includes:
   a. Two popular methods used to establish a connection
   b. Operational procedure to establish a connection
   c. How to use a DataSource object to establish a connection
   d. Compare two popular methods with the DataSource method in establishing a database connection

3. Explain the function of three different statement execution methods: executeQuery(), executeUpdate() and execute(). For each method, provide a way to retrieve the execution result.
4. Provide a brief introduction to the four types of JDBC drivers and their architecture.
5. Provide a brief introduction to the connection pooling API.

4 JDBC Applications and Design Considerations

This chapter discusses the application fundamentals of JDBC and the JDBC API, which include the application models and operational procedures of the JDBC API implemented in Java database applications.

4.1 JDBC APPLICATION MODELS

The JDBC API supports both two-tier and three-tier models for database accesses. In a two-tier model, a Java application or an applet can communicate directly with the database.

In a three-tier model, commands are sent to a middle tier, which sends the messages to the database. In return, the result of the database query is sent to the middle tier, which finally directs it to the application or applet. The presence of a middle tier has a number of advantages, such as tight control over changes made to the database.

4.1.1 Two-Tier Client-Server Model

In a two-tier client-server model, a Java application can directly communicate with the database. In fact, the so-called two-tier model means that the Java application and the target database can be installed in two components with two layers:

- Application layer, which includes the JDBC driver, the user interface and the whole Java application installed on a client machine.
- Database layer, which includes the RDBMS and the database installed on a database server.

Figure 4.1 shows a typical configuration of a two-tier model.

It can be seen from Figure 4.1 that both the Java application and JDBC API are located at the first layer, or the client machine, and the DBMS and database are located at the second layer, or the database server. A DBMS-related protocol is used as a tool to communicate between these two layers. The interface to the database is handled by a JDBC driver that is matched to the particular database management system being used. The JDBC driver has double-sided

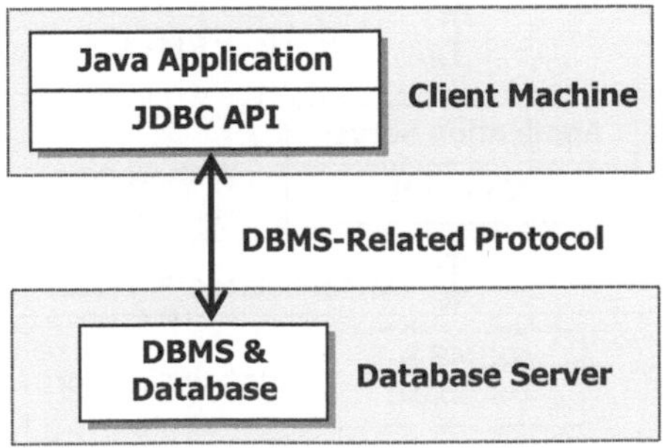

FIGURE 4.1 A typical configuration of a two-tier model.

DOI: 10.1201/9781003304029-4

functionality; it passes Oracle statements to the database when a data action request is sent from the client and returns the results of executing those statements to the client when the data action is done.

A client-server configuration is a special case of the two-tier model, where the database is located on another machine called the database server. The Java application program runs on the client machine that is connected to the database server through a network.

Most topics discussed in Chapters 5, 6 and 7 in this book are about two-tier model applications. Java application projects are built on the client machine and communicate with the database server through the network to perform all kinds of data actions. The inherent flexibility of Java JDBC approach to developing database applications enables you to access a variety of RDBMS systems, including Microsoft Access, SQL Server and Oracle.

4.1.2 Three-Tier Client-Server Model

In a three-tier client-server model, a data action request comes from an application GUI and is sent to the application server that can be considered a middle tier, and the application server that contains the JDBC API then sends Oracle statements to the database located on a database server. When the data action is processed, the database sends the results back to the application server, which then sends them to the client. The so-called three-tier model is common in Web applications, in which the client tier is implemented in a Web browser, the middle tier is a Web server and the database management system runs on a database server. This model can be represented by the following three layers:

- Client layer, which includes a Web browser with language-specific virtual machines, installed on a client machine.
- Application server layer, which includes Java Web applications or Java Web services, installed in a Web server. This layer is used to handle the business logic or application logic. This may be implemented using Java Servlet engines, JavaServer Pages or JavaServer Faces. The JDBC driver is also located in this layer.
- Database layer, which includes the RDBMS and the database, installed on a database server.

Figure 4.2 shows a typical configuration of a three-tier model.

Advantages of using a three-tier configuration over its two-tier counterpart include:

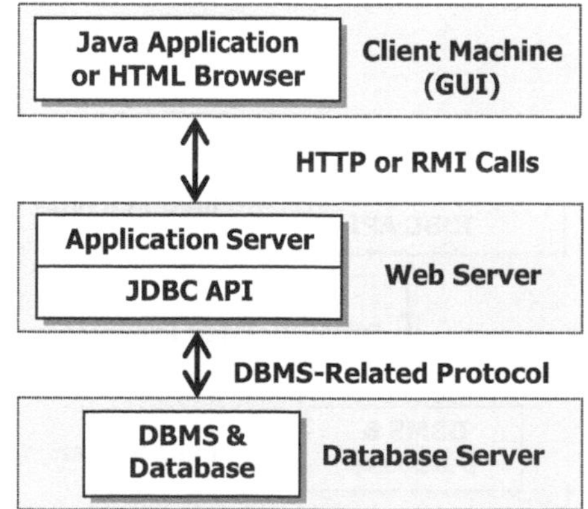

FIGURE 4.2 A TYPICAL CONFIGURATION OF A THREE-TIER MODEL.

- Application performance can be greatly improved by separating the application server and database server.
- Business logic is clearly separated from the database.
- Client applications can then use a simple protocol to access the server.

Topics discussed in Chapters 8 and 9 in this book are about three-tier applications that use a Web browser as the client, a JavaServer Face or JavaServer Page as the middle tier and a relational database management system as the database server.

Now that we have a clear picture of the Java application running models, next we need to dig a little deeper into Java database applications.

4.2 JDBC APPLICATION FUNDAMENTALS

As we discussed in Section 3.1 in Chapter 3, to run a Java database application to perform data actions against the selected database, the JDBC API needs to perform the following operations:

1) Establish a connection between your Java application and related databases.
2) Build and execute Oracle statements.
3) Process the results.

In fact, to successfully develop and run a Java database application, the previous three steps need to be further divided into the following seven steps:

1) Import necessary Java packages, such as `java.awt`, `java.util`, `javax.swing`, `java.sql` and `javax.sql`.
2) Load and register the JDBC driver.
3) Establish a connection to the database server.
4) Create an Oracle statement.
5) Execute the built statement.
6) Retrieve the execution results.
7) Close the statement and connection objects.

For all these steps, step 1 is a prerequisite since all JDBC-related components and interfaces are defined in the `java.sql` and `javax.sql` packages. All GUI-related components are defined in the `java.awt` and `javax.swing` packages, and all other application-related components are defined in the `java.util` package. In order to use any component defined in those packages, you must first import those packages into your program to provide namespaces and locations for those components. Otherwise, a compiling error may be encountered since the compiler cannot find and identify those components when you use them without providing the related packages.

In this and the following sections, we will provide a deeper and more detailed discussion about data actions in Java database applications based on these seven fundamental steps.

4.2.1 Loading and Registering Drivers

As we studied in Chapter 3, to establish a valid database connection, first you need to load and register a JDBC driver. Then you can call the `connect()` method to establish a database connection to your desired database.

We provided a brief discussion about the JDBC Driver and DriverManager components in Chapter 3. In fact, the core of the JDBC API is the JDBC Driver that can be accessed and called from the DriverManager class method. However, the Driver class is under the control of the DriverManager class, and the DriverManager is just that: a manager for the Driver class. When using this Driver class, you cannot call and run any method defined in the Driver class; instead, you need to call them via the DriverManager class methods.

The DriverManager class is a set of utility functions that work with the Driver methods together and manage multiple JDBC drivers by keeping them as a list of drivers loaded. Although loading a driver and registering a driver are two steps, only one method call is necessary to perform these two operations. The operational sequence of loading and registering a JDBC driver is:

1) Call class methods in the DriverManager class to load the driver into the Java interpreter.
2) Register the driver using the **registerDriver()** method.

When loaded, the driver will execute the **DriverManager.registerDriver()** method to register itself. These two operations will never be performed until a method in the **DriverManager** is executed, which means that even if both operations have been coded in an application, the driver cannot be loaded and registered until a method such as **connect()** is first executed.

To load and register a JDBC driver, two popular methods can be used:

1) Use the **Class.forName()** method:
   Class.forName("oracle.jdbc.OracleDriver");
2) Create a new instance of the Driver class:
   Driver oraDriver = new oracle.jdbc.OracleDriver;

Relatively speaking, the first method is more professional, since the driver is both loaded and registered when a valid method in the **DriverManager** class is executed. The second method cannot guarantee that the driver has been registered by using the DriverManager.

A piece of sample code used to load and register an Oracle 18c XE JDBC driver using the first method is shown in Figure 4.3.

In Figure 4.3, the first codeline is used to import the JDBC API package **java.sql.***.

Then a **try-catch** block is used to load and register an Oracle 18c XE JDBC Driver. The **Class.forName()** method is utilized to make sure that our JDBC Driver is not only loaded but also registered when it is connected by running the **getConnection()** method later. The argument of this method, **oracle.jdbc.OracleDriver**, is the name of this Oracle 18c XE JDBC Driver class, and it is created by NetBeans when it is added to a Java database application project.

The **catch** block is used to track any possible error in loading and registering. The related exception information will be displayed if any error occurs.

You can use the second method instead to perform the same driver loading and registering operation if you like.

```
import java.sql.*;
try
{
     //Load and register Oracle 18c XE driver
     Class.forName("oracle.jdbc.OracleDriver ");
}
catch (Exception e) {
     System.out.println("Class not found exception!" + e.getMessage());
}
```

FIGURE 4.3 Sample code for driver loading and registering.

4.2.2 Getting Connected

To establish a connection to the desired database, two methods can be used:

1) Using **DriverManager.getConnection()**
2) Using **Driver.connect()**

Before we can take a closer look at these two methods, first let's have a quick review of all methods defined in these two classes, **DriverManager** and **Driver**.

4.2.2.1 The DriverManager and Driver Classes

All 12 methods defined in the DriverManager class are shown in Table 4.1.

Four methods in the **DriverManager** class are widely applied in most database applications: **getConnection()**, **getDriver()**, **registerDriver()** and **deregisterDriver()**. Note that the **getConnection()** method has two more overloaded methods with different arguments.

All six methods defined in the Driver class are shown in Table 4.2.

The most popular methods in the Driver class are **acceptsURL()** and **connect()**.

Most methods defined in the Driver class will not be called directly in most Java database applications; instead, they will be called indirectly by using the DriverManager class.

Now let's have a closer look at these two methods.

4.2.2.2 Using the DriverManager.getConnection() Method

When using the first method, **DriverManager.getConnection()**, to establish a database connection, it does not immediately try to make this connection. Instead, in order to make this connection more robust, it performs a two-step process. The **getConnection()** method first checks the driver and uniform resource locator (URL) by running a method called **acceptsURL()** via the DriverManager class to test the first driver in the driver list. If no matching driver returns, the **acceptURL()** method will go to test the next driver in the list. This process continues until each driver is tested or a matchingdriver is found. If a matching driver is found, the **Driver.connect()** method will be executed to establish this connection. Otherwise, an exception is raised.

TABLE 4.1
Methods Defined in the DriverManager Class

Method	Function
deregisterDriver(Driver dr)	Remove a driver from the driver list
getConnection(String url, Properties login)	Attempt to establish a connection to the referenced database
getConnection(String url, String user, String pswd)	Attempt to establish a connection to the referenced database
getConnection(String url)	Attempt to establish a connection to the referenced database
getDriver(String url)	Locate an appropriate driver for the referenced URL from the driver list
getDrivers()	Get a list of all drivers currently loaded and registered
getLoginTimeout()	Get the maximum time (in seconds) a driver will wait for a connection
getLogStream()	Get the current PrintStream being used by the DriverManager
Println(String msg)	Print a message to the current LogStream
registerDriver(Driver dr)	Add the driver to the driver list. This is normally done automatically when the driver is instantiated
setLoginTimeout(int seconds)	Set the maximum time (in seconds) that a driver can wait when attempting to connect to a database before giving up
setLogStream(PrintStream out)	Set the PrintStream to direct logging message to

TABLE 4.2
Methods Defined in the Driver Class

Method	Function
acceptsURL(String url)	Return true if the driver is able to open a connection to the database given by the URL
connect(String url, Properties login)	Check the syntax of the URL and the matched drivers in the driver list. Attempt to make a database connection to the given URL
getMajorVersion()	Determine the minor revision number of the driver
getMinorVersion()	Determine the major revision number of the driver
getPropertyInfo(String url, Properties login)	Return an array of DriverPropertyInfo objects describing login properties accepted by the database
jdbcCompliant()	Determine if the driver is JDBC compliant

If it looks like this two-step connection is not efficient enough, a more robust connection can be set if more than one driver is available in the driver list.

The purpose of the **acceptsURL()** method is to check whether the current driver is able to open a valid connection to the given URL. This method does not create a real connection or test the actual database connections; instead, it merely examines the sub-protocol of the URL and determines if it understands its syntax. In this way, it can effectively reduce the chance of a misconnection and make sure of the correctness of an established connection.

4.2.2.3 Using the Driver.connect() Method

The **Driver.connect()** method enables you to create an actual connection to the desired database and returns an associated Connection object. This method accepts the database URL string and a Properties object as its argument. A URL indicates the protocol and location of a data source, while the Properties object normally contains the user login information. One point to be noted is that the only time you can use the **Driver.connect()** method directly is when you have created a new instance of the Driver class.

A null will be returned if an exception occurs when the **Driver.connect()** method is executed, which means that something went wrong during the connection operation.

Comparing the **DriverManager.getConnection()** method with the **Driver.connect()** method, the following conclusions can be obtained:

- The **DriverManager.getConnection()** method can perform checking and testing for each driver in the driver list automatically for all loaded drivers. As soon as a matching-driver is found, it can be connected to the database directly by using the **Driver.connect()** method. This automatic process will greatly reduce the processing time.
- The **DriverManager.getConnection()** method has looser requirements for the arguments passed. When applying the **Driver.connect()** method, you have to pass two arguments, the URL as a string and the login properties as a Properties object with strict syntax and grammar requirements. However, when using the **DriverManager.getConnection()** method, you can define login properties as either a String, a Properties object or even a null string, since the DriverManager can handle converting these arguments to the appropriate Properties object when it is applied.

From this comparison, it can be seen that the **DriverManager.getConnection()** method is better than the **Driver.connect()** method; therefore, we will use this method to makeour database connection in all example projects in this book.

After a driver has been loaded and registered, the next step is to establish a database connection using a URL. Before we can continue with the database connection, we need to have a clear picture and understanding of JDBC connection URLs.

4.2.2.4 The JDBC Connection URL

The JDBC URL provides all the information for applications to access a special resource, such as a database. Generally, a URL contains three parts or segments: protocol name, sub-protocol and subname for the database to be connected. Each of these three segments has different function, and they work together to provide unique information for the target database. The syntax for a JDBC URL is:

```
protocol:sub-protocol:subname
```

The protocol name works as an identifier or indicator to show what kind of protocol should be adopted when connecting to the desired database. For a JDBC driver, the name of the protocol should be **jdbc**. The protocol name is used to indicate what kind of items shouldbe delivered or connected.

The sub-protocol is generally used to indicate the type of the database or data source to be connected, such as **sqlserver** or **oracle**.

The subname is used to indicate the address to which the item supposed to be delivered or the location of the database. Generally, a subname contains the following information for an address of a resource:

- Network host name/IP address
- The database server name
- The port number
- The name of the database

An example of a subname for our Oracle Server database is:

```
localhost:1521:XE
```

The network host name is **localhost**, the server name is **XE** and the port number the server uses is **1521**. You need to use a double slash, either forward or back, to represent a normal slash in this URL string, since this is a DOS-style string.

By combining all three segments, we can get a full JDBC URL. An example URL that uses an Oracle 18c XE thin JDBC driver is:

```
jdbc:oracle:thin:@localhost:1521:XE
```

The database name works as an attribute of the connected database.

Now that we have a clear picture ofthe JDBC URL, next let's connect our application to our desired database.

4.2.2.5 Establish a Database Connection

Now we have a clear picture and understanding of the fundamentals in the **DriverManager** and Driver classes as well as the related database connection methods. As we discussed in the previous sections, to connect to a database, two methods, **DriverManager.getConnection()** and **Driver.connect()**, can be used. However, as we know, the first method is better than the second one; therefore, in this section, we will concentrate on the use of the first method to establish a database connection.

Figure 4.4 shows a piece of example code to establish a connection using the **DriverManager.getConnection()** method. This code is a follow-up to the code shown in Figure 4.3—in other words, a valid driver has been loaded and registered before the following connection can be established.

```
........
//A driver has been successfully loaded and registered

String url = "jdbc:oracle:thin:@localhost:1521:XE;";
//String url = "jdbc:oracle:thin:@localhost:1521:XE;
//            databaseName=CSE_DEPT;password=oracle_18c";
//Establish a connection
try {
      con = DriverManager.getConnection(url,"CSE_DEPT","oracle_18c");
      //con = DriverManager.getConnection(url);
      con.close();
    }
    catch (SQLException e) {
      System.out.println("Could not connect! " + e.getMessage());
      e.printStackTrace();
    }
```

FIGURE 4.4 Example code for the database connection.

Since the **DriverManager.getConnection()** method is an overloaded method with three different signatures, here we used two of them; the first one is highlighted in bold, and the second one is commented out.

To establish a database connection, a valid JDBC URL is defined in the first codeline with the following components:

- The protocol name **jdbc**
- The sub-protocol **oracle:thin**
- The subname **localhost:1521:XE**
- The database name **CSE _ DEPT**

Then a **try-catch** block is used to try to establish a connection using the **getConnection()** method with three arguments: URL, username and password. After a valid connection is established, a Connection object is returned, and this returned object has the following functions and properties:

1) The Connection object represents an Oracle session with the database.
2) The Connection object provides methods for the creation of Statement objects that will be used to execute Oracle statements in the next step.
3) The Connection object also contains methods for the management of the session, such as transaction locking, catalog selection and error handling.

By definition, the responsibility of a Connection object is to establish a valid database connection with your Java application, and that is all. The Connection object has nothing to do with Oracle statement execution. Oracle statement execution is the responsibility of the Statement, PreparedStatement and CallableStatement objects. As we mentioned, both PreparedStatement and CallableStatement are subclasses of the Statement class, and they play different roles in statement execution.

In the next codeline in Figure 4.4, a **close()** method that belongs to the Connection class is called to try to close a connection. In fact, it is unnecessary to close a connected database in actual applications. However, we use this method here to show users a complete picture of using the Connection object, which means that you must close a connection when it is no longer to be used in

TABLE 4.3
Methods Defined in the Connection Interface

Method	Function
close()	Close the connection to the database
createStatement()	Create a Statement object for the execution of static Oracle statements
getMetaData()	Retrieve all database related information stored in the DatabaseMetaData object for the current connection
isClosed()	Determine if the referenced connection has been closed—True = closed
prepareCall(String oraString)	Create a CallableStatement object for use with Oracle stored procedures
prepareStatement(String oraString)	Create a PreparedStatement object for use with Oracle dynamic queries
commit()	Immediately commits all transactions to the database. All updates and changes are made permanent

your application (even in the connection pooling situation, but it will not really be closed; instead, it is placed into a pool); otherwise, a runtime error may be encountered when you reuse this connection in the future. Therefore, this codeline is only for testing purposes and should be removed in a real application.

The `catch` block is used to detect any possible exceptions and display them if any occurred.

A Connection class contains 19 methods, and Table 4.3 lists the 7 most popular methods.

Now a valid database connection has been established, and the next step is to execute Oracle statements to perform data actions against our connected database.

4.2.3 Executing Statements

To successfully execute an appropriate Statement object to perform Oracle statements, the following operational sequence should be followed:

1) Creating a `Statement` object based on the requirements of the data actions
2) Calling the appropriate execution method to run the Oracle statements

In essence, the `Statement` object is used for executing a static Oracle statement and returning the results stored in a ResultSet object.

4.2.3.1 Overview of Statement Objects and Their Execution Methods

By using the `Connection` object, three separate statement objects can be created:

- `Statement` object
- `PreparedStatement` object
- `CallableStatement` object

The `Statement` object is used to execute static Oracle queries. So-called static statements do not include any IN or OUT parameters in the query string and do not contain any parameters passing to or from the database.

The `Statement` interface contains more than 18 methods, and Table 4.4 lists the 10 most popular methods.

Among these ten methods in the `Statement` interface, three execution methods, **`executeQuery()`**, **`executeUpdate()`** and **`execute()`**, and the **`getResultSet()`** method are often used in Java database applications.

TABLE 4.4
Methods Defined in the Statement Interface

Method	Function
close()	Close the Statement and release all resources, including the ResultSet associated with it
execute(String oraString)	Execute an Oracle statement that may have an unknown number of results. Returning True means that the first set of results from the oraString execution is a ResultSet. If the execution resulted in either no results or an update count, False is returned
executeQuery(String oraString)	Execute an Oracle Select statement. A ResultSet object that contains the query results from the database will be returned
executeUpdate(String oraString)	Execute an Oracle Update, Insert or Delete statement. An integer will be returned to indicate the number of rows that have been affected
getMaxRows()	Determine the maximum number of rows that can be returned in a ResultSet object
getMoreResults()	Move to the Statement's next result. Used only in conjunction with the Execute statement and where multiple results are returned by the Oracle statement. False is returned if the next result is null or the results are an update count
getResultSet()	Return the current result set for the statement. Only used in conjunction with execute() method. The current ResultSet object will be returned
getUpdateCount()	Return the number of rows affected by the last Oracle statement. Only meaningful for INSERT, UPDATE or DELETE statements
setCursorName(String name)	Set the cursor name to be used by the statement. Only useful for databases that support positional updates and deletes
setMaxRows(int rows)	Set the maximum number of rows that can be returned in a ResultSet. If more results are returned by the query, they are truncated

PreparedStatement is a subclass of **Statement**, and it is mainly used to execute dynamic Oracle queries that involve the IN parameter. These kinds of statements can be pre-parsed and pre-compiled by the database and therefore have faster processing speed and lower running loads for the database server.

The **PreparedStatement** interface contains more than 20 methods, and Table 4.5 lists the 17 most popular methods.

It can be seen from Table 4.5 that three execution methods, **execute()**, **executeQuery()** and **executeUpdate()**, look like duplicates of those methods defined in the Statement interface. However, a significant difference is that all three of these methods defined in the Statement interface have their query strings as an argument when they are executed, which means that the Oracle statements have to be defined in those query strings and should be passed into the database as the arguments of those methods. In contrast, all three methods defined in the PreparedStatement interface have no argument to be passed into the database when they are executed. This means that the Oracle statements have been built and passed into the database by using the **PreparedStatement** object before these three methods are executed.

Two methods belong to the getters that are used to retrieve the metadata for the **ResultSet** and the **ParameterMetaData** objects. Both methods are very useful when the developer wants to get more detailed structure and property information about a returned **ResultSet** or **ParameterMetaData** object.

More than ten methods defined in the **PreparedStatement** interface are setter methods, which means that these methods are used to set up an appropriate value to an input parameter with different data types. These methods are especially useful when a dynamic query is built with one or more dynamic input parameters that need to be determined in the Oracle statements.

TABLE 4.5
Methods Defined in the PreparedStatement Interface

Method	Function
clearParameters()	Clear all parameters associated with a PreparedStatement. After execution of this method, all parameters have the value null
execute()	Execute the associated Oracle statement when the number of results returned is unknown. False is returned if the returned result is null
executeQuery()	Execute an Oracle Select statement. A ResultSet object that contains the query results from the database will be returned
executeUpdate()	Execute an Oracle Update, Insert or Delete statement. An integer will be returned to indicate the number of rows that have been affected
getMetaData()	Return a set of metadata for the returned ResultSet object
getParameterMetaData()	Return the number, types and properties of this PreparedStatement object's parameters
setBoolean(int index, Boolean value)	Bind a Boolean value to an input parameter
setByte(int index, Byte value)	Bind a byte value to an input parameter
setDouble(int index, double value)	Bind a double value to an input parameter
setFloat(int index, float value)	Bind a floating point value to an input parameter
setInt(int index, int value)	Binds an integer value to an input parameter
setLong(int index, long value)	Bind a long value to an input parameter
setNull(int index, int oraType)	Bind a null value to an input parameter
setObject(int index, Object obj)	Bind an object to an input parameter. The object will be converted to an Oracle data type before being sent to the database
setShort(int index, short value)	Bind a short value to an input parameter
setString(int index, String value)	Bind a string value to an input parameter
setTime(int index, Time value)	Bind a time value to an input parameter

CallableStatement is also a subclass of the **Statement** and the **PreparedStatement** classes, and it is mainly used to execute stored procedures with both IN and OUT parameters. As we know, stored procedures are built and developed inside databases and therefore have higher run and response efficiency in data queries and processing.

This interface is used to execute Oracle stored procedures. The JDBC API provides a stored procedure escape syntax that allows stored procedures to be called in a standard way for all RDBMSs. This escape syntax has one form that includes a result parameter and one that does not. If used, the result parameter must be registered as an OUT parameter. The other parameters can be used for input, output or both. Parameters are referred to sequentially, by number or position, with the first parameter being 1.

```
{?= call <procedure-name>[(<arg1>,<arg2>, . . .)]}
{call <procedure-name>[(<arg1>,<arg2>, . . .)]}
```

The IN parameter values are set using the **setXXX()** methods inherited from the interface **PreparedStatement**. The type of all OUT parameters must be registered prior to executing the stored procedure; their values are retrieved after execution via the **getXXX()** methods defined in this **CallableStatement** interface.

A **CallableStatement** can return one ResultSet object or multiple ResultSet objects. Multiple ResultSet objects are handled using operations inherited from the **Statement** interface. The **CallableStatement** interface contains over 30 methods, and Table 4.6 lists the 15 most popular methods.

TABLE 4.6
Methods Defined in the CallableStatement Interface

Method	Function
getBigDecimal(int index, int scale)	Return the value of a parameter specified by the parameter index number as a BigDecimal
getBoolean(int index)	Return the value of a parameter specified by the parameter index number as a Boolean
getByte(int index)	Return the value of a parameter specified by the parameter index number as a byte
getBytes(int index)	Return the value of a parameter specified by the parameter index number as an array of bytes
getDouble(int index)	Return the value of a parameter specified by the parameter index number as a double
getFloat(int index)	Return the value of a parameter specified by the parameter index number as a floating point number
getInt(int index)	Return the value of a parameter specified by the parameter index number as an integer
getLong(int index)	Return the value of a parameter specified by the parameter index number as a long integer
getObject(int index)	Return the value of a parameter specified by the parameter index number as an object. The object type is determined by the default mapping of the Oracle data type to Java data type
getShort(int index)	Return the value of a parameter specified by the parameter index number as a short integer
getString(int index)	Return the value of a parameter specified by the parameter index number as a String object
getTime(int index)	Return the value of a parameter specified by the parameter index number as a Time object
registerOutParameter(int index, int sql Type)	Register the specified output parameter to receive the Oracle data type indicated by the argument passed
registerOutParameter(int index, int sql Type, int scale)	Register the specified output parameter to receive the Oracle data type indicated by the argument passed. If the output is registered as either DECIMAL or NUMERIC, the scale of the value may also be specified
wasNull()	Determine if the last value read by a **getXXX()** method was a Oracle null value. True is returned if the last read value contained a null value

The **registerOutParameter()** method is an overloaded method with two signatures, and these methods are used to declare what Oracle type the OUT parameter will return when a CallableStatement method is executed.

By default, only one ResultSet object per Statement object can be open at the same time. Therefore, if the reading of one ResultSet object is interleaved with the reading of another, each must have been generated by different Statement objects. All execution methods in the Statement interface implicitly close a Statement's current ResultSet object if an open one exists.

The Statement interface contains three important query methods with different functions: **executeQuery()**, **executeUpdate()** and **execute()**. For each method, different operations can be performed and different results will be returned.

Generally, query methods can be divided into two categories: 1) the query method that needs to perform a data query, such as **executeQuery()**, which returns an instance of **ResultSet** that contains the queried results, and 2) the query method that does not perform a data query and only returns an integer, such as **executeUpdate()**. An interesting method is **execute()**, which can be used either way.

Let's first concentrate on the creation of Statement objects based on the different requirements of data actions.

4.2.3.2 Using the Statement Object

As we discussed in the last section, three separate statement objects can be created based on three different data actions: **`Statement`**, **`PreparedStatement`** and **`CallableStatement`**. Let's discuss how to create a **`Statement`** object first.

4.2.3.2.1 Creating the Statement Object

The **`Statement`** object is the most common type of object and is easy to use in a static data query. The shortcoming of using this object is that all Oracle statements must be pre-defined with definite parameters when a Statement object is created. In other words, by using a Statement object to execute an Oracle statement, no parameter can be passed into or from the database.

The **`Statement`** object is created by using the **`createStatement()`** method defined in the **`Connection`** interface (refer to Table 4.3). Figure 4.5 shows an example of creation of a **`Statement`** object. The codeline that is used to create a **`Statement`** object is in bold. All other lines are prerequisite code used to load and register a driver, establish a connection using the URL and build an Oracle query string.

4.2.3.2.2 Executing the Statement Object

To execute the created **`Statement`** object to perform a data action, you need to call one of the execution methods defined in the **`Statement`** interface shown in Table 4.4. Figure 4.6 shows example code for the execution of an Oracle query with the **`Statement`** object.

The codeline that is used to execute the **`Statement`** object is in bold. All other lines are prerequisite code used to load and register a driver, establish a connection using the URL, build an Oracle query string and create a **`Statement`** object. It can be seen from this piece of code that no parameter can be passed to or from the database when this query is executed. Therefore, the **`Statement`** object can only be used to perform static queries.

To overcome this shortcoming, we need to use **`PreparedStatement`** objects to perform dynamic queries with varied input parameters.

4.2.3.3 Using the PreparedStatement Object

To perform dynamic Oracle statements, we need to use a **`PreparedStatement`** object. Generally, using a **`PreparedStatement`** object to perform a dynamic Oracle statement includes the following steps:

1) Create a **`PreparedStatement`** object.
2) Set data types and values to the associated input parameters in the query string.
3) Call an appropriate execution method to perform this dynamic query.

Let's first concentrate on the creation of a **`PreparedStatement`** object.

```
String url = "jdbc:oracle:thin:@localhost:1521:XE;";
try {
        con = DriverManager.getConnection(url,"CSE_DEPT","oracle_18c");    //Establish a connection
}
catch (SQLException e) {
        System.out.println("Could not connect! " + e.getMessage()); }
String query = "SELECT user_name, pass_word FROM LogIn";
try{
        Statement stmt = con.createStatement();
}
catch (SQLException e) {
        System.out.println("Error in Statement! " + e.getMessage()); }
```

FIGURE 4.5 Example code for the creation of a Statement object.

The first method is to set an input parameter, which is the second one in an Oracle statement, to an object (here an integer) with a value of 101. The next method is to set the same input to the same object; however, it needs to convert the object (integer) to a float data type. The final method performs the same operation as the previous one, but it indicates that the conversion result should contain at least twodigits.

Since set stream IN methods are not very popular in Java database applications, we skip that part in this section. If you want to get more detailed information for these methods, refer to some sections in Chapter 6.

Now let's begin to call some appropriate execution methods to run the PreparedStatement object to perform dynamic queries.

4.2.3.3.4 Executing the PreparedStatement Object

As we discussed in Section 3.3.2 in Chapter 3, three execution methods can be called to perform the data action against the database. Refer to Tables 4.4 and 4.5, where it can be seen that both the **`Statement`** and **`PreparedStatement`** interfaces contain these three methods:

- **`executeQuery()`**
- **`executeUpdate()`**
- **`execute()`**

The difference between these three methods in both interfaces is that all three execution methods defined in the Statement interface need an argument, which works as a query statement passed into the database. However, the three methods defined in the **`PreparedStatement`** interface have no argument, which means that the query statement has been built and passed to the database by using the **`PreparedStatement`** object when it is created.

Figure 4.7 shows example code for calling the **`executeQuery()`** method to perform a login process.

First, the query statement **`query`** is created in which two placeholders (?) are used since we have two dynamic parameters, username and password, to be passed into our sample database, **CSE _ DEPT**.

```
String url = "jdbc:oracle:thin:@localhost:1521:XE;";
//Establish a connection
try {
      con = DriverManager.getConnection(url,"cse","mack8000");
}
catch (Exception e) {
      System.out.println("Could not connect! " + e.getMessage()); }
String query = "SELECT user_name, pass_word FROM LogIn " +
               "WHERE user_name = ? AND pass_word = ?";
try{
      PreparedStatement pstmt = con.prepareStatement(query);
      pstmt.setString(1, "cse");
      pstmt.setString(2, "mack8000");
      ResultSet rs = pstmt.executeQuery();
}
catch (Exception e) {
      System.out.println("Error in PreparedStatement! " + e.getMessage()); }
```

FIGURE 4.7 Code example for the execution of a PreparedStatement.

Then, with a **try-catch** block, a **PreparedStatement** object is created with the **query** statement as an argument. Two **setString()** methods defined in the **PreparedStatement** interface are used to initialize these two dynamic parameters (user-name = "**cse**", password = "**mack8000**"). Finally, the **executeQuery()** method defined in the **PreparedStatement** interface is called to run this query statement, and the results are returned and stored in a **ResultSet** object.

In addition to using the **executeQuery()** method, the **PreparedStatement** object can also use another two methods, **executeUpdate()** and **execute()**, to perform a data action. However, those methods have different functionalities and should be applied in different situations. For more detailed information about these methods, refer to Section 4.2.3.8.

Compared with the **Statement** interface, the advantage of using a **PreparedStatement** interface is that it can perform a dynamic query with known or unknown dynamic parameters as inputs. Most of the time, those dynamic parameters are input parameters and can be defined as IN variables. However, you do not need to specify those parameters with an IN keyword when using a **PreparedStatement** interface.

4.2.3.4 Using the CallableStatement Object

As we discussed in the early part of this chapter, **CallableStatement** is a subclass of both **Statement** and **PreparedStatement**, and this interface is mainly used to call stored procedures to perform group data actions. The JDBC **CallableStatement** method provides a way to perform a complicated query. The speed and efficiency of a data query can be significantly improved by using the stored procedure, since it is built on the database side.

The difference between a **PreparedStatement** and a **CallableStatement** interface is: unlike the **PreparedStatement** interface, the **CallableStatement** interface has both input and output parameters, which are indicated with IN and OUT keywords, respectively. In order to set up values for input parameters or get values from output parameters, you have to use either a **setXXX()** method inherited from the **PreparedStatement** or a **getXXX()** method. However, the point is that before you can use any **getXXX()** method to pick up the values of output parameters, you must first register the output parameters to allow the **CallableStatement** interface to recognize them.

Generally, the sequence to run a **CallableStatement** to perform a stored procedure is:

1) Build a **CallableStatement** query string.
2) Create a **CallableStatement** object.
3) Set the input parameters.
4) Register the output parameters.
5) Execute **CallableStatement**.
6) Retrieve the run result by using a different **getXXX()** method.

Let's discuss these steps one by one in more detail in the following sections.

4.2.3.4.1 Building a CallableStatement Query String

The **CallableStatement** interface is used to execute Oracle stored procedures. The JDBC API provides a stored procedure escape syntax that allows stored procedures to be called in a standard way for all RDBMSs. This escape syntax has one form that includes an output parameter and one that does not. If used, the output parameter must be registered as an **OUT** parameter. The other parameters can be used for input, output or both. Parameters are referred to sequentially, by number, with the first parameter being 1.

```
{?= call <procedure-name>[<arg1>,<arg2>, . . .]}
{call <procedure-name>[<arg1>,<arg2>, . . .]}
```

```
String query = "{call FacultyCourse(?, ?)}";
cstmt = con.prepareCall(query);
cstmt.setString(1, "Jones");
cstmt.setString(2, "CSC-132B");
cstmt.registerOutParameter(2, java.sql.Types.VARCHAR);
```

FIGURE 4.9 A code example for the registering of output parameters.

```
String query = "{call FacultyCourse(?, ?)}";
cstmt = con.prepareCall(query);
cstmt.setString(1, "Jones");
cstmt.setString(2, "CSC-132B");
cstmt.registerOutParameter(2, java.sql.Types.VARCHAR);
cstmt.execute();
```

FIGURE 4.10 A code example for running the CallableStatement object.

An interesting point to the **registerOutParameter()** method is that all OUT parameters can be registered by using this syntax except those OUT parameters with the **NUMERIC** and **DECIMAL** data types. The syntax to register those OUT parameters looks like:

```
registerOutParameter(int position, data_type Oracle_data_type,
int scale);
```

The only difference is that a third parameter, **scale**, is added, and it is used to indicate the number of digits to the right of the decimal point for the OUT parameter.

4.2.3.4.5 Executing the CallableStatement Object

To run a **CallableStatement** object, three execution methods can be used: **executeQuery()**, **executeUpdate()** and **execute()**. As we discussed in Section 4.2.3.1, the **executeQuery()** method can return a **ResultSet** object that contains the run or query results, and the **executeUpdate()** method can return an integer to indicate the number of rows that have been inserted, updated or deleted against the target database. However, the **execute()** method cannot return any run result itself, and you need to use the associated **getXXX()** methods to pick up the query or run result. Another important point of using the **execute()** method is that it can handle an unknown result with an undefined data type. Refer to Section 4.2.3.5 to get more detailed information about the **execute()** method.

An example of using the **execute()** method to run the **CallableStatement** object is shown in Figure 4.10.

After finishing building the query string, creating the **CallableStatement** object, and setting and registering input and output parameters, the **execute()** method is called to execute the**CallableStatement** object to perform stored procedure processing.

Before we can continue withhow to retrieve the run result from the execution of a **Statement**, **PreparedStatement** or **CallableStatement** object, we need to have a closer look at three execution methods.

4.2.3.5 More about the Execution Methods

The three statement objects are used to perform different data actions against the target database, and the type of statement object to be used is determined by the parameters of the Oracle statements. To make it simple, the following strategy should be adopted for the given situation:

- For static statements without needing to pass any parameter into the database, a **Statement** object can be used.
- For dynamic statements with some input parameters that need to be passed into the target database, a **PreparedStatement** object should be used.
- For stored procedures with both input and output parameters that need to be passed into the target database, a **CallableStatement** object can be used.

Similarly to statement objects, the execute method to be used is determined by the expected output of the Oracle statement. There are three types of output that can be expected from an Oracle statement:

- A **ResultSet** containing data in tabular format with rows and columns.
- An integer indicating the number of rows affected by the Oracle statements.
- A combination of a **ResultSet** and an integer.

Each of these output types requires its own special output handling. Accordingly, three execute methods, **executeQuery()**, **executeUpdate()** and **execute()**, can be used for each type of statement object.

Generally, the execute methods can be divided into two categories: 1) execute methods that need to perform a data query, such as **executeQuery()**, which returns an instance of **ResultSet** that contains the queried results, and 2) execute methods that do not perform a data query and only return an integer, such as **executeUpdate()**. An interesting method is **execute()**, which can be used either way. In conclusion, the following points should be noted when using any of these execute methods:

- The **executeQuery()** method performs a data query and returns a **ResultSet** object that contains the queried results.
- The **executeUpdate()** method does not perform a data query; instead, it only performs either a data update, insert or delete action against the database and returns an integer that equals the number of rows that have been successfully updated, inserted or deleted.
- The **execute()** method is a special method, and it can be used either way. All the different data actions can be performed by using this method, such as data query, data insertion, data updating and data deleting. The most important difference between the **execute()** method and the two previous methods is that the former can be used to execute some Oracle statements that are unknown at compile time or return multiple results from stored procedures. Another difference is that the **execute()** method does not return any result itself, and one needs to use the **getResultSet()** or **getUpdateCount()** method to pick up the results. Both methods belong to the **Statement** interface.

Confusion may arise with the use of the **execute()** method. As we mentioned, since any Oracle statement, either known or unknown at compile time, can be used with the **execute()** method, how do we know the execution results? Yes, that indeed is a problem. However, fortunately, we can solve this problem by using some testing methods indirectly.

In fact, we can call either the **getResultSet()** or **getUpdateCount()** method to try to pick up the run results from execution of the **execute()** method. The key point is:

- The **getResultSet()** method will return a **null** if the run result is an integer, which is a number of rows that have been affected, either inserted, updated or deleted.
- The **getUpdateCount()** method will return a –1 if the run result is a **ResultSet**.

Based on these two key points, we can easily determine whether a result is a **ResultSet** or an integer. Figure 4.11 shows a piece of example code to illustrate how to distinguish what kind of result is returned by using these two methods.

```
PreparedStatement pstmt = con.prepareStatement(query);
pstmt.setString(1, "faculty_name");
pstmt.execute();
int updateCount = pstmt.getUpdateCount();
if (updateCount == -1)
    System.out.println("execute() method returned a ResultSet object!");
else
    System.out.println("execute() method returned an integer!");
```

FIGURE 4.11 A code example to distinguish the returned result.

A **PreparedStatement** object is created, the input parameter is initialized using the **setString()** method and then the **execute()** method is called to run the Oracle statement. In order to distinguish the run result, first we use the **getUpdateCount()** method to pick up the returned result. A **ResultSet** object is returned if a –1 is returned for the execution of the **getUpdateCount()** method. Otherwise, an integer is returned to indicate that a data update, insert or delete action has been executed, and the integer value is equal to the number of rows that have been affected.

Now that we know how to create and execute different execute methods, let's have a closer look at the creation and execution of Oracle statements using those methods.

4.2.3.6 Creating and Executing Oracle Statements

Executing any execution method we discussed in the previous sections is exactly the same as executing a string representing an Oracle statement. In fact, the Oracle statement and the JDBC representation are exactly the same thing from the point of view of the terminal execution results. However, in some cases, you have to modify the JDBC string to make sure that the database can receive the correct Oracle statement.

All Oracle statements can be divided into two categories:

- Data definition language (DDL) statements
- Data manipulation language (DML) statements

DDL statements are used to create and modify the structure of your database Tables and other objects related to the database. DML statements are used to work with and manipulate data in database Tables.

Let's discuss the creation and execution of Oracle statements based on these two categories in the following sections.

4.2.3.6.1 Creating and Executing DDL Statements

Since DDL statements are mainly used for the creation and modification of the structure of database Tables and related objects, they do not perform any queries and do not affect any rows in database-related Tables. Of course, they will never return any **ResultSet** object, either. However, in order to keep DDL statements consistent with other types of Oracle statements, DDL statements always return a 0 in an actual application.

A standard DDL protocol used to create the structure of a Table is:

```
CREATE Table <Table name>
(<attribute name 1><data type 1>,
. . . . . . .
<attribute name n><data type n>);
```

Figure 4.12 shows a piece of example code to illustrate how to create a **LogIn** Table using the JDBC statement.

First, the protocol used to create the **Login** Table is assigned to a JDBC statement string, **oraString**. The data type for both the **user _ name** and **pass _ word** columns is**VARCHAR2**, which is a variable-length char. The argument 10 is used to define the length of those chars. **login _ ID** is an integer. Then a **Statement** object is created, and the **execute()** method is called to perform the creation of this Table with **oraString** as the argument that is passed to the database.

To add data into a created Table, you need to use DML statements.

4.2.3.6.2 Creating and Executing DML Statements

DML statements are used to build and complete the body of database Tables. These statements include data query statements and insert, update and delete statements. All of these statements need to return execution results, either a **ResultSet** object or an integer.

A standard DML statement used to insert data into the created data Table looks like:

```
INSERT INTO <Table name>
VALUES (<value 1>, <value 2>, . . . <value n>);
```

A standard DML statement used to update data from a created data Table looks like:

```
UPDATE <Table name>
SET <attribute> = <expression>
WHERE <condition>;
```

Figure 4.13 shows a piece of example code to illustrate how to add data items to the created LogIn Table using the JDBC statement.

Figure 4.14 shows a piece of example code to illustrate how to perform a select query to retrieve the desired username and password from the **LogIn** Table.

4.2.3.6.3 JDBC Escape Syntax

When JDBC performs an Oracle statement, it does not check the Oracle grammar, and you can send any Oracle statement to your database. This gives you the flexibility to use some extended functions that are not included in the entry-level SQL92 standard provided by particular vendors. To support

```
String oraString = (" CREATE TABLE LogIn"
                  + "(user_name VARCHAR2(10), "
                  + " pass_word VARCHAR2(10), "
                  + " login_ID int )";
Statement stmt = con.createStatement();
stmt.execute(oraString);
```

FIGURE 4.12 A code example to create a LogIn Table using a JDBC statement.

```
String oraString = ("INSERT INTO LogIn"
                  + "VALUES ('Tom Baker', 'come123', 100078, 'David Tim', 'test55', 100080)";
Statement stmt = con.createStatement();
stmt.execute(oraString);
```

FIGURE 4.13 A code example to insert data into the LogIn Table using a JDBC statement.

```
String query = "SELECT user_name, pass_word FROM LogIn " +
               "WHERE user_name = ? AND pass_word = ?";
try{
      PreparedStatement  pstmt = con.prepareStatement(query);
      pstmt.setString(1, "cse");
      pstmt.setString(2, "mack8000");
      ResultSet rs = pstmt.executeQuery();
}
catch (Exception e) {
       System.out.println("Error in PreparedStatement! " + e.getMessage()); }
```

FIGURE 4.14 A code example to perform an Oracle query using a JDBC statement.

TABLE 4.7
Keywords and Their Syntax Supported by JDBC Escape Syntax

Keyword	Function	Syntax
Call	Execute stored procedures	{call procedure_name [arg1, . . .]}
? = call	Execute stored functions	{? = call function_name [arg1, . . .]}
d	Define a date	{d 'yyy-mm-dd'}
escape	Define the database's escape character	{escape 'escape character'}
fn	Execute a scalar function	{'fn function [arg1, . . .]}
oj	Define an outer join	{oj outer-join}
t	Define a time	{'hh:mm:ss'}
ts	Define a time stamp	{'yyyy-mm-dd hh:mm:ss.f. . . . '}

these extensions in a database-independent manner, JDBC implements an ODBC-style escape syntax for many of these extensions. By using escape syntax, applications can achieve total database independence and still take advantage of the additional functionalities provided by those extensions.

Escape syntax works much like the escape character, which contains a keyword and parameters, all enclosed in curly braces.

```
{keyword [parameter], . . . . }
```

WhenJDBC finds a set of curly braces in an execuTable string, the driver maps the enclosed keyword and parameters to the database-specified syntax, and the mapped syntax is then sent to the database for execution.

JDBC escape syntax supports seven keywords; each of them indicates the type of extension that is enclosed within the braces. Table 4.7 shows a collection of the keywords and their syntax.

So far we have discussed most Statement components and interfaces in JDBC data actions and applications. Now let's take care of retrieving the execution results.

4.2.4 Retrieving Results

Based on the different Oracle statements, three execution methods can be used to run an associated Oracle statement. As we discussed in Section 4.2.3.1, each execution method performs different data actions:

- The **`executeQuery()`** method is used to run a data query, and the expected returned result is a result set stored in a **`ResultSet`** object.

- The **executeUpdate()** method is used to perform a insert, update or delete data action, and the returned result should be an integer that equals the number of rows that have been affected by running this data manipulation.
- The **execute()** method can be used in either way, but this method never returns any result, and you need to use special methods to pick up the run results.

To pick up the run results for different methods, the following rules should be observed:

1) For the **executeQuery()** method, the **getResultSet()** method defined in the **Statement** interface should be used since the run result is a result set stored in a **ResultSet** object.
2) For the **executeUpdate()** method, the **getUpdateCount()** method defined in the **Statement** interface should be used since the run result is an integer that equals the number of rows that have been affected.
3) For the **execute()** method, since this method can handle both **ResultSet**s and integers, and it never returns any result, you need to use special methods to retrieve the run result for the execution of this method.

Relatively speaking, for the first two methods, it is relatively easy to pick up the run result, since the result is known and definite. The challenge is the third method, **execute()**, since the result of execution of this method can be either a **ResultSet** or an integer. Another challenge is that this method can be used where the Oracle statement to be executed is not known at compile time or there is a possibility of multiple results being returned by a stored procedure. Unlike the first two methods, the **execute()** method never returns any result, and you must use either the **getResultSet()** or **getUpdateCount()** method to retrieve the run results.

To distinguish what kind of result is returned, we can use the method we discussed in the last section. To handle multiple results, we need to use the **getMoreResults()** method defined in the **Statement** interface (refer to Table 4.4). When executing this method, **True** will be returned if a **ResultSet** object is returned. If the result retrieved is an integer, then the **getMoreResults()** method returns **False**. The confusing issue is that this method will also return **False** if no result is received. In order to solve this confusion, you must use the **getUpdateCount()** method to test the possible results. Table 4.8 shows a full picture of the associated test conditions and possible test results.

It is easy to get the result of the execution of the **execute()** method, since only an integer is returned as the result for this method. However, the result of the execution of the **executeQuery()** and **execute()** methods needs more work, since a **ResultSet** object that contains a tabular set is returned. We will concentrate on the methods used to retrieve and process the actual data contained in the **ResultSet** object. First let's have a closer look at the **ResultSet** interface.

TABLE 4.8
Methods Used to Determine the Type of Result Returned

Method	Return Value	Test Result
getUpdateCount()	> 0	The result is an update count
getUpdateCount()	= –1	The result is not an update count
getUpdateCount()	= 0	Either the update count is zero, or a data definition language statement is executed, such as CREATE Table
getResultSet()	= null	The result is not a ResultSet
getResultSet()	= –1	The result is a ResultSet
getUpdateCount()	!= null	

4.2.4.1 The ResultSet Interface

Data is stored in a **ResultSet** just as it is returned by the database: it is stored in tabular format. Each field of the database can be described by a unique combination of a row ID and a column ID. A column can be mapped to an array, since all data in a single column has the same data type. Similarly, a row can be mapped to a vector, since all elements in a single row may have different data types.

The **ResultSet** interface has more than 25 methods, and Table 4.9 lists some of the most often used methods.

All **getXXX()** methods defined in this **ResultSet** interface, except **getMetaData()**, are overloaded methods with two signatures, which means that all of these methods can pass two types of arguments, either a column index that is an integer or a column name that is a string. To save space, here we only list the first signature for each of those methods.

Now we have a clear picture of the **ResultSet** interface; next we need to get the run results from the execution of an execute method. First let's take care of how to get a **ResultSet** object after an execute method has been done.

TABLE 4.9
Methods Defined in the ResultSet Interface

Method	Function
close()	Close the ResultSet and release all resources associated with it
findColumn(String colName)	Return the column index number corresponding to the column name argument
getAsciiStream(int index)	Retrieve the value of the specified column from the current row as an ASCII stream. The column can be represented by either the column index or the column name
getBigDecimal(int index)	Return the value of the referenced column from the current row as a BigDecimal object
getBoolean(int index)	Return the value of the referenced column from the current row as a Boolean
getByte(int index)	Return the value of the referenced column from the current row as a byte
getBytes(int index)	Return the value of the referenced column from the current row as an array of bytes
getBlob(int column_Index)	Retrieve the value of the designated column in the current row of this ResultSet object as a Blob object in the Java programming language
getBlob(String column_Name)	Retrieve the value of the designated column in the current row of this ResultSet object as a Blob object in the Java programming language
getDouble(int index)	Return the value of the referenced column from the current row as a double
getFloat(int index)	Return the value of the referenced column from the current row as a floating point number
getInt(int index)	Return the value of the referenced column from the current row as an integer
getLong(int index)	Return the value of the referenced column from the current row as a long integer
getObject(int index)	Return the value of the referenced column from the current row as an Object. The object type is determined by the default mapping of the Oracle data type
getShort(int index)	Return the value of the referenced column from the current row as a short integer
getString(int index)	Return the value of the referenced column from the current row as a String object
getTime(int index)	Return the value of the referenced column from the current row as a java.sql.Time object
getMetaData()	Return a metadata object from the ResultSet object
next()	Move the ResultSet row cursor to the next row
wasNull()	Determine if the last value read by a getXXX() method was an Oracle null value. True is returned if the last read value contained a null value

4.2.4.2 Getting and Processing the ResultSet Object

When an Oracle data query is executed, the returned result is stored in a **ResultSet** object, and this **ResultSet** object can be created by one of the following two methods:

- The **executeQuery()** method
- The **getResultSet()** method

When an **executeQuery()** method is executed, the result of the queried data is stored in a **ResultSet** object and returned. However, when an **execute()** method is used to retrieve a data query result, it will not return any result directly; instead, you need to use the **getResultSet()** method to create a **ResultSet** to pick up the returned result.

Once the **ResultSet** object is created by using either method, an appropriate **getXXX()** method defined in the **ResultSet** interface can be used to access and retrieve data. Since the data is in a tabular format, any data can be retrieved by using the column and row ordinals. Two different ways can be used to select and access each column and row in a **ResultSet** object:

1) Using either the column index or column name to select the desired column
2) Using the cursor that points to the current row to select a desired row

In order to scan the entire Table in a **ResultSet** object, you can use the **next()** method defined in the **ResultSet** interface to move the cursor row by row until the last record. To pick up a specified column from a given row, you can use an appropriate **getXXX()** method defined in the **ResultSet** interface with a column index or column name as the argument.

Let's have a closer look at accessing and processing each row and column from a **ResultSet** object with a little more discussion in the following sections.

4.2.4.2.1 Fetching by Row

In a **ResultSet** object, a cursor is used as a pointer to point to each row, and each row of data must be processed in the order in which it can be returned. At the beginning time, after an execution method is executed and a **ResultSet** object is returned, the cursor points to the initial row, which is an empty row (refer to Figure 4.15). To move the cursor to point to the first row of data, as we mentioned, the **next()** method can be used. Then an appropriate **getXXX()** method can be used to pick up the desired column from the current row based on the column index or the column name as the argument of that method. Figure 4.15 shows a structure of a **ResultSet** object with a row pointer positioning diagram.

Figure 4.15a shows an initial cursor position of a **ResultSet** object in which an execution method has just completed and a **ResultSet** object is created. The cursor now points to the initial row, row 0, and it is an empty row with no data included.

To access and retrieve a row of data, the **next()** method is executed to move the cursor to point to the next row, row 1 (shown in Figure 4.15b), in which the first row of data is stored. An appropriate **getXXX()** method can be used to retrieve the desired column with the column index or column name as the argument. To navigate through the entire **ResultSet** and process each row, you can use the **next()** method again until the last row. A **true** will be returned from this **next()** method if it points to a row containing data, and a **false** will be returned if the cursor points to a null row, which means that the bottom of the **ResultSet** has been reached, and no more data is available in this object.

In an actual program development and coding process, a **while()** loop can be used to execute the **next()** method to advance the cursor from the current row to point to the next row until a **false** is returned, which means that the bottom of the **ResultSet** object has been reached.

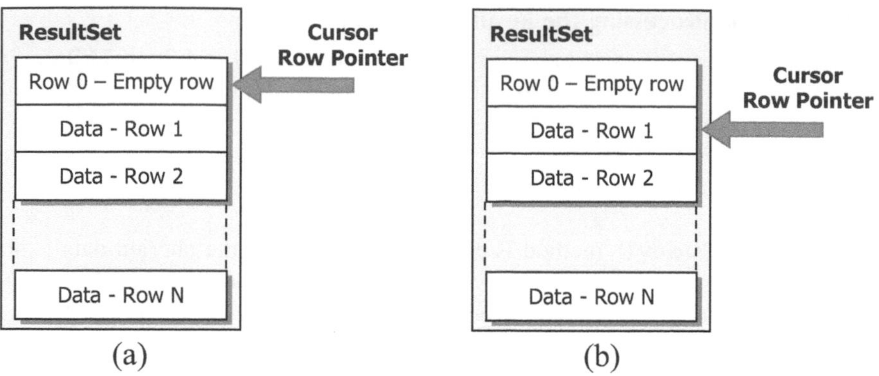

FIGURE 4.15 The structure of a ResultSet with a row pointer positioning diagram.

```
String query = "SELECT user_name, pass_word FROM LogIn " +
               "WHERE user_name = ? AND pass_word = ?";
PreparedStatement pstmt = con.prepareStatement(query);
pstmt.setString(1, "cse");
pstmt.setString(2, "mack8000");
ResultSet rs = pstmt.executeQuery();
while (rs.next()){
    username = rs.getString(1);          // username = rs.getString("user_name");
    password = rs.getString(2);          // password = rs.getString("pass_word");
}
```

FIGURE 4.16 Example code of using the looped next() method.

Figure 4.16 shows a piece of example code to illustrate how to use a **`while()`** loop with the **`next()`** method to retrieve the related username and password from the LogIn Table in our sample database, **CSE _ DEPT**.

The non-highlighted code is prerequisite code used to create an Oracle statement query string, create a **`PreparedStatement`** object and set input parameters for the query string. The code in bold is the key code used to create a **`ResultSet`** object and perform a **`while()`** loop with the **`next()`** method to retrieve all related usernames and passwords from the LogIn Table in our sample database. Since most **`getXXX()`** methods defined in the **`ResultSet`** interface are overloaded methods, alternatively, you can use the column name as an argument to pick up the desired column. This alternative code is shown on the right side with the comment-out symbol in front of it.

4.2.4.2.2 Fetching by Column

When a valid data row has been retrieved, we need to get each column from that row. To do that, a different **`getXXX()`** method should be used based on the different data type of the returned data. One can use either the name of a column or the index of that column to get the data value. Inside the **`while`** loop in Figure 4.16, we used a column index as the argument for the **`getString()`** method to retrieve the username and password columns from our **`LogIn`** Table. As you know, the data type for both the **`user _ name`** and the **`pass _ word`** are String in our **`LogIn`** Table; therefore, a **`getString()`** method is used with the index of each column. A point to be noted is that the first column has an index of 1, not 0. If the name of each column, not an index, is used for the **`getString()`** method in this **`while`** loop, the code can be rewritten as:

```
while (rs.next()){
username = rs.getString("user _ name");
password = rs.getString("pass _ word");
}
```

One of the most important methods in the **ResultSet** class is **getObject()**. The advantage of using this method is that a returned datum, which is stored in a **ResultSet** object with its data type unknown (a datum is dynamically created), can be automatically converted from its Oracle data type to the ideal Java data type. This method outperforms any other **getXXX()** method, since the data type of returned data must be known before a suiTable **getXXX()** method can be used to fetch the returned data.

The **findColumn()** method is used to find the index of a column if the name of that column is given, and the **close()** method is used to close a **ResultSet** instance.

One very useful method, or a pair of methods, **getBlob()**, is crucially important when retrieving an image object from a Table in a database. An image object is stored in a Table in BLOB format; thus, one needs to use this method to access the Table to retrieve any image object stored in a database.

The **getMetaData()** method is a very good and convenient method, and it allows users to have a detailed and clear picture of the structure and properties of data returned to a **ResultSet**. A **ResultSetMetaData** object, which contains all pieces of necessary information about the returned data stored in a **ResultSet** instance, is returned when this method is executed. By using different methods of the **ResultSetMetaData** interface, we can obtain a clear picture of the returned data. For example, by using the **getColumnCount()** method, we can find how many total columns have been retrieved and stored in the **ResultSet**. By using **getTableName()**, **getColumnName()** and **getColumnType()**, we can find the name of the data Table we queried, the name of column we just fetched and the data type of that column. A more detailed discussion about the **ResultSetMetaData** component will be given in the following sections.

4.2.5 Using JDBC MetaData Interfaces

In addition to general and popular data information provided by three statement interfaces and execution methods, JDBC also provides useful and critical information and descriptions ofthe database, run result sets and parameters related to JDBC drivers and database applications. All of these properties, structures and descriptions can be categorized into three interfaces, so-called metadata interfaces, or

1) **ResultSetMetaData** interface
2) **DatabaseMetaData** interface
3) **ParameterMetaData** interface

In the following sections, we will concentrate on these three interfaces to illustrate how to use them to retrieve detailed descriptions and structures as well as properties related to the data action components, such as **ResultSet**, database and parameters to facilitate database applications.

Let's start with the **ResultSetMetaData** interface.

4.2.5.1 Using the ResultSetMetaData Interface

In Section 4.2.4, we discussed how to retrieve run results stored in a **ResultSet** object and important methods of this interface. By using different fetching methods, either fetching by rows or columns, we can easily retrieve a whole set of returned results stored in a **ResultSet** object. However, in some applications, we may need more detailed information about and properties of the returned result set, such as the total number of columns returned and each column's name and data type, as well as other structure information related to the returned result set. By using this structure information and properties, we can get a clear and full picture of the returned **ResultSet**, which will enable us to retrieve our desired data more directly and conveniently. With the help of the metadata provided by **ResultSetMetaData**, you can develop entire database applications without even knowing what RDBMS, Table or type of data is being accessed.

The **ResultSetMetaData** interface provides a collection of information about the structure and properties related to the returned **ResultSet** object, and this gives us the ability to perform the functions we described previously. The **ResultSetMetaData** interface contains more than 20 methods, and Table 4.10 shows the 16 most popular methods.

It can be seen from Table 4.10 that the top ten methods in a **ResultSetMetaData** object are mainly used to retrieve the structure and properties for the specified column with the column index as an argument. The rest of methods that return a Boolean value are used to determine some important properties that describe special functions provided by the database engine for the selected column. One of the advantages of using this metadata is that you can build dynamic applications that are independent of the data source. One possible way to achieve this is to remove the need for all direct column name references.

Because of the space limitation, we can only provide a brief discussion of some important methods that are widely implemented in most database applications.

After a data query is executed and a **ResultSet** object is returned, before we can retrieve our desired data from the **ResultSet**, we may need to get some structure information and properties related to the columns we chose. One of the most important properties is the total number of columns returned in the **ResultSet** object. By using the **getColumnCount()** method, we can easily get not only the total number of columns but also the content of each column. Figure 4.17 shows example code to illustrate how to use this method to scan the entire **ResultSet** to retrieve each column from it.

The first code line is used to create a ResultSet object by executing the **executeQuery()** method. Then a **ResultSetMetaData** object, **rsmd**, is created by calling the **getMetaData()** method defined by the **ResultSet** interface. To pick up each returned column, a **while** loop is used combined with the **next()** method. By using this piece of code, you do not even need to know

TABLE 4.10
Methods Defined in the ResultSetMetaData Interface

Method	Function
getCatalogName(int index)	Determine the name of the catalog that contains the referenced column
getColumnCount()	Return the total number of columns contained in the ResultSet object
getColumnDisplaySize(int index)	Return the maximum display width for the selected column
getColumnLabel(int index)	Return the preferred display name for the selected column
getColumnName(int index)	Return the name of the column for the selected column
getColumnType(int index)	Return the Oracle data type for the selected column
getPrecision(int index)	Return the precision used for the selected column
getScale(int index)	Return the scale used for the selected column
getSchemaName(int index)	Return the name of the schema that contains the selected column
getTableName(int index)	Return the name of the Table that contains the selected column
isAutoIncrement(int index)	Determine if the column is automatically numbered by the database (auto-number)
isCurrency(int index)	Determine if the column represents currency
isNullable(int index)	Determine if the column is able to accept null values
isSigned(int index)	Determine if the column contains signed numbers
isWriTable(int index)	Determine if the column is wriTable by the user
isReadOnly(int index)	Determine if the column is read-only

```
ResultSet  rs = pstmt.executeQuery();
ResultSetMetaData  rsmd = rs.getMetaData();
While (rs.next()){
   for (int m = 1; m< rsmd.getColumnCount(); m ++)
   {
       System.out.println( rs.getString(m));
   }
}
```

FIGURE 4.17 A code example using the getColumnCount() method.

how many columns were returned in that **ResultSet** or the name for each column; in other words, you do not have to have prior knowledge about the Table and database: you can retrieve all the columns with their exact names! Yes, that is easy and fancy.

In some applications, you may need to know some other useful information about the columns, such as the data type of each column, the width of each column and the precision and scale of the selected column if a floating point or double data is stored in that column. To get those properties, you can call the appropriate methods, such as **getColumnType()**, **getColumnDisplaySize()**, **getPrecision()** and **getScale()**.

Also, to get some important information and properties about the returned ResultSet, sometimes we may need to get similar information for the connected database. In that case, you may need to use the **DatabaseMetaData** interface.

4.2.5.2 Using the DatabaseMetaData Interface

Compared with other metadata interfaces, the **DatabaseMetaData** is the largest, with over 150 methods. This interface is mainly used by developers who are building database applications that need to be fully RDBMS independent, which means that the developers do not need to know anything about the database or have prior knowledge about the database they are using. In this way, the users can discover and retrieve structures and properties of the RDBMS dynamically as the application runs.

To create a **DatabaseMetaData** object, one needs to call the **getMetaData()** method defined in the **Connection** interface.

Relatively speaking, the **ResultSetMetaData** interface allows you to discover the structure of Tables and properties of columns, but the **DatabaseMetaData** interface enables you to dynamically determine properties of the RDBMS. Table 4.11 shows the 16 most popular and important methods widely implemented by the **DatabaseMetaData** interface.

These 16 methods can be divided into seven groups based on their functionalities:

1) Catalog Identification Methods
2) Database Identification Methods
3) Driver Identification Methods
4) Stored Procedure–Related Methods
5) Schema Identification Methods
6) Table Identification Methods
7) Database-Related Parameter Methods

To get the name and version of the current database being used, the **getDatabaseProduct-Name()** and **getDatabaseProductVersion()** methods can be used. Similarly, to get the name and revision number of the JDBC driver being used, the **getDriverName()** and **getDriverVersion()** methods can be executed.

TABLE 4.11
Popular Methods Defined in the DatabaseMetaData Interface

Method	Function
getCatalogs()	Return a ResultSet containing a list of all catalogs available in the database
getCatalogTerm()	Determine what the database-specific name for Catalog is
getDatabaseProductName()	Return the name of the database product
getDatabaseProductVersion()	Return the database revision number
getDriverName()	Return the name of the driver
getDriverVersion()	Return the revision number of the driver
getPrimaryKeys(String catalog, String schema, String Table)	Return a ResultSet describing all of the primary keys within a Table
getProcedures(string catalog, String schPatt, String proPatt)	Return a ResultSet describing all stored procedures available in the catalog
getProcedureTerm()	Determine the database-specific term for procedure
getSchemas()	Return a ResultSet containing a list of all schemas available in the database
getSchemaTerm()	Determine the database-specific term for schema
getTables(String catalog, String schePatt, String TablePatt, String[] types)	Return a ResultSet containing a list of all Tables available matching the catalog, schema and Table type selection criteria
getTableTypes()	Return a ResultSet listing the Table types available
getTypeInfo()	Return a ResultSet describing all of the standard Oracle types supported by the database
getURL()	Return the current URL for the database
getUserName()	Return the current user name used by the database

In fact, the **DatabaseMetaData** interface provides methods that allow you to dynamically discover properties of a database as the project runs. Many methods in **DatabaseMetaData** return information in the **ResultSet** component, and one can get those pieces of information from the **ResultSet** object by calling related methods such as **getString()**, **getInt()** and **getXXX()**. An exception would be thrown if the queried item is not available in the **MetaData** interface.

Overall, the **DatabaseMetaData** interface provides an easy and convenient way to allow users to identify and retrieve important structure and property information about the database dynamically.

4.2.5.3 Using the ParameterMetaData Interface

Detailed information about the parameters passed into or from the database can be obtained by calling the **getParameterMetaData()** method that is defined in the **PreparedStatement** interface. Although this interface is not as popular as **ResultSetMetaData** and **DatabaseMetaData**, it is useful in some special applications.

Basically, the **ParameterMetaData** interface can be defined as an object that can be used to get information about the types and properties of the parameters in a **PreparedStatement** object. For some queries and driver implementations, the data that would be returned by a **ParameterMetaData** object may not be available until the **PreparedStatement** has been executed. Some driver implementations may not be able to provide information about the types and properties for each parameter marker in a **CallableStatement** object.

The **ParameterMetaData** interface contains seven fields and nine methods. Table 4.12 shows the ten most popular methods that are widely implemented in most database applications.

Figure 4.18 shows a piece of example code to illustrate how to retrieve the total number of parameters related to a **PreparedStatement** object.

TABLE 4.12
Popular Methods Defined in the ParameterMetaData Interface

Method	Function
getParameterCount()	Return the number of parameters in the PreparedStatement object for which this ParameterMetaData object contains information
getPrecision(int param)	Return the designated parameter's number of decimal digits
getScale(int param)	Return the designated parameter's number of digits to right of the decimal point
getParameterType(int param)	Return the designated parameter's Oracle type
getParameterTypeName(int param)	Return the designated parameter's database-specific type name
getParameterMode(int param)	Return the designated parameter's mode
isNullable(int param)	Determine whether null values are allowed in the designated parameter
isSigned(int param)	Determine whether values for the designated parameter can be signed numbers

```
String query = "SELECT user_name, pass_word FROM LogIn " +
               "WHERE user_name = ? AND pass_word = ?";
PreparedStatement pstmt = con.prepareStatement(query);
pstmt.setString(1, "cse");
pstmt.setString(2, "mack8000");
ResultSet  rs = pstmt.executeQuery();
ParameterMetaData  pmmd = pstmt.getParameterMetaData();
System.out.println( "The total number of parameter is " + pmmd.getParameterCount());
```

FIGURE 4.18 A code example of using the getParameterCount() method.

After a `PreparedStatement` instance is created, the `getParameterMetaData()` method is executed to retrieve the total number of parameters returned in the `ParameterMetaData` object.

Finally, let's handle closing the connection object and releasing used resources, including the statement objects.

4.2.6 Closing the Connection and Statements

After a set of data actions has been performed and the desired data has been acquired, the Connection object that is used to connect to our target database should be closed, and the related data operational resources, including all opened statement objects used for these data actions, should also be released. Otherwise, you may encounter some possible exceptions when you try to open a database that has been opened but without being closed in the previous applications. This cleanup is very easy with the piece of code shown in Figure 4.19.

To do a closing operation, a `try-catch` block should be used to track and monitor the closing process with possible exception warnings.

4.3 CHAPTER SUMMARY

The application fundamentals of JDBC and the JDBC API, which include the application models and operational procedures of the JDBC API implemented in Java database applications, are discussed in detail in this chapter.

```
try{
        stmt.close();
        if (!con.isClosed())
          con.close();
   }
catch(SQLException e){
   System.out.println("Could not close!" + e.getMessage());
   }
```

FIGURE 4.19 A code example of closing the Connection and Statement objects.

Starting with an introduction to two JDBC application models, two-tier and three-tier models, a detailed illustration and description of these two models is given in the first part of this chapter. A typical two-tier model contains an application server and a database server, in which a Java database application project resides on an application server and the target database is located on the database server. The so-called three-tier model places the application onto an application server that can be considered a middle tier and installs the database on a database server. To run this three-tier model application, the user needs to communicate with the application server by using a Web browser that can be considered a top tier, with a GUI installed in this browser. Then the application server can process requests sent from the browser via the target database via the database server. Finally, when requests have been sent, the results will be returned to the browser by the application server.

Following the application models, a complete operational procedure to perform a standard Java database application is discussed with some example code, including:

- Load and register a JDBC Driver.
- Connect to the target database using either the `DriverManager.getConnection()` method or `Driver.connect()` method.
- Execute an Oracle statement by creating and calling an appropriate `Statement` object, including:
    - **Statement** object
    - **PreparedStatement** object
    - **CallableStatement** object
- Distinguish different queries by running the associated execute method.
- Execute DDL and DML Oracle statements.
- Retrieve run results by creating and getting a `ResultSet` object.
- Develop sophisticated Java database applications using different JDBC metadata interfaces, including the `ResultSetMetaData`, `DatabaseMetaData` and `ParameterMetaData` interfaces.
- Close the connected database and opened statement objects to release data resources used byte application.

Combining the contents in this chapter and the last chapter, you should have a complete and clear picture of JDBC fundamentals and the application procedure. Beginning from the next chapter, we will introduce and discuss some development tools and actual techniques used in Java database applications.

HOMEWORK

I. True/False Selections

______1) JDBC applications are made of two models: two-tier and three-tier model.

_______2) In a three-tier model, the application is located on a Web server and the database is installed on a database server. The user can access the application server through a Web browser with a GUI installed in the browser.

_______3) To load and register a driver, creating a new instance of the Driver class method is better than using the **Class.forName**() method.

_______4) When establishing a database connection, the **DriverManager.getConnection**() method is a better method than the **Driver.connect**() method.

_______5) A JDBC URL is composed of three parts: network host name, database server name and port number.

_______6) By using three methods defined in the Connection interface, **createStatement**(), **prepareStatement**() and **prepareCall**(), one can create three statement objects: **Statement**, **PreparedStatement** and **CallableStatement**.

_______7) The **Statement** object can be used to perform both static and dynamic data queries.

_______8) To create a **ResultSet** object, you can either use the **getResultSet**() method or call the **executeQuery**() method.

_______9) The **executeQuery**() method returns an integer that equals the number of rows that have been returned, and the **executeUpdate**() method returns a **ResultSet** object containing the run results.

______10) The `next()` method defined in the `ResultSet` interface can be used to move the cursor that points to the current row to the next row in a `ResultSet`.

II. Multiple Choice

1) The __________ object provides methods for the creation of Statement objects that will be used to execute Oracle statements in the next step.
   a. Statement
   b. Connection
   c. DriverManager
   d. Driver

2) The relationship between three statement objects is: the __________ is a subclass of the __________ that is a subclass of the __________.
   a. CallableStatement, PreparedStatement, Statement
   b. Statement, CallableStatement, PreparedStatement
   c. PreparedStatement, Statement, CallableStatement
   d. Statement, PreparedStatement, CallableStatement

3) The __________ method returns a(n) __________, and the __________ method returns a(n) __________.
   a. execute(), ResultSet, executeQuery(), integer
   b. executeQuery(), integer, execute(), nothing
   c. executeUpdate(), integer, executeQuery(), ResultSet
   d. execute(), integer, executeUpdate(), ResultSet

4) The __________ object is used to execute a static Oracle query, but the __________ object is used to execute a dynamic Oracle query with IN and OUT parameters.
   a. PreparedStatement, Statement
   b. Statement, PreparedStatement
   c. CallableStatement, Statement
   d. Statement, CallableStatement

5) Both interfaces, PreparedStatement and CallableStatement, are used to perform dynamic Oracle statements; however, __________ performs queries with only

__________ parameters, but __________ calls stored procedures with both __________ and __________ parameters.

a. CallableStatement, OUT, PreparedStatement, IN, OUT
b. PreparedStatement, IN, CallableStatement, IN, OUT
c. CallableStatement, IN, PreparedStatement, IN, OUT
d. PreparedStatement, OUT, CallableStatement, IN, OUT

6) By using the __________ method, we can get a collection of information about the structure and properties of the returned ResultSet object.
   a. getResultSetMetaData()
   b. getResultSet()
   c. getMetaData()
   d. ResultSetMetaData()
7) To create a ____________ object, one needs to call the ___________ method defined in the **Connection** interface.
   a. ResultSet, getMetaData()
   b. Statement, getStatement()
   c. PreparedStatement, getPreparedStatement()
   d. DatabaseMetaData, getMetaData()
8) The ____________ interface allows you to discover the structure of Tables and properties of columns, but the _______________ interface enables you to dynamically determine properties of the RDBMS.
   a. ResultSet, DatabaseMetaData
   b. ParameterMetaData, ResultMetaData
   c. DatabaseMetaData, ParameterMetaData
   d. DatabaseMetaData, ResultSet
9) When using a CallableStatement object to run a stored procedure, you need to register the __________ parameters by using the _____________ method.
   a. IN/OUT, getParameters()
   b. IN, registerINParameter()
   c. OUT, registerOUTParameter()
   d. IN/OUT, registerINOUTParameter()
10) The placeholder used in the `setXXX()` and the `registerOUTParameter()` methods is used to ___________________.
   a. Indicate the location of the input or output parameters
   b. Reserve spaces for input or output parameters
   c. Inform the compiler to hold memory spaces for those parameters
   d. All of these

III. Exercises

1) Provide a brief description of the seven basic steps to use JDBC.
2) Translate the seven steps to Java code.
3) Provide a detailed description of the JDBC three-tier model and its function.
4) Provide a brief description of the JDBC URL.
5) Explain the operational sequence of retrieving results from a returned **ResultSet** object.
6) Explain the relationship between three Statement objects, and illustrate why and how the **CallableStatement** object can use the **setXXX()** methods defined in the **PreparedStatement** interface.
7) Explain the advantages of using JDBC metadata for Java database applications.

5 Introduction to Apache NetBeans IDE

Java was originally created by Sun Microsystems to try to overcome some complexities in C++ and to simplify the structure and architecture of applications developed by using object-oriented programming (OOP) languages such as C++. In the early days, Java developers needed to use separate tools to build, develop and run a Java application. The following tools are the most popular used when building a Java application:

- NotePad or WordPad—used to develop the Java source code
- Java Compiler—used to compile the Java source code to Java byte-code
- Java Interpreter—used to convert Java byte-code to machine code

There was no GUI or similar tools available in the early days, and developers had to use the Java layout manager to design and build the GUI by using different layouts with various components, such as buttons, labels, textfields, checkboxes and radio buttons. Even Web-related Java applications, such as applets, had to be built by using different tools. This created significant inconvenience and a complicated development environment for Java developers in that age.

As more sophisticated and advanced techniques developed, the Java development environment and tools greatly improved. By combining Java Software Development Kits (SDKs) and GUI components, such as the Abstract Windowing Toolkit (AWT) and Swing API, Sun integrated those components and tools to establish and build an integrated development environment. This IDE is very similar to Visual Studio. NET, in which all program development tools and components have been integrated and categorized into different packages. Developers can design, develop, build and run a Java stand-alone or Web application easily and conveniently inside this IDE without needing to use any other tools.

The Apache NetBeans IDE is one of the most current and updated IDEs and is widely implemented in a wide spectrum of Java applications. The Apache NetBeans IDE is actually written in Java and runs everywhere a Java Virtual Machine (JVM) is installed, including Windows, Mac OS, Linux and Solaris. A Java Development Kit is required for Java development functionality but is not required for development in other programming languages.

The Apache NetBeans project consists of an open-source IDE and an application platform that enables developers to rapidly create web, enterprise, desktop and mobile applications using the Java platform, as well as Java Page, JavaFX, PHP, JavaScript and Ajax, Ruby and Ruby on Rails, Groovy and Grails and C/C++.

The Apache NetBeans IDE, which was originally called NetBeans IDE and was released by Sun Microsystems and later taken over by Oracle, is a modular, standards-based integrated development environment written in the Java programming language. The NetBeans project consists of a full-featured open-source IDE written in the Java programming language and a rich client application platform, which can be used as a generic framework to build any kind of application.

5.1 OVERVIEW OF APACHE NETBEANS 12

Apache NetBeans, which contains two parts: the Apache NetBeans IDE and the Apache NetBeans Platform, is a top-level Apache project dedicated to providing rock-solid software development products that address the needs of developers, users and the businesses who rely on NetBeans as a basis for their products, particularly to enable them to develop these products quickly, efficiently and easily by leveraging the strengths of the Java platform and other relevant industry standards.

DOI: 10.1201/9781003304029-5

Like the NetBeans IDE, the Apache NetBeans IDE works as a free Java IDE and provides support for several other languages, such as Java, Maven, Ruby, PHP, JavaFX, JavaScript and C/C++, but the latter provides more support for Web and Internet applications.

Table 5.1 shows some of the most popular features provided by Apache NetBeans IDE 12.

TABLE 5.1
Most Popular Features Supported by Apache NetBeans IDE 12

Project Category	Features
Java Enterprise Edition 8	• Web projects with Java EE 8 and Java EE 8 Web profiles, EJBs in web applications. • EJB 3.1 support; EJB project file wizard also supports singleton session type. • RESTful web services (JAX-RS 2.1), GlassFish Metro 2.0 web services (JAX-WS 2.3), JAXB 2.2.8. • Java Persistence JPA 2.2, deployment, debugging profiling with GlassFish v5 application server.
Web Projects with JavaServer Faces 2.3 (Facelets)	• Code completion, error hints, namespace completion, documentation popups and tag auto-import for Facelets. • Editor support for Facelets libraries, composite components and expression language, including generators for JSF and HTML forms. • Customizable JSF components palette generates JSF forms and JSF data Tables from entities. • New File wizard generates customizable CRUD JSF pages from entities. • Broader usage of annotations instead of deployment descriptors.
JavaFX	• Added support for the latest JavaFX SDK 14. • Improved code completion. • Editor Hints: Fix Imports, Surround With, Implements Abstract Methods and more. • Improved navigation: Hyperlinks, Go to Type, Find Usages.
Kenai.com: Connected Developer	• Full JIRA support (plugin from update center). • Project dashboard with more member and project details, improved search and navigation, easier project sharing. • Improved instant messenger integration: Online presence, private and group chat with Kenai members, easy to add links to code/files/issues/stack traces to messages. • Improved issue tracker integration.
PHP	• Full PHP 7.4 support: namespaces, lambda functions and closures, syntax additions: NOWDOC, ternary conditions, jump labels, __callStatic(). • Symfony Framework support: Symfony projects, Symfony commands, shortcuts, PHP syntax coloring in YAML files. • Create a PHP project from a remote PHP application. • PHPUnit, Code Coverage, FTP/SFTP integration improvements, excluding PHP project folders from scanning/indexing.
Maven	• New Project from Maven archetype catalog and improved support for Java EE 6, Groovy, Scala projects. • Customizable dependency exclusion in dependency graph. Maven CheckStyle plugin. • "Update from Kenai" action for Kenai.com-hosted Maven projects.
Ruby	• Support for creating Rails 6.0 apps with dispatchers, JRuby 9.2.9, Ruby 2.7 debugging, and RSpec 3.7. • Improved rename refactoring, type inference and navigation. • Specifying arguments for Rails servers. • Run/Debug File with arguments, also for files not part of a project.
C and C++	• Profiling: New Microstate Accounting indicator, Thread Map view, Hot Spots view, Memory Leaks view, Sync Problems view. • Faster synchronization during remote development. • Support for gdbserver attach and easier attaching to already running processes.
Miscellaneous improvements	• Java Debugger: Mark an object in the variables tree with a name to refer to it in expressions. • Database integration: Code completion in SQL Editor now also for DELETE, DROP, UPDATE statements and for reserved keywords. • Groovy 2.0 and Grails: Improved code completion, including methods introduced via AST Transformations.

TABLE 5.2
Most Popular Techniques and Application Servers Supported by Apache NetBeans

Category	Supported Techniques and Application Servers
Supported technologies	Java EE 8 and higher JavaFX SDK 14 Java ME SDK 8.0 Struts 1.3.8 Spring 2.5 Hibernate 5.4 Java API for RESTful Web Services (JAX-RS) 2.1 PHP 7.4, 7.3, 7.1 Ruby 2.7 JRuby 9.2.9 Rails 2.3.4 Groovy 2.0 Grails 1.1 VCS • CVS: 1.11.23 • Subversion: 1.14 • Mercurial: 5.x • ClearCase V9.x
Tested application servers	• GlassFish v5 • Sun Java System Application Server PE 9.x • WebLogic 14c (14.1.1) • Tomcat 8 and 7 • Tomcat 9 • JBoss 7.2 and 7.3

The current version of the Apache NetBeans IDE is 12, and it offers complete support for the entire Java Enterprise Edition (EE) 8 and higher, with improved support for JSF 2.3/Facelets, Java Persistence 2.2, Enterprise JavaBean 3.1 including using EJBs in web applications, RESTful web services and GlassFish v3. It is also recommended for developing with the latest JavaFX SDK 14 and for creating PHP Web applications with the new PHP 7.4 release or with the Symfony Framework.

As we know, Apache NetBeans projects are composed of an open-source IDE and an application platform that enable developers to rapidly create Web, enterprise, desktop and mobile applications. Let's have a closer look at these two components to have a deeper understanding of this IDE.

Table 5.2 shows the most popular techniques supported by Apache NetBeans IDE 12 and application servers adopted by Apache NetBeans.

5.1.1 The Apache NetBeans Platform

The Apache NetBeans Platform is a broad Swing-based framework on which you can base large desktop applications. The IDE itself is based on the NetBeans Platform. The Platform contains APIs that simplify the handling of windows, actions, files and many other things typical in applications.

Each distinct feature in a NetBeans Platform application can be provided by a distinct NetBeans module, which is comparable to a plugin. An Apache NetBeans module is a group of Java classes that provides an application with a specific feature.

You can also create new modules for the Apache NetBeans IDE itself. For example, you can write modules that make your favorite cutting-edge technologies available to users of Apache NetBeans IDE. Alternatively, you might create a module to provide an additional editor feature.

The Apache NetBeans platform offers reusable services common to desktop applications, allowing developers to focus on the logic specific to their application. Among the features of the platform are:

- User interface management (e.g. menus and toolbars)
- User settings management
- Storage management (saving and loading any kind of data)
- Window management
- Wizard framework (supports step-by-step dialogs)
- NetBeans Visual Library

The second part of an Apache NetBeans is the NetBeans open-source IDE.

5.1.2 The Apache NetBeans Open-Source IDE

The Apache NetBeans IDE is an open-source integrated development environment, and it supports development of all Java application types, such as Java Standard Edition (Java SE) including JavaFX, Java Mobile Edition (Java ME), Web, Enterprise JavaBean (EJB) and mobile applications, out of the box. This IDE also allows users to quickly and easily develop Java desktop, mobile and Web applications, as well as HTML5 applications with HTML, JavaScript and CSS. The IDE provides a great set of tools for PHP and C/C++ developers. It is free and open source with a large community of users and developers around the world. Among other features are an Ant-based project system, Maven support, refactorings and version control.

All the functions of the IDE are provided by modules. Each module provides a well-defined function, such as support for the Java language, editing or support for the Concurrent Versions System (CVS) versioning system and Java Subversion(SVN). NetBeans contains all the modules needed for Java development in a single download, allowing the user to start working immediately. Modules also allow NetBeans to be extended. New features, such as support for other programming languages, can be added by installing additional modules. For instance, Sun Studio, Sun Java Studio Enterprise and Sun Java Studio Creator from Sun Microsystems are all based on the NetBeans IDE.

The three main modules included in the NetBeans IDE and most often used are shown in Table 5.3.

Users can choose to download NetBeans IDE bundles tailored to specific development needs.

Users can also download and install all other features at a later date directly through the NetBeans IDE. A complete set of bundles that can be used by users when they download and install NetBeans IDE onto their computers is shown in the following:

- Apache NetBeans Base IDE
- Java SE, JavaFX
- Web and Java EE
- Java ME
- Ruby
- C/C++
- PHP (version 6.5 and later)
- GlassFish
- Apache Tomcat

Figure 5.1 shows a typical structure and architecture of the Apache NetBeans IDE.

TABLE 5.3
Three Main Modules Included in the Apache NetBeans IDE

Module Name	Functions
NetBeans Profiler	This is a tool for the monitoring of Java applications: It helps you find memory leaks and optimize speed. Formerly downloaded separately, it has been integrated into the core IDE since version 12.1. The Profiler is based on a Sun Laboratories research project that was named JFluid. That research uncovered specific techniques that can be used to lower the overhead of profiling a Java application. One of those techniques is dynamic bytecode instrumentation, which is particularly useful for profiling large Java applications. Using dynamic bytecode instrumentation and additional algorithms, the NetBeans Profiler is able to obtain runtime information on applications that are too large or complex for other profilers. NetBeans also support Profiling Points that let you profile precise points of execution and measure execution time.
GUI design tool	The GUI design tool enables developers to prototype and design Swing GUIs by dragging and positioning GUI components. The GUI builder also has built-in support for JSR 296 (Swing Application Framework) and JSR 295 (Beans Binding technology).
NetBeans JavaScript Editor	This module provides extended support for JavaScript, Ajax and Cascading Style Sheets (CSS). JavaScript editor features comprise syntax highlighting, refactoring, code completion for native objects and functions, generation of JavaScript class skeletons, generation of Ajax callbacks from a template and automatic browser compatibility checks. CSS editor features comprise code completion for styles names; quick navigation through the navigator panel; displaying the CSS rule declaration in a List View and file structure in a Tree View; sorting the outline view by name, type or declaration order (List and Tree); creating rule declarations (Tree only); refactoring a part of a rule name (Tree only).

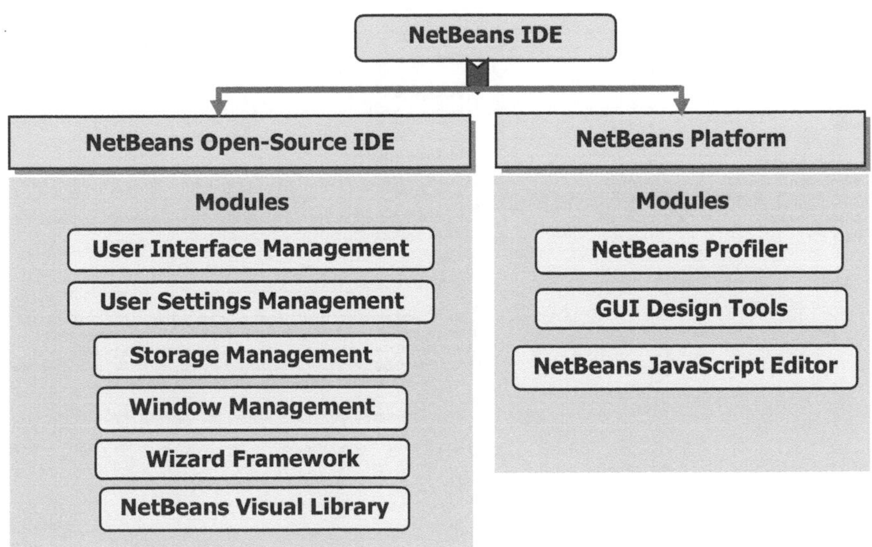

FIGURE 5.1 A typical structure of the Apache NetBeans IDE.

Now that we have a clear picture and understanding of the NetBeans IDE, next we need to conFigure the Apache NetBeans IDE and build actual projects on our computers.

5.2 INSTALLING AND CONFIRMING THE APACHE NETBEANS IDE

Refer to Appendices B and N to download and install Apache NetBeans 12.0 and the Java Development Kit (JDK) 14. Next we need to check and confirm the installed NetBeans IDE to make it our desired development environment.

To launch the installed Apache NetBeans IDE 12.0, double-click on the Apache NetBeans IDE 12.0 icon on the desktop. To conFigure this IDE, go to the `Tools|Plugins` item to check and confirm all installed components used in the Java applications, as shown in Figure 5.2.

As the `Plugins` wizard appears, click on the `Installed` tab and check all desired components installed by this IDE, as shown in Figure 5.2. The following components are needed for our projects:

- HTML5
- Java SE
- Tools
- PHP
- JavaFX 2
- Java Web and EE
- Developing NetBeans
- Groovy
- Service Registry
- Base IDE

From this installed list, it can be seen that most components or tools have been activated. The `Base IDE` has been activated by default, so leave this checked and click on the `Groovy` checkbox

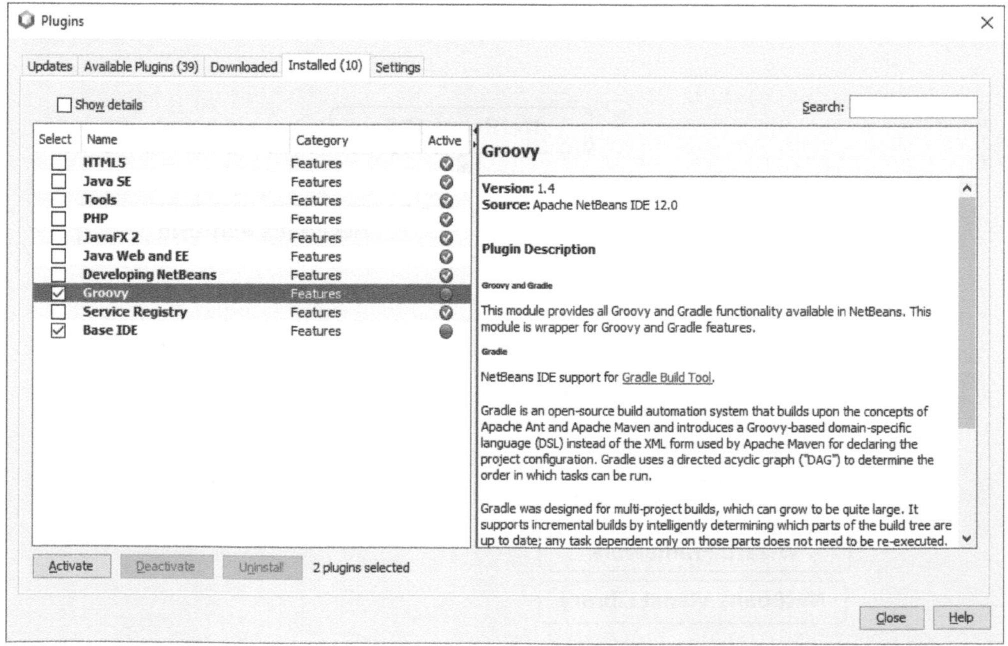

FIGURE 5.2 The launched NetBeans IDE 12.

to activate it as well. Click on the **Activate** button for the next two wizards and then the **Close** button to close this **Plugins** wizard.

Now that we have installed and confirmed the Apache NetBeans IDE 12, next we need to explore it to find all the useful features we will use to build our professional database applications in this integrated development environment.

5.3 EXPLORING THE APACHE NETBEANS IDE 12

By using the Apache NetBeans IDE, developers can design and build Java-related applications with different categories:

- Java applications
- JavaFX applications
- Java Web applications
- Java Enterprise applications
- PHP applications
- Maven applications
- Grails applications
- NetBeans modules

To get a clear picture and detailed description of this IDE, first let's have a workthrough overview for this product and its functionalities.

5.3.1 An Overview of the Apache NetBeans IDE 12 GUI

When you first launch the Apache NetBeans IDE 12, a main menu and some default windows are displayed, as shown in Figure 5.3.

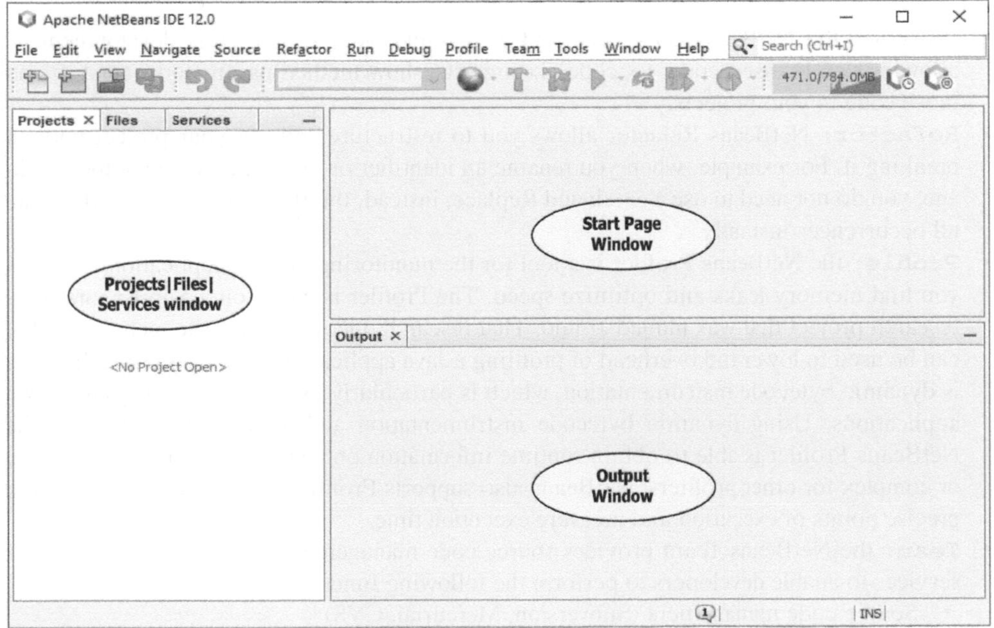

FIGURE 5.3 The opened Apache NetBeans IDE 12.

The first window or pane located at the upper-left corner is the **Projects|Files|Services** window and contains three different kinds of items:

1) All opened projects
2) All created files
3) All database services

These three different items can be displayed and switched between by clicking on the corresponding tab at the top of this window.

The second window, located at the lower-left corner, which is currently hidden, is the **Navigator** window that contains all components to enable users to scan and go through all the different objects or parts of a file. In fact, the Navigator window provides structured views of the file you are working with and lets you quickly navigate between different parts of the file.

The **Tasks** window, which is also hidden, is located at the bottom, and it is mainly used to list all the methods in your projects and allow you to enter code into those methods at any time when you are building your project.

The **Start Page** is the main window when the IDE is opened and displays all the recent projects you have developed. All updated news and tutorials related to NetBeans will also be displayed in this window.

Refer to Figure 5.3; among all the menu items, the following are special items with specific functionalities in the NetBeans IDE:

- **Navigate**: the NetBeans Navigator is used to navigate to any object, file, type of object or symbol you have created and built in your projects. With the name of each object or file, you can navigate to any of them at the development stage. Another important property of using the Navigate menu item is to enable you to inspect any member and hierarchy of those members defined in your project. The Inspect submenu item is used to inspect the members and hierarchy of any Java class in a convenient popup window that displays base classes, derived classes and interfaces. Use filters to control the level of detail that is displayed.
- **Source:** the NetBeans Source is used to facilitate your source code development by allowing you to insert code, fix code, fix imports, show method parameters and shift and move code in your projects.
- **Refactor:** NetBeans Refactor allows you to restructure code in your project without breaking it. For example, when you rename an identifier or move a class to another package, you do not need to use Search and Replace; instead, the IDE can identify and update all occurrences instantly.
- **Profile:** the NetBeans Profiler is a tool for the monitoring of Java applications. It helps you find memory leaks and optimize speed. The Profiler is based on a Sun Laboratories research project that was named JFluid. That research uncovered specific techniques that can be used to lower the overhead of profiling a Java application. One of those techniques is dynamic bytecode instrumentation, which is particularly useful for profiling large Java applications. Using dynamic bytecode instrumentation and additional algorithms, the NetBeans Profiler is able to obtain runtime information on applications that are too large or complex for other profilers. NetBeans also supports Profiling Points that let you profile precise points of execution and measure execution time.
- **Team:** the NetBeans Team provides source code management and connected developer services to enable developers to perform the following functions:
  - Source code management (Subversion, Mercurial, CVS)
  - Local file history
  - Integrated Connected Developer features for projects hosted on Kenai.com:

- Source code management (Subversion, Mercurial, and Git)
- Issue tracking (Jira and Bugzilla)
- Team wiki, forums, mailing lists
- Document and download hosting

In the NetBeans IDE, you always work inside of a project. In addition to source files, an IDE project contains metadata about what belongs on the **`Classpath`**, how to build and run the project and so on. The IDE stores project information in a project folder, which includes an Ant build script and properties file that control the building and running settings and a project.xml file that maps Ant targets to IDE commands.

Apache Ant is a Java-based building tool used to standardize and automate building and running environments for development. The IDE's project system is based directly on Ant. All of the project commands, like **`Cleanand Build Project`** and **`Debug`**, call targets in the project's Ant script. You can therefore build and run your project outside the IDE exactly as it is built and run inside the IDE.

It is not necessary to know Ant to work with the IDE. You can set all the basic compilation and runtime options in the project's **`Project Properties`** wizard, and the IDE automatically updates your project's Ant script. If you are familiar with Ant, you can customize a standard project's Ant script or write your own Ant script for a project.

The Apache NetBeans 12 IDE categorizes all Java-related applications into different groups based on the related template, such as Java with Ant, Java with Maven, HTML5/JavaScript and PHP. Under Java with Ant, there are another four subgroups:

1) JavaFX
2) Java Web
3) Java Enterprise
4) NetBeans Modules

Let's start with a new **`Java with Ant`** project, since this is a popular type of Java application.

5.3.2 Build a New Java with Ant Project

The NetBeans IDE allows you to create and build different projects based on different categories by selecting the right template for your project and completing the remaining wizard steps. First let's take care of creating a new Java with Ant project.

To create a new **`Java with Ant`** project under the Apache NetBeans IDE, go to the **`File|New Project`** menu item. A **`New Project`** wizard is displayed and shown in Figure 5.4.

Under the **`Javawith Ant`** category, the IDE contains the following standard project templates for Java desktop and Web applications:

- **`Java Application`**: Creates a new skeleton Java Standard Edition (SE) project with a main class
- **`Java Class Library:`** Creates a skeleton Java class library without a main class
- **`Java Project with Existing Sources:`** Creates a Java SE project based on your own Java sources
- **`Java Modular Project:`** Creates a new Java SE Modular Application in a standard IDE project. Multiple modules can be added into the project as standard projects using an IDE-generated Ant building script to build, run and debug the whole project. Java module is a new feature in Java 9 via the JavaPlatform Module System (JPMS)
- **`Java Free-Form Project:`** The free-form templates enable you to use an existing Ant script for a project but require manual configuration

Let's give a more detailed discussion of each of these projects one by one.

5.3.2.1.1 *Add a Graphical User Interface*

To proceed with building our interface, we need to create a Java container within which we will place the other required GUI components. Generally, the most popular Java GUI containers include:

- JFrame Form (Java Frame Form window)
- JDialog Form (Java Dialog Box Form window)
- JPanel Form (Java Panel Form window)

In this project, we will create a container using the **`JFrame`** component. We will place the container in a new package, which will appear within the **`Source Packages`** node.

Perform the following operations to complete this GUI adding process:

1) In the **`Projects`** window, right-click on our new created project, **`JavaAppProject`**, and choose the **`New > JFrame Form`** menu item from the popup menu.
2) Enter **`JavaAppFrame`** into the **`Class Name`** box as the class name, as shown in Figure 5.7.
3) Enter **`JavaAppPackage`** into the **`Package`** box as the package name (Figure 5.7).
4) Click on the **`Finish`** button.

Your finished **`New JFrame Form`** wizard should match the one that is shown in Figure 5.7.

The IDE creates the **`JavaAppFrame`** form and the JavaAppFrame class within the **`JavaAppProject`** application and opens the **`JavaAppFrame`** form in the GUI Builder. The **`JavaAppPackage`** package replaces the default package.

When we added the **`JFrame`** container, the IDE opened the newly created **`ContactEditorUI`** form in an Editor tab with a toolbar containing several buttons, as shown in Figure 5.8. The ContactEditor form opened in the GUI Builder's Design view, and three additional windows appeared automatically along the IDE's edges, enabling you to navigate, organize and edit GUI forms as you build them.

The GUI Builder's various windows include:

- **`Design Area`**: The GUI Builder's primary window for creating and editing Java GUI forms. The toolbar's Source and Design toggle buttons enable you to view a class's source code or a graphical view of its GUI components. The additional toolbar buttons provide convenient

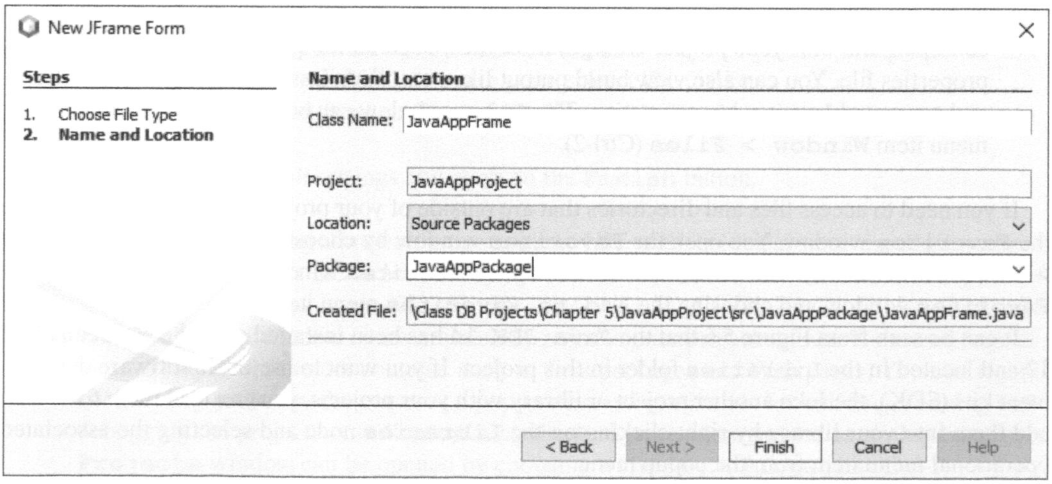

FIGURE 5.7 The finished New JFrame Form wizard.

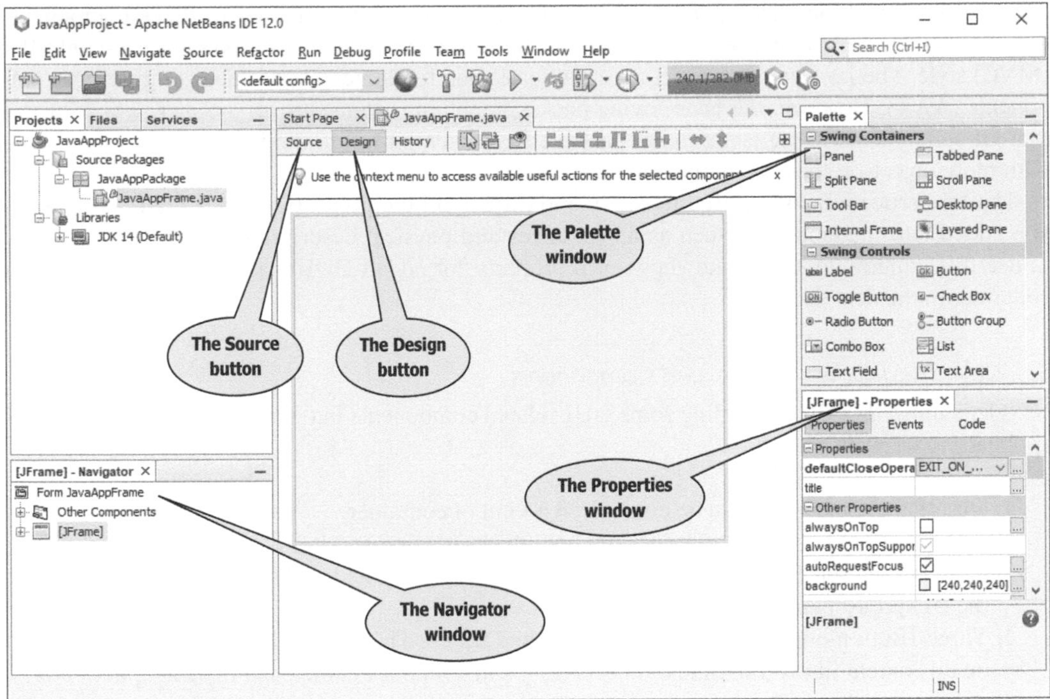

FIGURE 5.8 The opened ContactEditor form.

access to common commands, such as choosing between Selection and Connection modes, aligning components, setting component auto-resizing behavior and previewing forms.

- `Navigator Window`: Provides a representation of all the components, both visual and non-visual, in your application as a tree hierarchy. The Navigator API is good for clients that want to show some structure or outline of their document in dedicated window, allowing fast end-user navigation and control over the document. The Navigator API also allows its clients to plug in their Swing-based views easily, which then will be automatically shown in a specialized Navigator UI.
- `Palette Window`: A customizable list of available components containing tabs for JFC/Swing, AWT and JavaBeans components, as well as layout managers. In addition, you can create, remove and rearrange the categories displayed in the Palette using the customizer.
- `Properties Window`: Displays the properties of the component currently selected in the GUI Builder, Inspector window, Projects window or Files window.

Two more points to be emphasized are about the Palette and the Properties windows.

All Java GUI-related components are located in the Palette window and distributed in different packages or namespaces. This Palette window contains the following GUI-related components based on the different packages:

- Swing Containers: contains all Java container classes
- Swing Controls: contains all Swing-related GUI components
- Swing Menus: contains all Swing-related menu items
- Swing Windows: contains all Swing-related window classes
- AWT: contains all AWT-related GUI components
- Beans: contains all JavaBeans-related GUI components
- Java Persistence: contains all Java Persistence–related components

Relatively speaking, AWT-related GUI components are older compared to those components defined in the Swing package, in which all components are defined in a model-view-controller (MVC) style. The java.awt package contains all basic and fundamental graphic user interface components (AWT). However, the javax.swing package contains extensions of java.awt, which means that all components in the javax.swing package have been built into model-view-controller mode with more object-oriented properties (Swing).

The Properties window is used to set up and display all the properties of the GUI components you added into the container, such as appearances and physical descriptions. Let's illustrate how to use this window to set up and show each property for added GUI-related components on this container in the next section.

5.3.2.1.2 Add Other GUI-Related Components

Next let's finish this GUI by adding some GUI-related components into this GUI container. For this application, we want to add:

1) One JPanel object that can be considered a kind of container.
2) Two JTextField objects to retrieve and hold the user's first and last name.
3) Four JLabel objects to display the caption for each JTextField and the user's full name as the **Display** button is clicked.
4) Three JButton objects, **Display**, **Clear** and **Exit**. The **Clear** button is used to clean up all content in two JTextField objects (user's first and last name), and the **Exit** button is used to exit the application.

Now let's begin to add those components one by one by dragging them from the Palette window. If you do not see the Palette window in the upper-right corner of the IDE, choose the Windows > IDE Tools > Palette menu item to open it.

Let's add the JPanel object first in the following operational sequence:

1) Start by selecting a **Panel** from the Palette window and drop it onto the **JFrame**.
2) While the **Panel** is highlighted, go to the Properties window and click on the ellipsis (. . .) button next to the Border property to choose a border style.
3) In the Border dialog, select TitledBorder from the list, type in Display Full Name in the Title field and click on OK to save the changes and exit the dialog.
4) You should now see an empty titled JFrame that says Display Full Name JPanel object. Now add the rest of GUI-related components, including four JLabels, two JTextFields and three JButtons, into this JPanel object as you see in Figure 5.9.

Next let's rename all added components and modify **JLabel4** by setting the appropriate property for that label in the Properties window. Perform the following operational sequence:

1) Double-click on **jLabel1** and change the text property to **First Name**.
2) Double-click on **jLabel2** and change the text to **Last Name**.
3) Double-click on **jLabel3** and change the text to **Full Name**.
4) Click on **jLabel4** and click on the ellipsis (. . .) button next to the Border property to choose a border style. In the Border dialog, select Line Border, change the border color to dark blue by clicking on the ellipsis (. . .) button next to the Color property and click on the **OK** to save the changes and exit the dialog. Then go to the Text property to delete the default text JLabel4 to make this an empty label. Set the **preferredSize** property to [100, 20] if you like.

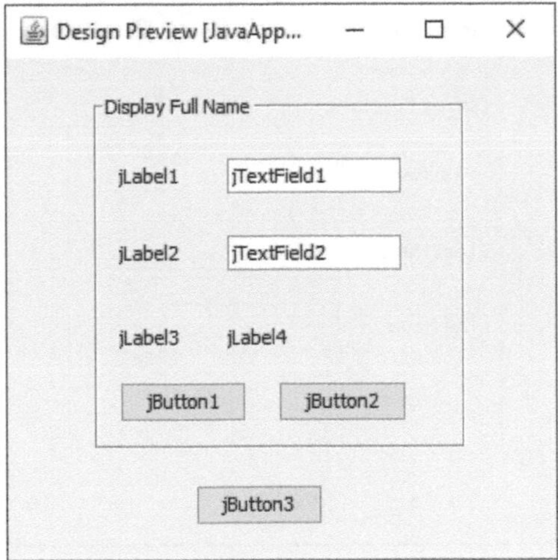

FIGURE 5.9 A design preview of the GUI Window Form.

5) Delete the sample text from **`jTextField1`**. You can make the display text ediTable by clicking on the Text field, pausing and then clicking the Text field again. You may have to resize the **`jTextField1`** to its original size. Repeat this step for **`jTextField2`**.
6) Change the **`name`** of **`jTextField1`** to FirstTextField. To make that change, right-click on the **`jTextField1`** object and select the Change Variable Name menu item from the popup menu, then enter FirstTextField into the New Name box. Click on **`OK`** to complete this rename operation.
7) Perform a similar operation to change the Name property of the **`jTextField2`** to LastTextField and the Name property of the **`jLabel4`** to FullNameLabel.
8) Rename the display text of **`jButton1`** to Display. You can edit a button's Text property by right-clicking on the button and choosing the Edit Text menu item from the popup menu. Or you can click on the button, pause, and then click again.
9) Rename the display text of **`jButton2`** to Clear.
10) Rename the display text of **`jButton3`** to Exit.
11) Change the Name property of the **`jButton1`** to DisplayButton, **`jButton2`** to ClearButton and **`jButton3`** to ExitButton.

Your finished GUI should now look like the one that is shown in Figure 5.10.

Next let's develop the code for each component to connect our GUI-related components with our code to process and respond to user input and display the run result.

5.3.2.1.3 Develop the Code for Three Buttons

In fact, only three JButton objects need to be coded, since both TextField objects are used to retrieve and hold the user's input without any other actions in this application. A similar situation holds for JLabel4, which is used to display the run result of this application.

In order to give a function to any button, we need to assign an event handler to each to respond to events. In our case, we want to know what happens when a button is pressed either by mouse clicking or keyboard pressing. So we will use ActionListener to respond to ActionEvent.

In the early days, developers had to make the connection between ActionListener and ActionEvent manually in an application. Thanks to NetBeans IDE, the Listener and Event model has been set up and conFigured. To set up that connection, what the developer needs to do is just double-click

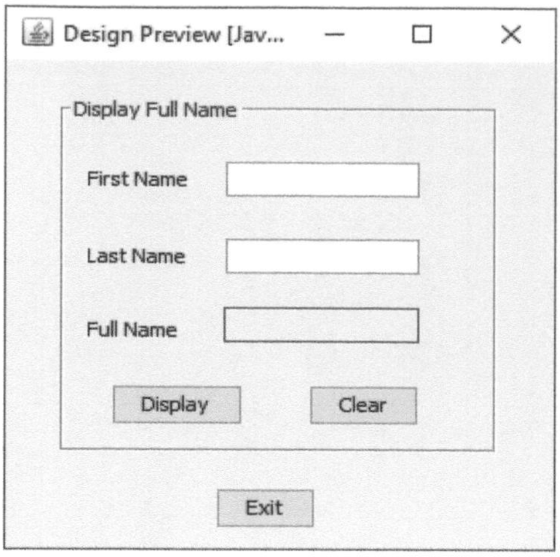

Design Preview [Jav...

Display Full Name

First Name

Last Name

Full Name

Display Clear

Exit

FIGURE 5.10 The finished GUI design window.

```
private void DisplayButtonActionPerformed(java.awt.event.ActionEvent evt) {
    // TODO add your handling code here:
    FullNameLabel.setText(FirstTextField.getText() + " " + LastTextField.getText());
}
```

FIGURE 5.11 The code for the DisplayButtonActionPerformed() event handler.

on the selected button. Is that easy? Yes, it is. Now let's create the Event-Listener action connection with our first button—DisplayButton.

5.3.2.1.3.1 Code for the Display Button

The function of the Display button is to concatenate the first and the last names entered by the user and stored in the FirstTextField and LastTextField TextFields and display this in the FullNameLabelwhen the Display button is clicked by the user as the project runs.

Double-click on the Display button, and you can open its callback method or event handler, DisplayButtonActionPerformed(). Enter the code shown in Figure 5.11 into the event handler to concatenate the first and last names entered by the user and display them in the FullNameLabel.

Usually, for most events and the associated event handler methods, you can make that connection by right-clicking on the source object (DisplayButton in this application) and selecting the Events menu item from the popup menu. All events that can be triggered by this source object will be displayed in a popup menu. By moving your cursor to the desired event, all event handlers responding to this event will be displayed in a popup submenu, and you can select the desired event handler to open it, and a connection between that event and event handler will be set up simultaneously.

The code for the `Display` button ActionPerformed() event handler is simple, and the setText() method is used to display the concatenated first and last name with a plus symbol.

5.3.2.1.3.2 Code for the Clear Button

The function of the Clear button is to clean up all the content in the two TextFields,

FirstTextField and LastTextField allow the user to enter a new name. Double-click on the Clear button to open its event handler, and enter the code shown in Figure 5.12 into the event handler.

```
private void ClearButtonActionPerformed(java.awt.event.ActionEvent evt) {
    // TODO add your handling code here:
    FirstTextField.setText(null);
    LastTextField.setText(null);
    FullNameLabel.setText(null);
}
```

FIGURE 5.12 The code for the ClearButtonActionPerformed() event handler.

```
private void ExitButtonActionPerformed(java.awt.event.ActionEvent evt) {
    // TODO add your handling code here:
    System.exit(0);
}
```

FIGURE 5.13 The code for the ExitButtonActionPerformed() event handler.

When this button is clicked by the user, the setText() method is executed with a null as the argument to clean up the three objects' contents, FirstTextField, LastTextField and FullNameLabel.

5.3.2.1.3.3 Code for the Exit Button

The function of this button is to stop the running of this project and exit from this application. To open its event handler, this time, we use another method. Perform the following operations to finish this coding process.

1) Right-click on the Exit button. From the pop-up menu, choose Events > Action > ActionPerformed. Note that the menu contains many more events you can respond to! When you select the actionPerformed event, the IDE will automatically add an ActionListener to the Exit button and generate a handler method for handling the listener's actionPerformed method.
2) The IDE will open up the Source Code window and scroll to where you implement the action you want the button to do when it is pressed.
3) Enter the code shown in Figure 5.13 into this event handler.

A system method, exit(), is executed as this button is clicked by the user, and a 0 is used as an argument to be returned to the operating system to indicate that the application has been completed successfully. A returned non-zero value indicates that some exceptions may have been encountered when the application ran.

Before we can run the project to test the functions we have built, we need to do one more piece of code, which is to locate the GUI window in the center when the project runs.

The NetBeans IDE has a default location for each GUI window, the upper-left corner, and will display windows in that location as the project runs. To place our GUI window in the center of the screen as the project runs, we need to put one line of code into the constructor of this class, since the first thing we need to do is to display our GUI window after the project runs. Open the code window by clicking on the Source button and enter one code line into the constructor of this class, which is shown in Figure 5.14.

A system method, setLocationRelativeTo(), is used to set this form at the center of the screen as the project runs. A null argument means that no object can be referenced or relatedto, and the JFrame Form is set to the center.

```
public class JavaAppProjectFrame extends javax.swing.JFrame {
   /** Creates new form JavaAppProjectFrame */
   public JavaAppProjectFrame() {
      initComponents();
      this.setLocationRelativeTo(null);          // set the GUI form at the center
   }
   ........
}
```

FIGURE 5.14 The code for the constructor of the class JavaAppProjectFrame.

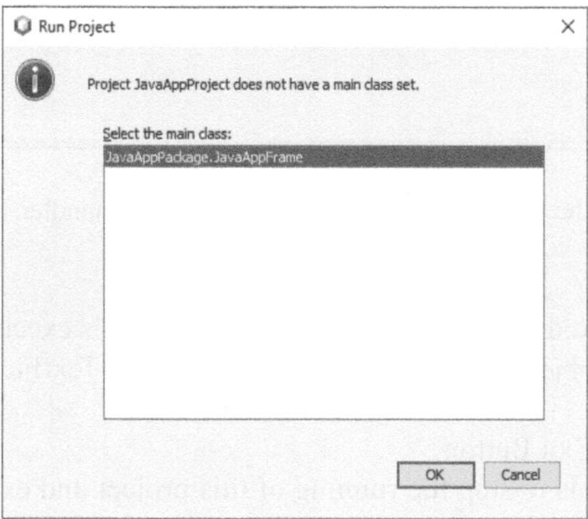

FIGURE 5.15 Add the JFrame as the main class.

Now we have finished the building process for this project, and we are ready to run it to test the functions we have built.

5.3.2.1.4 Run the Project

Perform the following operations to run our project:

1) Click on the Clean and Build Main Project button to compile and build our project.
2) Choose the Run > Run Main Project menu item.
3) If you get a window informing you that project JavaAppProject does not have a main class set, then you should select JavaAppPackage.JavaAppFrame as the main class in the same window and click the **OK** button, as shown in Figure 5.15.

A sample of running our project is shown in Figure 5.16.

Enter your first and last name in the First Name and Last Name TextFields, respectively, and click on the Display button. Your full name will be displayed in the Full Name label, as shown in Figure 5.16. Try to click on the Clear button. See what happened? Then you can click on the Exit button to stop our project. Yes, that is all for a typical Java application project.

A complete Java application project, **JavaAppProject**, is located in the folder **Students\Class DB Projects\Chapter 5**, which is located at the CRC Press ftp site (refer to Figure 1.2 in Chapter 1).

5.3.2.2 Build a Java Class Library

As we mentioned, a Java class library is only a skeleton Java class library without a main class, and it cannot be executed itself; instead, it must be called or used by other Java applications. Similarly

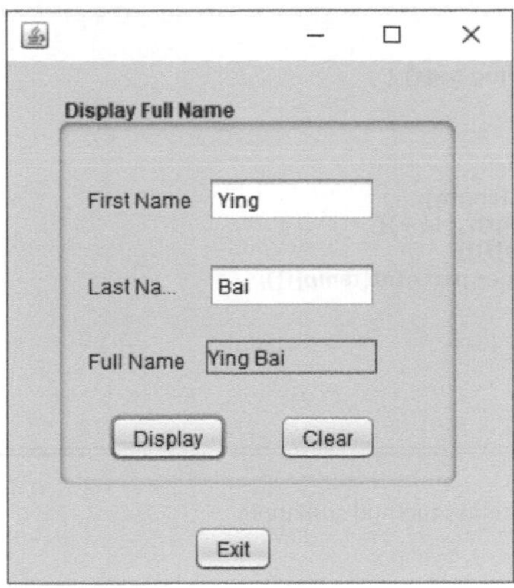

FIGURE 5.16 The run result of our project.

to other general libraries, a Java class library can be statically or dynamically bound or connected to an application and used as a utility class.

Since a Java class library cannot be executed itself, we need to create a Java application project to call or use that Java class library. Therefore, we need to create two projects to illustrate how to use a Java class library from a Java application:

- A Java class library project in which you will create a utility class.
- A Java application project with a main class that implements a method from the library project's utility class.

The function of this Java class library is simple, which is just to add two integers together and return the sum result to the Java application project, and the result will be displayed in the application project by calling some methods defined in the Java application project.

First let's create a Java class library project named **`SumLib()`**.

5.3.2.2.1 Create a Java Class Library Project

Perform the following operations to create the new Java class library project:

1) Choose the File > New Project menu item. Under Categories, select Java with Ant. Under Projects, select Java class library, and then click on the **`Next`** button.
2) Enter **`SumLib`** into the Project Name field as the name of this class library. Change the Project Location to any directory as you want on your computer. From now on, this directory is **`C:\Oracle DB Programming\Class DB Projects\Chapter 5`**.
3) Click the Finish button. The **`SumLib`** project opens in both the **`Projects`** window and the **`Files`** window.

Next we need to create a new Java package and our class file. The Java package is used as a container or a namespace to hold the class file.

Perform the following operations to finish this Java package and class file:

1) Right-click on the **`SumLib`** project node in the **`Projects`** window and choose the New > Java Class item. Type **`SumLibClass`** as the name for the new class, type **`org.`**

```
public class SumLibClass {
  public static int sumapp(String args) {
    int sum = 0;

    String[] temp;
    temp = args.split(",");
    int num[] = new int[temp.length];
    for(int i = 0; i < temp.length ; i++){
      System.out.println(temp[i]);
      num[i] = java.lang.Integer.parseInt(temp[i]);
      sum = sum + num[i];
    }
    return sum;
  }
}
```

FIGURE 5.17 The code for the class method sumapp().

me.sumlib in the **Package** field as the package name for this class file and click on the **Finish** button. The SumLibClass.java opens in the Source Editor.

2) In the opened SumLibClass.java file, place the cursor on the line after the class declaration, public classSumLibClass {.
3) Type or paste the code shown in Figure 5.17 as a new method, **sumapp()**.
4) If the code that you pasted in is not formatted correctly, press **Alt-Shift-F** to reformat the entire file.
5) Go to the File > Save All menu item to save this file.

This piece of code is simple and straightforward. The input argument to this method should be a sequence of integers separated with commas (,), which can be considered a String entered by the user as the project runs.

Let's have a closer look at this piece of code to see how it works.

First, a temporary String array, temp, is created, and it is used to hold the split input integers. Then the split() method is executed to separate the input argument into each separate number string. A for loop is used to display each separated number string and convert each of them to the associated integer using the parseInt() method. Since this method is defined in the java.lang.Integer package, the full name of the method must be used. A sum operation is performed to add all integers together and return to the main() method in the Java application project SumApp.

Now that a Java class library project has been created and a Java class file has been coded, next we need to create our Java application project to call or use that class library to perform a two-integer addition operation.

5.3.2.2.2 Create a Java Application Project

Perform the following operations to create a new Java application project:

1) Choose the File > New Project menu item. Under Categories, select Java with Ant. Under Projects, select Java Application. Then click on the **Next** button.
2) Enter **SumApp** into the Project Name field. Make sure the Project Location is set to **C:\Oracle DB Programming\Class DB Projects\Chapter 5**.
3) Enter **sumapp.Main** as the main class.
4) Ensure that the Create Main Class checkbox is checked.
5) Click the **Finish** button. The **SumApp** project is displayed in the Projects window, and Main.java opens in the Source Editor.

Now we have finished creating two Java projects.

After these two projects have been created, you need to add the Java class library project to the *classpath* of the Java application project. Then you can code the application. The library project will contain a utility class with a **sumapp()** method. This method takes two integers as arguments and then generates a sum based on those integers. The **SumApp** project will contain a main class that calls the **sumapp()** method and passes the integers that are entered as arguments when the application runs.

Now let's conFigure the compilation class path in the Java application project to enable the application to know the location of the class library and execute it to perform the integer addition operation when the project runs.

5.3.2.2.3 ConFigure the Compilation Classpath

Since the **SumApp** Java application is going to depend on a class in **SumLib**, you have to add **SumLib** to the classpath of **SumApp**. Doing so also ensures that classes in the **SumApp** project can refer to classes in the **SumLib** project without causing compilation errors. In addition, this enables you to use code completion in the **SumApp** project to fill in code based on the **SumLib** project. In the Apache NetBeans IDE 12, the classpath is visually represented by the Libraries node.

Perform the following operations to add the **SumLib** library's utility classes to the application **SumApp** project classpath:

1) In the Projects window, right-click the Libraries node under the **SumApp** project and choose Add Project, as shown in Figure 5.18.
2) Browse to the folder **C:\Oracle DB Programming\Class DB Projects\Chapter 5** and select the **SumLib** project folder, as shown in Figure 5.19. The Project JAR Files pane shows the JAR files that can be added to the project. Notice that a JAR file for **SumLib** is listed even though you have not actually built the JAR file yet. This JAR file will get built when you build and run the SumApp project.
3) Click on the **Add Project JAR Files** button.
4) Now expand the Libraries node. The **SumLib** project's JAR file has been added to the **SumApp** project's classpath.

Before we can run our Java application project to call the Java class library, we need to add some code to the **Main.java** tab in our Java application project.

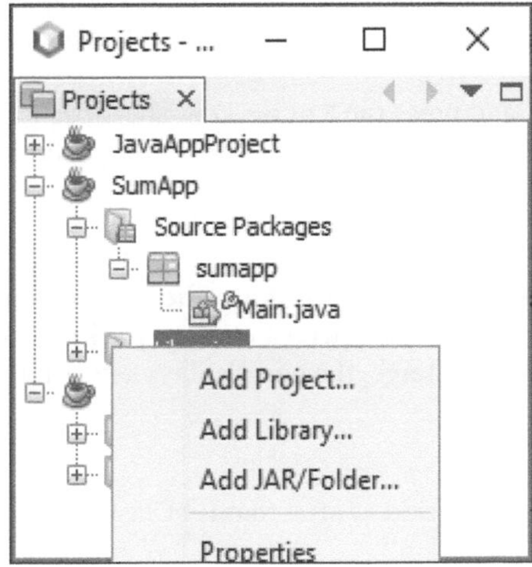

FIGURE 5.18 Adding the SumLib class to the classpath of the SumApp project.

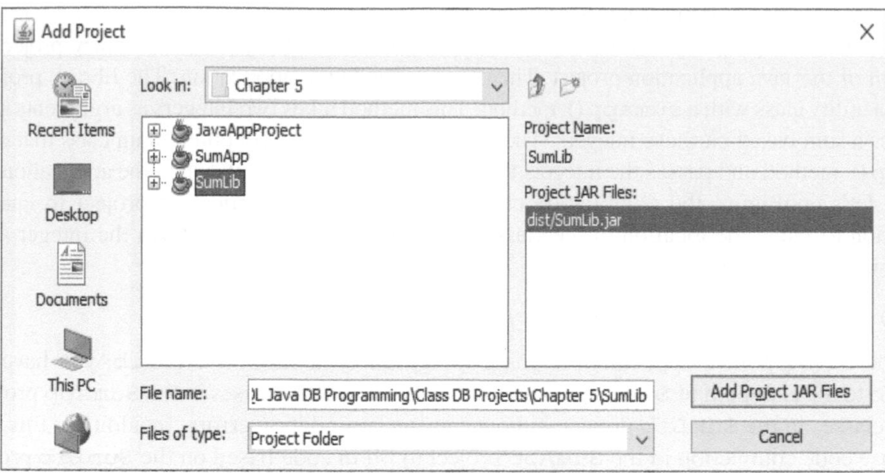

FIGURE 5.19 The Add Project dialog box.

5.3.2.2.4 Add Code to the Main.java Tab in the Java Application Project

Now we need to add some code to **`Main.java`**. In doing so, you will see the Source Editor's code completion and code template (abbreviation) features.

1) Select the **`Main.java`** tab in the Source Editor. If it isn't already open, expand **`SumApp > Source Packages > sumapp`** in the Projects window and double-click on the item **`Main.java`**.
2) Inside the **`main()`** method, replace the comment //TODO code application logic here with the following:

```
int result = Sum
```

3) Leave the cursor immediately after **`Sum`**. In the next step, you will use code completion to turn **`Sum`** into **`SumLibClass`**.
4) Press Ctrl-Space to open the code completion box. A short list of possible ways to complete the word appears. However, the class that you want, **`SumLibClass`**, might not be there.
5) Press Ctrl-Space again to display a longer list of possible matches. **`SumLibClass`** should be in this list.
6) Select **`SumLibClass`** and press the **`Enter`** key. The Apache NetBeans IDE fills in the rest of the class name and also automatically creates an import statement for the class.

Note: The IDE also opens a box above the code completion box that displays Javadoc information for the selected class or package. Since there is no Javadoc information for this package, the box displays a "Cannot find Javadoc" message.

7) In the main method, type a period (.) after SumLibClass. The code completion box opens again.
8) Select the **`sumapp(String args) int`** method and press the Enter key. The IDE fills in the **`sumapp()`** method and highlights the input parameters.

9) Press the **Enter** key to accept args as the parameter, and change this null to args[0]. Type a semicolon (;) at the end of this code line. The final line should look like the following:

```
int result = SumLibClass.sumapp(args[0]);
```

10) Press the Enter key to start a new line. Then type the following code line.

```
System.out.println("The sum = "+ result);
```

11) Go to the File > Save All menu item to save the file.

At this point, we are ready to run our Java application project, **SumApp**, to test its calling function to our Java library file **SumLibClass**.

5.3.2.2.5 Run the Application Project to Call the Java Library

The output of this application program, **SumApp.java**, is based on arguments that you provide when you run the application. As arguments, you can provide two or more integers, from which the added result will be generated. The adding process will be executed by the Java library file **sumapp()** located in the **SumLibClass** library, and the execution result will be returned to and displayed in the **main()** method in the Java application project **SumApp.java**.

Now let's run the application. Since this application needs arguments as inputs to the **main()** method, we have to use an alternative way to run it. First let's perform the following operations to add the arguments for the IDE to use when running the application:

- Right-click on the **SumApp** project node, choose the Properties item and select the **Run** node in the dialog's left pane. The main class should already be set to **sumapp.Main**.
- Enter some integers as input arguments to the Arguments field. Each integer should be separated with a comma, such as 12, 34, 56.Click on the **OK** button.

Your finished Project Properties window should match the one that is shown in Figure 5.20.

Now that we have created the application and provided runtime arguments for the application, we can test and run the application in two ways: run the application inside the Apache NetBeans IDE 12, or run the application outside the NetBeans IDE 12.

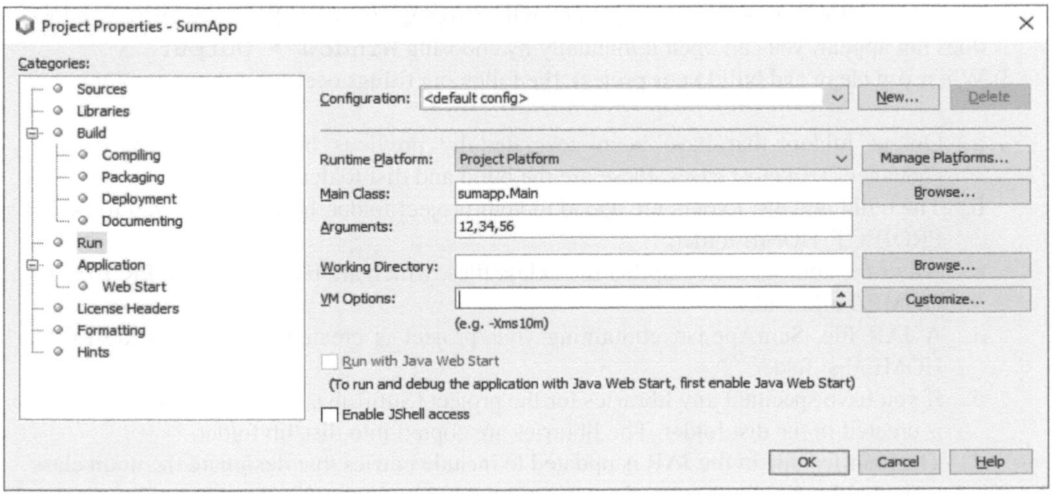

FIGURE 5.20 The completed Project Properties window.

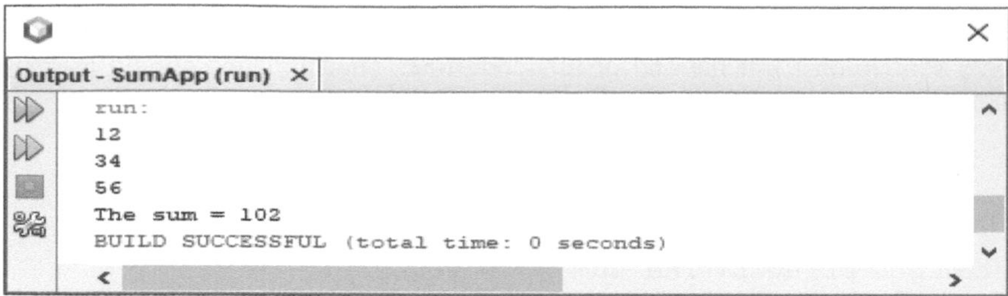

FIGURE 5.21 The run result shown in the Output window.

To run the application inside the Apache NetBeans IDE 12, Click on the **`Run`** button in the menu item (or press the **`F6`** key). In the **`Output`** window shown in Figure 5.21, you should see both input arguments (12, 34 and 56) and the output result from the program (the sum = 102).

To run this application outside of the NetBeans IDE, you need first to build and deploy the application into a JAR file and then run the JAR file from the command line.

5.3.2.2.6 Build and Deploy the Application

The main build command in the NetBeans IDE is the **`Clean and Build Main Project`** command. This command deletes previously compiled classes and other build artifacts and then rebuilds the entire project from scratch.

Notes: There is also a Build Main Project command, which does not delete old building artifacts, but this command is disabled by default.

Perform the following operations to build the application:

1) Click on the **`Run > Clean and Build Main Project(SumApp)`** menu item (Shift-F11).
2) Output from the Ant build script appears in the **`Output`** window. If the **`Output`** window does not appear, you can open it manually by choosing **`Window > Output`**.
3) When you clean and build your project, the following things occur:

a. Output folders that have been generated by previous build actions are deleted ("cleaned"). In most cases, these are the build and dist folders.
b. The build and dist folders are added to your project folder, hereafter referred to as the PROJECT_HOME folder.
c. All of the sources are compiled into. class files, which are placed into the PROJECT_HOME/build folder.
d. A JAR file, SumApp.jar, containing your project is created inside the PROJECT_HOME/dist folder.
e. If you have specified any libraries for the project (SumLib.jar in this case), a lib folder is created in the dist folder. The libraries are copied into dist/lib folder.
f. The manifest file in the JAR is updated to include entries that designate the main class and any libraries that are on the project's classpath.

Note: You can view the contents of the manifest in the IDE's Files window. After you have built your project, switch to the Files window and navigate to SumApp/dist/SumApp.jar. Expand the node for the JAR file, expand the META-INF folder and double-click MANIFEST.MF to display the manifest in the Source Editor.

```
Manifest-Version: 1.0
Ant-Version: Apache Ant 1.10.4
Created-By: 14.0.1+7 (Oracle Corporation)
Class-Path: lib/SumLib.jar
X-COMMENT: Main-Class will be added automatically by build
Main-Class: sumapp.Main
```

After building and deploying the application, now we can run this application outside the NetBeans IDE. To do that, perform the following operations:

1) On your system, open a command prompt or terminal window.
2) At the command prompt, change directories to the **SumApp/dist** directory.
3) At the command line, type the following statement:

```
java -jar SumApp.jar 12, 34, 56
```

The application then executes and returns the output, as shown in Figure 5.22.

5.3.2.2.7 Distribute the Application to Other Users

Now that you have verified that the application works outside of the IDE, you are ready to distribute the application and allow other users to use it.

To distribute the application, perform the following operations:

1) On your system, create a zip file that contains the application JAR file (**SumApp.jar**) and the accompanying lib folder that contains **SumLib.jar**.
2) Send the file to the people who will use the application. Instruct them to unpack the zip file, making sure that the **SumApp.jar** file and the **lib** folder are in the same folder.
3) Instruct the users to follow the steps listed in the last section to run this application outside the Apache NetBeans IDE.

Two complete Java projects, Java class library project **SumLib** and Java Application project **SumApp**, can be found from the folder **Students\Class DB Projects\Chapter 5**, which is located at the CRC Press ftp site (refer to Figure 1.2 in Chapter 1).

```
Command Prompt
C:\SQL Java DB Programming\Class DB Projects\Chapter 5\SumApp\dist>java -jar SumApp.jar 12,34,56
12
34
56
The sum = 102

C:\SQL Java DB Programming\Class DB Projects\Chapter 5\SumApp\dist>
```

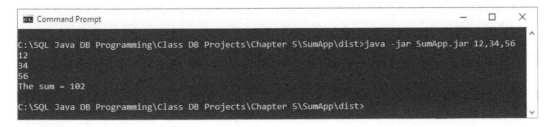

FIGURE 5.22 The run result shown in the Command window.

You can download these two projects and test them by calling the Java class library **SumLib** from the Java application project **SumApp**.

Next let's develop and build a Java project with existing sources.

5.3.2.3 Build a Java Project with Existing Sources

Building a Java project with existing sources is mainly done for development of a new Java project, but some existing sources, either GUIs or source code that was built in early Java or the current Java JDK, must be involved in this new Java project to save development efforts or time. For Java projects developed outside of NetBeans, you can use an "Existing Sources" template in the New Project wizard to make a NetBeans project. In the wizard, you identify the location of the sources and specify a location for the NetBeans project metadata. You then use the Project Properties dialog box to conFigure the project.

Perform the following operations to set up a NetBeans project for an existing Java application:

1) Choose **File > New Project** (Ctrl-Shift-N).
2) Choose **Java with Ant > Java Project with Existing Sources**, then click on **Next**.
3) In the **Name and Location** page of the wizard, perform these steps:
   a. Type a project name as you like.
   b. (Optional) Change the location of the project folder.
   c. (Optional) Change the name of the build script used by the IDE. This might be desirable if there is already a build script called build.xml that is used to build the sources.
   d. (Optional) Select the **Use Dedicated Folder for Storing Libraries** checkbox and specify the location for the libraries folder.
4) Click on **Next** to advance to the **Existing Sources** page of the wizard.
5) In the **Source Packages Folder** pane, click **Add Folder**. Then navigate to your sources and select the source roots.
6) When you add a folder containing source code, you must add the folder that contains the highest folder in your package tree. For example, in the **com.mycompany.myapp.ui** package, you add the folder that contains the **com** folder.
7) (Optional) In the **Test Package Folders** pane, click **Add Folder** to select the folder containing the **JUnit** package folders. Click on the **Next** button to continue.
8) (Optional) In the **Includes & Excludes** page of the wizard, enter file name patterns for any files that should be included or excluded from the project. By default, all files in your source roots are included.
9) Click on the **Finish** button to complete this process.

The new built project is displayed in both the **Projects** window and the **Files** window.

Because of the simplicity of this kind of Java project, no example project is given in this chapter.

5.3.2.4 Build a Free-Form Java Project

There are also project templates available for free-form Java projects. In so-called free-form projects, the NetBeans IDE uses targets in an existing Ant script to build, run, clean, test and debug your application. If the Ant script does not contain targets for some of these functions, the functions are unavailable for the project. To implement these functions, you write targets either in your Ant script or in a secondary Ant script.

In general, it is better to use standard **With Existing Sources** project templates for importing projects. For Eclipse projects, it is best to use the Import Project feature, which creates and conFigures a standard project for you. Standard projects are easier to maintain in the long term. However, the free-form project templates can be useful if you have an existing Ant-based project with a complex or idiosyncratic configuration that cannot be replicated within a standard project. For example, if you are importing a project with multiple source roots, each of which has a different classpath, and you cannot split the source roots into different projects, it might be necessary to use a free-form project template.

Because the scope of this book is about database programming with Java, for more detailed information on setting up free-form projects, refer to advanced free-form project configuration.

5.3.3 Build a Java Web Application Project

The Java platform, either Standard Edition or Enterprise Edition, provides rich and flexible tools and components to support Web applications and Web services development. With Java EE, developers can build professional, multitier, porTable applications that can be run in cross-platform environments with improved efficiency.

We will provide a detailed discussion of Java Web applications development in Chapter 8 with real project examples. Refer to that chapter to get more detailed information on building this kind of application in NetBeans IDE.

5.4 SET UP THE ENVIRONMENT FOR THE APACHE NETBEANS IDE 12 TO BUILD OUR CUSTOMER PROJECTS

To successfully develop and build our Java database projects, we need to use some additional Java Development Kits, JDBC drivers and web servers, as well as some tools, which include:

1) Java Development Kit (JDK14)
2) Oracle 18c Express Edition (XE) database
3) Java Database Connection Driver for Oracle 18c XE
4) Oracle SQL Developer
5) GlassFishWeb server
6) Tomcat Web server

The first component, JDK 14, was installed when we downloaded and installed the Apache NetBeans IDE 12 based on Appendices B and N in Section 5.2.

Refer to Appendix A to download and install the Oracle 18c Express Edition (XE) database. For the JDBC driver used for the Oracle 18c XE database, we will discuss the download and installation process for this tool in Section 6.2 in Chapter 6.

Refer to Appendix C to download and install Oracle SQL Developer. The GlassFish Web server was installed when the Apache NetBeans IDE 12 was installed. The Tomcat Web server may be needed later when we build Java Web application projects.

5.5 CHAPTER SUMMARY

Basic and fundamental knowledge about and implementations of the Apache NetBeans IDE 12 are discussed and presented, with some real example projects, in this chapter. The components and architecture of the Apache NetBeans IDE 12 are introduced and analyzed in detail at the beginning of this chapter. Following an overview of Apache NetBeans IDE 12, a detailed discussion and introduction of the Apache NetBeans IDE 12 platform is given. A detailed introduction to and illustration of how to download and install the Apache NetBeans IDE 12 are provided in this chapter.

Most popular technologies and applications supported by the Apache NetBeans IDE 12 are discussed, which include:

- Java Ant applications
- Java Class Library
- Build a Java project with existing sources

- Build a free-form Java project
- Build a Java Web Application project

Each of these technologies and implementations is discussed and analyzed in detail with real project examples and line-by-line code illustrations and explanations. Each real sample project has been compiled and built in the NetBeans IDE and can be downloaded and run at a user's computer easily and conveniently.

All of these technologies and their implementations are discussed and illustrated by using real project examples in this chapter step by step and line by line. By following these example projects, users can learn and master those key techniques easily and conveniently with lower learning curves.

All actual example projects discussed and developed in this chapter have been compiled and built successfully and are stored in the folder **`Class DB Projects\Chapter 5`** located in the **`Students`** folder at the CRC Press ftp site (refer to Figure 1.2 in Chapter 1).

HOMEWORK

I. True/False Selections

_______1. The Apache NetBeans Platform is a broad Swing-based framework on which you can base large desktop applications.

_______2. Each distinct feature in a NetBeans Platform application can be provided by a distinct NetBeans module, which is comparable to a plugin.

_______3. An Apache NetBeans module is a group of Java classes that provides an application with a specific feature.

_______4. The NetBeans IDE is an open-source integrated development environment, and it only supports development of all Java application types.

_______5. Three main modules included in the NetBeans IDE are: NetBeans Profiler, GUI Design Tool and NetBeans JavaScript Editor.

_______6. The Apache NetBeans IDE is mainly composed of NetBeans Open-Source IDE and NetBeans Platform.

_______7. A Java Class Library is only a skeleton Java class library without a main class, but it can be executed itself.

_______8. JavaFX, which is a kind of script language, is a Java platform for creating and delivering rich Internet applications. But starting from JDK 9, this platform has been removed from the JDK and no longer belongs to any JDK.

_______9. Like VisualStudio. NET, one can build a Java Ant application by adding a JFrame Form and use the Palette to add any GUI component to that form.

_______10. The Java EE differs from the Java SE in that it adds libraries that provide functionality to deploy fault-tolerant, distributed, multi-tier Java software, based largely on modular components running on an application server.

II. Multiple Choice

1. Each distinct feature in a NetBeans Platform application can be provided by a distinct NetBeans module, and an Apache NetBeans module is a: ____________.
   a. Java SE application
   b. Group of classes with specific features
   c. Java EE application model and specifications
   d. Enterprise JavaBeans and Java Persistence API (JPA)

2. The Apache NetBeans IDE is an open-source integrated development environment, and it supports development of all Java application types, which include ____________.
   a. Java desktop applications

b. Mobile and Web applications
c. HTML5 and Java Script applications
d. All of them

3. Three main modules included in the Apache NetBeans IDE are ____________.
   a. JEUS 7 application server, JBoss Application Server 6, Caucho Resin 4.0
   b. Java EE, Java SE, Maven
   c. NetBeans Profiler, GUI design tool, NetBeans JavaScript Editor
   d. PHP, JavaScript, GlassFish

4. The major Java Bean used to handle or process messages is called ____________.
   a. Session Bean
   b. Notification Bean
   c. Message-Driven Bean
   d. Manager Bean

5. The ____________ just works as a view for the GlassFish application server and sets up a connection between the application server and the Session Bean in the Web tier.
   a. Java EE 8
   b. Enterprise Java Beans
   c. JavaServer Faces (JSFs)
   d. Java Persistence API

6. To add new components or tools into the NetBeans IDE, one can use ____________.
   a. The JFrame tool
   b. Plugins
   c. The PHP tool
   d. JavaFX

7. The Apache NetBeans IDE is composed of two components, which are: ____________.
   a. NetBeans Platform and NetBeans modules
   b. NetBeans modules and Java EE
   c. NetBeans Profiler and GUI design tools
   d. NetBeans open-source IDE and NetBeans platform

8. The most popular Java GUI containers include: ____________.
   a. JFrame Form, JDialog Form, JPanel Form
   b. JPanel Form, JPlugins Form, JCanvas Form
   c. JPanel Form, JMaven Form, PHP Form
   d. JFrame Form, JField Form, JDialog Form

9. To display an image in JFrame Form, one needs to use a ____________ object.
   a. JImage
   b. JPanel
   c. Canvas
   d. JPicture

10. A module can be considered a(n) ____________ object or unit that can be combined or bound together to form a ____________ application.
    a. Dependent, big and complex
    b. Dependent, small and easier
    c. Independent, big and complex
    d. Independent, small and easier

III. Exercises
1. Explain the advantages of using the NetBeans Module for Java project development.
2. Provide a brief discussion of Apache NetBeans Platform.
3. Provide a brief description of the Apache NetBeans Open Source IDE.
4. Refer to Section 5.3.2, and build a similar Java Ant application named `SumTwoNumbers` with the following functions:
   a) Build a GUI by adding a JFrame Form with two TextFields, **Num1Field** and **Num2Field**; one Label, **ResultLabel**; and two buttons, **CalculateButton** and **ExitButton**.
   b) Code the **CalculateButton** and **ExitButtons**' ActionPerformed() event handlers to perform summing of two input integers, display the result on the **ResultLabel** and exit the project.

Part I

Building Two-Tier Client-Server Applications

6 Querying Data from Databases

Similarly to querying data in Visual Studio. NET, when querying data in the Java NetBeans IDE environment, one of the most efficient ways is to use a so-called runtime object method. Using this method, users can access and manipulate databases by building a sequence of code, starting from creating a DriverManager to load the database driver, setting up a connection using the Driver, creating a query statement object, running the executeQuery object and processing the received data using a ResultSet object. The advantage is that this method allows users to develop code to directly access and control all operations against the target database and, furthermore, provides a direct and easy learning strategy to enable users to better understand the detailed code development process in how to access and manipulate target databases manually. For this purpose, in this chapter, we introduce this method to perform database queries in the NetBeans IDE 12 environment.

6.1 INTRODUCTION TO RUNTIME OBJECT METHOD

The Java runtime object method is to develop and build database-accessing operations using runtime Java code without touching JPA Wizards and Entity classes. In other words, no object-to-relational database mapping is needed, and the project can directly access the database using Java code.

As we discussed in Chapter 4, to access a database to perform a data query, the following operational sequence should be followed:

1) Load and register the database driver using the **DriverManager** class and Driver methods.
2) Establish a database connection using the **Connection** object.
3) Create a data query statement using the **createStatement()** method.
4) Execute the data query statement using the **executeQuery()** method.
5) Retrieve the queried result using the **ResultSet** object.
6) Close the statement and connection using the **close()** method.

In the following sections, we will use some example projects, such as **OracleSelectFaculty**, to illustrate how to use the Java runtime object method to develop and build database query projects to access Oracle databases. To make these developments easy, we still use NetBeans 12 as our development IDE.

6.2 CONNECT TO THE ORACLE DATABASE 18C EXPRESS EDITION CSE_DEPT

The first thing we need to do is download an Oracle JDBC thin driver, since we need this driver to connect to our sample database, **CSE _ DEPT**.

The Oracle JDBC thin driver is a Type IV JDBC driver, meaning that it is platform independent and does not require any extra Oracle software on the client side to interact with an Oracle database. So you can download the JAR file containing the classes of an appropriate thin driver version from the JDBC Driver Downloads page and then install the driver on your machine without having to install and upgrade any other Oracle software.

DOI: 10.1201/9781003304029-7

Refer to Appendix H to finish the download and installation process for the JDBC Driver for Oracle Database 18c XE. The downloaded driver, `ojdbc8.jar`, should be located in the `C:\Temp` folder on our machine (copy the downloaded driver file, `ojdbc8.jar`, to that folder).

There are two ways to make this database connection; one way is to use the **`Services`** window in the Apache NetBeans IDE 12 environment, and the other is to use Java code to make that connection in real time during the project development stage later.

Now let's use the first way to test and confirm the database connection process. The second way will be built later when we build our database query project.

Perform the following operations to set up the database connection:

1) Launch Apache NetBeans IDE 12 to open its Start Page.
2) Click on the **`Services`** tab to open the **`Services`** window shown in Figure 6.1.
3) Right-click on the **`Databases`** icon and select the **`New Connection`** menu item to open the New Connection Wizard, which is shown in Figure 6.2.

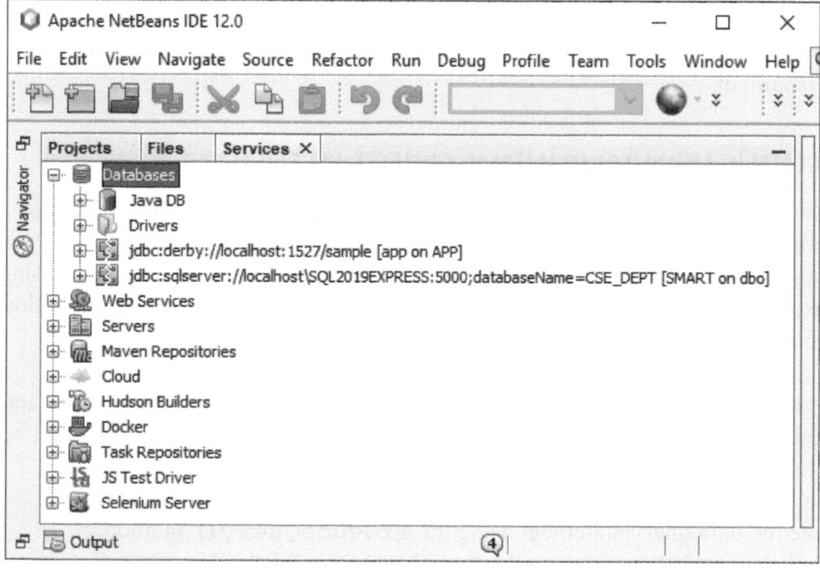

FIGURE 6.1 The opened Services window.

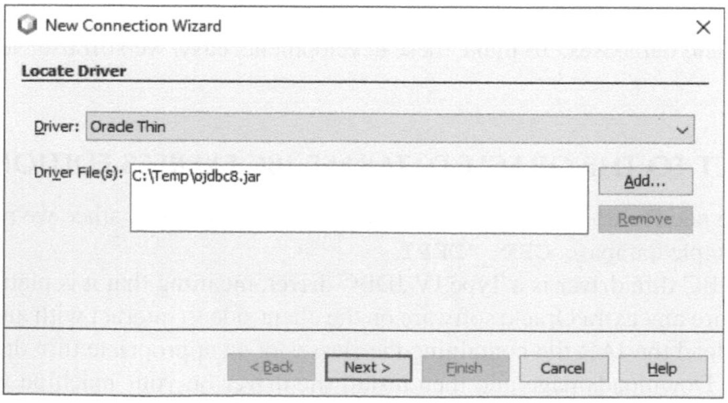

FIGURE 6.2 The opened New Connection Wizard.

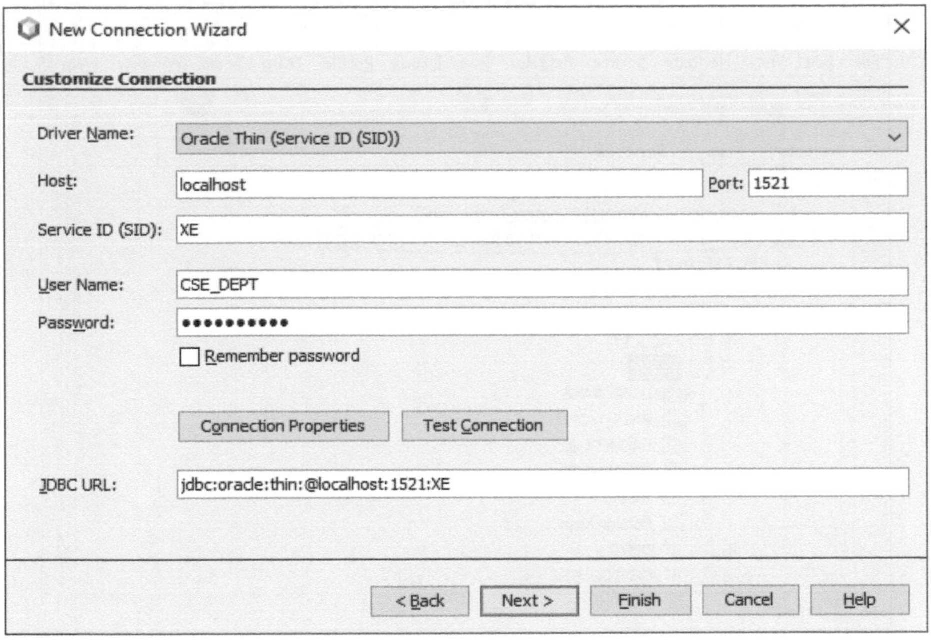

FIGURE 6.3 The sample database connection parameters.

4) Click on the drop-down arrow from the `Driver` box and select the `Oracle Thin` item from the `Driver` list.
5) Click on the **Add** button to scan and browse to the folder under which our new downloaded Oracle JDBC driver, `ojdbc8.jar`, is located (`C:\Temp`); select that driver file; and click on the `Open` button to add this driver to our driver list. Your finished `New Connection Wizard` should match the one in Figure 6.2.
6) Click on the `Next` button to open the Customize Connection sub-wizard, as shown in Figure 6.3.
7) Enter the following parameters into the associated boxes as the connection elements:
   a. Enter **localhost** in the **Host** box as the host name, since we are using our local machine as the database server.
   b. Enter **1521** in the **Port** box, since we used this as our port number when we installed our Oracle Database 18c XE (refer to Appendix A).
   c. Enter **XE** in the **Service ID** box, since we used this as our server name (refer to the **tnsnames.ora** file, which provided a description for the Oracle database after it was installed in our machine).
   d. Enter **CSE_DEPT**, which is the name of our database created in Chapter 2, in the **User Name** box.
   e. Enter **oracle_18c** in the **Password** box, since we used this as our password when we created our sample Oracle database, **CSE_DEPT** (refer to Appendix A).
   f. You can test this database connection by clicking on the **Test Connection** button.
   g. Click the **Next** button to try to establish the connection.
   h. Keep the default database schema, **CSE_DEPT**, in the next wizard with no change, and click on the **Next** button to continue.
   i. Click on the `Finish` button in the next wizard to complete the database connection-establishing process, unless you want to change the connection name.

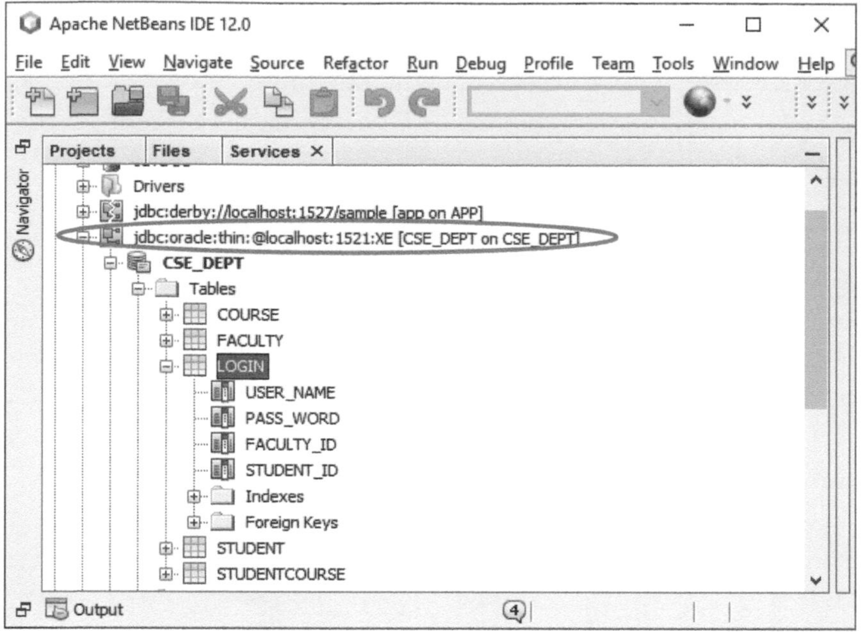

FIGURE 6.4 The connected and opened sample database, **`CSE _ DEPT`**.

Immediately, you can see that a new Oracle database connection URL icon, **`jdbc:oracle:thin:@localhost:1521:XE [CSE _ DEPT on CSE _ DEPT]`**, has been set up in the **`Services`** window, which is shown in Figure 6.4. Expand this icon, our sample database **`CSE _ DEPT`** and **`Tables`** folder, and you can find all five of our data Tables. Expand any of those Tables, such as the **`LogIn`** Table, you can find that all the columns we created for this Table are displayed under that Table folder.

You can expand all five Tables, such as **`Faculty`**, **`Course`**, **`Student`** and **`StudentCourse`**, to check them and confirm the correctness of each. You can even open each Table by right-clicking on it and select the **`View Data`** item to open that Table to check all the data columns and records.

One possible bug or error is: when you try to test this connection, an Oracle 10072 error may occur. This means that the XE server did not listen to any server connection requests. To solve this bug, do the following:

1. Press the Windows + R buttons.
2. Type **services.msc** into the box and press the Enter button.
3. Find the service named**OracleOraDB18Home1TNSListener**.
4. Right-click on that service, and select **Start** item to run the listener.

6.3 CREATE A JAVA APPLICATION PROJECT TO ACCESS THE ORACLE DATABASE

First let's create a new Java application project named **`OracleSelectFaculty`** using the NetBeans IDE 12. Go to the **`File|New Project`** menu item to start this process.

- Select **`Java with Ant`** from the **`Categories`** panel and **`Java Application`** from the **`Projects`** panel, and then click on the **`Next`** button.

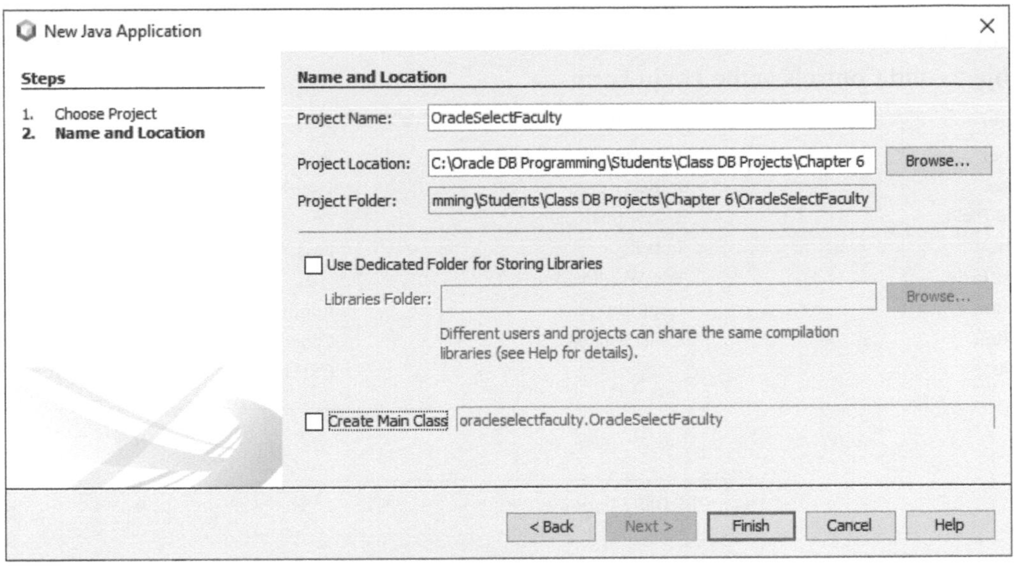

FIGURE 6.5 The finished New Java Application wizard.

- Enter **OracleSelectFaculty** into the **Project Name** box and select a desired location to store this project. A suggested location on your machine is **C:\Class DB Project\Chapter 6**. Uncheck the **Create Main Class** checkbox, since we need to use our frame to start the project.

Your finished New Java Application wizard is shown in Figure 6.5. Click on the **Finish** button to create this new Java application project, **OracleSelectFaculty**.

Next we need to create five JFrame Forms as our graphical user interfaces, LogInFrame, SelectionFrame, FacultyFrame, CourseFrame and StudentFrame, to perform the data queries to five data Tables in our sample database. We also need to create a JDialog as our message box.

6.3.1 Create Graphic User Interfaces

First let's create the LogInFrame Form window.

Right-click on our new project, **OracleSelectFaculty**, and select the **New|JFrame Form** item from the popup menu to open the New JFrame Form panel. Enter the following values in this panel to create the new JFrame Form:

1) **LogInFrame** in the Class Name box.
2) **OracleSelectFacultyPackage** in the Package box.
3) Click on the **Finish** button.

Add the GUI components with the appropriate properties shown in Table 6.1 into this form. You need to drag each component from the Palette Windows and place it in the LogInFrame Form and set up each property in the Properties Windows.

When setting up the property for each component, you need first to click on that component to select it and then go the Properties Window to set up an appropriate property for that component. To set up a **Variable Name** for each component, you need to right-click on that component and select the **Change Variable Name** item from the pop-up menu, then enter the desired name in the **New Name** box for that object. Your finished LogInFrame Form is shown in Figure 6.6.

TABLE 6.1
Objects and Controls in the LogIn Form

Type	Variable Name	Text
Label	Label1	Welcome to CSE Department
Label	Label2	User Name
Text Field	UserNameField	
Label	Label3	Pass Word
Text Field	PassWordField	
Button	LogInButton	LogIn
Button	CancelButton	Cancel
Title		CSE DEPT LogIn

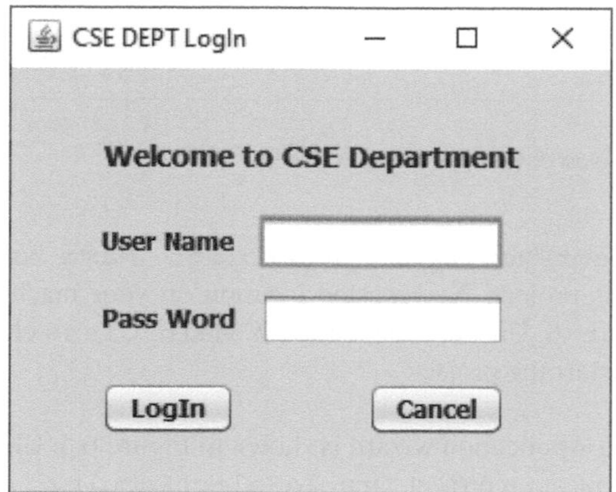

FIGURE 6.6 The finished LogInFrame Form.

Now let's create the SelectionFrame Form window.

As we did for the **LogIn** Form, right-click on our project, **OracleSelectFaculty**, in the Projects window and select the **New|JFrame Form** item from the popup menu to open the New JFrame Form panel. Enter **SelectionFrame** in the **Class Name** box as the name of our new Frame Form class, and select **OracleSelectFacultyPackage** from the Package box. Click on the **Finish** button to complete this creation.

Add the following objects and controls, which are shown in Table 6.2, into this SelectionFrame Form. One point to be noted is that you need to remove all default items located inside the model property of the Combo Box **ComboSelection**. To do that, click on the **ComboSelection** combo box from the Design View, and then go the **model** property and click on the three-dot button to open the model panel. Select all four default items, and press the **Delete** button from the keyboard to remove all of those items. A preview of the completed **SelectionFrame** Form should match the one that is shown in Figure 6.7.

Next let's create our **FacultyFrame** Form window.

Right-click on our new project, **OracleSelectFaculty**, in the Projects window and select the **New|JFrame Form** item to open the New JFrame Form pane. Enter **FacultyFrame** in the Class Name box as the name of our new Frame Form class, and then select the **OracleSelectFacultyPackage** from the Package box. Click on the **Finish** button to complete this creation.

Add the following objects and controls, which are shown in Table 6.3, into the FacultyFrame Form.

TABLE 6.2
Objects and Controls in the SelectionFrame Form

Type	Variable Name	Text	Model	Title
Label	Label1	Make Your Selection		
ComboBox	ComboSelection			
Button	cmdOK	OK		
Button	cmdExit	Exit		
SelectionFrame				CSE DEPT Selection

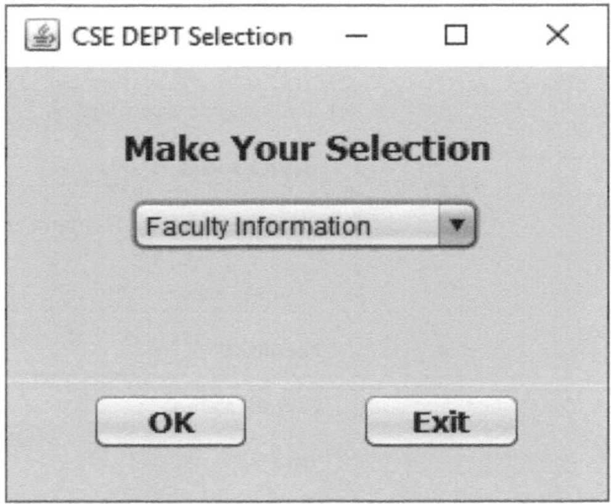

FIGURE 6.7 A preview of the created SelectionFrame Form.

TABLE 6.3
Objects and Controls in the FacultyFrame Form

Type	Variable Name	Text	Border	Title
Canvas	ImageCanvas			
Panel	jPanel1		Titled Border	Faculty Name and Query Method
Label	Label1	Faculty Name		
ComboBox	ComboName			
Label	Label2	Query Method		
ComboBox	ComboMethod			
Panel	jPanel2		Titled Border	Faculty Information
Label	Label3	Title		
Label	Label4	Office		
Label	Label5	Phone		
Label	Label6	College		
Label	Label7	Email		
Text Field	TitleField			
Text Field	OfficeField			
Text Field	PhoneField			
Text Field	CollegeField			
Text Field	EmailField			

(Continued)

TABLE 6.3 *(Continued)*

Type	Variable Name	Text	Border	Title
Button	cmdSelect	Select		
Button	cmdInsert	Insert		
Button	cmdUpdate	Update		
Button	cmdDelete	Delete		
Button	cmdBack	Back		
FacultyFrame Form	FacultyFrame			CSE DEPT Faculty Form

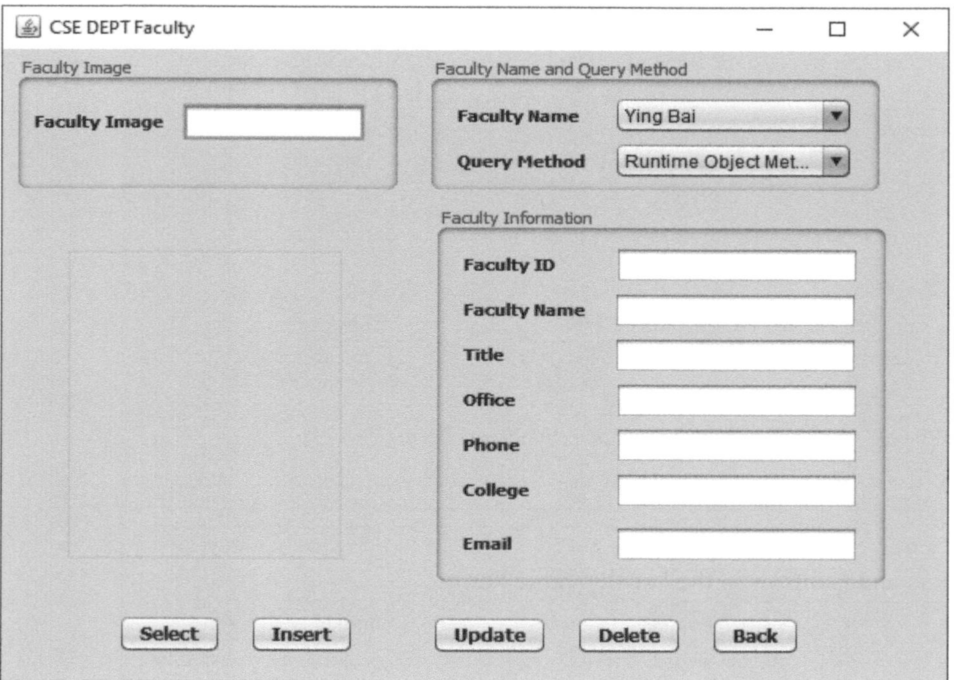

FIGURE 6.8 A preview of the finished FacultyFrame Form window.

One point to be noted is that you need to remove all default items located inside the model property of the Combo Box **`ComboName`** and **`ComboMethod`**. To do that, click on the **`ComboName`** combo box from the **`Design`** View, and then go the **`model`** property and click on the three-dot extension button to open the **`model`** pane. Select all four default items, and press the **`Delete`** button from the keyboard to remove all of those items. Perform similar operations for the **`ComboMethod`**. A preview of the completed FacultyFrame Form should match the one shown in Figure 6.8.

A point to be noted is that when you drag a Canvas control from the Palette and place it in the FacultyFrame Form window, first you need to click on the Canvas from the Palette. Then you need to click the location where you want to place it in the FacultyFrame. A Canvas icon is displayed in the location you clicked. You must drag the Canvas icon in the upper-left direction, never in the lower-right direction, to enlarge it.

Next let's build our **`CourseFrame`** Form window.

TABLE 6.4
Objects and Controls in the CourseFrame Form

Type	Variable Name	Text	Border	Title
Panel	jPanel1		Titled Border	Faculty Name and Query Method
Label	Label1	Faculty Name		
ComboBox	ComboName			
Label	Label2	Query Method		
ComboBox	ComboMethod			
Panel	jPanel2		Titled Border	Course ID List
ListBox	CourseList			
Panel	jPanel3		Titled Border	Course Information
Label	Label3	Course		
TextField	CourseField			
Label	Label4	Schedule		
TextField	ScheduleField			
Label	Label5	Classroom		
TextField	ClassRoomField			
Label	Label6	Credits		
TextField	CreditField			
Label	Label7	Enrollment		
TextField	EnrollField			
Button	cmdSelect	Select		
Button	cmdInsert	Insert		
Button	cmdBack	Back		
JFrame	CourseFrame			CSE DEPT Course Form

Right-click on our project, **OracleSelectFaculty**, in the **Projects** window, and select the **New|JFrame Form** item to open the **New JFrame Form** panel. Enter **CourseFrame** in the **Class Name** box, and select **OracleSelectFacultyPackage** from the **Package** box. Click on the **Finish** button to create the new **CourseFrame** class.

Add the objects and controls shown in Table 6.4 into the CourseFrame Form window to finish the GUI design for this form.

Your finished CourseFrame Form window should match the one shown in Figure 6.9.

Let's continue to complete the creation of the StudentFrame Form window.

As we did for the other JFrame Forms, right-click on our project, **OracleSelectFaculty**, in the **Projects** window, and then select the **New|JFrame Form** item from the popup menu to open the **New JFrame Form** dialog box. Enter **StudentFrame** in the **Class Name** box as the name for our new class, select **OracleSelectFacultyPackage** from the **Package** box and click on the **Finish** button to create the new **StudentFrame** class.

Add the objects and controls shown in Table 6.5 into the StudentFrame Form window to finish the GUI design for this form.

Your finished StudentFrame Form window should match the one shown in Figure 6.10.

6.3.2 Create a Message Box with JDialog Form Class

In the opened project, right-click on our project, **OracleSelectFaculty**, in the Projects window and select the **New|OK/Cancel Dialog Sample Form** item from the popup menu to open the New JDialog Form dialog box. Enter **MsgDialog** in the **Class Name** box as our dialog

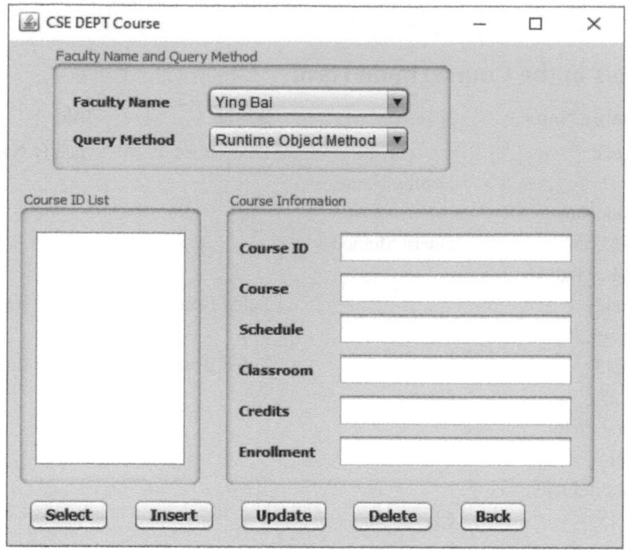

FIGURE 6.9 The Finished CourseFrame Form window.

TABLE 6.5
Objects and Controls in the StudentFrame Form

Type	Variable Name	Text	Border	Title
Canvas	ImageCanvas			
Panel	jPanel1		Titled Border	Student Name and Query Method
Label	Label1	Student Name		
ComboBox	ComboName			
Label	Label2	Query Method		
ComboBox	ComboMethod			
Panel	jPanel2		Titled Border	Course Selected
ListBox	CourseList			
Panel	jPanel3		Titled Border	Student Information
Label	Label3	Student ID		
Text Field	StudentIDField			
Label	Label4	School Year		
Text Field	SchoolYearField			
Label	Label5	GPA		
Text Field	GPAField			
Label	Label6	Major		
Text Field	MajorField			
Label	Label7	Credits		
Text Field	CreditsField			
Label	Label8	Email		
Text Field	EmailField			
Button	cmdSelect	Select		
Button	cmdInsert	Insert		
Button	cmdExit	Exit		
StudentFrame Form	StudentFrame			CSE DEPT Student Form

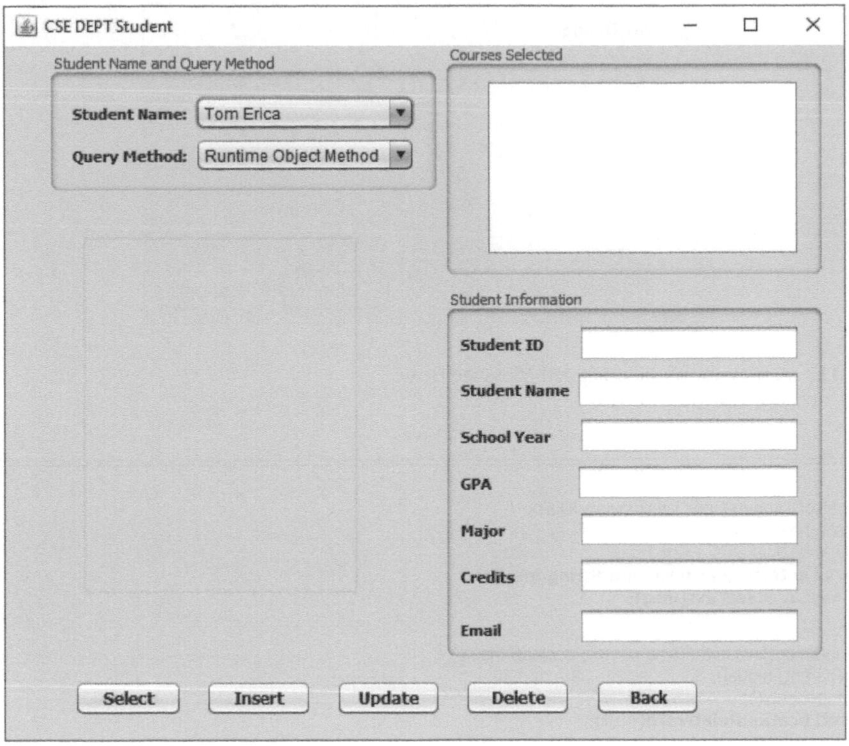

FIGURE 6.10 Finished StudentFrame Form window.

box's name and select **OracleSelectFacultyPackage** from the **Package** box to select it as our package in which our **MsgDialog** will be developed. Your finished New JDialog Form dialog box should match the one shown in Figure 6.11.

Click on the Design tab from the top to open the Design View of our newly created **MsgDialog** box. Reduce the size to an appropriate one, and add one label control to this dialog by dragging a **Label** control from the Palette window and placing it on our dialog box. Right-click on this label and select the **Change Variable Name** item from the popup menu to change it to **MsgLabel**. Go to the **text** property to remove the default text. A preview of this dialog box is shown in Figure 6.11.

In order to use this dialog box as our MessageBox, we need to add some code to this class. First we need to add code to the constructor of this class to make this dialog display at the center of the screen as the project runs. To do that, open the Code Window by clicking on the **Source** tab from the top, and enter **this.setLocationRelativeTo(null);** just under the **initComponents();** method in the constructor.

Then, move your cursor just under the line: **public static final int RET_OK = 1;** and enter the code shown in Figure 6.12 to create a new method, **setMessage()**. Your finished code for these two code-adding processes, which have been highlighted, is shown in Figure 6.12.

At this point, we have completed building all the graphical user interfaces we need in this project. Next let's concentrate on the code development to perform the data query for each different data Table in our sample database.

Before we can access our sample database to perform any query, first let's take care of loading and registering the JDBC Driver for Oracle database.

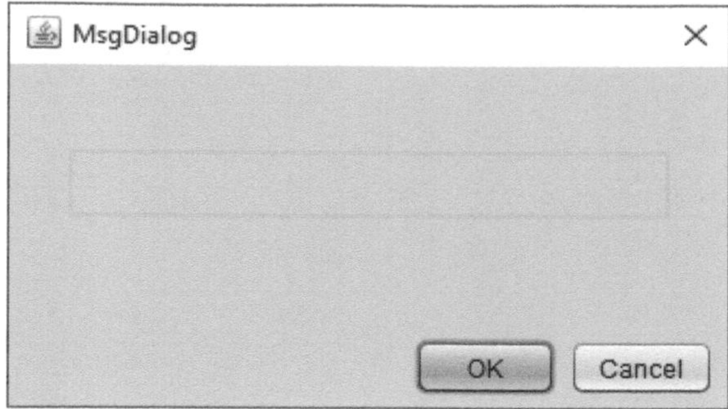

FIGURE 6.11 A preview of the designed Message Box.

```
......
public class MsgDialog extends javax.swing.JDialog {
    public static final int RET_CANCEL = 0;
    public static final int RET_OK = 1;
    public void setMessage(java.lang.String msg){
            MsgLabel.setText(msg);
        }
    public MsgDialog(java.awt.Frame parent, boolean modal) {
        super(parent, modal);
        initComponents();
        this.setLocationRelativeTo(null);
    ......
```

FIGURE 6.12 Code for the constructor and the setMessage() method.

6.3.3 Add Oracle JDBC Driver to the Project

Before we can load and register a JDBC driver, first we need to add the Oracle JDBC Driver we downloaded and installed on our machine as a library file into our current project's **`Libraries`** node to enable our project to find it when it is loaded and registered. Refer to Appendix H to get more details about downloading this JDBC driver.

Perform the following steps to finish the JDBC library adding process:

1) Right-click on our project, **`OracleSelectFaculty`**, in the **`Projects`** window, and select the **`Properties`** item from the popup menu to open the Project Properties wizard.
2) In the **`Categories`** panel (left), select the **`Libraries`** node by clicking on it.
3) Then click on the plus (+) icon on the right of the **`Classpath`** item under the Compile-time Libraries, and select the **`Add JAR/Folder`** item by clicking on it.
4) In the opened **`Add JAR/Folder`** wizard, browse to the location where we installed the **`Oracle JDBC Driver`**, which is **`C:\Temp`** (refer to Appendix H). Click on the driver **`ojdbc8.jar`**, and click on the **`Open`** button to select this driver. The finished Project Properties wizard is shown in Figure 6.13.
5) Click on the **`OK`** button to add this driver to our project's **`Libraries`** node.

The reason we add this JDBC driver to the **`Classpath`**, instead of the **`Modulepath`**, is that we need to use the **`Class.forName()`** method later in our LogInFrame code window to find this driver class first and to enable us to use DriverManager to connect to our sample database.

Next let's begin to load and register the Oracle JDBC Driver in our project.

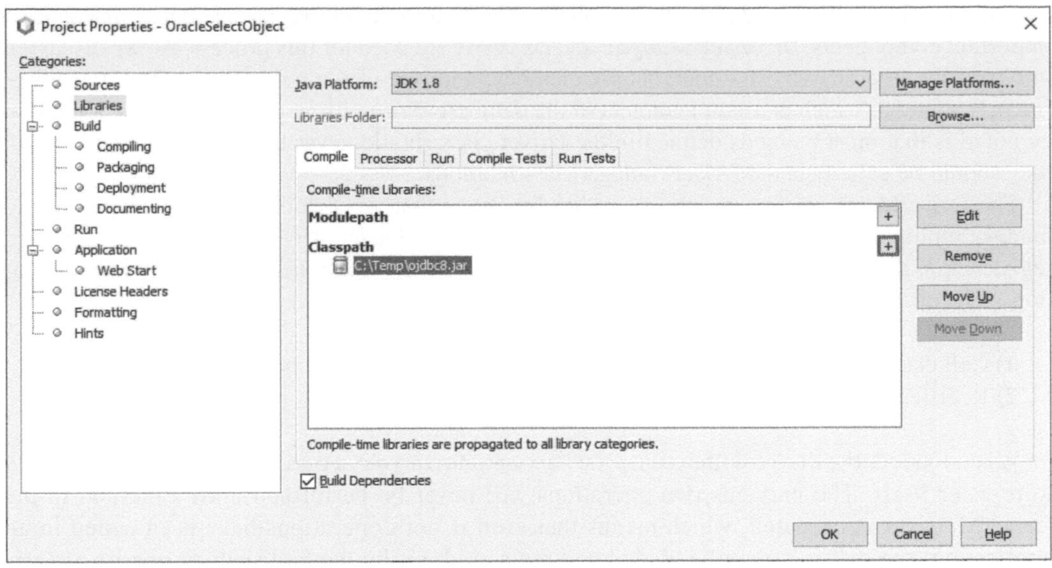

FIGURE 6.13 The finished Project Properties wizard.

6.3.3.1 Load and Register the Oracle JDBC Driver

As we discussed in Chapter 3, the core component or interface of accessing databases in Java is the Java Database Connectivity API, which is composed of two parts in two packages: the JDBC 2.0 core API in **java.sql** and the JDBC Standard Extension in **javax.sql**. Both parts are combined to provide necessary components and classes to build database applications using Java.

Similarly to other general JDBC packages, the Oracle core JDBC implementation includes two packages:

- **oracle.sql**: this package includes classes and interfaces that provide Java mappings to SQL data types, such as **OracleTypes**.
- **oracle.jdbc**: this package contains implementations and extended functions provided by the **java.sql** and **javax.sql** interfaces, such as **OraclePreparedStatement** and **oracleCallableStatement**.

Generally, the JDBC API enables users to access virtually any kind of tabular data source, such as spreadsheets or flat files, from a Java application. It also provides connectivity to a wide scope of Oracle databases. One of the most important advantages of using JDBC is that it allows users to access any kind of relational database in the same way with code, which means that the user can develop one program with the same code to access either an Oracle database or a MySQL database without code modification.

The JDBC 3.0 and JDBC 4.0 specifications contain additional features, such as extensions to support various data types, metadata components and improvements to some interfaces.

The JDBC API is composed of a set of classes and interfaces used to interact with databases from Java applications. As we discussed in Chapter 3, the basic components of JDBC are located in the package **java.sql**, and the Standard Extension of JDBC, which provides additional features, such as the Java Naming and Directory Interface and Java Transaction Service, is in the **javax.sql** package.

The first step to build a Java database application is to load and register a JDBC driver. Two important components, **DriverManager** and **Driver**, are used for this process. As we discussed in Chapter 4, the Driver class contains six methods, and one of the most important is the **connect()** method, which is used to connect to the database. When using the Driver class, a point to be noted is that most methods defined in the Driver class should never be called directly; instead, they should be called via the DriverManager class methods.

The DriverManager class is a set of utility functions that work with the Driver methods and manage multiple JDBC drivers by keeping them as a list of loaded drivers. Although loading and registering a driver are two steps, only one method call is necessary to perform these two operations. The operational sequence of loading and registering a JDBC driver is:

1) Call class methods in the DriverManager class to load the driver into the Java interpreter.
2) Register the driver using the **registerDriver()** method.

When loaded, the driver will execute the **DriverManager.registerDriver()** method to register itself. The previous two operations will never be performed until a method in the DriverManager is executed, which means that even if both operations have been coded in an application, the driver cannot be loaded and registered until a method such as **connect()** is first executed.

To load and register an Oracle JDBC driver, two popular methods can be used:

1) Use the **Class.forName()** method: **Class.forName("oracle.jdbc.OracleDriver");**
2) Create a new instance of the Driver class: **Driver oraDriver = new oracle.jdbc.OracleDriver;**

Relatively speaking, the first method is more professional, since the driver is both loaded and registered when a valid method in the DriverManager class is executed. The second method cannot guarantee that the driver has been registered by using the DriverManager. We prefer to use the first method in this application.

6.3.3.2 JDBC Uniform Resource Locators (URLs)

A JDBC **url** provides all information for applications to access a special resource, such as a database. Generally, a **url** contains three parts: protocol name, sub-protocol and subname for the database to be connected. Each of these three segments has a different function when they work together to provide unique information for the target database.

The syntax for a JDBC **url** can be presented as:

```
protocol:sub-protocol:subname
```

The protocol name works as an identifier to show what kind of protocol should be adopted when connecting to the desired database. For a JDBC driver, the name of the protocol should be **jdbc**. The protocol name is used to indicate the kind of items to be delivered or connected.

The sub-protocol is generally used to indicate the type of the database or data source to be connected, such as **oracle** or **sqlserver**.

The subname is used to indicate the address to which the item supposed to be delivered or the location where the database resides. Generally, a subname contains the following information for an address of a resource:

- Network host name/IP address
- The database server name
- The port number
- The name of the database

As we discussed in Section 6.2, a JDBC **url** can be considered a string used to define the address of the Oracle database to which we need to connect from our Java application. The protocol of this string, especially for an Oracle database, can be represented as:

```
jdbc:oracle:driver _ type:@database
```

where

- **driver _ type**: indicates the type of JDBC driver to be used for the database connection. Three options exist for Oracle JDBC drivers:
  - **oci**: for Oracle9i and 10g OCI drivers
  - **thin**: for the Oracle thin driver
  - **kprb**: for the Oracle internal driver
- **database**: indicates the address to which the database will be connected. The following options exist:
  - ***host:port:sid***: this option works for thin and OCI drivers. The host is the host name or IP address of a database server, and the port is the port number of the Oracle listener. Both are similar to those in the SQL Server database. The **sid** is the Oracle system identifier or Oracle service name of the database.
  - ***Net service name***: this is only used for the OCI driver. It is a **tnsnames.ora** file entry that resolves to a connect descriptor.
  - ***Connect descriptor***: this is only used for the OCI or thin driver. It is the Net8 address specification.

In our application, the **driver _ type** is **thin**, since we are using a thin driver. The database is represented as: **localhost:1521:XE**. The database server is built on our host computer; therefore, the name is **localhost**. The listener port number is 1521, which can be found from the Oracle database configuration file **tnsnames.ora**, which is located at the folder **C:\app\yingb\product\18.0.0\dbhomeXE\NETWORK\ADMIN** in my case. The path after **C:\app**, **yingb**, is the user name on the author's computer, and it should be replaced by your user name on your computer.

After a target database has been connected, the next job is to build a database query to requestor retrieve information or records from the selected Table in that database. In Java database applications, the statement class is one of the most popular components and widely used to access and manipulate the target database.

6.3.3.3 Create and Manage the Statement and PreparedStatement Objects

The Statement class contains three important query methods with different functions: **executeQuery()**, **executeUpdate()** and **execute()**. For each method, different operations can be performed and different results can be returned. Generally, the execute methods can be divided into two categories: 1) execute methods that need to perform a data query, such as **executeQuery()**, which returns an instance of **ResultSet** that contains the queried results, and 2) execute methods that do not perform a data query and only return an integer, such as **executeUpdate()**. An interesting method is **execute()**, which can be used either way.

- The **executeQuery()** method performs a data query and returns a **ResultSet** object that contains the queried results.
- The **executeUpdate()** method does not perform a data query; instead, it only performs either a data update, insert or delete action against the database and returns an integer that equals the number of rows that have been successfully updated, inserted or deleted.
- The **execute()** method is a special method, and it can be used either way. All different data actions can be performed by using this method, such as data query, data insertion, data updating and data deleting. The most important difference between the **execute()**

method and the other two methods is that the former can be used to execute Oracle statements that are unknown at compile time or return multiple results from stored procedures. Another difference is that the **execute()** method does not return any result itself, and one needs to use the **getResultSet()** or **getUpdateCount()** method to pick up the results. Both methods belong to the **Statement** interface.

Confusion may arise when using the **execute()** method. As we mentioned, since any Oracle statement, either known or unknown at compile time, can be used with the **execute()** method, how do we know the execution results? Yes, that is indeed a problem. However, fortunately, we can solve this problem by using some testing methods indirectly.

In fact, we can call either the **getResultSet()** or **getUpdateCount()** method to try to pick up the run results from execution of the **execute()** method. The key point is that:

- The **getResultSet()** method will return a null if the run result is an integer, which is the number of rows that have been affected, either inserted, updated or deleted.
- The **getUpdateCount()** method will return a –1 if the run result is a ResultSet.

Based on these two key points, we can easily determine whether a result is a ResultSet or an integer.

As we mentioned, a static statement does not contain any parameters passing into or from the database; therefore, this kind of statement does not meet our requirements, since we need to pass parameters, such as username and password, into our sample database to perform the login process. To make a data query to our **LogIn** Table to perform the login process, we need to use the second type of statement, **PreparedStatement**.

The advantages of using a PreparedStatement object to build and perform a dynamic query are that both the query flexibility can be increased and the query execution speed and efficiency can be significantly improved since the prepared statement can be pre-compiled and re-run again for a multiple query situation.

6.3.3.4 Use ResultSet Object

The ResultSet class contains 25 methods, and the most popular methods used are:

- **getXXX()**
- **getMetaData()**
- **next()**
- **findColumn()**
- **close()**

The ResultSet object can be created by either executing the **executeQuery()** or **getResultSet()** method, which means that the ResultSet instance cannot be created or used without executing a query operation first. Similarly to a Statement object, a Connection object must be first created, and then the Statement component can be created and implemented based on the Connection object to perform a query.

The queried result or data is stored in the ResultSet with a certain format, generally in a 2D tabular form with columns and rows. Each column can be mapped onto an array, and each row can be considered a Vector. Therefore, the easiest way to map a ResultSet is to create an array of Vectors.

When a query operation is performed and a ResultSet instance is created, next we need to retrieve the queried result from the ResultSet object by using a suiTable **getXXX()** method. Depending on the returned data type of the queried result, different methods should be used, such as **getInt()**, **getString()**, **getByte()**, **getDouble()**, **getShort()** and **getObject()**.

Two different methods can be used to get returned data from a ResultSet instance: fetching by row and fetching by column.

6.3.3.4.1 Fetching by Row:

Since the returned data can be stored in a ResultSet in tabular form, the data can be picked up row by row. The **next()** method in the ResultSet class is specially used for this purpose. Each row can be selected by using a cursor that can be considered a pointer to point to each row. The **next()** method can move the row pointer from the current position to the next row. When a login query is executed, a ResultSet instance, **rs**, can be created and returned. Initially the cursor points to a row that is just above the first row, and you have to run the **next()** method once to make it point to the first data row; then you can repeat running this method by using a **while()** loop to scan the whole Table until the last row. A true is returned by the **next()** method if a valid row has been found and pointed to, and a false is returned if the cursor points to a null row, which means that no more valid rows can be found and the bottom of the ResultSet has been reached.

6.3.3.4.2 Fetching by Column:

When a valid data row has been retrieved, we need to get each column from that row. To do that, a different **getXXX()** method should be used based on the different data type of the returned data. One can use either the name of the column or the index of that column to get the data value. For example, in our LogIn Table, both the **user _ name** and the **pass _ word** are Strings; therefore, a **getString()** method should be used with the index of each column. A point to be noted is that the first column has an index of 1, not 0. If the name of each column, not an index, is used for the **getString()** method, the code can be written as

```
while (rs.next()){
username = rs.getString("user _ name");
password = rs.getString("pass _ word");
}
```

One of the most important methods in the ResultSet class is **getObject()**. The advantage of using this method is that a returned datum, which is stored in a ResultSet object with its data type unknown (a datum is dynamically created), can be automatically converted from its Oracle data type to the ideal Java data type. This method outperforms any other **getXXX()** method, since the data type of returned data must be known before a suiTable **getXXX()** method can be used to fetch the returned data.

The **findColumn()** method is used to find the index of a column if the name of that column is given, and the **close()** method is used to close a ResultSet instance.

The **getMetaData()** method is a very good and convenient method, and it allows users to have a detailed and clear picture of the structure and properties of data returned to a ResultSet. A **ResultSetMetaData** object, which contains all pieces of necessary information about the returned data stored in a ResultSet instance, is returned when this method is executed. By using different methods of the ResultSetMetaData class, we can obtain a clear view of the returned data. For example, by using the **getColumnCount()** method, we can find how many columns in all have been retrieved and stored in the ResultSet. By using **getTableName()**, **getColumnName()** and **getColumnType()**, we can find the name of the data Table we queried, the name of column we just fetched and the data type of that column. A more detailed discussion of the ResultSetMetaData component will be given in later sections.

Now that we have some basic and necessary understanding of the Java JDBC driver, statement class, execution methods and ResultSet components, we are ready to develop our project to perform some data queries from our sample database.

Let's start from the LogIn Table.

6.3.4 Develop Code for the LogIn Table to Connect to Our Sample Database

Now let's develop the code to load and register the Oracle JDBC Driver in our LogInFrame class. Open the Code Window of the LogInFrame by clicking on the **`Source`** tab at the top of the window, and enter the code shown in Figure 6.14 into this window.

Let's have a closer look at this piece of code to see how it works.

A. Since all JDBC-related classes and interfaces are located in the **`java.sql`** package, we first need to import this package.
B. A class instance, **`con`**, is declared here since we need to use this connection object in our whole project. A MsgDialog object is also created, and we need to use it in this form.
C. The **`setLocationRelativeTo()`** method is called to set up theLogInFrame Form at the center of the screen as the project runs. A **`null`** argument means that no object can be referenced or relatedto, and the JFrame Form is set to the center.
D. A **`try-catch`** block is used to load and register our Oracle JDBC Driver. The default method, **`Class.forName()`**, is utilized to make sure that our JDBC Driver is not only loaded but also registered when it is connected by running the **`getConnection()`** method in step 7 later. The argument of this method is the name of our Oracle JDBC Driver class, and it was created by NetBeans when we added this driver to our project in Section 6.2.
E. The **`catch`** block is used to track any possible error in loading and registering. The related exception information will be displayed if any error occurs.
F. The connection **`url`**, which includes the protocol, subprotocol and subname of the data source, is created to define a full set of information for the database to be connected.

```
    package OracleSelectFacultyPackage;
A   import java.sql.*;
    public class LogInFrame extends javax.swing.JFrame {
B       static Connection con;
        MsgDialog msgDlg = new MsgDialog(new javax.swing.JFrame(), true);
        /** Creates new form LogInFrame */
        public LogInFrame() {
            initComponents();
C           this.setLocationRelativeTo(null);
            try
            {
                //Load and register SQL Server driver
D               Class.forName("oracle.jdbc.OracleDriver");
            }
E           catch (Exception e) {
                msgDlg.setMessage("Class not found exception!" + e.getMessage());
                msgDlg.setVisible(true);
            }
F           String url = "jdbc:oracle:thin:@localhost:1521:XE";
            //Establish a connection
            try {
G           con = DriverManager.getConnection(url,"CSE_DEPT","oracle_18c");
           // Testing purpose for this database closing
H           con.close();
            }
I           catch (SQLException e) {
                msgDlg.setMessage("Could not connect! " + e.getMessage());
                msgDlg.setVisible(true);
J               e.printStackTrace();
            }
    }
```

FIGURE 6.14 Code for loading and registering a JDBC Driver.

G. Another **try-catch** block is used to perform the database connection by calling the **getConnection()** method. Three arguments are passed into this method: **url**, username and password.
H. The connected database is disconnected by calling the **close()** method. This instruction is only for testing purposes for this LogInFrame Form, and it will be removed later when we build the formal project, since we need to keep this single database connection active during the entire running period of our project until the project is terminated.
I. If any possible exception occurred during this connection process, it would be displayed by using this **catch** block.
J. This prints the **Throwable** and its backtrace to the standard error stream. This method prints a stack trace for the **Throwable** object on the error output stream that is the value of the field **System.err**. The first line of output contains the result of the **toString()** method for this object. The remaining lines represent data previously recorded by the method **fillInStackTrace()**.

The reason we put the piece of code that includes the loading, registering and connection to our JDBC Driver inside the constructor of the LogInFrame class is that we need to set up and complete these operations first, before other data actions can be performed, since a valid database connection is a prerequisite for any database query operation.

Next let's use the PreparedStatement component to build our dynamic query to our LogIn Table in our sample database.

6.3.5 Use the PreparedStatement Object to Perform Dynamic Query for the LogIn Table

In the Design View of the LogInFrame Form window, double-click on the **LogIn** button to open its event handler, and enter the code shown in Figure 6.15 into this event handler.

Let's have a closer look at this piece of code to see how it works.

A. Two local string variables, username and password, are declared first, since we need to use them to hold the returned query results later.
B. An instance of the next Java Frame Form, **selFrame**, is generated, and this frame form will be displayed if the login process is successful to enable users to select a valid query form to perform the desired query for the selected Table.
C. The login query string is created with two dynamic parameters that are represented by using the positional parameter mode.
D. A **try-catch** block is used to perform the data query. First, a PreparedStatement object, **pstmt**, is created based on the Connection object with the query string as an argument.
E. The **setString()** method of the PreparedStatement class is used to set up two dynamic parameters. The position of each parameter is indicated with the associated index of each parameter. The **getText()** method is used to get the username and password entered by the user from two text fields, **UserNameField** and **PassWordField**, respectively. A point to be noted is that different **setXXX()** methods should be used to perform this setup operation for the different types of dynamic parameters. For example, here, both the username and password are Strings, so the **setString()** method is used. If the type of the parameter is integer, the **setInt()** method should be used to finish this parameter setting, where **XXX** means the data type used for the dynamic parameter.
F. The **executeQuery()** method that belongs to the PreparedStatement class is called to perform this data query, and the query result is returned to the ResultSet object **rs**.
G. The **next()** method of the ResultSet class is utilized with a **while** loop to point to the next available queried row. This method returns a Boolean value, and a **true** indicates that a valid queried row is fetched and stored in the ResultSet. A **false** means that there

```
  private void LogInButtonActionPerformed(java.awt.event.ActionEvent evt) {
      // TODO add your handling code here:
A     String username = new String();
      String password = new String();
B     SelectionFrame  selFrame = new SelectionFrame().getSelectionFrame();
C     String query = "SELECT user_name, pass_word FROM LogIn " +
                     "WHERE user_name = ? AND pass_word = ?";
D     try{
          PreparedStatement pstmt = con.prepareStatement(query);
E         pstmt.setString(1, UserNameField.getText());
          pstmt.setString(2, PassWordField.getText());
F         ResultSet rs = pstmt.executeQuery();
G         while (rs.next()){
            username = rs.getString(1);
            password = rs.getString(2);
          }
      }
H     catch (SQLException e) {
        msgDlg.setMessage("Error in Statement! " + e.getMessage());
        msgDlg.setVisible(true);
      }
I     if (UserNameField.getText().isEmpty() || PassWordField.getText().isEmpty()) {
        msgDlg.setMessage("Enter valid LogIn Information...");
        msgDlg.setVisible(true);
      }
J     else if ((username.equals(UserNameField.getText())) && (password.equals(PassWordField.getText()))) {
        selFrame.setVisible(true);
        this.setVisible(false);
        this.dispose();
      }
K     else {
        msgDlg.setMessage("LogIn is failed!");
        msgDlg.setVisible(true);
      }
  }
```

FIGURE 6.15 The code for the LogIn button Click event handler.

are no more queried rows in the ResultSet. The **getString()** method is used to pick up each column from the ResultSet until a false is returned from the **next()** method. Similarly to the **setString()** method discussed in step 5, different **getXXX()** methods should be used to pick up queried columns with different data types. The argument **index** in the **getString()** method is used to indicate the position of the queried column in the ResultSet, which starts from 1, not 0.

H. The **catch** block is used to catch and display any possible error for this data query process.
I. If either the UserName or PassWord text field is empty, a warning message should be displayed to allow the user to enter valid login information.
J. If the queried username and password both match those entered by the user, the login process is successful. The next frame form, SelectionFrame Form, will be displayed to enable users to select a valid query form to perform the desired query for the selected Table.
K. Otherwise, the login process fails, and a warning message will be displayed to indicate the situation.

Before we can move to the next section, we need to finish developing the code for the **Cancel** button Click event handler. The function of this button is to close the LogInFrame Form window and the database connection if this button is clicked by the user. Open the Design View of the LogInFrame Form, double-click on the **Cancel** button to open its event handler and enter the code shown in Figure 6.16 into this event handler.

```
  private void CancelButtonActionPerformed(java.awt.event.ActionEvent evt) {
A       this.setVisible(false);
        this.dispose();
B       try {
            con.close();
        }
C       catch (SQLException e) {
            msgDlg.setMessage("Could not close!" + e.getMessage());
            msgDlg.setVisible(true);
        }
  }
```

FIGURE 6.16 The code for the Cancel button Click event handler.

```
  package OracleSelectFacultyPackage;
A import java.sql.*;
  public class SelectionFrame extends javax.swing.JFrame {
B     MsgDialog dlg = new MsgDialog(new javax.swing.JFrame(), true);
      public SelectionFrame() {
          initComponents();
C         this.setLocationRelativeTo(null);
D         this.ComboSelection.addItem("Faculty Information");
          this.ComboSelection.addItem("Course Information");
          this.ComboSelection.addItem("Student Information");
      }
```

FIGURE 6.17 The code for the constructor of the SelectionFrame class.

Let's have a closer look at this piece of code to see how it works.

A. The **`setVisible()`** and **`dispose()`** methods are called to remove the LogInFrame Form window from the screen when this button is clicked by the user.
B. Also, a **`try-catch`** block is used to try to close the database connection. A point to be noted is that a **`try-catch`** block must be used if one wants to perform a close action to a connected database.
C. The **`catch`** block will track and display any possible exception that occurs for the close action.

Now we have completed the coding process for the LogInFrame Form. However, before we can run the project to test this login process via the LogInFrame Form class, we prefer to complete the coding process for the SelectionFrame Form class, since a tie relationship exists between these two frame form classes.

6.3.6 Develop the Code for the SelectionFrame Form

The function of this frame form is to enable users to select a desired query form to perform the related query to the selected Table in our sample database if the login process is successful. Select the SelectionFrame class by clicking on it in the **`Projects`** window and open its code window, enter the codes shown in Figure 6.17 into this window.

Let's have a closer look at this piece of code to see how it works.

A. The Java JDBC Driver package is imported first, since we need to use some classes located in that package to perform the data query.
B. A class-level object of the JDialog class **`dlg`** is created here, since we need to use this **`dlg`** to display debug and warning messages as the project runs.

```
    private void OKButtonActionPerformed(java.awt.event.ActionEvent evt) {
        // TODO add your handling code here:
A       FacultyFrame facultyFrame = new FacultyFrame();
        CourseFrame courseFrame = new CourseFrame();
        StudentFrame studentFrame = new StudentFrame();

B       if (ComboSelection.getSelectedItem()== "Faculty Information"){
          facultyFrame.setVisible(true);
        } else if (ComboSelection.getSelectedItem()== "Course Information"){
          courseFrame.setVisible(true);
        } else {
          studentFrame.setVisible(true);
        }
    }
```

FIGURE 6.18 Code for the OK button Click event handler.

C. The **setLocationRelativeTo()** method is called to locate the SelectionFrame Form at the center of the screen as the project runs. A **null** argument means that no object can be referenced or relatedto, and the JFrame Form is set to the center.
D. Three **addItem()** methods are executed to add three pieces of information into the Combo Box **ComboSelection** to allow users to choose one of them as the project runs. Another method to add these three pieces of information is to directly add those pieces of information into the **model** box under the Combo Box Model Editor, which can be considered a static addition (before the project runs). That way, you do not need to enter these three lines of code in this constructor. However, we prefer to call the **addItem()** method to add those pieces of information, since it belongs to a dynamic addition.

Next let's build the code for the **OK** and **Exit** command buttons or, more precisely, for the event handlers of those two buttons. The function of the SelectionFrame Form, as we mentioned before, is to allow users to select a desired choice from the Combo Box, and after users click the **OK** button, the related information frame, such as **FacultyFrame Form**, **CourseFrame Form** or **StudentFrame Form**, will be displayed to enable users to make related queries.

Now let's open the Design View of the SelectionFrame Form by clicking on the **Design** tab from the top and double-clicking on the **OK** button to open its event handler. Enter the code shown in Figure 6.18 into this handler.

Let's have a closer look at this piece of code to see how it works.

A. Three objects are created at the beginning of this handler, FacultyFrame, CourseFrame and StudentFrame, since we need to direct the program to the different frame when an associated frame is selected by the user.
B. An **if** selection structure is used to identify each selected item from the **ComboSelection** combo box. The selected frame form window will be displayed if it has been selected by the user by setting the **Visible** property to **true** via the **setVisible()** method.

The rest of the code includes two parts: code for the **Exit** button Click event handler and code for creating a **getter()** method. As you know, in object-oriented programming, to use a unique object created in a project, a popular way is to create a **setter()** and a **getter()** method in the target class. In this way, when other objects, such as JFrames, JDialogs or JWindows, in the same project want to use the target object, they can call this **getter()** to get the desired object.

Let's build code for the **getter()** method and the **Exit** button Click event handler by entering the code shown in Figure 6.19 into this SelectionFrame class.

Let's have a closer look at this piece of code to see how it works.

```
A  public SelectionFrame getSelectionFrame(){
      return this;
   }
   private void ExitButtonActionPerformed(java.awt.event.ActionEvent evt) {
        // TODO add your handling code here:
B       try{
            if (!LogInFrame.con.isClosed()){ LogInFrame.con.close(); }
        }
C       catch(SQLException e){
           dlg.setMessage("Could not close!" + e.getMessage());
           dlg.setVisible(true);
           }
D       this.setVisible(false);
        this.dispose();
        System.exit(0);
   }
```

FIGURE 6.19 Code for the getter() method and the Exit button Click event handler.

A. The function of the **`getter()`** method is: as it is called, the current SelectionFrame object is obtained by returning the **`this`** component that is a pointer to the current Frame object. A point to be noted is that the access mode of this method must be **`public`**, since we want this method to be called by other objects to get the SelectionFrame object as the project runs.
B. In the **`Exit`** button Click event handler, a **`try-catch`** block is used to check whether the database connection we created in the LogInFrame Form window is still connected to our database by using the **`isClosed()`** method. A **`true`** will be returned if that connection has been closed. Otherwise, a **`false`** is returned to indicate that the connection is still active. The **`close()`** method of the Connection class is called to close the connection if a **`false`** is returned. As you may remember, the Connection object, **`con`**, we created in the LogInFrame class is a class instance; therefore, we can directly use the class name to access that instance without needing to create a new instance.
C. The **`catch`** block is used to track and display any errors for the close process.
D. Then the SelectionFrame Form object is removed from the screen by calling the **`setVisible()`** and **`dispose()`** methods. The object **`this`** indicates the current Frame Form object, which is the SelectionFrame. A system **`exit()`** method is called to allow the project to officially exit from the current process. An argument of 0 means that no error for this exit operation has occurred.

At this point, we have completed all code development for the LogInFrame and SelectionFrame Forms windows. Before we can run the code to test the functions for both the LogInFrame and SelectionFrame Forms, make sure to remove or comment out the code in step H in Figure 6.14, which is to close the connection to our sample database, because when we build the connection code in Figure 6.14, we need to close any connection to our sample database if a connection is successful to avoid possible multiple connections to our database. However, now we want to perform data queries; therefore, we need to keep that connection active for the whole time our project is running, since no data query can be performed if no database connection has been made.

After we remove or comment out the **`close()`** code line in Figure 6.14, we can build and run this project to test our code. Click on the **`Clean and Build Main Project`** button from the toolbar to build our project. Then click on the **`Run`** button (green arrow on the top) to run this object. In the opened **`Run Project`** wizard, select the **`OracleSelectFacultyPackage.`**

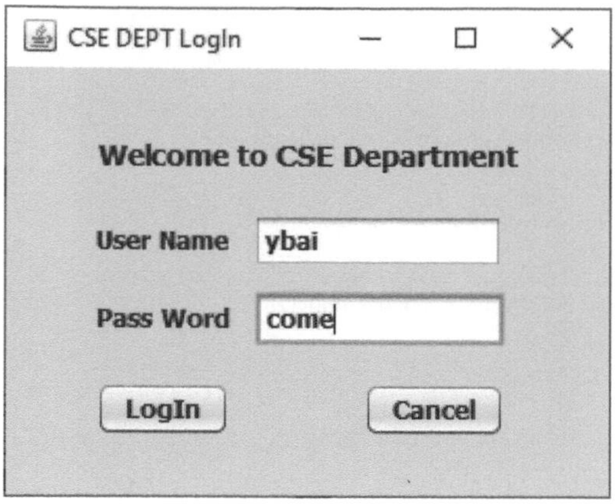

FIGURE 6.20 A running sample of the LogInFrame Form.

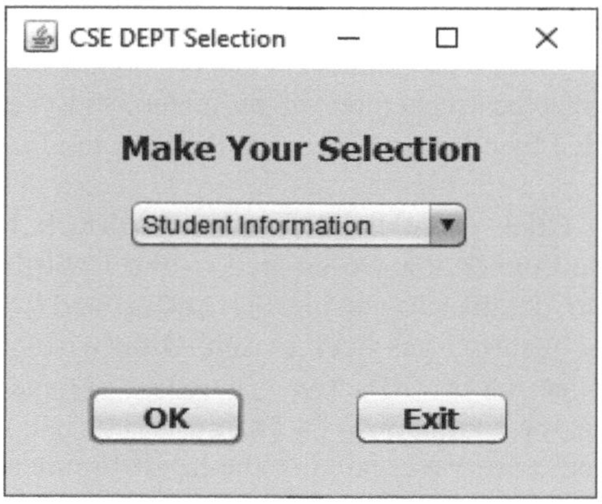

FIGURE 6.21 The run status of the SelectionFrame Form.

LogInFrame item from the list to use this frame as our start frame, and click on the **OK** button to start this running process. A sample of the run result is shown in Figure 6.20.

Enter a valid username and password, such as **ybai** and **come**, and click on the **LogIn** button to begin the login process. The SelectionFrame Form window should be displayed if the login process is successful, as shown in Figure 6.21.

Now you can select any desired query frame from the selection combo box in the SelectionFrame Form and click on the **OK** button to open that selected frame form window to test the code function of the SelectionFrame Form class.

Click on the **Close** button located at the upper-right corner of any opened frame form, such as **FacultyFrame**, **CourseFrame** or **StudentFrame**, to close that frame window, and finally, click on the **Exit** button in the SelectionFrame Form to terminate our project.

In the following sections, we will discuss how to perform data queries to our **Faculty** Table using the FacultyFrame Form class.

6.3.7 Perform a Data Query for the Faculty Table

The function of this frame form is: when the user selects a faculty member from the **ComboName** combo box and clicks the **Select** button, detailed information with an image of the selected

```
  package OracleSelectFacultyPackage;
A import java.awt.*;
  import java.sql.*;
  import javax.swing.*;
  import java.io.FileNotFoundException;
  import java.io.FileOutputStream;
  import java.io.IOException;
  import java.util.logging.Level;
  import java.util.logging.Logger;
  public class FacultyFrame extends javax.swing.JFrame {
B   MsgDialog msgDlg = new MsgDialog(new javax.swing.JFrame(), true);
    /** Creates new form FacultyFrame */
    public FacultyFrame() {
      initComponents();
      this.setLocationRelativeTo(null);   // set the faculty Form at the center
C     ComboMethod.addItem("Java executeQuery Method");
      ComboMethod.addItem("Java execute Method");
      ComboMethod.addItem("Java Callable Method");
D     ComboName.addItem("Ying Bai");
      ComboName.addItem("Davis Bhalla");
      ComboName.addItem("Black Anderson");
      ComboName.addItem("Steve Johnson");
      ComboName.addItem("Jenney King");
      ComboName.addItem("Alice Brown");
      ComboName.addItem("Debby Angles");
      ComboName.addItem("Jeff Henry");
  }
```

FIGURE 6.22 Initialization code for the FacultyFrame class.

faculty member should be displayed in seven text fields and a canvas. The code development of this query can be divided into the following six parts:

1) Add the necessary Java packages and code for the constructor of the FacultyFrame class to perform the initialization processes.
2) Build code for the **`Select`** button Click event handler to run the **`executeQuery()`** method to query data from the **`Faculty`** Table in our sample database using the **`DatabaseMetaData`** interface and **`ResultSetMetaData`** interface.
3) Code the **`Select`** button Click event handler to run the **`execute()`** method to query data from our **`Faculty`** Table in our sample database.
4) Code the **`Select`** button Click event handler to run the **`Java Callable`** method to query data from our **`Faculty`** Table in our sample database.
5) Add a user-defined method, **`ShowFaculty()`**, to display an image for the selected faculty member in the FacultyFrame Form window.
6) Code the **`Back`** button Click event handler to close the FacultyFrame Form window and return control to the SelectionFrame Form.

Steps 2, 3 and 4 include using three different methods to perform this query. Now let's start with the first part.

6.3.7.1 Add Java Package and Code for the Constructor

Since we need to display an image for the selected faculty member when a data query is executed, the **`java.awt.*`** package should be imported, since some image-related classes, such as **`Image`**, **`Graphics`** and **`MediaTracker`**, are located in this package.

Open the Code Window of the FacultyFrame class by clicking on the **`Source`** tab at the top of the window and add the code shown in Figure 6.22 into this source file.

Let's have a closer look at this piece of code to see how it works.

A. Some useful java packages, including two important packages, **`java.awt.*`** and **`java.sql.*`**, are imported at the beginning of this file, since we need to use some classes defined in those packages.
B. A JDialog object, **`msgDlg`**, is created here as a class-level object because we need to use it in the whole class of the FacultyFrame to display debug or warning messages.
C. The **`addItem()`** method is used to add all three query methods into the **`Query Method`** combo box.
D. Also, the **`addItem()`** method is utilized to add all eight faculty members into the **`Faculty Name`** combo box.

Now let's first have a quick look at some popular JDBC MetaData Interfaces, since we need to use some of them in this faculty query operation.

6.3.7.2 Introduction to Some Popular JDBC MetaData Interfaces

In Section 6.3.3.4, we discussed how to use the ResultSet component to retrieve the queried result. Relatively speaking, there are some limitations on using the ResultSet object to get the returned query result. In other words, it is hard to get a clear and detailed picture of the queried result, such as the structure and properties of the data stored in the ResultSet. For example, no information about the returned result, such as the name of the data Table, the total number of columns and each column's name and data type, would be available when using a ResultSet object to pick up the queried result. In order to solve this problem and get detailed knowledge about the data Table structure, we need to use the ResultSetMetaData component.

The JDBC MetaData Interface provides detailed information about the database and its contents via the JDBC API, and it can be divided into the following three categories:

1) The DatabaseMetaData interface
2) The ResultSetMetaData interface
3) The ParameterMetaData interface

Each class has special functions and operation sequences, and some of them are related when they are utilized in specific ways.

6.3.7.2.1 The DatabaseMetaData Interface

The DatabaseMetaData interface contains more than 150 methods and provides detailed information about the database as a whole, such as:

- General information about the database
- Data source limitations
- Levels of transaction support
- Feature support
- Information about the SQL objects that source includes

In fact, the DatabaseMetaData interface provides methods that allow you to dynamically discover properties of a database as the project runs. Many methods in DatabaseMetaData return information in the ResultSet component, and one can get those pieces of information from the ResultSet object by calling related methods such as **`getString()`**, **`getInt()`** and **`getXXX()`**. A SQLException will be thrown if the queried item is not available in the MetaData interface.

6.3.7.2.2 The ResultSetMetaData Interface

Detailed information about the structure of a queried data Table can be obtained by calling the **getMetaData()** method that belongs to the ResultSetMetaData class, and a ResultSetMetaData object will be created when the **getMetaData()** method is executed. Some popular methods included in the ResultSetMetaData class are:

- **getColumnCount()**—returns the total number of columns in the ResultSet
- **getColumnName()**—returns the column name
- **getColumnType()**—returns the column data type
- **getTableName()**—returns the data Table name

Similar to the DatabaseMetaData interface, the ResultSetMetaData interface allows users to find the structure of data Tables and properties of columns in Tables.

6.3.7.2.3 The ParameterMetaData Interface

Detailed information about parameters passed into or from the database can be obtained by calling the **getParameterMetaData()** method that belongs to the PreparedStatement class. Although this interface is not as popular as ResultSetMetaData and DatabaseMetaData, it is useful in some special applications.

In this section, we will use the DatabaseMetaData and the ResultSetMetaData interfaces to illustrate how to improve data queries for our **Faculty** Table.

Now let's develop code for the **Select** button Click event handler to perform a data query.

6.3.7.3 Use Java executeQuery() with the DatabaseMetaData Interface to Query the Faculty Table

Open the **Select** button Click event handler if it has not been opened, and enter the code shown in Figure 6.23 into this event handler as the first part of code.

Let's take a closer look at this added piece of code to see how it works.

A. First, an Oracle image BLOB object, **fimgBlob**, is generated, and it is used to hold the retrieved faculty image to be displayed later on the canvas.
B. Then a TextField array is created, since we need to combine all seven TextField objects, **FacultyIDField**, **FacultyNameField**, **TitleField**, **OfficeField**, **PhoneField**, **CollegeField** and **EmailField**, in this array and assign the queried results to the TextField objects one by one later to improve the assignment efficiency. A point to be noted is that the definition for this TextField class is different in the basic **java.awt** package and the **javax.swing** package, and the TextField used here belongs to the latter.
C. The query string is declared here to query all columns from the **Faculty** Table based on the selected faculty name that works as a position parameter.
D. An **if** selection structure is used to identify which query method will be used for this query. If the **Java executeQuery Method** is selected by the user, the related code will be built in this section. Otherwise, the program will be branched to another query method.
E. A **try-catch** block is utilized to perform adatabase-related information query using the DatabaseMetaData interface. A DatabaseMetaData object, **dbmd**, is created by calling the **getMetaData()** method that belongs to the Connection class, and detailed information about the connected database is returned and assigned to the **dbmd** object.
F. Two system methods, **getDriverName()** and **getDriverVersion()**, are executed to pick up the retrieved driver name and version and assign them to the associated String variables, **drName** and **drVersion**, respectively. Both variables' values will be displayed

```
   private void SelectButtonActionPerformed(java.awt.event.ActionEvent evt) {
       // TODO add your handling code here:
A      Blob fimgBlob = null;
B      JTextField[] f_field = {FacultyIDField,FacultyNameField,TitleField,OfficeField,PhoneField,CollegeField, EmailField};
C      String query = "SELECT faculty_id, faculty_name, title, office, phone, college, email, fimage " +
                      "FROM Faculty WHERE faculty_name = ?";
D      if (ComboMethod.getSelectedItem()=="Java executeQuery Method"){
          try{
E              DatabaseMetaData dbmd = LogInFrame.con.getMetaData();
F              String drName = dbmd.getDriverName();
               String drVersion = dbmd.getDriverVersion();
               System.out.println("DriverName is: " + drName + ", Version is: " + drVersion);
G              PreparedStatement pstmt = LogInFrame.con.prepareStatement(query);
H              pstmt.setString(1, ComboName.getSelectedItem().toString());
I              ResultSet rs = pstmt.executeQuery();
J              ResultSetMetaData rsmd = rs.getMetaData();
K              while (rs.next()){
L                 for (int i = 1; i <=rsmd.getColumnCount(); i++) {
                     if (i == rsmd.getColumnCount()){
                       fimgBlob = rs.getBlob("fimage");
                       break;
                     }
M                    f_field[i-1].setText(rs.getString(i));
                  }
               }
N          }catch (SQLException e) {
               msgDlg.setMessage("Error in Statement!" + e.getMessage());
               msgDlg.setVisible(true);
           }
       }
       ......
```

FIGURE 6.23 The first part of the code for the Select button event handler.

in the **Output** window by calling the system method **System.out.println()** as a debug message as the project runs.

G. A prepared query statement is then created to query the detailed information for the selected faculty member.
H. The **setString()** method is used to set up the dynamic positional parameter in the preparedquery statement. The actual value of this parameter, which is the faculty member selected by the user from the ComboName combo box, can be obtained by calling the **getSelectedItem()** method.
I. The **executeQuery()** method is executed to perform the prepared statement to get the queried result, which is assigned to the ResultSet object **rs**.
J. The **getMetaData()** method is executed to query detailed information about the structure of the **Faculty** Table and properties of the columns in that Table. The returned result is assigned to the ResultSetMetaData object **rsmd**.
K. As we discussed in Section 6.3.3.4 for fetching by row, a **while** loop is used with the **next()** method as the argument to move the data Table cursor from the initial position to the first row position in the ResultSet object. This allows us to pick up each record one by one.
L. A **for** loop is used to pick up the first seven columns and assign them to the related TextFields to display the queried faculty information, which really happensin step M, until it gets to the last column by using the system method **getColumnCount()**, which is the faculty image column. Then we need to use the **getBlob()** method to retrieve this image as a binary large object and assign it to our local object **fimgBlob**. A break occurs to finish this **for** loop when the desired faculty image is obtained.
N. Any possible exception or error will be caught by the **catch** block and displayed in our **msgDlg** dialog.

Now let's handle the query to the Faculty Table by using another method, the Java execute() method.

6.3.7.4 Use the Java execute() Method to Query the Faculty Table

As we discussed in Section 6.3.3.3, unlike the Java **executeQuery()** and Java **executeUpdate()** methods, the Java **execute()** method is a more popular query operation, and it can be used for both selecting queries and data-manipulating queries to an Oracle database. The **execute()** method will not return any result itself, and one needs to use either **getResultSet()** or **getUpdateCount()** method to pick up the results. Both methods belong to the Statement class. The key point is:

- The **getResultSet()** method will return a null if the run result is an integer, which is the number of rows that have been affected, either inserted, updated or deleted.
- The **getUpdateCount()** method will return a –1 if the run result is a ResultSet.

Based on these two key points, we can easily determine whether a result is a ResultSet or an integer value.

In this section, we will discuss how to use this method to perform data query operation to our **Faculty** Table. In fact, we will add another **if** selection block with the code into the **Select** button Click event handler to use the **execute()** method to perform this data query.

Open the **Select** button Click event handler and add the code highlighted in bold and shown in Figure 6.24 into this event handler.

Let's have a closer look at this new piece of added code to see how it works.

A. If the user selected the **Java execute() Method** from the Query Method combo box, a **try-catch** block is used to create a prepared statement using the **prepareStatement()** method with the query string as the argument. Then the **setString()** method is used to set up the positional dynamic parameter, which is obtained from the ComboName combo box and selected by the user.
B. The Java **execute()** method is executed to perform this data query. The advantage of using this method is that both a query-related action and a non-query-related action can be performed by using this method. The disadvantage of using this method is that the run result cannot be determined when this method is used, since this method can only execute either a data query by returning a ResultSet object or a manipulating action, such as updating, inserting and deleting, by returning an integer.
C. Suppose we do not know what kind of data will be returned by running the **execute()** method; we assume that a manipulating action has been performed by calling this method. So we try to use the **getUpdateCount()** method to pick up the run result, which is supposed to be an integer.
D. If the returned result of calling of the **getUpdateCount()** method is –1, this means that the result of the **execute()** method is not an integer; instead, it is a ResultSet object. The **getResultSet()** method should be used to pick up that result. The following code is identical to that used in the Java **executeQuery()** method to get the query result.
E. Otherwise, if the run result of this **execute()** method returns an integer, it means that a data manipulation action has been performed. Of course, this is impossible, since we used this method to perform a data query, not a data manipulation. Thus, an error would have occurred if that had really happened, and this error would be displayed with a message.
F. The **catch** block is used to track and monitor any possible error during this query operation and display it if any error has occurred.

Next let's take care of using the Java **CallableStatement()** method to query our Faculty Table.

```
private void SelectButtonActionPerformed(java.awt.event.ActionEvent evt) {
   Blob fimgBlob = null;
   JTextField[] f_field = {FacultyIDField,FacultyNameField,TitleField,OfficeField, PhoneField, CollegeField, EmailField};
   String query = "SELECT faculty_id, faculty_name, title, office, phone, college, email, fimage " +
                  "FROM Faculty WHERE faculty_name = ?";
   if (ComboMethod.getSelectedItem()=="Java executeQuery Method"){
      try{
            DatabaseMetaData dbmd = LogInFrame.con.getMetaData();
            String drName = dbmd.getDriverName();
            String drVersion = dbmd.getDriverVersion();
            System.out.println("DriverName is: " + drName + ", Version is: " + drVersion);
            PreparedStatement pstmt = LogInFrame.con.prepareStatement(query);
            pstmt.setString(1, ComboName.getSelectedItem().toString());
            ResultSet rs = pstmt.executeQuery();
            ResultSetMetaData rsmd = rs.getMetaData();
            while (rs.next()){
              for (int i = 1; i <=rsmd.getColumnCount(); i++) {
                 if (i == rsmd.getColumnCount()){
                    fimgBlob = rs.getBlob("fimage");
                    break;
                 }
                 f_field[i-1].setText(rs.getString(i));
              }
            }
      } catch (SQLException e) {
           msgDlg.setMessage("Error in Statement!" + e.getMessage());
           msgDlg.setVisible(true);
      }
   }
A  if (ComboMethod.getSelectedItem()=="Java execute Method"){
      try{
            PreparedStatement pstmt = LogInFrame.con.prepareStatement(query);
            pstmt.setString(1, ComboName.getSelectedItem().toString());
B           pstmt.execute();
C           int updateCount = pstmt.getUpdateCount();
D           if (updateCount == -1){
               ResultSet rs = pstmt.getResultSet();
               ResultSetMetaData rsmd = rs.getMetaData();
               while (rs.next()){
                  for (int i=1; i <=rsmd.getColumnCount(); i++){
                     if (i == rsmd.getColumnCount()){
                      fimgBlob = rs.getBlob("fimage");
                      break;
                     }
                     f_field[i-1].setText(rs.getString(i));
                  }
               }
            }
E           else{
               msgDlg.setMessage("execute() method returned an integer!");
               msgDlg.setVisible(true);
            }
         }
F        catch (SQLException e) {
            msgDlg.setMessage("Error in Statement!" + e.getMessage());
            msgDlg.setVisible(true);
         }
   }
}
```

FIGURE 6.24 The added code for the Java execute() method.

6.3.7.5 Use the Java CallableStatement Method to Query the Faculty Table

The JDBC CallableStatement method provides a way to allow us to call a stored procedure to perform a complicated query. The speed and efficiency of a data query can be significantly improved by using the stored procedure, since it is built in the database side. An example of using the

CallableStatement method to query detailed information for a selected faculty member is provided in the FacultyFrame class with an Oracle stored procedure named **FacultyInfo**. A more detailed discussion of developing and implementing the CallableStatement method will be given in the next section for the CourseFrame class.

Generally, the sequence to run a CallableStatement to call a stored procedure is:

1) Build and formulate the CallableStatement query string.
2) Create a CallableStatement object.
3) Set the input parameters.
4) Register the output parameters.
5) Execute CallableStatement.
6) Retrieve the run result by using a different **getXXX()** method.

Let's discuss this issue in more detail in the following sections.

6.3.7.5.1 Build and Formulate the CallableStatement Query String

The CallableStatement interface is used to execute Oracle stored procedures. The JDBC API provides a stored procedure escape syntax that allows stored procedures to be called in a standard way for all RDBMSs. This escape syntax has one form that includes an output parameter and one that does not. If used, the output parameter must be registered as an **OUT** parameter. The other parameters can be used for input, output or both. Parameters are referred to sequentially by number, with the first parameter being 1.

```
{?= call <procedure-name>[<arg1>,<arg2>, . . .]}
{call <procedure-name>[<arg1>,<arg2>, . . .]}
```

Two syntaxes are widely used to formulate a CallableStatement string: the SQL92 syntax and the Oracle syntax. The SQL92 syntax is more popular in most applications. We will concentrate on the SQL92 syntax in this section.

For a stand-alone stored procedure or packaged procedure, the SQL92 syntax can be represented as:

```
{call [schema.][package.]procedure _ name[(?,?, . . .)]}
```

For stand-alone or packaged functions, the SQL92 syntax looks like:

```
{? = call [schema.][package.]function _ name[(?,?, . . .)]}
```

The meanings of the elements used in these syntaxes are:

- All elements enclosed inside the square brackets [] are optional.
- The curly braces {} are necessary in building a CallableStatement string, and they must be used to enclose the whole string.
- The schema indicates the schema in which the stored procedure is created.
- The package indicates the name of the package if the stored procedure is from it.
- The **procedure _ name** or **function _ name** indicates the name of the stored procedure or the function.
- The question mark (?) is a placeholder for either an **IN**, **IN/OUT** or **OUT** parameter used in the stored procedure or the returned value of a function. The order of these placeholders, which starts from 1, is very important, and it must be followed exactly when using either a **setXXX()** method to set up input parameters or register the output parameters for the built CallableStatement string later.

A CallableStatement can either return a ResultSet object and multiple ResultSet objects by using the **executeQuery()** method or return nothing by using the **execute()** method. Multiple

ResultSet objects are handled using operations inherited from Statement. A suiTable **getXXX()** method is needed to pick up the run result from the execution of a CallableStatement.

6.3.7.5.2 Create a CallableStatement Object

To create a CallableStatement object, you need to use one of methods defined in the Connection class, **prepareCall()**. When the SQL92 syntax is used to create the CallableStatement object, it will look like:

```
CallableStatement cstmt = null;
try{
String query = "{call FacultyCourse(?,?)}";
cstmt = LogInFrame.con.prepareCall(query);
. . .
```

The operation sequence of this piece of code to create a new CallableStatement object is:

1) A new null CallableStatement object, **cstmt**, is first declared.
2) A **try** block is used to create the query string with the SQL92 syntax. The name of the stored procedure to be called is **FacultyCourse()** with two arguments; the first one is an input parameter, **faculty _ name**, and the second one is an output parameter used to store all **course _ id** taught by the selected faculty. Both parameters are represented by placeholders, and they are positional parameters.
3) The CallableStatement object is created by calling the **prepareCall()** method, which belongs to the Connection class with the query string as the argument.

Next let's take a look at how to set up the input parameters for this object.

6.3.7.5.3 Set the Input Parameters

All input parameters used for a CallableStatement interface must be clearly bound to the associated **IN** parameters in a stored procedure by using a **setXXX()** method. This **setXXX()** method can be divided into three categories based on the different data types:

1) The primitive data type method
2) The object method
3) The stream method

For the primitive and the object method, the syntax is identical, and the difference between them is the type of value that is assigned. For the stream method, both the syntax and the data types are different.

Set Primitive Data Type and Object IN Values

The primitive data type means all built-in data types used in the Java programming language. The syntax of setting a primitive data type or an object value method is,

```
setXXX(int position, data _ type value);
```

where **XXX** means the associated value type to be assigned, **position** is an integer used to indicate the relative position of the **IN** parameter in the query statement or the stored procedure and **value** is the actual data value to be assigned to the **IN** parameter.

Some popular **setXXX()** methods are:

```
setBoolean(), setByte(), setInt(), setDouble(), setFloat(), setLong(),
setShort(), setString(),
setObject(), setDate(), setTime(), setTimeStamp()
```

An example of using the **setXXX()** method is:

```
String query = "SELECT product, order _ date FROM Order "+
"WHERE order _ id =? AND customer =?";
PreparedStatement pstmt = con.prepareStatement(query);
setInt(1, 101);
setString(2, "Tom Johnson");
```

Two dynamic parameters are used in the query string, and both of them are **IN** parameters. The data type of the first **IN** parameter is an integer; the second one is a String; and both are represented by a placeholder,?. The first setting method, **setInt(1, 101)** is to assign an integer value of 101 to the first **IN** parameter, which is indicated with a position number of 1, and the second setting method, **setString(2, "Tom Johnson")**, is to assign a String value, "**Tom Johnson**", to the second **IN** parameter, which is indicated with a position number of 2.

From this example, you can see that there is no difference between setting a primitive parameter and an object value to the **IN** parameters in a query statement.

Set Object Methods

The **setObject()** method has three protocols, which are:

```
setObject(int position, object _ type object _ value);
setObject(int position, object _ type object _ value, data _ type
desired _ data _ type);
setobject(int position, object _ type object _ value, data _ type
desired _ data _ type, int scale);
```

The first one is straightforward, and it contains two parameters; the first one is the relative position of the **IN** parameter in the query statement, and the second one is the value of a desired object to be assigned to the **IN** object.

The second one adds one more input parameter, **desired _ data _ type**, and it is used to indicate a data type to convert the object to.

The third one adds the fourth input parameter, **scale**, and it is used to make sure that the object conversion result contains a certain number of digits.

An example of the **setObject()** method is shown here,

```
pstmt.setObject(2, 101);
pstmt.setObject(2, 101, Type.FLOAT);
pstmt.setObject(2, 101, Type.FLOAT, 2);
```

The first method is to set an input parameter, which is the second one in a query statement, to an object (here an integer) with a value of 101. The next method is to set the same input to the same object; however, it needs to convert the object (integer) to a float data type. The final method performs the same operation as the previous one, but it indicates that the conversion result should contain at least two digits.

Set Stream IN Methods

When transferring images between an application and a database, the **IN** parameters need to have large sizes. In that situation, an **InputStream()** method should be used. The syntax of this method is:

```
setXXXStream(int position, data _ type input _ stream, int number _
of _ bytes);
```

where **XXX** means the InputStream type: ASCII, Binary or Unicode. The first parameter is the relative position of the **IN** parameter in the query statement, and the second parameter is the data stream to be read from. The third parameter indicates the number of bytes to be read from the data stream at a time.

A simple example of using the **InputStream()** method is:

```
FileInputStream picFile = new FileInputStream("new _ file");
String query = "INSERT INTO picture (image) VALUES (?) WHERE pic _
id = 101 ";
PreparedStatement pstmt = prepareStatement(query);
pstmt.setUnicodeStream(1, picFile, 2048);
```

This piece of code is used to set the first **IN** parameter to read 2KB bytes from a picture file, which is a Unicode file named **picFile**, at a time.

6.3.7.5.4 Register the Output Parameters

As we discussed in Section 6.3.7.5, after a CallableStatement interface is executed, you need to use the associated **getXXX()** method to pick up the run result from the CallableStatement object, since it cannot return any result itself. However, before you can do that, you must first register any output parameter in the query statement to allow the CallableStatement to know that an output result is involved and stored in the related output parameters in the query statement.

Once an output parameter is registered, the parameter is considered an **OUT** parameter, and it can contain run results that can be picked up by using the associated **getXXX()** method.

To register an output parameter, the **registerOutParameter()** method that belongs to the **CallableStatement** interface should be used to declare what kind of Oracle type the **OUT** parameter will return. A point to be noted is that a parameter in a query statement can be defined as both an **IN** and an **OUT** at the same time, which means that you can set up this parameter as an **IN** by using the **setXXX()** method, and you can also register this parameter as an **OUT** using the **registerOutParameter()** method at the same time. In this way, this parameter can be considered an **IN/OUT** parameter with both input and output functions.

The syntax to register an output parameter is:

```
registerOutParameter(int position, data _ type Oracle _ data _ type);
```

where **position** is still the relative position of the **OUT** parameter in the query statement, and **Oracle _ data _ type** is the Oracle data type of the **OUT** parameter, which can be found from the JDBC API class **java.sql.TYPE**.

An example of using this method is shown here:

```
String query = "{call FacultyCourse(?,?)}";
cstmt = LogInFrame.con.prepareCall(query);
cstmt.setString(1, ComboName.getSelectedItem().toString());
cstmt.setString(2, "CSC-230A");
cstmt.registerOutParameter(2, oracle.jdbc.OracleTypes.VARCHAR);
```

There are two parameters in the CallableStatement interface in this example. The first one is an **IN** parameter, which is set by using the **setString()** method. The second one is an **IN/OUT** parameter, which is first set up by using the **setString()** method and then registered by using the **registerOutParameter()** method with the data type of **VARCHAR**. The Oracle data type **VARCHAR** can be mapped to a data type of String in Java.

An interesting point to the**registerOutParameter()** method is that all **OUT** parameters can be registered by using this syntax except those **OUT** parameters with **NUMERIC** and **DECIMAL** data types. The syntax to register those **OUT** parameters looks like:

```
registerOutParameter(int position, data _ type Oracle _ data _ type,
int scale);
```

The only difference is that the third parameter, **scale**, is added, and it is used to indicate the number of digits to the right of the decimal point for the **OUT** parameter.

6.3.7.5.5 Execute CallableStatement

To run a CallableStatement object, three methods can be used: **executeQuery()**, **executeUpdate()** and **execute()**. As we discussed in Section 6.3.3.3, the **executeQuery()** method can return a ResultSet object that contains the run or query results; however, the **execute()** method cannot return any run result byitself, and you need to use the associated **getXXX()** methods to pick up the query or run result. Another important point of using the **execute()** method is that it can handle an unknown result with undefined data type. Refer to Section 6.3.3.3 to get more detailed information about the **execute()** method.

An example of using the **execute()** method to run the CallableStatement object is:

```
String query = "{call FacultyCourse(?,?)}";
cstmt = LogInFrame.con.prepareCall(query);
cstmt.setString(1, ComboName.getSelectedItem().toString());
cstmt.registerOutParameter(2, oracle.jdbc.OracleTypes.VARCHAR);
cstmt.execute();
```

Now let's handle how to retrieve the result from running a CallableStatement object.

6.3.7.5.6 Retrieve the Run Results

To pick up the run results from the execution of a CallableStatement object, one needs to use the associated **getXXX()** method. Two popular ways to get a run result from a CallableStatement are the **getXXX()** method and the **getObject()** method. The former is based on the returned data type of the result, and the latter is more general to get any kind of result.

All of the **getXXX()** and **getObject()** methods use the same syntax, which looks like:

```
getXXX(int position);
getObject(int position);
```

where **XXX** indicates the **OUT** value Java data type, and the position is the relative position of the **OUT** parameter in the query statement. The same syntax is used for the **getObject()** method.

An example of using the **getXXX()** method to pick up the run result from the execution of a CallableStatement object is shown here:

```
String query = "{call FacultyCourse(?,?)}";
cstmt = LogInFrame.con.prepareCall(query);
cstmt.setString(1, ComboName.getSelectedItem().toString());
cstmt.registerOutParameter(2, oracle.jdbc.OracleTypes.VARCHAR);
cstmt.execute();
String cResult = cstmt.getString(2);
```

Since the **OUT** parameter is a String and is located at position of 2, an argument of 2 is used in the **getString()** method to pick up the run result. An alternative way to get the same result is to use the **getObject()** method, which looks like:

```
String cResult = (String)cstmt.getObject(2);
```

The returned result must be cast by using the String data type, since an object can be any data type.

Ok, that is enough for the theoretical discussions. Now let's getto our real stuff, developing the code for the **Select** button Click event handler to perform the CallableStatement object to call an Oracle stored procedure to query a faculty record from our Faculty Table in our sample database.

6.3.7.5.7 The Syntax of Creating Stored Procedures in the Oracle Database

The syntax of creating a stored procedure in the Oracle database is shown in Figure 6.25.

The keyword **REPLACE** is used for the modified stored procedures. Recall that in SQL Server, the keyword **ALTER** is used for any stored procedure that has been modified since it was created. In Oracle, the keyword **CREATE OR REPLACE** is used to represent any procedure that is either newly created or modified.

Following the procedure's name, all input or output parameters are declared inside the braces. After the keyword **AS**, the stored procedure's body is displayed. The body begins with the keyword **BEGIN** and ends with the keyword **END**. Note that a semicolon must follow each query statement and the keyword **END**.

An example of creating a stored procedure in an Oracle database is shown in Figure 6.26.

The length of data type for each parameter is not necessary, since this allows parameters of varying length.

6.3.7.5.8 The Syntax of Creating Packages in the Oracle Database

To create a stored procedure that returns data, one needs to embed the stored procedure into a package. The syntax of creating a package is shown in Figure 6.27.

The syntax of creating a package contains two parts: the package definition part and the package body part. The returned data type, **CURSOR**, is defined first, since the cursor can be used to return a group of data. Following the definition of the cursor, the stored procedure, or, more precisely, the protocol of the stored procedure, is declared with the input and output parameters (the cursor works as the output argument).

Following the package definition part is the body part. The protocol of the stored procedure is re-declared at the beginning, and then the body begins with the opening of the cursor and assigns

```
CREATE OR REPLACE PROCEDURE Procedure name
{
        Param1's name       Param1's data type,
        Param2's name       Param2's data type,
        .......
}
AS
    BEGIN
    (Your query Statements, such as INSERT, UPDATE or DELETE);
    END;
```

FIGURE 6.25 The syntax of creating a stored procedure in the Oracle database.

```
CREATE OR REPLACE PROCEDURE InsertProcedure
{
        studentId           VARCHAR2,
        name                VARCHAR2,
        credit              NUMBER
}
AS
    BEGIN
    INSERT INTO Student(student_id, s_name, s_credit)
    VALUES(studentId, name, credit);
    END;
```

FIGURE 6.26 An example of creating a stored procedure in the Oracle database.

```
CREATE OR REPLACE PACKAGE Package name
AS
        Definition for the returned Cursor;
        Definition for the stored procedure
END;
CREATE OR REPLACE PACKAGE BODY Package name
AS
    Stored procedure prototype
    AS
    BEGIN
      OPEN Returned cursor FOR
      (Your SELECT Statements);
    END;
END;
```

FIGURE 6.27 The syntax of creating a package in the Oracle database.

```
CREATE OR REPLACE PACKAGE FacultyPackage
AS
     TYPE CURSOR_TYPE IS REF CURSOR;
     PROCEDURE SelectFacultyID (FacultyName IN CHAR, FacultyID OUT CURSOR_TYPE);
END;
CREATE OR REPLACE PACKAGE BODY FacultyPackage
AS
    PROCEDURE SelectFacultyID (FacultyName IN CHAR, FacultyID OUT CURSOR_TYPE)
    AS
    BEGIN
      OPEN FacultyID FOR
      SELECT faculty_id, title, office, email FROM Faculty
      WHERE faculty_name = FacultyName;
    END;
END;
```

FIGURE 6.28 An example of creating a Faculty Package in the Oracle database.

the returned result of the following **SELECT** statement to the cursor. Similarly, each statement must end with a semicolon, including the **END** command.

An example of creating a **FacultyPackage** in the Oracle database is shown in Figure 6.28.

The stored procedure is named **SelectFacultyID** and has two parameters: the input parameter **FacultyName** and the output parameter **FacultyID**. The keywords **IN** and **OUT** following the associated parameters are used to indicate the input/output direction of the parameter. The length of the stored procedure name is limited to 30 letters in Oracle. Unlike stored procedure names created in SQL Server, there is no prefix applied for each procedure's name.

Unlike Server Explorer provided by Visual Studio. NET, Oracle Database 18c XE does not provide a valid GUI to assist users to build customized databases, including stored procedures and packages. Fortunately, one of the powerful tools used to support various developments for Oracle databases, Oracle SQL Developer, provides all kinds of GUIs and components to enable users to build those elements in a very friendly environment.

In this section, we will use Oracle SQL Developer as a tool to build our Oracle packages and stored procedures, since this tool provides a GUI to allow users to create and manipulate database components, including packages and stored procedures, directly in the Developer environment.

6.3.7.5.9 Create an Oracle Package FacultyInfo

As we discussed, a stored procedure is divided into two categories in the Oracle database, package and procedure, which are defined as:

- A stored procedure that never returns any data is called a procedure
- A stored procedure that always returns something is called a package

In this application, we need to call an Oracle stored procedure to fetch a record from the **Faculty** Table based on the selected faculty name. Therefore, we need to build an Oracle package, since we need our procedure to return a matching faculty record.

Open Oracle SQL Developer and perform the following operations to create this package:

1) In the opened Oracle SQL Developer, click on the **XE** service under the **Recent** tab.
2) In the popup wizard, enter our password, **oracle _ 18c**, into the Password box, and click on the **OK** button to connect to our service and our sample database.
3) Then expand the two folders **XE** and **Other Users** and our sample database folder, **CSE _ DEPT**.
4) Right-click on the **Packages** folder and select the **New Package** item.
5) In the opened Create Package wizard, enter the package name **FACULTYINFO** into the Name box, as shown in Figure 6.29. Click on the **OK** button.

Each package has two parts: the definition or specification part and the body part. First let's create the specification part by entering the code shown in Figure 6.30.

The coding language we used in this section is called Procedural Language Extension for SQL, or PL/SQL, which is a popular language widely used in Oracle database programming.

Refer to line 2 in Figure 6.30, where we define the returned data type as a **CURSOR _ TYPE** by using:

```
TYPE CURSOR _ TYPE IS REF CURSOR;
```

since we must use a cursor to return a group of data—a faculty record.

The prototype of the procedure **SelectFacultyInfo()** is declared in line 3. Two arguments are used for this procedure. The input parameter facultyName is indicated as an input by using the keyword **IN**, followed by the data type of **VARCHAR2**. The output parameter is a cursor named **Faculty _ Info**, followed by the keyword **OUT**. Each PL/SQL statement must end with a semicolon, and this rule also applies to the **END** statement.

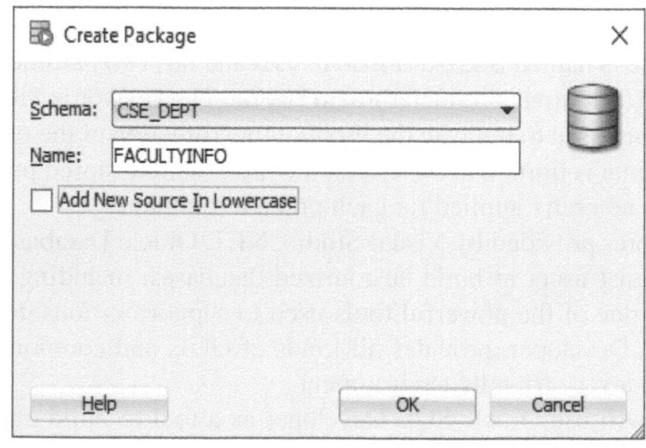

FIGURE 6.29 The opened new package wizard.

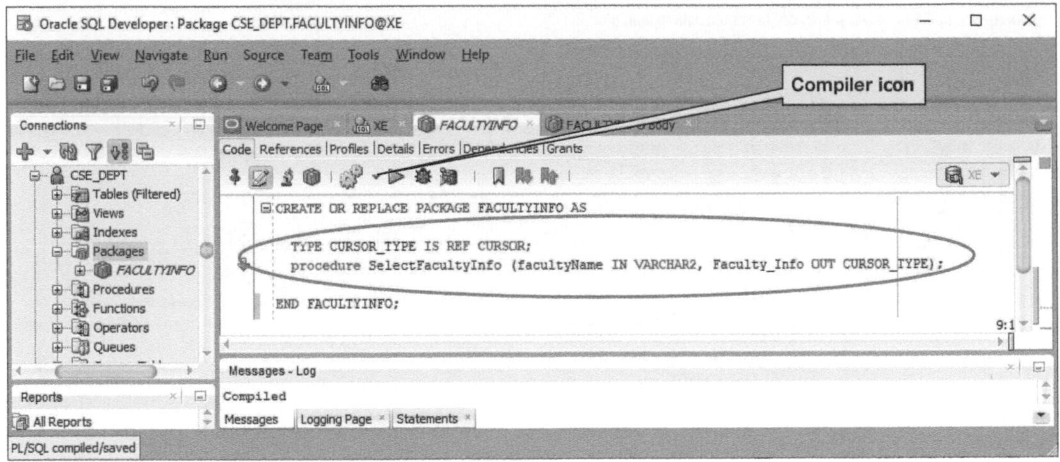

FIGURE 6.30 The opened package definition wizard (Copyrighted by Oracle and used with permission).

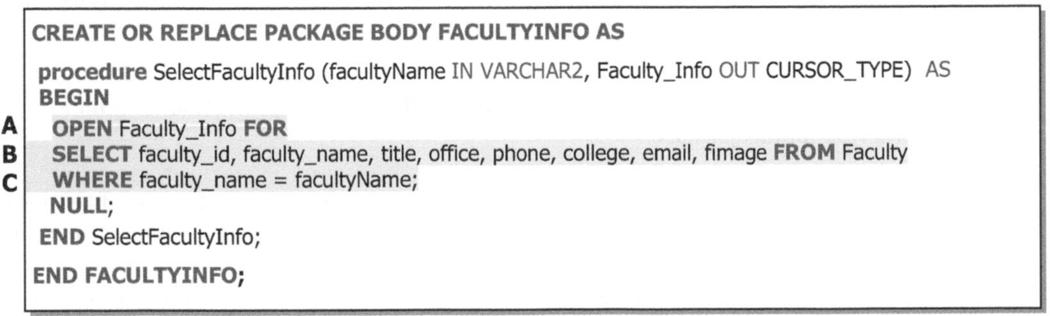

```
  CREATE OR REPLACE PACKAGE BODY FACULTYINFO AS
   procedure SelectFacultyInfo (facultyName IN VARCHAR2, Faculty_Info OUT CURSOR_TYPE)  AS
   BEGIN
A    OPEN Faculty_Info FOR
B    SELECT faculty_id, faculty_name, title, office, phone, college, email, fimage FROM Faculty
C    WHERE faculty_name = facultyName;
    NULL;
   END SelectFacultyInfo;
  END FACULTYINFO;
```

FIGURE 6.31 The finished Package Body wizard.

Now let's continue to build the body part for this package. Perform the following operations to create this body part:

1) Click on the drop-down arrow and select `Compile` to compile this package. A `Compiled` message should be displayed in the Message-Log window if the compile is successful.
2) Now right-click on our new created package, **`FACULTYINFO`**, under the **`Packages`** folder in the left and select the **`Create Body`** item to add a package body into this package.
3) In the opened Package Body wizard, enter the code that is highlighted and shown in Figure 6.31.
4) Click on the drop-down arrow and select `Compile` to compile this package body. A `Compiled` message should be displayed in the Message-Log window if the compile is successful, as shown in Figure 6.32.
5) Your finished package, **`FACULTYINFO`**, is shown in Figure 6.32.

Let's have a closer look at this piece of code to see how it works.

A. The **`OPEN Faculty_Info FOR`** command is used to assign the returned data columns from the following query to the cursor variable **`Faculty_Info`**.
B. The **`SELECT`** query is executed to get all columns from the **`FACULTY`** Table.

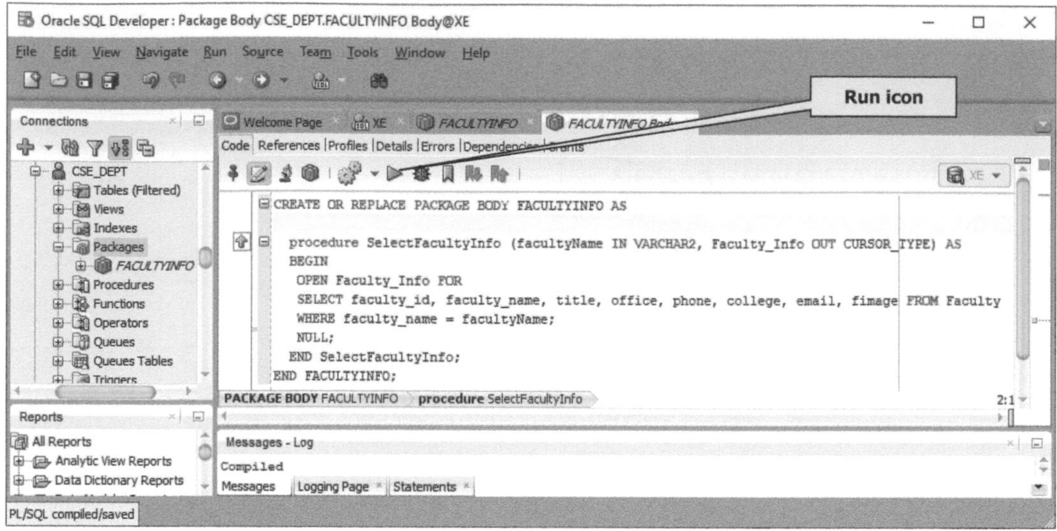

FIGURE 6.32 The finished FACULTYINFO package (Copyrighted by Oracle and used with permission).

C. The input argument, **facultyName**, is assigned to the **faculty _ name** column as a query criterion for this package.

If for some reason the compile process fails, a debug process is needed, and one of the most likely errors is the misspelling of variables used in either the definition part or body part or inconsistent spellings for variables used in the definition part and body part.

In fact, it is unnecessary to build this query as a package due to its simplicity, but here we prefer to use this query as an example to illustrate the building process for an Oracle package.

Now we can test this package in the Oracle SQL Developer environment to confirm its correctness. Click on the green arrow (**Run**) button on the task bar, as shown in Figure 6.32, to run this package. The opened Run PL/SQL wizard is shown in Figure 6.33.

Enter a desired faculty member's name, such as **Ying Bai**, into the **Input Value** box (Figure 6.33), and click on the **OK** button to run this package.

To check the run result, click on the **Output Variables** tab at the lower-right corner, and all eight queried columns related to the faculty member named **Ying Bai** in the **FACULTY** Table are displayed under the **Value** tab in the **Output Variables** window at the bottom, as shown in Figure 6.34.

Now let's go to the **File|Save All** menu item to save this package, close Oracle SQL Developer and return to our Java application to develop the code to try to call this package to perform the data query using the CallableStatement method.

6.3.7.5.10 Develop the Code to Perform the CallableStatement Query

Open the **Select** button click event handler in the FacultyFrame Form window, move to the **Java Callable Method** block and add the code shown in Figure 6.35 to this part. The newly added parts are in bold.

Let's have a closer look at this piece of modified code to see how it works.

A. An **else if** block is added immediately after the **if** block for the **Java execute** method block.
   This block is used to execute the Java Callable method.
B. A CallableStatement object, **cstmt**, is generated and initialized first.

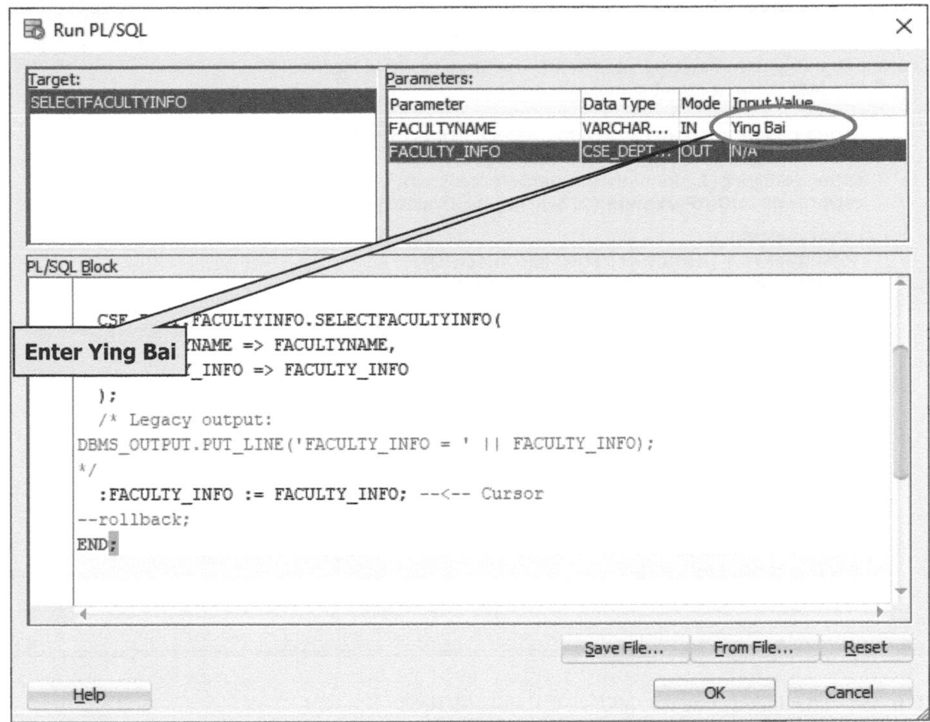

FIGURE 6.33 The opened Run PL/SQL wizard (Copyrighted by Oracle and used with permission).

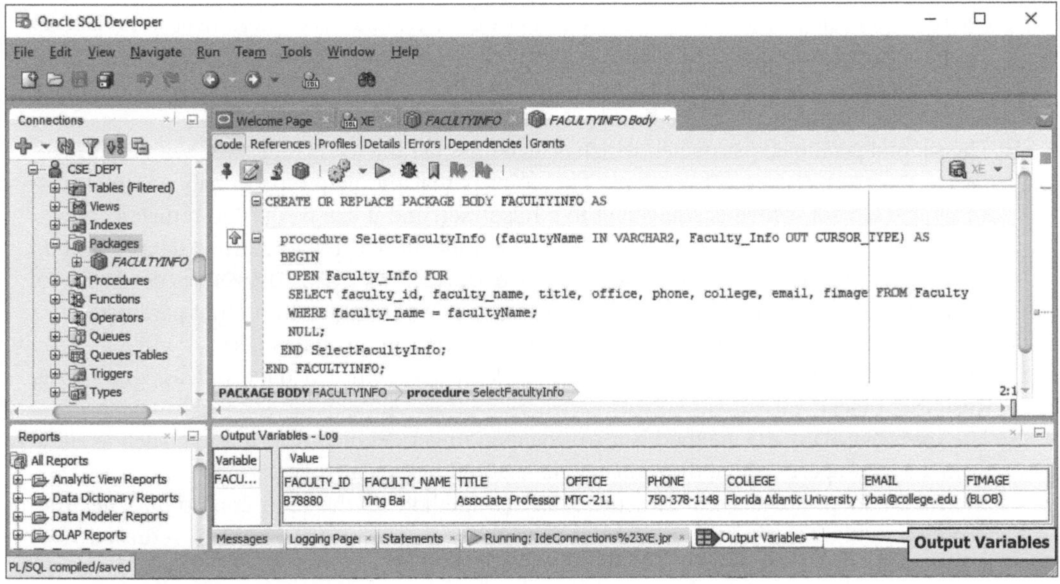

FIGURE 6.34 The run result of the package FACULTYINFO (Copyrighted by Oracle and used with permission).

C. A query statement is created with SQL92 syntax, which is used to call the Oracle package we built in the last section with an embedded stored procedure. The stored procedure, **`SelecteFacultyInfo()`**, must be prefixed with the package name **`FacultyInfo`**, and

```
    .................
A   else if (ComboMethod.getSelectedItem()=="Java Callable Method"){
B       CallableStatement cstmt = null;
        try{
C           String cquery = "{call FacultyInfo.SelectFacultyInfo(?, ?)}";
D           cstmt = LogInFrame.con.prepareCall(cquery);
E           cstmt.setString(1, ComboName.getSelectedItem().toString());
F           cstmt.registerOutParameter(2, oracle.jdbc.OracleTypes.CURSOR);
G           cstmt.execute();
H           ResultSet rs = (ResultSet)cstmt.getObject(2);
I           ResultSetMetaData rsmd = rs.getMetaData();
J           while (rs.next()){
              for (int i=1; i <=rsmd.getColumnCount(); i++) {
K               if (i == rsmd.getColumnCount()){
L                 fimgBlob = rs.getBlob("fimage");
                  break;
                }
M               f_field[i-1].setText(rs.getString(i));
              }
            }
N       } catch (SQLException e){
            msgDlg.setMessage("Error in CallableStatement! " + e.getMessage());
            msgDlg.setVisible(true);
        }
    .........
```

FIGURE 6.35 The added code for the Java Callable Method.

this is required by Oracle databases. Two dynamic positional parameters, the first one an input and the second an output, are represented by two question marks as the arguments for this call.

D. Then the **prepareCall()** method is executed to create a CallableStatement object.
E. A system setter method, **setString()**, is used to set up the input parameter, which is a selected faculty name from the Faculty Name combo box by the user.
F. The second positional parameter, which is an output parameter, is registered with the **registerOutParameter()** method. The point is that the data type of this parameter is an Oracle Cursor, which is equivalent to a ResultSet, and it can be used to return a collection of queried data; it can be considered a data Table in which the returned data is stored. An Oracle extension Java type, **oracle.jdbc.OracleTypes.CURSOR**, is used here to define this returned data type. This is a necessary step to register this output parameter.
G. Then the CallableStatement object is executed to perform this data query.
H. The **getObject(2)** method is used to pick up the returned data and assigned to a ResultSet object, **rs**.
I. The **getMetaData()** method is also executed to get detailed information, such as data format and property, about the returned data stored in the Cursor.
J. A **while** loop is executed with the **next()** method as the loop condition. The first **next()** method moves the cursor one step down to point to the current returned row (exactly one row is returned).
K. Inside the **while** loop, a **for** loop is used to pick up all seven columns and assign them to the related TextFields to display the queried faculty information, which really happens in step M, until it gets the last column, which can be identified by using a system method, **getColumnCount()**, and this column stores the queried faculty image.
L. Then we need to use **getBlob()** to retrieve this image as a binary large object and assign it to our local object, **fimgBlob**. A **break** instruction is executed to finish this **for** loop when the desired faculty image has been obtained.

M. The first seven columns, which store the queried faculty information, are picked up one by one and assigned to the related TxtField via the **f _ field[]** array.
N. Any possible exception or error will be caught by the **catch** block and displayed in our **msgDlg** dialog.

Now we need to Figure out how to select and display the queried faculty image involved in this data query in this FacultyFrame Form with related code.

6.3.7.6 Display an Image for the Selected Faculty Member in Canvas

There are different ways to store and display images in a database-related project. One professional way is to store all images as binary files in a database with all queried data together. As we did in Chapter 2 when we built our sample database, **CSE _ DEPT**, all faculty images have been stored in the **fimage** column as a sequence of binary data in our sample database, in the **Faculty** Table.

Unlike Visual Studio. NET, in environments such as Visual Basic.NET and Visual C#.NET, there is no PictureBox class available in Java to display an image or a picture. One needs to use a Canvas object as an image holder, a Graphics object as a tool to display an image and a MediaTracker class as a monitor to coordinate image processing.

In Java, the main package containing the key image processing classes, such as **Image**, **Toolkit**, **Graphics** and **MediaTracker**, is **java.awt**. Currently, the Java graphics programming library (AWT) supports GIF and JPEG images. Format considerations include local color palettes, feature restrictions (compression, color depth and interlacing, for example) and dithering.

We divide this section into the following three parts to make image displaying in Java more illustrative and straightforward:

1) Show the operational sequence to display an image in Java.
2) Create a user-defined method, **ShowFaculty()**, to select and display a desired faculty image.
3) Develop the additional code to coordinate this image display.

Now let's start with the first part.

6.3.7.6.1 Operational Sequence to Display an Image in Java

Usually, to display an image in Java, two steps should be performed:

1) Load an image from an image file.
2) Display that image by drawing it in a Graphics context.

For example, to load an image named "**faculty.jpg**", use the **getImage()** method that belongs to the Toolkit class, which looks like:

```
Image img = myWindow.getToolkit().getImage("faculty.jpg");
```

where **MyWindow** is a Java GUI container, such as a JFrame, JDialog or JWindow, in which the image will be displayed. The **getToolkit()** method that belongs to the Java GUI container is used to get the Toolkit object. One point to be noted when this instruction is executed is that both the **Image** and **Toolkit** classes are abstract classes, which means that you cannot directly create new instances by invoking those classes' constructors. Instead, you have to use methods related to those abstract classes.

After an image is loaded, display the image by drawing it in a Graphics context using

```
g.drawImage(img, x, y, width, height, imageObserver);
```

where the object **g** is an instance of the Graphics class.

As we know, every AWT component object has a Graphics context, and the real drawing is done in the **paint()** method of a component because **paint()** is called by AWT automatically when the image is finished loading. However, an important issue is that image loading is an asynchronous process, which means that loading does not necessarily occur until you attempt to display the image via **drawImage()**. The last parameter to **drawImage()** specifies which component to repaint when the image is finally ready. This is normally the component that calls **drawImage()** in the Java GUI container.

In fact, when the first step, loading an image, starts, the **getImage()** method kicks off a new thread to load and fetch the image, and this thread does not start immediately or synchronously when you run the loading method. Instead, this thread will not begin its process until the **drawImage()** method is called. Therefore, it is not guaranteed that the required image will be loaded and ready to be displayed when **drawImage()** is executed.

In order to solve this asynchronous problem in image loading and display, another image-related class, **MediaTracker**, is used to monitor and track the run status of the image loading process. MediaTracker is a utility class designed to track the status of media objects. In theory, media objects could include audio clips and other media as well as images. You can use a media tracker object by instantiating an instance of MediaTracker for the component that you want to monitor and invoking its **addImage()** method for each image that you want to track. Each image can be assigned a unique identifier starting from 1, or groups of images can be assigned the same identifier. You can determine the status of an image or group of images by invoking one of several methods on the MediaTracker object and passing the identifier as a parameter to the method.

Another way you can use the MediaTracker object is to block and wait until a specified image or group of images completes loading. We will use this approach in this project to make certain that a desired faculty image has completed loading before we attempt to draw it.

Before we can start this image-displaying process with code, we need first to create a user-defined method to include our code in this customer-made or user-defined method to identify, select and display the desired faculty image via the **FileOutputStream** object defined in the **Java Swing** windows group.

6.3.7.6.2 Create a User-Defined Method to Select and Display Desired Faculty Image

Open the Code Window of the **FacultyFrame** class by clicking on the **Source** tab from the top of the window and enter the code shown in Figure 6.36 to create the new method, **ShowFaculty()**. Let's have a closer look at this piece of code to see how it works.

A. Some local variables and objects used in this method are declared and defined first. **imgId** and **timeout** are used as the ID of the tracked image and the maximum waiting time for that tracking process. A local Image object, **img**, which is used to temporarily hold the selected faculty image, is created and initialized here. Since we need to retrieve our faculty image and store it in output stream format, a **FileOutputStream** object, **imgOutputStream**, is declared here and initialized to null. A new instance of the MediaTracker class, **tracker**, is created since we need to use it in the ShowFaculty() method.
B. In order to store our retrieved faculty image in our current project folder, the system method **getProperty()**, with our current directory (**user.dir**), is used, and this current folder is assigned to a local string variable, **imgPath**.
C. To get the selected faculty image, we need to get the current selected or queried faculty name from the Faculty Name combo box, convert this item to a string and attach a "**.jpg**" as the image file name. We need to use this faculty image name later to store and display the selected faculty image in the Canvas.
D. A **try-catch** block is used to activate and initialize a new instance for the **FileOutputStream** class **imgOutputStream** by attaching our current project

```
  private boolean ShowFaculty(Blob bimg) throws SQLException, IOException{
A       Image img;
        int imgId = 1, timeout = 1000;
        FileOutputStream imgOutputStream = null;
        MediaTracker tracker = new MediaTracker(this);
B       String imgPath = System.getProperty("user.dir");
C       String fimgName = ComboName.getSelectedItem().toString() + ".jpg";
D       try {
              imgOutputStream = new FileOutputStream(imgPath + "/" + fimgName);
E         }catch (FileNotFoundException ex) {
                Logger.getLogger(FacultyFrame.class.getName()).log(Level.SEVERE, null, ex);
        }
F       imgOutputStream.write(bimg.getBytes(1, (int)bimg.length()));
G       imgOutputStream.close();
H       img = this.getToolkit().getImage(fimgName);
        Graphics g = ImageCanvas.getGraphics();
I       tracker.addImage(img, imgId);
J       try{
          if(!tracker.waitForID(imgId, timeout)){
             msgDlg.setMessage("Failed to load image");
             msgDlg.setVisible(true);
             return false;
          }
K         }catch(InterruptedException e){
            msgDlg.setMessage(e.toString());
            msgDlg.setVisible(true);
            return false;
          }
L         g.drawImage(img, 0, 0, ImageCanvas.getWidth(), ImageCanvas.getHeight(), this);
          return true;
  }
```

FIGURE 6.36 Detailed code for the user-defined method ShowFaculty().

folder to the name of the selected faculty image, since we need to store this image file in that folder and later retrieve it to display it on our Canvas in the **FacultyFrame** Form. The forward slash, "/", is necessary to separate the current folder from the image name.

E. Any possible error, including the **file not found** exception, is collected by this catch block.
F. If the **imgOutputStream** instance is initialized successfully, our retrieved faculty image, **bimg**, which is a Blob and passed argument to the **ShowFaculty()** method, is written or stored into our current folder with the selected faculty image name, **fimgName**. This writing operation is performed by executing a method, **getBytes()**, with the length of the Blob, which means that the entire Blob is retrieved and written byte by byte into our current folder with the image name.
G. The**imgOutputStream** should be closed when the write operation is completed.
H. To display the selected faculty image, the **getImage()** method that belongs to the abstract class Toolkit is executed to load the selected image. Since the Toolkit class is an abstract class, we use the **getToolkit()** method to create it instead of generating it by invoking its constructor. The **getGraphics()** method is called to get a Graphics context, and our **ImageCanvas** works as an image holder for this faculty image.
I. The **addImage()** method that belongs to the MediaTracker class is called to add our image with its ID into the tracking system.
J. A **try catch** block is used to begin this tracking process, and the **waitForID()** method is called to execute the tracking. If a timeout occurs for this tracking process, which means that the selected faculty image has not been loaded into the project, a warning message is displayed using our MsgDialog object.

K. Any possible exception or error will be caught by the **catch** block and displayed in our **msgDlg** dialog.

L. If no timeout error happens, which means that the selected faculty image has been loaded into our project and is ready to be displayed, the **drawImage()** method is executed to display it in the FacultyFrame Form window. We want to display this image starting from the origin of the Canvas object, which is the upper-left corner of the canvas (0, 0), with a width and height that are identical to those of the canvas. Therefore, the **getWidth()** and **getHeight()** methods are called to get both of these from the canvas object. A **true** is returned to the main program to indicate that the execution of this method is successful.

Now we have finished the coding process for this method. Next let's finish the coding process to call the user-defined method to select and display the selected faculty image by adding the additional code into the **Select** button event handler.

6.3.7.6.3 Develop Additional Code to Coordinate theImage Display

Open the Design View of our **FacultyFrame** Form by clicking on the **Design** tab from the top of the window, and double-click on the **Select** button to open its event handler. Add the code in bold in Figure 6.37 into this handler.

```
  private void SelectButtonActionPerformed(java.awt.event.ActionEvent evt) {
    Blob fimgBlob = null;
    JTextField[] f_field = {FacultyIDField,FacultyNameField,TitleField,OfficeField, PhoneField, CollegeField, EmailField};
    String query = "SELECT faculty_id, faculty_name, title, office, phone, college, email, fimage " +
                   "FROM Faculty WHERE faculty_name = ?";
    if (ComboMethod.getSelectedItem()=="Java executeQuery Method"){
      try{
          PreparedStatement pstmt = LogInFrame.con.prepareStatement(query);
          pstmt.setString(1, ComboName.getSelectedItem().toString());
          .........
    if (ComboMethod.getSelectedItem()=="Java execute Method"){
      try{
          PreparedStatement pstmt = LogInFrame.con.prepareStatement(query);
          pstmt.setString(1, ComboName.getSelectedItem().toString());
          pstmt.execute();
          .........
    else if (ComboMethod.getSelectedItem()=="Java Callable Method")
      {
         CallableStatement cstmt = null;
         .........

      } catch (SQLException e) {
          msgDlg.setMessage("Error in CallableStatement!" + e.getMessage());
          msgDlg.setVisible(true);
      }
    }
A   try {
        if (!ShowFaculty(fimgBlob)){
            msgDlg.setMessage("No matched faculty image found!");
            msgDlg.setVisible(true);
        }
B     } catch (SQLException | IOException ex) {
          Logger.getLogger(FacultyFrame.class.getName()).log(Level.SEVERE, null, ex);
      }
  }
```

FIGURE 6.37 The new added code to the Select button Click event handler.

Let's have a closer look at the new added code to see how it performs.

A. A **try-catch** block pair is used for the faculty image-displaying operation. First, the user method **ShowFaculty()** is called with the selected faculty image, **fimgBlob**, as the argument to pick up and display the selected faculty image in the Canvas. This method should return a Boolean value to indicate whether it executes successfully. A **true** means that the method executed successfully; otherwise, a returned **false** means that the method failed, and that is displayed in our **MsgDialog**.
B. The **catch** block is used to monitor any possible SQLException or IOException during the execution of this user-defined method and to log them into a log file.

The final coding job for the FacultyFrame class is the **Back** button Click event handler. This code is very easy; the FacultyFrame object should be closed and disposed when the user clicks on this button, and control should be directed back to the SelectionFrame Form to allow the user to continue selecting other functions.

6.3.7.7 Develop the Code for the Back Button Click Event Handler

The coding process for this event handler is simple. The FacultyFrame Form window should be closed and removed from the screen when this button is clicked by the user. Open the **Back** button Click event handler and enter the code shown in Figure 6.38 into this event handler.

6.3.7.8 Build and Run the Project to Test Functions of the FacultyFrame Form

Now we can build and run our project to test the functionalities of most FrameForm classes, including the **LogInFrame** Form, **SelectionFrame** Form and **FacultyFrame** Form.

Click on the **Clean and Build Main Project** button on the toolbar to build our project, and click on the **Run Main Project** button from the toolbar to run our project. Select **OracleSelectFaculty-Package.LogInFrame** as the starting class for our project if a MessageBox appears, and click on the **OK** button to run our project.

Enter the correct username and password, such as **jhenry** and **test**, to the **LogInFrame** to complete the login process. Select the **Faculty Information** from the **SelectionFrame** Form window to open the **FacultyFrame** Form window. Select the default faculty member **Ying Bai** from the Faculty Name combo box and the **Java executeQuery Method** from the Query Method combo box, and click on the **Select** button to get detailed information for this selected faculty member.

Immediately, detailed information about the selected faculty member is displayed in seven text fields with the faculty image, which is shown in Figure 6.39. You can try other methods, such as **Java execute Method** or **Java Callable Method**, with any other faculty members to perform different queries to test the function of this form.

Click on the **Back** and the **Exit** buttons to terminate our project to finish this test. Next let's discuss how to query data from the **Course** Table in our sample database.

A completed project, **OracleSelectFaculty**, can be found in the **Class DB Projects\Chapter 6** folder in the **Students** folder on the CRC Press ftp site (refer to Figure 1.2 in Chapter 1).

```
private void BackButtonActionPerformed(java.awt.event.ActionEvent evt) {
      // TODO add your handling code here:
      this.setVisible(false);
      this.dispose();
}
```

FIGURE 6.38 The code for the Back button Click event handler.

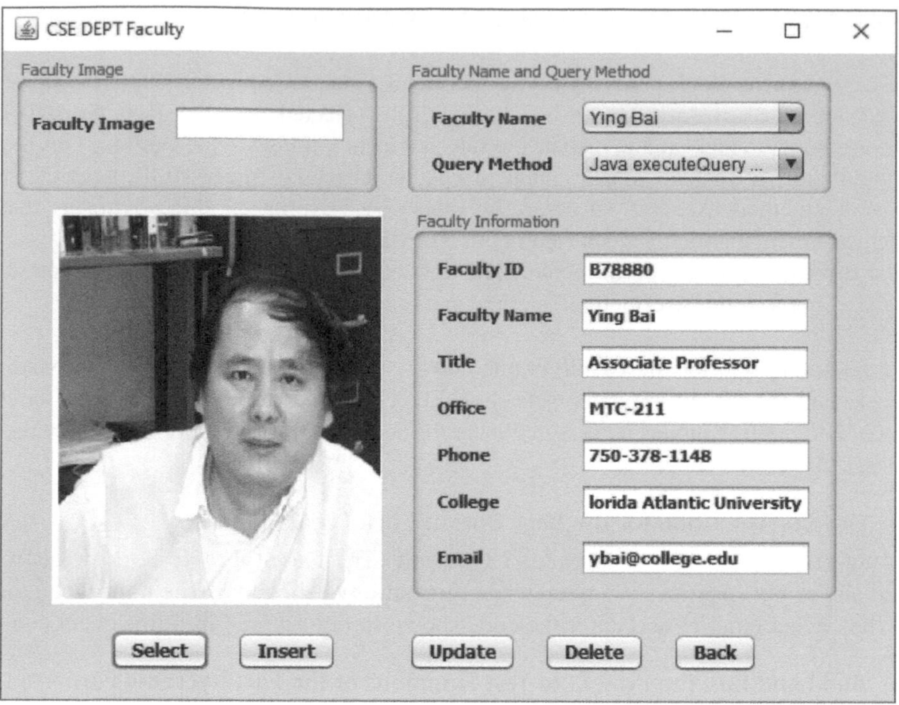

FIGURE 6.39 A run result of the project.

6.3.8 Perform the Data Query for the Course Table

The function of this CourseFrame Form is to allow users to get all courses taught by the selected faculty member and detailed information for each course. First, all courses, that is, all `course_id` values, taught by the selected faculty member from the Faculty Name combo box will be displayed in the `Course ID` List list box when the user clicks on the `Select` button. Second, detailed information for each course (`course_id`) selected from the Course ID List box will be displayed in six text fields as each `course_id` is clicked by the user.

Let's modify the project `OracleSelectFaculty` and make it our new project, `OracleSelectCourse`. Just right-click that project, and select `Copy` item. Then enter `OracleSelectCourse` in the Project Name box in the opened Copy Project wizard, and click on the `Copy` button.

Now open our new project, `OracleSelectCourse`, in the `Projects` window. In this section, only two buttons, `Select` and `Back`, are used for the `CourseFrame` Form to get course data, and other buttons will be used later for data-manipulating query actions.

The code development in this section can be divided into the following five parts:

1) Importing the necessary Java packages and building code for the constructor of the `CourseFrame` class to perform the initialization processes.
2) Building the Java package named `FacultyCourse` via Oracle SQL Developer.
3) Coding for the `Select` button Click event handler to perform a `CallableStatement` query to run a stored procedure to query data from the `Course` Table in our sample database.
4) Coding for the `CourseList` box to handle an event when a `course_id` in the CourseList box is selected to display the detailed information for that `course_id` in six text fields.
5) Coding for the `Back` button Click event handler to close the `CourseFrame` Form window and return control to the `SelectionFrame` Form.

```
   package OracleSelectFacultyPackage;
A  import java.sql.*;
   import javax.swing.*;
   public class CourseFrame extends javax.swing.JFrame {
B    MsgDialog msgDlg = new MsgDialog(new javax.swing.JFrame(), true);
     /** Creates new form CourseFrame */
     public CourseFrame() {
       initComponents();
       this.setLocationRelativeTo(null);
C      ComboMethod.addItem("Java Callable Method");
D      ComboName.addItem("Ying Bai");
       ComboName.addItem("Davis Bhalla");
       ComboName.addItem("Black Anderson");
       ComboName.addItem("Steve Johnson");
       ComboName.addItem("Jenney King");
       ComboName.addItem("Alice Brown");
       ComboName.addItem("Debby Angles");
       ComboName.addItem("Jeff Henry");
     }
```

FIGURE 6.40 The code for the constructor of the CourseFrame class.

6.3.8.1 Import Java Packages and Code for the CourseFrame Constructor

Open the Code Window of the **CourseFrame** class by clicking on the **Source** tab from the top of the window and add the code shown in Figure 6.40 into this source file.

Let's have a closer look at this piece of code to see how it works.

A. Two packages, **java.sql.*** and **javax.swing.***, are added into this file, since we need to use some JDBC API classes and interfaces that are located in these packages.
B. A class-level object, **msgDlg**, which is an instance of the JDialog class, is created, since we need to use it to display debug and exception information to track and monitor the run status of our project as it runs.
C. A query method is added into the **Query Method** combo box to enable users to perform a query with it. In this project, we only use one method, **Java Callable Method**.
D. Eight faculty members are also added into the **Faculty Name** combo box to allow users to select one of them to query all courses taught by the selected faculty member.

Now let's build our Java package, **FacultyCourse**, with the Oracle SQL Developer as we did in the last section for calling the **Faculty** Table.

6.3.8.2 Create an Oracle Package, FacultyCourse

When a faculty member has been selected from the Faculty Name combo box and the **Select** button is clicked by the user, all courses (**course _ id**) taught by the selected faculty member should be displayed in the Course ID List listbox. As we know, there is no **faculty _ name** column available in the **Course** Table; instead, the only connection between each course and the faculty member who teaches that course is the **faculty _ id**, which is a foreign key in the **Course** Table. Therefore, in order to get the **course _ id** that is taught by the selected faculty member, two queries are needed:

1) First, we need to perform a query to the **Faculty** Table to get the **faculty _ id** based on the selected faculty name.
2) Second, we need to perform another query to the **Course** Table to get all **course _ id** values based on the **faculty _ id** obtained from the first query.

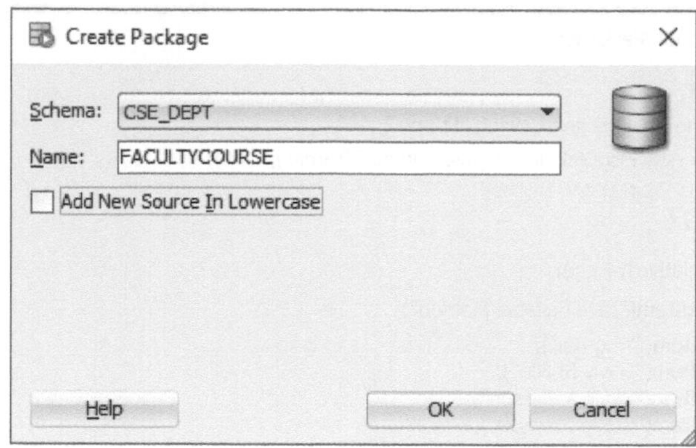

FIGURE 6.41 The finished new package wizard.

To save time and space, a good solution for these two queries is to combine both of them into a stored procedure. As you know, stored procedures are developed and built inside a database. The execution speed and efficiency of stored procedures can be significantly better than those of a normal query. In the JDBC API, a CallableStatement interface is used for this purpose.

As we discussed in the last section, compared with the Statement interface, the advantage of using a **PreparedStatement** interface is that it can perform a dynamic query with known or unknown dynamic parameters as inputs. Most of the time, those dynamic parameters are input parameters and can be defined as **IN** variables. However, you do not need to specify those parameters with an **IN** keyword when using a PreparedStatement interface.

The difference between the **PreparedStatement** and **CallableStatement** interfaces is: unlike the PreparedStatement interface, the CallableStatement interface has both input and output-parameters, which are indicated with **IN** and **OUT** keywords, respectively. In order to set up values for input parameters or get values for the output parameters, you have to use either a **setXXX()** method or a **getXXX()** method. However, the point is that before you can use any **getXXX()** method to pick up the values of output parameters, you must first register the output parameters to allow the **CallableStatement** interface to recognize them.

Just as we did in Section 6.3.7.5.9, open the Oracle SQL Developer and perform the following operations to create this package:

1) In the opened Oracle SQL Developer, click on the **XE** service under the **Recent** tab.
2) In the popup wizard, enter our password, **oracle _ 18c**, into the Password box, and click on the **OK** button to connect to our service and sample database.
3) Then expand the two folders **XE** and **Other Users** and our sample database folder, **CSE _ DEPT**.
4) Right-click on the **Packages** folder and select the **New Package** item.
5) In the opened Create Package wizard, enter the package name, **FACULTYCOURSE**, into the **Name** box, as shown in Figure 6.41. Click on the **OK** button.

Each package has two parts: the definition or specification part and the body part. First let's create the specification part by entering the code shown in Figure 6.42.

The prototype of the procedure **SelectFacultyCourse()** is declared in line 3. Two arguments are used for this procedure. The input parameter **facultyName** is indicated as an input by using the keyword **IN**, followed by the data type of **VARCHAR2**, which is equivalent to a String in Java. The output parameter is a cursor named **Faculty _ Course** followed by a keyword, **OUT**. Each PL/SQL statement must end with a semicolon, and this rule also applies to the **END** statement.

```
CREATE OR REPLACE PACKAGE FACULTYCOURSE AS
  TYPE CURSOR_TYPE IS REF CURSOR;
  procedure SelectFacultyCourse(facultyName IN VARCHAR2, Faculty_Course OUT CURSOR_TYPE);
END FACULTYCOURSE;
```

FIGURE 6.42 The definition code for the Oracle package FacultyCourse.

```
  CREATE OR REPLACE PACKAGE BODY FACULTYCOURSE AS
    procedure SelectFacultyCourse(facultyName IN VARCHAR2, Faculty_Course OUT CURSOR_TYPE) AS
A   facultyID VARCHAR2(10);
    BEGIN
B    SELECT faculty_id INTO facultyID FROM Faculty WHERE faculty_name = facultyName;
C    OPEN Faculty_Course FOR SELECT course_id FROM Course
     WHERE faculty_id = facultyID;
     NULL;
    END SelectFacultyCourse;
  END FACULTYCOURSE;
```

FIGURE 6.43 The code for the body part of the Oracle package FacultyCourse.

Click on the **Compile** button to compile this specification block. A successful compile message should be displayed in the Messages box at the bottom if it is completes successfully.

Next we need to create the body block for this package. Perform the following operations to create this body part:

1) Right-click on our new created package, **FACULTYCOURSE**, under the **Packages** folder in the left, and select the **Create Body** item to add a package body into this package.
2) In the opened Package Body wizard, enter the code that is highlighted in Figure 6.43.
3) Click on the drop-down arrow and select **Compile** to compile this package body. A **Compiled** message should be displayed in the Messages window if the compile is successful, as shown in Figure 6.44.
4) Your finished package, **FACULTYCOURSE**, is shown in Figure 6.44.

```
create or replace package FacultyInfo
AS
  TYPE CURSOR_TYPE IS REF CURSOR;
  procedure SelectFacultyInfo ( FacultyName IN VARCHAR2,
                                Faculty_Info OUT CURSOR_TYPE);
END;
```

Two queries are included in this stored procedure; the first one is to query a **faculty_id** from the **Faculty** Table based on the input **faculty_name**, and the second one is to query all **course_id** values from the **Course** Table based on the queried **faculty_id** from the first query. As we know, there is no **faculty_name** column available in the **Course** Table, and the only relationship between each **course_id** and the associated faculty member is **faculty_id**, which is a primary key in the **Faculty** Table but a foreign key in the **Course** Table. In order to get all **course_id** values related to a faculty member, we have to perform two queries from two Tables. The advantage of using a stored procedure is that we can combine these two queries into a single procedure to speed up this process.

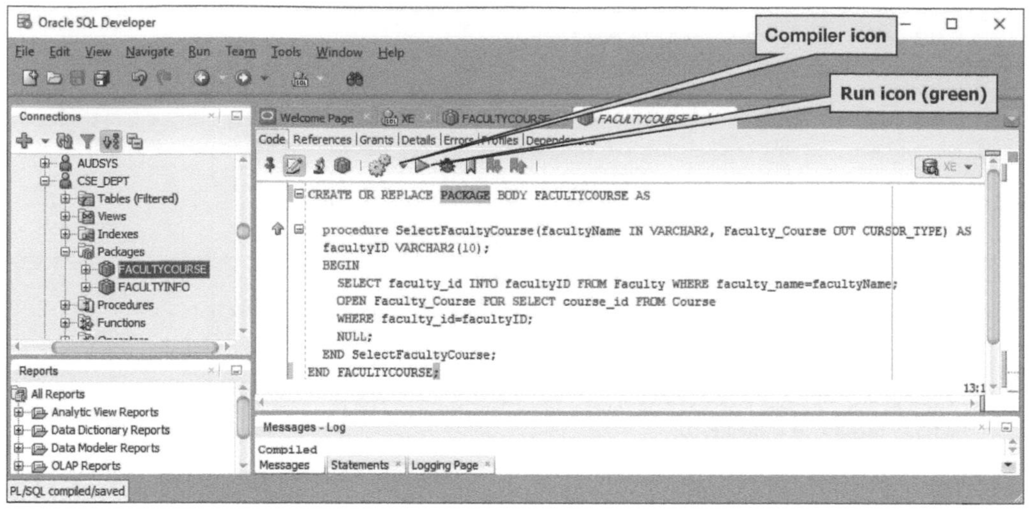

FIGURE 6.44 The completed Oracle FacultyCoursepackage (Copyrighted by Oracle and used with permission).

Let's have a closer look at this piece of code to see how it works (Figure 6.43).

A. A local variable, **facultyID**, which will work as an intermediate variable to hold the returned **faculty _ id** from the first query, is declared with a data type of **VARCHAR2**(10).
B. Starting from **BEGIN**, our first data query statement is generated. It is used to get the **faculty _ id** from the **Faculty** Table based on the input parameter **facultyName**, which is the first argument of this procedure. An **SELECT . . . INTO** statement is utilized to temporarily store the returned **faculty _ id** into the local variable **facultyID**.
C. The **OPEN Faculty _ Course FOR** command is used to assign the returned data columns from the second query to the cursor variable **Faculty _ Course**. Starting from this line, the second query is declared, and it is to get all **course _ id** values taught by the selected faculty member from the **Course** Table based on the local variable's value, **facultyID**, which is obtained from the first query previously. The queried results are assigned to the cursor variable **Faculty _ Course**.

Now let's run our package by clicking the **Run** button (green arrow), as shown in Figure 6.44. A Run PL/SQL wizard is displayed, as shown in Figure 6.45.

Enter the desired faculty name, such as **Ying Bai**, into the **Input Value** box, as shown in Figure 6.45, and click on the **OK** button to run this package. To check the run result, click on the **Output Variables** tab on the bottom. One can find that all courses taught by this faculty member are retrieved and displayed in the **Output Variables—Log** wizard, as shown in Figure 6.46.

The development of our Oracle package is complete, and now we can close Oracle SQL Developer and return to our Java application program to call this package to perform our course query to our **Course** Table.

6.3.8.3 Develop the Code to Perform the CallableStatement Query

Open the **Select** button click event handler in the CourseFrame Form window, and add the code shown in Figure 6.47 to this event handler.

Let's have a closer look at this piece of modified code to see how it works.

A. An **if** selection structure is used to check whether the query method is the **Java Callable Method**. If it is, a local CallableStatement object, **cstmt**, is generated.

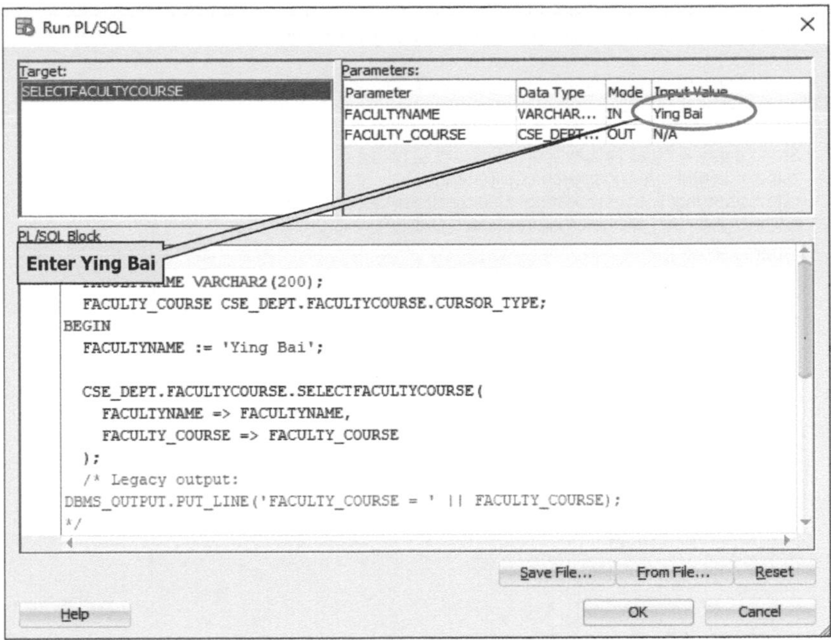

FIGURE 6.45 The opened Run PL/SQL wizard (Copyrighted by Oracle and used with permission).

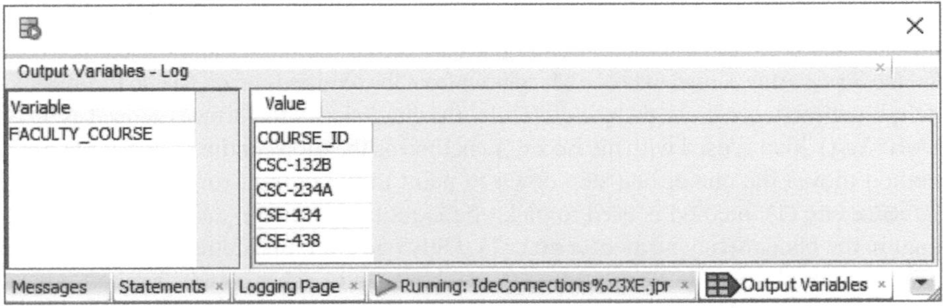

FIGURE 6.46 The run result for our FacultyCourse package (Copyrighted by Oracle and used with permission).

B. A **try-catch** block with SQL92 syntax is used to call the Oracle package, **Faculty Course**, we built in the last section. The point is that the stored procedure **Select FacultyCourse()** must be prefixed with the package name when this procedure is called. Two positional parameters are involved in this call. The first one is an input, **faculty _ name**, and the second is an output, a cursor in which all **course _ id** values are stored and returned.
C. The first dynamic positional parameter, **faculty _ name**, which is selected by the user from the Faculty Name combo box, is initialized with a system method, **setString()**.
D. The second parameter, which is an output cursor, is registered by calling the **registerOut-Parameter()** method. The data type of this parameter is a cursor, and it must be clearly indicated with an Oracle extension Java type, **oracle.jdbc.OracleTypes.CURSOR**.
E. The CallableStatement method is executed by calling the **execute()** method to access our Oracle package and stored procedure to perform this course data query.
F. The **getObject()** method is used to pick up the returned result that is stored in a returned cursor when this CallableStatement is done and assign it to a ResultSet object.

```
  private void SelectButtonActionPerformed(java.awt.event.ActionEvent evt) {
      // TODO add your handling code here:
A     if (ComboMethod.getSelectedItem()=="Java Callable Method"){
        CallableStatement cstmt;
        try{
B         String query = "{call FacultyCourse.SelectFacultyCourse(?, ?)}";
          cstmt = LogInFrame.con.prepareCall(query);
C         cstmt.setString(1, ComboName.getSelectedItem().toString());
D         cstmt.registerOutParameter(2, oracle.jdbc.OracleTypes.CURSOR);
E         cstmt.execute();
F         ResultSet rs = (ResultSet)cstmt.getObject(2);
G         int index = 0;
          String[] cResult = new String[9];
H         while (rs.next()){
            cResult[index] = rs.getString(1);
            index++;
          }
I         CourseList.setListData(cResult);
        }
J       catch (SQLException e){
          msgDlg.setMessage("Error in CallableStatement! " + e.getMessage());
          msgDlg.setVisible(true);
        }
      }
  }
```

FIGURE 6.47 The added code for the Java Callable Method.

G. A local integer variable, **index**, and a blank String array, **cResult[]**, are created. The first one is used as a loop number for a **while()** loop to be executed later to pick up each returned column, and the String array is used to hold each column from the returned cursor. Due to the upperbound of the number of courses taught by each faculty, the dimension of this array is defined as 9.
H. A **while()** loop is used with the **next()** method as the loop condition. First, the **next()** method moves the cursor one step down to point to the current row or a valid row. The **getString(1)** method is used to pick up the returned column and assign it to one element in the blank String array **cResult[]**. Only one column is returned (this is indicated by the index of 1 in the **getString()** method), and each **next()** method is used to move and point to the next row until all rows have been selected and picked up.
I. All collected **course_id** values are assigned to the Course ID List box by calling the method **setListData()**, and all of them are displayed there.
J. The **catch** block is used to monitor and display any possible exception during the project's run.

Before we can build and run this project to test the functionality of the CallableStatement interface, we need to do one more thing, which is to develop code for the event handler **CourseListValueChanged()** to display detailed information for each selected **course_id** from the Course ID List box.

Open the Design View of the CourseFrame Form window by clicking on the **Design** tab at the top of the window, and then right-click on the Course ID List box and select the item **Events|ListSelection|valueChanged** to open this event handler. Enter the code shown in Figure 6.48 into this event handler.

Let's have a closer look at this piece of code to see how it works.

A. A text field array, **c_field**, is created here, since we need to assign the queried detailed course information to six text fields to display it; therefore, it is easy to use an array to do that assignment.

```
  private void CourseListValueChanged(javax.swing.event.ListSelectionEvent evt) {
      // TODO add your handling code here:
A     JTextField[] c_field = {CourseIDField, CourseField, ScheduleField, ClassRoomField, CreditsField, EnrollField};
B     if(!CourseList.getValueIsAdjusting() ){
        String courseid = (String)CourseList.getSelectedValue();
C       if (courseid != null){
            String cQuery = "SELECT course_id, course, schedule, classroom, credit, enrollment FROM Course " +
                            "WHERE course_id = ?";
D       try{
            PreparedStatement pstmt = LogInFrame.con.prepareStatement(cQuery);
E           pstmt.setString(1, courseid);
F           ResultSet rs = pstmt.executeQuery();
G           ResultSetMetaData rsmd = rs.getMetaData();
H           while (rs.next()){
                for (int index =1; index <=rsmd.getColumnCount(); index++) {
                    c_field[index - 1].setText(rs.getString(index));
                }
            }
        }
I        catch (SQLException e) {
            msgDlg.setMessage("Error in Statement!" + e.getMessage());
            msgDlg.setVisible(true);
        }
      }
    }
  }
```

FIGURE 6.48 The code for the CourseListValueChanged() event handler.

B. Since the **JList** component belongs to the **javax.swing** package, not the **java.awt** package, any click on an entry in the **CourseList** box causes the **itemStateChanged**() method to fire twice, once when the mouse button is pressed, and once again when it is released.

   Therefore, the selected **course _ id** will appear twice when it is selected. To prevent this from occurring, the **getValueIsAdjusting()** method is used to make sure that no item is allowed to be displayed twice. Then the selected **course _ id** is assigned to a local String variable, **courseid**, by calling the **getSelectedValue()** method of the **CourseList** Box class.
C. Before we can proceed to the query operation, first we need to confirm that the selected **courseid** is not a null value. A null value would be returned if the user did not select any **course _ id** from the **CourseList** box, that is, if the user just clicked on the **Select** button to try to find all **course _ id** values taught by other faculty members. Even if the user only clicked on the **Select** button without entering any **course _ id** in the **CourseList** box, the system still considers that a null **course _ id** has been selected, and thus a null value will be returned. To avoid that situation, an **if** selection structure is used to make sure that no null value has been returned from the **CourseList** box. The course query string is created if no null value has been returned.
D. A **try-catch** block is used to perform the PreparedStatement query operation. First, a PreparedStatement object is created with the query string as the argument.
E. The **setString()** method is executed to use the real query criterion, **courseid**, to replace the nominal position parameter.
F. The dynamic query is actually executed by calling the **executeQuery()** method, and the query result is returned and stored in a ResultSet object.
G. The **getMetaData()** method is called to return the detailed information about the returned ResultSet object, including the column number, column name and data type.

```
private void BackButtonActionPerformed(java.awt.event.ActionEvent evt) {
        // TODO add your handling code here:
        this.setVisible(false);
        this.dispose();
}
```

FIGURE 6.49 The code for the Back button Click event handler.

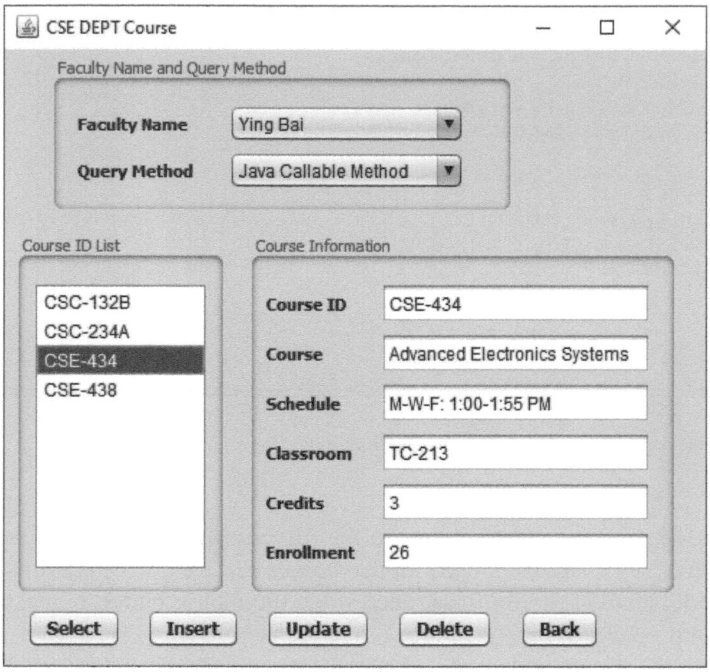

CSE DEPT Course

Faculty Name and Query Method

Faculty Name	Ying Bai
Query Method	Java Callable Method

Course ID List: CSC-132B, CSC-234A, CSE-434, CSE-438

Course Information

Course ID	CSE-434
Course	Advanced Electronics Systems
Schedule	M-W-F: 1:00-1:55 PM
Classroom	TC-213
Credits	3
Enrollment	26

Select Insert Update Delete Back

FIGURE 6.50 The run result of the CourseFrame Form window.

H. **while()** and **for()** loops are used to retrieve the queried columns from the ResultSet object and assign them one by one to the associated Text Field to display them.

I. The **catch** block is used to track the run status of this piece of code. An error message will be displayed if any exception occurs.

The final coding process is to build the code for the **Back** button event handler. The function of this event handler is to close the current CourseFrame Form window and direct control back to the SelectFrame Form window to enable users to select a desired item to perform another data query action. Open that event handler and enter the code shown in Figure 6.49 into it.

Now we can build and run our project to test its function. As the project runs, enter an appropriate username and password, such as **jhenry** and **test**, to the LogInFrame Form to finish the login process. Then select the Course Information from the SelectionFrame Form to open the CourseFrame Form window, as shown in Figure 6.50.

Select a desired faculty member, such as **Ying Bai**, from the Faculty Name combo box, and click on the Select button to try to retrieve all courses (**course _ id**) taught by that faculty member. All four courses (**course _ id**) are fetched and displayed in the CourseList box. Click on any **course _ id** from that CourseList box, and the details for that course are displayed in six TextFields on the right, as shown in Figure 6.50.

One can try to select other faculty members to do the related data query to test the function of this Form window. Click on the **Back** and **Exit** buttons to terminate our project when you are done.

A completed project, **OracleSelectCourse**, can be found in the folder **Class DB Projects\Chapter 6** in the **Students** folder on the CRC Press ftp site (refer to Figure 1.2 in Chapter 1).

Next we'll discuss how to perform data queries to our **Student** Table via the Java RowSet method.

6.3.9 Query Data from the Student Table Using the Java RowSet Object

A RowSet object is one of the JavaBeans components with multiple support from JavaBeans, and it is a new feature in the **java.sql** package. By using the RowSet object, a database query can be performed automatically with the data source connection and query statement creation.

In this section, we will show readers how to use this new feature to reduce the code load and improve the efficiency of the data query with the help of this RowSet object.

6.3.9.1 Introduction to Java RowSet Object

The JDBC 4.0 API includes many new features in the java.sql package as well as the new Standard Extension package, **javax.sql**. This new JDBC API moves Java applications into the world of heavy-duty database computing. One of the important features is the RowSet object.

A RowSet object contains a set of rows from a result set or some other source of tabular data, like a file or spreadsheet. Because a RowSet object follows the JavaBeans model for properties and event notification, it is a JavaBeans component that can be combined with other components in an application. As it is compatible with other Beans, application developers can use a development tool to create a RowSet object and set its properties.

RowSets may have many different implementations to fill different needs. These implementations fall into two broad categories, connected and disconnected:

1) A connected RowSet is equivalent to a ResultSet, and it maintains a connection to a data source as long as the RowSet is in use.
2) A disconnected RowSet works as a DataSet, and it can connect to a data source to perform data updates periodically. Most of the time, it is disconnected from the data source and uses a mapping memory space as a mapped database.

While a RowSet is disconnected, it does not need a JDBC driver or the full JDBC API, so its footprint is very small. Thus, a RowSet is an ideal format for sending data over a network to a thin client.

Because it is not continually connected to its data source, a disconnected RowSet stores its data in memory. It needs to maintain metadata about the columns it contains and information about its internal state. It also needs a facility for making connections, for executing commands and for reading and writing data to and from the data source. A connected RowSet, by contrast, opens a connection and keeps it open for as long as the RowSet is being used.

To make writing an implementation easier, the Java Software division of Oracle, Inc., plans to provide reference implementations for five different styles of RowSets. The following list of planned implementations gives you an idea of some of the possibilities.

1) A CachedRowSet class—a disconnected RowSet that caches its data in memory; not suiTable for very large data sets but an ideal way to provide thin Java clients, such as a personal digital assistant or network computer, with tabular data.
2) A JDBCRowSet class—a connected RowSet that serves mainly as a thin wrapper around a ResultSet object to make a JDBC driver look like a JavaBeans component.
3) A WebRowSet class—a connected RowSet that uses the HTTP protocol internally to talk to a Java Servlet that provides data access; used to make it possible for thin web clients to retrieve and possibly update a set of rows.

4) A FilteredRowSet is an extension to WebRowSet that provides programmatic support for filtering its content. This enables you to avoid the overhead of supplying a query and the processing involved. The SQL implementation of FilteredRowSet is **`javax.sql.rowset.FilteredRowSet`**. The Oracle implementation of FilteredRowSet is **`oracle.jdbc.rowset.OracleFilteredRowSet`**. The OracleFilteredRowSet class in the **`ojdbc14.jar`** file implements the standard JSR-114 interface javax.sql.rowset.FilteredRowSet.
5) A JoinRowSet is another extension to WebRowSet that consists of related data from different RowSets. There is no standard way to establish a SQL **`JOIN`** between disconnected RowSets without connecting to the data source. A JoinRowSet addresses this issue. The SQL implementation of JoinRowSet is the **`javax.sql.rowset.JoinRowSet`** class. The Oracle implementation of JoinRowSet is the **`oracle.jdbc.rowset`**. OracleJoinRowSet class. This class, which is in the **`ojdbc14.jar`** file, implements the standard JSR-114 interface **`javax.sql.rowset.JoinRowSet`**. Any number of RowSet objects, which implement the Joinable interface, can be added to a JoinRowSet object, provided they can be related in a SQL **`JOIN`**. All five types of RowSet support the Joinable interface. The Joinable interface provides methods for specifying the columns based on which the **`JOIN`** will be performed, that is, the match columns.

Next, let's have a closer look at the operational sequence for the RowSet object.

6.3.9.2 The Operational Procedure of Using the JDBC RowSet Object

A compliant JDBC RowSet implementation must implement one or more standard interfaces specified in this package and may extend the BaseRowSet abstract class. For example, a CachedRowSet implementation must implement the CachedRowSet interface and extend the BaseRowSet abstract class. The BaseRowSet class provides the standard architecture on which all RowSet implementations should be built, regardless of whether the RowSet objects exist in a connected or disconnected environment. The BaseRowSet abstract class provides any RowSet implementation with its base functionality, including property manipulation and event notification, that is fully compliant with JavaBeans component requirements. As an example, all implementations provided in the reference implementations (contained in the **`com.sun.rowset`** package) use the BaseRowSet class as a basis for their implementations.

TABLE 6.6
Features of the BaseRowSet Abstract Class

Feature	Details
Properties	Provides standard JavaBeans property manipulation mechanisms to allow applications to get and set RowSet command and property values. Refer to the documentation of the javax.sql.RowSet interface (available in the JDBC 3.0 specification) for more details on the standard RowSet properties.
Event notification	Provides standard JavaBeans event notifications to registered event listeners. Refer to the documentation of javax.sql.RowSetEvent interface (available in the JDBC 3.0 specification) for more details on how to register and handle standard RowSet events generated by compliant implementations.
Setters for a RowSet object's command	Provides a complete set of setter methods for setting RowSet command parameters.
Streams	Provides fields for storing of stream instances in addition to providing a set of constants for stream type designation.

Table 6.6 illustrates the features that the BaseRowSet abstract class provides.

In this application, we will concentrate on the implementation of the CachedRowSet component, since we prefer to use a disconnected RowSet.

Generally, the operational procedure of using a RowSet object to query data can be divided into the following four steps:

1) Set up and conFigure a RowSet object.
2) Register the RowSet Listeners.
3) Set input and output parameters for the query command.
4) Traverse through the result rows from the ResultSet.

The first step is to set up and conFigure the static or dynamic properties of a RowSet object, such as the connection **`url`**, username, password and run command, to allow the RowSet object to connect to the data source, pass user parameters into the data source and perform data queries.

The second step allows users to register different Listeners for the RowSet object with different event sources. The RowSet feature supports registering multiple listeners with the RowSet object. Listeners can be registered using the **`addRowSetListener()`** method and unregistered through the **`removeRowSetListener()`** method. A listener can implement the **`javax.sql.RowSetListener`** interface to register itself as the RowSet listener. Three types of events are supported by the RowSet interface:

1) **`cursorMoved event`**: Generated whenever there is a cursor movement, which occurs when the **`next()`** or **`previous()`** method is called.
2) **`rowChanged event`**: Generated when a new row is inserted, updated or deleted from the row set.
3) **`rowsetChanged event`**: Generated when the whole row set is created or changed.

In our applications, the Apache NetBeans IDE 12 is used, and the event-listener model has been set up by NetBeans IDE. So we can skip this step.

Step 3 allows users to set up all static or dynamic parameters for the query statement of the RowSet object. Depending on the data type of the parameters used in the query statement, suiTable **`setXXX()`** method should used to perform this parameter setup process.

The fourth step is used to retrieve each row from the ResultSet object.

A point to be noted when using any RowSet object to perform data query is that most RowSet classes are abstract classes, and they cannot be instantiated directly. One needs to use a suiTable RowSet Implementation class to create a RowSet implementation object to perform a data query. Also, a RowSet can be implemented in two ways: direct implementation and distributed implementation via a ResultSet. We will use the first way in our project.

Let's modify the project **`OracleSelectCourse`** and make it our new project, **`OracleSelectStudent`**. Just right-click that project, and select **Copy** item. Then enter **`OracleSelectStudent`** into the Project Name box in the opened Copy Project wizard, and click on the **Copy** button.

6.3.9.3 Coding for the Constructor of the StudentFrame Class

Now open our new project, **`OracleSelectStudent`**, and the Code Window of the **`StudentFrame`** class, and enter the code shown in Figure 6.51 in the top of this window and the constructor of this class. Let's have a closer look at this piece of code to see how it works.

A. Ten useful Java packages are added first, since we need to utilize some classes defined in these packages. The first package, **`java.sql.*`**, provides all classes and interfaces used in JDBC API for SQL Server expressions. The next two packages contain all related classes and interfaces used for the CachedRowSet component and CachedRowSet Implementation

```
  package OracleSelectFacultyPackage;
A import java.sql.*;
  import javax.sql.rowset.*;
  import java.util.logging.Level;
  import java.util.logging.Logger;
  import java.awt.Graphics;
  import java.awt.Image;
  import java.awt.MediaTracker;
  import java.io.IOException;
  import java.io.FileNotFoundException;
  import java.io.FileOutputStream;
  public class StudentFrame extends javax.swing.JFrame {
B    MsgDialog msgDlg = new MsgDialog(new javax.swing.JFrame(), true);
    /** Creates new form StudentFrame */
     public StudentFrame() {
       initComponents();
       this.setLocationRelativeTo(null);
C      ComboMethod.addItem("CachedRowSet Method");
D      ComboName.addItem("Tom Erica");
       ComboName.addItem("Ashly Jade");
       ComboName.addItem("Holes Smith");
       ComboName.addItem("Andrew Woods");
       ComboName.addItem("Blue Valley");
  }
```

FIGURE 6.51 The code for the constructor of the StudentFrame class.

classes. As we mentioned, the CachedRowSet is an abstract class, and we have to use its implementation class to perform any data query.

B. One class-level variable is declared here, since we need to use it in our whole class. The variable **msgDlg** is used to track and display any debug and warning information if any error is encountered during our project's run.
C. The query method is added into the Query Method combo box. In this application, we only use one method, **CachedRowSet Method**.
D. Five students' names are added into the Student Name combo box.

Next let's Figure out the code for the **Select** button Click event handler. When this button is clicked, detailed information about the selected student should be displayed in both the seven text fields and the Course Selected Listbox.

6.3.9.4 Coding for the Select Button Event Handler to Query Data Using the CachedRowSet

Open this event handler and enter the code shown in Figure 6.52 into this handler. Let's have a closer look at this new added piece of code to see how it works.

A. Two local objects, **simgBlob** and **rowSet**, are declared first; the first one is used to hold the retrieved student image, and the second is used to create a CachedRowSet object.
B. Then a new **CachedRowSet** object is created with the **RowSetFactory** class, **newFactory()**, which is created by a **RowSetProvider**. One point to be noted is that the old syntax used to create this CachedRowSet object, **CachedRowSet rowSet = new Cached RowSetImpl();**, is no longer available after JDBC 9.0. A **try-catch** block is used for this creation.
C. As we know, there is no **student _ name** column available in the **StudentCourse** Table, and the only relationship between a student and a course taken by that student is the **student _ id**, which is a primary key in the **Student** Table but a foreign key in the

```
  private void SelectButtonActionPerformed(java.awt.event.ActionEvent evt) {
A       Blob simgBlob = null;
        CachedRowSet rowSet = null;
B       try{
          rowSet = RowSetProvider.newFactory().createCachedRowSet();
        }catch (SQLException ex) {
          Logger.getLogger(StudentFrame.class.getName()).log(java.util.logging.Level.SEVERE, null, ex); }
C       String strStudent = "SELECT student_id, student_name, gpa, credits, major, schoolYear, email, simage " +
                            "FROM Student  WHERE student_name = ?";
D       String strStudentCourse = "SELECT course_id FROM StudentCourse WHERE student_id = ?";
E       if (ComboMethod.getSelectedItem()== "CachedRowSet Method"){
          try{
            String url = "jdbc:oracle:thin:@localhost:1521:XE";
            rowSet.setUrl(url);
            rowSet.setUsername("CSE_DEPT");
            rowSet.setPassword("oracle_18c");
            rowSet.setCommand(strStudent);
F           rowSet.setString(1, ComboName.getSelectedItem().toString());
G           rowSet.execute();
H           while (rowSet.next()){
              StudentIDField.setText(rowSet.getString(1));
              StudentNameField.setText(rowSet.getString(2));
              GPAField.setText(Float.toString(rowSet.getFloat(3)));
              CreditsField.setText(Integer.toString(rowSet.getInt(4)));
              MajorField.setText(rowSet.getString(5));
              SchoolYearField.setText(rowSet.getString(6));
              EmailField.setText(rowSet.getString(7));
            } // end while
I           rowSet.setCommand(strStudentCourse);
            rowSet.setString(1, StudentIDField.getText());
J           rowSet.execute();
K           int index = 0;
            String Result[] = new String[9];
L           while (rowSet.next()){
              String sResult = rowSet.getString(1);
              Result[index] = sResult;
              index++;
            }
M           CourseList.setListData(Result);
N           rowSet.close();
O           PreparedStatement pstmt = LogInFrame.con.prepareStatement(strStudent);
            pstmt.setString(1, ComboName.getSelectedItem().toString());
            ResultSet rs = pstmt.executeQuery();
P           while(rs.next()) simgBlob = rs.getBlob("simage");
          }
Q         catch(SQLException e){
            msgDlg.setMessage("RowSet is wrong!" + e.getMessage());
            msgDlg.setVisible(true);
            System.exit( 1 );
          }
        }
R       try {
          if (!ShowStudent(simgBlob)){
            msgDlg.setMessage("No matched student image found!");
            msgDlg.setVisible(true);
          }
S       } catch (SQLException | IOException ex) {
          Logger.getLogger(FacultyFrame.class.getName()).log(Level.SEVERE, null, ex);
      }
  }
```

FIGURE 6.52 The code for the Select button Click event handler.

StudentCourse Table. In order to pick up all courses taken by the selected student, we need to perform two queries; first, we need to perform a query to the **Student** Table to get a **student _ id** based on the selected **student _ name**, and then we can perform another query to the **StudentCourse** Table based on the **student _ id** to get all courses taken by the selected student. The first query string, **strStudent**, is created here with a positional parameter, **student _ name**.

D. The second query string, **strStudentCourse**, is also created, with another positional parameter, **student _ id**.

E. If the user selectsthe CachedRowSet Method, a **try-catch** block is used to perform this query using the CachedRowSet implementation component. First, a database connection with parameters, such as **url**, **username** and **password**, isset up since we are using a direct implementation with a direct connection to our sample database. The **setCommand()** method is used to create an execuTable command with the first query string, **strStudent**, as the argument.

F. The **setString()** method is used to set up the real value for the positional parameter, **student _ name**, which is obtained from the Student Name combo box, **ComboName**.

G. The query is then executed by calling the **execute()** method to perform the first query using the CachedRowSet instance.

H. A **while()** loop is used to repeatedly pick up all seven pieces of information related to the selected student. The **next()** method works as the loop condition, and it returns a **true** as long as a valid row can be found from the returned data by the execution of the CachedRowSet object. The result of running the**next()** method is to move the cursor from the initial position to the first row in the returned data stored in the RowSet. In fact, only one row is returned and stored in the CachedRowSet object for the first query, and a sequence of **getXXX()** methods is used to pick up each column from the RowSet and assign each of them to the associated text field to be display on the StudentFrame Form.

I. To execute the second query, the **setCommand()** method is called again to create an execuTable Command object with the second query string as the argument. Then the **setString()** method is called to set up the positional parameter, **student _ id**, for the second query statement. The actual value for this parameter can be obtained from the Student ID text field, and it is retrieved and filled by the first query.

J. The query is executed by calling the **execute()** method to perform the second query using the CachedRowSet instance.

K. In order to pick up the second query result, which contains multiple rows with one column, we need to declare a local integer variable, **index**, and a String array, **Result[]**, and initialize them. This step is necessary; otherwise, a **NullPointer** exception may be encountered if this array has not been initialized when the project runs later.

L. A **while()** loop is used with the **next()** method as the loop condition. Each time the **next()** method is executed, the cursor in the CachedRowSet object is moved down one step to point to the next returned row. The **getString()** method is used to pick up that row and assign it to the local String variable, **sResult**, and, furthermore, to the String array **Result[]**. The input number used in the **getString()** method indicates the current column's number (only one column is collected), and this process will be continued until all rows have been collected and assigned to the **Result[]** array.

M. All courses, that is, all **course _ id** values, are collected and stored in the **Result[]** array and assigned to the Course Selected Listbox to be displayed in there. The **setListData()** method is a very useful method, and the argument of this method must be an array when this method is executed.

N. The CachedRowSet object must be closed when it has finished its mission. A **close()** method is used to perform this job.

O. To retrieve the student's image, we still need to use the ResultSet object, since the CachedRowSet cannot get any **Blob** from a database; it only can retrieve an Object via the **getObject()** method. An issue is that this Object data type cannot be converted to a Blob type, so we cannot use the CachedRowSet to directly get a Blob. For that purpose, a ResultSet object, **rs**, is generated, and the first query is executed again to pick up all eight pieces of a student's information.

P. A **while()** loop is executed to pick up the selected student's image and assign it to our local Blob variable, **simgBlob**, which will be used later by the **ShowStudent()** method.

Q. The **catch** block is used to collect any possible exception and display it if it did occur.

R. Another **try-catch** block is used to call our user-defined method, **ShowStudent()**, whose code will be built later, to display the selected student's image in the Canvas in our StudentFrame Form.

S. Another **catch** block is used to collect any possible exceptions and display them if they did occur.

Next let's build a user-defined method to display a student picture for the selected student.

6.3.9.5 Display a Student Picture for the Selected Student

As we did for the FacultyFrame Form class, we can display a student picture as a part of the student information in the Canvas component. The code is identical to that in our user-defined method, **ShowFaculty()**, in Section 6.3.7.6.2; refer to that section to get more detailed information about this piece of code. Figure 6.53 shows the detailed code for this method. Only one modification is made for this method, which is to change **fimgName** to **simgName**, as shown in the highlighted code in lines B, C and F in Figure 6.53.

```
  private boolean ShowStudent(Blob bimg) throws SQLException, IOException{
A       Image img;
        int imgId = 1, timeout = 1000;
        FileOutputStream imgOutputStream = null;
        MediaTracker tracker = new MediaTracker(this);
B       String imgPath = System.getProperty("user.dir");
        String simgName = ComboName.getSelectedItem().toString() + ".jpg";
C       try {
              imgOutputStream = new FileOutputStream(imgPath + "/" + simgName);
           }catch (FileNotFoundException ex) {
                 Logger.getLogger(StudentFrame.class.getName()).log(Level.SEVERE, null, ex);
        }
D       imgOutputStream.write(bimg.getBytes(1, (int)bimg.length()));
E       imgOutputStream.close();
F       img = this.getToolkit().getImage(simgName);
        Graphics g = ImageCanvas.getGraphics();
G       tracker.addImage(img, imgId);
H       try{
           if(!tracker.waitForID(imgId, timeout)){
              msgDlg.setMessage("Failed to load image");
              msgDlg.setVisible(true);
              return false;
           }
I       }catch(InterruptedException e){
           msgDlg.setMessage(e.toString());
           msgDlg.setVisible(true);
           return false;
        }
J       g.drawImage(img, 0, 0, ImageCanvas.getWidth(), ImageCanvas.getHeight(), this);
        return true;
  }
```

FIGURE 6.53 The code for the ShowStudent() method.

```
private void BackButtonActionPerformed(java.awt.event.ActionEvent evt) {
    // TODO add your handling code here:
    this.setVisible(false);
    this.dispose();
}
```

FIGURE 6.54 The code for the Back button Click event handler.

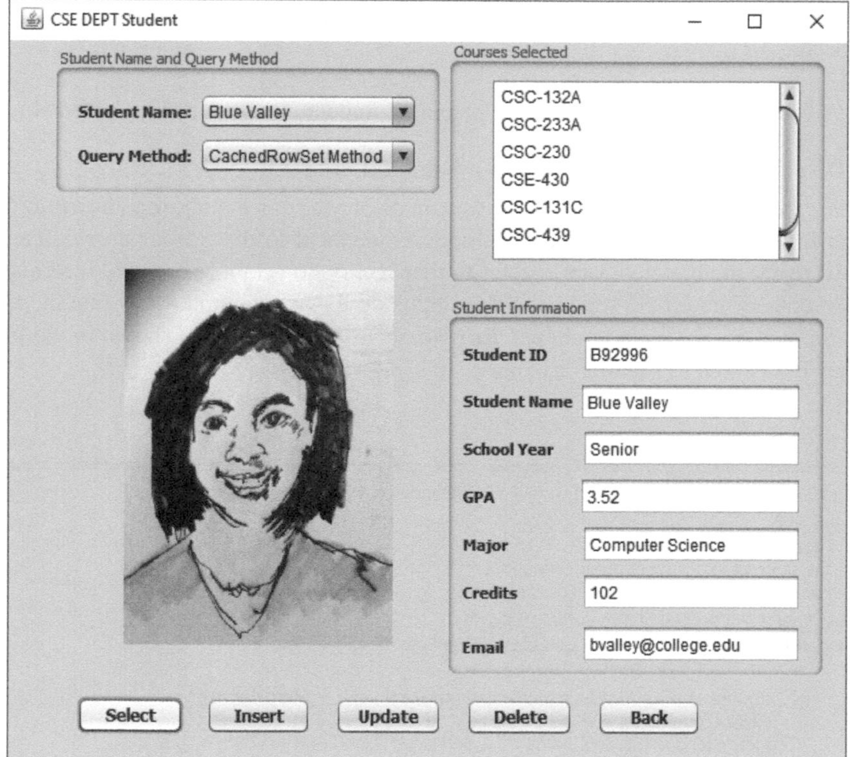

FIGURE 6.55 A running sample of the StudentFrame Form window.

The final coding process is to build the code for the `Back` button event handler. The function of this event handler is to close the current StudentFrame Form window and direct control back to the SelectFrame Form window to enable users to select a desired item to perform another data query action.

Open that event handler and enter the code shown in Figure 6.54 into it. Due to the simplicity of this piece of code, no explanation is given for it.

At this point, we have finished the code development for the StudentFrame Form class. Now let's build and run our project. Click on the `Clean and Build Main Project` button from the toolbar to build the project. Then click on the `Run Project` button (green arrow button) on the tool bar to run the project.

Complete the login process by entering `jhenry` and `test` into the Username and Password box, respectively, and select the `Student Information` item from the Selection combo box to open the StudentFrame Form, as shown in Figure 6.55.

Select a desired student from the Student Name combo box, and then click on the **Select** button to try to retrieve all pieces of information related to the selected student. A sample run result is shown in Figure 6.55.

Click on the **Back** button to return to the **SelectionFrame** Form to allow users to perform other queries from other Forms, or click on the **Exit** button to terminate the project.

A complete project, **OracleSelectStudent**, can be found in the folder **Class DB Projects\Chapter 6** that is located in the **Students** folder at the CRC Press ftp site (see Figure 1.2 in Chapter 1).

6.4 CHAPTER SUMMARY

A popular Java database programming method, the runtime object method, is discussed in detail in this chapter.

This method is discussed with a real sample project, **OracleSelectFaculty**. With a lot of code development and dynamic parameter setups, some advanced and complicated techniques in Java database programming are discussed and analyzed, which include:

- How to perform a dynamic data query using standard JDBC drivers, such as
  1) Load and register database drivers
  2) Connect to databases and drivers
  3) Create and manage a PreparedStatement object to perform a dynamic query
  4) Use a ResultSet object to pick up the queried result
  5) Query data using the JDBC MetaData interface
  6) The ParameterMetaData interface
  7) Use the DatabaseMetaData interface
  8) Use the ResultSetMetaData interface
  9) Query data using the CallableStatement method
- Query data using the Java RowSet object

The key novel technique discussed in this part is the interface between an Oracle package with a stored procedure and a Java CallableStatement interface. Usually, there is no mapped partner for the cursor data type in the JDBC data type. In other words, a cursor applied in the Oracle stored procedure cannot be returned to a Java database application, since the cursor cannot be mapped to a valid JDBC data type. In order to solve that problem, we developed a special Oracle stored procedure to perform the conversion between a VARCHAR string and a cursor inside the Oracle stored procedure and return a VARCHAR string to the Java database application.

Very detailed discussions of how to build Oracle packages and Oracle stored procedures are provided in this chapter to give readers a clear global picture of how to build an interface between a CallableStatement interface and a database stored procedure. One of the most popular databases, Oracle Database 18c XE, is used in the entire chapter.

HOMEWORK

I. True/False Selections

_______1. A static query is called a Named Query, and it is defined statically with the help of annotation or XML before the entity class is created.

_______2. Dynamic queries belong to queries in which the query strings are provided at runtime or created dynamically. All calls of EntityManager.createQuery(queryString) are actually creating dynamic query objects.

_______3. The **java.awt** package contains all basic and fundamental graphic user interface components. However, the javax.swing package contains extensions of

java.awt, which means that all components in the **javax.swing** package have been built in model-view-controllermode.

_______4. Only one method can be used to load and register a JDBC Driver during a project runs, which is to use the **Class.forName**() method.

_______5. When using the **getConnection**() method in the DriverManager class to perform a database connection, the connection is made as soon as this instruction runs.

_______6. The **executeQuery**() method will definitely return a query result, but the **executeUpdate**() method will never return any result.

_______7. When a query is performed and a ResultSet is created, you need to retrieve the queried result from the ResultSet object by using a suiTable **getXXX**() method.

_______8. The advantage of using the **getObject**() method is that a returned datum, which is stored in a ResultSet object with an unknown data type, can be automatically converted from its Oracle data type to the ideal Java data type.

_______9. The SQL92 syntax can only be used for calling an Oracle stored procedure, not for an Oracle package or stored procedure.

______10. One has to use the **registerOutParameter**() method to register any output parameter in a query statement to allow the CallableStatement to know that there is an **OUT** parameter in that query, and the returned value should be stored in that parameter.

______11. When using a Java RowSet object to query data, one has to create an instance of the RowSet Implementation class, not the RowSet class itself, since all RowSet classes are abstract classes.

______12. One can run and test any Oracle package with a stored procedure directly in the Oracle SQL Developer environment.

II. Multiple Choice

1. The sequence to perform a data query from a database using a JDBC driver is ___________
   a. Connect to database, load JDBC driver, perform the query, get result from ResultSet
   b. Perform the query, connect to database, load JDBC driver, get result from ResultSet
   c. Get result from ResultSet, connect to database, load JDBC driver, perform the query
   d. Load JDBC driver, connect to database, perform the query, get result from ResultSet

2. One needs to use a ___________ object as an image holder, a ___________ object as a tool to display an image and a ___________ class as a monitor to coordinate image processing.
   a. Canvas, MediaTracker, Graphics
   b. Graphics, MediaTracker, Canvas
   c. Canvas, Graphics, MediaTracker
   d. MediaTracker, Graphics, Canvas

3. Generally, a connection **url** contains three parts, ___________, ___________ and ___________, for the database to be connected.
   a. Subname, sub-protocol, sub-protocol name
   b. Protocol name, sub-protocol, subname
   c. Protocol name, sub-protocol name, subname
   d. Protocol, sub-protocol, subname

4. The execute() method can ___________.
   a. Not return any result
   b. Return some results
   c. Be used either to return a result or not return any result
   d. None of above
5. To identify the data type returned by the execute() method, one needs to ___________.
   a. Use the getResultSet() method
   b. Use the getUpdateCount() method
   c. Use either of them
   d. Use both of them
6. The ResultSet object can be created by either executing the ___________ or ___________ method, which means that the ResultSet instance cannot be created or used without executing a query operation first.
   a. executeQuery(), getResultSet()
   b. getResultSet(), execute()
   c. createResultSet(), getResultSet()
   d. buildResultSet(), executeQuery()
7. The cursor in a ResultSet object can be moved by executing the ___________ method.
   a. move()
   b. first()
   c. next()
   d. last()
8. A cursor in the Oracle database can be mapped to a(n) ___________ data type.
   a. jdbc.oracle.CURSOR
   b. oracle.jdbc.OracleTypes.CURSOR
   c. oracle.jdbc.CURSOR
   d. jdbc.CURSOR
9. A ___________ object, which contains all pieces of necessary information about the returned data stored in a ResultSet instance, is returned when the ___________ method is executed.
   a. getMetaData(), ResultSetMetaData
   b. ResultSet, getMetaData()
   c. getResultSet, ResultSet
   d. ResultSetMetaData, getMetaData()
10. A CallableStatement can either return a ___________ object and multiple ResultSet objects by using the executeQuery() method or return nothing by using the ___________ method.
    a. ResultSetMetaData, getResultSet()
    b. Cursor, getCursor()
    c. Object, getObject()
    d. ResultSet, execute()
11. There are two parts in an Oracle Package: ___________ and ___________
    a. Specification, body
    b. Definition, specifications
    c. Body, specification
    d. Specification, execution

12. The reason of using ResultSet, instead of CachedRowSet, to get a column with the `Blob` data type from an Oracle database is ___________
    a. The former is easy
    b. The latter is faster
    c. The former cannot return any column with the **Blob** data type
    d. The latter cannot return any column with the **Blob** data type

III. Exercises

1. List five steps to build a data query from a Java database application project to a relational database using the Java runtime object method.
2. Develop a method by adding code into the LogIn button Click event handler in the LogInFrame class in the project **OracleSelectFaculty** to allow users to try the login process only three times. A warning message should be displayed and the project should exit after three failed login attempts.
3. UsePL-SQL to create a package, **Student_Course**, in the Oracle SQL Developer. The package contains a stored procedure named**SelectStudentCourse()** with two positional parameters,

    a. The input student name, **studentName**, with **VARCHAR2** data type.
    b. The output cursor, **StudentCourse**, containing all **course_id** values selected by that student.

    Two queries are involved in this stored procedure; the first one is used to query the **student_id** from the **Student** Table based on the input student name, and the second is to query all **course_id** values taken by the selected student from the **StudentCourse** Table based on the **student_id** retrieved from the first query.
    Compile and run this package after it is created to confirm that it works.
4. Use the Java CallableStatement method to develop a data query from the Student and StudentCourse Tables with the StudentFrame class in the `OracleSelectFaculty` project (the project file can be found in the folder `ClassDB Projects\Chapter 6` that is located in the `Students` folder at the accompanying CRC Press ftp site [see Figure 1.2 in Chapter 1]). The procedures to develop this data query include the following steps:

    a. Build two packages, **Student_Info** and **Student_Course**, using Oracle SQL Developer. For the second package, **Student_Course**, one can use the one built in Exercise 3.
    b. Develop the code for the StudentFrame class to perform the data query to these Oracle packages (adding an **else if** block to the **Select** button Click event handler).
    c. Add a new query method by using: **ComboMethod.addItem("Java Callable Method");** in the StudentFrame constructor.

7 Insert, Update and Delete Data from Databases

Similarly to manipulating data in Visual Studio. NET, when manipulating data in the Java NetBeans IDE environment, a popular method is always utilized, the Java runtime object method. Java code enables users to access Oracle databases with a sequence of code, starting from creating a DriverManager to load an Oracle JDBC database driver, setting up a connection using the Driver, creating a query statement object, running the **`executeQuery`** object and processing the data using a ResultSet object. In this chapter, we introduce and use this method to perform database manipulations to perform data insert, update and delete queries.

In the following sections, we will concentrate on inserting, updating and deleting data against our Oracle sample database using the Java runtime method.

7.1 PERFORM DATA MANIPULATIONS TO ORACLE DATABASE USING THE JAVA RUNTIME OBJECT

As we did for data query operations, in this section, we will discuss how to perform data manipulations using the Java runtime object method. Relatively speaking, there are some limitations in using Java API wizards to do data manipulations. For instance, after the mapped entity has been built and the entity manager object has been created, data manipulation can only be performed for that specified entity object or data Table. In other words, a defined or mapped entity object cannot perform data manipulation for any other entity object or data Table.

A good solution to those limitations is to use the Java runtime object to perform the data manipulation, and this will provide much more flexibility and control of data manipulation against the Oracle database and allow a single object to perform multiple data manipulations against the target database.

Let's first concentrate on data insertion to our Oracle database using the Java runtime object method.

7.2 PERFORM DATA INSERTION TO ORACLE DATABASE USING THE JAVA RUNTIME OBJECT METHOD

We have provided a very detailed and clear discussion about the Java runtime object method in Section 6.1 in Chapter 6. Refer to that section to get more details on this topic. Generally, to use the Java runtime object to perform data manipulations against our target database, the following six steps should be followed:

1) Load and register the database driver using the DriverManager class and Driver methods.
2) Establish an Oracle database connection using the Connection object.
3) Create a data manipulation statement using the **`createStatement()`** method.
4) Execute the data manipulation statement using the **`executeUpdate()`** or **`execute()`** method.
5) Retrieve and check the execution result of the data manipulation.
6) Close the statement and the database connection using the **`close()`** method.

DOI: 10.1201/9781003304029-8

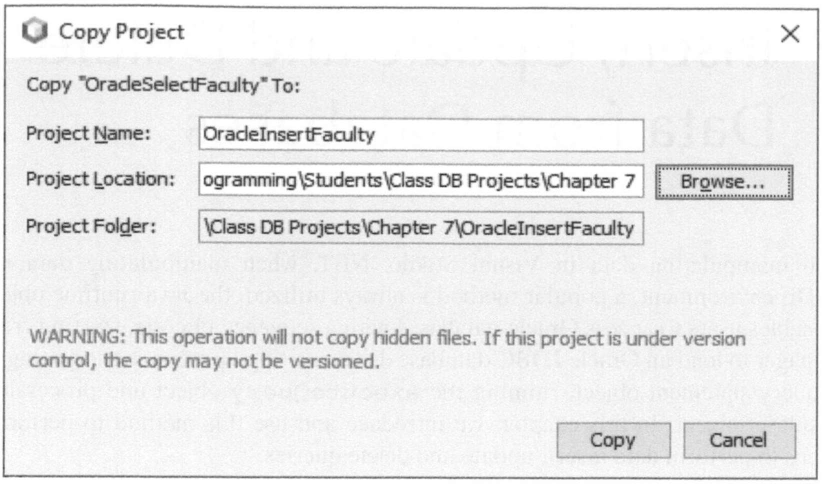

Copy Project

Copy "OracleSelectFaculty" To:

Project Name: OracleInsertFaculty

Project Location: ogramming\Students\Class DB Projects\Chapter 7 Browse...

Project Folder: \Class DB Projects\Chapter 7\OracleInsertFaculty

WARNING: This operation will not copy hidden files. If this project is under version control, the copy may not be versioned.

Copy Cancel

FIGURE 7.1 The finished Copy Project wizard.

Generally, the Oracle database is a popular database system and has been widely implemented in most commercial and industrial applications. In this and the following sections in this chapter, we will concentrate on this database system to discuss how to perform data insert, update and delete operations.

To save time and space, we can use and modify a project we built in Chapter 6, **OracleSelectFaculty**, to perform data manipulations against the Faculty Table in our target database. Perform the following operations to complete this project transfer:

1) Open the Windows Explorer and create a new folder, such as **Class DB Project\Chapter 7**, in your root drive.
2) Open Apache NetBeans 12.0, and find the project we built in Chapter 6, **OracleSelectFaculty**, in the **Projects** window. Otherwise, find this project in the folder **Class DB Projects\Chapter 6** in the **Students** folder on the CRC Press ftp site.
3) Right-click on that project and select the **Copy** item from the popup menu to open the **Copy Project** wizard.
4) Change the project name to **OracleInsertFaculty** in the Project Name box.
5) Browse to the folder, **Class DB Projects\Chapter 7**, which was created in step 1, and click on the **OK** button to select this location as your project location.
6) Your finished **Copy Project** wizard should match the one shown in Figure 7.1.
7) Click on the **Copy** button to complete the copy process.

Now you can find this copied project, **OracleInsertFaculty**, in the **Project** window. With this project, we are ready to build our data insertion query to perform data manipulations on our Oracle sample database **CSE_DEPT**.

In Section 6.3.1 in Chapter 6, we created a **FacultyFrame** class and Faculty JFrame window, **FacultyFrame**. Also, the following components have been added into that project:

- A JDBC driver for the Oracle 18c XE database has been loaded and registered.
- A valid database connection to that project has been established.
- A **PreparedStatement** instance has been created and implemented in the **Select** button click event handler to perform the data selection query.

In this section, we want to use the **Insert** button that has been built in the FacultyFrame window to perform the data insertion function. The data insertion action includes inserting a new faculty record with a new or default faculty image.

7.2.1 Develop the Code for the Insert Button Event Handler

In Section 6.3.3.3 in Chapter 6, we gave a detailed discussion of dynamic data query using the PreparedStatement object method. Refer to that section to get more details about that method. In this section, we will use that object to perform a dynamic faculty member insertion into the **Faculty** Table in our sample database.

Open the **Insert** button click event handler and enter the code shown in Figure 7.2. Let's have a closer look at this piece of code to see how it works.

A. Some local variables and objects are declared first, which include a local integer variable, **numInsert**, which is used to hold the returned number of inserted rows as the data insert action is performed, and a byte array, **fImage**, which is used to hold the selected faculty image to be inserted into the database later.
B. Prior to performing a data insertion, one needs to make sure that all TextFields that contain the seven pieces of new faculty information are filled. To do that, a user-defined method, **chkFaculty()**, is called to check all pieces of information to make sure that this insertion is valid. A warning message will be displayed if any field is empty.

```
  private void InsertButtonActionPerformed(java.awt.event.ActionEvent evt) {
      // TODO add your handling code here:
A     int numInsert = 0;
      byte[] fImage;
B     if (!chkFaculty()) {
         msgDlg.setMessage("Fill all TextFields for a new record!");
         msgDlg.setVisible(true);
         return;
      }
C     fImage = getFacultyImage();
D     String InsertQuery = "INSERT INTO Faculty (faculty_id, faculty_name, title, office, phone, " +
                          "college, email, fimage) VALUES (?, ?, ?, ?, ?, ?, ?, ?)";
E     try {
           PreparedStatement pstmt = LogInFrame.con.prepareStatement(InsertQuery);
F          pstmt.setString(1, FacultyIDField.getText());
           pstmt.setString(2, FacultyNameField.getText());
           pstmt.setString(3, TitleField.getText());
           pstmt.setString(4, OfficeField.getText());
           pstmt.setString(5, PhoneField.getText());
           pstmt.setString(6, CollegeField.getText());
           pstmt.setString(7, EmailField.getText());
           pstmt.setBytes(8, fImage);
G          numInsert = pstmt.executeUpdate();
      }
H     catch (SQLException e) {
           msgDlg.setMessage("Error in Statement!" + e.getMessage());
           msgDlg.setVisible(true);
      }
I     System.out.println("The number of inserted row = " + numInsert);
J     ComboName.addItem(FacultyNameField.getText());
K     InsertButton.setEnabled(false);
L     clearFaculty();
  }
```

FIGURE 7.2 The added code for the Insert button click event handler.

C. Another user-defined method, **getFacultyImage()**, is executed to select and obtain a selected faculty image to be inserted into the **Faculty** Table in our sample database.
D. An insert query string is created with eight positional dynamic parameters, which are associated with the eight pieces of inserted faculty information. One point to be noted is that the order of these parameters must be identical to the order of columns defined in the **Faculty** Table. Otherwise, an exception may occur when this insertion is performed.
E. A **try-catch** block is used to initialize and execute the data insertion action. First, a **PreparedStatement** instance is created using the **Connection** object that is located at the **LogInFrame** class with the insert query string as the argument.
F. The **setString()** method is used to initialize the seven pieces of inserted faculty information, which are obtained from the seven text fields entered by the user as the project runs. Also, the **setBytes()** method must be used to set the faculty image column, **fimage**, to insert a new selected faculty image into the database.
G. The data insertion function is performed by calling the **executeUpdate()** method. The run result of this method, which is an integer that equals the number of rows that have been inserted into the database, is assigned to the local variable **numInsert**.
H. The **catch** block is used to track and collect any possible exception encountered when this data insertion is executed.
I. The run result is printed out for debugging purposes.
J. The new inserted faculty name is attached to the **Faculty Name** combo box to enable users to validate this data insertion later.
K. After data insertion, the **Insert** button must be disabled to avoid any possible duplicated insertion operation. To do that, a system method, **setEnable()**, with a **false** argument is used.
L. Finally, another user-defined method, **clearFaculty()**, is called to clean up all pieces of inserted information to make it ready for a validation of this insertion later.

Before we can build and run the project to test the data insertion function, we should first Figure out how to check and validate this data insertion. First let's take care of the data checking to make sure that all pieces of new inserted faculty information are valid prior to this insertion.

7.2.2 Develop a Method for Data Checking Prior to Data Insertion

Create a new method named **chkFaculty()** and enter the code shown in Figure 7.3 in this method. Let's take a closer look at this piece of code to see how it works.

A. A Java TextField array, **f _ field[]**, is declared and initialized with seven TextFields that will be filled by seven pieces of faculty information later. The purpose of this setting is to simplify the data checking process later.
B. A **for** loop is used to check all TextFields, that is, to use a system method, **getText()**, to do this check to make sure that all of them are filled, without any empty ones. A **false** is returned if any field is empty to indicate this error.

Next, let's take care of how to insert a selected faculty image into the database.

7.2.3 Develop a Method for Selecting a Valid Faculty Image

When performing this data insertion, in addition to the seven pieces of a new faculty information, a new or a default faculty image should also be included. It is crucial to get this image in a simple way to speed up this insertion action. To that purpose, create another user-defined method, **getFacultyImage()**, and enter the code shown in Figure 7.4 for this method.

```
  private boolean chkFaculty() {
A   JTextField[] f_field = {FacultyIDField, FacultyNameField, TitleField, OfficeField, PhoneField, CollegeField, EmailField};
B   for (int loop = 0; loop <f_field.length; loop++) {
       if (f_field[loop].getText() == "") {
          return false;
       }
    }
    return true;
  }
```

FIGURE 7.3 The detailed code for the user-defined method chkFaculty().

```
  private byte[] getFacultyImage() {
A     byte[] fimage = null;
      File imgFile = null;
B     JFileChooser imgChooser = new JFileChooser();
C     imgChooser.setCurrentDirectory(new File(System.getProperty("user.home")));
D     int result = imgChooser.showOpenDialog(this);
E     if (result == JFileChooser.APPROVE_OPTION) {
         imgFile = imgChooser.getSelectedFile();
F        System.out.println("Selected path: " + imgFile.getAbsolutePath());
         System.out.println("Selected file: " + imgFile.toString());
       }
G     try {
         fimage = Files.readAllBytes(imgFile.toPath());
H     } catch (IOException ex) {
        Logger.getLogger(FacultyFrame.class.getName()).log(Level.SEVERE, null, ex);
      }
I     return fimage;
  }
```

FIGURE 7.4 The detailed code for the user-defined method getFacultyImage().

Let's take a closer look at this piece of code to see how it works.

A. Some local variables are declared first, which include a byte array, **fimage**, and a File object, **imgFile**. The former is used to hold the selected faculty image, and the latter is used to keep the selected faculty image in a file format.
B. A **JFileChooser** object, **imgChooser**, is created, and it is used to assist users to select a desired faculty image via a File Dialog.
C. To get and save a selected faculty image or a file, the current folder with the path is necessary, and this folder is our current project folder. The selected faculty image is stored in that folder to enable the system to pick it up and display it later.
D. A **JFileChooser** dialog is opened to allow users to select the desired faculty image.
E. If this dialog is opened successfully and a faculty image is selected, the property **APPROVE _ OPTION** is returned with a result whose value is non-zero. Then a system method, **getSelectedFile()**, is executed to return the selected image and assign it to the File object, **imgFile**, which is to be used in next step.
F. For debugging purposes, the file name and its path are displayed here.
G. A **try-catch** block is used to convert the image from the File format to the byte array format, since this is the allowed format for the **fimage** column in the database. To do that, a system method, **readAllBytes()**, is used. The argument of this method is the path of the selected image file.

H. A catch block is used to catch and report any possible exceptions if they occur.
I. Finally, the converted faculty image in byte array format is returned.

Before we can handle the last user-defined method, **clearFaculty()**, let's take a look at an issue related to the **Insert** button. As we know, this button is disabled after a data insertion is done to avoid any possible duplicated insertion in step K in Figure 7.2. One question is: When should this button be enabled to allow users to begin a new insertion?

7.2.4 Find a Way to Enable the Insert Button to Begin a New Data Insertion

Now let's try to answer the previous question of when the **Insert** button should be enabled again to allow users to insert another new record. Based on the fact that when a new record is to be inserted into a database, the **Faculty ID** should be a new value and should not be identical to any current **faculty _ id** in the database, this gives us an idea: as long as a new faculty record is to be inserted, the Faculty ID TextField, that is, its content, should be updated with a new value. Yes, that is true and a good solution to this question.

The answer is: the **Insert** button should be enabled again as long as the content of the Faculty ID TextField has been changed, and this kind of change can be reflected and triggered by a TextField event, **FacultyIDFieldKeyTyped**.

Perform the following steps to open this event handler:

1) Click on the **Design** tab on the top to open the Design View of the FacultyFrame Form.
2) Right-click on the **Faculty ID** TextField and select the item **Events > Key > key-Typed** to open this event handler.

Then enter the code shown in Figure 7.5 into this event handler.

Only one code line is built here, and it is to call the system method **setEnabled()** with **true** as an argument to enable the **Insert** button when the content of the Faculty ID TextField is changed. With this code, we solved this issue, and let's continue to the next step.

7.2.5 Develop a Method for Clearing Original Faculty Information

In order for us to perform validation for this new inserted faculty record in the **Faculty** Table in our sample database, we need to clean up all pieces of original faculty information stored in the seven TextFields in the FacultyFrame Form. To do that, we need to build another user-defined method, **clearFaculty()**, and enter the code shown in Figure 7.6 into this method.

Let's have a closer look at this piece of code to see how it works.

A. A JTextField array is declared and initialized by adding seven TextFields into it. Each TextField in this array is associated with a TextField used to store and display a piece of selected faculty information. The purpose of using this array is to simplify the cleaning process with a **for()** loop, shown in the following.

```
  private void FacultyIDFieldKeyTyped(java.awt.event.KeyEvent evt) {
      // TODO add your handling code here:
A     InsertButton.setEnabled(true);
  }
```

FIGURE 7.5 The code inside the FacultyIDFieldKeyTyped event handler.

```
  private void clearFaculty() {
A   JTextField[] f_field = {FacultyIDField, FacultyNameField, TitleField, OfficeField, PhoneField, CollegeField, EmailField};
B   for (int loop = 0; loop < f_field.length; loop++){
      f_field[loop].setText("");
    }
  }
```

FIGURE 7.6 The code in the method clearFaculty().

B. A **for()** loop is used to scroll through all seven TextFields and to set empty strings to them to clean up each.

Next let's handle the validation process for the data insertion.

7.2.6 Develop the Code for the Validation of the Data Insertion

To confirm and validate the data insertion, we can use the code we built inside the **Select** button click event handler without any modifications.

Now we are ready to build and run the project to test the data insertion function.

7.2.7 Build and Run the Project to Test the Data Insertion

Click on the **Clean and Build Main Project** button from the toolbar to build the project. Make sure that our sample SQL Server database, **CSE _ DEPT**, has been connected to our project.

Now click on the **Run Main Project** button to run the project. Enter a suiTable username and password, such as jhenry and test, in the **LogIn** frame form and select **Faculty Information** from the SelectFrame window to open the FacultyFrame form window. Make sure that the **Runtime Object Method** has been selected from the **Query Method** combo box. Then click on the **Select** button to query the default faculty information.

Modify the contents of the seven text fields by entering the following credentials into these TextFields, which is equivalent to creating a new record fora faculty member:

- Faculty ID: **J28544**
- Faculty Name: **James Carson**
- Title: **AssociateProfessor**
- Office: **MTC-118**
- Phone: **750-378-1134**
- College: **University of Miami**
- Email: **jcarson@college.edu**

Then click on the **Insert** button to select the desired faculty image for this insertion.

The **JFileChooser** dialog appears, as shown in Figure 7.7. Browse to the desired folder on your computer where all the faculty images are stored, and click on the **Open** button to select that image. In our case, this folder is **C:\Oracle DB Programming\Students\Images\Faculty**. You may select a default faculty image file, **Default.jpg**, as we did in this example. All faculty images can be found in the folder **Students\Images\Faculty** at the CRC Press ftp site (refer to Figure 1.2 in Chapter 1). You can copy them to your desired folder on your computer.

Now all TextFields containing the original faculty information become blank. To confirm or validate this data insertion, just go to the **Faculty Name** combo box and scroll down; you

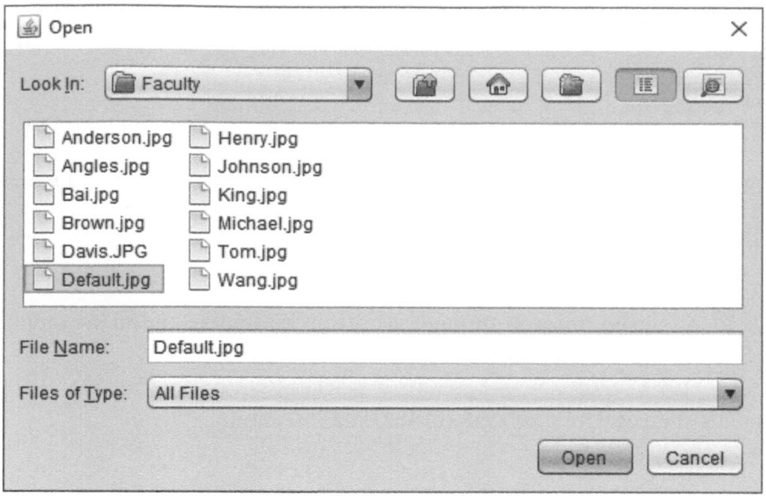

FIGURE 7.7 The opened JFileChooser dialog.

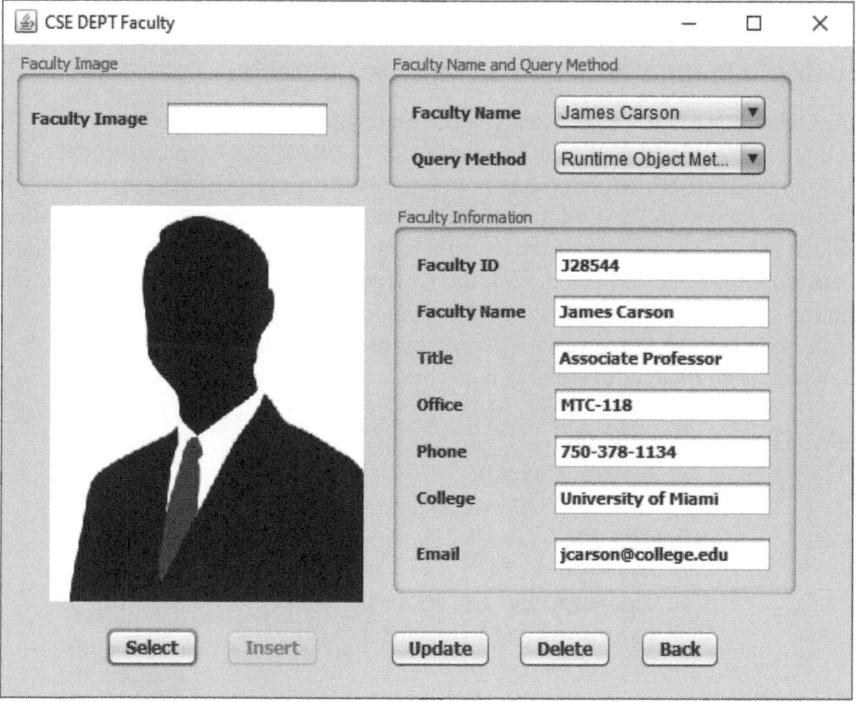

FIGURE 7.8 The validation result for the new inserted faculty member.

can see that our new inserted faculty member, **`James Carson`**, has been added there. Click that faculty member to select it, and click on the **`Select`** button to try to retrieve all pieces of information for this inserted faculty member. Immediately you can see that all pieces of information for the inserted faculty member are displayed in the FacultyFrame Form, as shown in Figure 7.8.

Generally it is recommended to remove the new inserted faculty member from the **Faculty** Table to keep our sample database neat and clean. But right now, just keep this record, since we may need to delete it when we build and test our delete query later. Next, let's perform the data update action against our sample database using the Java runtime object method.

7.3 PERFORM DATA UPDATE TO ORACLE DATABASE USING THE JAVA RUNTIME OBJECT METHOD

Usually, we do not need to update a **faculty _ id** when we update a faculty record, since a better way to do that is to insert a new faculty record and delete the old one. The main reason for this is that a very complicated operational process would be performed if the **faculty _ id** were updated, since it is a primary key in the **Faculty** Table and foreign key in the **Course** and the **LogIn** Tables. To update a primary key, one needs to update foreign keys first in the child Tables and then update the primary key in the parent Table. This will make our update process very complicated and proneto confusion. In order to avoid this confusion, in this section, we will update a faculty record by changing any column except the **faculty _ id**, and this is a popular way to update a Table and widely implemented in most database applications.

We still want to work with the **Faculty** Table in our sample database via the FacultyFrame Form; thus, we do not need to create a brand new project to perform this data update action, but instead we can modify an existing project, **OracleInsertFaculty**, to make it our new project, **OracleUpdateFaculty**. Perform the following operations to make our new project:

1) Open Windows Explorer and create a new folder, such as **Class DB Project\Chapter 7**, on your root drive if you did not already do this.
2) Open Apache NetBeans 12.4; one can find the project we built in the last section, **OracleInsertFaculty**, in the **Projects** window. The other way to find this project is to go to CRC Press ftp site, where it is located in the **Class DB Projects\Chapter 7** folder in the **Students** folder (refer to Figure 1.2 in Chapter 1). You can copy and paste that project to any folder, such as **Class DB Projects\Chapter 7**, on your computer.
3) Right-click on the project and select the **Copy** item from the popup menu to open the **Copy Project** wizard.
4) Change the project name to **OracleUpdateFaculty** in the Project Name box.
5) Browse to the folder **Class DB Projects\Chapter 7**, which was created in step 1, and click on the **OK** button to select this location as your project location.
6) Click on the **Copy** button to complete the copy process.

Before we can build code for the **Update** button event handler, first let's perform some modification for the code in the **FacultyFrame** constructor.

7.3.1 Modify the Code Inside the FacultyFrame Constructor

The reason we need to do this modification is that some faculty records in the **Faculty** Table will be changed after the update action. Thus, we need to update the faculty members in the **Faculty Name** combobox, **ComboName**, to enable users to check and validate the related update action based on the updated faculty records. One of the most important updates is the faculty name stored in that combobox.

Open our new project, **OracleUpdateFaculty**, and the **FacultyFrame** Form, and enter the code shown in Figure 7.9 into the constructor of this class.

The only modification is to replace original eight code lines, which are used to add eight faculty members into the **Faculty Name** combobox **ComboName**, with a new user-defined method, **CurrentFaculty()**, as shown in step A in Figure 7.9.

```
  public class FacultyFrame extends javax.swing.JFrame {
    MsgDialog msgDlg = new MsgDialog(new javax.swing.JFrame(), true);
    /**
     * Creates new form FacultyFrame
     */
    public FacultyFrame() {
      initComponents();
      this.setLocationRelativeTo(null);   // set the faculty Form at the center

      ComboMethod.addItem("Runtime Object Method");
      ComboMethod.addItem("Java execute() Method");
      ComboMethod.addItem("Java Callable Method");
A     CurrentFaculty();
    }
    ......
  }
```

FIGURE 7.9 The modified code in the FacultyFrame constructor.

```
  private void CurrentFaculty() {
A     ResultSet rs;
B     try {
        PreparedStatement pstmt = LogInFrame.con.prepareStatement("SELECT faculty_name FROM Faculty");
C       rs = pstmt.executeQuery();
D       ComboName.removeAllItems();
E       while (rs.next()){
          ComboName.addItem(rs.getString(1));
        }
F       rs.close();
G     } catch (SQLException ex) {
        Logger.getLogger(FacultyFrame.class.getName()).log(Level.SEVERE, null, ex);
      }
  }
```

FIGURE 7.10 The detailed code in the user-defined method CurrentFaculty().

The detailed code for this method is shown in Figure 7.10. Let's have a closer look at the code in this method to see how it works.

A. A local **ResultSet** object, **rs**, is declared first, since we need to use this object to hold our queried faculty member result.
B. A **try-catch** block is used to perform this data query. A database connection is established via the **LogInFrame** class, and a new **PreparedStatement** object, **pstmt**, is created with a query string to retrieve all faculty names from our **Faculty** Table.
C. The query is executed by calling the **executeQuery()** method, and the query result is assigned to our local **ResultSet** object, **rs**.
D. Prior to updating all faculty names in the **ComboName** box, it is cleared to make this update action ready with a system method, **removeAllItems()**.
E. A **while()** loop is used to repeatedly pick up each faculty name with the **next()** method. The retrieved faculty name, **rs.getString(1)**, is added into the **ComboName** box by using a system method, **addItem()**. Since only one column, **faculty _ name**, is queried from the **Faculty** Table, the column number is 1.
F. The **ResultSet** object is closed after this query.
G. A **catch** block is used to collect and report any possible exceptions during that query.

Now let's develop the code for the **Update** button even handler to perform the data update action to the **Faculty** Table via the FacultyFrame Form in this project.

7.3.2 Develop the Code for the Update Button Event Handler

We want to use the **Update** button built in the FacultyFrame form window to perform the faculty update function; therefore, no other modification to the FacultyFrame form window needs to be made. Now let's develop the code for the **Update** button click event handler.

Open this event handler and enter the code shown in Figure 7.11 into this event handler. Let's have a closer look at this piece of code to see how it works.

A. A local variable, **numUpdated**, and a byte array object, **fImage**, are created first. The variable **numUpdated** holds the run result of the data updating, and the byte array is used to hold a returned faculty image by calling the **getFacultyImage()** method later.
B. The user-defined method **getFacultyImage()** is executed to obtain an updated faculty image that can be selected by the user. The detailed code and an introduction to that user-defined method can be found in Section 7.2.3.
C. The update query string is created with eight positional parameters. The query criterion is the faculty ID, which is the eighth parameter and placed after the **WHERE** clause.
D. A **try-catch** block is used to assist this data update action. First, a **PreparedStatement** instance is created using the **Connection** object that is located in the **LogInFrame** class with the update query string as the argument.
E. A set of **setString()** methods is used to initialize the six pieces of updated faculty information, which are obtained from six TextFields and entered by the user as the project runs.
F. A **setBytes()** method is used to assign a byte array, **fImage**, to the **fimage** column in the **Faculty** Table as an updated faculty image. This method is very important, and only

```
   private void UpdateButtonActionPerformed(java.awt.event.ActionEvent evt) {
     // TODO add your handling code here:
A    byte[] fImage;
     int numUpdated = 0;
B    fImage = getFacultyImage();
C    String query = "UPDATE Faculty SET faculty_name=?, title=?, office=?, phone=?, college=?, email=?, fimage=? " +
                    "WHERE faculty_id= ?";
D    try {
          PreparedStatement pstmt = LogInFrame.con.prepareStatement(query);
E         pstmt.setString(1, FacultyNameField.getText());
          pstmt.setString(2, TitleField.getText());
          pstmt.setString(3, OfficeField.getText());
          pstmt.setString(4, PhoneField.getText());
          pstmt.setString(5, CollegeField.getText());
          pstmt.setString(6, EmailField.getText());
F         pstmt.setBytes(7, fImage);
G         pstmt.setString(8, FacultyIDField.getText());
H         numUpdated = pstmt.executeUpdate();
       }
I     catch (SQLException e) {
              msgDlg.setMessage("Error in Statement!" + e.getMessage());
              msgDlg.setVisible(true);
       }
J     System.out.println("The number of updated row = " + numUpdated);
K     CurrentFaculty();
   }
```

FIGURE 7.11 The developed code for the Update button click event handler.

a byte array can be used to hold an image to be stored to the related image column in the database.

G. The eighth input parameter in the query string, **faculty _ id**, is assigned to the query criterion that is located after the **WHERE** clause.
H. The data update action is performed by calling the **executeUpdate()** method. The update result, which is an integer that is equal to the number of rows that have been updated by this data update action, is returned and assigned to the local integer variable **numUpdated**.
I. The **catch** block is used to track and collect any possible exception encountered when the data update is executed.
J. The run result is printed out for debugging purposes.
K. The user-defined method **CurrentFaculty()** is executed to retrieve all updated faculty names and add them into the Faculty Name combo box to enable users to validate this data update later.

Now let's build and run the project to test the data update action.

7.3.3 Build and Run the Project to Test the Data Update

Click on the **Clean and Build Main Project** button from the toolbar to build our project. Then click on the **Run Main Project** button to run the project.

Enter a suiTable username and password, such as **jhenry** and **test**, to complete the login process and select Faculty Information from the SelectFrame window to open the FacultyFrame window. Make sure that the **Runtime Object Method** has been selected from the **Query Method** combo box. Then click on the **Select** button to query any faculty information. As an example, here select the faculty member **Ying Bai** from the ComboName box and display all pieces of information for this example faculty member.

To update this faculty record, enter the following information into six Text Fields (no **Faculty ID** Text Field) in the Faculty Information panel as an updated faculty record:

- Faculty Name: **Susan Bai**
- Title: **Professor**
- Office: **MTC-218**
- Phone: **750-378-1248**
- College: **Duke University**
- Email: **sbai@college.com**

Click on the **Update** button to select a desired image for this updated faculty member, such as **White.jpg**. All example faculty image files, including this faculty image, can be found in the folder **Students\Images\Faculty** on the CRC Press ftp site (refer to Figure 1.2 in Chapter 1). You can copy and paste those image files to your desired folder on your computer.

Now, if you go to the Faculty Name combobox, **ComboName**, it can be seen that the updated faculty name, **Susan Bai**, has been added into the Faculty Name combobox, and the original faculty member, **Ying Bai**, has been removed from this box.

One way to validate this data update is to go to the **Output** window. You can find that a success message is displayed in that window, as shown in Figure 7.12.

Similar to the data insert action, here we have another two ways to validate the data update. One way is to open our **Faculty** Table in our sample database to confirm the data update, and the other way is to use the **Select** button (that is, the code inside that button's click event handler). We prefer to use the second way. Click on the **Select** button to try to retrieve this updated faculty record, and the run result is shown in Figure 7.13. Our data update action is successful!

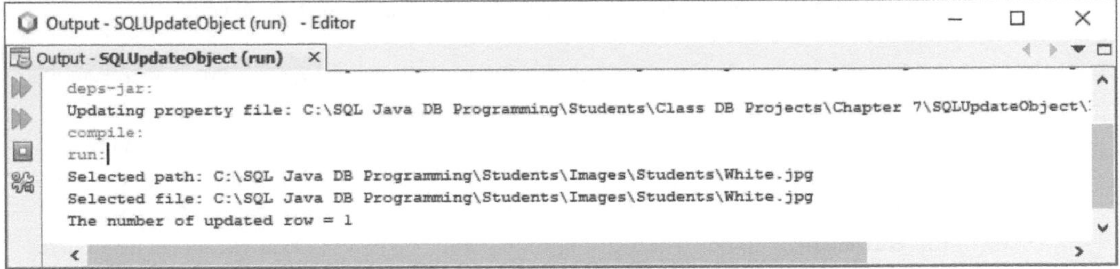

FIGURE 7.12 The successful data update message.

FIGURE 7.13 The data update result.

It is highly recommended to recover the updated faculty record to the original one to keep our database clean and neat. One can perform a similar update action to do this recovery job. Of course, you can also perform this data recovery job by using the Oracle SQL Developer if you like.

Next let's handle the data deletion action against our sample database.

7.4 PERFORM DATA DELETE TO ORACLE DATABASE USING THE JAVA RUNTIME OBJECT

We still want to work with the `Faculty` Table in our sample database via the FacultyFrame Form, sowe do not need to create a brand new project to perform this data update action, and instead we can use an existing project, `OracleUpdateFaculty`, and make it our new project to do the data delete action.

Perform the following operations to make our new project based on that project:

1) Open Windows Explorer and create a new folder, such as **`Class DB Project\Chapter 7`**, on your root drive if you did not already do this.
2) Open Apache NetBeans 12.4, and one can find the project **`OracleUpdateFaculty`** we built in the last section in the **`Projects`** window. The other way to find this project is to go to the CRC Press ftp site, where it is located inthe **`Class DB Projects\Chapter 7`** folder in the **`Students`** folder (refer to Figure 1.2 in Chapter 1). You can copy and paste that project to any folder, such as **`Class DB Projects\Chapter 7`**, on your computer.
3) Right-click on that project and select the **`Copy`** item from the popup menu to open the **`Copy Project`** wizard.
4) Change the project name to **`OracleDeleteFaculty`** in the Project Name box.
5) Browse to the folder, **`Class DB Projects\Chapter 7`**, which was created in step 1, and click on the **`OK`** button to select this location as your project location.
6) Click on the **`Copy`** button to complete this copy process.

Basically, there is no significant difference between data update and deletion using the Java runtime object method. In this section, we try to use the **`Delete`** button we built in the FacultyFrame Form window to perform this data deletion operation.

7.4.1 Develop the Code for the Delete Button Event Handler

Open our new project, **`OracleDeleteFaculty`**, and the **`Delete`** button click event handler, and enter the code shown in Figure 7.14 into this event handler. Let's have a closer look at this piece of code to see how it works.

A. Two local variables, **`numDeleted`** and **`cFacultyName`**, are created first, and these two variables are used to hold the run result of the data delete action and the current faculty name.
B. The delete query string is created with one positional parameter. The query criterion is the faculty name that is placed after the **`WHERE`** clause.
C. A **`try-catch`** block is used to assist this data delete action. First, a **`PreparedStatement`** instance is created using the Connection object that is located in the LogInFrame class with the delete query string as the argument.

```
  private void cmdDeleteActionPerformed(java.awt.event.ActionEvent evt) {
A     int numDeleted = 0;
      String cFacultyName = null;
B     String query = "DELETE FROM Faculty WHERE faculty_name = ?";
      try {
C          PreparedStatement  pstmt = LogInFrame.con.prepareStatement(query);
D          pstmt.setString(1, ComboName.getSelectedItem().toString());
E          cFacultyName = (String)ComboName.getSelectedItem();
F          numDeleted = pstmt.executeUpdate();
      }
G     catch (SQLException e) {
            msgDlg.setMessage("Error in Statement!" + e.getMessage());
            msgDlg.setVisible(true);
      }
H     System.out.println("The number of deleted row = " + numDeleted);
I     CurrentFaculty();
  }
```

FIGURE 7.14 The developed code for the Delete button click event handler.

D. The **setString()** method is used to initialize the positional parameter, which is the faculty name to be deleted from the Faculty Name combo box.
E. After this faculty record has been deleted, we need to remove the faculty name from the Faculty Name combo box. In order to remember the current faculty name, we need to temporarily store it in our local string variable, **cFacultyName**.
F. The data delete action is performed by calling the **executeUpdate()** method. The delete result, which is an integer that is equal to the number of rows that have been deleted by the data delete action, is returned and assigned to the local integer variable **numDeleted**.
G. The **catch** block is used to track and collect any possible exception encountered when the data delete is executed.
H. The run result is printed out for debugging purposes.
I. The **CurrentFaculty()** method is executed to update the Faculty Name combo box.

Now we are ready to build and run the project to test the data deletion function.

7.4.2 Build and Run the Project to Test the Data Deletion

Now click on the **Clean and Build Main Project** button from the toolbar to build our project. Then click on the **Run Main Project** button to run the project.

Enter a suiTable username and password, such as **jhenry** and **test**, to complete the login process and select the Faculty Information from the SelectFrame window to open the FacultyFrame window. Make sure that the **Runtime Object Method** has been selected from the **Query Method** combo box. Then click on the **Select** button to query the default faculty information. The default faculty information is displayed.

To test the data deletion function, we can try to delete one faculty member, **James Carson**, which was inserted into our database in Section 7.2.7. To do that, select this faculty member from the Faculty Name combo box, and click on the **Delete** button. Immediately, you can see that this faculty name has been removed from the Faculty Name combo box. Also, the run result is shown in the **Output** window, as shown in Figure 7.15.

To confirm this data deletion, one can open the Faculty Name combo box, and there is no faculty member named **James Carson** in there. Another way to do this validation is to click on the **Back** and the **Exit** button to stop our project. Then open our **Faculty** Table by going to the **Services** window and expand the **Databases** node; our connection URL; and finally our sample database, **CSE _ DEPT**. Right-click on the **Faculty** Table and select the **View Data** item from the popup menu to open it. In the opened **Faculty** Table, you can see that the faculty member **James Carson** has been removed from the Table.

However, the story is not finished. If an original faculty member, such as **Ying Bai**, is deleted, not only is that faculty record deleted from the **Faculty** Table, but other records related to that deleted faculty member located in the child Tables, such as **LogIn**, **Course** and **StudentCourse**, will also be deleted due to the cascading delete option we selected when we built this database. Therefore, we need to recover all of those deleted records to keep our sample database in good shape.

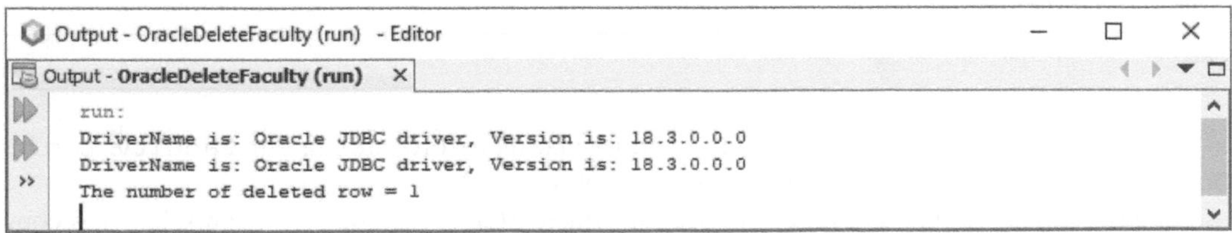

FIGURE 7.15 The successful data deletion message.

TABLE 7.1
The Deleted Faculty Record in the Faculty Table

faculty_id	faculty_name	title	office	phone	college	email	fimage
B78880	Ying Bai	Associate Professor	MTC-211	750–378–1148	Florida Atlantic University	ybai@college.edu	NULL

TABLE 7.2
The Deleted Course Records in the Course Table

course_id	course	credit	classroom	schedule	enrollment	faculty_id
CSC-132B	Introduction to Programming	3	TC-302	T-H: 1: 00–2:25 PM	21	B78880
CSC-234A	Data Structure & Algorithms	3	TC-302	M-W-F: 9:00–9:55 AM	25	B78880
CSE-434	Advanced Electronics Systems	3	TC-213	M-W-F: 1:00–1:55 PM	26	B78880
CSE-438	Advd Logic &Microprocessor	3	TC-213	M-W-F: 11:00–11:55 AM	35	B78880

TABLE 7.3
The Deleted Login Records in the Login Table

user_name	pass_word	faculty_id	student_id
ybai	come	B78880	NULL

TABLE 7.4
The Deleted Records in the StudentCourse Table

s_course_id	student_id	course_id	credit	major
1005	T77896	CSC-234A	3	CS/IS
1009	A78835	CSE-434	3	CE
1014	A78835	CSE-438	3	CE
1016	A97850	CSC-132B	3	ISE
1017	A97850	CSC-234A	3	ISE

In order to recover this deleted faculty member and related records in our **Faculty**, **LogIn**, **Course** and **StudentCourse** Tables, refer to Tables 7.1~7.4.

An easy way to do this recovery is to use the Oracle SQL Developer. One can select and copy data from each Table (Tables 7.1~7.4) and paste it into the bottom line of each opened Table with Oracle SQL Developer.

Three points to be noted when recovering the data are:

1) The order to perform the row recovery. The faculty record in the parent Table must be recovered first. In our case, the record in the **Faculty** Table must be recovered first, since it is a parent Table. The records in the child Tables can be recovered after the record in the parent Table has been completed. Otherwise, an error may be encountered.
2) To recover the deleted faculty member **Ying Bai**, one can run this project again to insert it back into our sample database based on data shown in Table 7.1 by using the **Insert** button.
3) Then one can perform the recovery job by adding all deleted records into the other Tables by using the Oracle SQL Developer based on the data in Tables 7.2~7.4.
4) When you finish your recovery operations for all the rows, click **File > Save All** in Oracle SQL Developer to save all the additions.

As we discussed in Section 6.3.3.5 in Chapter 6, in addition to using the **executeUpdate()** method to perform data manipulations such as data insert, update and delete actions, one can use the **execute()** method to perform the similar data manipulations. It is preferred to leave this optional method as homework and allow students to handle this issue.

A complete sample project, **OracleDeleteFaculty**, can be found in the folder **Class DB Projects\Chapter 7** that is located in the **Students** folder on the CRC Press ftp site (refer to Figure 1.2 in Chapter 1).

Next let's take care of the data manipulations against the Oracle database using the Java UpdaTable ResultSet method.

7.5 PERFORM DATA MANIPULATION USING UPDATABLE RESULTSET

As we discussed in Section 6.3.3.4 in Chapter 6, a ResultSet object can be considered a Table of data representing a database result set, which is usually generated by executing a statement that queries the database.

The **ResultSet** interface provides **getXXX()** methods for retrieving column values from the current row. Values can be retrieved using either the index number of the column or the name of the column. In general, using the column index will be more efficient. Columns are numbered from 1. For maximum portability, result set columns within each row should be read in left-to-right order, and each column should be read only once.

A default ResultSet object is not updaTable with a cursor that moves forward only. Thus, it is possible to iterate through it only once from the first row to the last row. New methods in the JDBC 4.0 API make it possible to produce ResultSet objects that are scrollable and/or updaTable.

Before we can use the ResultSet object to perform data manipulation against our sample database, let's first get a clear picture of the ResultSet additional functionalities and categories supported in JDBC 4.0.

7.5.1 Introduction to ResultSet Enhanced Functionalities and Categories

ResultSet functionality in JDBC 4.0 includes enhancements for scrollability and positioning, sensitivity to changes by others and updatability.

- **Scrollability**: the ability to move backward as well as forward through a ResultSet object. Associated with scrollability is the ability to move to any particular position in the ResultSet through either relative positioning or absolute positioning.
- **Positioning**: the ability to move a specified number of rows forward or backward from the current row. Absolute positioning enables you to move to a specified row number, counting from either the beginning or the end of the ResultSet.

TABLE 7.5
The ResultSet Type and Concurrency Type

ResultSet Type	Functions
Forward-only	This is a JDBC 1.0 functionality. This type of ResultSet is not scrollable, not positionable and not sensitive
Scroll-sensitive	This type of ResultSet is scrollable and positionable. It is also sensitive to underlying database changes.
Scroll-insensitive	This type of result set is scrollable and positionable but not sensitive to underlying database changes.
Concurrency Type	**Functions**
UpdaTable	Data update, insert and delete can be performed on the ResultSet and copied to the database.
Read-only	The result set cannot be modified in any way.

- **`Sensitivity`**: the ability to see changes made to the database while the ResultSet is open, providing a dynamic view of the underlying data. Changes made to the underlying column values of rows in the ResultSet are visible.

Two parameters can be used to set up the properties of a ResultSet object when it is created: ResultSet Type and Concurrency Type of a ResultSet. Table 7.5 lists these types and their functions. Under JDBC 4.0, the **`Connection`** class has the following methods that take a ResultSet type and a concurrency type as input to define a new created ResultSet object:

- Statement createStatement(int resultSetType, int resultSetConcurrency)
- PreparedStatementprepareStatement(Stringsql,intresultSetType,intresultSetConcurrency)
- CallableStatement prepareCall(String sql, int resultSetType, int resultSetConcurrency)

You can specify one of the following static constant values for ResultSet type:

- **`ResultSet.TYPE _ FORWARD _ ONLY`**
- **`ResultSet.TYPE _ SCROLL _ INSENSITIVE`**
- **`ResultSet.TYPE _ SCROLL _ SENSITIVE`**

And you can specify one of the following static constant values for concurrency type:

- **`ResultSet.CONCUR _ READ _ ONLY`**
- **`ResultSet.CONCUR _ UPDATABLE`**

The following code fragment, in which **`conn`** is a valid Connection object and **`ora`** is a defined query string, illustrates how to make a ResultSet that is scrollable, sensitive to updates by others and updaTable.

```
PreparedStatement pstmt = conn.prepareStatement (ora, ResultSet.TYPE _
SCROLL _ SENSITIVE,
ResultSet.CONCUR _ UPDATABLE);
```

Now that we have a basic understanding of the ResultSet and its enhanced functionalities, we can go ahead to perform data manipulation against our sample database using the **`UpdaTable ResultSet`** object.

TABLE 7.6
The Steps of Data Manipulation Using UpdaTable ResultSet

Manipulation Type	Steps
Data Deletion	Single step: Use the **deleteRow()** method of the ResultSet class.
Data Updating	Two steps: 1. Update the data in the ResultSet using the associated **updateXXX()** methods. 2. Copy the changes to the database using the **updateRow()** method.
Data Insertion	Three steps: 1. Move to the insert row by calling the ResultSet **moveToInsertRow()** method. 2. Use the appropriate **updateXXX()** methods to update data in the insert row. 3. Copy the changes to the database by calling the ResultSet **insertRow()** method.

7.5.2 Perform Data Manipulation Using the UpdaTable ResultSet Object

Generally, performing data manipulation using the updaTable ResultSet can be divided into the following three categories:

- Data insertion
- Data updating
- Data deleting

Different data manipulations need different steps, and Table 7.6 lists the most popular steps for these data manipulations.

It can be seen from Table 7.6 that data deletion is the easiest way to remove a piece of data from the database, since it only takes one step to delete data from both the ResultSet and the database. The other two data manipulations, data update and insertion, need at least two steps to complete.

The point to be noted is that in the data insertion action, the first step, **`moveToInsertRow()`**, is moved to a blank row that is not a part of the ResultSet but related to the ResultSet. The data insertion actually occurs when the **`insertRow()`** method is called and the next **`commit`** command is executed.

Let's start with the data insertion against our sample database first. In the following sections, we will use the Oracle database as our target database and build code to perform data manipulations against our target sample database.

7.5.2.1 Insert a New Row Using the UpdaTable ResultSet

To save time and space, we want to use and modify a project, **`OracleDeleteFaculty`**, we built in Section 7.4 to make it our new project to perform this data insertion action. Perform the following operations to make it our project:

1) Create a new folder, **`ClassDB Projects\Chapter 7`**, on your computer if you did not already do that, launch Apache NetBeans IDE 12 and open the **`Projects`** window.
2) Right-click on the project **`OracleDeleteFaculty`** we built in Section 7.4 and select the **`Copy`** item from the popup menu to open the **`Copy Project`** wizard.
3) Change the project name to **`OracleUpdaTableInsert`** in the Project Name box.
4) Browse to the folder **`Class DB Projects\Chapter 7`**, which was created in step 1, and click on the **`OK`** button to select this location as your project location.
5) Click on the **`Copy`** button to complete the copy process.

Perform the following code modifications to the FacultyFrame Form:

1) Open the constructor of this class and add one more statement into this constructor,

   ComboMethod.addItem("Java UpdaTable ResultSet");

   Your modified code in this constructor should match that shown in Figure 7.16. The modified part is in bold.
2) Click on the **Design** button to switch back to the design view of the FacultyFrame form window, and double-click on the **Insert** button to open its event handler. Enter the code shown in Figure 7.17 into this handler to perform the data insertion action against our sample database.

Let's have a closer look at this piece of modified code to see how it works.

A. First, we add an **if** block to distinguish between the **Java UpdaTable ResultSet** method and other query methods to perform this data insertion.
B. An **else if** block is added with the same objective as step A.
C. The query string is created, and it is used to help the UpdaTable ResultSet object do the data insertion action. One point to be noted is that because of a limitation of the UpdaTable ResultSet under JDBC 4.0, you cannot use a star (*) following the **SELECT** to query all columns from the target Table; instead, you have to explicitly list all columns for this query. An option is to use Table aliases, such as **SELECT f.* FROM Table f** ... to do this kind of query.
D. A **try-catch** block is used to perform the data insertion. A **PreparedStatement** is created with two ResultSet parameters, **TYPE_SCROLL_SENSITIVE** and **CONCUR_UPDATable**, to define the ResultSet object to enable it to be scrollable and updaTable and to perform data manipulation.
E. The **setString()** method is used to initialize the positional parameter in the query string.
F. The **executeQuery()** method is called to perform this query and return the query result to a new created ResultSet object.
G. In order to insert a new row into the ResultSet, the **moveToInsertRow()** method is executed to move the cursor of the ResultSet to a blank row that is not a part of the ResultSet but is related to the ResultSet.
H. A sequence of **updateString()** methods is executed to insert the desired columns into the associated columns in the ResultSet. The point to be noted is that different **updateXXX()** methods should be used if the target columns have different data types, and the **XXX** indicates the associated data type, such as **Int**, **Float** or **Double**.

```
public FacultyFrame() {
    initComponents();
    this.setLocationRelativeTo(null);   // set the faculty Form at the center
    ComboMethod.addItem("Java executeQuery Method");
    ComboMethod.addItem("Java execute Method");
    ComboMethod.addItem("Java Callable Method");
    ComboMethod.addItem("Java Updatable ResultSet");
    CurrentFaculty();
}
```

FIGURE 7.16 The modified code for the constructor of the FacultyFrame class.

```
    private void InsertButtonActionPerformed(java.awt.event.ActionEvent evt) {
        int numInsert = 0;
        byte[] fImage;
        if (!chkFaculty()) {
            msgDlg.setMessage("Fill all TextFields for a new record!");
            msgDlg.setVisible(true);
            return;
        }
        fImage = getFacultyImage();
        String InsertQuery = "INSERT INTO Faculty (faculty_id, faculty_name, title, office, phone, " +
                             "college, email, fimage) VALUES (?, ?, ?, ?, ?, ?, ?, ?)";
A       if (ComboMethod.getSelectedItem()=="Java executeQuery Method") {
        try {
            PreparedStatement pstmt = LogInFrame.con.prepareStatement(InsertQuery);
            pstmt.setString(1, FacultyIDField.getText());
            pstmt.setString(2, FacultyNameField.getText());
            pstmt.setString(3, TitleField.getText());
            pstmt.setString(4, OfficeField.getText());
            pstmt.setString(5, PhoneField.getText());
            pstmt.setString(6, CollegeField.getText());
            pstmt.setString(7, EmailField.getText());
            pstmt.setBytes(8, fImage);
            numInsert = pstmt.executeUpdate();
        }
        catch (SQLException e) {
            msgDlg.setMessage("Error in Statement!" + e.getMessage());
            msgDlg.setVisible(true);
        }
      }
B       else if (ComboMethod.getSelectedItem()=="Java Updatable ResultSet"){
C       String query = "SELECT faculty_id, faculty_name, title, office, phone, college, email, fimage " +
                       "FROM Faculty WHERE faculty_name = ?";
D       try {
            PreparedStatement pstmt = LogInFrame.con.prepareStatement(query,
                            ResultSet.TYPE_SCROLL_SENSITIVE, ResultSet.CONCUR_UPDATABLE);
E           pstmt.setString(1, ComboName.getSelectedItem().toString());
F           ResultSet rs = pstmt.executeQuery();
G           rs.moveToInsertRow();
H           rs.updateString(1, FacultyIDField.getText());
            rs.updateString(2, FacultyNameField.getText());
            rs.updateString(3, TitleField.getText());
            rs.updateString(4, OfficeField.getText());
            rs.updateString(5, PhoneField.getText());
            rs.updateString(6, CollegeField.getText());
            rs.updateString(7, EmailField.getText());
I           rs.updateBytes(8, fImage);
J           rs.insertRow();
K           rs.moveToCurrentRow(); // Go back to where we came from...
          }
L         catch (SQLException e){
            msgDlg.setMessage("Error in Updatable ResultSet! " + e.getMessage());
            msgDlg.setVisible(true);
          }
        }
        System.out.println("The number of inserted row = " + numInsert);
        ComboName.addItem(FacultyNameField.getText());
        InsertButton.setEnabled(false);
        clearFaculty();
    }
```

FIGURE 7.17 The modified code for the Insert button click event handler.

I. For the image column, the system method `updateBytes()` must be used to insert or update a faculty image in the `Faculty` Table.

J. The `insertRow()` method is executed to update this change to the database. That is, this data update will not happen until the next Commit command is executed.

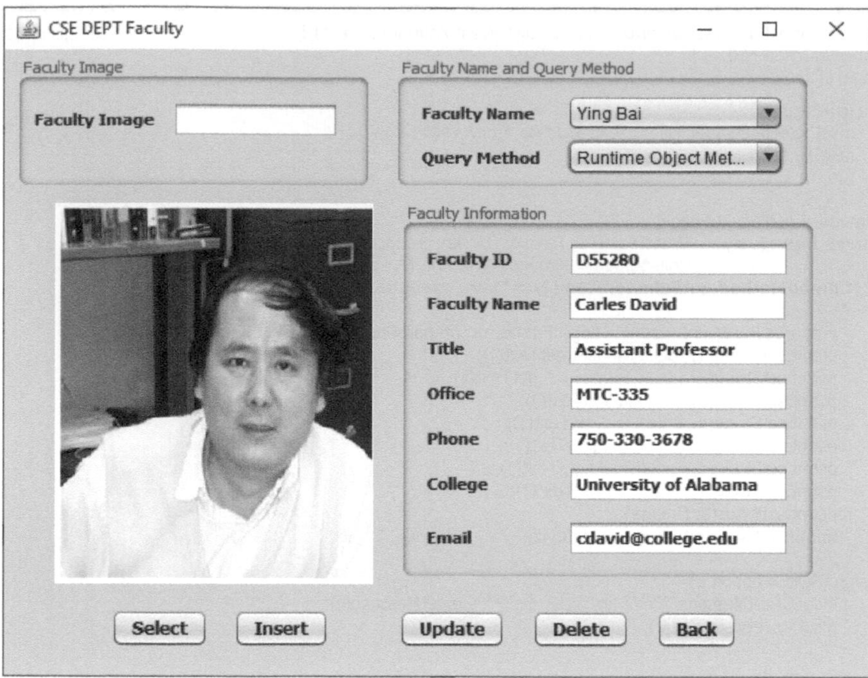

FIGURE 7.18 The new inserted faculty record.

K. The **`moveToCurrentRow()`** method is optional, and it returns the cursor of the ResultSet to its original position before this data insertion was performed.
L. The **`catch`** block is used to track and collect any possible exception for this data insertion action.

Now let's build and run the project to test the data insertion function. Click on the **`Clean and Build Main Project`** button to build the project, and click on the **`Run Main Project`** button to run it.

Enter a suiTable username and password, such as **`jhenry`** and **`test`**, to complete the login process and open the FacultyFrame form window. Make sure that the **`Java executeQuery Method`** has been selected from the **`Query Method`** combo box. Then click on the **`Select`** button to query a faculty record. For example, select the faculty member **`Ying Bai`** to query and display this record.

Modify the content of the seven text fields, as shown in Figure 7.18, which is equivalent to a new faculty record:

- Faculty ID: `D55280`
- Faculty Name: **`Charles David`**
- Title: **`Assistant Professor`**
- Office: `MTC-335`
- Phone: `750-330-3678`
- College: **`University of Alabama`**
- Email: **`cdavid@college.edu`**
- fimage: **`David.jpg`**

To insert this new record using the **`JavaUpdaTable ResultSet`** method, select the **`Java UpdaTable ResultSet`** from the Query Method combo box. Then click on the **`Insert`** button to perform this data insertion. Browse to the faculty image folder to select the desired image, **`David.jpg`**.

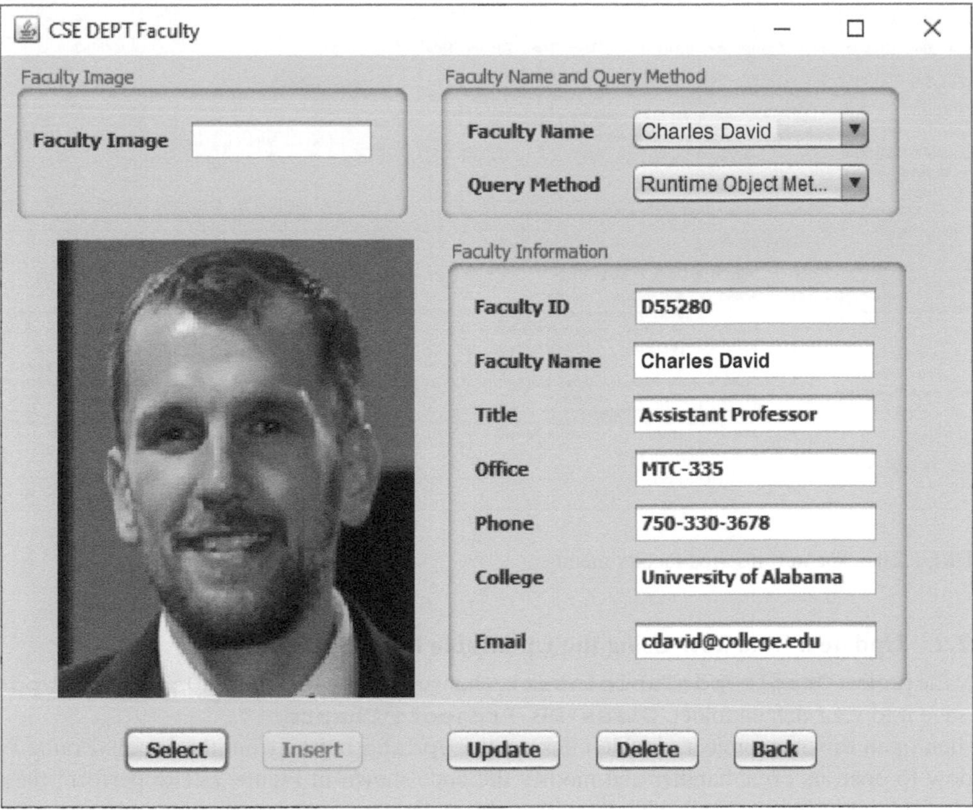

FIGURE 7.19 The retrieved new inserted faculty record.

To confirm and validate this data insertion, the easiest way is to use the **Select** button in the FacultyFrame form. Go to the Faculty Name combo box, and you will find that the new inserted faculty name, **Charles David**, has been added into this box. Select this new inserted faculty member from that box and select **Java executeQuery Method** from the Query Method combo box followed by clicking on the **Select** button to try to retrieve this new inserted faculty record. The returned faculty record is displayed, as shown in Figure 7.19.

Another way to confirm this data insertion is to open the **Faculty** Table in our sample database. Open the **Services** window in the NetBeans IDE, expand the **Databases** node and right-click on our Oracle database connection URL, then select the **Connect** item to connect to our sample database. You may need to use the password **oracle _ 18c** to do this connection. Then expand the connected database, **CSE _ DEPT**, and the **Tables** node, and right-click on the **Faculty** Table and select the **View Data** item. In the opened **Faculty** Table, you can see that the new inserted faculty member, **Charles David**, which is highlighted in the **Faculty** Table, is there, as shown in Figure 7.20.

Click on the **Back** and the **Exit** buttons to terminate our project. Generally, it is recommended to remove the new inserted faculty record to keep our database clean and neat, but for now, just keep it, and we can delete this record later when we test our data delete actions with the Java UpdaTable ResultSet method.

Next let's take care of the data update action using the UpdaTable ResultSet object.

As we did for the data insertion, we still want to use the FacultyFrame form window to update one of faculty members in the **Faculty** Table in our sample database, **CSE _ DEPT**.

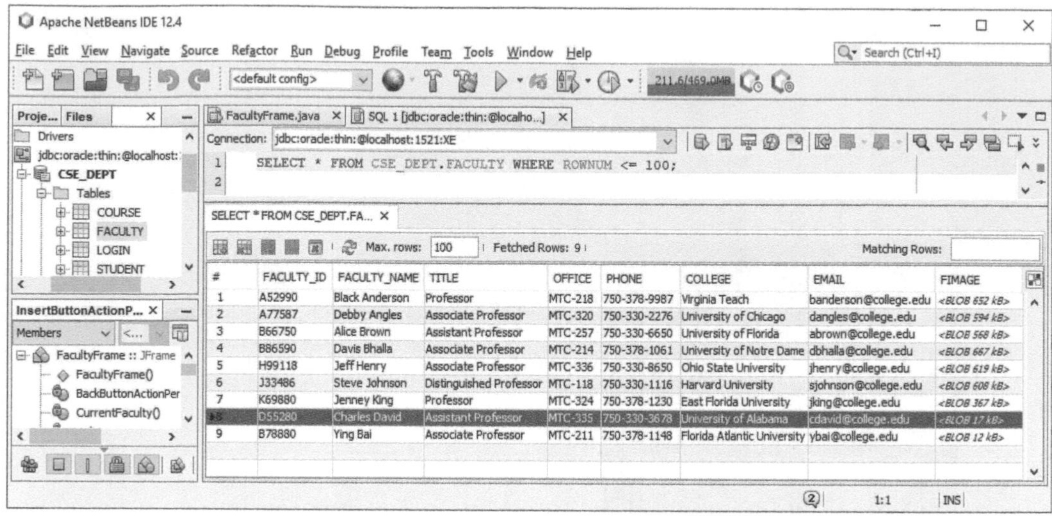

FIGURE 7.20 The new inserted faculty member.

7.5.2.2 Update a Data Row Using the UpdaTable ResultSet

Copy the project **OracleUpdaTableInsert**, change its name to **OracleUpdaTableUpdate** and save it to your default folder, **Class DB Projects\Chapter 7**.

Then open this new project, double-click on the **Update** button from the FacultyFrame Form window to open its event handler and modify the code shown in Figure 7.21 to perform the data update function using the UpdaTable ResultSet object.

Let's have a closer look at this piece of modified code to see how it works.

A. First, we add an **if** block to distinguish the **Java executeQuery Method** and the **Java UpdaTable ResultSet** method to perform this data update action.
B. An **else if** block is added with the same objective as step A.
C. The query string is created, and it is used to help the UpdaTable ResultSet object do this data update action.
D. A **try-catch** block is used to perform this data update action. A **PreparedStatement** is created with two ResultSet parameters, **TYPE _ SCROLL _ SENSITIVE** and **CONCUR _ UPDATable**, to define the ResultSet object to enable it to be scrollable and updaTable and to perform data manipulations.
E. The **setString()** method is used to initialize the positional parameter in the query string.
F. The **executeQuery()** method is called to perform this query and return the query result to a new created ResultSet object.
G. First we need to identify the location of the row to be updated. There is only one row that has been retrieved from our **Faculty** Table and saved in the ResultSet, which may be any default faculty member, and this row will be updated in this data update action. Therefore, the absolute position for this row is 1. Then a sequence of **updateString()** methods is executed to update the desired columns to the associated columns in the ResultSet. The point to be noted is that different **updateXXX()** methods should be used if the target columns have the different data types, and the **XXX** indicates the associated data type, such as **Int**, **Float**or**Double**.
H. For the image column, the system method **updateBytes()** must be used to update a faculty image in the **Faculty** Table.

```
    private void UpdateButtonActionPerformed(java.awt.event.ActionEvent evt) {
      byte[] fImage;
      int  numUpdated = 0;
      fImage = getFacultyImage();
A     if (ComboMethod.getSelectedItem()=="Java executeQuery Method") {
      String query = "UPDATE  Faculty SET faculty_name=?, title=?, office=?, phone=?, college=?, email=?, fimage=? " +
                      "WHERE  faculty_id= ?";
      try {
           PreparedStatement pstmt = LogInFrame.con.prepareStatement(query);
           pstmt.setString(1, FacultyNameField.getText());
           pstmt.setString(2, TitleField.getText());
           pstmt.setString(3, OfficeField.getText());
           pstmt.setString(4, PhoneField.getText());
           pstmt.setString(5, CollegeField.getText());
           pstmt.setString(6, EmailField.getText());
           pstmt.setBytes(7, fImage);
           pstmt.setString(8, FacultyIDField.getText());
           numUpdated = pstmt.executeUpdate();
        }
       catch (SQLException e) {
              msgDlg.setMessage("Error in Statement!" + e.getMessage());
              msgDlg.setVisible(true);
        }
       System.out.println("The number of updated row = " + numUpdated);
      }
B     else if (ComboMethod.getSelectedItem()=="Java Updatable ResultSet") {
C         String query = "SELECT faculty_name, title, office, phone, college, email, fimage " +
                          "FROM Faculty WHERE faculty_id = ?";
D         try {
            PreparedStatement pstmt = LogInFrame.con.prepareStatement(query,
                                   ResultSet.TYPE_SCROLL_SENSITIVE, ResultSet.CONCUR_UPDATABLE);
E           pstmt.setString(1, FacultyIDField.getText());
F           ResultSet rs = pstmt.executeQuery();
G           if (rs.absolute(1)) {
              rs.updateString(1, FacultyNameField.getText());
              rs.updateString(2, TitleField.getText());
              rs.updateString(3, OfficeField.getText());
              rs.updateString(4, PhoneField.getText());
              rs.updateString(5, CollegeField.getText());
              rs.updateString(6, EmailField.getText());
H             rs.updateBytes(7, fImage);
I             rs.updateRow();
            }
          }
J         catch (SQLException e){
            msgDlg.setMessage("Error in Updatable ResultSet! " + e.getMessage());
            msgDlg.setVisible(true);
          }
        }
        CurrentFaculty();
    }
```

FIGURE 7.21 The modified code for the Update button click event handler.

I. The `updateRow()` method is executed to update this change to the database. That is, this data update will not happen until the next Commit command is executed. Be aware that by default, the auto-commit flag is set to `true` so that any operation run is committed immediately.

J. The `catch` block is used to track and collect any exception for this data update action.

Now let's build and run the project to test the data update function. Click on the `Clean and Build Main Project` button to build the project, and click on the `Run Main Project` button to run it.

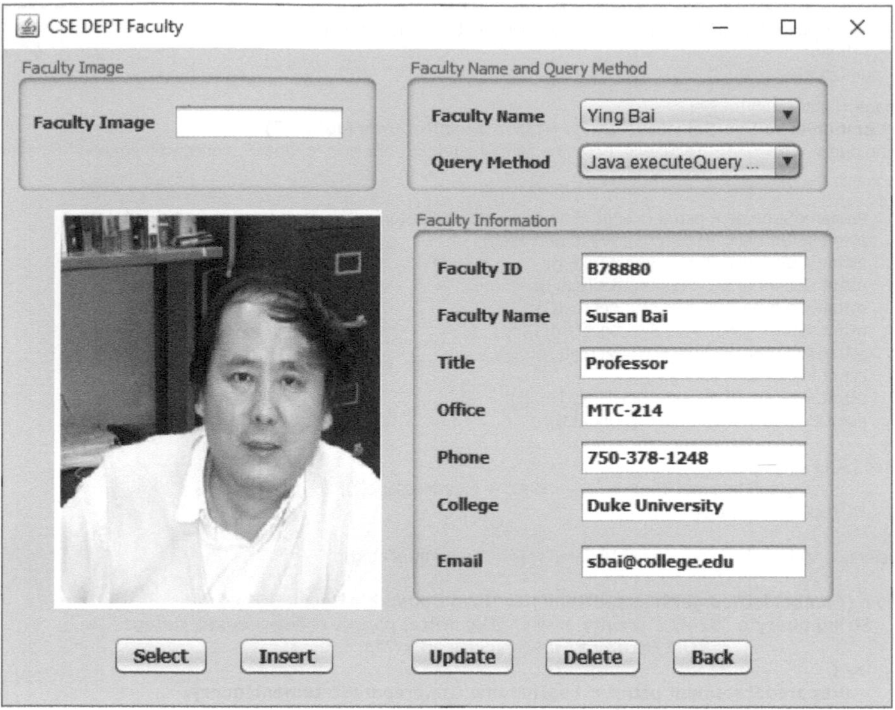

FIGURE 7.22 The updated faculty information.

Enter a suitable username and password, such as **`jhenry`** and **`test`**, to complete the login process and open the FacultyFrame form window. Make sure that the **`Java executeQuery Method`** has been selected from the **`Query Method`** combo box. Then click on the **`Select`** button to query any faculty information.

To perform the update action with the **`Java UpdaTable ResultSet`** method, select this method from the **`Query Method`** combo box, and change the content of the six text fields (without the Faculty ID field); for example, update faculty member **`Ying Bai`** to another faculty member, **`Susan Bai`**, as shown in Figure 7.22, and click on the **`Update`** button to select her image file, **`White.jpg`**. Your finished update screen should match the one shown in Figure 7.22.

To confirm the data update function using the UpdaTable ResultSet, select either **`Java executeQuery Method`** or **`Java execute Method`** from the Query Method combo box, and go to the **`Faculty Name`** combo box. You can see that the updated faculty member **`Susan Bai`** is there. Select this faculty name, and then click on the **`Select`** button to get the updated result back and displayed in the Form. The returned faculty record is displayed, as shown in Figure 7.23.

Click on the **`Back`** and the **`Exit`** buttons to terminate our project.

Now let's try to confirm this data update the second way, which is to open the **`Faculty`** Table to confirm the data manipulation. Open the **`Services`** window in the NetBeans IDE, expand the **`Databases`** node and right-click on our sample database URL. Select the **`Connect`** item to connect to our sample database. Then expand this connected database, **`CSE _ DEPT`**, and the **`Tables`** node; right-click on the **`Faculty`** Table; and select the **`View Data`** to open this Table. In the opened **`Faculty`** Table, you can see that the updated faculty member, who has been highlighted, is there, as shown in Figure 7.24. Our data update function is successful.

It is highly recommended to recover this updated faculty record back to the original one in our sample database to keep our database clean and neat. One can perform another update action to do this.

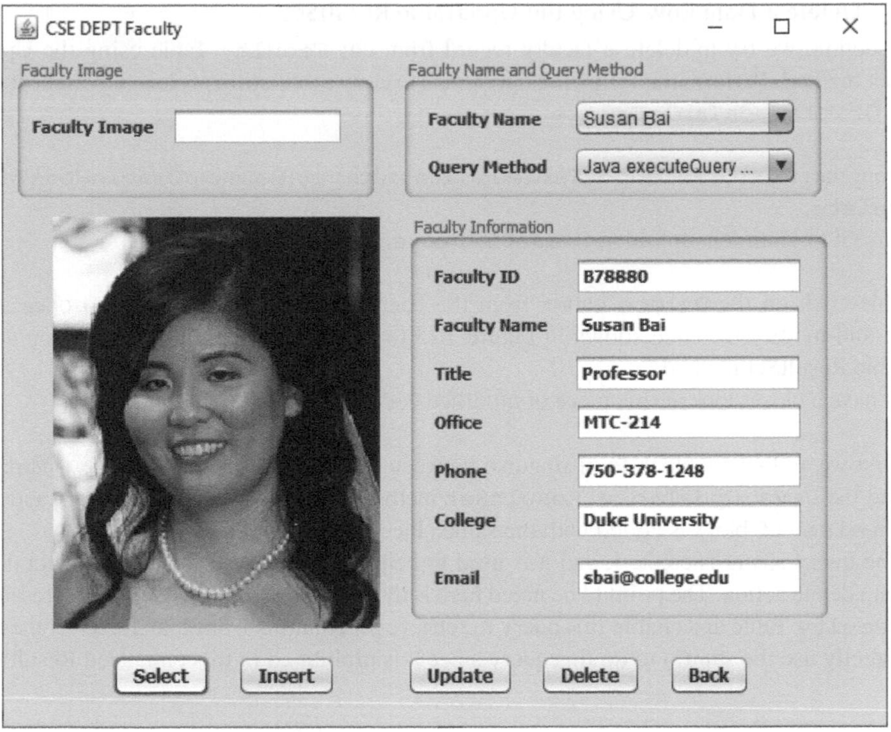

FIGURE 7.23 The retrieved updated faculty record.

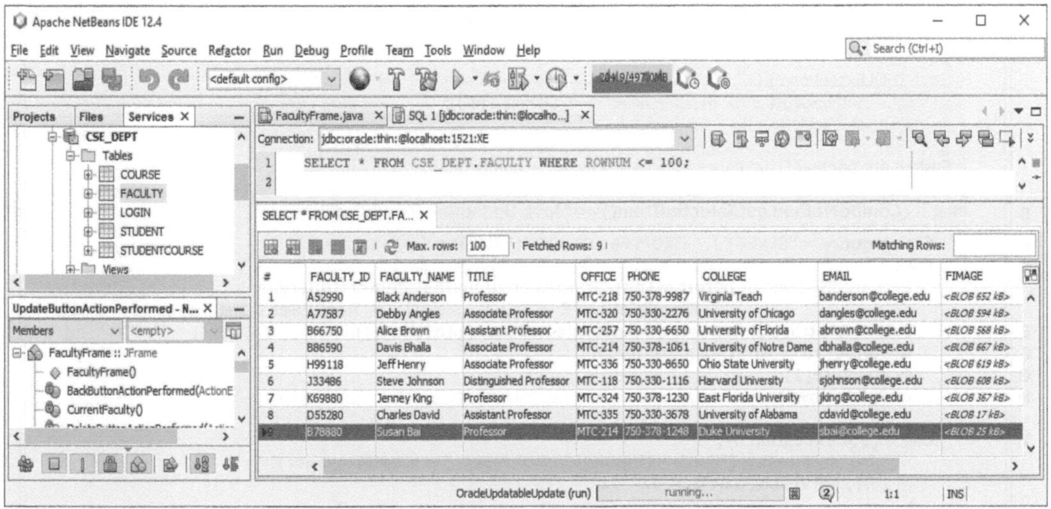

#	FACULTY_ID	FACULTY_NAME	TITLE	OFFICE	PHONE	COLLEGE	EMAIL	FIMAGE
1	A52990	Black Anderson	Professor	MTC-218	750-378-9987	Virginia Teach	banderson@college.edu	<BLOB 652 kB>
2	A77587	Debby Angles	Associate Professor	MTC-320	750-330-2276	University of Chicago	dangles@college.edu	<BLOB 594 kB>
3	B66750	Alice Brown	Assistant Professor	MTC-257	750-330-6650	University of Florida	abrown@college.edu	<BLOB 568 kB>
4	B86590	Davis Bhalla	Associate Professor	MTC-214	750-378-1061	University of Notre Dame	dbhalla@college.edu	<BLOB 667 kB>
5	H99118	Jeff Henry	Associate Professor	MTC-336	750-330-8650	Ohio State University	jhenry@college.edu	<BLOB 619 kB>
6	J33486	Steve Johnson	Distinguished Professor	MTC-118	750-330-1116	Harvard University	sjohnson@college.edu	<BLOB 608 kB>
7	K69880	Jenney King	Professor	MTC-324	750-378-1230	East Florida University	jking@college.edu	<BLOB 367 kB>
8	D55280	Charles David	Assistant Professor	MTC-335	750-330-3678	University of Alabama	cdavid@college.edu	<BLOB 17 kB>
9	B78880	Susan Bai	Professor	MTC-214	750-378-1248	Duke University	sbai@college.edu	<BLOB 25 kB>

FIGURE 7.24 The updated faculty record in the Faculty Table.

Next let's take care of the data delete action using the UpdaTable ResultSet object. As we did for the data update, we still want to use the FacultyFrame form window to delete one of the faculty members in the **Faculty** Table in our sample database, **CSE _ DEPT**.

7.5.2.3 Delete a Data Row Using the UpdaTable ResultSet

In this section, we try to delete a faculty record from our **Faculty** Table using the UpdaTable ResultSet method. Perform the following operations to copy an existing project and make it our new project, **OracleUpdaTableDelete**:

- Copy the project **OracleUpdaTableUpdate** and change its name to **OracleUpdaTable Delete**.
- Save it to your default folder, **ClassDB Projects\Chapter 7**.

Double-click on the **Delete** button from the FacultyFrame Form window to open its event handler, and modify the code shown in Figure 7.25 to perform the data delete function using the UpdaTable ResultSet method.

Let's have a closer look at this piece of modified code to see how it works.

A. First we add an **if** block to distinguish between the **Java executeQuery Method** and the **Java UpdaTable ResultSet** method to perform the data deletion action.
B. An **else if** block is added with the same objective as step A.
C. The query string is created, and it is used to help the UpdaTable ResultSet object do the data delete action. The point to be noted here is that a Table alias, **f**, is used to represent the **Faculty** Table and enable this query to retrieve all columns from that Table. You cannot directly use the star (*) to do this query since it is prohibited in this enhanced ResultSet.

```
    private void DeleteButtonActionPerformed(java.awt.event.ActionEvent evt) {
        int numDeleted = 0;
A       if (ComboMethod.getSelectedItem()=="Java executeQuery Method") {
        String query = "DELETE FROM Faculty WHERE faculty_name = ?";
        try {
              PreparedStatement  pstmt = LogInFrame.con.prepareStatement(query);
              pstmt.setString(1, ComboName.getSelectedItem().toString());
              numDeleted = pstmt.executeUpdate();
          }
          catch (SQLException e) {
              msgDlg.setMessage("Error in Statement!" + e.getMessage());
              msgDlg.setVisible(true);
          }
          System.out.println("The number of deleted row = " + numDeleted);
        }
B       else if (ComboMethod.getSelectedItem()=="Java Updatable ResultSet"){
C           String query = "SELECT f.* FROM Faculty f WHERE f.faculty_name = ?";
D           try {
              PreparedStatement pstmt = LogInFrame.con.prepareStatement(query,
                                  ResultSet.TYPE_SCROLL_SENSITIVE, ResultSet.CONCUR_UPDATABLE);
E             pstmt.setString(1, ComboName.getSelectedItem().toString());
F             ResultSet rs = pstmt.executeQuery();
G             rs.absolute(1);
H             rs.deleteRow();
              }
I           catch (SQLException e){
              msgDlg.setMessage("Error in Updatable ResultSet! " + e.getMessage());
              msgDlg.setVisible(true);
              }
          }
J       else {
             msgDlg.setMessage("Only executeQuery & Updatable ResultSet methods available! ");
             msgDlg.setVisible(true);
          }
K         CurrentFaculty();
    }
```

FIGURE 7.25 The modified code for the Delete button click event handler.

D. A **try-catch** block is used to perform the data delete action. A **PreparedStatement** is created with two ResultSet parameters, **TYPE _ SCROLL _ SENSITIVE** and **CONCUR _ UPDATable**, to define the ResultSet object to enable it to be scrollable and updaTable and furthermore enable it to perform data manipulation.
E. The **setString()** method is used to initialize the positional parameter in the query string.
F. The **executeQuery()** method is called to perform this query and return the query result to a new created ResultSet object.
G. We need first to identify the location of the row to be deleted. In fact, there is only one row that has been retrieved from our **Faculty** Table and saved in the ResultSet, which is the selected faculty member to be removed, and this row will be deleted with the data delete action. Therefore, the absolute position for this row is 1.
H. The **deleteRow()** method is executed to delete this record from the ResultSet and the database. In fact, the data delete will not happen until the next Commit command is executed. Be aware that by default, the auto-commit flag is set to **true** so that any operational run is committed immediately.
I. The **catch** block is used to track and collect any possible exception for this data deletion.
J. Otherwise, if another method is selected by the user, a warning message is displayed to remind the user to select a valid method.
K. Finally, the user-defined method, **CurrentFaculty()**, is called to update the Faculty Name combo box to enable users to confirm this delete action later.

Now let's build and run the project to test the data delete function.

Click on the **Clean and Build Main Project** button to build the project, and click on the **Run Main Project** button to run it.

Enter a suiTable username and password, such as **jhenry** and **test**, to complete the login process and open the FacultyFrame form window. Make sure that the **Java executeQuery Method** has been selected from the **Query Method** combo box. Then click on the **Select** button to query any faculty record or information, such as a faculty member named **Charles David**.

To test the data delete function using the UpdaTable ResultSet, select the **Java UpdaTable ResultSet** from the Query Method combo box. Then click on the **Delete** button to try to delete this selected faculty member from our sample database. To simplify this data delete action and avoid a completed recovery process, in this case, we try to delete a faculty member, **Charles David**, since this faculty member is a new one inserted in Section 7.5.2.1 without other related records in any child Tables. Select that faculty member from the **Faculty Name** combo box, and click on the **Delete** button to remove this faculty member from our sample database.

Click on the **Back** and the **Exit** buttons to terminate our project.

To confirm and validate this data delete action, one can go to the Faculty Name combo box to check this faculty member. It can be seen that this faculty member has been removed from the faculty name list.

Another way to confirm the data delete is to open the **Faculty** Table in our sample database **CSE _ DEPT**. To do that, first open the **Services** window in the NetBeans IDE, expand the **Databases** node, right-click on our Oracle database connection URL and select the **Connect** item to connect to our sample database. You may need to use our password, **oracle _ 18c**, to do this connection. Then expand the connected database, **CSE _ DEPT**, and the **Tables** node; right-click on the **Faculty** Table; and select **View Data** for this Table. In the opened **Faculty** Table, you can find that the faculty member **Charles David** has been deleted from the **Faculty** Table.

Our data delete function is successful.

A complete project, **OracleUpdaTableDelete**, that contains the data insert, update and delete functions using the UpdaTable ResultSet object can be found in the folder **Class DB Projects\Chapter 7** located in the **Students** folder at the CRC Press ftp site (refer to Figure 1.2 in Chapter 1).

Next let's discuss how to perform data manipulation using the Callable statement.

7.6 PERFORM DATA MANIPULATION USING CALLABLE STATEMENTS

In Section6.3.7.5 in Chapter 6, we provided a very detailed discussion of the data query from the **Faculty** Table in our sample database using the CallableStatement method. Some basic and fundamental ideas and techniques using the CallableStatement method and stored procedures were given in detail, with some real sample projects. Refer to that section to get a clear picture and understanding of the CallableStatement object. In this section, we will use this method to perform data manipulations against the **Course** Table in our sample database, **CSE _ DEPT**.

First let's take care of the data insertion to the **Course** Table in our sample Oracle 18c XE database using the CallableStatement method.

7.6.1 INSERT DATA TO THE COURSE TABLE USING CALLABLE STATEMENTS

In Section 6.3.8 in Chapter 6, we built a project, **OracleSelectCourse**, with a graphical user interface, including the CourseFrame Form window, and we want to use that CourseFrame Form window from that project with some modifications in our new project. You can find that project in the folder **Class DB Projects\Chapter 6** in the **Students** folder at the CRC Press ftp site. Copy that project and change its name to **OracleCallableInsert** and save it to the folder **Class DB Projects\Chapter 7** on your computer. We will build the data insertion function with the CallableStatement method in the following procedures:

1) Build our stored procedure, **InsertNewCourse**, using the Oracle SQL Developer.
2) Develop the code for the **Insert** button in the CourseFrame Form window to execute the CallableStatement method to call our stored procedure **InsertNewCourse** to insert the new course record into the **Course** Table in our sample database.
3) Confirm and validate the new course insertion using the code we built for the **Select** button event handler.

Now let's start from the first step.

7.6.1.1 Develop the Oracle Stored Procedure InsertNewCourse()

Recall that when we built our sample database, **CSE _ DEPT**, in Chapter 2, there was no faculty name column in the **Course** Table, and the only relationship between the **Faculty** and the **Course** Tables was the **faculty _ id**, which is a primary key in the **Faculty** Table but a foreign key in the **Course** Table. As the project runs, the user needs to insert new course records based on the faculty name, not the faculty ID. Therefore, for this new course data insertion, we need to perform two queries with two Tables: first we need to make a query to the **Faculty** Table to get the desired **faculty _ id** based on the faculty name selected by the user, and second we can insert a new course record based on the **faculty _ id** we obtained from our first query into the **Course** Table. These two queries can be combined into a single stored procedure.

We provided a very detailed discussion about Oracle stored procedures and their generation procedures in Section 6.3.7.5.7 in Chapter 6. Refer to that section to get more details about building a stored procedure with Oracle SQL Developer.

Perform the following steps to build the Oracle stored procedure **InsertNewCourse** with Oracle SQL Developer:

1) Open the Oracle SQL Developer and click on the system database, **XE**, under **Recent** to connect to the Oracle database by entering the system password, **oracle _ 18c**. Then expand the **Other Users** folder and our sample database folder, **CSE _ DEPT**.
2) Right-click on the **Procedures** folder and select the **New Procedure** item.

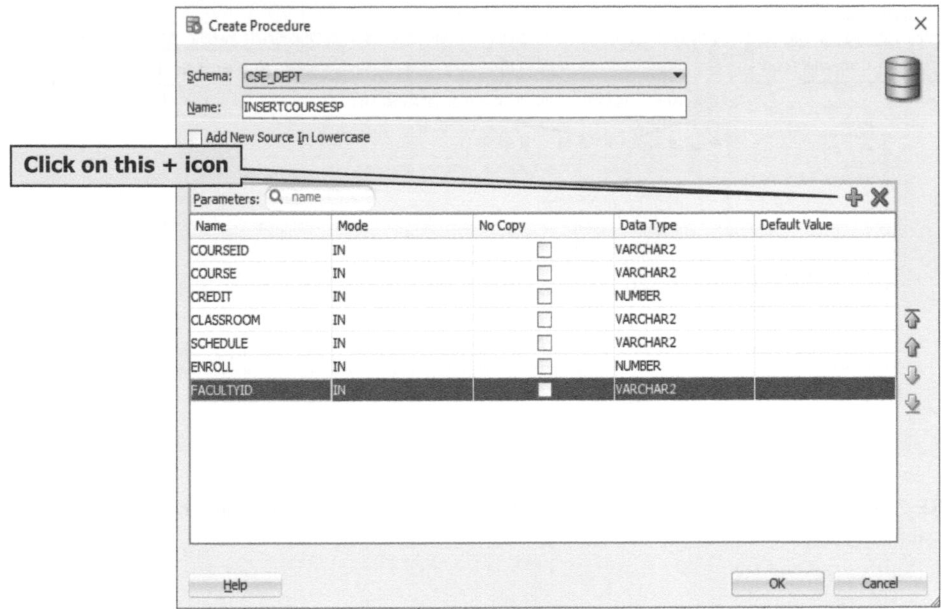

FIGURE 7.26 The Create Procedure wizard (Copyrighted by Oracle and used with permission).

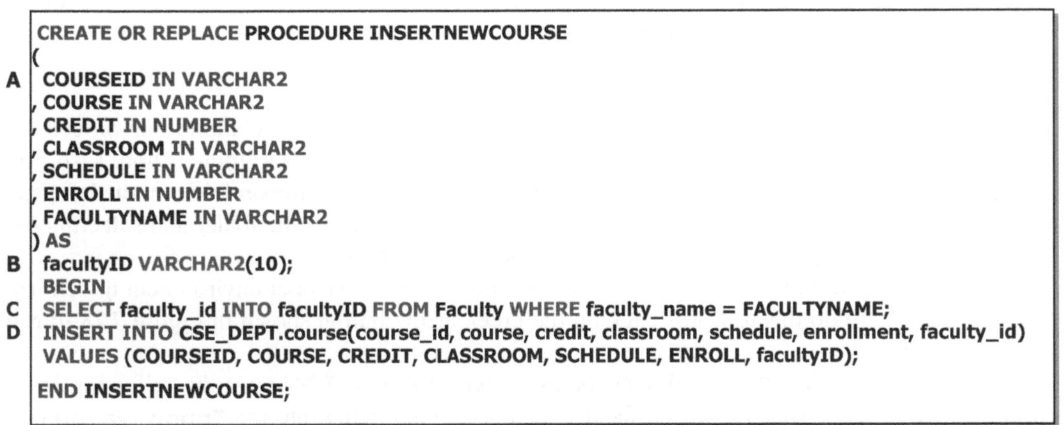

```
  CREATE OR REPLACE PROCEDURE INSERTNEWCOURSE
  (
A  COURSEID IN VARCHAR2
  , COURSE IN VARCHAR2
  , CREDIT IN NUMBER
  , CLASSROOM IN VARCHAR2
  , SCHEDULE IN VARCHAR2
  , ENROLL IN NUMBER
  , FACULTYNAME IN VARCHAR2
  ) AS
B  facultyID VARCHAR2(10);
   BEGIN
C  SELECT faculty_id INTO facultyID FROM Faculty WHERE faculty_name = FACULTYNAME;
D  INSERT INTO CSE_DEPT.course(course_id, course, credit, classroom, schedule, enrollment, faculty_id)
   VALUES (COURSEID, COURSE, CREDIT, CLASSROOM, SCHEDULE, ENROLL, facultyID);
  END INSERTNEWCOURSE;
```

FIGURE 7.27 The code body for the procedure.

3) In the opened Create Procedure wizard, enter **INSERTNEWCOURSE** into the **Name:** box as the procedure's name, as shown in Figure 7.26.
4) Click on the green plus symbol (+) in the upper-right corner to add all seven input parameters one by one with the data type shown in Figure 7.26.
5) Click on the **OK** button to open the procedure code window.

In the opened procedure code window, enter the code shown in Figure 7.27 into the procedure body section, which is just under the **BEGIN** command. Let's have a closer look at this piece of code to see how it works.

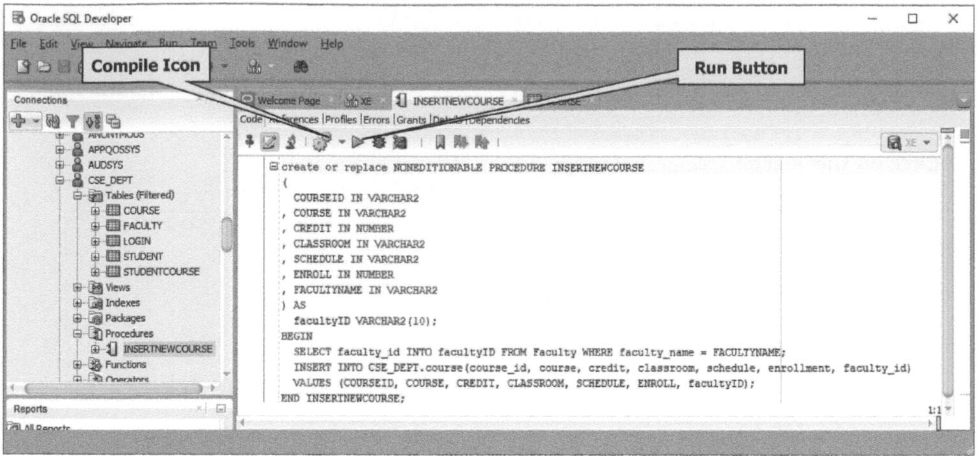

FIGURE 7.28 The completed procedure, INSERTNEWCOURSE() (Copyrighted by Oracle and used with permission).

A. The top seven items are the input parameters we added into this procedure.
B. A local variable, **facultyID**, is declared, and we need to use it as an intermediate variable to hold the query result from the first query from the **Faculty** Table.
C. The first query is executed to get the faculty_id based on the input **FACULTYNAME**.
D. The second query, **INSERT INTO**, is created with seven nominal input data columns followed by associated seven input parameters.

Your completed stored procedure is shown in Figure 7.28.

Now expand the **Compile** icon and click on the **Compile** item to compile our procedure. A **Compiled** statement should be displayed in the Message window if everything is fine. Also, you can find our procedure, **INSERTNEWCOURSE**, is just under the **Procedures** folder in the left pane (Figure 7.28). You may need to refresh that folder by right-clicking on the folder and selecting the **Refresh** item in the popup menu if you cannot find our procedure.

We can directly test the stored procedure in the Oracle SQL Developer environment to confirm its performance. To do this test, just click on the green arrow button shown in Figure 7.28 to run this procedure.

When the **Run PL/SQL** wizard appears, as shown in Figure 7.29, enter the following input parameters as a new course record for faculty member Jenney King into the **Input Value** column, as shown in Figure 7.29:

Course_ID:	**CSE-668**
Course:	**Neural Network**
Credit:	**4**
Classroom:	**TC-303**
Schedule:	**T-H: 2:00-4:00 PM**
Enroll:	**26**
FacultyName:	**Jenney King**

To check this run result, one can open the **COURSE** Table in the Oracle SQL Developer environment to check the insertion. To do this, expand the **Tables** folder just under our user database, **CSE _ DEPT**; right-click on our **COURSE** Table; and select **Open** item. In the opened **COURSE** Table, click on the **Data** tab on the top to open the data view for all courses. Scroll down along the

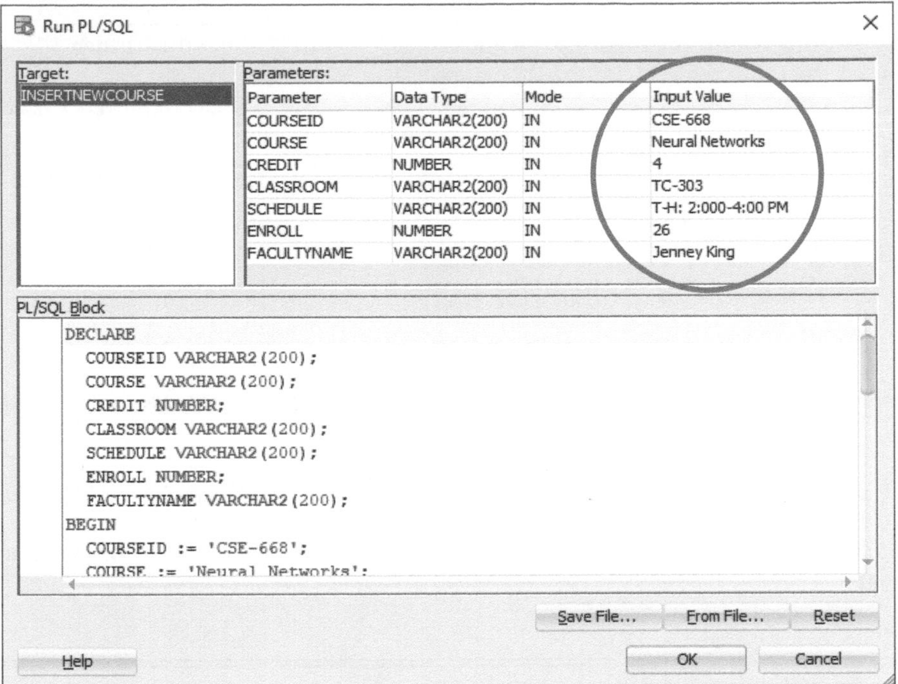

FIGURE 7.29 The run status of the procedure INSERTNEWCOURSE() (Copyrighted by Oracle and used with permission).

Table, and you will find that our new inserted course, **CSE-668**, with all related fields, has been inserted into this Table, as shown in the highlighted line in Figure 7.30.

It is highly recommended to remove this new inserted course from the **Course** Table, since we may need to perform this insert action again later when we test this function in the NetBeans environment.

Now close the Oracle SQL Developer, and we can continue to develop the code for the CallableStatement method in our project to call this stored procedure to perform a new course insertion action against our sample database.

7.6.1.2 Develop the Code for the Insert Button Click Event Handler

The function of this piece of code is to call the stored procedure we built in the last section to perform a new course insertion to the **Course** Table in our sample database. The insertion criterion is the faculty member selected from the Faculty Name combo box. The new inserted course record can be retrieved and displayed in the CourseList listbox by clicking on the **Select** button to confirm the data insertion.

Generally, the sequence to run a CallableStatement to perform a stored procedure is:

1) Build and formulate the CallableStatement query string.
2) Create a CallableStatement object.
3) Set the input parameters.
4) Register the output parameters.
5) Execute CallableStatement.
6) Retrieve the run result by using different **getXXX()** method.

Since we do not have any output result to be returned from this stored procedure, we can skip steps 4 and 6.

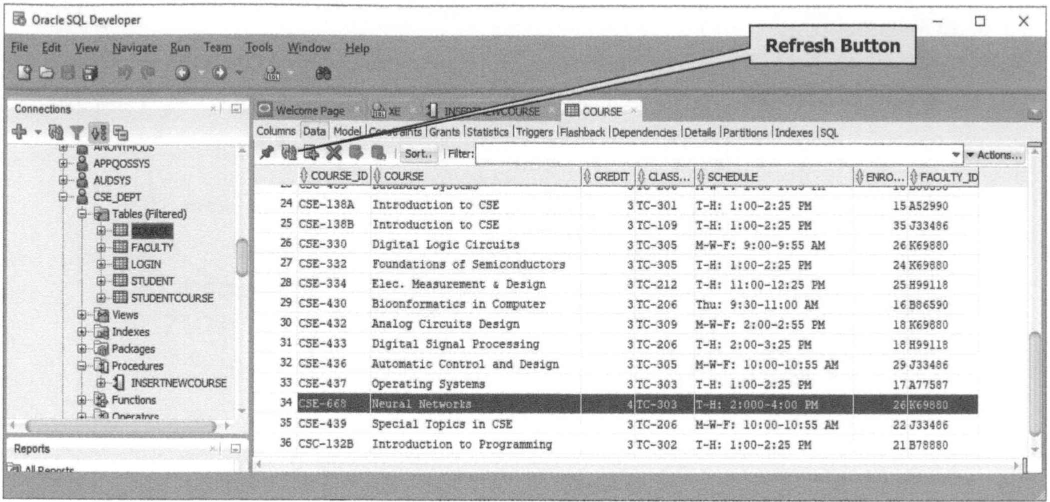

FIGURE 7.30 The run result of procedure INSERTNEWCOURSE() (Copyrighted by Oracle and used with permission).

```
  package OracleSelectFacultyPackage;
  import java.sql.*;
  import javax.swing.*;
  private void InsertButtonActionPerformed(java.awt.event.ActionEvent evt) {
A    if (ComboMethod.getSelectedItem()=="Java Callable Method"){
B         CallableStatement cstmt;
C      try{
          String query = "{call InsertNewCourse(?, ?, ?, ?, ?, ?, ?)}";
D         cstmt = LogInFrame.con.prepareCall(query);
E         cstmt.setString(1, CourseIDField.getText());
          cstmt.setString(2, CourseField.getText());
          cstmt.setInt(3, Integer.valueOf(CreditsField.getText()));
          cstmt.setString(4, ClassRoomField.getText());
          cstmt.setString(5, ScheduleField.getText());
          cstmt.setInt(6, Integer.valueOf(EnrollField.getText()));
          cstmt.setString(7, ComboName.getSelectedItem().toString());
F         cstmt.execute();
          }
G      catch (SQLException e){
          msgDlg.setMessage("Error in CallableStatement! " + e.getMessage());
          msgDlg.setVisible(true);
          }
     }
H    else {
          msgDlg.setMessage("Only Java Callable Method is available!");
          msgDlg.setVisible(true);
     }
  }
```

FIGURE 7.31 The code for the Insert button click event handler.

Now let's develop the code for this event handler to perform the calling of the stored procedure we built in the last section to perform this data insertion function.

Double-click on the `Insert` button on the CourseFrame form window to open its event handler, and enter the code shown in Figure 7.31 into this handler.

Let's have a closer look at this piece of code to see how it works.

A. An **if** block is used to distinguish whether the **Java Callable Method** has been selected.
B. If it is, a new CallableStatement instance is declared.
C. A **try-catch** block is used to perform this data insertion using the CallableStatement method. The CallableStatement query string is created. Refer to Section 6.3.7.5.1 in Chapter 6 to get more detailed information about the structure and protocol of a CallableStatement query string. This is a dynamic query string with seven pieces of positional insertion information related to the new course; therefore, seven question marks are used as the position holders for those parameters.
D. A new CallableStatement instance is created by calling the **prepareCall()** method that is defined in the Connection class.
E. The dynamic query string is initialized with seven positional parameters, and the values of those parameters are entered by the user into the associated course-related text fields.
F. The CallableStatement instance is executed to call the stored procedure we built in the last section to insert a new course record into the **Course** Table in our sample database.
G. The **catch** block is used to track and collect any possible exception for this data insertion process.
H. If some other method is selected by the user, a warning message is displayed.

Two points to be noted are in step E, where all seven input parameters, including **Credit** and **Enrollment**, are initialized and assigned to the stored procedure:

1) The order of these input parameters must be exactly identical to the order used in the stored procedure **InsertNewCourse()**. Otherwise data type mismatch errors may be encountered as the project runs.
2) For two parameters, **Credit** and **Enrollment**, both data types are **Integer**, so the collected contents from these two TextFields must be converted to integers, and then they can be assigned to the stored procedure. Both the **parseInt()** and **valueOf()** methods, which belong to the Integer class, are available for this kind of conversion.

Now let's build and run the project to test the data insertion function. Click on the **Clean and Build Main Project** button to build the project, and click on the **Run Main Project** button to run the project.

Enter a suiTable username and password, such as **jhenry** and **test**, to the LogIn frame form and select **Course Information** from the SelectFrame window to open the CourseFrame form window. Make sure that the **Java Callable Method** has been selected from the **Query Method** combo box. Also make sure that the desired faculty member, **Ying Bai**, is selected from the Faculty Name combo box. Click on the **Select** button to query all courses (**course _ id**) taught by the selected faculty member, Ying Bai. All queried courses (**course _ id**) are displayed in the CourseList box. Click on **CSE-434** from that list to get all details for that course, which are displayed in six TextFields on the right.

Now enter the following data into the six text fields as a new course record for the selected faculty member, **Ying Bai**:

Course ID:	`CSE-549`
Course:	`Fuzzy Systems`
Schedule:	`T-H: 1:30-2:45 PM`
Classroom:	`TC-302`
Credit:	`3`

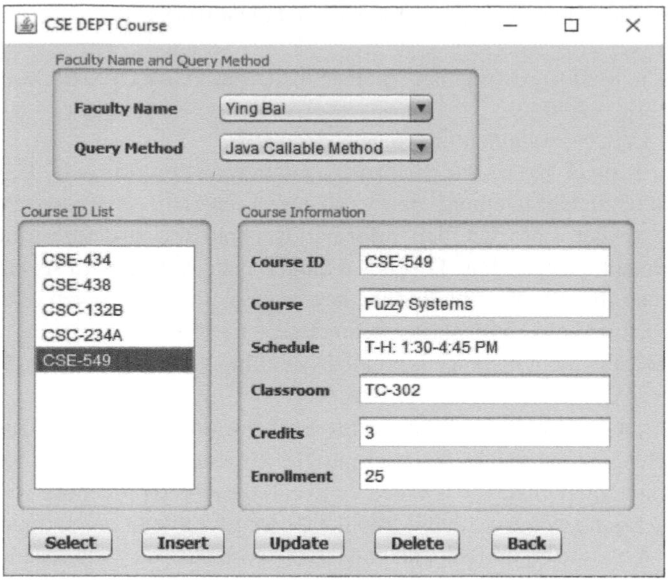

FIGURE 7.32 The confirmation result for new course insertion.

Enrollment: **25**

Then click on the **Insert** button to insert this course record into the **Course** Table in our sample database. To check and confirm this data insertion, two methods could be used:

1) Click on the **Select** button to get all courses (**course _ id**), including the new added course, and display them in the CourseList box. One can see that the new inserted course, **CSE-549**, is retrieved and displayed at the bottom in the CourseList box. Click on that course from that list, and all details about that course are displayed in the six TextFields on the right, as shown in Figure 7.32.
2) Open the **Services** window inside the NetBeans IDE, expand the **Databases** node, connect to our Oracle sample database by right-clicking on the URL, enter the password**oracle _ 18c** and select the **Connect** item. Then expand our **CSE _ DEPT** database node and **Tables** nodes. Right-click on the **Course** Table and select **View Data** to open the Table. Scroll down along the Table, and you can see that course **CSE-549** has been inserted to the last line on this **Course** Table, as shown in Figure 7.33.

Now click on the **Back** and **Exit** buttons to terminate our project.

Our data insertion using the CallableStatement object is successful.

A complete project, **OracleCallableInsert**, that contains the data insertion functions using the CallableStatement object can be found in the folder **ClassDB Projects\Chapter 7** located in the **Students** folder at the CRC Press ftp site (refer to Figure 1.2 in Chapter 1).

Next let's handle the data update using the CallableStatement object method.

7.6.2 Update Data to the Course Table Using Callable Statements

Copy the project **OracleCallableInsert**, change its name to **OracleCallableUpdate** and save it to the folder **Class DB Projects\Chapter 7** on your computer. We will build the data update function with the CallableStatement method in the following procedures:

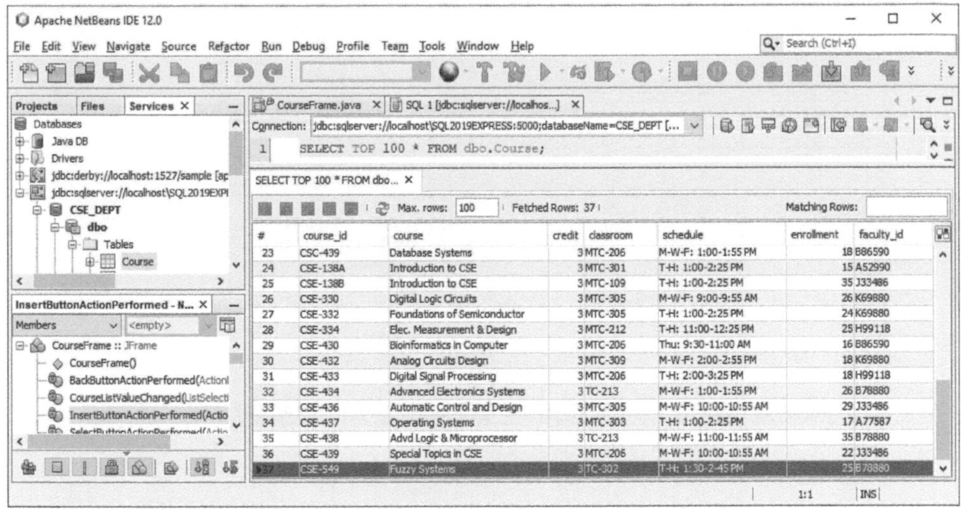

FIGURE 7.33 The new inserted course, CSE-549.

1) Build our stored procedure, **UpdateCourse**, using the Oracle SQL Developer.
2) Develop the code for the **Update** button in the CourseFrame Form window to execute the CallableStatement method to call our stored procedure **UpdateCourse** to update a course record in the **Course** Table in our sample database.
3) Confirm and validate this course update action using the code we built for the **Select** button event handler.

Now let's start from the first step.

7.6.2.1 Develop the Oracle Stored Procedure UpdateCourse()

Generally, we do not need to update a **course _ id** when we update a course record in the **Course** Table, since a better way to do that is to insert a new course record and delete the old one. The main reason for this is that a very complicated cascade operation would be performed if the **course _ id** were updated, since it is a primary key in the **Course** Table and foreign key in the **StudentCourse** Table. To update a primary key, one needs to update the foreign key first in the child Tables and then update the primary key in the parent Table. This will make our update operation much more complicated and potentially confusing. In order to avoid this confusion, in this section, we will update a course record by changing any column other than **course _ id**, and this is a popular way to update a Table and is widely implemented in most database applications.

Perform the following steps to build the Oracle stored procedure **DeleteCourse** with Oracle SQL Developer:

1) Open Oracle SQL Developer and click on the system database, **XE**, under **Recent** to connect to the Oracle database by entering the system password, **oracle _ 18c**. Then expand the **Other Users** folder and our sample database folder, **CSE _ DEPT**.
2) Right-click on the **Procedures** folder and select the **New Procedure** item.
3) In the opened Create Procedure wizard, enter **UPDATECOURSE** in the **Name:** box as the procedure's name.
4) Click on the green plus symbol (+) in the upper-right corner to add all seven input parameters one by one with the data type shown in Figure 7.34.
5) Click on the **OK** button to open the procedure code window.

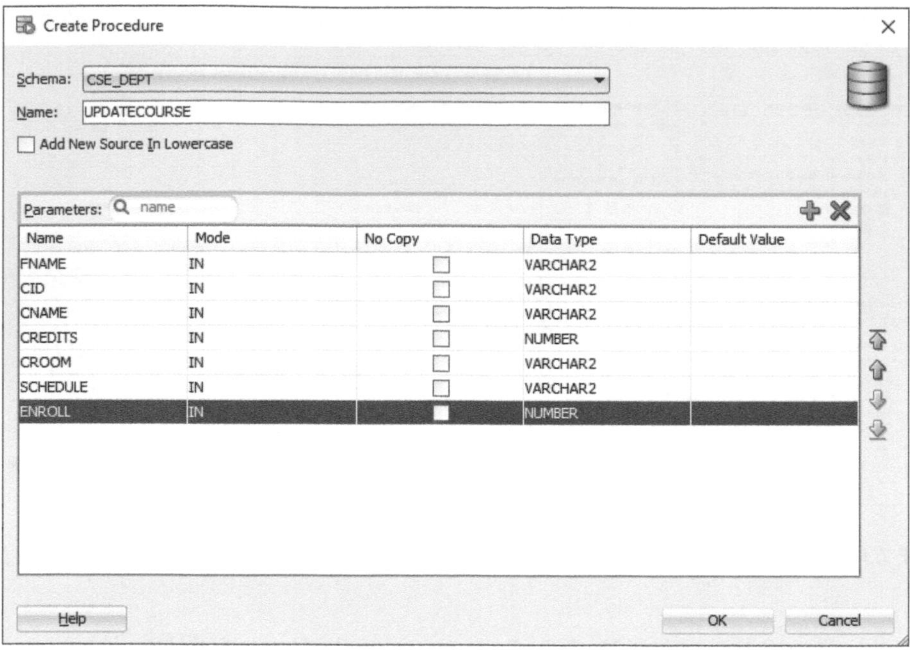

FIGURE 7.34 The finished Create Procedure wizard (Copyrighted by Oracle and used with permission).

```
  CREATE OR REPLACE PROCEDURE UPDATECOURSE
  (
A   FNAME IN VARCHAR2
  , CID IN VARCHAR2
  , CNAME IN VARCHAR2
  , CREDITS IN NUMBER
  , CROOM IN VARCHAR2
  , SCHED IN VARCHAR2
  , ENROLL IN NUMBER
  ) AS
B FID VARCHAR2(20);
  BEGIN
C   SELECT faculty_id INTO FID FROM FACULTY WHERE faculty_name = FNAME;
D   UPDATE CSE_DEPT.course
    SET course=CNAME, credit=CREDITS, classroom=CROOM, schedule=SCHED, enrollment=ENROLL,
        faculty_id=FID WHERE course_id=CID;
  END UPDATECOURSESP;
```

FIGURE 7.35 The finished code body for the procedure.

In the opened procedure code window, enter the code shown in Figure 7.35 into the procedure body section, which is just under the **BEGIN** command. Let's have a closer look at this piece of code to see how it works.

A. Seven input parameters to this stored procedure are declared first with the associated data types. These parameters must be identical to the parameters in the CallableStatement query string we will build later to enable the CallableStatement to recognize them when it is executed to perform the data update action in our project.

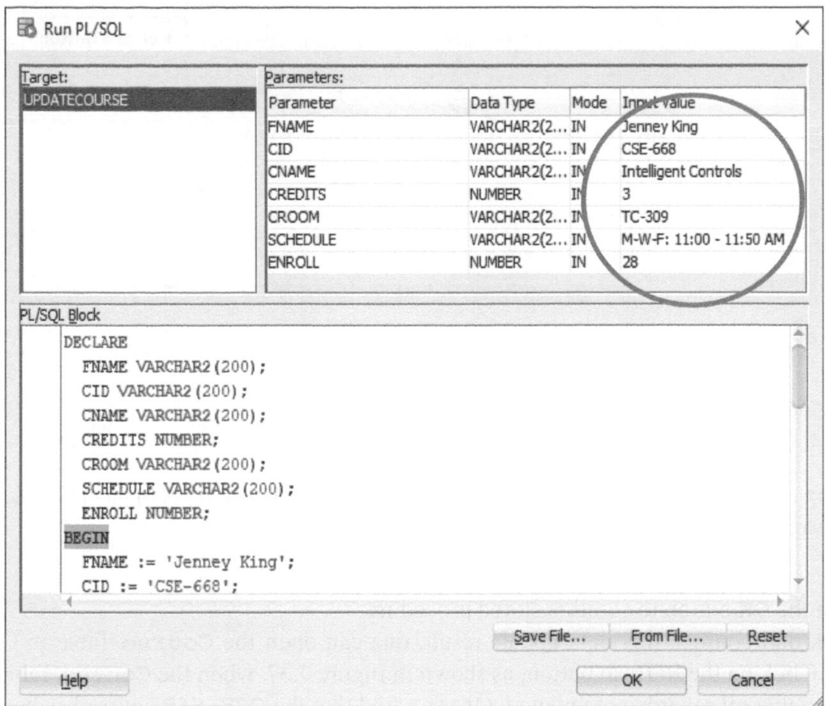

FIGURE 7.36 The run status of the stored procedure UPDATECOURSE (Copyrighted by Oracle and used with permission).

B. A local variable, **FID**, that works as an intermediate-level variable is declared, and it is used to hold the queried **faculty _ id** from the first query to the **Faculty** Table since we do not have **faculty _ name** column available in the **Course** Table.
C. The first query to the **Faculty** Table is executed to get a matching **faculty _ id** based on the input faculty name **FNAME**.
D. The **UPDATE** statement is executed here, and the query criterion **course _ id** is the input parameter **CID**.

Now expand the **Compile** icon and click on the **Compile** item to compile our procedure. A **Compiled** statement should be displayed in the Message window if everything is fine. Also, you can find our procedure, **UPDATECOURSE**, just under the **Procedures** folder in the left pane. You may need to refresh that folder by right-clicking on the folder and selecting the **Refresh** item on the popup menu if you cannot find our procedure.

We can directly test the stored procedure in the Oracle SQL Developer environment to confirm its performance. To do this test, just click on the green arrow button to run the procedure. When the **Run PL/SQL** wizard appears, enter the following input parameters as an updated course record for the faculty member **Jenney King** in the **Input Value** column, as shown in Figure 7.36:

- FNAME: **Jenney King**
- CID: **CSE-668**
- CNAME: **Intelligent Controls**
- CREDITS: **3**
- CROOM: **TC-309**
- SCHEDULE: **M-W-F: 11:00-11:50 AM**
- ENROLL: **28**

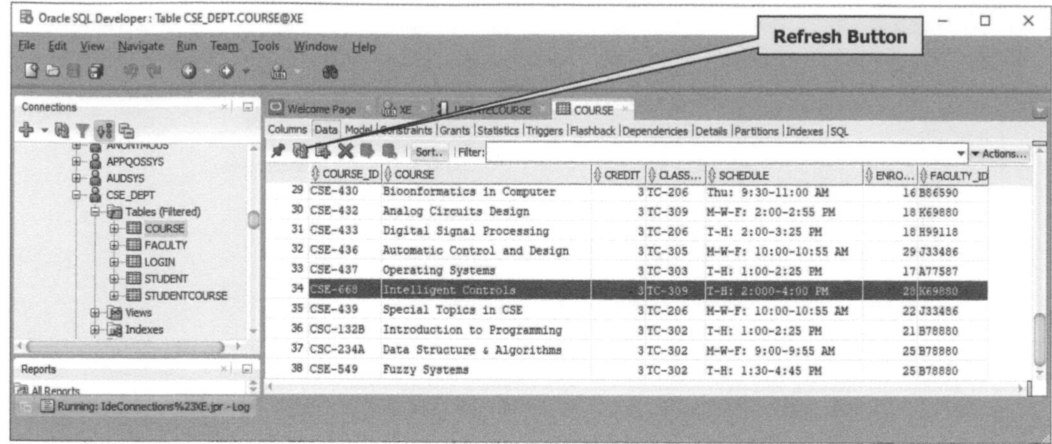

FIGURE 7.37 The run result of the stored procedure UPDATECOURSE (Copyrighted by Oracle and used with permission).

Click on the **OK** button to run this stored procedure.

To check and confirm this data update result, one can open the **Course** Table in Oracle SQL Developer. Click on the Refresh button, as shown in Figure 7.37, when the **Course** Table is opened to make sure that all records are updated. One can find that the **CSE-668** course has been updated, as shown in a highlighted line in Figure 7.37.

It is highly recommended to recover this updated course record to its original values, since we need to call the CallableStatement object to run this stored procedure again when we test our project later. You can do this recovery by performing another update action using this stored procedure. Refer to Section 7.6.1.1 to get more details for this course record to recover the course **CSE-668**.

Now close the Oracle SQL Developer, since we have finished building and testing this stored procedure. Now let's build our code for the **Update** button click event handler in the CourseFrame form to call this stored procedure to perform the data update action.

7.6.2.2 Develop the Code for the Update Button Click Event Handler

Open our project, **OracleCallableUpdate**, and the CourseFrame Form window in Design View; double-click on the **Update** button to open its event handler; and enter the code shown in Figure 7.38 into this handler.

Let's have a closer look at this piece of code to see how it works.

A. An **if** block is used to distinguish whether the **Java Callable Method** has been selected.
B. If it is, a new CallableStatement instance is declared.
C. A **try-catch** block is used to perform the data update action using the CallableStatement method. The CallableStatement query string is created. Refer to Section 6.3.7.5.1 in Chapter 6 to get more detailed information about the structure and protocol of a CallableStatement query string. This is a dynamic query string with seven pieces of positional update information related to a new course; therefore, seven question marks are used as the position holders for those parameters.
D. A new CallableStatement instance is created by calling the **prepareCall()** method that is defined in the **Connection** class.
E. The dynamic query string is initialized with seven positional parameters, and the values of those parameters are entered by the user into the associated course-related text fields. The point to be noted is for two parameters, the credits (**Integer**) and enrollment (**integer**), both are

```
  private void UpdateButtonActionPerformed(java.awt.event.ActionEvent evt) {
A     if (ComboMethod.getSelectedItem()=="Java Callable Method"){
B     CallableStatement cstmt;
      try{
C         String query = "{call UpdateCourse(?, ?, ?, ?, ?, ?, ?)}";
D         cstmt = LogInFrame.con.prepareCall(query);
E         cstmt.setString(1, ComboName.getSelectedItem().toString());
          cstmt.setString(2, CourseList.getSelectedValue());
          cstmt.setString(3, CourseField.getText());
          cstmt.setInt(4, java.lang.Integer.valueOf(CreditsField.getText()));
          cstmt.setString(5, ClassRoomField.getText());
          cstmt.setString(6, ScheduleField.getText());
          cstmt.setInt(7, java.lang.Integer.parseInt(EnrollField.getText()));
F         cstmt.execute();
        }
G     catch (SQLException e){
          msgDlg.setMessage("Error in CallableStatement! " + e.getMessage());
          msgDlg.setVisible(true);
        }
    }
H     CourseIDField.setText(CourseList.getSelectedValue());
  }
```

FIGURE 7.38 The code for the Update button click event handler.

defined as numbers. Therefore the associated **setXXX()** methods need to be used to initialize these two parameters. Since the **Integer** class belongs to the **java.lang** package, here a full name is used for these classes. You can import the **Java.lang** package at the top of the code window under the **Package** clause to remove those package names if you like.

F. The CallableStatement instance is executed to call the stored procedure to update the selected course record in the **Course** Table in our sample database.
G. The **catch** block is used to collect any possible exception for this data update process.
H. Finally, the selected **course _ id** from the **CourseList** Listbox is assigned to the **Course ID** field to indicate the updated course.

Now let's build and run the project to test the data update function. Click on the **Clean and Build Main Project** button to build the project, and click the **Run Main Project** button to run the project.

Enter a suiTable username and password, such as **jhenry** and **test**, to the LogIn frame form and select the **Course Information** from the SelectFrame window to open the CourseFrame form window. Make sure that the **Java Callable Method** has been selected from the **Query Method** combo box. Then click on the **Select** button to query the default course information for the selected faculty member, **Jenney King**.

Now select course **CSE-668** from the CourseList listbox and enter the following data into the seven text fields as an updated course record for the selected course, **CSE-668**:

- Faculty Name: **Jenney King**
- Course ID: **CSE-668**
- Course Name: **Intelligent Controls**
- Credits: **3**
- Classroom: **TC-309**
- Schedule: **M-W-F: 11:00-11:50 AM**
- Enrollment: **28**

Then click on the **Update** button to update this course record in the **Course** Table in our sample database. To confirm and validate this data update, click on the **Select** button to try to retrieve all courses taught by the selected faculty member, **Jenney King**. Click on **course _ id CSE-668**

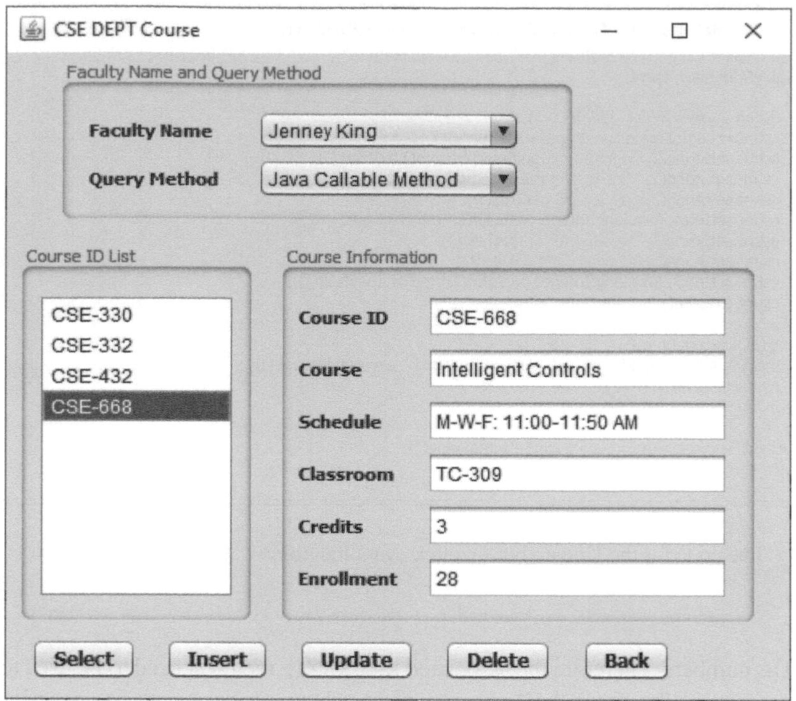

FIGURE 7.39 The run result of the data update action.

from the CourseList box; all details about this updated course are displayed in six TextFields on the right, as shown in Figure 7.39.

Another way to confirm this data update action is to open the **Course** Table using the **Services** window in the NetBeans IDE. To do that, open the **Services** window, expand the **Databases** node and connect to our sample database by right-clicking on that URL and selecting the **Connect** item. Then expand that connected URL and our **CSE _ DEPT** database node and **Tables** nodes. Right-click on the **Course** Table and select **View Data** to open the Table. Scroll down along this Table, and you can see that course **CSE-668** has been updated and is displayed on the last line of this **Course** Table.

It is highly recommended to recover this updated course record to its original values, since we want to keep our database clean and neat. You can do this by performing another update action using the **Update** button event handler in this project. Refer to Section 7.6.1.1 to get more details about the course record to recover course **CSE-668**.

A complete project, **OracleCallableUpdate**, that contains the data update functions using the CallableStatement object can be found in the folder **Class DB Projects\Chapter 7** located in the **Students** folder at the CRC Press ftp site (refer to Figure 1.2 in Chapter 1).

Next let's handle the data deletion using the CallableStatement object method.

7.6.3 Delete Data from the Course Table Using Callable Statements

Copy the project **OracleCallableUpdate**, change its name to **OracleCallable Delete** and save it to the folder **Class DB Projects\Chapter 7** on your computer. We will build the data delete function with the CallableStatement method in the following procedures:

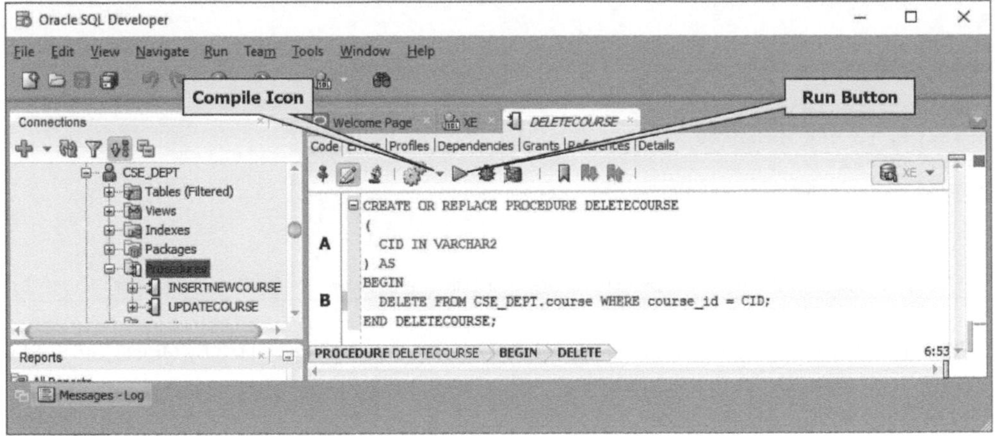

FIGURE 7.40 The codes for the stored procedure DeleteCourse() (Copyrighted by Oracle and used with permission).

1) Build our stored procedure, **DeleteCourse**, using the Oracle SQL Developer.
2) Develop the code for the **Delete** button in the CourseFrame Form window to execute the CallableStatement method to call our stored procedure, **DeleteCourse**, to delete a course record from the **Course** Table in our sample database.
3) Confirm and validate this course delete action using the code we built for the **Select** button event handler.

Now let's start from the first step.

7.6.3.1 Develop the Stored Procedure DeleteCourse()

Perform the following steps to build the Oracle stored procedure **DeleteCourse** with Oracle SQL Developer:

1) Open the Oracle SQL Developer and click on the system database, **XE**, under **Recent** to connect to the Oracle database by entering the system password, **oracle _ 18c**. Then expand the **Other Users** folder and our sample database folder, **CSE _ DEPT**.
2) Right-click on the **Procedures** folder and select the **New Procedure** item.
3) In the opened Create Procedure wizard, enter **DELETECOURSE** into the **Name:** box as the procedure's name.
4) Click on the green + icon to add only one input parameter, **CID**, which is equivalent to an input (**IN**) parameter **course _ id** with the **VARCHAR2** data type, and click on the **OK** button to continue.
5) In the opened code wizard, enter the code shown in Figure 7.40 into the code window as the body of this procedure.
6) Click on the **Compile** icon (Figure 7.40) to compile this procedure. A **Compiled** statement should be displayed in the **Message** window if everything is fine.

Your finished stored procedure should match the one shown in Figure 7.40. Let's have a closer look at this piece of code to see how it works.

A. The only input to this stored procedure is the **course _ id** that is a primary key to the **Course** Table. Here we use **CID** as a dynamic parameter for this stored procedure.
B. The **DELETE** statement is created with **CID** as this deleting criterion.

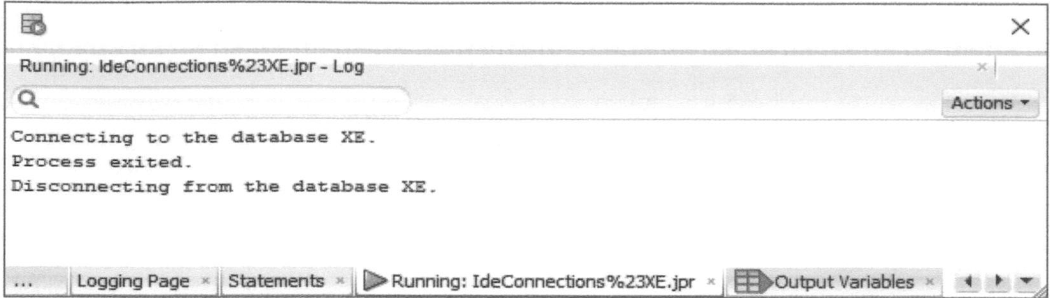

FIGURE 7.41 The run result of the stored procedure DeleteCourse() (Copyrighted by Oracle and used with permission).

TABLE 7.7
The Deleted Course Record in the Course Table

course_id	course	credit	classroom	schedule	enrollment	faculty_id
CSE-549	Fuzzy Systems	3	TC-302	T-H: 1:30–2:45 PM	25	B78880

To run and test the stored procedure, click on the green arrow button on the top to open the Run PL/SQL wizard. Enter **CSE-549** into the associated **Value** column in this wizard and click on the **OK** button to run this procedure. The run result is shown in Figure 7.41.

To confirm the data delete action, you can open the **COURSE** Table in this Oracle SQL Developer to check it. Go to the **COURSE** Table located under the **Tables** folder in our sample database, **CSE _ DEPT**, in Developer, expand the **Tables** folder and click on the **COURSE** Table to open it. You may need to refresh the Table by clicking on the **Refresh** icon in the upper-left corner. Then you can see that course **CSE-549** has been deleted from this Table.

It is highly recommended to recover this deleted course record to its original values, since we need to call the CallableStatement object to run this stored procedure again when we test our project later. You can do this inside the Oracle SQL Developer by opening the **Course** Table and inserting this course record at the bottom line of that Table. When it is done, right-click on the new inserted data line and select the **Commit Changes** item from the popup menu to make this insertion effective.

Refer to Table 7.7 to get more details to recover this deleted course record.

Before you can close the Oracle SQL Developer, go to **File > Save All** to save there covered job and any other modifications to the Table.

Next we need to build code for the **Delete** button click event handler in the CourseFrame form to call this stored procedure to perform the data delete action.

7.6.3.2 Develop the Code for the Delete Button Click Event Handler

Open the Design View of our project, **OracleCallableDelete**, and double-click on the **Delete** button in the CourseFrame form window to open its event handler and enter the code shown in Figure 7.42 into this handler. Let's have a close look at this piece of code to see how it works.

A. An **if** block is used to distinguish whether the **Java Callable Method** has been selected.
B. If it is, a new **CallableStatement** instance is declared.

```
  private void cmdDeleteActionPerformed(java.awt.event.ActionEvent evt) {
A    if (ComboMethod.getSelectedItem()=="Java Callable Method"){
B      CallableStatement cstmt;
       try{
C         String query = "{call DeleteCourse(?)}";
D         cstmt = LogInFrame.con.prepareCall(query);
E         cstmt.setString(1, CourseList.getSelectedValue());
F         cstmt.execute();
       }
G      catch (SQLException e){
          msgDlg.setMessage("Error in CallableStatement! " + e.getMessage());
          msgDlg.setVisible(true);
       }
     }
H    CourseIDField.setText(null);
  }
```

FIGURE 7.42 The code for the Delete button click event handler.

C. A **try-catch** block is used to perform the data delete action using the CallableStatement method. The CallableStatement query string is created. Refer to Section 6.3.7.5.1 in Chapter 6 to get more detailed information about the structure and protocol of a CallableStatement query string. This is a dynamic query string with one positional parameter related to a new course; therefore, a question mark is used as the position holder for this parameter.
D. A new CallableStatement instance is created by calling the **prepareCall()** method that is defined in the **Connection** class.
E. The dynamic query string is initialized with a positional parameter, and the value of the parameter is selected by the user from the **CourseList** Listbox.
F. The CallableStatement instance is executed to call the stored procedure we built in the last section to delete the selected course record in the **Course** Table from our sample database.
G. The **catch** block is used to track and collect any possible exception for the data delete.
H. The deleted **course _ id** is removed from the Course ID field to indicate this delete action.

Let's build and run the project to test the data delete function. Click on the **Clean and Build Main Project** button to build the project, and click on the **Run Main Project** button to run the project.

Enter a suitable username and password, such as **jhenry** and **test**, to the LogIn frame form and select the **Course Information** from the SelectFrame window to open the CourseFrame form window. Make sure that the **Java Callable Method** has been selected from the **Query Method** combo box. Then click on the **Select** button to query the default course information for the selected faculty member, **Ying Bai**.

Now select course **CSE-549** from the **CourseList** Listbox and click on the **Delete** button to try to delete this course from the **Course** Table in our sample database.

To confirm and validate this data deletion action, click on the **Select** button again to try to retrieve all courses taught by the default faculty member, **Ying Bai**. It can be seen that there is no **CSE-549** course in the **CourseList** Listbox, and this means that course **CSE-549** has been deleted from the **Course** Table. You can also confirm this data delete action by opening the **Course** Table using the **Services** window in the Apache NetBeans IDE.

At this point, we have finished developing and building a data manipulation project using the CallableStatement object method. A complete project, **OracleCallableDelete**, can be found in the folder **Class DB Projects\Chapter 7** in the **Students** folder at the CRC Press ftp site (refer to Figure 1.2 in Chapter 1).

7.7 CHAPTER SUMMARY

Three popular data manipulation methods against the Oracle database have been discussed and analyzed in detail, with quite a few real project examples in this chapter.

This chapter is divided into three parts based on three different data query methods: insert, update and delete data in our sample database using the Java runtime object method. This method provides more flexibility and efficiency in data actions against Oracle databases. Also in this chapter, two more data manipulation methods, UpdaTable ResultSet and CallableStatement, are discussed with real projects for the Oracle database.

Detailed introductions to and illustrations of building stored procedures under the Oracle database system with Oracle SQL Developer are provided with real and step-by-step examples. After finishing this chapter, readers will be able to:

- Design and build professional data actions against an Oracle database system using the Java runtime objects method.
- Design and build popular stored procedures for the Oracle database system.
- Design and build professional data actions against the Oracle database system using UpdaTable ResultSet methods.
- Design and build professional data actions against the Oracle database system using CallableStatement methods.

Starting with the next chapter, we will discuss how to build Java Web applications to access and manipulate Oracle databases.

HOMEWORK

I. True/False Selections

_______1. To use the Java runtime method to insert an image into the Oracle database, the **setString**() method should be used.

_______2. When using the **JFileChooser** object to select an image, the returned image is a Java File object, and one needs to convert it to a **Byte[]** array to be inserted into a column in a database Table.

_______3. When converting an image file to a **Byte[]** array, one can use a system method, **readAllBytes**().

_______4. To avoid possible duplicated records being inserted into a database, the **Insert** button on a Frame Form should be enabled after a desired record has been inserted.

_______5. By setting the Concurrency Type property as **UpdaTable** to a ResultSet object, that ResultSet object can be used to perform data insert, update and delete actions to a database.

_______6. To use the UpdaTable ResultSet object to delete a record from a database, only one step is enough, which is to use the **deleteRow**() method of the ResultSet class.

_______7. When using the UpdaTable ResultSet object to update a record in a database, only one step is enough, which is to call the **updateRow**() method.

_______8. When perform data manipulation using the Java runtime object method, one can use either the **executeUpdate**() or **execute**() method.

_______9. A default ResultSet object is updaTable and has a cursor that can move either forward or backward.

______10. To insert a new record into a database using the UpdaTable ResultSet method, one needs first to move the cursor to an insert row that is a blank row and is not a part of the ResultSet but related to the ResultSet.

II. Multiple Choice

1. When using the UpdaTable ResultSet object to update a record in a database, two steps are needed: ___________.
   a. Insert data in ResultSet, update the data in database
   b. Update data in ResultSet, copy change to database
   c. Delete data from ResultSet, copy change to database
   d. Select data in ResultSet, update the data in database

2. When finished building a stored procedure with Oracle SQL Developer, one needs to save the stored procedure by ___________.
   a. Going to the **File > Save All** menu item
   b. Building the procedure
   c. Executing the procedure
   d. Updating the procedure

3. When using an UpdaTable ResultSet to perform data manipulations, two parameters can be used to setup properties of a ResultSet object: ___________.
   a. Forward-only, UpdaTable
   b. Scroll-sensitive, Read-only
   c. ResultSet Type, Concurrency Type of a ResultSet
   d. ResultSet Type, UpdaTable Type

4. Which of the following create ResultSet protocols is correct? ___________
   a. Statement createStatement(int resultSetType, int resultSetConcurrency).
   b. PreparedStatement prepareStatement(String sql, int resultSetType, int resultSet Concurrency).
   c. CallableStatement prepareCall(String sql, int resultSetType, int resultSet Concurrency).
   d. All of them.

5. To update a record using the UpdaTable ResultSet, one needs to use ___________ steps, and they are: ___________.
   a. 1, UpdateXXX()
   b. 2, UpdateXXX() and UpdateRow()
   c. 3, UpdateXXX(), UpdateCursor() and UpdateRow()
   d. 4, MoveToRow(), UpdateXXX(), UpdateCursor() and UpdateRow()

6. To insert a new record using the UpdaTable ResultSet, one needs to use ___________ steps, and they are: ___________.
   a. 1, insertRow()
   b. 2, moveToInsertRow(), insertRow()
   c. 3, moveToInsertRow(), updateXXX(), insertRow()
   d. 4, moveToCursor(), moveToInsertRow(), updateXXX(), insertRow()

7. When building a stored procedure to perform a data insertion action, the order of the input parameters must be ___________ with the order of the related ___________.
   a. Identical, data column
   b. Different, data column
   c. Same or different, data row
   d. Identical, data Table

8. By using which of the following static constant values can we set an UpdaTable Result object that has a cursor that can move either forward or backward?
   a. ResultSet.TYPE_FORWARD_ONLY
   b. ResultSet.TYPE_SCROLL_INSENSITIVE

c. ResultSet.CONCUR_UPDATable
d. ResultSet.TYPE_SCROLL_SENSITIVE

9. By using which of the following static constant values can we set an UpdaTable Result object whose contents can be updated?
   a. ResultSet.TYPE_FORWARD_ONLY
   b. ResultSet.TYPE_SCROLL_INSENSITIVE
   c. ResultSet.CONCUR_UPDATable
   d. ResultSet.TYPE_SCROLL_SENSITIVE
10. When building an Oracle stored procedure to update a record in a database, each input parameter ____________.
   a. Can have a different name from the associated column name in the database
   b. Can have the same name as the associated column name in the database
   c. Must have the same name as the associated column name in the database
   d. Must have a different name from the associated column name in the database

III. Exercises

1. List six steps to use the Java runtime object to perform data manipulations against our target database.
2. List three steps to insert a new record into a database using the UpdaTable ResultSet method.
3. Build a new project, **OracleInsertStudent**, and develop code for the StudentFrame Form window to insert a new student record into the **Student** Table in our sample database using the Java runtime object method. The new student's record is:
   - Student ID: `F78569`
   - Student Name: `Williams Ford`
   - GPA: `3.42`
   - Credits: `97`
   - Major: `Computer Engineering`
   - SchoolYear: `Junior`
   - Email: `wford@college.edu`
   - simage: `Default.jpg`

   Hint1:

   Copy and modify a project, **OracleSelectStudent**, which can be found in the folder **Class DB Projects\Chapter 6** in the **Students** folder on the CRC Press ftp site (refer to Figure 1.2 in Chapter 1). Based on that project and referring to another project, **OracleInsertFaculty**, which can be found in the folder **Class DB Projects\Chapter 7** in the **Students** folder on the CRC Press ftp site, build your code in the **Insert** button event handler on the StudentFrame Form.

   Hint2:

   1) Add one more method, **Java Runtime Method**, into the StudentFrame constructor.
   2) Add one **if** block in the **Insert** button event handler to identify the **Java Runtime Method**, and build and add your code inside this block.
   3) You may need to use three user-defined methods in the project, **OracleInsertFaculty**, **chkFaculty()**, **clearFaculty()** and **getFacultyImage()**, which you can obtain from the **Insert** button event handler in the Facultyframe class in the same project. It is recommended to change their names to **chkStudent()**, **clearStudent()** and **getStudentImage()**, respectively.

```
create or replace NONEDITIONABLE PROCEDURE UPDATESTUDENT
(
 SID IN VARCHAR2
, SNAME IN VARCHAR2
, SGPA IN NUMBER
, SCREDITS IN NUMBER
, SMAJOR IN VARCHAR2
, SSCHOOLYEAR IN VARCHAR2
, SEMAIL IN VARCHAR2
, SSIMAGE IN BLOB
) AS
BEGIN
 UPDATE Student
 SET student_name=SNAME, gpa=SGPA, credits=SCREDITS, major=SMAJOR,
    schoolYear=SSCHOOLYEAR, email=SEMAIL, simage=SSIMAGE
    WHERE student_id=SID;
END UPDATESTUDENT;
```

FIGURE 7.43 A completed stored procedure, UPDATESTUDENT.

4. Figure 7.43 shows a stored procedure, **UpdateStudent**. Develop and build a new project, **OracleUpdateStudent**, and add code into the **Update** button event handler on the StudentFrame form class to call this stored procedure to update a student record for the **Student** Table in our sample Oracle database using the CallableStatement method. A default student photo, **Default.jpg**, can be used for this update action. The updated student record is:
   - Student ID: `B92996`
   - Student Name: `Black Jackson`
   - GPA: `3.12`
   - Credits: `42`
   - Major: `Computer Science`
   - SchoolYear: `Sophomore`
   - Email: `bjackson@college.edu`
   - simage: `Default.jpg`

   Hint1:

   Copy and modify a project, **OracleSelectStudent**, which can be found inthe folder **Class DB Projects\Chapter 6** in the **Students** folder on the CRC Press ftp site (refer to Figure 1.2 in Chapter 1). Based on that project and referring to two other projects, **OracleUpdateFaculty** and **OracleCallableUpdate**, which can be found in the folder **Class DB Projects\Chapter 7** in the **Students** folder on the CRC Press ftp site, build your new project, **OracleUpdateStudent**.

   Hint2:

   Add one **if** block in the **Update** button event handler to identify the **Java Callable Method**, and build and add your code inside this block.

   Hint3:

   Refer to the code in the `Update` button event handler in the FacultyFrame Form in the project `OracleCallableUpdate` located in the folder `Class DB Projects\Chapter 7` in the `Students` folder on the CRC Press ftp site (refer to Figure 1.2 in Chapter 1). You may also need to use two user-defined methods, `getFaculty-Image()` and `CurrentFaculty()`, developed in that project and change them to `getStudentImage()` and `CurrentStudent()`.

Part II

Building Three-Tier Client-Server Applications

8 Develop Java Web Applications to Access Databases

With the rapid development of Java Web application techniques, today, Java Web applications are closely related to the Java Enterprise Edition platform, and the latter provides rich and powerful APIs to support developers to build and develop more efficient and productive Web applications with less complexity and development effort.

The Java EE platform uses a simplified programming model. XML deployment descriptors are optional. Instead, a developer can simply enter the information as an annotation directly into a Java source file, and the Java EE server will conFigure the component at deployment and runtime. These annotations are generally used to embed data in a program that would otherwise be furnished in a deployment descriptor. With annotations, specification information is put directly in your code next to the program element that it affects.

In order to have a clear idea of Java Web applications and their developments, let's first have a quick historical review on this topic. This review is absolutely necessary for beginners who have never built and developed any Java Web application before. You are not required to understand all the details of the code in the following review sections, but we expect that you can understand it based on its function.

8.1 A HISTORICAL REVIEW ABOUT JAVA WEB APPLICATION DEVELOPMENT

Java Web applications are based on the Servlet technique, and the Servlet works as a Web server that provides all support, such as receiving requests from the client and sending responses back to the client. That is, a Servlet is a server class built in the Java language with all the functionalities of a server engine. A Servlet performs its job in the following ways:

- When a Servlet is created, the **`init()`** method is called to do the initialization for the Web server.
- When a request is received by the Servlet, it creates two objects: request and response.
- Then the Servlet sends these two objects to the **`service()`** method.
- The request object encapsulates the information passed from the HTTP request coming from the client.
- The **`service()`** method is the main responding body and will be used to process the request and send the response that has been embedded into the response object back to the client.

Conventional Web applications are built with a Servlet as a Web container and HTML pages as Web clients.

8.1.1 Using Servlet and HTML Web Pages for Java Web Applications

The main purpose of using the Servlet is to compensate for the shortcomings of using a common gateway interface (CGI). Unlike the CGI, the Servlet can be used to create dynamic Web pages during the server-client communication processes. Two methods, **`doGet()`** and **`doPost()`**, are the main channels to communicate between the server and clients.

DOI: 10.1201/9781003304029-10

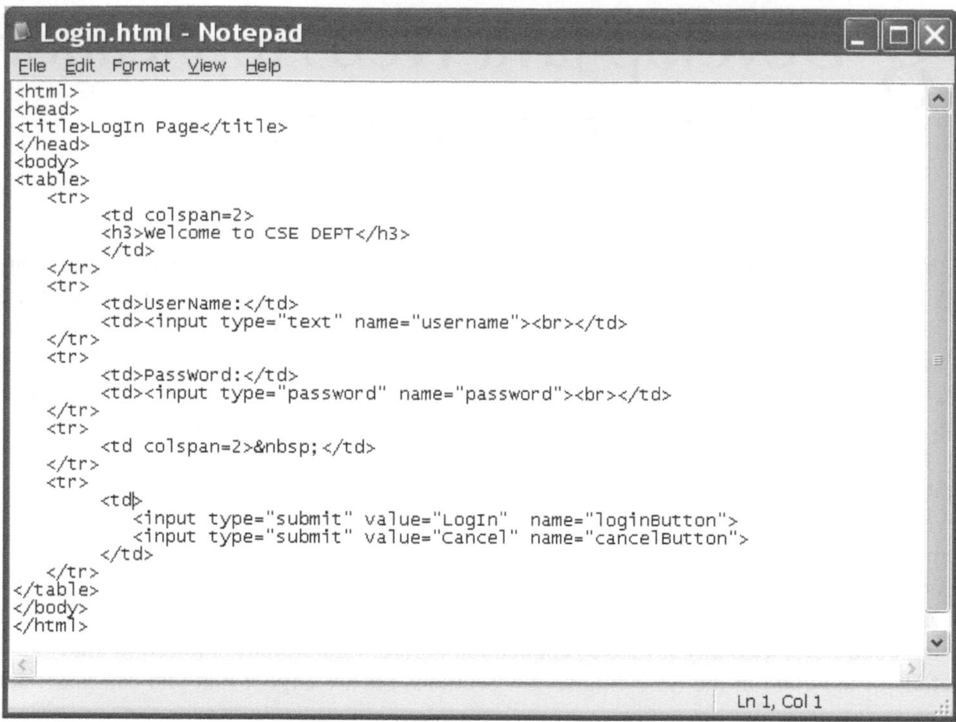


```
<html>
<head>
<title>LogIn Page</title>
</head>
<body>
<table>
   <tr>
        <td colspan=2>
        <h3>Welcome to CSE DEPT</h3>
        </td>
   </tr>
   <tr>
        <td>UserName:</td>
        <td><input type="text" name="username"><br></td>
   </tr>
   <tr>
        <td>Password:</td>
        <td><input type="password" name="password"><br></td>
   </tr>
   <tr>
        <td colspan=2> </td>
   </tr>
   <tr>
        <td>
          <input type="submit" value="LogIn"  name="loginButton">
          <input type="submit" value="Cancel" name="cancelButton">
        </td>
   </tr>
</table>
</body>
</html>
```

FIGURE 8.1 The finished Login.html file.

General uses of Servlets include:

- Processing requests received from clients and responses back to clients
- Creating dynamic Web pages
- Managing state information for applications
- Storing data and information for clients

Generally, client pages can be divided into two categories: reading pages and posting pages. The former is used to read data from the user, and the latter is used for displaying feedback from the server. To interface to the client to get user data, most often, the server calls the **`getParameter()`** method that belongs to the **`request`** object. To send feedback to the client, the server usually uses the **`println()`** method that belongs to the **`out`** object. With this pair of methods, a server can easily communicate with the client and transfer data between them.

By using an example that utilizes these methods to transfer login information between a Servlet and a client Web page, we can get a much clearer picture and deeper understanding of this topic.

Open Notepad and enter the code shown in Figure 8.1 to build the **`Login.html`** file. Save this file with the name of "**`Login.html`**" to make it an HTML file. You have to use double quotation marks to enclose this file name with the. html extension to let Notepad know that you want to save it as an HTML file.

Double-click on this file to run it. The run result is shown in Figure 8.2.

Two input text fields are used by users to enable them to enter the desired username and password. The key is the identifier for both text fields, **`username`** and **`password`**, which is the name

FIGURE 8.2 The Login.html run result.

```
public void doGet(HttpServletRequest request, HttpServletResponse response)
{
    response.setContentType("text/html");
    PrintWriter out = new PrintWriter(response.getWriter());

    String uname = request.getParameter("username");
    String pword = request.getParameter("password");

    // process the received uname and pword
```

FIGURE 8.3 Using the getParameter() method to get data from the client.

property or attribute of these two text fields. When a server needs these two pieces of login information, it uses the `getParameter()` method defined in the `request` object with the names of two text fields as identifiers to get them. Figure 8.3 shows a piece of code developed on the server side to perform this login information pick-up operation.

Two variables, `uname` and `pword`, are used on the server side to hold the picked-up username and password entered by the user from the client Web page. The `getParameter()` method is used to do this pick-up operation. The identifiers for these two parameters are the names of two text fields on the HTML page.

With this simple example, you can see how easy it is for the server and client to communicate with each other. The server can send feedback or post any desired information in the client by using the `out` object that is obtained by creating a new `PrintWriter` instance in the first two codelines.

OK, now we have a clear picture of using a Servlet and a client to build and implement a Java Web application in the early days. To deploy this login Servlet, we need to locate the Servlet class file in the suiTable directory.

One of the shortcomings of this kind of application is that the server and client use two different languages, and a converter or renderer is necessary to perform a conversion between the two. This will reduce the run speed and efficiency of the Web application. A solution to this issue is the JavaServer Pages technique, which was developed by Sun. With the help of the JSP, server code can be extended and embedded on the client side to facilitate communications between a server and a client.

8.1.2 Using JavaServer Pages Technology for Java Web Applications

In fact, the JavaServer Pages technique provides a way of using Java code within an HTML page, which means that you can embed a piece of Java code or part of Servlet's functions into the code on the client side with appropriate tags.

The embedded Java code will be compiled and executed by the JSP engine on the server side as the application runs. From this point of view, the JavaServer Pages can be considered as a part of a Servlet or as an extension of an application server located at the client side. Although the JSP provides a lot of advantages over Servlets, it is actually a subclass of the Servlet class and built based on Servlets technology.

JavaServer Pages can be implemented not only in HTML files but also in the following files:

- Script language files, which allow you to specify a block of Java code
- JSP directives, which enable you to control the JSP structure and environment
- Actions, which allow you to specify executing commands such as loading a parameter from a client page

The JSP provides some useful built-in or implicit objects to perform most interfacing functions with clients and servers. The so-called implicit objects in JSP are objects that are automatically available in JSP. Implicit objects are Java objects that the JSP Container provides to a developer to access in their applications using JavaBeans and Servlets. These objects are called implicit objects because they are automatically instantiated. Some popular implicit JSP objects include:

- request
- response
- out
- session
- application
- pageContext
- page
- exception

Among those objects, **request**, **response** and **session** are most popular objects and are often used in the interface between clients and servers. Some other objects, such as **out** and **pageContext**, are mainly used to write output to the client and to access most built-in objects.

Figure 8.4 shows an example of using the **out** and **pageContext** objects to write feedback to the client (top section) and to get a session object (bottom section).

Two popular tags used by JSP to distinguish it from other languages are:

- `<% . . . . %>`
- `<jsp: . . . . />`

```
out.println("<HTML>");
out.println("<HEAD>Hello World</HEAD>");
out.println("</HTML>");
out.close();
```

```
HttpSession session = pageContext.getSession();
```

FIGURE 8.4 An example of using the out and pageContext objects.

```
<HTML>
<HEAD>
<TITLE>Welcome to CSE DEPT LogIn Page</TITLE>
</HEAD>
<BODY>
<%@ Page language="java" %>
<%
     String uname = request.getParameter("username");
     String pword = request.getParameter("password");
%>
User Name = <%=uname%><br>
Pass Word  = <%=pword%><br>
</BODY>
</HTML>
```

FIGURE 8.5 An example of a JavaServer Page file.

Between these two tags, you can put any Java code you want to improve the execution of Servlet techniques for Java Web applications.

In fact, you can get a JSP file or page easily by just changing the extension of the **Login.html** file, such as from **Login.html** to **Login.jsp**. Yes, it is this easy to get a JSP file.

An example of using a JSP file to display the received user login data is shown in Figure 8.5.

Within the tags **<% . . .%>**, two lines of Java code are written, and they are used to call the **getParameter()** method to pick up the username and password entered by the user from the client Web page. You can directly display the received login data on the client side with the Java local variables **uname** and **pword** enclosed within the JSP tags.

In fact, JavaServer Pages can handle more complicated jobs, such as business logic, JDBC-related database connections, data processing and JSP switching. Generally, a main or controller JSP takes charge of passing parameters between the server and clients, forwarding the user to the other target JSP or Web pages based on the run result of the Servlet.

The example code shown in Figure 8.6 illustrates how to use JSP to handle multiple jobs, including parameter collection from the client page, database accessing and data processing and forwarding from the current page to the target Java Server Pages based on the run results of data processing. Let's have a closer look at this code to see how it works.

A. The **getParameter()** method is called to pick up two pieces of login information, username and password, which are entered by the user from the client page and assigned to two local variables, uname and pword, in the Servlet.
B. These two pieces of login data are displayed on the client side with the JSP tags.
C. Starting from the JSP tag **<%**, a piece of Java code is developed. An Oracle JDBC database driver is loaded, and this is a Type IV JDBC driver.
D. The Oracle JDBC URL is assigned to the local variable **url**.
E. The **getConnection()** method is executed to establish the database connection.
F. A query string is created and used to query a matching username and password from the **LogIn** Table.
G. The **createStatement()** method is called to create a Statement object.
H. The **executeQuery()** method is executed to perform the query, and the returned result is assigned to the ResultSet object **rs**.
I. A **while** loop is used to pick up any possible matching username and password. In fact, only one row is returned, and therefore this loop can run only one time.
J. If a matching username and password pair is found, **nextPage** is assigned to **Selection.jsp**.

```
  <HTML>
  <HEAD>
  <TITLE>Welcome to CSE DEPT LogIn Page</TITLE></HEAD>
  <BODY>
  <%@ Page language="java" %>
  <%
A     String uname = request.getParameter("username");
      String pword = request.getParameter("password");
  %>
B User Name = <%=uname%><br>
  Pass Word  = <%=pword%><br>
  <%
      try {
C         Class.forName("oracle.jdbc.OracleDriver");
      }
      catch (Exception e) {
        msgDlg.setMessage("Class not found exception!" + e.getMessage());
        msgDlg.setVisible(true);
      }
D     String url = "jdbc:oracle:thin:@localhost:1521:XE";
      try {
E       con = DriverManager.getConnection(url,"CSE_DEPT","oracle_18c");
      }
      catch (SQLException e) {
        msgDlg.setMessage("Could not connect!" + e.getMessage());
        msgDlg.setVisible(true);
        e.printStackTrace();
      }

      Statement  stmt = null;
      ResultSet  rs = null;
F     String query = "SELECT user_name, pass_word FROM LogIn " +
                     "WHERE user_name = '" + uname + "'" + " AND pass_word = '"+pword+"';";
G     stmt = con.createStatement();
H     rs = stmt.executeQuery(query);
I     while (rs.next()) {
        String c_uname = rs.getString("user_name");
        String c_pword = rs.getString("pass_word");
      }
J     if (c_uname.equals(uname) && c_pword.equals(pword)) {
        String  nextPage = "Selection.jsp";
      }
K     else {
        String  nextPage = "LoginError.jsp";
      }
  %>
L <jsp:forward  page = "<%=nextPage%>" />
```

FIGURE 8.6 A piece of example code.

K. Otherwise, `nextPage` is assigned to `LoginError.jsp`.

L. `<jsp:forward />` is used to direct the page to an appropriate page based on the match result.

A good point of using this JSP technique to handle a lot of JDBC-related code or business logic in JavaServer Pages is that the Servlet processing speed and efficiency can be improved. However, you may find that, at the same time, a shortcoming also comes with this benefit, which is relatively complex code development. Quite a lot of code for JDBC database access and data processing as well as business logic is involved in JSP and therefore makes it a big mess during code development.

To solve this problem, separate the business logic and JDBC-related database processing from the results displayed in Web pages and make our coding process easy and clear, three possible methods can be used:

1) Using a Java help class to handle all business logic and database-related processing. In this way, we can separate the login process into two different parts: the data display Web page and JDBC-related database processing or business logic to make the process more objective and clear based on its functionality. This Java help class file works just like a bridge or intermediate layer to help JavaServer Pages perform business-related jobs in a separate file to allow the JSP to concentrate on the data display process. You will see that this Java help class file can be translated to a Java Bean later.
2) Using the session implicit object provided by JSP to store and transfer data between clients and server. This method still belongs to the Java help class category. That is, session objects are used in the Java help class to help with data storage and retrieval between clients and clients and between clients and the server.
3) Using Java Beans techniques to cover and handle JDBC-related database access, data processing and business logic such as data matching and comparison processes. The main role of JavaServer Pages is to provide a view to display the results. JSP can also need to load Java Beans, pass the necessary parameters between a Servlet and clients and forward users to the different target pages based on the run result.

Let's have a detailed discussion of these methods one by one.

8.1.3 Using Java Help Class Files for Java Web Applications

To distinguish between database-related data processing and display of run results, we can separate a Java Web application into two parts: JDBC-related database processing and business logic, such as checking and confirming a username and password pair located in a Java help class file, and the data and run results displayed in a Web or JavaServer page.

Take a look at the code in Figure 8.6, and you can see that about 80% of this code is JDBC-related database processing code, and 10% is data-processing code. In all, about 90% of the code is used to access the database, query for the data and perform data-matching functions. Only about 10% is HTML code.

To separate these two kinds of code into two different files, we can pick up all JDBC-related code and put it in a Java help class file, **LogInQuery.java**, as shown in Figure 8.7.

Let's have a closer look at this piece of code to see how it works.

A. Some member data or attributes are defined first inside this class, which includes two private String member data variables, **user _ name** and **pass _ word**; a class-level connection variable, **con**; and a dialog box that is used to display debug information.
B. Inside the class constructor, an Oracle JDBC database driver is loaded, and itis a type IV JDBC driver.
C. The Oracle JDBC URL is assigned to the local variable **url**.
D. The **getConnection()** method is executed to establish the database connection.
E. The Java help method **checkLogIn()** is declared inside the help class. This method is a main function to perform JDBC-related data query and data matching operations.
F. Some local variables used in this method are defined first, which include the Statement and ResultSet objects.
G. A query string is created, and it is used to query a matching username and password from the **LogIn** Table.
H. The **createStatement()** method is called to create a Statement object.

```
  import java.sql.*;
  public class LogInQuery {
A     private String user_name = null;
      private String pass_word = null;
      static Connection con;
      MsgDialog msgDlg = new MsgDialog(new javax.swing.JFrame(), true);
      public LogInQuery() {
         try {
B           Class.forName("oracle.jdbc.OracleDriver");
         }
         catch (Exception e) {
            msgDlg.setMessage("Class not found exception!" + e.getMessage());
            msgDlg.setVisible(true);
         }
C        String url = " jdbc:oracle:thin:@localhost:1521:XE";
         try {
D           con = DriverManager.getConnection(url,"CSE_DEPT","oracle_18c");
         }
         catch (SQLException e) {
            msgDlg.setMessage("Could not connect!" + e.getMessage());
            msgDlg.setVisible(true);
            e.printStackTrace();
         }
      }
E     public String checkLogIn(String uname, String pword) {
F        String c_uname = null, c_pword = null;
         Statement stmt = null;
         ResultSet rs = null;
G        String query = "SELECT user_name, pass_word FROM LogIn " +
                        "WHERE user_name = '" + uname + "' " + " AND pass_word = '"+pword+"';";
H        stmt = con.createStatement();
I        rs = stmt.executeQuery(query);
J        while (rs.next()) {
            c_uname = rs.getString("user_name");
            c_pword = rs.getString("pass_word");
         }
K        if (c_uname.equals(uname) && c_pword.equals(pword)) {
            user_name = c_uname;
            pass_word = c_pword;
            return "Matched";
         }
L        else {
            return "UnMatched";
         }
      }
  }
```

FIGURE 8.7 The code for the Java Web help class LogInQuery.java.

I. The `executeQuery()` method is executed to perform the query, and the returned result is assigned to the ResultSet object `rs`.

J. A `while` loop is used to pick up any possible matching username and password. In fact, only one row is returned, and thus this loop can run only one time. The `getString()` method is used to pick up the queried username and password. A point to be noted is that the arguments of this method, `user _ name` and `pass _ word`, both are column names in the LogIn Table in our database `CSE _ DEPT`, and they are different from those member data variables declared at the beginning of this class, even though they have the same names. The retuned username and password are assigned to two local variables, `c _ uname` and `c _ pword`, respectively.

```
  <html>
    <head>
        <meta http-equiv="Content-Type" content="text/html; charset=UTF-8">
        <title>LogIn Page</title>
    </head>
     <body>
     <%@page language="java" %>
A    <form method="POST" action=".\LogInQuery.jsp">
     <table>
       <tr>
             <td colspan=2>
             <h3>Welcome to CSE DEPT</h3>
             </td>
       </tr>
       <tr>
             <td>UserName:</td>
             <td><input type="text" name="username"><br></td>
       </tr>
       <tr>
             <td>PassWord:</td>
             <td><input type="password" name="password"><br></td>
       </tr>
       <tr>
             <td colspan=2> </td>
       </tr>
       <tr>
             <td>
               <input type="submit" value="LogIn"  name="loginButton">
B              <input type="button" value="Cancel" name="cancelButton" onclick="self.close()">
             </td>
       </tr>
     </table>
C    </form>
     </body>
  </html>
```

FIGURE 8.8 The modified Login.html file (now it is index.jsp).

K. If a matching username and password pair is found, they are assigned to the two member data variables `user_name` and `pass_word` and return a "`Matched`" string to indicate that the `checkLogIn()` method is successful and matching results were found.
L. Otherwise, an "`UnMatched`" string is returned to indicate that no matching login information can be found.

Now let's do a little modification to our `Login.html` file and break this file into two JSP files: `index.jsp` and `LogInQuery.jsp`. The reason for us to make it into two JSP files is that we want to process and display data in two separate files to make it clear and easy. Generally, `index.jsp` can be considered a starting or home page as a Web application runs. Figure 8.8 shows the modified code for our original `Login.html` file that will be renamed to `index.jsp`, and the modified parts are in bold.

Let's have a closer look at this piece of modified code to see how it works.

A. The first modification is that a Form tag is added to this page with a `POST` method and an `action` attribute. Generally, a Form tag is used to create an HTML form to collect user information and send all that collected information to the server when a submit button on this Form is clicked. Therefore, a Form and all submit buttons on that Form have a coordinating relationship. If a button is defined as a `submit` button by its `type` attribute, all Form data

```
  <html>
    <head>
      <meta http-equiv="Content-Type" content="text/html; charset=UTF-8">
      <title>LogIn Query Page</title>
    </head>
    <body>
A   <%@page language="java" %>
    <%
B     String nextPage = null;
      LogInQuery lquery = new LogInQuery();
C     String u_name = request.getParameter("username");
      String p_word = request.getParameter("password");
D     String result = lquery.checkLogIn(u_name, p_word);
E     if (result.equals("Matched")) {
        nextPage = "Selection.jsp";
        }
F     else { out.println("LogIn is failed"); }
    %>
G   <jsp:forward page = "<%=nextPage%>" />
    </body>
  </html>
```

FIGURE 8.9 The code for the LogInQuery.jsp page.

will be sent to the server whose URL is defined in the **action** attribute on the Form tag when this button is clicked by the user. Here we use a JavaServer Page, **.\LogInQuery.jsp**, as the URL for our target page. That is, this target page is used to access our Java help class file to handle all JDBC- and data-related processing and business logic. The **.** symbol is used to indicate that our JSP file is located in the relatively current folder, since this page is a part of the server functions and will be run on the server side when the whole project runs.

B. The second modification is to change the **type** of our Cancel button from **submit** to **button** and add one more attribute, **onclick**, for this button. The reason for us to do this is that we want to close our **Login.jsp** page when the Cancel button is clicked when the project runs, but we do not want to forward this button-click event to the server to allow the server to do a close action. Therefore, we have to change the type of the button to **button** (not **submit**) to avoid triggering the **action** attribute in the Form tag. We also need to add a **self.close()** method to the **onclick** attribute of the button to call the system **close()** method to terminate our application. **self** means the current page.
C. The Form close tag is also added when the form arrives at its bottom.

Now let's build our **LogInQuery.jsp** page, which works as a part of the server, to receive and handle the Form data, including the login information sent by the **index.jsp** page. Figure 8.9 shows the code for this page. Let's have a closer look at this piece of code to see how it works.

A. A JSP directive tag is to indicate that this page uses the Java language and is a JSP file.
B. Some local variables and objects are declared first. The string variable **nextPage** is used to hold the URL of the next page, and **lquery** is a new instance of our Java help class, LogInQuery, we built at the beginning of this section.
C. The **getParameter()** method is used to pick up the login information entered by the user in the **index.jsp** page. The collected login information, including the username and password, is assigned to two local string variables, **u_name** and **p_word**, respectively.
D. The **checkLogIn()** method defined in our Java help class file is called to perform the database query and the login matching processing. The collected login information is used

as arguments and passed into this method. The run result of this method is a string, and it is assigned to the local string variable `result`.

E. An `if` block is used to check the run result of the `checkLogIn()` method. The program will be forwarded to a success page (`Selection.jsp`) if the login process is successful.
F. Otherwise, an error message is printed to indicate that the login process failed.
G. A JSP forward directive is used to direct the program to the next page.

In summary, to use a JavaServer Page to assist a Java Web application, the following components should be considered and used:

1) The whole Web application can be divided into two parts:

   a. The JDBC- and database processing–related functions and business logic—Java help class file (**LogInQuery.java**).
   b. The user data input and run result output functions—HTML or JavaServer Pages (`index.jsp` and `LogInQuery.jsp`).

2) The relationships between these three pages are:

   a. **index.jsp**, which runs on the client side, works as a starting or home page as the Web application runs, and it is used to collect user information and send it to the Web server.
   b. **LogInQuery.jsp**, which can be considered a part of the application server and runs on the server side, provides information passing or transformation functions between the home page and other target pages to collect user information, call the Java help class to perform data and business logic processing and direct the program to the different target pages based on the data processing results.
   c. The Java help class file `LogInQuery.java`, which provides the JDBC and database processing functions and business logic processing abilities, works as an intermediate layer between the server and clients to support the previoustwo JSP files. Since this help class file will be called by `LogInQuery.jsp`, it also belongs to the server-side software.

These components and their relationships are illustrated in Figure 8.10.

Compared with our first Java Web application that utilized the Java Servlet and HTML page, the Web application that used the JavaServer Pages techniques has great improvements in simplification of data collection and processing by using different function-related pages and a help class file. However, one defect is that JDBC- and database-related functions make the Java help class file `LogInQuery.java` very complicated because too many database-related functions must be involved and executed, such as loading database drivers, connecting to the database, creating query-related objects, building the data query and collecting the queried results. All of these operations make this file longer and increase the complexity of operations. A good solution to this is to use the JSP Sessions to simplify these operations and make the file short and simple.

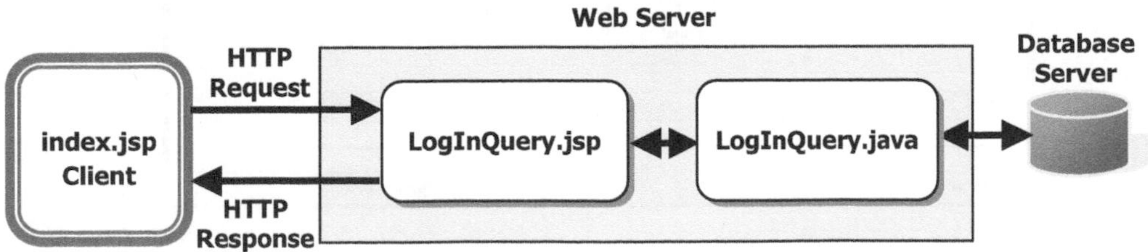

FIGURE 8.10 The components and their relationships in a JSP Web application.

8.1.4 Using the JSP Implicit Object Session for Java Web Applications

As we mentioned in Section 8.1.2, the session is a JSP implicit object used to help developers build professional Java Web applications. “Implicit” means that those objects, including the session object, can be created automatically when a new JSP is executed. The specific property of using a session object is that you can save user data in some Web pages and retrieve it from other Web pages. This provides a great and convenient way to transfer data between clients and clients and also between clients and a server.

In this section, we will use this session object to help us to build our Faculty page to query and display the desired faculty information from the Faculty Table in our sample database. The structure or architecture of using the session object to coordinate the data query from the Faculty Table is shown in Figure 8.11.

Basically, this structure is identical to that we discussed in the last section, and the only difference is that we use a new Java help class file, **`FacultyBean.java`**, that is not a real Java Bean class but is very similar to a JavaBean. The reason we do this is that we do not want to have a big jump between the help class and JavaBean to make this design difficult.

`FacultyPage.jsp`, our Web client page, is shown in Figure 8.12. Because of its complex HTML and JSP code, we will leave the building and coding of this page to our real project later. In

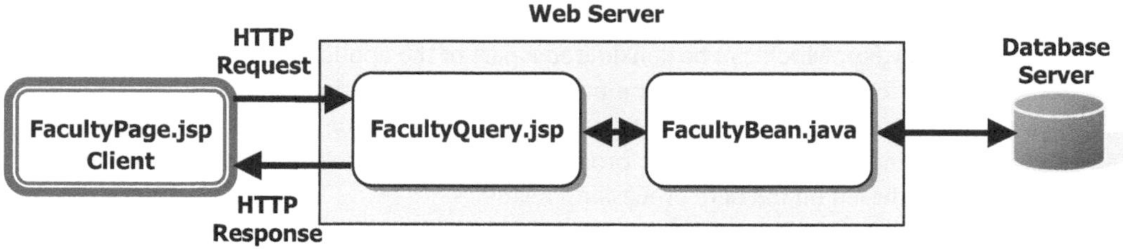

FIGURE 8.11 The architecture of using session objects in Web applications.

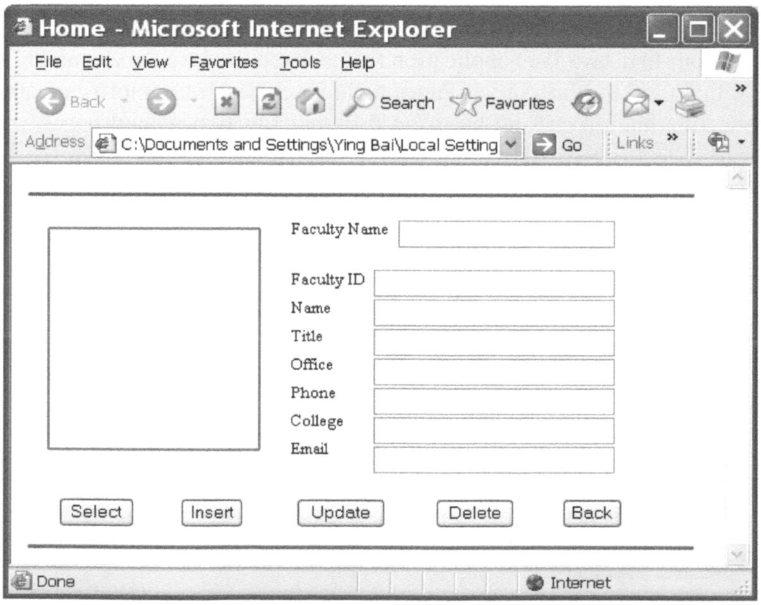

FIGURE 8.12 Preview of the FacultyPage.jsp page.

fact, we need to use Microsoft Office Publisher 2007 to build a **FacultyPage.html** file first and then convert it to a **FacultyPage.jsp** file. Now we just assume that we have built this page and want to use it in our **Faculty** Table query process.

Now let's modify **FacultyPage.jsp** to use a session object to perform data storage and retrieval functions between this page and the help class file **FacultyQuery.jsp**.

8.1.4.1 Modify the FacultyPage JSP File to Use the Session Object

Perform the modifications shown in Figure 8.13 to the **FacultyPage.jsp** file to use the session object to store and pick up data between client pages. All modified code is in bold.

In step A, we add an action attribute to forward all information collected from this page to our model and controller page, **FacultyQuery.jsp**, that will call our FacultyBean file to perform the faculty data query process.

Starting from step B until step H, we use the embedded JSP code to assign the real queried faculty columns from our Faculty Table to the value tag of each text field in the **Facultypage.jsp** using the **getAttribute()** method of the session class. In this way, as long as the queried faculty row has any change, the modification will be immediately updated and reflected to each text field in our **FacultyPage.jsp** page. In this way, a direct connection or binding between the text fields in our **Facultypage.jsp** page and the queried Faculty columns in our help class is established.

Now let's take a look at our model and controller page, **FacultyQuery.jsp**.

```
  <html>
    <head>
      <meta http-equiv="Content-Type" content="text/html; charset=UTF-8">
      <title>LogIn Query Page</title>
    </head>
    <body>
    <%@page language="java" %>
A   <form method=post action=".\FacultyQuery.jsp">
    <input name=FacultyNameField maxlength=255 size=24
B    value="<%=session.getAttribute("facultyName") %>" type=text v:shapes="_x0000_s1109">
    .........
    <input name=FacultyIDField maxlength=255 size=26
C    value="<%=session.getAttribute("facultyId") %>" type=text  v:shapes="_x0000_s1110">
    .........
    <input name=NameField maxlength=255 size=26
D    value="<%=session.getAttribute("facultyName") %>" type=text  v:shapes="_x0000_s1106">
    .........
    <input name=OfficeField maxlength=255 size=26
E    value="<%=session.getAttribute("office") %>"  type=text  v:shapes="_x0000_s1104">
    .........
    <input name=PhoneField maxlength=255 size=26
F    value="<%=session.getAttribute("phone") %>"  type=text  v:shapes="_x0000_s1116">
    .........
    <input name=CollegeField maxlength=255 size=26
G    value="<%=session.getAttribute("college") %>" type=text  v:shapes="_x0000_s1117">
    .........
    <input name=EmailField maxlength=255 size=26
H    value="<%=session.getAttribute("email") %>" type=text  v:shapes="_x0000_s1118">
    .........
    </body>
  </html>
```

FIGURE 8.13 The modifications to the FacultyPage.jsp file.

8.1.4.2 Build the Transaction JSP File, FacultyQuery.jsp

The purpose of this file is to transfer data and information between our main display page, **FacultyPage.jsp**, and our working help class file, FacultyBean, which performs all JDBC- and database-related operations and business logic. The code for this file is shown in Figure 8.14.

Let's take a closer look at this piece of code to see how it works.

A. You can embed any import directory using the JSP directive in a HTML or a JSP file. The format is **<%@ page import="java package" %>**. On this page, we embed two packages: **java.util.***, since we need to use the List class, and **JavaWebHibDBOraclePackage.***, since we build our FacultyBean help class in that package.
B. The **getParameter()** method is executed to get the faculty name entered by the user to the Faculty Name text field on the **FacultyPage.jsp** page, and this faculty name is assigned to a local String variable, **fname**.
C. A new instance of our help class, FacultyBean, is created.
D. The main help method, **QueryFaculty()**, we built in the FacultyBean is called to query a faculty record based on the faculty name we obtained from step B.
E. The **setAttribute()** method in the session class is executed to store each column of the queried faculty row from the Faculty Table with a given name. The **getter()** methods defined in the FacultyBean class are executed to pick up each queried column. The point to be noted is that later on when we need to pick up these queried columns from the session object in other pages, we need to use names identical to those we used here for each column, such as facultyId, facultyName, title and so on.
F. Finally, since we need to display all queried columns in the associated text fields on the **FacultyPage.jsp** page, we use the **sendRedirect()** method to return to that page.

Finally let's take care of the help class file, **FacultyBean**.

```
A   <%@ page import="java.util.*" %>
    <%@ page import="JavaWebHibDBOraclePackage.*" %>
    <html>
      <head>
        <meta http-equiv="Content-Type" content="text/html; charset=UTF-8">
        <title>FacultyQuery JSP Page</title>
      </head>
      <body>
        <h1>This is the FaculrtQuery JSP Page!</h1>
        <%
B       String fname = request.getParameter("FacultyNameField");
C       FacultyBean fBean = new FacultyBean();
D       List fList = fBean.QueryFaculty(fname);
E       session.setAttribute("facultyId", fBean.getFacultyID());
        session.setAttribute("facultyName", fBean.getFacultyName());
        session.setAttribute("office", fBean.getOffice());
        session.setAttribute("title", fBean.getTitle());
        session.setAttribute("college", fBean.getCollege());
        session.setAttribute("phone", fBean.getPhone());
        session.setAttribute("email", fBean.getEmail());
F       response.sendRedirect("FacultyPage.jsp");
        %>
      </body>
    </html>
```

FIGURE 8.14 The code for the model and controller page, FacultyQuery.jsp.

8.1.4.3 Build the Help Class FacultyBean

This class is a help class but is very similar to a real Java bean class. The code for this class is shown in Figure 8.15.

```
  @Stateless
  public class FacultyBean {
A    private String facultyID;
     private String facultyName;
     private String office;
     private String title;
     private String phone;
     private String college;
     private String email;
B    public Session session = null;
     public FacultyBean() {
C       this.session = HibernateUtil.getSessionFactory().getCurrentSession();
     }
D    public List QueryFaculty(String fname) {
E       List<Faculty> facultyList = null;
        MsgDialog msgDlg = new MsgDialog(new javax.swing.JFrame(), true);
        try {
F          org.hibernate.Transaction tx = session.beginTransaction();
G          Query f = session.createQuery ("from Faculty as f where f.facultyName like '"+fname+"'");
H          facultyList = (List<Faculty>) f.list();
I       } catch (Exception e) {
           msgDlg.setMessage("Query is failed and no matched found!");
           msgDlg.setVisible(true);
           e.printStackTrace();
        }
J       facultyID = facultyList.get(0).getFacultyId();
        facultyName = facultyList.get(0).getFacultyName();
        office = facultyList.get(0).getOffice();
        title = facultyList.get(0).getTitle();
        phone = facultyList.get(0).getPhone();
        college = facultyList.get(0).getCollege();
        email = facultyList.get(0).getEmail();
        return facultyList;
     }
K    public String getFacultyID() {
        return this.facultyID;
     }
     public String getFacultyName() {
        return this.facultyName;
     }
     public String getOffice() {
        return this.office;
     }
     public String getTitle() {
        return this.title;
     }
     public String getPhone() {
        return this.phone;
     }
     public String getCollege() {
        return this.college;
     }
     public String getEmail() {
        return this.email;
     }
  }
```

FIGURE 8.15 The code for the FacultyBean help class.

Let's have a closer look at this piece of code to see how it works.

A. At the beginning of this class, seven member data or properties of this class are defined. This is very important in a Java bean class, since all data-related transactions between the client pages and Java bean are dependent these properties. In other words, all clients could pick up data from a Java bean using those properties, and a one-to-one relationship exists between each property in the Java bean class and each queried column in the data Table. According to convention, all of these properties should be defined as a private data type and can be accessed by using the **getter()** methods provided in the Java bean class.
B. A new instance of the Hibernate session class is created and initialized. The point to be noted is that this Hibernate session object is different from the JSP implicit session object.
C. The **getCurrentSession()** method is executed to get the default Hibernate session object.
D. The detailed definition of the **QueryFaculty()** method starts from here with the method header.
E. A new **java.util.List** instance is created and initialized, since we need this object to pick up and hold our queried faculty result. The MsgDislog instance is used to display error information in case an exception is encountered during this query operation.
F. A **try . . . catch** block is used to perform our data query. First a new Transaction instance, **tx**, is created with the **beginTransaction()** method.
G. Then a query string built with Hibernate Query Language (HQL) is created, and this query string will be used to perform the faculty information query later.
H. The **list()** method is executed to perform a query to the Faculty Table in our sample database to try to retrieve a matching faculty record based on the selected faculty name **fname**. The query result is assigned to and held in a local variable, **facultyList**, that has a **List<Faculty>** data type.
I. The **catch** block is used to track and collect any possible exception during the query process. An error message will be displayed if the query encounters any problem.
J. The **facultyList.get(0)** method is used to retrieve the first matching row from the query result. In fact, only one faculty row should be queried and retrieved, since all faculty names are unique in our sample database. A sequence of **getter()** methods is used to pick up the associated columns and assign them to the associated properties in the FacultyBean class. Finally, the query result is returned to the **FacultyQuery.jsp** page.
K. Seven **getter()** methods are defined at the bottom of this class, and they can be used to pick up all properties defined in this class.

The operational sequence and data transformation structure of the Faculty Name are shown in Figure 8.16, where the faculty name is used as an example to illustrate how to transfer data between the client and the help class. The operational sequence is:

1) First the desired faculty name is entered by the user into the Faculty Name text field on the **FacultyPage.jsp** page. This piece of data will be transferred to the **FacultyQuery.jsp** page when the Select button is clicked by the user.
2) In the **FacultyQuery.jsp** page, the **getParameter()** method is used to pick up the transferred Faculty Name.
3) Then the help method **QueryFaculty()** in the help class FacultyBean is called to query a matching faculty record from the **Faculty** Table based on the transferred faculty name, **fname**.
4) When the **getter()** method in the FacultyBean class is executed, the queried faculty name is returned to the **FacultyQuery.jsp** page.
5) One of session methods, **setAttribute()**, is called to stored the queried faculty name in the JSP implicit object session.

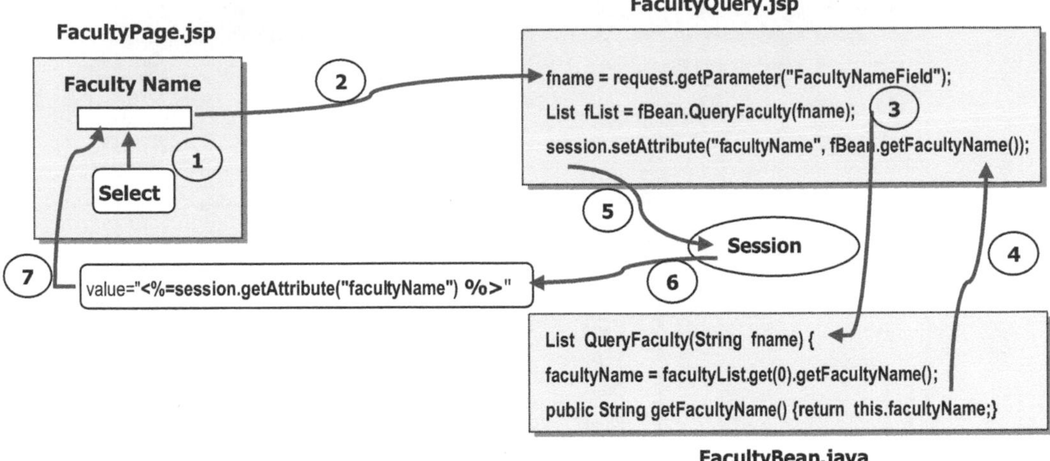

FIGURE 8.16 The operational sequence and data transfer structure using the session object.

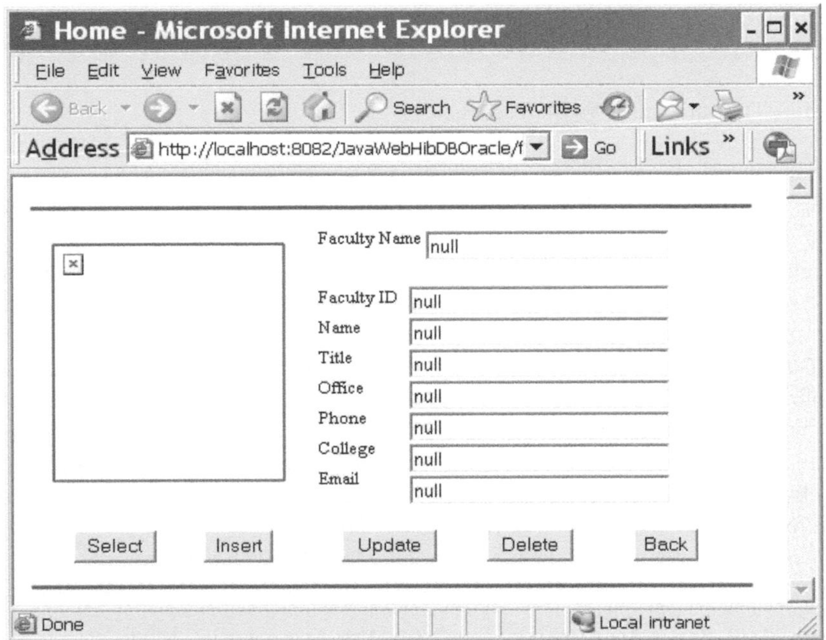

FIGURE 8.17 The run status of FacultyPage.jsp.

6) The **getAttribute("facultyName")** method that is assigned to the value tag of the FacultyName text field will pick up the queried faculty name and display it in the text field in step 7.

By referring to Figure 8.16, we can get a clear and complete picture of the data storage and transfer between different pages.

Now if you compile and run these three files, **FacultyPage.jsp**, **FacultyQuery.jsp** and **FacultyBean.java**, you can get the start page shown in Figure 8.17. Enter a desired faculty name

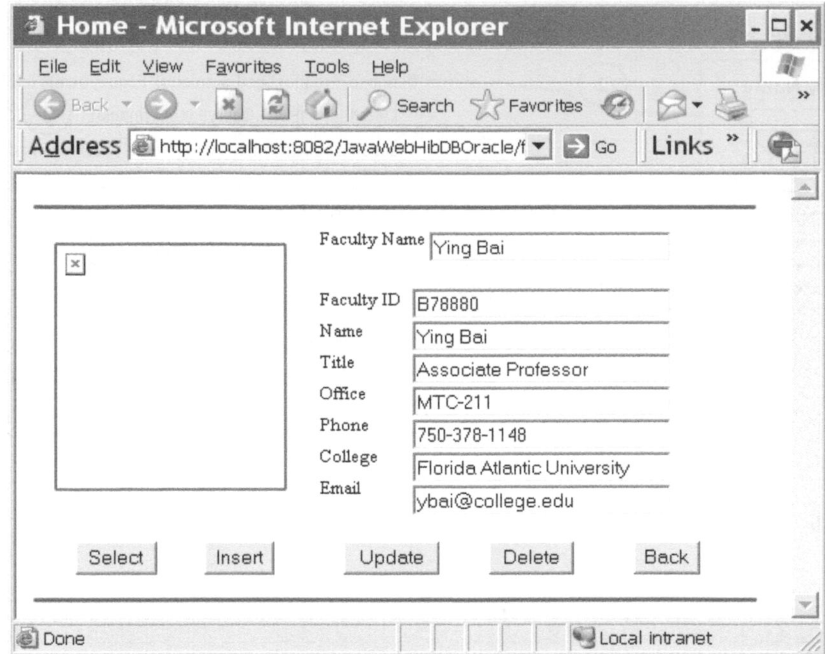

FIGURER 8.18 The run result of FacultyPage.jsp.

such as **Ying Bai** into the Faculty Name text field and click on the **Select** button. The run result is shown in Figure 8.18.

As we mentioned at the beginning of this chapter, Java EE provides a set of powerful tools and support to Java Web applications to access and manipulate databases. One of the most important components provided by Java EE is the Java bean that works as a separate component to perform database-related operations and business logic. By combining JavaServer Faces techniques and Java beans, a professional Java Web database application can be divided into two separate parts: the GUI that is built with JSF tags in JavaServer Pages isused for data presentation and displaying results, and Java managed beans are used for database-related operations and business logic. By dividing a Web application into these two sections, it greatly reduces the development efforts and complexities in code development and organization of the whole application.

Now let's take care of using Java beans technology for Java Web applications.

8.1.5 Using Java Beans Technology for Java Web Applications

In recent years, the Java beans technique has been widely applied in Java Web applications. In fact, a Java bean can be considered an extended Java help class, as we discussed in the previous sections, and the main purpose of a Java bean is to handle JDBC- and database-related operations as well as business logic in a Web application.

In fact, Java beans are reusable components, and the main purpose of using Java beans is to separate business logic from presentation.

That is, a Java bean is just an instance of a class.

Once a JavaBean is created and loaded, it can be used by all parts of your application based on its scope. The so-called scope defines the section of your application that can access and use this bean. Generally, there are four popular scopes available to a Java Bean object. The default scope is **page** scope.

- **page scope**: The bean is accessible within a JSP page with the **<jsp: useBean>** tag or any of the page's static include files until the page sends a response to the client or forwards a request to another page. In other words, as long as the process is on the current page, the bean can be accessed and used until the process is transferred to other pages.
- **request scope**: The bean is accessible from any JSP page as long as the same request is processed in that page until a JSP page sends a response to the client or forwards the request to another page. In other words, the bean can be used until a different request has been forwarded or a response for that request has been received, which means that the lifetime or scope of that request has been completed.
- **session scope**: The bean is accessible from any JSP page in the same session as the JSP page that creates the bean. A session can be considered a common place where many JSP pages can exist and share. The JSP page in which you create the Java bean must have a JSP page directive <%@ page %> with the session = true.
- **application scope**: The bean can be accessed from any JSP page in the same application as the JSP page that creates the bean. In other words, any JSP page can use the bean as long as that page is included in the application in which the JSP page that creates the bean is included.

There is no difference between creating a help class and creating a Java bean class. In fact, the help class **FacultyBean.java** we created in the last section is a Java bean class.

The JSP provide three basic tags for working with beans.

<jsp:useBean id="**bean name**" class="**bean class**" scope = "**page | request | session |application**"/>

The definitions for these three tags are:

1) The **bean name** is just a given name to refer to the Java bean. You can use any valid name for this tag.
2) The **bean class** is the full name of the Java bean class you created. The so-called full name means that you need to use both the bean class name and the package name in which the bean is located. For example, this bean class should be **mypackage.mybeanclass** if the bean class named **mybeanclass** is located in the package **mypackage**.
3) The **scope** indicates the range or the lifetime the bean can be used. Refer to the four scopes we discussed previously to get more detailed information about them.

A very useful JSP directive used for Java bean classes is **<jsp:setProperty />**. The protocol of this directive is:

<jsp:setProperty name = "**id**" property = "**someProperty**" value = "**someValue**" />

The three arguments for this directive are:

1) The **id** is the bean name as we discussed in step 1 previously.
2) **someProperty** is the property name defined inside the Java bean class, such as **faculty Id** and **facultyName** we defined in our **FacultyBean.java** class in the last section.
3) **someValue** is the initialized value assigned to a property in the bean class.

A variant for this tag is that the property attribute can be replaced by an "*". What this does is accept all the form parameters and thus reduce the need for writing multiple **setProperty** tags. The only point to be remembered when you use this variant is that the form parameter names must be the same as the bean property names.

An example of using the **setProperty** tag is:

<jsp:setProperty name="dbFaculty"property="*" />

```
@Stateless
public class FacultyBean {
    private String facultyID;
    private String facultyName;
    private String office;
    private String title;
    private String phone;
    private String college;
    private String email;

    public Session session = null;
    public FacultyBean() {
        this.session = HibernateUtil.getSessionFactory().getCurrentSession();
    }
    public List QueryFaculty(String fname) {
        List<Faculty> facultyList = null;
        MsgDialog msgDlg = new MsgDialog(new javax.swing.JFrame(), true);
        .........
        return facultyList;
    }
    public String getFacultyID() {
        return this.facultyID;
    }
    .........
A   public void setFacultyID(String facultyID) {
        this.facultyID = facultyID;
    }
B   public void setFacultyName(String facultyName) {
        this.facultyName = facultyName;
    }
C   public void setOffice(String office) {
        this.office = office;
    }
D   public void setTitle(String title) {
        this.title = title;
    }
E   public void setPhone(String phone) {
        this.phone = phone;
    }
F   public void setCollege(String college) {
        this.college = college;
    }
G   public void setEmail(String email) {
        this.email = email;
    }
}
```

FIGURE 8.19 The modified help class—now it is a Java bean class.

In the `setProperty` tag, the `id` of the Java bean class is `dbFaculty`. The * in the property value means that all parameters transferred from another page can be assigned to the associated properties in the Java bean class.

Now let's modify `FacultyBean.java` to make it a Java bean class to replace the help class file `FacultyBean.java` we built in the last section.

8.1.5.1 Modify the Help Class FacultyBean to Make It a Java Bean Class

First we need to create a new Java Session Bean class named FacultyBean in the NetBeans IDE. Then we need to add seven `setter()` methods into this bean class. Your finished Java bean class, `FacultyBean.java`, is shown in Figure 8.19. All modified code is in bold.

Let's have a closer look at this piece of modified code to see how it works.

```
<%@ page import="java.util.*" %>
<%@ page import="JavaWebHibDBOraclePackage.*" %>
<%@ page import="csedept.entity.Faculty" %>
<html>
  <head>
    <meta http-equiv="Content-Type" content="text/html; charset=UTF-8">
    <title>FacultyBeanQuery Page</title>
  </head>
  <body>
    <h1>This is the FacultyBeanQuery Page</h1>
A   <jsp:useBean id="dbFaculty" scope="session" class="JavaWebHibDBOraclePackage.FacultyBean" />
B   <jsp:setProperty name="dbFaculty" property="*" />
    <%
C     String fname = request.getParameter("FacultyNameField");
D     List<Faculty> facultyList = dbFaculty.QueryFaculty(fname);
E     response.sendRedirect("FacultyBeanPage.jsp");
    %>
  </body>
</html>
```

FIGURE 8.20 The code for the FacultyBeanQuery.jsp page.

From step A to step G, seven **setter()** methods are added into this Java bean class. All of these **setter()** methods are used to setup the initial values for the seven properties in this bean.

Next we need to create a new transaction JSP page **FacultyBeanQuery.jsp** to transfer data between our new starting page **FacultyBeanPage.jsp** and our Java bean class **FacultyBean.java**. Basically, the **FacultyBeanQuery.jsp** file has no significant difference from the **FacultyQuery.jsp** we built in the last section. The only different part is the way to execute the JDBC- and database-related queries or business logic. In the **FacultyQuery.jsp** file, we called a Java help class, **FacultyBean.java**, to do those functions. However, in **FacultyBeanQuery.jsp**, we will call a modified help class that has been converted to a Java bean, **FacultyBean.java**, to perform these functions.

The code for the **FacultyBeanQuery.jsp** file is shown in Figure 8.20.

Now let's have a closer look at this piece of code to see how it works.

Some system- or user-related packages are imported at the beginning of this page. The JSP directive <%@ page /> is used to convert those packages and embedded in this page. Three packages are imported here: the **java.util.*** package contains the List class, the **JavaWebHibDBOraclePackage** contains our Java bean class FacultyBean and the **csedept.entity.Faculty** is a Hibernate class mapping for the Faculty Table in our sample database, **CSE _ DEPT**.

A. The Java bean class is declared with the JSP tag **<jsp:useBean />** with the three tags we discussed at the beginning of this section. The referenced name for this bean is **dbFaculty**, which is assigned to the **id** of the bean. The scope of this bean is **session**, and the full name of the bean class is **JavaWebHibDBOraclePackage.FacultyBean**.
B. The **setProperty** tag is used to setup all parameters passed from the **FacultyBeanPage.jsp** page to the associated properties in the bean class FacultyBean.
C. The Java code starting from the JSP tag and faculty name parameter is retrieved by using the **getParameter()** method and assigned to a local String variable, **fname**.
D. The main bean method, **QueryFaculty()**, is executed to query a faculty record based on the retrieved faculty name from the FacultyBeanPage.jsp page. The result is assigned to a local List variable. In fact, this result is not important in this application since the columns in the query result have been assigned to the associated properties in the bean class, and later on we can pick up those columns by calling the **getter()** methods in the bean class.
E. Since we want to fill those text fields in our starting page **FacultyBeanPage.jsp** with the queried result, we used the **sendRedirect()** method to return the process back to that page.

Now let's take a look at a new starting page, **FacultyBeanPage.jsp**, that will be used to call the transaction JSP page and Java bean to perform the faculty data query and display the query result in this page. Because of the complexity of building this page with HTML code, we leave this coding job to our project development stage later.

8.1.5.2 Build a New Starting Web Page, FacultyBeanPage

The preview of this page is shown in Figure 8.21.

The difference between this starting page and the **FacultyPage.jsp** starting page we built in the last section is: in **FacultyPage.jsp**, we used a JSP built-in or implicit object session to transfer data between the page and the help class. However, in the new starting page, **FacultyBeanPage.jsp**, we need to use the properties defined in the Java bean class to transfer data.

That is, we need to use the Java bean's **getter()** method to replace the **session.getAttribute()** methods embedded in the value tag of each text field to retrieve and display the associated column queried from the Faculty Table in our sample database in each text field in the new starting page.

The code for the new starting page is shown in Figure 8.22. The modified parts are in bold.

Let's have a closer look at this piece of code to see how it works.

A. A JSP tag declared to use a Java bean is put at the beginning of this page to indicate that a Java bean will be called to perform JDBC- and database-related queries or business logic, and the result will be retrieved and reflected in this starting page.
B. The next page is changed to **FacultyBeanQuery.jsp** in the action tag of the form, which means that the page and all data in this starting page will be forwarded to the next page if the submit button is clicked by the user from this page.
C. From step C to step I in the Figure, the different Java bean's **getter()** methods are executed to retrieve the matching columns from the queried result and display them one by one in each associated text field.

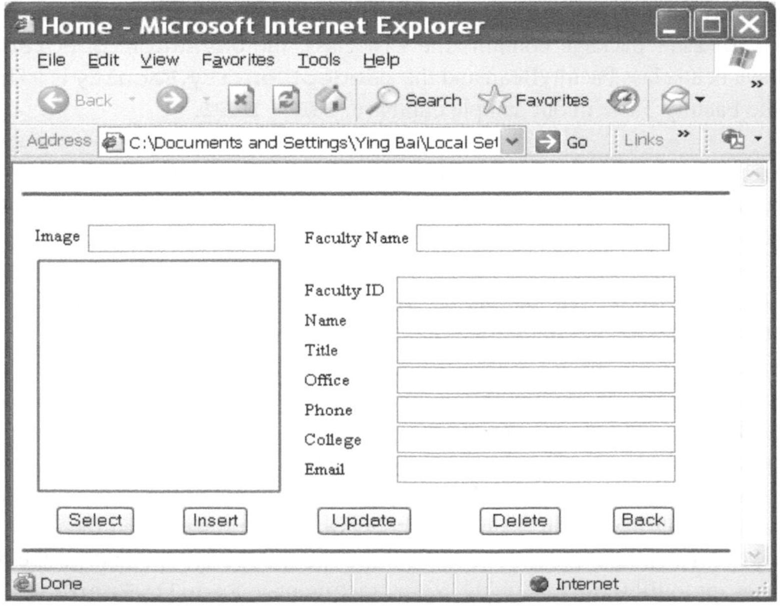

FIGURE 8.21 The new starting Web page, FacultyBeanPage.jsp.

```
A  <jsp:useBean id="dbFaculty" scope="session" class="JavaWebHibDBOraclePackage.FacultyBean" />
   <html>
     <head>
       <meta http-equiv="Content-Type" content="text/html; charset=UTF-8">
       <title>Faculty Query Page</title>
     </head>
     <body>
     <%@page language="java" %>
B    <form method=post action=".\FacultyBeanQuery.jsp">
     <input name=FacultyNameField maxlength=255 size=24
C     value="<%=dbFaculty.getFacultyName() %>" type=text v:shapes="_x0000_s1109">
     .........
     <input name=FacultyIDField maxlength=255 size=26
D     value="<%=dbFaculty.getFacultyID() %>" type=text  v:shapes="_x0000_s1110">
     .........
     <input name=NameField maxlength=255 size=26
E     value="<%=dbFaculty.getFacultyName() %>" type=text  v:shapes="_x0000_s1106">
     .........
     <input name=OfficeField maxlength=255 size=26
F     value="<%=dbFaculty.getOffice() %>"  type=text  v:shapes="_x0000_s1104">
     .........
     <input name=PhoneField maxlength=255 size=26
G     value="<%=dbFaculty.getPhone() %>"  type=text  v:shapes="_x0000_s1116">
     .........
     <input name=CollegeField maxlength=255 size=26
H     value="<%=dbFaculty.getCollege() %>" type=text  v:shapes="_x0000_s1117">
     .........
     <input name=EmailField maxlength=255 size=26
I     value="<%=dbFaculty.getEmail() %>" type=text  v:shapes="_x0000_s1118">
     .........
     </body>
   </html>
```

FIGURE 8.22 The code for the new starting page, FacultyBeanPage.jsp.

From this piece of code, you can see how easy it is to transfer data between the starting Web page written in either HTML or JSP and Java bean class by using the Java bean's properties.

From the examples discussed previously, it can be seen that the JavaServer Pages technology provides good communication and data passing methods between the Servlet and client Web pages; however, it does not provide direct binding and mapping between the Web page's components and the server-side code. This kind of binding and mapping plays a more important role in today's complicated and multi-tier Web applications. To meet this need, a new technology has been introduced in recent years, JavaServer Faces technology.

With this new technology, all Web components can be installed and distributed in a Web page by using JSF tags. Also, more importantly, all of these components can be bound to the server-side properties and functions using the so-called backing beans or Java managed beans. By using a Unified Expression Language (EL) value expression, the value of the property of a mapped or bound Web component can be easily picked up from a backing bean on the server side.

8.1.6 Using JavaServer Faces Technology for Java Web Applications

JavaServer Faces provides new techniques and components for building user interfaces (UIs) for server-side applications. In fact, JSF is a server-side technology for developing Web applications with rich user interfaces. Before JavaServer Faces, developers who built Web applications had to rely on building HTML user interface components with Servlets or JavaServer Pages. This is mainly because HTML user interface components are the lowest common denominator that Web browsers support. One of the defects of using HTML or JSP techniques to build Web applications is that such Web applications do not have rich user interfaces compared with standalone fat clients and therefore have less functionality and/or poor usability. One of the possible solutions is to use Applets to develop rich user interfaces; however, in most cases, Web application developers do not always know whether those Applets are signed or unsigned or whether they can access the local database files. This greatly limits the implementation of Applets in Java Web database applications.

A good solution is to use JavaServer Faces technique that provides a set of rich GUI components and can be installed and run on the server side. The GUI components provided by JSF are represented by a collection of component tags. All component tags are defined and stored in the UIComponent class. A model-view-controller model is applied to the JSF technique.

The JSF technology consists of the following main components:

- JSF APIs used to represent UI components, manage state, handle events and validate input. The UI components are represented and implemented using JSF tags. The API has support for internationalization and accessibility.
- A special Servlet class, FacesServlet, that is located on the server side and works as a controller to handle all JSF-related events.
- JSP pages that contain rich user interface components represented by customer tags that work as views. The GUI of a JSF page is one or more JSP pages that contain JSF component tags.
- Two JSP custom tag libraries used for expressing JSF user interface components within a JSP page and wiring components to server-side objects. Page authors can easily add UI components to their pages.
- Java bean components used to work as model objects.
- An application configuration resource file, **faces-config.xml**, used to define the navigation rules between JSP pages and register Java backing beans.
- Web deployment descriptor file, **web.xml**, used to define the FaceServlet and its mapping.

JavaServer Faces technology is basically built based on JavaServer Pages and Servlet techniques. It uses JSP pages as the GUI and FacesServlet as the Web container. A high-level architecture of JSF is shown in Figure 8.23.

It can be seen from Figure 8.23 that a JSF Web application is composed of JSP pages representing the user interface components using the JSF custom tag library and FacesServlet Web container that can be considered part of the Servlet class and takes care of the JSF-related events.

JSF defines two standard tag libraries (Core and HTML) that you have to declare in your JSP pages with the **<%@taglib%>** directive. The two tag libraries are:

- **html _ basic.tld**: A JSP custom tag library for building JSF applications that render to an HTML client.
- **jsf _ core.tld**: A JSP custom tag library for representing core actions independently of a particular render kit.

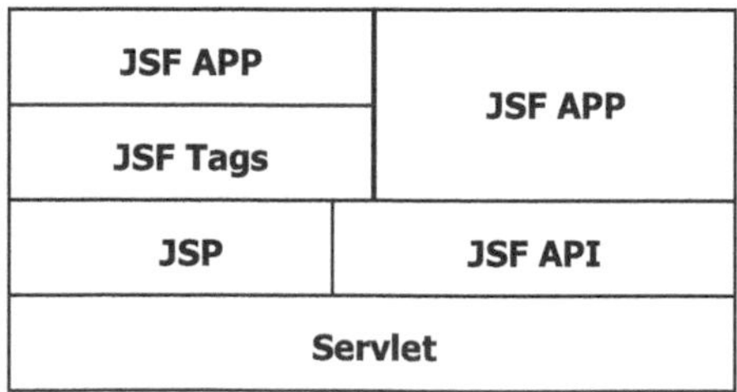

FIGURE 8.23 High-level architecture of JSF.

The JSF core library contains tags that do not depend on any markup language, while the JSF HTML library was designed for pages that are viewed in a Web browser. The standard prefixes of the two tag libraries are **f** for the JSF Core and **h** for the JSF HTML. All JSF tags must be nested inside an**<f:view>** element. The **<f:view>** tag allows the JSF framework to save the state of the UI components as part of the response to a HTTP request.

To use these customer tags to represent JSF components in JSP pages, one needs to indicate them by using the following two taglib directives at the top of each JSF file:

- **<%@ taglib uri="http://java.sun.com/jsf/html" prefix="h" %>**
- **<%@ taglib uri="http://java.sun.com/jsf/core" prefix="f" %>**

The **uri** is used to indicate the location of the customer tag library.

JavaServer Faces pages are just regular JSP pages that use the standard JSF tag libraries or other libraries based on the JSF API. When using JSF tag components to build a JavaServer Page, a component tree or view is created in the server side memory, and this tree will be used by the JSF framework to handle requests coming from clients and send responses to the clients. Each JSF tag component is mapped to a component class defined in the UIComponent class. In fact, each tag is an instance of the mapped class in the UIComponent.

JSF utilizes a model-view-controller architecture, which means that it uses Java beans as models to stored application data, JSF GUI as the view and the Servlet as the controller.

8.1.6.1 The Application Configuration Resource File, faces-config.xml

Navigation from one page to another can be done in two ways. One way is to use code directly by writing a JSP tag such as **<jsp:forward />** or an HTML hyperlink in the JSF file. Another way that is provided by JSF is to use the application configuration resource file faces-config.xml to build navigation rules. The task of defining navigation rules involves defining which page is to be displayed after the user clicks on a button or a hyperlink. Each **<navigation-rule>** element defines how to get from one page as defined by the **<form-view-id>** to the other pages of the application. A **<navigation-rule>** element can contain any number of **<navigation-case>** elements that define the page to open next using the **<to-view-id>** based on a logical outcome defined by the **<from-outcome>**. This outcome is defined by the **action** attribute of the component that submits the form (such as the command Button).

An application configuration resource file, faces-config.xml, is used to define your Java managed beans, validators, converters and navigation rules.

Figure 8.24 shows a part of an example of an application configuration resource file. The configuration resource file is composed of a sequence of tags: Starting from the**<navigation-rule>** tag, a new navigation rule is defined. The **<from-view-id>**tag is used to define the navigation source, which is the current page (**Current.jsp**). The **<navigation-case>** tag is used to define one of the navigation destinations defined by the **<to-view-id>** tag based on the output of clicked buttons or links triggered by the **action** tag in the current page. Those outputs are defined by the **<from-outcome>** tag.

```
<navigation-rule>
<from-view-id>/Current.jsp</from-view-id>
  <navigation-case>
  <from-outcome>clickAction</from-outcome>
  <to-view-id>/Next.jsp</to-view-id>
  </navigation-case>
</navigation-rule>
```

FIGURE 8.24 A part of the application configuration resource file.

You can use design tools such as PageFlow to do this navigation plan graphically and directly. Refer to Section 5.3.5.12 in Chapter 5 to get more detailed information about using design tools to build this configuration file graphically.

8.1.6.2 Sample JavaServer Face Page Files

Two JSF files are shown in Figures 8.25 and 8.26. In Figure 8.25, a **Current.jsp** page that works as a receiving page to get the username is shown. In Figure 8.26, **Next.jsp**, which works as a responding page to select and return a matching password based on the username to the **Current.jsp** page, is shown.

The function of the **Current.jsp** page is:

A. In order to use JSF tags, you need to include the **taglib** directives to the html and core tag libraries that refer to the standard HTML render kit tag library and the JSF core tag library, respectively.
B. A **body** tag with the **bgcolor** attribute is defined.
C. A page containing JSF tags is represented by a tree of components whose root is **UIViewRoot**, which is represented by the **view** tag. All component tags must be enclosed in the **view** tag. Other content such as HTML and other JSP pages can be enclosed within that tag.
D. A typical JSP page includes a **form**, which is submitted to the next page when a button is clicked. The tags representing the form components (such as text fields and buttons) must be nested inside the **form** tag.
E. The **inputText** tag represents an input text field component. The **id** attribute represents the ID of the component object represented by this tag, and if it is missing, then the implementation will generate one. The **validator** attribute refers to a method-binding expression pointing to a Java backing bean method that performs validation on the component's data. The Java backing bean's property **userName** is bound to the **value** attribute by using the Unified Expression Language value expression.

```
  <html>
    <head>
      <title>Current Page</title>
    </head>
A   <%@ taglib uri="http://java.sun.com/jsf/html" prefix="h" %>
    <%@ taglib uri="http://java.sun.com/jsf/core" prefix="f" %>
B   <body bgcolor="white">
C       <f:view>
D       <h:form id="QueryForm" >
E       <h:inputText id="userName" value="#{QueryBean.userName}"
            validator="#{ QueryBean.validate}"/>
F       <h:commandButton id="Query"  action="success"
            value="Query" />
G       <h:message style="color: red; font-family: 'New Century Schoolbook',
            serif; font-style: oblique; text-decoration: overline"
            id="QueryError" for="userName"/>
        </h:form>
      </f:view>
    </body>
  </html>
```

FIGURE 8.25 The code for the Current.jsp page.

F. The **commandButton** tag represents the button used to submit the data entered in the text field. The **action** attribute helps the navigation mechanism decide which page to open next. That is, the next page is defined in the application configuration resource file faces-config.xml using the <to-view-id> tag, which is **Next.jsp**.
G. The **message** tag displays an error message if the data entered is not valid. The **for** attribute refers to the component whose value failed validation.

An interesting thing in step E in this piece of sample code is that an embedded backing bean property, **userName**, has been bound to the **value** attribute of the **inputText** tag. Recall that we used either the **getAttribute()** method of a JSP implicit object **session (session.getAttribute())** or the **getProperty()** method of a Java bean to hook to the **value** attribute of this text field tag in the previous sample code to enable this text field's value to be updated automatically. However, in this JSF file, we directly bind one of the backing bean's properties, **userName**, with the **value** attribute of this text field by using the value-binding expression in the expression language (EL) with the syntax **#{bean-managed-property}** to update the data. One point to be noted is that the JSF EL bindings are bi-directional when it makes sense. For example, the UI component represented by the **inputText** tag can get the value of the bean property **userName** and present it to the user as a default value. When the user submits the **QueryForm** data, the UI component can automatically update the bean property **userName** so that the application logic can process the new value. You can see how easy it is now to setup a connection between a component in a JSF page and the related property in the backing bean object when using this binding for a JSF file. In fact, you can bind not only the bean's properties but also the bean's methods to certain UI components in JSP pages.

The code for the **Next.jsp** file is shown in Figure 8.26. The detailed function of this piece of code is:

A. The form **id** is defined as a Response Form.
B. An image is added into this page with the image id and the image URL. The forward slash, "/", before the image name, **Response.jpg**, indicates that this image is located in the current project folder.
C. An **outputText** tag is equivalent to a label in a Web page. The selected password is assigned to the **value** attribute using a value-binding expressions with the syntax

```
  <html>
    <head>
      <title>Next Page</title>
    </head>
    <%@ taglib uri="http://java.sun.com/jsf/html" prefix="h" %>
    <%@ taglib uri="http://java.sun.com/jsf/core" prefix="f" %>
    <body bgcolor="white">
        <f:view>
A       <h:form id="ResponseForm" >
B       <h:graphicImage id="ResponseImg" url="/Response.jpg" />
C       <h:outputText id="QueryResult" value="#{QueryBean.passWord}" />
D       <h:commandButton id="Back" action="success"
          value="Back" />
        </h:form>
       </f:view>
    </body>
  </html>
```

FIGURE 8.26 The code for the Next.jsp page.

#{bean-managed-property}. In fact, this value is bound with a property password in the backing bean QueryBean class.

D. The command Button **Back** is used to direct the page to return to the **Current.jsp** page when it is clicked by the user. This return function has been defined in the application configuration source file, faces-config.xml, we discussed previously.

The real tracking issue is no username-password matching process occurs in either of these two pages. Yes, that is true! All of the data-matching processes, or, as we called them business logic, occur in the backing Java bean QueryBean class.

When user enters a valid username into the input textbox and clicks the **Submit** button in the **Current.jsp** page, all input data is sent to the next page, **Next.jsp**. Of course, you can handle the data matching on the **Next.jsp** page based on the passed username. However, in order to separate the presentation from business logic, JSF uses JSF pages as views and assigns the business logic to the Java beans that work as controllers to handle the data-matching jobs. In fact, since the **userName** has been bound to the **value** attribute of the input Text tag by using a value-binding expression with the syntax **#{bean-managed-property}**, any change to this data item will be immediately reflected to the associated property, **userName**, defined in the Java bean QueryBean class. The Java bean will perform the password-matching process based on that username and send the matching password to the **passWord** property in that bean class. As soon as the Java bean finishes the password-matching processing and sends the matching password to the **passWord** property, it can be immediately updated and displayed in the output Text **QueryResult** in the **Next.jsp** page using the value-binding expression**#{QueryBean.passWord}**.

8.1.6.3 The Java Bean Class File

The Java bean class used in JSF pages is very similar to the **FacultyBean** class we built in Section 8.1.5.1. Like most Java bean classes, it should contain setter and getter methods as well as some special methods to process the business logic.

In addition, Java beans need to be conFigured in the application configuration resource file **faces-config.xml** so that the implementation can automatically create new instances of the beans as needed. The **<managed-bean>** element is used to create a mapping between a bean name and class. The first time the QueryBean is referenced, the object is created and stored in the appropriate scope. You can use the code elements shown in Figure 8.27 to register a Java bean in the **faces-config.xml** file: Besides registering the Java bean class, you also need to use the configuration file to conFigure and define all properties created inside the Java bean. In this example, only two properties, **userName** and **passWord**, have been defined in this Java bean. Therefore, you need to use the **<managed-property>** element to do the configuration, as shown in Figure 8.28.

In fact, you do not need to worry about the configuration if you are using an IDE such as the NetBeans IDE, which can do the configuration automatically for you as you build the Java bean class file.

Next let's take a look at the Web deployment descriptor file.

8.1.6.4 The Web Deployment Descriptor File, web.xml

Before you can use and access a Servlet such as FacesServlet on the server side from a Web browser, you need to map the **FacesServlet** to a path in your deployment descriptor file, **web.xml**. By

```
<managed-bean-name>QueryBean</managed-bean-name>
<managed-bean-class>LogInQuery.QueryBean</managed-bean-class>
<managed-bean-scope>session</managed-bean-scope>
```

FIGURE 8.27 A piece of sample code to register a Java bean.

```
<managed-property>
<property-name>userName</property-name>
<property-class>string</property-class>
<value>null</value>
</managed-property>
<managed-property>
<property-name>passWord</property-name>
<property-class>string</property-class>
<value>null</value>
</managed-property>
```

FIGURE 8.28 A piece of code to define all properties in a Java bean class.

```
<web-app>
<display-name>JSF LogIn Application</display-name>
<description>JSF LogIn Application</description>
<!-- Faces Servlet -->
<servlet>
<servlet-name>Faces Servlet</servlet-name>
<servlet-class>javax.faces.webapp.FacesServlet</servlet-class>
<load-on-startup> 1 </load-on-startup>
</servlet>
<!-- Faces Servlet Mapping -->
<servlet-mapping>
<servlet-name>Faces Servlet</servlet-name>
<url-pattern>/login/*</url-pattern>
</servlet-mapping>
```

FIGURE 8.29 Example code for the Web deployment descriptor file.

using this deployment descriptor file, you can register Servlet and FacesServlet, register listeners and map resources to URLs. Figure 8.29 shows a piece of example code used in the `web.xml` file for the `FacesServlet` class.

Most code in this file will be created automatically if you are using the NetBeans IDE to build your Web application.

As we discussed in section 8.1.6.1, usually, JSP pages use the `<jsp:useBean>` tag to instantiate JavaBeans. When using the JSF framework, you do not have to specify the Java bean class names in your Web pages anymore. Instead, you can conFigure your bean instances in the application configuration resource file `faces-config.xml` using the `<managed-bean>` element. You may use multiple configuration files if you develop a large application. In that case, you must add a `javax.faces.CONFIG _ FILES` parameter in the deployment descriptor file, `web.xml`.

Now that we have worked through all the main techniques of JSF, let's get a full picture of the complete run procedure of JSF Web applications.

8.1.6.5 A Complete Run Procedure of JSF Web Applications

As we mentioned, a UI component represented by a JSF tag in a JSP page can be bound to a Java bean's property or method. To separate the presentation and business logic, we can use JSP pages to present our GUI and Java beans to store our data to perform business-related logic. Therefore, we can divide methods into two categories: data access methods (business methods) and action methods. Data access methods should be located at the Java bean side, and action methods should be located at the JSF page side. Each data access method defined in the Java bean can be called by an associated action method defined in an **action** attribute of a submit button tag in the JSP page if that submit button has been bound to the **action** attribute.

Here, we use a login process to illustrate the operational procedure using the JSF technique. Two JSP pages, **LogIn.jsp** and **Selection.jsp**, and a Java bean class, **LogInBean.java**, are involved in this procedure. Two JSP pages work as views and are used to display the input and output login information, and the Java bean works as a model to handle the database-related processing and business logic. The functional procedure of this example application is:

1) When the user enters a username/password pair into the Username/Password input text fields in the **LogIn.jsp** page and clicks on the LogIn button, a query request is sent to the Web server with all form data (Username and Password) for processing.
2) After the server receives the request, if the validation passes, all form data (Username and Password) will be stored in the associated properties of the Java bean.
3) The action method that is bound to the LogIn button will call the data access method defined in the Java bean to perform the database query to find the matching login information in the LogIn Table.
4) If the data access method is successful, the next page, Selection.jsp, should be displayed.

To run this procedure using the JSF technique, we need to have a clear picture of JSF pages and Java beans and the page-to-page navigation schedule.

8.1.6.5.1 The Java Bean–JSF Page Relationship and Page Navigation

Table 8.1 lists all data access methods and action methods used in this example.

A Java bean can be connected to a JSF page by using the **value** attribute of a UI component represented by a JSF tag in that page. That is, a property or method defined in a Java bean class can be mapped to a **value** attribute of a UI component in a JSF page. This relationship can be triggered and setup when a submit button in the JSF page is clicked by the user and all form data sent to the Web server. Refer to Figure 8.30. The operational procedure of executing a request is:

1) The data access method **LogInQuery()** is defined in the Java bean class LogInBean and will be called by the action method **LogInBean.LogInAction()** defined in the JSF page **LogIn.jsp** when the user clicks the **LogIn** button. Since the action method **LogInBean.LogInAction()** has been bound to the **LogIn** command button, all form data, including the Username and Password entered by the user on the JSF page, will be submitted to the FacesServlet when the **LogIn** button is clicked by the user.
2) After the FacesServlet receives the form data, it will validate it and return the form back to the client if any error is encountered.
3) Otherwise, the validated form data, including the Username and Password, will be stored to the associated properties in the Java bean class. Then JSF engine will call the action method **LogInBean.LogInAction()** that has been bound to the LogIn button and in turn call the data access method **LogInQuery()** to perform the database-related query to find the matching login information.

TABLE 8.1
The Relationship between the Data Access Method and the Action Method

Data Access Method	Action Method	JSF Page
LogInQuery()	LogInBean.LogInAction()	LogIn.jsp

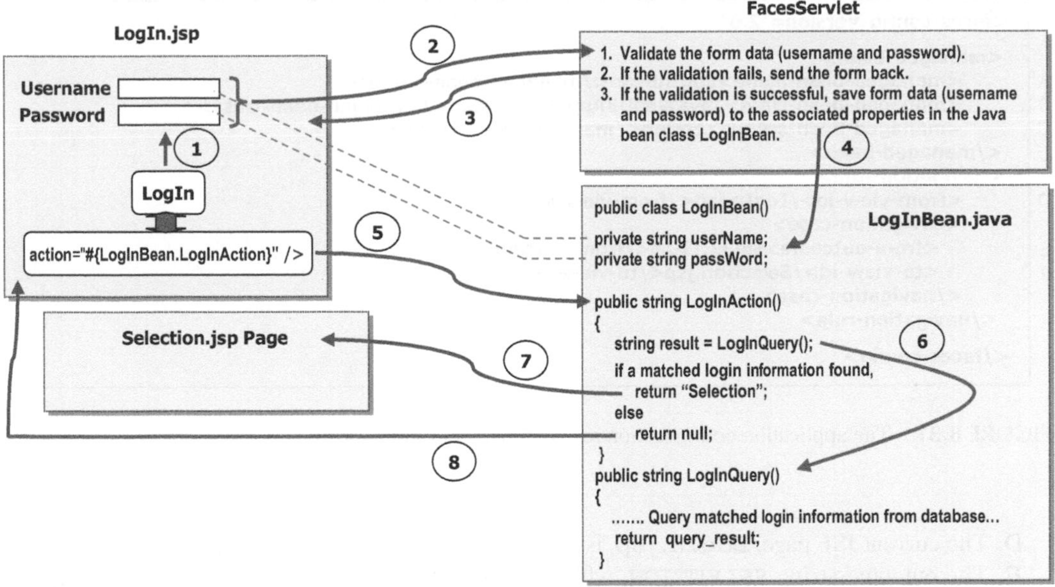

FIGURE 8.30 The operational procedure of executing a request using JSF.

4) After a piece of matching login information has been found, the associated properties, **userName** and **passWord**, which are defined inside the Java bean class, will be updated by assigning the matching username and password to them. This update occurs on the Java bean side and will be immediately reflected to the **value** attributes of the Username and Password input Text fields in the JSF page, since they have been bound together. Therefore, the content of each input Text tag will also be updated.
5) The action method **LogInAction()** defined in the LogInBean class will also be called when the LogIn button is clicked by the user since it is bound to the LogIn button.
6) The data access method **LogInQuery()** will be executed to perform database-related queries and business logic.
7) Each action method returns a string called "outcome". JSF uses a navigation handler to determine what it is supposed to do for each outcome string. If an action method returns a **null**, it means that the execution of that method encountered problems and the same page must be redisplayed. Otherwise, the desired next page should be displayed, depending on the returned outcome string. The default JSF navigation handler uses a set of navigation rules that are specified in the JSF application configuration file **faces-config.xml**, which is shown in Figure 8.31. In this example, if a piece of matching login information is found, the action method will return an outcome string "**SELECTION**" and the next page, **Selection.jsp**, should be displayed.
8) Otherwise, the query fails and no matching login user information can be found. The **LogInAction()** method returns a **null** to the JSF engine to redisplay the LogIn page.

A detailed explanation of the code shown in Figure 8.31 follows:

A. Our Java managed bean **LogInBean** is defined using the <managed-bean-name> tag.
B. The full class name, including the package name and the bean class name, is defined by the <managed-bean-class> tag.
C. The scope of this Java bean is defined by using the <managed-bean-scope> tag.

```
  <faces-config version="2.0"
   <managed-bean>
A      <managed-bean-name>LogInBean</managed-bean-name>
B      <managed-bean-class>JavaWebDBApp. LogInBean</managed-bean-class>
C      <managed-bean-scope>session</managed-bean-scope>
   </managed-bean>
   <navigation-rule>
D      <from-view-id>/LogIn.jsp</from-view-id>
       <navigation-case>
E        <from-outcome>SELECTION</from-outcome>
F        <to-view-id>/Selection.jsp</to-view-id>
       </navigation-case>
    </navigation-rule>
  </faces-config>
```

FIGURE 8.31 The application configuration resource file faces-config.xml.

D. The current JSF page, **`LogIn.jsp`**, is defined by using the <from-view-id> tag.
E. The outcome string **`SELECTION`**, which is mapped to the next page **`Selection.jsp`**, is defined by using the <from-outcome> tag and should be returned by the action method **`LogInAction()`** if a matching login user has been found.
F. The name of the next page, **`Selection.jsp`**, is defined by using the <to-view-id> tag.

The points to be noted for this configuration file are:

1) Both the outcome string and the next page should be defined inside the <navigation-case> tag, and all navigation pages should be defined inside the <navigation-rule> tag.
2) The forward-slash symbol "/" before each page name is used to indicate that those pages are located at the current location where the JSF project is located.
3) You can create and edit this configuration file using either the XML editor or the PageFlow design tool.

In order to use the PageFlow design tool to build the navigation rules in the faces-config.xml file, sometimes you need to close and reopen the NetBeans IDE.

The code for a sample **`LogIn.jsp`** page is shown in Figure 8.32. Let's have a closer look at this piece of code to see how it works.

A. Two JSF standard customer tag libraries, one for building JSF applications that render to an HTML client and another for representing core actions independently of a particular render kit, are declared first at this page using the **`<%@taglib%>`** directive. The **`uri`** is used to indicate the valid sites where both libraries are located.
B. All JSF tag components are represented by a tree of components whose root is **`UIViewRoot`**, which is represented by the **`<f:view>`** tag. All JSF component tags must be enclosed in this **`<f:view>`** tag.

```
  <html>
    <head>
      <meta http-equiv="Content-Type" content="text/html; charset=UTF-8">
      <title>LogIn Page</title>
    </head>
A   <%@ taglib uri="http://java.sun.com/jsf/html" prefix="h" %>
    <%@ taglib uri="http://java.sun.com/jsf/core" prefix="f" %>
    <body>
B     <f:view>
C       <h:form id="LogInForm">
D         <h:inputText id="userName" required="true" value="#{LogInBean.userName}"
          size="10" maxlength="40">
E         <f:validateLength minimum="1" maximum="40"/>
          </h:inputText>
F         <h:inputSecret id="passWord" required="true" value="#{LogInBean.passWord}"
          size="10" maxlength="20">
G         <f:validateLength minimum="6" maximum="20"/>
           </h:inputSecret>
H         <h:commandButton id="LogIn" action="#{LogInBean.LogInAction}"
          value="LogIn" />
        </h:form>
      </f:view>
    </body>
  </html>
```

FIGURE 8.32 The code of a sample LogIn.jsp page.

C. A JSP **form**, which is submitted to the Web server when a button is clicked, is represented by the **<h:form>** tag. The tags representing the form components, such as text fields and buttons, must be nested inside this **form** tag. The form is identified by its **id**; here it is a LogInForm.
D. An inputText tag is used to represent an input field to allow the user to enter one line of text string, such as a username in this example. This inputText tag is identified by its **id**, and the **required** attribute is set to true. This means that the inputText cannot be empty and must be filled in by the user when the project runs. The **value** attribute of the inputText tag is bound to the property **userName** in the Java bean class, LogInBean, by using the EL value expression. Two points to be noted for this tag are: (1) the value of this tag's **id** must be identical to the property name **userName** defined in the Java managed bean LogInBean, and (2) the **value** attribute of this tag must be bound to the same **username** property defined in the Java managed bean LogInBean class. In this way, any update made to the **username** property in the Java bean can be immediately reflected to the **value** of the inputText tag and, furthermore, displayed in the input field.
E. A **<f:validateLength>** tag is used to make sure that the length of the username is in the range defined by the **minimum** and **maximum** attributes.
F. A similar tag is used for the passWord inputText, and it is bound to the **passWord** property defined in the Java managed bean LogInBean class. The only difference between this tag and the userName inputText tag is that a **<h:inputSecret>** tag is used to replace the **<h:inputText>** tag, since this is a way to present a password input style.
G. A **<f:validateLength>** tag is also used to validate the length of the passWord to make sure that it is in the required range.
H. A **<h:commandButton>** tag is used to present a submit button component, and its **action** attribute is bound to the action method defined in the Java managed bean LogInBean using the EL value expression "**#{LogInBean.LogInAction}**".

Next let's have a closer look at the code for our Java Bean class.

8.1.6.5.2 The Detailed Code for the Java Bean Class

The code for the Java bean class **`LogInBean.java`** is shown in Figure 8.33. The functionality of each part of the code is illustrated in the following.

A. Two properties, **`userName`** and **`passWord`**, are defined first, and these two properties must be identical to the **`id`** attributes defined in the inputText and inputSecret tags in the JSF page **`LogIn.jsp`** we discussed previously.
B. The associated getter methods for these two properties are declared and defined in steps B and D, respectively.
C. The associated setter methods for these two properties are defined in steps C and E.
F. The action method **`LogInAction()`** is defined, and this method is bound to the **`action`** attribute of the LogIn commandButton tag in the **`LogIn.jsp`** page. This method will be executed when the LogIn button is clicked by the user.
G. The data access method **`LogInQuery()`** is defined, and this method is used to perform the database-related query and business logic and return a outcome string to the JSF page. The JSF page will use its handler to search the returned outcome string to determine the next page to navigate.

So far, we have provided a very detailed introduction to and review of the development history of Java Web applications using different components, such as Java Servlet and HTML pages, JavaServer Pages and help classes and JavaServer Pages and Java beans, as well as JavaServer Faces

```
  @ManagedBean(name="LogInBean")
  @SessionScoped
  public class LogInBean {
     /** Creates a new instance of LogInBean */
     public LogInBean() {
     }
A    private String userName;
     private String passWord;
B    public String getPassWord() {
        return passWord;
     }
C    public void setPassWord(String passWord) {
        this.passWord = passWord;
     }
D    public String getUserName() {
        return userName;
     }
E    public void setUserName(String userName) {
        this.userName = userName;
     }
F    public String LogInAction()
     {
        String result=null;
        result = LogInQuery();
        return result;
     }
G    public String LogInQuery()
     {
        // query username from database and assign the queried value to the userName property
        // query password from database and assign the queried value to the passWord property
        return "SELECTION";
     }
  }
```

FIGURE 8.33 The code for the Java bean class LogInBean.

and Java bean techniques. In the following sections, we will provide more detailed discussion for each component and technique. Following these discussions, we will begin to build and develop real Java Web application projects to perform data actions against our sample database.

8.2 JAVA EE WEB APPLICATION MODEL

The Java EE application model begins with the Java programming language and the Java virtual machine. The proven portability, security and developer productivity they provide form the basis of the application model. Java EE is designed to support applications that implement enterprise services for customers, employees, suppliers, partners and others who make demands on or contributions to the enterprise. Such applications are inherently complex, potentially accessing data from a variety of sources and distributing applications to a variety of clients.

The Java EE application model defines an architecture for implementing services as multitier applications that deliver the scalability, accessibility and manageability needed by enterprise-level applications. This model partitions the work needed to implement a multitier service into two parts: the business and presentation logic to be implemented by the developer and the standard system services provided by the Java EE platform. The developer can rely on the platform to provide solutions for the hard systems-level problems of developing a multitier service.

The Java EE platform uses a distributed multi-tier application model for enterprise applications. Application logic is divided into components according to function, and the various application components that make up a Java EE application are installed on different machines depending on the tier in the multi-tier Java EE environment to which the application component belongs.

Most Java Web database applications are three-tier client-server applications, which means that this kind of application can be built in three tiers or three containers: client container, Web server container and database server container. Java Enterprise Java Beans plays an additional role in business data management and processing in this three-tier architecture. However, in recent years, because of its complexity and time-consuming development cycles as well as undesirable output performances, some researchers recommend using Java EE without EJB.

In order to get a clearer picture of these two kinds of architectures, let's first concentrate on the difference between them.

8.2.1 Java EE Web Applications with and without EJB

Most Java Web applications can be divided into three tiers: a client tier composed of client machines, Web tier consisting of Java EE Server and Enterprise Information System (EIS) tier made of the database server. Java Enterprise Java Beans also works as a business tier attached to the Java server layer. This relationship can be represented by the different tiers shown in Figure 8.34.

In fact in recent years, because of undesirable output results and complicated development processes, some developers have changed their minds and moved to Java EE without EJB. This simplification can be illustrated by the architecture shown in Figure 8.35.

Compared with the two architectures shown in Figures 8.34 and 8.35, it can be seen that the business tier, Enterprise Java Bean, has been removed from the Web layer, and this greatly simplifies communications and data transformations between those related tiers. From a practical application viewpoint, this will also significantly reduce code development cycles and improve the efficiency of program executions in real time.

As we know, the popular Java EE components are:

- Application clients and Applets are components that run on the client machine.
- Java Servlet, JavaServer Faces and JavaServer Pages technology components are web components that run on the server.
- Enterprise JavaBeans components are business components that run on the server.

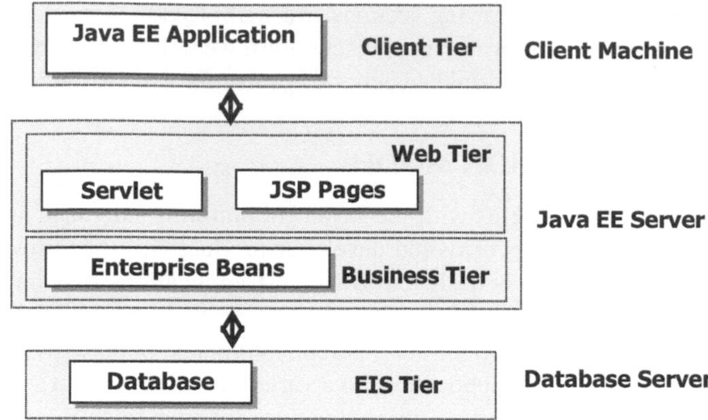

FIGURE 8.34 An illustration of Java EE three-tier application with EJB.

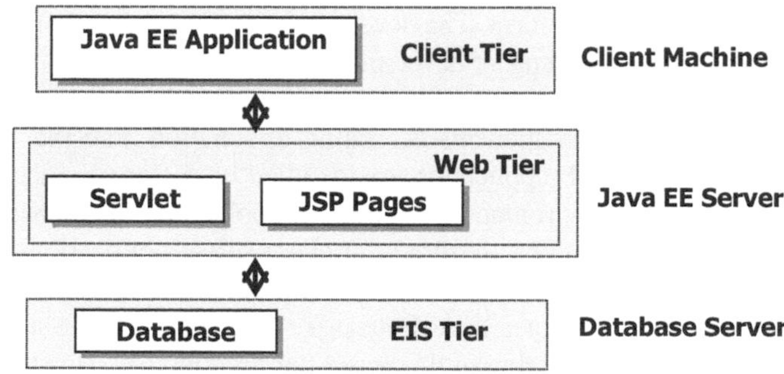

FIGURE 8.35 An illustration of Java EE three-tier application without EJB.

As we build a Java Web application using the architecture shown in Figure 8.35, the third component, EJB, can be removed from this three-tier architecture.

When building a Java Web application, different modules can be adopted based on the different applications. A Java EE module consists of one or more Java EE components for the same container type and, optionally, one component deployment descriptor of that type. An enterprise bean module deployment descriptor, for example, declares transaction attributes and security authorizations for an enterprise bean. A Java EE module can be deployed as a stand-alone module.

The four types of Java EE modules are:

1) EJB modules, which contain class files for enterprise beans and an EJB deployment descriptor. EJB modules are packaged as JAR files with a `.jar` extension.
2) Web modules, which contain Servlet class files, Web files, supporting class files, GIF and HTML files and a Web application deployment descriptor. Web modules are packaged as JAR files with a. `war` (Web ARchive) extension.
3) Application client modules, which contain class files and an application client deployment descriptor. Application client modules are packaged as JAR files with a `.jar` extension.
4) Resource adapter modules, which contain all Java interfaces, classes, native libraries and other documentation, along with the resource adapter deployment descriptor. Together, these implement the Connector architecture for a particular EIS. Resource adapter modules are packaged as JAR files with a `.rar` (resource adapter archive) extension.

We will concentrate on deeper discussion of Java EE Web applications in the following sections.

8.3 THE ARCHITECTURE AND COMPONENTS OF JAVA WEB APPLICATIONS

A Web application is a dynamic extension of a web or application server. There are two types of Web applications:

- `Presentation-Oriented`: A presentation-oriented Web application generates interactive Web pages containing various types of markup language (HTML, XHTML, XML and so on) and dynamic content in response to requests. We will cover how to develop presentation-oriented Web applications in this chapter.
- `Service-Oriented`: A service-oriented Web application implements the endpoint of a Web service. Presentation-oriented applications are often clients of service-oriented Web applications. We will discuss how to develop service-oriented Web applications in the next chapter.

On the Java EE platform, Web components provide the dynamic extension capabilities for a Web server. Web components can be either Java Servlets, Web pages, Web service endpoints or JSP pages. The interaction between a Web client and a Web application is illustrated in Figure 8.36.

Based on Figure 8.36, a complete request-response message transformation for a Java Web application between a client and a Web server can be illustrated as follows:

1) The client sends an HTTP request to the Web server.
2) A Web server that implements Java Servlet and JavaServer Pages technology converts the request into an HTTPServletRequest object.
3) The Web component can then generate an HTTPServletResponse, or it can pass the request to another Web component.
4) Eventually a Web component generates an HTTPServletResponse object.
5) The Web server converts this object to an HTTP response and returns it to the client.

The dashed lines between the Web components and Java Beans components and between Java Beans components and the database, are alternative ways to interact with database via the business layer that is supported by the Java Beans components.

In order to get a clear and complete picture of how to control and transmit these request and response messages between Java EE Web components, we first need to have a basic understanding of Java EE containers.

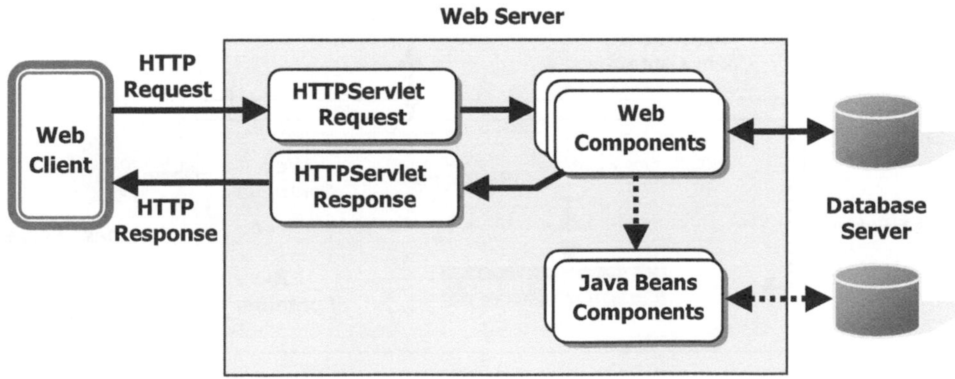

FIGURE 8.36 An illustration of the Java Web application.

8.3.1 Java EE Containers

Java EE containers are the interfaces between a component and the low-level platform-specific functionality that supports the component. Before a Web, enterprise bean or application client component can be executed, it must be assembled into a Java EE module and deployed into its container. Refer to Section 8.2 for a detailed discussion of the four types of Java EE module.

The assembly process involves specifying container settings for each component in the Java EE application and for the Java EE application itself. Container settings customize the underlying support provided by the Java EE server, including services such as security, transaction management, JavaNaming and Directory Interface lookups and remote connectivity.

The deployment process installs Java EE application components in the Java EE containers, as illustrated in Figure 8.37.

The function of each container is listed in the following:

- `Java EE server`: The runtime portion of a Java EE product. A Java EE server provides EJB and web containers.
- `Enterprise JavaBeans container`: Manages the execution of enterprise beans for Java EE applications. Enterprise beans and their containers run on the Java EE server.
- `Web container`: Manages the execution of Web pages, Servlets and some EJB components for Java EE applications. Web components and their containers run on the Java EE server.
- `Application client container`: Manages the execution of application client components. Application clients and their containers run on the client.

All Web components are under the control of the associated containers, and the containers take charge of collecting, organizing and transmitting requests and responses between those components. Java EE Web components can be implemented with multiple APIs. Let's have a brief review of these APIs.

8.3.2 Java EE 8 APIs

In this section, we will give a brief summary of the most popular technologies required by the Java EE platform and the APIs used in Java EE applications.

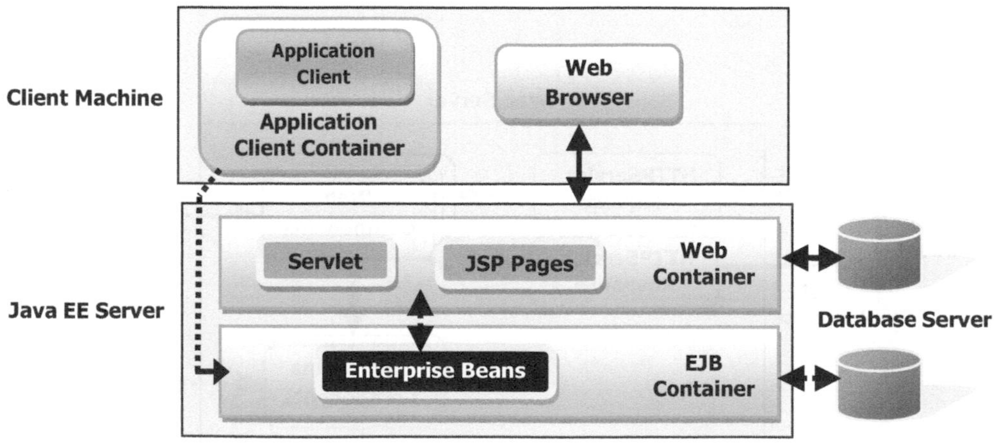

FIGURE 8.37 Java EE server and containers.

8.3.2.1 Enterprise Java Beans API Technology

An Enterprise Java Beans component, or enterprise bean, is a body of code with fields and methods to implement modules of business logic. You can think of an enterprise bean as a building block that can be used alone or with other enterprise beans to execute business logic on the Java EE server.

There are two kinds of enterprise beans: *session beans* and *message-driven beans*. A session bean represents a transient conversation with a client. When the client finishes executing, the session bean and its data are gone. A message-driven bean combines features of a session bean and a message listener, allowing a business component to receive messages asynchronously. Commonly, these are JavaMessage Service (JMS) messages. Refer to Figure 5.58 in Chapter 5 to get more detailed information about the EJB.

In the Java EE 8 platform, new enterprise bean features include the following:

1) The ability to package local enterprise beans in a. WAR file.
2) Singleton session beans, which provide easy access to shared states.
3) A lightweight subset of Enterprise Java Beans functionality that can be provided within Java EE Profiles such as the Java EE Web Profile.

8.3.2.2 Java Servlet API Technology

A Servlet is a class defined in Java programming language, and it is used to extend the capabilities of servers that host applications accessed by means of a request-response programming model. Although Servlets can respond to any type of request, they are commonly used to extend the applications hosted by Web servers. For such applications, Java Servlet API technology defines HTTP-specific Servlet classes.

The **`javax.servlet`** and **`javax.servlet.http`** packages provide interfaces and classes for writing Servlets. All Servlets must implement the Servlet interface, which defines life-cycle methods. When implementing a generic service, you can use or extend the GenericServlet class provided with the Java Servlet API. The HttpServlet class provides methods, such as **`doGet()`** and **`doPost()`**, for handling HTTP-specific services.

The life cycle of a Servlet is controlled by the container in which the Servlet has been deployed. When a request is mapped to a Servlet, the container performs the following steps.

1) If an instance of the Servlet does not exist, the Web container
   a. Loads the Servlet class.
   b. Creates an instance of the Servlet class.
   c. Initializes the Servlet instance by calling the **`init()`** method.
2) Invokes the service method, passing request and response objects.

If the container needs to remove the Servlet, it finalizes the Servlet by calling the Servlet's **`destroy()`** method.

You can monitor and react to events in a Servlet's life cycle by defining listener objects whose methods get invoked when life-cycle events occur. To use these listener objects, you must define and specify the listener class.

8.3.2.3 JavaServer Pages API Technology

JavaServer Pages is Java technology that helps software developers serve dynamically generated web pages based on HTML, XML or other document types. Released in 1999 as Sun's answer to ASP and PHP, JSP was designed to address the perception that the Java programming environment didn't provide developers with enough support for the Web.

Architecturally, JSP may be considered a high-level abstraction of Java Servlets. JSP pages are loaded in the server and operated from a structured special installed Java server packet called a Java EE Web Application, often packaged as a `.war` or `.ear` file archive.

JSP allows Java code and certain pre-defined actions to be interleaved with static Web markup content, with the resulting page being compiled and executed on the server to deliver an HTML or XML document. The compiled pages and any dependent Java libraries use Java byte-code rather than a native software format and must therefore be executed within a Java Virtual Machine (JVM) that integrates with the host operating system to provide an abstract platform-neutral environment.

JSP syntax is a fluid mix of two basic content forms: *scriptlet elements* and *markup*. Markup is typically standard HTML or XML, while scriptlet elements are delimited blocks of Java code which may be intermixed with the markup. When the page is requested, the Java code is executed and its output is added, in situ, with the surrounding markup to create the final page. Because Java is a compiled language, not a scripting language, JSP pages must be compiled to Java byte-code classes before they can be executed, but such compilation is needed only when a change to the source JSP file has occurred.

Java code is not required to be complete (self contained) within its scriptlet element block but can straddle markup content provided the page as a whole is syntactically correct (for example, any Java **`if/for/while`** blocks opened in one scriptlet element must be correctly closed in a later element for the page to successfully compile). This system of split inline code sections is called *step over scripting* because it can wrap around the static markup by stepping over it. Markup which falls inside a split block of code is subject to that code, so markup inside an **`if`** block will only appear in the output when the **`if`** condition evaluates to true; likewise, markup inside a loop construct may appear multiple times in the output depending upon how many times the loop body runs.

The JSP syntax adds additional XML-like tags, called JSP actions, to invoke built-in functionality. Additionally, the technology allows for the creation of JSP tag libraries that act as extensions to the standard HTML or XML tags. JVM-operated tag libraries provide a platform-independent way of extending the capabilities of a Web server. Note that not all commercial Java servers are Java EE specification compliant.

JavaServer Pages (JSP) technology lets you put snippets of Servlet code directly into a text-based document. A JSP page is a text-based document that contains two types of text: static data (which can be expressed in any text-based format such as HTML, WML and XML) and JSP elements, which determine how the page constructs dynamic content.

The JavaServer Pages Standard Tag Library (JSTL) encapsulates core functionality common to many JSP applications. Instead of mixing tags from numerous vendors in your JSP applications, you employ a single, standard set of tags. This standardization allows you to deploy your applications on any JSP container that supports JSTL and makes it more likely that the implementation of the tags is optimized.

JSTL has an iterator and conditional tags for handling flow control, tags for manipulating XML documents, internationalization tags, tags for accessing databases using SQL and commonly used functions.

JSP pages are compiled into Servlets by a JSP compiler. The compiler either generates a Servlet in Java code that is then compiled by the Java compiler, or it may compile the Servlet to byte code which is directly execuTable. JSPs can also be interpreted on the fly, reducing the time taken to reload changes.

JSP simply puts Java inside HTML pages using JSP tags. You can take any existing HTML page and change its extension to **`.jsp`** instead of **`.html`**.

Regardless of whether the JSP compiler generates Java source code for a Servlet or emits the byte code directly, it is helpful to understand how the JSP compiler transforms the page into a Java Servlet. For example, consider the input JSP page shown in Figure 8.38. This JSP page can be compiled to create its resulting generated Java Servlet. The JSP tags `<% . . . %>` or `<jsp . . . />` enclose Java expressions, which are evaluated at runtime by JVM.

```
A  <%@ page myPage="mypage.jsp" %>
   <%@ page import="com.foo.bar" %>
   <html>
   <head>
B  <%! int serverInstanceVariable = 1;%>
   <% int localStackBasedVariable = 1; %>
   <table>
   <tr><td><%= toStringOrBlank( "expanded inline data " + 1 ) %></td></tr>
```

FIGURE 8.38 An example of JSP pages.

Refer to Figure 8.38. In step A, two JSP code lines declare a JSP page and an import component. Then, in step B, two Java integer variables are created; one is an instance variable, and the other is a Stack-based variable.

8.3.2.4 JavaServer Faces API Technology

JavaServer Faces technology is a server-side component framework for building Java technology-based Web applications. JavaServer Faces technology consists of the following:

- An API for representing components and managing their state; handling events, server-side validation and data conversion; defining page navigation; supporting internationalization and accessibility; and providing extensibility for all these features
- Tag libraries for adding components to Web pages and for connecting components to server-side objects

JavaServer Faces technology provides a well-defined programming model and various tag libraries. These features significantly ease the burden of building and maintaining Web applications with server-side UIs. With minimal effort, you can complete the following tasks:

1) Create a Web page
2) Drop components onto a Web page by adding component tags
3) Bind components on a page to server-side data
4) Wire component-generated events to server-side application code
5) Save and restore application state beyond the life of server requests
6) Reuse and extend components through customization

The functionality provided by a JavaServer Faces application is similar to that of any other Java Web application. A typical JavaServer Faces application includes the following parts:

A set of Web pages in which components are laid out.

- A set of tags to add components to the Web page.
- A set of *backing beans*, which are JavaBeans components that define properties and functions for components on a page.
- A Web deployment descriptor (**`web.xml`** file).
- Optionally, one or more application configuration resource files, such as a **`faces-config.xml`** file, which can be used to define page navigation rules and conFigure beans and other custom objects, such as custom components.
- Optionally, a set of custom objects created by the application developer. These objects can include custom components, validators, converters or listeners.
- A set of custom tags for representing custom objects on the page.

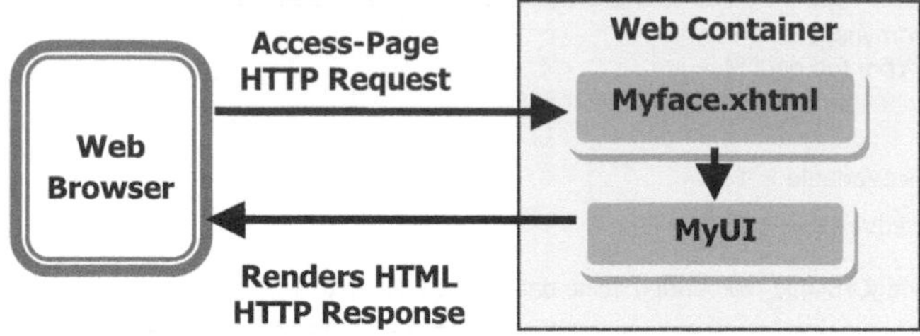

FIGURE 8.39 Responding to a client request for a JavaServer Faces page.

Figure 8.39 shows the interaction between client and server in a typical JavaServer Faces application. In response to a client request, a Web page is rendered by the Web container that implements JavaServer Faces technology.

The Web page, `Myface.xhtml`, is built using JavaServer Faces component tags. Component tags are used to add components to the view (represented by `MyUI` in the diagram), which is the server-side representation of the page. In addition to components, the Web page can also reference objects such as the following:

1) Any event listeners, validators and converters that are registered on the components
2) The JavaBeans components that capture the data and process the application-specific functionality of the components

On request from the client, the view is rendered as a response. Rendering is the process whereby, based on the server-side view, the Web container generates output such as HTML or XHTML that can be read by the browser.

8.3.2.5 Java Transaction API

The Java Transaction API (JTA) provides a standard interface for demarcating transactions.

The Java EE architecture provides a default auto commit to handle transaction commits and rollbacks. An `auto commit` means that any other applications that are viewing data will see the updated data after each database read or write operation. However, if your application performs two separate database access operations that depend on each other, you will want to use the JTA API to demarcate where the entire transaction, including both operations, begins, rolls back and commits.

In Section 7.1 in Chapter 7, we provided a very detailed discussion of the Java Persistence API on Transaction mechanism and its implementation with some data manipulations in real projects, such as data insertion, update and deletion, using the JPA wizard. Refer to that section to get more information about this API.

8.3.2.6 Java Message Service API

The JavaMessage Service (JMS) API is a messaging standard that allows Java EE application components to create, send, receive and read messages. It enables distributed communication that is loosely coupled, reliable and asynchronous.

Now that we have a basic and clear understanding of the Java EE architecture and components, let's take a look at the Java Web application life cycle.

8.3.3 Java Web Application Life Cycle

A Web application consists of Web components, static resource files such as images and helper classes and libraries. The Web container provides many supporting services that enhance the capabilities of Web components and make them easier to develop. However, because a Web application must take these services into account, the process for creating and running a Web application is different from that of traditional stand-alone Java classes.

The process for creating, deploying and executing a Web application can be summarized as follows:

1) Develop the Web component code.
2) Develop the Web application deployment descriptor.
3) Compile the Web application components and helper classes referenced by the components.
4) Optionally package the application into a deployable unit.
5) Deploy the application into a Web container.
6) Access the URL that references the Web application.

We will illustrate how to use this life cycle module to develop and build some professional Java Web applications in Section 8.4.

8.3.4 Java Web Modules

As we discussed in Section 8.2.1, four Java EE Web modules are available, and the Web module is one of them. In the Java EE architecture, Web components and static Web content files such as images are called **web resources**. A **web module** is the smallest deployable and usable unit of Web resources. A Java EE Web module corresponds to a Web application as defined in the Java Servlet specification.

In addition to Web components and Web resources, a Web module can contain other files:

- Server-side utility classes (database beans, shopping carts and so on). Often these classes conform to the JavaBeans component architecture.
- Client-side classes (applets and utility classes).

A Web module has a specific structure. The top-level directory of a Web module is the **document root** of the application. The document root is where XHTML pages, client-side classes and archives and static Web resources, such as images, are stored.

The document root contains a subdirectory named WEB-INF, which contains the following files and directories:

- **web.xml**: The Web application deployment descriptor
- Tag library descriptor files
- **classes**: A directory that contains server-side classes: Servlets, utility classes and JavaBeans components
- **tags**: A directory that contains tag files, which are implementations of tag libraries
- **lib**: A directory that contains JAR archives of libraries called by server-side classes

If your Web module does not contain any Servlets, filter or listener components, then it does not need a Web application deployment descriptor. In other words, if your Web module only contains XHTML pages and static files, you are not required to include a **web.xml** file.

You can also create application-specific subdirectories (that is, package directories) in either the document root or the WEB-INF/classes/ directory.

A Web module can be deployed as an unpacked file structure or can be packaged in a JAR file known as a Web archive (WAR) file. Because the contents and use of WAR files differ from those of JAR files, WAR file names use a **.war** extension. The Web module just described is porTable; you can deploy it into any Web container that conforms to the Java Servlet specification.

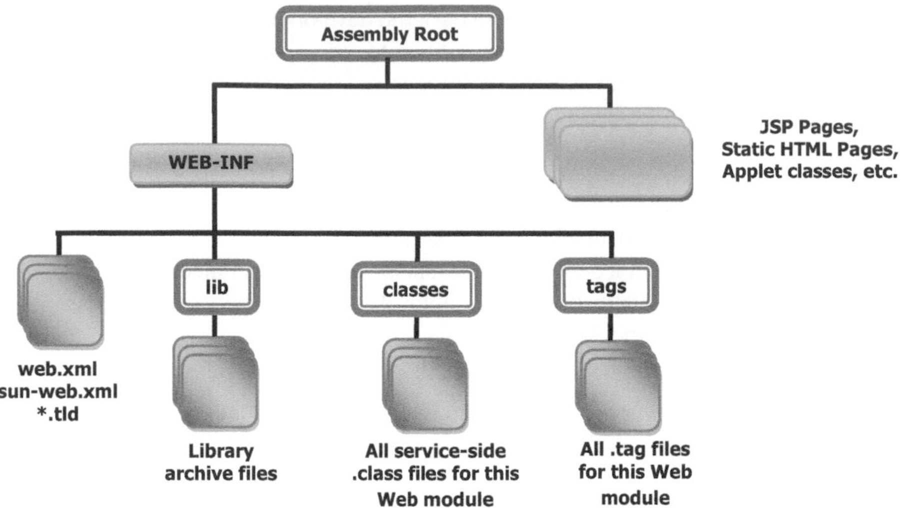

FIGURE 8.40 A Web module structure.

To deploy a WAR on the Enterprise Server, the file must also contain a runtime deployment descriptor. The runtime deployment descriptor is an XML file that contains information such as the context root of the Web application and the mapping of the porTable names of an application's resources to the Enterprise Server's resources. The Enterprise Server Web application runtime DD is named **`sun-web.xml`** and is located in the WEB-INF directory along with the Web application DD. The structure of a Web module that can be deployed on the Enterprise Server is shown in Figure 8.40.

To successfully build and implement a Java Web application, one needs to perform the following operations to make it a distribuTable application:

- Packaging Web modules
- Deploying a WAR file
- Testing deployed Web modules
- Listing deployed Web modules
- Updating Web modules
- Undeploying Web modules

We will discuss these operations in more detail in the following sections with some real Java Web application projects.

8.3.5 Java Web Frameworks

A Web application framework is a software framework that is designed to support the development of dynamic websites, Web applications and Web services. The framework aims to alleviate the overhead associated with common activities performed in Web development. For example, many frameworks provide libraries for database access, template frameworks and session management, and they often promote code reuse, too.

As we know, all Web components, such as Java Servlets, Web pages or JSP pages, are under the control of the associated Web containers. The question is: who controls those Web containers? The answer is the Web framework. A Web framework is a software framework that provides all the support to develop and organize dynamic sites. Some main features of a Web framework include:

- Provides user-friendly graphical user interfaces to Web applications
- Provides management of Web containers to coordinate request and response transmission between Web server and clients
- Provides security support to Web servers
- Provides support to database accessing and mapping
- Provides support to URL mapping
- Provides support to update Web templates

Almost all modern Web-development frameworks follow the model-view-controller (MVC) design. Business logic and presentation are separated, and a controller of logic flow coordinates requests from clients and actions taken on the server. This approach has become a popular style of Web development.

All frameworks use different techniques to coordinate navigation within the Web application, such as the XML configuration file, java property files or custom properties. All frameworks also differ in the way the controller module is implemented. For instance, EJBs may instantiate classes needed in each request, or Java reflection can be used to dynamically invoke an appropriate action class. Also, frameworks may differ conceptually.

Java frameworks are similar in the way they structure data flow. After a request, an action takes place on the application server, and data-populated objects are always sent to the JSP layer with the response. Data is then extracted from those objects, which could be simple classes with setter and getter methods, Java beans, value objects or collection objects. Modern Java frameworks also simplify a developer's tasks by providing automatic session tracking with easy APIs, database connection pools and even database call wrappers. Some frameworks either provide hooks into other J2EE technologies, such as JMS or Java Messaging XML (JMX), or have these technologies integrated. Server data persistence and logging also could be part of a framework.

The most popular Web frameworks include:

- JavaServer Faces
- Apache Wicket
- JBoss Seam
- Spring MVC and WebFlow
- Adobe Flex
- Hibernate
- PHP
- Perl
- Ruby
- ASP.NET
- Struts 2

Two popular Java frameworks used in the NetBeans IDE are JavaServer Faces and Hibernate.

Now that we've had a historical review and detailed discussion of each part of Java Web applications, let's concentrate on building and developing real Java Web database application project starting from the next section.

8.4 BUILD JAVA WEB PROJECT TO QUERY ORACLE DATABASE

It's time for us to do some practical work to build our Web application projects to show users how to apply the knowledge we discussed previously in real applications. First let's build some useful Web pages to begin our development.

8.4.1 Create Five Web Pages Using Microsoft Office Publisher 2007

In this section, we will create five Web pages, **LogIn**, **Selection**, **Faculty**, **Course** and **Student**, as the GUIs to access and manipulate our sample database via Web server.

When a Web application starts, the default starting page is **index.jsp**. However, in this application, we want to use the **LogIn.jsp** page as our starting page. Because of the relative complexity of our five pages, we need to use Microsoft Office Publisher 2007 as a tool to help us to do this job.

Let's first handle the LogIn page.

8.4.1.1 Create the LogIn Page

The purpose of this page is to allow users to login to our sample Oracle database to perform data actions on the five Tables in our sample database. That is, this page is related to the **LogIn** Table to enable users to login and enter this database.

Launch Microsoft Office Publisher 2007 and click on the **Web Sites** icon to open the **Web Sites** wizard. Scroll down to the bottom of this wizard and double-click on the **Web 984 × 4608px** item under the **Blank Sizes** category as the template of this page. Perform the following operations to build this page:

1) Go to **Insert > Text Box** to add a textbox to the top of this page. Enter **Welcome to CSE DEPT LogIn Page** into this textbox as a label for this page.
2) Highlight the text of the label and select **Arial Black** as the font type and **12** as the font size.
3) Perform similar steps to step 1 to create another two textboxes and enter **User Name** and **Pass Word** as another two labels. Locate these two labels just under the top label, as we did in step 1.
4) Go to **Insert > Form Control > TextBox** to add two textboxes, and align each of them with each of the two labels, **User Name** and **Pass Word**, respectively.
5) Right-click on the first textbox we added in step 4 and select the **Format Form Properties** item. Enter **UserNameField** into the text field under **Return data with this label** as the name of this textbox. Click the OK button to complete this naming process.
6) Perform a similar operation for the second textbox we added in step 4 and name it **PassWordField**.
7) Go to **Insert > Form Control > Submit** to add a command button into this page. Uncheck the **Button text is same as button type** checkbox and enter **LogIn** in the **Button text** field. Locate this button under two textboxes we added in steps 4 through 6. Click on the OK button to close this dialog box.
8) Perform a similar operation to add another button and use **Cancel** as the button text for this button.
9) Go to **File > Save As** to save this page as an HTML file. In the opened **Save As** dialog, select **Web Page, Filtered (*.htm, *.html)** from the **Save as type** combo box and enter **LogIn.html** in the **File name** field. Click on the **Save** button to save this HTML file to a location in your root drive, such as **C:\Temp**. Click **Yes** in the message box and **OK** in the **Form Properties** dialog to complete the save.

Now go to **File > Web Page Preview** and select a browser, such as Internet Explorer or Microsoft Edge, to take a look at the LogIn page. Your finished LogIn page should match the one shown in Figure 8.41. To convert the HTML page to a JSP page, open Notepad and perform the following operations:

1) In Notepad, go to **File > Open** to open the Open dialog box. Make sure to select **All Files** from the **Files of type** combo box at the bottom of this dialog.

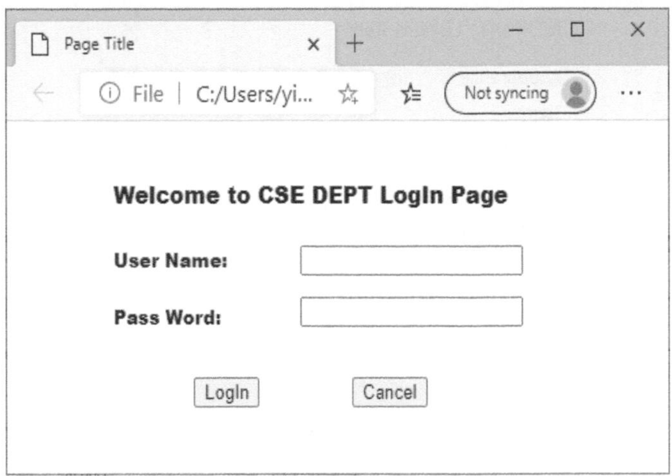

FIGURE 8.41 The finished LogIn page.

2) Browse to the folder where you saved the **LogIn.html** file, such as **C:\Temp**; select it; and click on the **Open** button to open it.
3) Go to **File > Save As** to open the **Save As** dialog box. Then enter "**LogIn.jsp**" into the **File name** field as the name of this page. The point to be noted is that you must use double quotation marks around the file name to enable Notepad to save it as a JSP file. Click on the **Save** button to save the JSP file to your desired folder, such as **C:\Temp**.
4) Close Notepad, and we have completed creating our **LogIn.jsp** file.

Next let's create our Selection JSP file.

8.4.1.2 Create the Selection Page

The purpose of this page is to allow users to choose other Web pages to perform related data actions with different data Tables in our sample database. Therefore, this page can be considered a main or control page to enable users to browse to other pages to perform data actions against the related data Table in our sample database.

Launch Microsoft Office Publisher 2007 and click on the **Web Sites** icon to open the **Web Sites** wizard. Scroll down to the bottom of this wizard and double-click on the **Web 984 × 4608px** item under the **Blank Sizes** category as the template of this page. Click on the **Change Page Size** button under the **Web Site Options** tab if you cannot find this item. Perform the following operations to build this page:

1) Go to **Insert > Text Box** to add a textbox to the top of this page. Enter **Make Your Selection** into this textbox as a label for this page.
2) Highlight the text of the label and select **Arial Black** as the font type and **12** as the font size.
3) Go to **Insert > Form Control > List Box** to add a listbox control. Locate this listbox just under the top label, as we did in step 1.
4) Right-click on the new added listbox and select **Format Form Properties** to open the **List Box Properties** dialog. Enter **ListSelection** in the **Return data with this label** field as the name of this listbox.
5) In the **Appearance** list, click on the **Remove** button three times to delete all default items from the list.

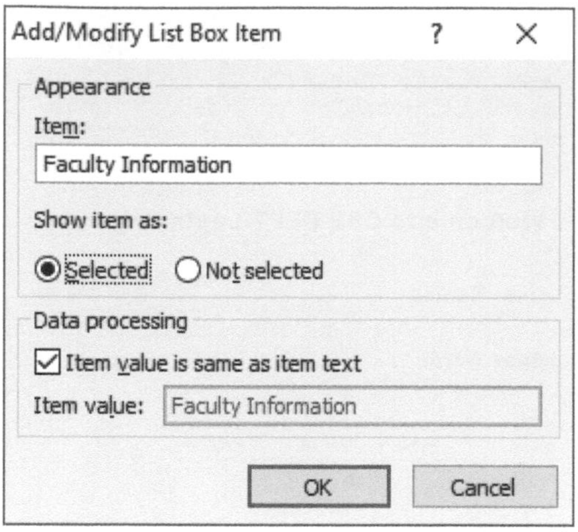

FIGURE 8.42 The finished Add/Modify List Box Item dialog box.

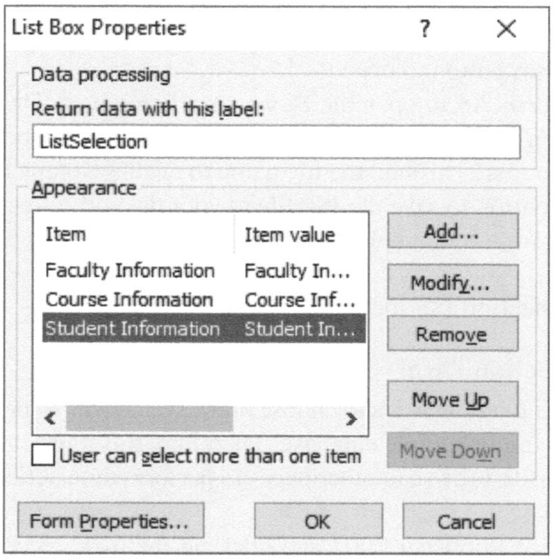

FIGURE 8.43 The finished List Box Properties dialog box.

6) Click on the **Add** button to add the first item to this list. In the opened dialog, enter **Faculty Information** in the **Item** field and check the **Selected** radio button. Make sure that the **Item value is same as item text** checkbox is checked. Your finished **Add/Modify List Box Item** dialog should match the one shown in Figure 8.42. Click on the **OK** button to close this dialog box.
7) Click on the **Add** button to add our second item into this listbox. In the opened **Add/Modify List Box Item** dialog, enter **Course Information** into the **Item** field, and make sure that both the **Not selected** radio button and **Item value is same as item text** checkbox are checked. Click on the **OK** button to close this dialog box.
8) Perform the steps we did in step 7 to add the third item, **Student Information**, to this listbox.
9) Your finished **List Box Properties** dialog should match the one shown in Figure 8.43. Click on the **OK** button to complete the listbox setup process.

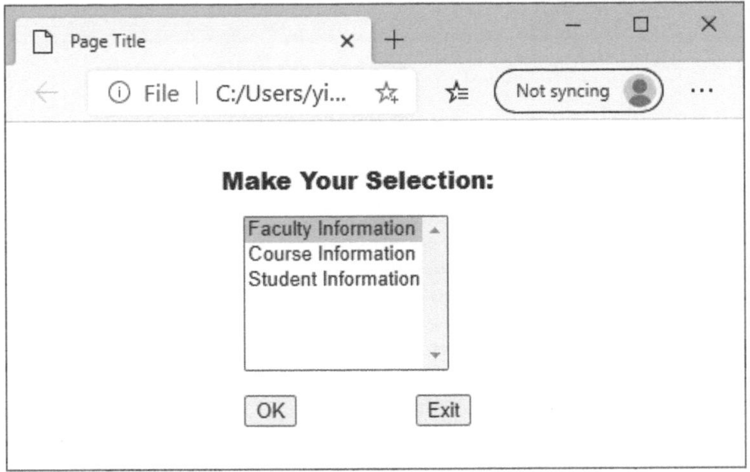

FIGURE 8.44 The preview of the Selection page.

10) Go to **Insert > Form Control > Submit** to add a command button to this page. Uncheck the **Button text is same as button type** checkbox and enter **OK** in the **Button text** field. Locate this button under the listbox we added previously. Click on the **OK** button to close the dialog box.
11) Perform a similar operation to add another button, and use **Exit** as the button text for this button.
12) Go to **File > Save As** to save this page as an HTML file. In the opened **Save As** dialog, select **Web Page, Filtered (*.htm, *.html)** from the **Save as type** combo box and enter **Selection.html** in the **File name** field. Click on the **Save** button to save the HTML file to your root drive, such as **C:\Temp**. Click **Yes** in the message box and **OK** in the **Form Properties** dialog to complete this save.
13) Now go to **File > Web Page Preview** to take a look at the Selection page. Your finished Selection page should match the one shown in Figure 8.44.

To convert the HTML page to a JSP page, open Notepad and perform the following operations:

1) In Notepad, go to **File > Open** to open the **Open** dialog box. Make sure to select **All Files** from the **Files of type** combo box at the bottom of this dialog.
2) Browse to the folder where you saved the **Selection.html** file, such as **C:\Temp**; select it; and click on the **Open** button to open it.
3) Go to **File > Save As** to open the **Save As** dialog box. Enter "**Selection.jsp**" in the **File name** field as the name of this page. The point to be noted is that you must use double quotation marks around the file name to enable Notepad to save it as a JSP file. Click on the **Save** button to save the JSP file to your desired folder, such as **C:\Temp**.
4) Close Notepad, and we have completed creating our **Selection.jsp** file.

Next, let's create our Faculty JSP file.

8.4.1.3 Create the Faculty Page

The purpose of this page is to allow users to access the **Faculty** Table in our sample database to perform data actions via this page, such as data query, new faculty record insertion, faculty member updating and deleting. Because the HTML and JSP did not provide any combo box control, in this

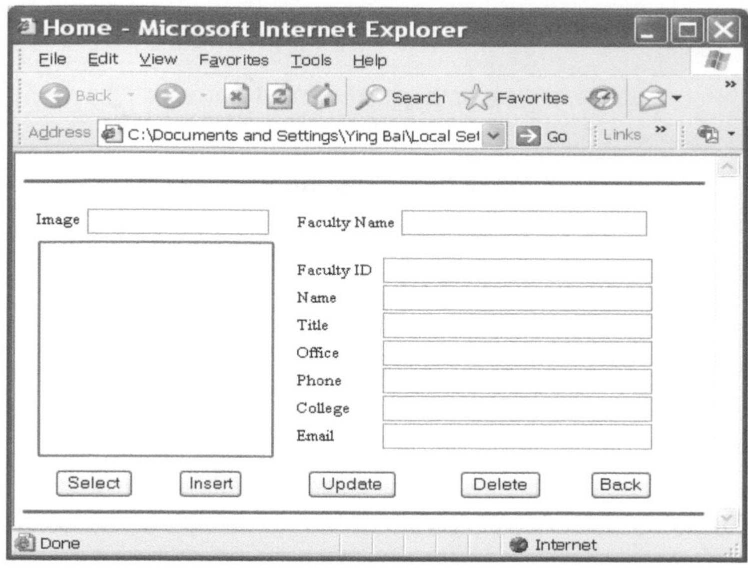

FIGURE 8.45 The preview of the Faculty page.

application, we have to use text box control to replace the combo box control and apply it in this page.

A preview of the Faculty page is shown in Figure 8.45.

Now let's start to build this page using Microsoft Office Publisher 2007.

Launch Microsoft Office Publisher 2007 and click on the `Web Sites` icon to open the `Web Sites` wizard. Scroll down to the bottom of this wizard and double-click on the `Web 984 × 4608px` item under the `Blank Sizes` category as the template of this page. Perform the following operations to build this page:

1) Go to `Insert > Text Box` to insert a textbox on this page, and enter `Image` into the textbox as an image label.
2) Go to `Insert > Form Control > Textbox` to insert a textbox into this page and locate this textbox just to the right of the `Image` label we added in step 1.
3) Right-click on the inserted textbox and select the `Format Form Properties` item to open the `Text Box Properties` dialog, as shown in Figure 8.46a. Then enter `FacultyImageField` in the `Return data with this label` field, as shown in Figure 8.46a. Click on the `OK` button to close this dialog.
4) Go to `Insert > Picture > Empty Picture Frame` to insert a blank picture on this page. Locate this picture under the `FacultyImageField` textbox we added in step 2.
5) Go to `Insert > Text Box` to insert a new textbox and move it to the right of the picture. Type `Faculty Name` in this inserted textbox as the `Faculty Name` label.
6) Go to `Insert > Form Control > Textbox` to insert a textbox on this page, and locate this textbox to the right of the `Faculty Name` label.
7) Right-click on the inserted textbox and select the `Format Form Properties` item to open the `Text Box Properties` dialog. Enter `FacultyNameField` in the `Return data with this label` field, as shown in Figure 8.46b. Click on the `OK` button to close this dialog.
8) Go to `Insert > Text Box` again to insert another textbox, and move it to the right of the picture under the `Faculty Name` textbox. Type `Faculty ID` into this textbox and use it as the `Faculty ID` label.

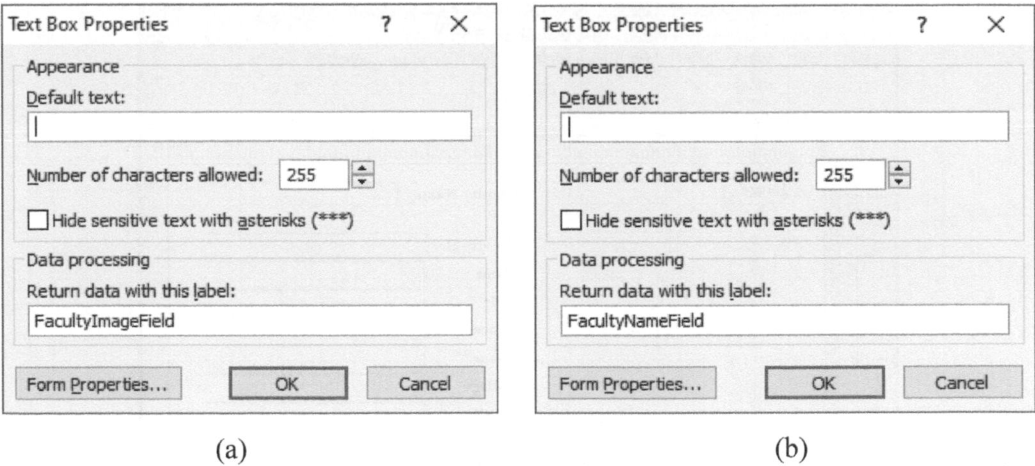

FIGURE 8.46 The FacultyImageField and FacultyNameField textboxes.

9) Go to **`Insert > Form Control > Textbox`** to insert a textbox into this page, and move this textbox to the right of the **`Faculty ID`** label.
10) Change this textbox's name to **`FacultyIDField`**, as we did in step 7.
11) In a similar way, you can finish adding another six textboxes and the associated labels, as shown in Figure 8.45. Use step 7 to change these six textboxes' names to:

    a. NameField
    b. TitleField
    c. OfficeField
    d. PhoneField
    e. CollegeField
    f. EmailField

12) You can use the **`Format > Paragraph > Line spacing > Between lines`** menu property to modify the vertical distance between each label. In this application, set the distance to 0.6sp.
13) Go to **`Insert > Form Control > Submit`** to insert five buttons at the bottom of this page. In the opened **`Command Button Properties`** dialog, uncheck the **`Button text is same as button type`** checkbox, and enter text in the **`Button text`** field for these five buttons one by one. Click on the **`OK`** button to complete the button creation process.

    a. Select
    b. Insert
    c. Update
    d. Delete
    e. Back

14) Your finished **`Faculty`** page in Microsoft Publisher 2007 should match the one shown in Figure 8.47.
15) Go to **`File > Save As`**to save this page as an HTML file. In the opened Save As dialog, select **`Web Page, Filtered (*.htm, *.html)`** from the **`Save as type`** combo box and enter **`Faculty.html`** in the **`File name`** field. Click on the **`Save`** button to save this HTML file to a location on your root drive, such as **`C:\Temp`**. Click **`Yes`** in the message box and **`OK`** in the **`Form Properties`** dialog to complete this save.

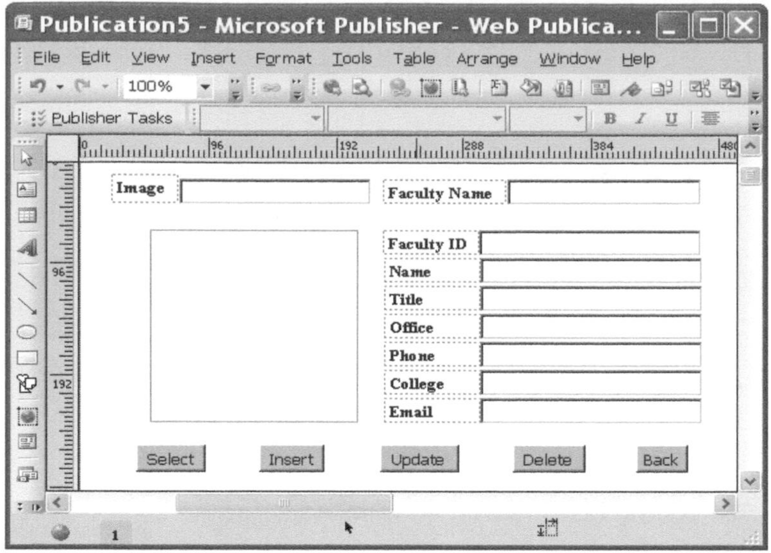

FIGURE 8.47 The finished Faculty page.

To convert the HTML page to a JSP page, open Notepad and perform the following operations:

1) In Notepad, go to **File > Open** to open the Open dialog box. Make sure to select **All Files** from the **Files of type** combo box at the bottom of this dialog.
2) Browse to the folder where you saved the **Faculty.html** file, such as **C:\Temp**; select it; and click on the **Open** button to open it.
3) Go to **File > Save As** to open the **Save As** dialog box. Enter "**Faculty.jsp**" in the **File name** field as the name of this page. The point to be noted is that you must use double quotation marks around file name to enable Notepad to save it as a JSP file. Click on the **Save** button to save the JSP file to your desired folder, such as **C:\Temp**.
4) Close Notepad, and we have completed creating our **Faculty.jsp** file.

Next, let's create our Course JSP file.

8.4.1.4 Create the Course Page

The purpose of using this page is to allow users to access and manipulate data in the Course Table in our sample database via the Web server, such as course query, new course insertion, course updating and deleting, based on the selected faculty member from the Faculty Name textbox.

The finished **Course** page is shown in Figure 8.48.

Now let's start to build this page using Microsoft Office Publisher 2007.

Launch Microsoft Office Publisher 2007 and click on the **Web Sites** icon to open the **Web Sites** wizard. Scroll down to the bottom of this wizard and double-click on the **Web 984 × 4608px** item under the **Blank Sizes** category as the template of this page. Perform the following operations to build this page:

1) Go to **Insert > Picture > Clip Art** to open the **Clip Art** dialog box. Make sure to select **geometry** in the **Search for** field and click on the **Go** button to display all clip art related to geometry. Click on the first one and add it to the upper-left corner of this page.

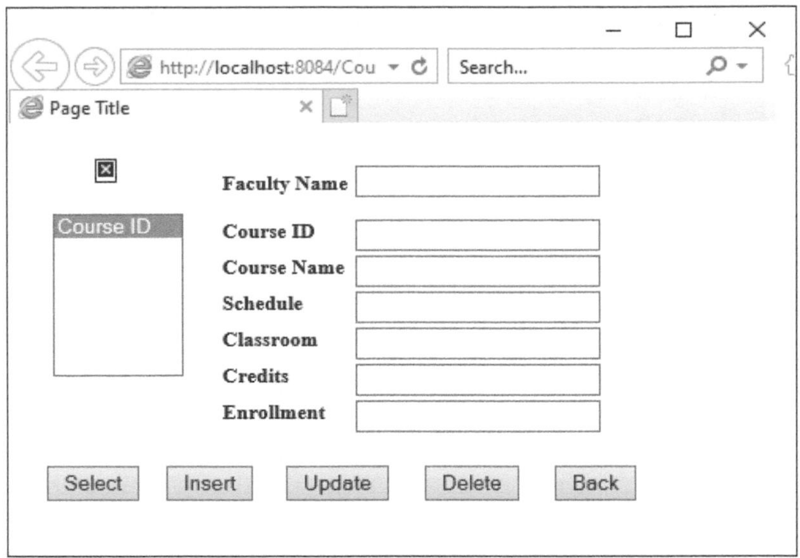

FIGURE 8.48 The preview of the Course page.

2) Go to **Insert > Text Box** to insert a textbox into this page and enter **Faculty Name** in this textbox as the **Faculty Name** label.
3) Go to **Insert > Form Control > Textbox** to insert a textbox into this page, and locate this textbox just to the right of the **Faculty Name** label we added in step 1.
4) Right-click on the inserted textbox and select the **Format Form Properties** item to open the **Text Box Properties** dialog. Then enter **FacultyNameField** in the **Return data with this label** field. Click on the **OK** button to close this dialog.
5) Go to **Insert > Form Control > List Box** to add a listbox control. Locate this listbox just under the top label, as we did in step 1.
6) Right-click on the new added listbox and select **Format Form Properties** to open the **List Box Properties** dialog. Enter **CourseList** in the **Return data with this label** field as the name of this listbox.
7) In the **Appearance** list, click on the **Remove** button three times to delete all default items from this list.
8) Right-click on the new added listbox **CourseList** and select **Format Form Properties** to open the **List Box Properties** dialog. Click on the **Add** button to open the **Add/Modify List Box Item** dialog box. Enter **Course ID** in the **Item** field and check the **Selected** radio button, and click on the **OK** button.
9) Go to **Insert > Text Box** to insert a new textbox and move it to the right of the listbox. Type **Course ID** in this textbox as the **Course ID** label.
10) Go to **Insert > Form Control > Textbox** to insert a textbox into this page, and locate this textbox to the right of the **Course ID** label.
11) Right-click on the inserted textbox and select the **Format Form Properties** item to open the **Text Box Properties** dialog. Enter **CourseIDField** into the **Return data with this label** field. Click on the **OK** button to close this dialog.
12) In a similar way, you can finish adding another five textboxes and the associated labels, as shown in Figure 8.48. Use step 10 to change these five textboxes' names to:

a. CourseNameField
b. ScheduleField

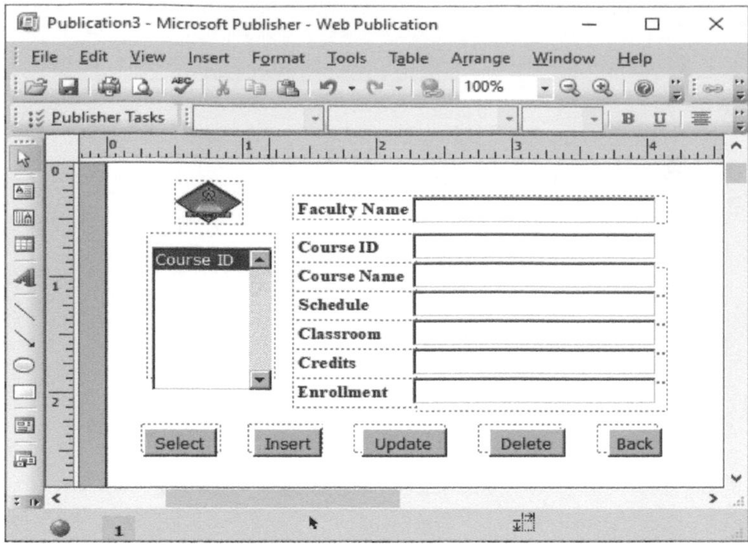

FIGURE 8.49 The finished Course page.

c. ClassroomField
d. CreditField
e. EnrollmentField

13) You can use **`Format > Paragraph > Line spacing > Between lines`** to modify the vertical distance between each label. In this application, set this distance to 0.6sp.
14) Go to **`Insert > Form Control > Submit`** to insert five buttons at the bottom of this page. In the opened **`Command Button Properties`** dialog, uncheck the **`Button text is same as button type`** checkbox, and enter text in the **`Button text`** field for these buttons one by one. Click on the **`OK`** button to complete the button creation process.

a. Select
b. Insert
c. Update
d. Delete
e. Back

15) Your finished Faculty page in Microsoft Publisher 2007 is shown in Figure 8.49.

To convert the HTML page to a JSP page, open Notepad and perform the following operations:

1) In Notepad, go to **`File > Open`** to open the Open dialog box. Make sure to select **`All Files`** from the **`Files of type`** combo box at the bottom of this dialog.
2) Browse to the folder where you saved the **`Course.html`** file, such as **`C:\Temp`**; select it; and click on the **`Open`** button to open it.
3) Go to **`File > Save As`** to open the Save As dialog box. Enter "**`Course.jsp`**" in the **`File name`** field as the name of this page. The point to be noted is that you must use double quotation marks around the file name to enable Notepad to save it as a JSP file. Click on the **`Save`** button to save the JSP file to your desired folder, such as **`C:\Temp`**.
4) Close Notepad, and we have completed creating our **`Course.jsp`** file.

Next, let's create our last page, Student JSP file.

8.4.1.5 Create the Student Page

Because of the similarity between the **Student** page and the other pages we have discussed, here we only provide the necessary information for the names of those controls to be added to this page. A preview of the Student page is shown in Figure 8.50.

Table 8.2 lists the name of each control in the **Student** page.

Refer to discussions in the previous sections to build the **Student** page and convert it to the **Student.jsp** page.

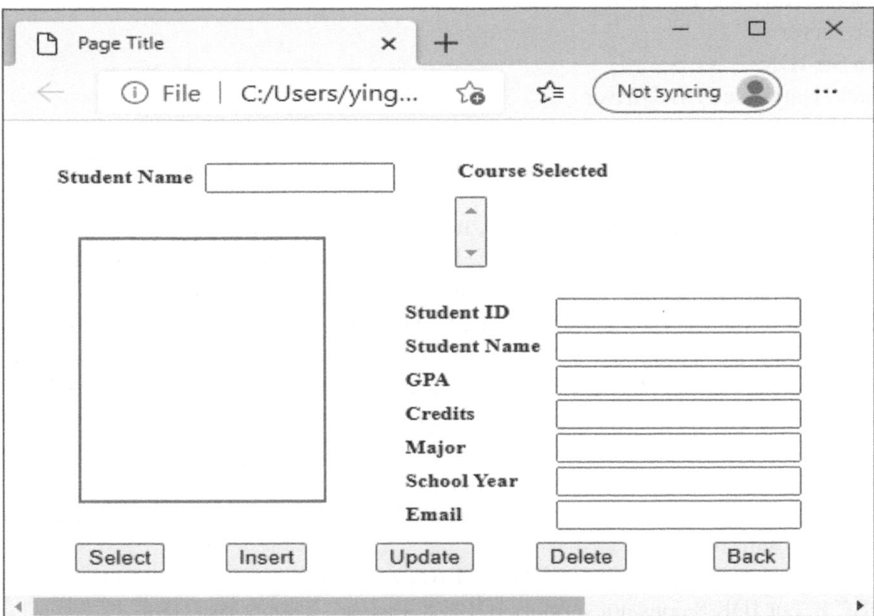

FIGURE 8.50 The preview of the Student page.

TABLE 8.2
All Controls in the Student Page

Control	Name
Student Name Textbox	StudentNameField
Course Selected Listbox	CourseList
The Item in the Course Selected Listbox	Course ID
Student ID Textbox	StudentIDField
Student Name Textbox	NameField
GPA Textbox	GPAField
Credits Textbox	CreditsField
Major Textbox	MajorField
School Year Textbox	SchoolYearField
Email Textbox	EmailField
Select Button	Select
Insert Button	Insert
Update Button	Update
Delete Button	Delete
Back Button	Back

At this point, we have finished the design and building process for all five Web pages. Next we will begin to code these Web pages and the associated help class or Session object to perform data queries against our database.

8.4.2 Setup Environments for NetBeans IDE to Build Java Web Applications

To build Java Web application projects, some basic components are required, including:

1) Apache NetBeans IDE 12.4
2) Web server
3) Java SE JDK
4) Oracle Database JDBC driver

Because of some compatibility issues, the following must be given special attention:

1) Starting with Apache NetBeans IDE 9, no support is provided or continued for building Web-related projects, including Java EE. In order to build Web applications, an additional Web server and components must be installed and conFigured by users.
2) In Apache NetBeans IDE 12.4, which is the latest version of the IDE, only the GlassFish server is bundled, but the latest version of the server is GlassFish 5, which only supports JDK 8, not the current JDK 14, which was installed and added into the NetBeans 12.0 and used to build all projects in the previous chapters.
3) A possible solution is to use another popular server, Tomcat. But the issue is that Apache NetBeans 12.4 only bundled the GlassFish server with it, and users must download, install and conFigure the Tomcat server under the NetBeans 12.4 environment if they want to use this server with NetBeans 12.4.
4) Another problem is the JDK and JDBC driver compatibility issue. JDK 14 only supports JDBC 8, but JDK 8 does not support JDBC 8; instead, it supports JDBC 4.

Based on all of these facts, we have to perform the following configuration to our NetBeans IDE with related components to meet ourneeds to build Web applications:

1) To continue to use Apache NetBeans IDE 12.4, we need to download and install the Tomcat Web server to replace the GlassFish server in this IDE.
2) To match to the requirements of Apache NetBeans IDE 12.4, we need to download and install JDK 8 to replace JDK 14 and use that JDK in our Web application projects.
3) To match JDK 8, an appropriate JDBC driver for Oracle database 18c XE, **`ojdbc8.jar`**, should be used as an interface between our Java program and the Oracle database.

Thus, starting from this chapter, we will change our development environment:

- Use Apache NetBeans IDE 12.4 to replace Apache NetBeans IDE 12.0.
- Use JDK 8 to replace JDK 14.
- Use Tomcat Web server to replace GlassFish Web server.

Now let's begin our setup process to download, install and conFigure these components one by one.

8.4.2.1 Download and Install Required Components

Refer to Appendix L to download and install Apache NetBeans IDE 12.4. Refer to Appendix H and Section 6.3.3 in Chapter 6 for the JDBC driver for Oracle 18c XE, **`ojdbc8.jar`**. This driver

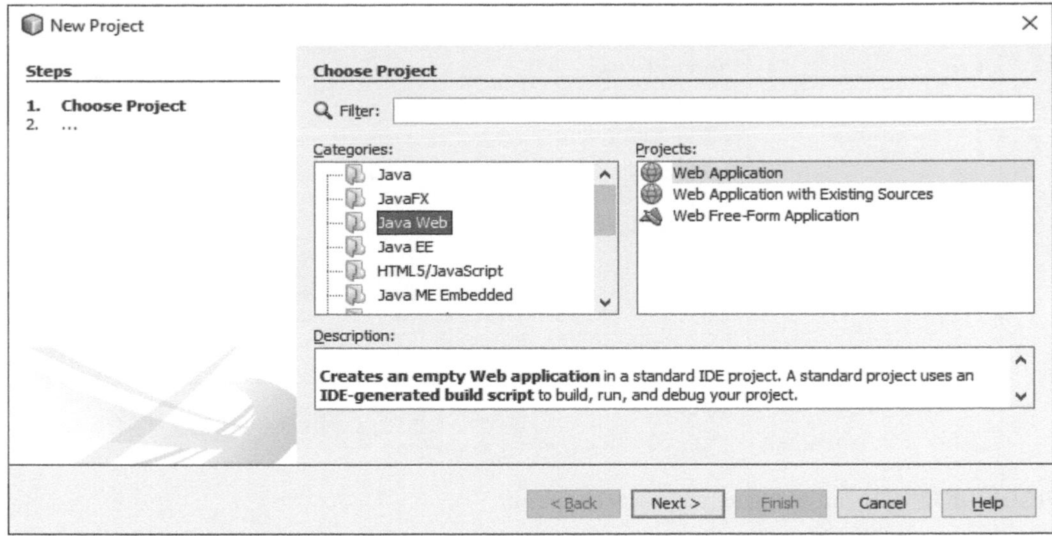

FIGURE 8.51 The opened New Project wizard.

was downloaded and installed on our computer based on Appendix H and was added in one project in that chapter. Refer to Appendix J to complete the download and installation process for JDK 8. Refer to Appendix I to download and install the Tomcat 8.0.27 Web server on your computer.

Now that we have completed the download and installation process for all our required components, we are ready to build our Web application projects. However, before we can continue, we need first to conFigure our Apache NetBeans IDE 12.4 to make it ready for us to start our project development process.

8.4.2.2 ConFigure Apache NetBeans IDE 12 and Create Our First Web Application Project

In order to conFigure the NetBeans IDE to meet the requirements to build Java Web applications, we need to first create a new Web project. Perform the following steps to create our first Web application project, **`JavaWebOracleSelect`**, in the default folder **`C:\Class DB Projects\Chapter 8`**:

1) Open the Apache NetBeans IDE 12.4 in **`Administrator`** mode by right-clicking on the IDE icon on the desktop and selecting the **`Run as administrator`** item (we *must* run in this mode).
2) In the opened NetBeans IDE, go to **`File|New Project`** to open the **`New Project`** wizard.
3) In the opened **`New Project wizard`**, select **`Java Web`** from the Categories list and **`Web Application`** from the Projects list, as shown in Figure 8.51. Click on the **`Next`** button.
4) Enter **`JavaWebOracleSelect`** into the **`Project Name`** box, as shown in Figure 8.52, and click on the **`Next`** button.
5) In the next wizard, **`Server and Settings`**, which is shown in Figure 8.53, keep the default Web server, **`Apache Tomcat or TomEE`**, in the Server box with no changes, and click on the **`Add`** button to add a new Tomcat Web server, which is our downloaded and installed Tomcat 8.0.27 from the last section. The reason this server needs to be added is because the default Tomcat server, **`Apache Tomcat or TomEE`**, does not work for our applications.
6) The next wizard, **`Choose Server`**, is opened, as shown in Figure 8.54. Select the server type, **`Apache Tomcat or TomEE`**, from the Server Listbox, and change the server name to **`Apache Tomcat`** in the **`Name`** box. Your finished **`Choose Server`** wizard should match the one shown in Figure 8.54. Click on the **`Next`** button to open the next wizard, **`Installation and Login Details`**, as shown in Figure 8.55.

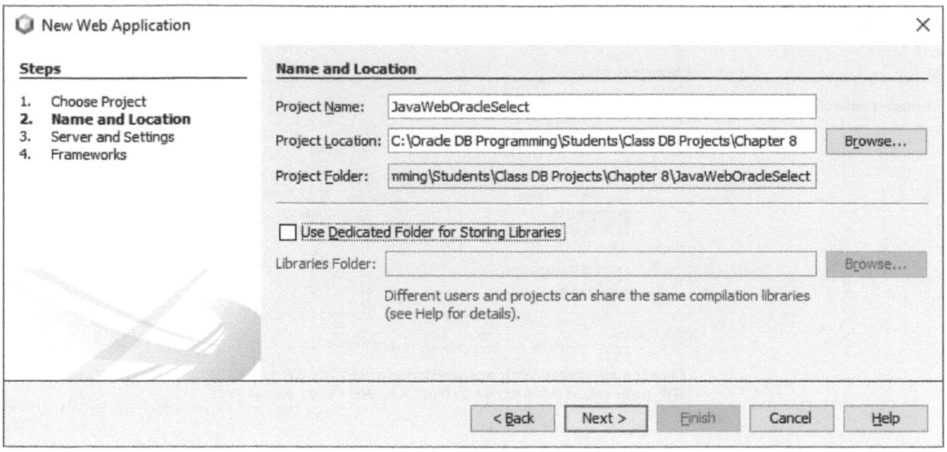

FIGURE 8.52 The finished Name and Location wizard.

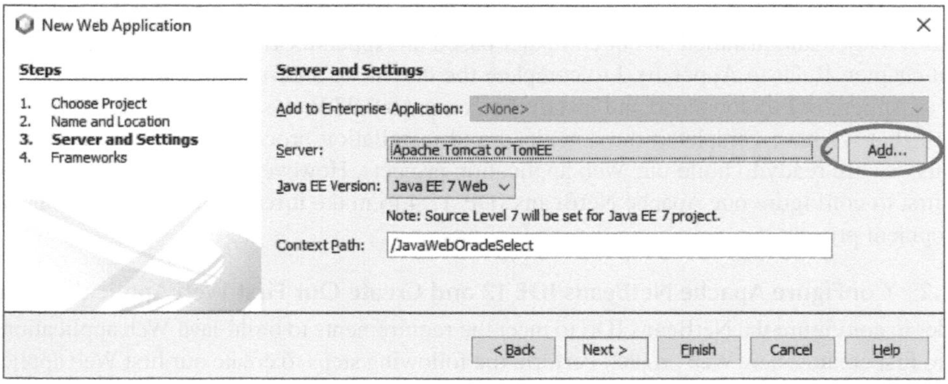

FIGURE 8.53 The opened Server and Settings wizard.

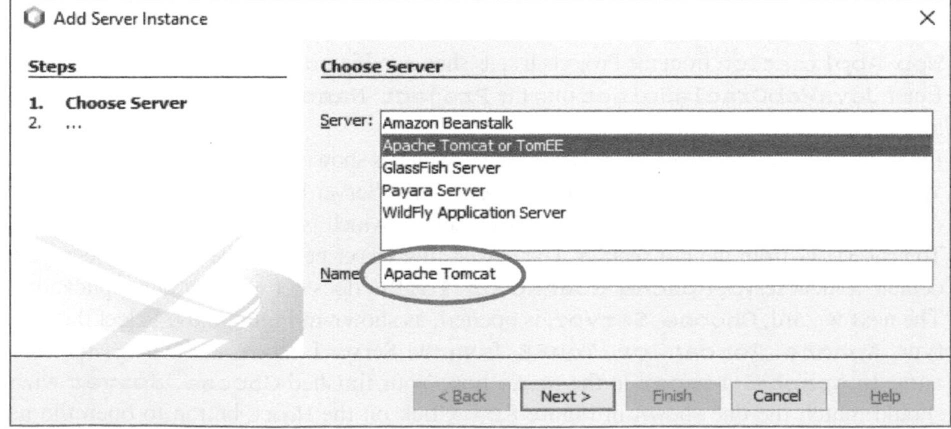

FIGURE 8.54 The finished Add Server Instance wizard.

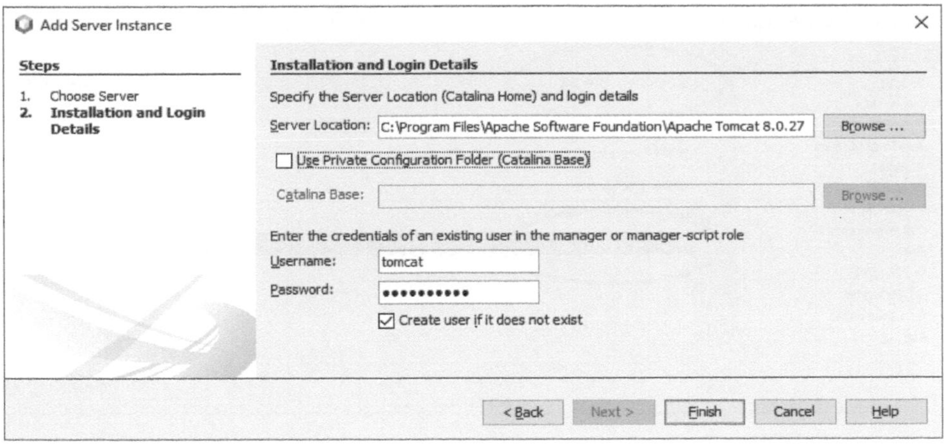

FIGURE 8.55 The finished Installation and Login Details wizard.

7) Click on the **Browse** button on the right of the **Server Location** box to locate our downloaded Tomcat 8.0.27 Web server from Section 8.4.2.1, which is at **C:\Program Files\Apache Software Foundation**, and select our Web server folder **Apache Tomcat 8.0.27** by clicking on it, and click on the **Open** button to select this server.
8) You can enter any desired username and password in the **Username** and **Password** box if you'd like to get more protection for this server. In our case, just enter **tomcat** and **oracle_18c** in those two boxes as the username and password for this server.
9) Keep the **Create user** checkbox checked to generate the new user for this server. Your finished **Installation and Login Details** wizard is shown in Figure 8.55.
10) Click on the **Finish** button to complete the process of adding the Tomcat Web server.

Now return to the **Server and Settings** wizard, as shown in Figure 8.53. Keep the default **Java EE 7 Web** in the **Java EE Version** box with no changes, and click on the **Next** button.

In the next wizard, **Frameworks**, just click on the **Finish** button to complete creation of the Web application, since we do not need to use a framework for this project.

Now we need to perform the following steps to complete configuration of our new project.

8.4.2.2.1 Setup the Correct JDBC Driver and Java Platform

Perform the following steps to complete the setup process:

1) Right-click on our project, **JavaWebOracleSelect**, in the **Projects** window and select the **Properties** item to open the project properties wizard, as shown in Figure 8.56.
2) Click on the **Libraries** node and click on the **Add JAR/Folder** button to open the Windows Explorer to locate our installed JDBC Driver for Oracle 18c XE, **ojdbc8.jar**.
3) In the opened Windows Explorer, browse to the location where we installed the JDBC Driver (refer to Appendix H to download and install this driver). In our case, it is **C:\Temp**. Click on the JAR file **ojdbc8.jar** to select it, and click on the **Open** button to add it into our project.
4) Click on the dropdown arrow on the right of the **Java Platform** box, select **JDK 1.8** and click on the **Change Platform** button in the popup menu to make this change valid.

Your finished **Project Properties** wizard should match the one shown in Figure 8.56. Click on the **OK** button to complete the JDBC driver addition.

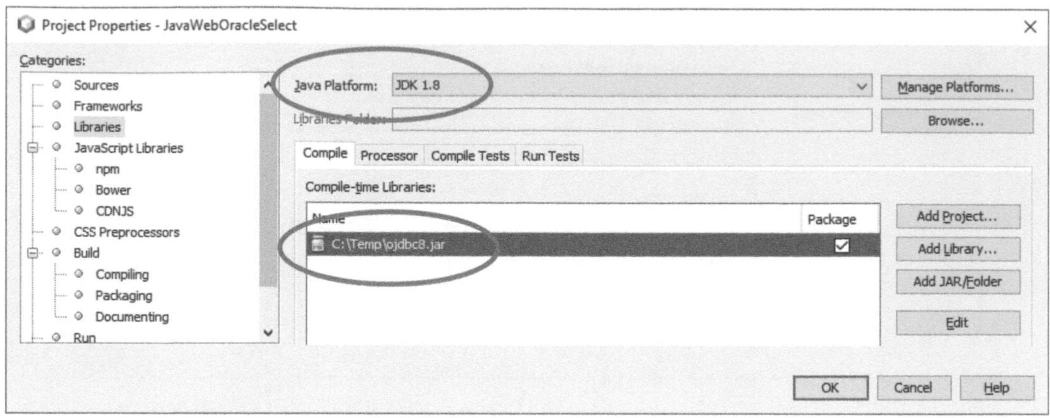

FIGURE 8.56 The finished Project Properties wizard.

Now we can continue to build our first Web application project by adding other required components.

8.4.3 Access and Query the LogIn Table Using JavaServer Pages and Help Class Files

First let's use JavaServer Pages and a help class file to access and query data from the LogIn Table in our sample Oracle database, **CSE _ DEPT**, via the **LogIn.jsp** page we built in Section 8.4.1.1 in this chapter.

We have provided a very detailed discussion about building and developing Java Web applications using JavaServer Pages and Java help class files in Sections 8.1.2 and 8.1.3. Now let's follow those discussions to code the LogIn page and create the Java help class file **LogInQuery.java** to perform data queries from the LogIn Table.

Now we need to add all five Web pages we built in Sections 8.4.1.1–8.4.1.5 into this new project. Perform the following operations to complete the Web page addition process:

1) Launch the Windows Explorer and go to the folder where we stored those five Web pages; in this application, it is **C:\Temp**. Copy all five pages, **LogIn.jsp**, **Selection.jsp**, **Faculty.jsp**, **Course.jsp** and **Student.jsp**, and then paste them to our new Web project folder, **C:\Class DB Projects\Chapter 8\JavaWebOracleSelect**.
2) Launch the NetBeans IDE 12.4 in Administrator mode and open our new Web project, **JavaWebOracleSelect**. Click on the **Files** tab to open the **Files** window, and browse to our Web project folder **JavaWebOracleSelect**. You can find that all five Web pages have been added into this project. Select all five pages using the **Shift** key, right-click on the five selected pages and click on the **Copy** item from the popup menu.
3) Click on the **Projects** tab to open the **Projects** window, browse to our project folder and right-click on the **Web Pages** folder and select the **Paste** item to paste these five Web pages to the **Web Pages** folder.

Next we need to do a little modification to our **LogIn.jsp** file and break this file into two JSP files: **LogIn.jsp** and **LogInQuery.jsp**. The reason for us to make it two JSP files is that we want to process and display data in two separate files to make these operations clear and easy.

8.4.3.1 Modify the LogIn.jsp Page and Create LogInQuery.jsp File

Now let's first modify the **LogIn.jsp** page by double-clicking on **LogIn.jsp** to open it and perform the following modifications to this page. The modified parts are in bold and are shown in Figure 8.57.

```
  <html xmlns:v="urn:schemas-microsoft-com:vml"
  .........
  <body style='margin:0'>
  <div style='position:absolute;width:10.-2040in;height:1.-1423in'>
  <![if !pub]>
A <form method=post action=".\LogInQuery.jsp">
  .........
  <input name=UserNameField maxlength=255 size=21 value="" type=text
   v:shapes="_x0000_s1028">
  .........
  <input name=PassWordField maxlength=255 size=21 value="" type=text
   v:shapes="_x0000_s1029">
  .........
B <input type=submit value=LogIn name="LogInButton" v:shapes="_x0000_s1030">
C <input type=button value=Cancel name="cancelButton" onclick="self.close()" v:shapes="_x0000_s1031">
  .........
  </form>
  </body>
  </html>
```

FIGURE 8.57 The modifications to the LogIn.jsp page.

Let's have a closer look at these modifications to see how they work.

A. The first modification is to the form tag, and an **action** attribute has been added into this tag. Generally a form tag is used to create a HTML form to collect user information and send all pieces of collected information to the server when a submit button on the Form is clicked. Therefore a form and all submit buttons on that form have a coordinating relationship. If a button is defined as a **submit** button by its **type** attribute, all Form data will be sent to the server whose URL is defined in the **action** attribute in the form tag when this submit button is clicked by the user. Here we use a JavaServer Page, **.\LogInQuery.jsp**, as the URL for our target page. That is, this target page is used to access our Java help class file to handle all JDBC- and database-related processing and business logic. The **.** symbol is used to indicate where our next JSP file is located relative to the current folder since this page is part of the server functions and will be run on the server side when the whole project runs.

B. The second modification is to add a `name` attribute to the LogIn button in order for it to be identified on the server side later.

C. The third modification is to change the `type` of our Cancel button from `submit` to `button` and add a `name` and `onclick` attribute for this button. The reason for these modifications is that we want to close our `LogIn.jsp` page when the Cancel button is clicked when the project runs, but we do not want to forward this button-click event to the server to allow the server to do the close action. Therefore, we have to change the type of this button to `button` (not `submit`) to avoid triggering the `action` attribute in the Form tag. We also need to add a `self.close()` method to the `onclick` attribute of this button to call the system `close()` method to terminate our application. `self` means the current page.

Go to `File > Save` item to save these modifications.

Now let's create and build our `LogInQuery.jsp` page, which works as a part of server, to receive and handle the Form data, including the login information sent by the `LogIn.jsp` page. Right-click on our project folder, `JavaWebOracleSelect`, in the `Projects` window and select the `New > JSP` item from the popup menu to open the `New JSP File` wizard. If you cannot find

```
A   <%@page import="JavaWebOracleSelectPackage.LogInQuery"%>
    <%@page contentType="text/html" pageEncoding="UTF-8"%>
    <!DOCTYPE html>
    <html>
      <head>
        <meta http-equiv="Content-Type" content="text/html; charset=UTF-8">
        <title>LogIn Query Page</title>
      </head>
      <body>
      <%@page language="java" %>
      <%
B       LogInQuery lquery = new LogInQuery();
C       String u_name = request.getParameter("UserNameField");
        String p_word = request.getParameter("PassWordField");
D       boolean result = lquery.checkLogIn(u_name, p_word);
E       if (result)
           response.sendRedirect("Selection.jsp");
F       else
           response.sendRedirect("LogIn.jsp");
G       lquery.CloseDBConnection();
      %>
      </body>
    </html>
```

FIGURE 8.58 The code for the LogInQuery.jsp page.

the **JSP** item under the **New** menu item, go to **Other** and select **Web** from the **Categories** list and then the **JSP** item from the **File Types** list. Click on the **Next** button to open the wizard.

Enter **LogInQuery** in the **File Name** field in the opened **New JSP File** wizard and keep all other default settings unchanged. Then click on the **Finish** button to create the JSP file. Enter the code shown in Figure 8.58 into the **<body> . . . </body>** tags in this page.

Let's have a closer look at this piece of code to see how it works.

A. A JSP page import tag is used to indicate that this JSP page uses a Java help class file named **LogInQuery.java** that will be built later.
B. A new instance of our Java help class or Java Bean model, **LogInQuery.java**, that we will build in the next section is first generated since we need to use some methods involved in that model to perform related login query operations.
C. The **getParameter()** method is used to pick up the login information entered by the user on the **LogIn.jsp** page. The collected login information, the username and password, is assigned to two local string variables, **u_name** and **p_word**, respectively.
D. The **checkLogIn()** method defined in our Java help class file is called to perform the database query and the login matching processing. The collected login information is used as arguments and passed into this method. The run result of this method is a Boolean value, and it is assigned to the local Boolean variable **result**.
E. An **if** block is used to check the run result of the **checkLogIn()** method. The program will be directed to a successful page (**Selection.jsp**) if a matching login record is found.
F. Otherwise, the LogIn page will be refreshed to indicate that the login process failed.
G. The **CloseDBConnection()** method defined in the Java help class is called to disconnect the connection to our sample database.

Next let's create and build our Java help class file **LogInQuery.java** to perform JDBC- and database-related operations and actions.

8.4.3.2 Create the Java Help Class File LogInQuery.java

The purpose of this help class file is to handle JDBC-related operations and database-related actions. As we discussed in Section 8.1.3, to distinguish between database-related dataprocessing and display of run results, we can separate a Java Web application into two parts: JDBC-related database processing and business logic such as checking and confirming a matching username and password pair located in a Java help class file and the data and run results displayed in a Web or JavaServer page.

We can use the Java persistence API to access the database and query our LogIn Table. However, because the Java persistence API can only be implemented in a limited number of Java EE containers that provide the Resource Injection function, we cannot inject the Java persistence API into our normal Java help class file. Therefore, in this part, we have to use the Java runtime object method to perform database-related actions to check the username and password from the **LogIn** Table in our sample database. We can include these database-related actions in the Java help class file.

Right-click on our project folder, **JavaWebOracleSelect**, in the **Projects** window and select the **New > Java Class** item from the popup menu to open the **New Java Class** wizard. If you cannot find the **Java Class** item under the **New** menu item, go to **Other** and select the **Java** item from the **Categories** list and the **Java Class** item from the **File Types** list. Click on the **Next** button to open this wizard.

In the opened wizard, enter **LogInQuery** into the **Class Name** field and enter or select **JavaWebOracleSelectPackage** in the **Package** box, as shown in Figure 8.59. Click on the **Finish** button to create the help class file.

Before we can develop the code for this help class, we first need to create a dialog box in this project. This dialog box works as a message box to provide possible debug information as the project runs.

8.4.3.3 Create a Dialog Box as the Message Box

To create a new dialog box form window, perform the following operations:

1) Right-click on our project, **JavaWebOracleSelect**, in the **Projects** window and select the **New > Other** item from the popup menu to open the **New File** wizard. Select **Swing GUIForms** from the Categories list and **OK/CancelDialog Sample Form** from the File Types list. Click on the **Next** button to open a new dialog box form.

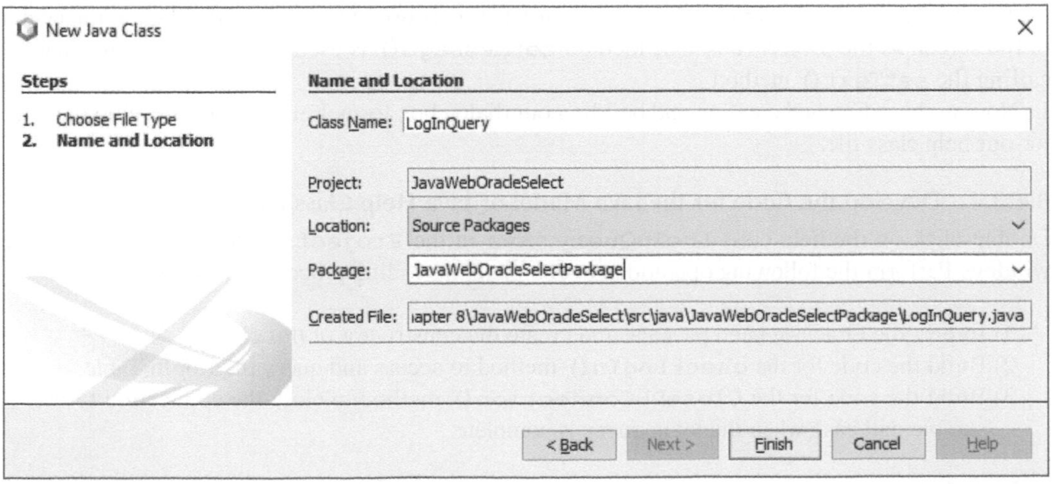

FIGURE 8.59 The completed New Java Class wizard.

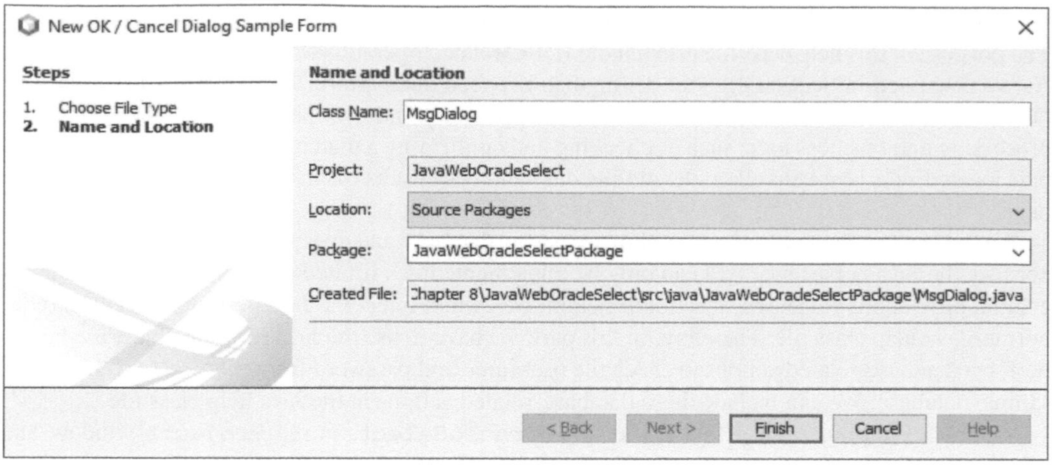

FIGURE 8.60 The finished New OK/Cancel Dialog Form wizard.

2) Enter **MsgDialog** in the Class Name field and select **JavaWebOracleSelectPackage** from the Package field. Your finished **NewDialog Form** wizard should match the one shown in Figure 8.60. Click on the **Finish** button to create the new dialog box.
3) A new Java dialog box class file, **MsgDialog.java**, is created and located under the **JavaWebOracleSelectPackage** folder in the **Projects** window. Click on the **Design** button to open its dialog form window. Add a label to this dialog form window by dragging a **Label** control from the Palette window, that is, from the AWT sub-window, and placing it in the dialog form window.
4) Resize this label to an appropriate size, as shown in Figure 8.61. Right-click on the label and select the **Change Variable Name** item from the popup menu to open the Rename dialog. Enter **MsgLabel** into the New Name field and click on the **OK** button.
5) Go to the **text** property and remove the default text **label1** for this label.

Now click on the **Source** button to open the code window for this dialog box, and we need to add some code to this class to enable it to display some necessary messages as the project runs. In the opened code window, add the code in bold shown in Figure 8.62.

The **setLocationRelativeTo(null)** instruction is used to set this dialog box at the center of the screen as the project runs. The method **setMessage()** is used to setup a user message by calling the **setText()** method.

Now we have finished creating and building our dialog box form. Let's begin to develop the code for our help class file.

8.4.3.4 Develop the Code for the Java Model or Java Help Class File

Double-click on the help class **LogInQuery.java** in the **Projects** window to open its code window. Perform the following operations to complete the coding process for this class:

1) Import the Oracle-related package and create the constructor of this class.
2) Build the code for the **checkLogIn()** method to access and query the LogIn Table.
3) Build the code for the **CloseDBConnection()** method to close the connection to our sample database when the login query is complete.

Let's do these steps one by one in the following sections.

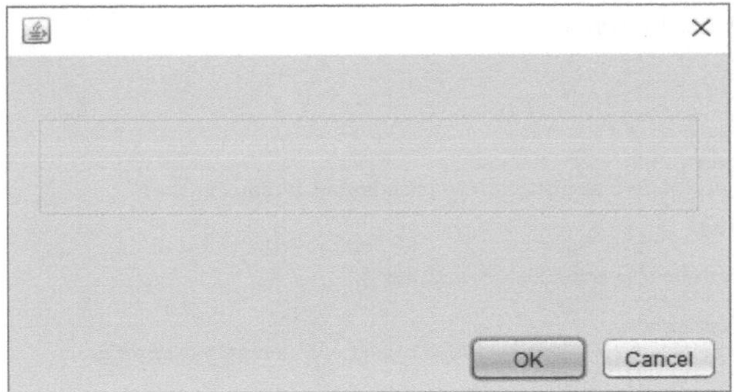

FIGURE 8.61 The preview of the dialog box.

```
public MsgDialog(java.awt.Frame parent, boolean modal) {
      super(parent, modal);
      initComponents();
      this.setLocationRelativeTo(null);
 }
public void setMessage(String  msg){
    MsgLabel.setText(msg);
}
```

FIGURE 8.62 The added code to the MsgDialog.java class.

8.4.3.4.1 Import Oracle-Related Package and Create the Class Constructor

Since we need to query our sample Oracle database, we need to import the Oracle data-related package. The class constructor is used to build a valid connection to our sample database. The detailed code is shown in Figure 8.63.

Let's have a closer look at this piece of code to see how it works.

A. The JDBC Oracle-related package is imported first, since we need to use some JDBC classes defined in that package.
B. Some attributes or properties of the help class are defined first inside this class, including two private String properties, **`user_name`** and **`pass_word`**; a class-level connection variable, **`con`**; and a dialog box that is used to display debug information.
C. Inside the class constructor, a **`try-catch`** block is used to load the JDBC Oracle driver, which is a Type IV JDBC driver. Refer to Section 6.3.3.3 in Chapter 6 to get more detailed information about this driver.
D. The **`catch`** block is used to collect any possible exceptions during the driver loading process.
E. The JDBC Oracle URL is assigned to the local variable **`url`**. Refer to Section 6.3.3.3.1 in Chapter 6 to get more detailed information about this URL.
F. A **`getConnection()`** method embedded in a **`try`** block is executed to establish the database connection.
G. The **`catch`** block is used to collect any possible exceptions that occur during the database connection process.

Now let's build the code for our two user-defined methods, **`checkLogIn()`** and **`CloseDBConnection()`**. First let's start with the **`checkLogIn()`** method to try to query the LogIn Table to find a matching username and password pair.

```
  package JavaWebOracleSelectPackage;
A import java.sql.*;
  public class LogInQuery {
B    String user_name;
     String pass_word;
     static Connection con;
     MsgDialog msgDlg = new MsgDialog(new javax.swing.JFrame(), true);
     public LogInQuery() {
C       try {
              Class.forName("oracle.jdbc.OracleDriver");
          }
D         catch (Exception e) {
             msgDlg.setMessage("Class not found exception!" + e.getMessage());
             msgDlg.setVisible(true);
          }
E         String url = "jdbc:oracle:thin:@localhost:1521:XE";
          try {
F            con = DriverManager.getConnection(url,"CSE_DEPT","oracle_18c");
          }
G         catch (SQLException e) {
             msgDlg.setMessage("Could not connect!" + e.getMessage());
             msgDlg.setVisible(true);
             e.printStackTrace();
          }
     }
  .........
```

FIGURE 8.63 The code of the class constructor.

8.4.3.4.2 Build the Code for the checkLogIn() Method

The function of this method is to query the `LogIn` Table in our sample database to try to find a matching username and password pair based on the username and password entered by the user from the `LogIn.jsp` page. A Boolean value `true` will be returned to the `LogInQuery.jsp` page if a matching username and password pair is found. Otherwise, a `false` is returned. Based on this returned Boolean value, the `LogInQuery.jsp` will determine the next page to be opened. If a matching pair is found, the `Selection.jsp` page will be displayed to allow users to select different information to access and query different Tables in our sample database. Otherwise, an error message will be displayed to indicate that the login process failed since no matching login information could be found in our sample database.

In the opened code window of the help class `LogInQuery.java`, enter the code shown in Figure 8.64 under the class constructor and make it the body of our `checkLogIn()` method.

Let's have a closer look at this piece of code to see how it works.

A. The query string, which is a standard Oracle statement, is created first with the actual column name as the query column. The positional parameter is only used for username as an dynamic input.
B. If either the input username or password is blank, a `false` is returned to indicate an error.
C. Starting from a `try` block, the `prepareStatement()` method is called to create a PreparedStatement object, `pstmt`.
D. The setter method is used to set the positional parameter in the positional order. Here only one parameter, `user _ name`, is used, since it is a primary key in the `LogIn` Table.
E. The `executeQuery()` method is executed to perform this query, and the returned result is assigned to the ResultSet object `rs`.
F. A `while()` loop is used to pick up any possible matching username and password. In fact, only one row is returned; therefore, this loop can only run one time. The `getString()` method is used to pick up the queried username and password. The retuned username and password are assigned to two properties, `user _ name` and `pass _ word`, respectively.

```
  public boolean checkLogIn(String uname, String pword) {
A       String query = "SELECT user_name, pass_word FROM LogIn " + "WHERE user_name = ?";
B       if (uname.isEmpty() || pword.isEmpty()) return false;
C       try{
            PreparedStatement pstmt = con.prepareStatement(query);
D           pstmt.setString(1, uname);
E           ResultSet rs = pstmt.executeQuery();
F           while (rs.next()){
              user_name = rs.getString(1);
              pass_word = rs.getString(2);
            }
        }
G       catch (SQLException e) {
          msgDlg.setMessage("Error in Statement! " + e.getMessage());
          msgDlg.setVisible(true);
        }
H       if (user_name.equals(uname) && pass_word.equals(pword))
            return true ;
I       else
            return false ;
  }
```

FIGURE 8.64 The code for the checkLogIn() method.

G. The **catch** block is used to collect any possible exceptions during the database query process.
H. If a matching username-password pair is found, the Boolean value **true** will be returned to the **LogInQuery.jsp** page.
I. Otherwise, a **false** value is returned to indicate that the login query failed.

Next let's build the code for the **CloseDBConnection()** method.

8.4.3.4.3 Build the Code for the CloseDBConnection() Method

This method is necessary when a data query is finished and no more data actions are needed for a database application. A runtime error may be encountered if one forgets to disconnect the established database connection to a target database and exit the project.

In the opened code window of the help class **LogInQuery.java**, enter the code shown in Figure 8.65 under the **checkLogIn()** method to create our **CloseDBConnection()** method.

Let's have a closer look at this piece of code to see how it works.

A. A **try** block is used to handle the database disconnection function. First we need to check whether a valid connection object exists, which means that the database is still connected. The **isClosed()** method is executed to do this check. A false will be returned if a valid connection object exists, which means that the database is still connected. In that case, the **close()** method is called to disconnect this connection.
B. The **catch** block collects any possible exceptions during the disconnection process.

Now we have finished all code development for the login process.

Prior to doing building and running this project, we need to setup our **LogIn.jsp** page as the starting page when the project runs. Perform the following operations to do this:

1) Right-click our project folder, **JavaWebOracleSelect**, in the **Projects** window and select **Properties** on the bottom to open the Project Properties wizard, as shown in Figure 8.66.
2) Then click on the **Run** node on the left panel and enter **/LogIn.jsp** in the **Relative URL** box, as shown in Figure 8.66. Click on the **OK** button to complete the setup process.

```
  public void CloseDBConnection()
  {
A     try{
        if (con != null)
          con.close();
B     }catch (SQLException e) {
        msgDlg.setMessage("Error in close the DB! " + e.getMessage());
        msgDlg.setVisible(true);
      }
  }
```

FIGURE 8.65 The code for the CloseDBConnection() method.

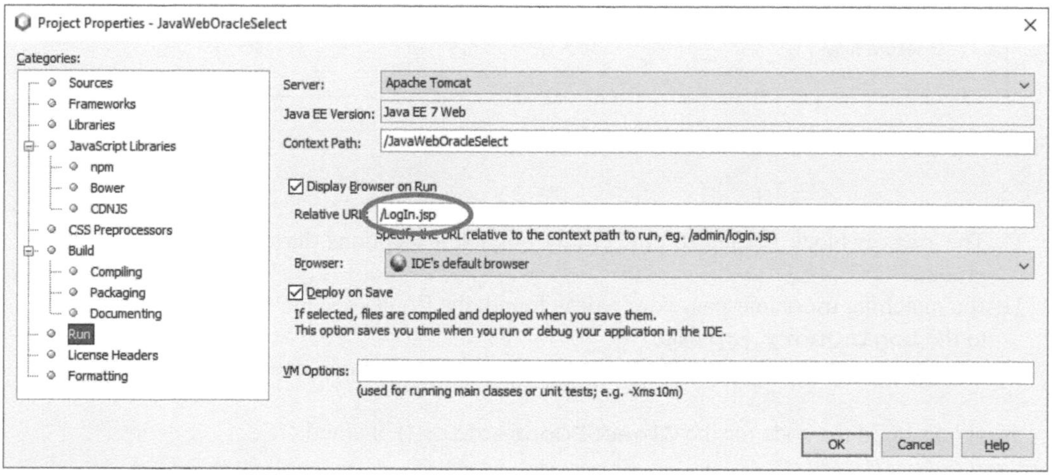

FIGURE 8.66 The completed Project Properties wizard.

The Relative URL means that the current folder is our project folder, **`JavaWebOracleSelect`**, and **`/LogIn.jsp`** is attached under that folder to make a partial project running URL, which is **`JavaWebOracleSelect/LogIn.jsp`**. The completed project running URL is: **`http://localhost:8080/JavaWebOracleSelect/LogIn.jsp`**. The **`localhost`** is the running Web server with port **`8080`**.

Now click on the **`Clean and Build Main Project`** button to build our project. Then click on the **`Run`** button (green arrow on the top taskbar) to run our project.

When **`LogIn.jsp`** is displayed, enter a valid username and password, such as **`jhenry`** and **`test`**, into the associated fields, as shown in Figure 8.67.

Click on the **`LogIn`** button to call the **`checkLogIn()`** method to perform a login query. If this login process is successful, the **`Selection.jsp`** page is displayed to indicate that a matching username and password have been found, as shown in Figure 8.68.

Now just click on the **`Exit`** button to terminate our project, since we have not built any code for any of the query Forms, such as FacultyFrame, CourseFrame or StudentFrame.

When running this project, one possible bug you may encounter is an Oracle database connection or server listener error. In that case, you need to open the **`System Services`** wizard to check that all components are working and running.

Perform the following steps to do this check:

1. Press the **Windows + R** keys.
2. Type **services.msc** in the box and click the **Enter** button.
3. Check that all services named**OracleOraDB18Home1TNSListener**, **Oracle ServiceXE** and **OracleJobSchedulerXE** are in Running status.
4. If not, right-click on that service, and select **Start** to run the listener.

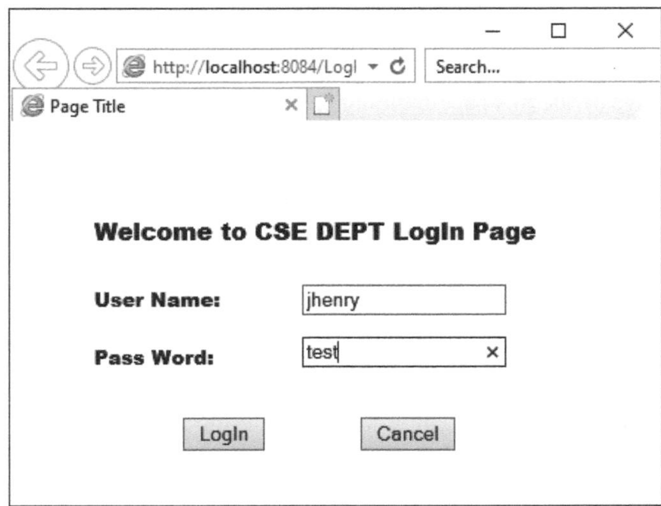

FIGURE 8.67 The displayed LogIn.jsp page.

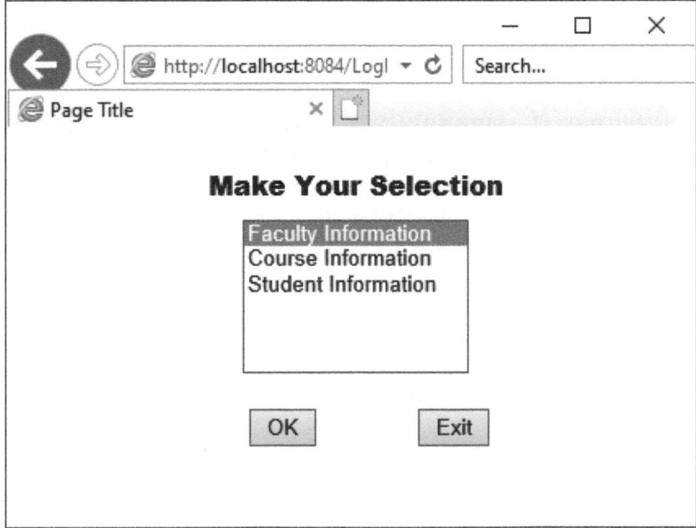

FIGURE 8.68 The successful Selection.jsp page.

Next let's build and code the **Selection.jsp** page. As we mentioned, this page can be considered the control page, and it will direct users to different pages to perform different database query functions based on the users' choices.

8.4.4 Develop the Code for the Selection Page

To handle user input and direct it to different target pages, we still want to use model-view-controller (MVC) mode to build this page. We can use the **Selection.jsp** page as a **view** to display the input and output and create another JSP page, **SelectionProcess.jsp**, as the **Model** and **Controller** to process the users' input and direct them to the target page.

Also, you can combine MVC mode to display and process pages in a single JSP page file. However, you need to add a hidden field to the page and use that hidden field as an identifier to indicate whether the page has been submitted. That will make the **Selection.jsp** page complex in the coding process. We divide this page-building process into two steps: modify the **Selection.jsp** page and create the **SelectionProcess.jsp** page. Let's first perform some necessary modifications to the **Selection.jsp** page.

Launch the NetBeans IDE 12.4 in Administrator mode and open the **Selection.jsp** page by double-clicking on it in the **Projects** window, and perform the modifications shown in Figure 8.69 to this page. All modifications are in bold.

Let's have a closer look at these modifications to see how they work.

A. An **action** attribute is added to the Form tag, and the destination of this action is the **SelectionProcess.jsp** page. The ".\" operator is used to indicate to the Web controller that the next page, **SelectionProcess.jsp**, is located in the current folder.
B. The type of the second button, **Exit**, is changed from **submit** to **button**, since we do not want to submit any form data to the next page when this button is clicked. Instead, we want a system method, **self.close()**, to be executed when this button is clicked to exit our project. Therefore, an **onclick** attribute is used to direct control to this method when this button is clicked.

Now let's create the selection process page, **SelectionProcess.jsp**.

Open our project, **JavaWebOracleSelect**, in the **Projects** window. Perform the following operations to create this page:

1) Right-click on our project, **JavaWebOracleSelect**, in the **Projects** window and select the **New >JSP** item from the popup menu. If you cannot find the **JSP** item in the popup menu, go to the **Other** item to open the **New File** wizard. Select **Web** from the **Categories** list and **JSP** from the **File Types** list to do this.

```
  .........
  <div style='position:absolute;width:10.-2040in;height:2.047in'>
  <![if !pub]>
A <form method=post action=".\SelectionProcess.jsp">
  .........
  <input type=submit value=OK v:shapes="_x0000_s1028">
  .........
B <input type=button value=Exit onclick="self.close()" v:shapes="_x0000_s1029">
  <![if !pub]></span><![endif]><![if !pub]>
  </form>
  .........
```

FIGURE 8.69 The code modifications to the Selection.jsp page.

```
  <html>
    <head>
      <meta http-equiv="Content-Type" content="text/html; charset=UTF-8">
      <title>Selection Process Page</title>
    </head>
    <body>
A    <%@page language="java" %>
     <%
B     String nextPage = null;
C     String userSel = request.getParameter("ListSelection");
D     if (userSel.equals("Faculty Information"))
        nextPage = "Faculty.jsp";
      else if (userSel.equals("Course Information"))
        nextPage = "Course.jsp";
      else
         nextPage = "Student.jsp";
     %>
E    <jsp:forward page = "<%=nextPage%>" />
    </body>
  </html>
```

FIGURE 8.70 The code for the SelectionProcess.jsp page.

2) In the opened **New JSP File** wizard, enter **SelectionProcess** into the **File Name** field and click on the **Finish** button.

Now let's develop the code for this page. Double-click on our new created page, **SelectionProcess.jsp**, in the **Projects** window to open its code window. In the opened code window, perform the modifications shown in Figure 8.70. All modifications are in bold.

Let's have a closer look at this piece of code to see how it works.

A. A JSP directive tag is used to indicate that this page uses the Java language and is a JSP file.
B. A local string variable, **nextPage**, is declared first. This variable is used to hold the URL of the next page, which we will use later to direct control to the associated page.
C. The **getParameter()** method is used to pick up item selected by the user from the selection list in the **Selection.jsp** page. The argument of the **getParameter()** method is the name of the selection list in the **Selection.jsp** page. The selected item is then assigned to another local string variable, **userSel**.
D. An **if** selection structure is used to check the user's selection and assign the associated next page to the local variable **nextPage**.
E. Finally a JSP forward directive is used to direct the program to the next page.

Now we can build and run this page to test its function.

Click on the **Clean and Build Main Project** button to compile and build our project. Click on the **Run** button on the task bar to run the project. Enter appropriate login information, such as **jhenry** and **test**, to the username and password boxes to complete the login process. **Selection.jsp** is displayed, as shown in Figure 8.68.

Select a desired item, such as **Faculty Information**, from the Selection listbox and click on the **OK** button. You can see that the **Faculty.jsp** page is displayed, as shown in Figure 8.71. You can try to select other items from the listbox to open other related pages.

Click on the **Exit** button to terminate our project now.

Our Selection page is successful!

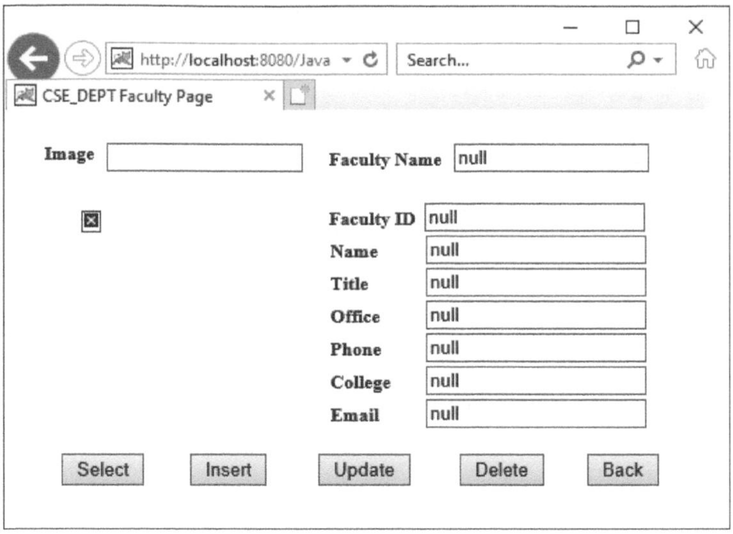

FIGURE 8.71 The run status of the Faculty.jsp page.

8.4.5 Query the Faculty Table Using JavaServer Pages and JSP Implicit Session Object

In this section, we will discuss how to access and query data from the **Faculty** Table in our sample database using the JavaServer Pages and JSP implicit session object.

In Section 8.1.4, we provided a detailed discussion on how to use the JSP implicit session object to query our **Faculty** Table. In this part, we will build a real project to perform a data query using this object. In fact, we will build three layers or components to complete any query to our sample Oracle database.

1) **Faculty.jsp page**—working as a View
2) **FacultyProcess.jsp**—working as a transaction layer or Controller
3) **FacultyQuery.java**—working as a Java Bean or Model to access our Oracle database

These three components are the model-view-controller mode we discussed in previous sections. As we mentioned, **Faculty.jsp** is equivalent to a View page on the client side, and **FacultyProcess.jsp** and **FacultyQuery.java** work as a Controller and a Java Model to coordinate data queries to our sample database via an Oracle database server. Both of the latter components are located on a Web server; in our project, it is a Tomcat server.

A key issue in querying our **Faculty** Table in our sample database is that a faculty image is involved in this query, and it will eventually be displayed in our View, the **Faculty.jsp** page. This makes our code development more complicated and difficult since retrieving an image from a database via a Web server and displaying it on a JSP page in a client is not an easy job. To make this issue clear and easy to understand, we need to emphasize some important ideas and connections behind this query.

8.4.5.1 Query Faculty Records with Image via Web Server and Display Them in JSP Pages

The working procedure for this kind of query can be summarized as follows:

1) The **Faculty.jsp** page, which is located on the client side, works as a View to contain both input and output information. This page allows users to provide any input and passes those inputs to the Controller, **FacultyProcess.jsp** page, to be further processed.

2) The Controller, **FacultyProcess.jsp** page, takes charge of transferring the input to the Java Model or Java Bean, **FacultyQuery.java**, and performs necessary operations to call related functions or methods located in that Java Model to execute actual database queries to get required records. This Controller also takes care of collecting retrieved records from the database and sending them back to the View, **Faculty.jsp** page, to display them in that View.
3) The Java Model or Java Bean class, **FacultyQuery.java**, provides all methods or functions to access our database server as well as to our sample Oracle database, to retrieve all required records from the related data Tables and make them ready to be picked up by the Controller later.

The situation is more complicated if an image is involved in these queries. Basically, the following three major steps should be taken if an image is involved in a data query via a Web server and displayed on a JSP page:

1) Access the database server and the queried database to get the desired image in Blob (Binary Large Object) format.
2) Convert that image to a Binary Array format and furthermore to a String Array in Base64 format.
3) Display that image in a JSP page using the **<img>** tag, with the image source in Base64 string format.

As they say, a picture is worth a thousand words. Let's have a closer look at the structure or functional block diagram of these steps shown in Figure 8.72.

1) The **Select** button, which is an input on the View or **Faculty.jsp** page, is first triggered by a user click.

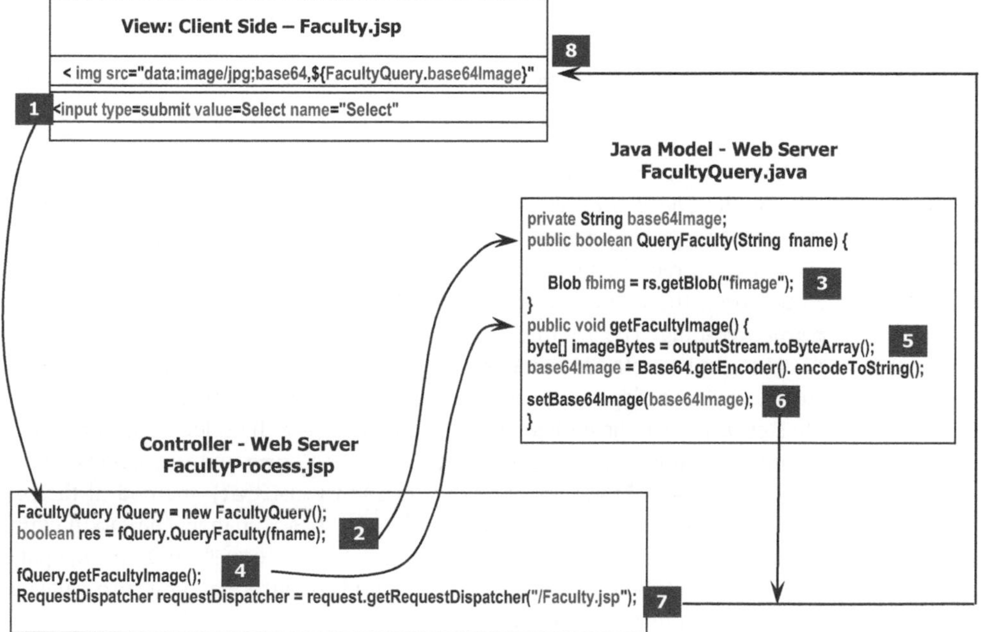

FIGURE 8.72 A functional block diagram of displaying an image on a JSP page.

2) This click is transferred to the Controller or the **FacultyProcess.jsp** page to create a new instance of the FacultyQuery class that is located in the Java Model **FacultyQuery.java**. The Controller then calls a query method, **QueryFaculty()**, in the Java Model to start the data query process with a selected faculty name as the argument.
3) At the end of that data query, a faculty image is queried and retrieved in Blob format.
4) The Controller calls another method, **getFacultyImage()**, that is located in the Java Model, to convert the image from Blob format to the desired format.
5) First, the image is converted to a byte array by using the **outputStream.toByteArray()** method. Then it is further converted to a **base64Image** string format.
6) Eventually the converted **base64Image** is stored in the FacultyQuery class since it is a private variable in that class.
7) A system method, **getRequestDispatcher()**, that belongs to the RequestDispatcher class is executed to setup a connection between the Java Model and the View to enable the latter to recognize the Java Bean with attached **base64Image** string.
8) Finally, steps 6 and 7 are combined to setup the **<img>** tag in the View or **Faculty.jsp** page to enable the page to recognize and display the faculty image on the client side.

Based on this analysis, we divide this code process into the following three parts:

1) Modify the **Faculty.jsp** page and use it as a view.
2) Create a new **FacultyProcess.jsp** page and use it as a controller page.
3) Create a Java Model **FacultyQuery.java** to handle data query and related business logic.

First let's modify our view class, the **Faculty.jsp** page.

8.4.5.2 Modify the Faculty.jsp Page

The **Faculty.jsp** page works as a view to provide a display function for input and output. We need to modify this page to enable it to forward user input to the controller page and, furthermore, to call the Java Model to process our data query. Also, this client page needs to return to the **Selection.jsp** page if the user clicks on the **Back** button on that page.

Open this page by double-clicking on it in the **Projects** window, and perform the modifications shown in Figure 8.73. All modified code is in bold. Let's have a closer look at this piece of modified code to see how it works.

A. An **action** attribute is added to the Form tag to forward all information collected from this page to the model and controller page, **FacultyProcess.jsp**, that will call our help class file, **FacultyQuery.java**, to perform the faculty data query process.
B. In order to select the correct faculty image based on the faculty member selected by the user, we need to assign the **session.getAttribute()** method to the **src** attribute under the **imagedata** tag. The argument of this method should be defined as a property in our help class file, and a method, **getFacultyImage()**, defined in that help class file will be used to select the appropriate faculty image and assign it to this property.
C. From step C to step J, we use the embedded JSP code to assign the selected faculty image and queried faculty columns from our **Faculty** Table to the **src** and **value** tags of the associated text field in **Faculty.jsp** using the **getAttribute()** method of the session class. In this way, as long as the queried faculty row has a change, the modification will be immediately updated and reflected in each text field in our **Faculty.jsp** page. Thus, a direct connection or binding between the text fields in our **Faculty.jsp** page and the queried Faculty columns in our help class is established.
K. From steps K to O, a **name** attribute is added to each **Submit** button tag. This attribute is very important, since we need to use it to identify each submit button on the next page,

```
A  <form method=post action=".\FacultyProcess.jsp">
   .........
   <v:imagedata src="" o:title="&lt;EMPTY&gt;"/><v:shadow color="#ccc [4]"/>
   .........
   left:47px;top:67px;width:154px;height:166px'><img width=154 height=166
B  src=" data:image/jpg;base64,${FacultyQuery.base64Image}" v:shapes="_x0000_s1027"></span><![endif]>
   ..........
   <input name=FacultyNameField maxlength=255 size=18
C   value="<%=session.getAttribute("facultyName") %>" type=text v:shapes="_x0000_s1029">
   .........
   <input name=FacultyIDField maxlength=255 size=21
D   value="<%=session.getAttribute("facultyId") %>" type=text v:shapes="_x0000_s1031">
   .........
   <input name=NameField maxlength=255 size=21
E   value="<%=session.getAttribute("facultyName") %>" type=text v:shapes="_x0000_s1033">
   .........
   <input name=TitleField maxlength=255 size=21
F   value="<%=session.getAttribute("title") %>" type=text v:shapes="_x0000_s1035">
   .........
   <input name=OfficeField maxlength=255 size=21
G   value="<%=session.getAttribute("office") %>" type=text v:shapes="_x0000_s1037">
   .........
   <input name=PhoneField maxlength=255 size=21
H   value="<%=session.getAttribute("phone") %>" type=text v:shapes="_x0000_s1039">
   .........
   <input name=CollegeField maxlength=255 size=21
I   value="<%=session.getAttribute("college") %>" type=text v:shapes="_x0000_s1041">
   .........
   <input name=EmailField maxlength=255 size=21
J   value="<%=session.getAttribute("email") %>" type=text v:shapes="_x0000_s1043">
   .........
K  <input type=submit value=Select name="Select" v:shapes="_x0000_s1044">
   .........
L  <input type=submit value=Insert name="Insert" v:shapes="_x0000_s1045">
   .........
M  <input type=submit value=Update name="Update" v:shapes="_x0000_s1046">
   .........
N  <input type=submit value=Delete name="Delete" v:shapes="_x0000_s1047">
   .........
O  <input type=submit value=Back name="Back" v:shapes="_x0000_s1048">
   .........
```

FIGURE 8.73 The modified code for the Faculty.jsp page.

our controller page, **FacultyProcess.jsp**, using the **getParameter()** method of the **request** object to direct control to the different pages to handle different data query and data manipulation actions in the **Faculty** Table in our sample Oracle database, **CSE _ DEPT**.

Now let's take a look at our controller page, **FacultyProcess.jsp**.

8.4.5.3 Create the FacultyProcess.jsp Page

The purpose of this page is to direct control to the different help class files based on the button clicked by the user on the **Faculty.jsp** page. The following help class files will be triggered and executed based on the button clicked by the user:

1) If the user clicked the **Select** button, control will be directed to the faculty data query help class file **FacultyQuery.java** to perform the faculty record query function.
2) If the user clicked the **Insert** button, control will be directed to the faculty data insertion help class file **FacultyInsertBean.java** to do the faculty record insertion.

3) If the user clicked the **Update** or **Delete** button, control will be directed to the faculty record update and delete help class file **FacultyUpdateDeleteBean.java** to perform the associated data manipulation.
4) If the user clicked the **Back** button, control will be returned to the **Selection.jsp** page to enable users to perform other information query operations.

Now let's create the **FacultyProcess.jsp** page.

Right-click on our project, **JavaWebOracleSelect**, in the **Projects** window and select the **New > JSP** item from the popup menu to open the **New JSP File** wizard. Enter **FacultyProcess** in the **File Name** field and click on the **Finish** button.

Double-click on our new created **FacultyProcess.jsp** page in the **Projects** window, under the **Web Pages** folder, to open this page. Enter the code shown in Figure 8.74 on this page. The new entered code is in bold.

```
A   <%@ page import="JavaWebOracleSelectPackage.*" %>
    <html>
      <head>
        <meta http-equiv="Content-Type" content="text/html; charset=UTF-8">
        <title>Faculty Process Page</title>
      </head>
      <body>
       <%
B      String[] F_Field = {"facultyName","facultyId","facultyName","title","office","college","phone","email"};
C      FacultyQuery fQuery = new FacultyQuery();
D      if (request.getParameter("Select")!= null) {
       //process the faculty record query
E      String fname = request.getParameter("FacultyNameField");
F      boolean res = fQuery.QueryFaculty(fname);
G      if (!res) {
           for (int index = 1; index < 8; index++)
               session.setAttribute(F_Field[index], null);
               response.sendRedirect("Faculty.jsp");
       }
H      else {
               session.setAttribute("facultyId", fQuery.getFacultyID());
               session.setAttribute("facultyName", fQuery.getFacultyName());
               session.setAttribute("office", fQuery.getOffice());
               session.setAttribute("title", fQuery.getTitle());
               session.setAttribute("college", fQuery.getCollege());
               session.setAttribute("phone", fQuery.getPhone());
               session.setAttribute("email", fQuery.getEmail());

I              fQuery.getFacultyImage();
J              request.setAttribute("FacultyQuery", fQuery);
K              RequestDispatcher requestDispatcher = request.getRequestDispatcher("/Faculty.jsp");
L              requestDispatcher.forward(request, response);
           }
M     } else if (request.getParameter("Insert")!= null) {
             //process the faculty record insertion
           }
N       else if (request.getParameter("Update")!= null) {
            //process the faculty record updating
           }
O       else if (request.getParameter("Delete")!= null) {
            //process the faculty record deleting
           }
P       else if (request.getParameter("Back") != null) {
           fQuery.CloseDBConnection();
           response.sendRedirect("Selection.jsp");
           }
       %>
      </body>
    </html>
```

FIGURE 8.74 The code for the FacultyProcess.jsp page.

Now let's have a close look at this code to see how it works.

A. You can embed any import directory using the JSP directive in a HTML or a JSP file. The format is **<%@ page import="java package" %>**. On this page, we embed one package, **JavaWebOracleSelectPackage.***, since we will build our Java help class file **FacultyQuery.java** under that package in the next section.
B. Here a String array, **F _ Field[]**, is generated, and its purpose is to map to eight fields in the **Faculty.jsp** page. In fact, we will use this array to clean up all those fields when users forget to input any faculty name for the data query. Do not be confused by the duplicated **facultyName** items, since we use two faculty name fields in the **Faculty.jsp** page; one is for **Faculty Name** at the top, and the other is for the **Name** in the lower part.
C. A new instance of our help class, **FacultyQuery**, which will be created in the next section, **fQuery**, is created since we need to use properties and methods defined in that class to perform faculty data and faculty image query functions.
D. The **getParameter()** method defined in the session class is executed to identify which submit button has been clicked by the user in the **Faculty.jsp** page. As you know, in all, we have five buttons on the **Faculty.jsp** page. All **Faculty.jsp** form data, including all text fields, image boxes and submit buttons, will be submitted to the **FacultyProcess.jsp** page when any of five buttons is clicked. If a button is clicked, the **getParameter()** method with the name of that clicked button as the argument will return a non-null value. In this way, we can identify which button has been clicked. We use a sequence of **if-else if** selection structures to check all five buttons to identify the clicked button.
E. If the **Select** button is clicked by the user, the **getParameter()** method with this button's name as argument will return a non-null value. This means that the user wants to perform a faculty record query from the **Faculty** Table in our sample database. Again, the **getParameter()** method with the name of the faculty name field, **FacultyNameField**, is used to pick up a desired faculty name that is entered by the user from the **Faculty.jsp** page. The picked-up faculty name is assigned to the local String variable **fname**.
F. Then the method **QueryFaculty()** defined in the help class file **FacultyQuery.java** is called to execute the faculty data query based on the selected faculty name **fname** obtained instep E.
G. If the **QueryFaculty()** method is executed unsuccessfully, which means that no matching faculty record has been found or a blank **fname** is used, a **false** is returned to indicate this situation. In that case, we need to cleanup all fields by setting them to **null** with a **for()** loop. The system method **setAttribute()** and the string array **F _ Field[]** are used for that purpose. Also, we need to refresh the **Faculty.jsp** page to enable users to re-enter new faculty data to do another query using the **sendRedirect()** method defined in the **response** class.
H. Otherwise, the query is successful. The **setAttribute()** method is used to set up all properties defined in the help class file using the associated getter methods in that class.
I. The **getFacultyImage()** method, which is defined in the help class file **FacultyQuery.java** that will be developed in the next section, is executed to pick up and convert the retrieved faculty image from Blob format to a byte[] array and then to a base64Image String format and store it in that class.
J. The system method **setAttribute()** is used again to setup a mapping relationship between the class **FacultyQuery** and the instance **fQuery**. This step is necessary to enable the class **FacultyQuery** as a global class to be recognized by all other objects in this project.
K. A system method **getRequestDispatcher()** that belongs to the RequestDispatcher class is executed to setup a connection between the Java Model and the View to enable the latter to recognize a Java Bean with attached **base64Image** string.

L. The **forward()** method is used to setup a connection between the client (request) and the server (response).
M. If the **getParameter("Insert")** method returns a non-null value, this means that the **Insert** button has been clicked by the user on the **Faculty.jsp** page and the user wants to insert a new faculty record into the **Faculty** Table in our sample database. We will build a Java bean class to handle this faculty data insertion later.
N. Similarly, if the **getParameter("Update")** method returns a non-null value, it means that the **Update** button has been clicked by the user in the **Faculty.jsp** page and the user wants to update an existing faculty record in the **Faculty** Table in our sample database. We will build a Java bean class to handle this faculty data update action later.
O. If the **getParameter("Delete")** method returns a non-null value, it means that the **Delete** button has been clicked by the user in the **Faculty.jsp** page and the user wants to delete an existing faculty record from the **Faculty** Table in our sample database. We will build a Java bean class to handle this faculty data delete action later.
P. If the **getParameter("Back")** method returns a non-null value, it means that the **Back** button has been clicked by the user in the **Faculty.jsp** page and the user wants to return to the **Selection.jsp** page to perform other data query operations. The **CloseDBConnection()** method is first executed to close the connection to our sample database, and then the **sendRedirect()** method is called to do this return function.

Now let's build our Java help class or Java model file, **FacultyQuery.java**, to handle all data query actions, getter methods, class properties and related business logic.

8.4.5.4 Create the Help Class or Java Model File, FacultyQuery.java

To create our Java help class file, **FacultyQuery.java**, to handle faculty record queries, right-click on our project, **JavaWebOracleSelect**, in the **Projects** window and select the **New > Java Class** item from the popup menu to open the **New Java Class** wizard. Enter **FacultyQuery** in the **Class Name** field and select the **JavaWebOracleSelectPackage** from the **Package** combo box. Click on the **Finish** button to create the new Java help class file.

Now let's develop the code for this new Java help class file. Double-click on our new created Java help class file, **FacultyQuery.java**, in the **Projects** window to open the file, and enter the code shown in Figure 8.75 into this file. Because of the large size of this piece of code, we divide this coding process into two parts. The first part is shown in Figure 8.75, and the second part is shown in Figure 8.76. The new entered code is in bold.

Let's have a close look at this new added code in Figure 8.75 to see how it works.

A. A group of packages is imported first, since all Oracle database-related classes and data operation methods are defined in those packages.
B. Seven local properties related to the associated columns in the **Faculty** Table in our sample database are declared first. These properties are very important, since they are directly mapped to the associated columns in the **Faculty** Table. All of these properties can be accessed by using the associated **getter()** method defined at the bottom of this class.
C. A special String variable, **base64Image**, which is a String array, is defined, since we need to use it to store our converted faculty image later. A local Blob variable, **fbimg**, is declared here, and it is used to hold our retrieved faculty image later. A class-level database connection object is created, and a Dialog object is also created. We will use the latter as a message box to display debug information as the project runs.
D. A **try-catch** block is used to load the database JDBC driver. The **catch** block is used to track and collect any possible exception during the database driver loading process.
E. The Java database connection URL is defined. Refer to Section 6.3.3.2 in Chapter 6 to get more detailed information about this URL definition.

```
  package JavaWebOracleSelectPackage;
A import java.io.ByteArrayOutputStream;
  import java.io.IOException;
  import java.io.InputStream;
  import java.sql.*;
  import java.util.Base64;
  import java.util.logging.Level;
  import java.util.logging.Logger;
  public class FacultyQuery {
B    private String facultyID;
     private String facultyName;
     private String office;
     private String title;
     private String phone;
     private String college;
     private String email;
C    private String base64Image;
     Blob fbimg = null;
     static Connection con;
     MsgDialog  msgDlg = new  MsgDialog(new javax.swing.JFrame(), true);
  public FacultyQuery() {
D      try {
              Class.forName("oracle.jdbc.OracleDriver");
         }
         catch (Exception e) {
             msgDlg.setMessage("Class not found exception!" + e.getMessage());
             msgDlg.setVisible(true);
         }
E        String url = "jdbc:oracle:thin:@localhost:1521:XE";
F        try {
             con = DriverManager.getConnection(url,"CSE_DEPT","oracle_18c");
         }
         catch (SQLException e) {
             msgDlg.setMessage("Could not connect!" + e.getMessage());
             msgDlg.setVisible(true);
             e.printStackTrace();
       }
  }
G public boolean QueryFaculty(String  fname) {
    String query = "SELECT faculty_id, faculty_name, title, office, phone, college, email, fimage FROM Faculty "+
                   "WHERE faculty_name = ?";
H   if (fname.isEmpty()) return false;
I   try{
           PreparedStatement pstmt = con.prepareStatement(query);
J          pstmt.setString(1, fname);
K          ResultSet rs = pstmt.executeQuery();
L          while (rs.next()){
              facultyID = rs.getString(1);
              facultyName = rs.getString(2);
              title = rs.getString(3);
              office = rs.getString(4);
              phone = rs.getString(5);
              college = rs.getString(6);
              email = rs.getString(7);
              fbimg = rs.getBlob("fimage");
           }
M          return true;
       }
N      catch (SQLException e) { System.out.println("Error in Statement! " + e.getMessage());
           return false;
       }
  }
```

FIGURE 8.75 The first part of the code for the Java help class file.

F. Another `try-catch` block is used to connect to our Oracle sample database with the desired username and password. The `catch` block is used to track and collect any possible exception during the database connection process.

G. The main query method, **QueryFaculty()**, is defined with the selected faculty name as the argument. The query statement is first created with the faculty name as the positional dynamic parameter.
H. First, let's check whether the input faculty name is a blank string. If it is, no data action is needed; just return a **false** to indicate this case to the calling function. One point to be noted is that a **null** value is a value, not a blank string; thus, do not try to use code like: **if (fname == null)** to do this kind of checking in the program. This is a potential bug.
I. Starting from a **try** block, the **prepareStatement()** method is called to create a PreparedStatement object, **pstmt**.
J. The setter() method is used to set the positional parameter in the positional order.
K. The **executeQuery()** method is executed to perform this query, and the returned result is assigned to the ResultSet object **rs**.
L. A **while()** loop is used to pick up a matching faculty record. In fact, only one row is returned, and therefore this loop can run only one time. The **getString()** method is used to pick up each queried column and assign the associated property defined at the beginning of this help class. The index used for the **getString()** method should be matched to the order of the queried columns in the query statement built in step G.
M. A **true** is returned to the **FacultyProcess.jsp** page to indicate that the execution of this query method is successful.
N. The **catch** block is used to collect any possible exception that may occur during this query process. A **false** is returned to the **FacultyProcess.jsp** page to indicate that the query failed if this happens.

Now let's handle the second part of the code of this help class file, which is shown in Figure 8.76. Let's have a closer look at this code to see how it works.

A. The user-defined method **CloseDBConnection**() is defined here, and this method is used to close the connection to our sample database. Prior to closing this connection, we need first to check whether a valid database connection object exists. If the connection object **con** is not equal to null, it means that a valid connection exists. In that case, we need to close it by calling the system method **close**(). Otherwise, we need to do nothing, since no database has been connected to our project.
B. The **catch** block is used to check, collect and display any possible bug during the disconnection process.
C. Starting from step C, including steps D through K, all getter methods are defined and used to pick up all related properties defined at the beginning of this class. Pay attention to steps J and K; these **getter()** and **setter()** methods are used to get and set a special String array, **base64Image**, which will be used for display in the View class.
L. The user-defined method **getFacultyImage()** is defined starting from here, throwing a possible **SQLException**.
M. First we need to check the retrieved faculty image to make sure that it is not a **null** object.
N. Then a **try-catch** block is used to convert the image object from Blob format to a byte[] array format. Meanwhile, both the **InputStream** and **ByteArrayOutputStream** classes are used to assist this conversion.
O. A byte[] array object, **fbuffer**, is generated with a upperboundsize of 4096. The termination condition of this reading operation, –1, is also defined here.
P. A **while()** loop is utilized to read out all data items and write them into a byte[] array, **fbuffer**.
Q. A system method, **encoderToString()**, is used to convert the byte[] array **fbuffer** to a String array with **base64Image** format.
R. Some cleaning jobs are performed to close inputStream and outputStream objects.

```
A   public void CloseDBConnection()
      {
         try{
            if (con != null)
               con.close();
B        }catch (SQLException e) {
            msgDlg.setMessage("Error in close the DB! " + e.getMessage());
            msgDlg.setVisible(true);
         }
      }
C    public String getFacultyID() {
         return this.facultyID;
      }
D    public String getFacultyName() {
         return facultyName;
      }
E    public String getOffice() {
         return office;
      }
F    public String getTitle() {
         return title;
      }
G    public String getPhone() {
         return phone;
      }
H    public String getCollege() {
         return college;
      }
I    public String getEmail() {
         return email;
      }
J    public String getBase64Image() {
         return base64Image;
      }
K    public void setBase64Image(String base64Image) {
         this.base64Image = base64Image;
      }
L    public void getFacultyImage() throws SQLException{
M        if (fbimg != null)
         {
            try {
N              InputStream inputStream = fbimg.getBinaryStream();
               ByteArrayOutputStream outputStream = new ByteArrayOutputStream();
O              byte[] fbuffer = new byte[4096];
               int bytesRead = -1;
P              while ((bytesRead = inputStream.read(fbuffer)) != -1) {
                  outputStream.write(fbuffer, 0, bytesRead);
               }
               byte[] fimageBytes = outputStream.toByteArray();
Q              base64Image = Base64.getEncoder().encodeToString(fimageBytes);
R              inputStream.close();
               outputStream.close();
S           } catch (IOException ex) {
               Logger.getLogger(FacultyQuery.class.getName()).log(Level.SEVERE, null, ex);
            }
T           setBase64Image(base64Image);
         }
      }
}
```

FIGURE 8.76 The second part of the code for the Java help class file.

S. The `catch` block is used to check, collect and display any possible bug during the disconnection process.
T. Finally, the `setter()` method is utilized to store the converted String array image object.

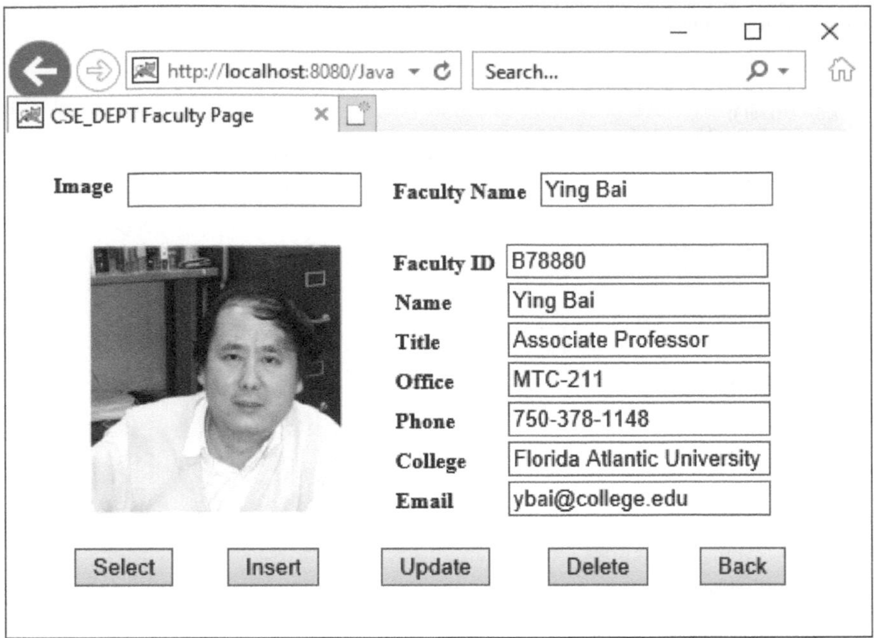

FIGURE 8.77 The run result of the Faculty.jsp page.

Now we have finished all code for the Faculty Information query operations.

Click on the **Clean and Build Main Project** button to build our project. Then click on the **Run** button to run our project.

In the opened **LogIn** page, enter an appropriate username and password, such as **jhenry** and **test**, and click on the **LogIn** button to perform the login process. If the login process is successful, select **Faculty Information** from the **Selection.jsp** page to open the **Faculty.jsp** page. On the opened **Faculty.jsp** page, enter a desired faculty name, such as **Ying Bai**, into the **Faculty Name** field, and click on the **Select** button to try to query the detailed information for the selected faculty member.

If a matching faculty record is found, the detailed information about that faculty member with a faculty image is displayed in the seven fields and Image box, as shown in Figure 8.77.

You can try to enter other faculty names, such as **Jenney King** or **Davis Bhalla**, into the **Faculty Name** field to query the information related to those faculty members.

Click on the **Back** and then **Exit** button on the **Selection.jsp** page to terminate our Web project.

Our Web project and faculty information query are successful!

A complete Web application project, **JavaWebOracleSelect**, that includes the login, selection and faculty information query processes can be found in the folder **Class DB Projects\Chapter 8** in the **Students** folder on the CRC Press ftp site (refer to Figure 1.2 in Chapter 1).

Next let's handle inserting new records into the **Faculty** Table using JavaServer Pages and Java beans technologies.

8.5 BUILD A JAVA WEB PROJECT TO MANIPULATE DATA IN THE ORACLE DATABASE

Now let's take care of manipulating data against our Oracle 18c XE database by using different methodologies, which include inserting, updating and deleting records from our sample database, **CSE _ DEPT**, via our Web application project.

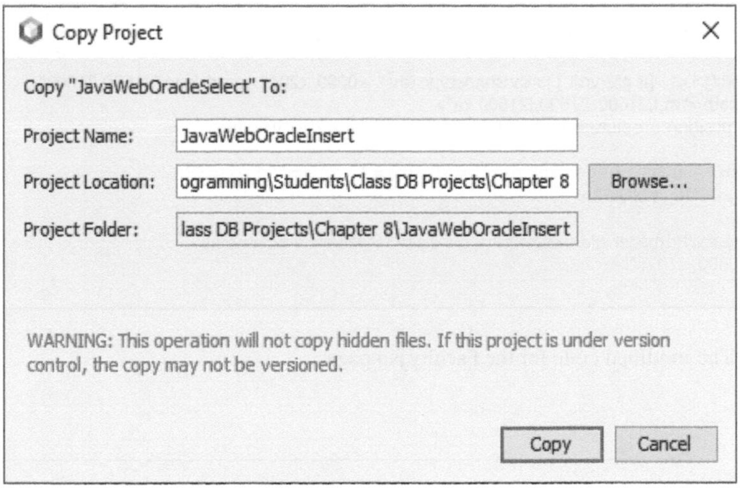

FIGURE 8.78 The opened Copy Project wizard.

First let's take care of inserting a new record into our **Faculty** Table in our sample database, **CSE _ DEPT**. To do that, we need to create a new Web project, **JavaWebOracleInsert**. In order to save time and space, we can copy and modify the project **JavaWebOracleSelect** that we built in the last section and make it our new project.

Perform the following steps to create this new project:

1) In the **Projects** window, right-click on the project **JavaWebOracleSelect** and select the **Copy** item from the popup menu to open the **Copy Project** wizard, as shown in Figure 8.78.
2) Enter our new project name, **JavaWebOracleInsert**, into the **Project Name** box, and browse to the default project folder, **C:\Class DB Projects\Chapter 8**, as the **Project Location**, which is shown in Figure 8.78, and click on the **Copy** button.

A new project, **JavaWebOracleInsert**, is generated and added into our **Projects** window. Next let's build the code for the related pages to insert some new records into the **Faculty** Table in our sample database.

8.5.1 Modify the Faculty.jsp Page by Adding a File Selection Function

In order to insert a new faculty record, especially to insert a new faculty image, into our sample database, a File Selection function should be added to the **Faculty.jsp** page to provide a way to enable users to select a desired faculty image for the new inserted faculty member. Perform the following steps to add this function:

1) On the opened **Faculty.jsp** page, scroll down to find one of the input tags, which should be around line 381:

```
<input name=FacultyImageField maxlength=255 size=18 value=""type=text
v:shapes=" _ x0000 _ s1026">
```

2) Enter the following tag located just above the previous tag:

```
<input name=Faculty_Image maxlength=50 size=4 value=""type=file
v:shapes=" _ x0000 _ s1026">
```

```
<form method=post action=".\FacultyProcess.jsp">
........
</span><![endif]><!--[if gte vml 1]><v:shapetype id="_x0000_t201" coordsize="21600,21600"
 o:spt="201" path="m,l,21600r21600,l21600,xe">
 <span style='position:absolute;top:18.0pt; left:54.0pt;z-index:2'><![endif]>

A <input name=Faculty_Image maxlength=50 size=4 value="" type=file
  v:shapes="_x0000_s1026">

<input name=FacultyImageField maxlength=255 size=18 value="" type=text
v:shapes="_x0000_s1026">
...........
```

FIGURE 8.79 The modified code for the Faculty.jsp page.

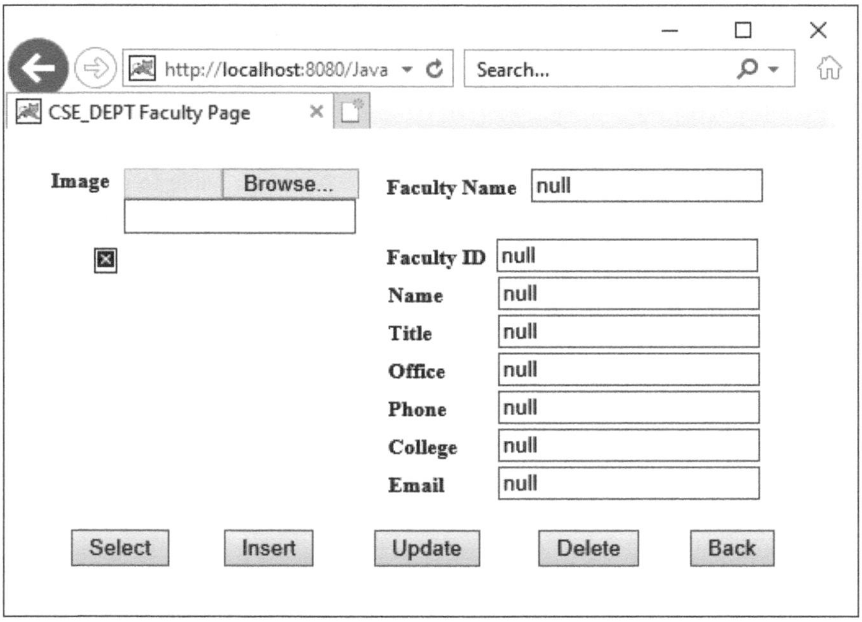

FIGURE 8.80 The run result of modified Faculty.jsp page.

Your modified **Faculty.jsp** page should match the one shown in Figure 8.79. The new added tag part is in bold.

Now go to the **Projects** window and right-click on our modified **Faculty.jsp** file, and click on the **Clean and Build Main Project** button to build our project. Then click on the **Run** button to run our project. Complete the login process and select the **Faculty Information** item from the **Selection.jsp** page to open the **Faculty.jsp** page. The run result of that page is shown in Figure 8.80. One File Selection tag is added at the top of the **Faculty Image** TextField, which can be used to select a faculty image to be inserted.

Next we can begin our code development for this data insertion action.

8.5.2 Insert New Records to the Faculty Table Using JavaServer Pages and Java Beans

To use JavaServer Pages and Java bean techniques to insert a new record into the **Faculty** Table, we need to perform the following operations:

1) Create a new Java bean class file, **FacultyInsertBean.java**, to handle the new faculty record insertion actions.
2) Modify the model controller page, **FacultyProcess.jsp**, to handle faculty data collection and assist with data insertion operations.

First let's create a new Java bean class file, **FacultyInsertBean.java**, to handle the new faculty record insertion actions.

8.5.2.1 Create a New Java Help Class File, FacultyInsertBean.java

To create our Java bean class file, **FacultyInsertBean.java**, to handle faculty record insertion, right-click on our project, **JavaWebOracleInsert**, in the **Projects** window and select the **New > Java Class** item from the popup menu to open the **New Java Class** wizard. Enter **FacultyInsertBean** in the **Class Name** field and select the **JavaWebOracleSelectPackage** from the **Package** combo box. Click on the **Finish** button to create the new Java bean class file.

Now open the code window of the new **FacultyInsertBean.java** class file by clicking on the **Source** button at the top and enter the code shown in Figure 8.81 into this window.

Let's have a closer look at this code to see how it works.

A. Some necessary Java libraries are imported first, since we need to use some components located in those libraries.
B. The constructor of this bean class is generated with the database connection operations included, which are identical to the code in the **FacultyQuery.java** constructor.
C. A new method, **InsertFaculty()**, is generated with a String array as the argument that contains a new record to be inserted into the **Faculty** Table in our sample database.
D. A local integer variable, **numInsert**, is used to hold the returned insertion result. Usually, it is equal to the number of records that have been inserted into the **Faculty** Table. A FileInputStream object, **fis**, is also created and works as a handler for converting our faculty image to a FileInputStream before it can be written or inserted into our database. A new File object, **fimage**, is declared with the name of our faculty image file as the target since the String variable, **new Faculty [7]**, contains the name of a selected faculty image to be inserted into the database.
E. The insert string is created with eight positional parameters represented by question marks in the query string.
F. A **try-catch** block is used to perform the faculty record insertion action. First a Prepared-Statement object is created with the query string as the argument.
G. Then seven elements in the String array **newFaculty[]**, which are equivalent to seven pieces of new faculty information, are assigned to seven positional parameters. The point to be noted is that the order of those seven elements must be identical to the order of columns represented in the query string and in the **Faculty** Table in our sample database.
H. Another **try-catch** block is used to create a new handler for the converted FileInputStream object with our faculty image as the input.
I. The faculty image is inserted by calling the **setBinaryStream()** method with the handler of our FileInputStream as the source.
J. The **executeUpdate()** method is executed to perform the new record insertion action. The run result, which equals the number of records that have been successfully inserted into the **Faculty** Table, is returned and assigned to the local integer variable **numInsert**.
K. The **catch** block is used to track and collect any possible exceptions during the data insertion action.
L. Finally, the run result is returned to the calling method on the **FacultyProcess.jsp** page.

Next let's modify the model controller page **FacultyProcess.jsp** to handle the faculty data collection and insertion operations.

```
  package JavaWebOracleSelectPackage;
A import java.io.File;
  import java.io.FileInputStream;
  import java.io.FileNotFoundException;
  import java.io.InputStream;
  import java.sql.*;
  import java.util.logging.Level;
  import java.util.logging.Logger;
  public class FacultyInsertBean {
     static Connection con;
B    public FacultyInsertBean() {
       try {
            Class.forName("oracle.jdbc.OracleDriver");
         }
         catch (Exception e) {
            System.out.println("Class not found exception!" + e.getMessage());
         }
         String url = "jdbc:oracle:thin:@localhost:1521:XE";
         try {
            con = DriverManager.getConnection(url,"CSE_DEPT","oracle_18c");
         }
         catch (SQLException e) {
            System.out.println("Could not connect!" + e.getMessage());
            e.printStackTrace();
       }
     }
C public int InsertFaculty(String[]  newFaculty) {
D      int  numInsert = 0;
       FileInputStream fis = null;
       File fimage= new File(newFaculty[7]);
E      String  InsertQuery = "INSERT INTO Faculty (faculty_id, faculty_name, title, office, phone, " +
                             "college,  email,  fimage)  VALUES  (?, ?, ?, ?, ?, ?, ?, ?)";
F      try{
           PreparedStatement pstmt = con.prepareStatement(InsertQuery);
G          pstmt.setString(1, newFaculty[0]);
           pstmt.setString(2, newFaculty[1]);
           pstmt.setString(3, newFaculty[2]);
           pstmt.setString(4, newFaculty[3]);
           pstmt.setString(5, newFaculty[4]);
           pstmt.setString(6, newFaculty[5]);
           pstmt.setString(7, newFaculty[6]);
H          try {
                fis = new FileInputStream(fimage);
         } catch (FileNotFoundException ex) {
           Logger.getLogger(FacultyInsertBean.class.getName()).log(Level.SEVERE, null, ex);
         }
I          pstmt.setBinaryStream(8, (InputStream)fis, (int)(fimage.length()));
J          numInsert = pstmt.executeUpdate();
       }
K      catch (SQLException e) {
         System.out.println("Error in Insert Statement! " + e.getMessage());
       }
L      return numInsert;
     }
  }
```

FIGURE 8.81 The code for the new created bean, FacultyInsertBean.java.

8.5.2.2 Modify the FacultyProcess.jsp Page to Handle Faculty Data Collection and Insertion

Double-click on the **FacultyProcess.jsp** page in the **Projects** window in our new project, and perform the following modifications and additions to this page to use the Java bean class file

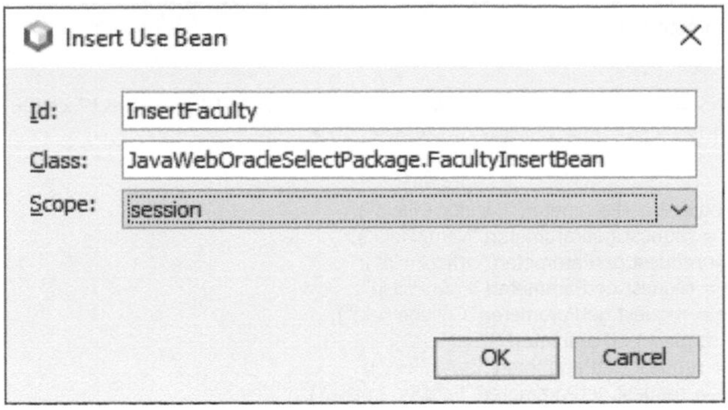

FIGURE 8.82 The finished Insert Use Bean dialog box.

FacultyInsertBean.java to perform a new faculty record insertion:

1) Move the cursor to the **else if (request.getParameter("Insert")!= null)** block; then type a JSP ending tag, **%>**, under the **else if** statement; and click on the **Enter** key on the keyboard to get a new line under the **else if** block.
2) Open the **Palette** window by going to **Window > IDE Tools > Palette**. In the opened **Palette** window, browse to the **JSP** tab, expand it and drag the **Use Bean** icon and place it under the JSP ending tag,**%>**.
3) In the opened **Insert Use Bean** dialog, enter **InsertFaculty** in the **ID** field and **JavaWebOracleSelectPackage.FacultyInsertBean** in the **Class** filed. Select **session** from the **Scope** combo box. Your finished **Insert Use Bean** dialog is shown in Figure 8.82. Click on the **OK** button to close this dialog box. A JSP directive that contains the bean id, bean scope and class is added to this block.
4) Add a JSP directive just under the previous JSP directive to setup all properties for the Java bean class **FacultyInsertBean.java** shown subsequently:

   <jsp:setProperty name="InsertFaculty" property="*" />

5) Add an opening JSP directive,**<%**, to start our Java code, to be built in the following.

The code related to steps 1~5 is shown in steps 1~4 in Figure 8.83. Add the Java code shown in steps A~G in Figure 8.83 into this block.

Let's have a closer look at this code to see how it works.

A. A local integer variable, **res**, is created and used to hold the run result of executing the **InsertFaculty()** method in the Java bean class **FacultyInsertBean** with the bean id of **InsertFaculty**.
B. Eight **getParameter()** methods are used to pick up eight pieces of new inserted faculty information stored in the eight fields in the **Faculty.jsp** page. The eight collected pieces of new faculty information are assigned to eight local String variables.
C. A new String array, **fnew**, is created and used to hold eight pieces of new faculty information stored in the eight local String variables.
D. The **InsertFaculty()** method defined in our Java bean is executed to insert these eight pieces of faculty information as a new faculty record into the **Faculty** Table. The eight pieces of new faculty information are stored in the String array **fnew** that works as the argument for this method. The run result of this method is returned and assigned to the local integer variable **res**.

```
  else if (request.getParameter("Insert")!= null) {
     //process the faculty record insertion
1    %>
2       <jsp:useBean id="InsertFaculty" scope="session" class="JavaWebOracleSelectPackage.FacultyInsertBean" />
3       <jsp:setProperty name="InsertFaculty" property="*" />
4    <%
A       int res = 0;
B       String fid = request.getParameter("FacultyIDField");
        String fname = request.getParameter("NameField");
        String office = request.getParameter("OfficeField");
        String phone = request.getParameter("PhoneField");
        String college = request.getParameter("CollegeField");
        String title = request.getParameter("TitleField");
        String email = request.getParameter("EmailField");
        String fImage = request.getParameter("Faculty_Image");
C       String[] fnew = {fid, fname, title, office, phone, college, email, fImage };
D       res = InsertFaculty.InsertFaculty(fnew);
E       if (res == 0) {
           response.sendRedirect("Faculty.jsp");
          }
F       else {
           for (int index = 1; index < 8; index++)
              session.setAttribute(F_Field[index], null);
G          response.sendRedirect("Faculty.jsp");
           }
   }
   %>
```

FIGURE 8.83 The modified and added code for the Insert block in FacultyProcess.jsp.

E. If the run result is 0, it means that no record has been inserted into the **Faculty** Table, and this data insertion action fails. In that case, we need to re-display the **Faculty.jsp** page to enable users to re-insert that faculty record.
F. If the run result is non-zero, it means that the new faculty record has been inserted into the **Faculty** Table. We need to clean up all seven fields that contain seven pieces of new inserted faculty information in the **Faculty.jsp** page to enable users to either test the insertion or insert another faculty record. A **for()** loop is used for that purpose.
G. Also, we need to re-display the **Faculty.jsp** page to enable users to perform the next action.

At this point, we have finished all code development for this data manipulation or data insertion action to the **Faculty** Table in our sample Oracle database. Prior to building and running this Web application, make sure that the new faculty image to be selected and inserted into our database has been stored in a default folder in your local machine. All faculty images can be found in the folder **Images\Faculty** in the **Students** folder on the CRC Press ftp site. One can copy and paste them to the default folder in your computer.

Now we can build and run our project to test the new faculty record insertion function. Click on the **Clean and Build Main Project** button to perform cleaning up and building our project. Then click on the **Run** button to run our project. Enter the appropriate username and password, such as **jhenry** and **test**, to finish the login process, and select the **Faculty Information** item from the **Selection.jsp** page to open the **Faculty.jsp** page.

First enter a faculty member, such as **Ying Bai**, into the **Faculty Name** box and click on the **Select** button to query the record for this faculty member, then enter seven pieces of desired new faculty information into the associated seven fields as a new faculty record, and click on the **Browse** button on the File Selection box (above the **Image** TextField) to select a desired faculty

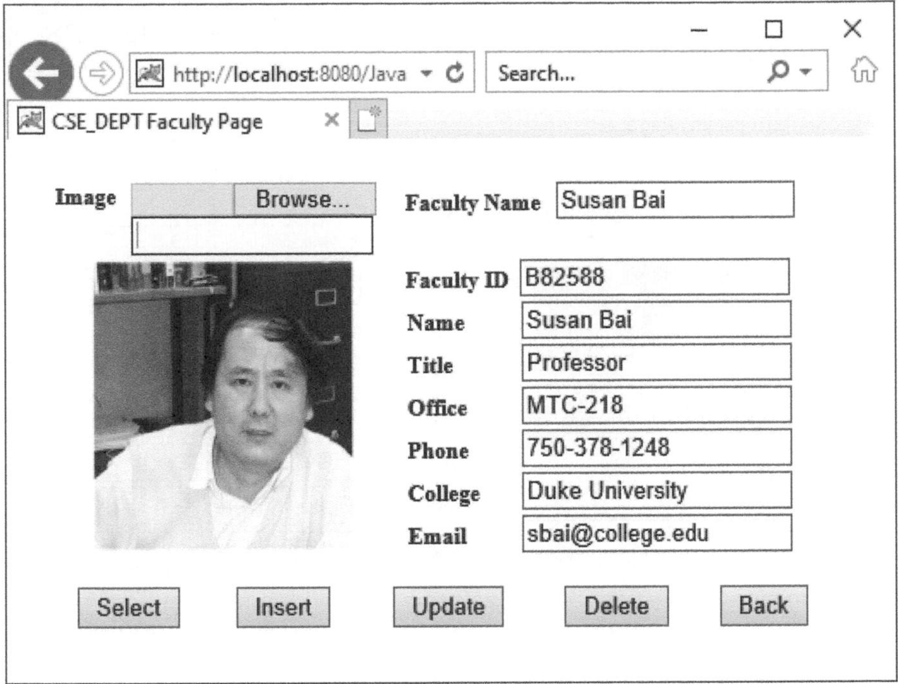

FIGURE 8.84 The entered new faculty information.

image, **White.jpg**, which is located in our default project image folder and belongs to the new inserted faculty member, **Susan Bai**. The finished new faculty record is shown in Figure 8.84.

Click on the **Insert** button to try to insert this new faculty record into the **Faculty** Table in our sample database. Immediately you can see that all TextFields, including the Faculty Name, become blank or null, which means that this data insertion is successful.

To confirm this insertion, two methods could be used. The first is to use the **Select** button on the **Faculty.jsp** page to retrieve this new inserted record from the **Faculty** Table. To do that, enter **Susan Bai** in the **Faculty Name** field and then click on the **Select** button. You can see that the new inserted record is retrieved and displayed in the seven fields with the new faculty image, as shown in Figure 8.85. Now click on the **Back** and **Exit** buttons to terminate our project.

The second way to confirm this data insertion is to open the **Faculty** Table by using either the Oracle SQL Developer or our connected database, **CSE_DEPT**, under the **Services** window in the NetBeans IDE. Here we prefer to use the second way to confirm this insertion.

To use the second way to check the data insertion, first we need to connect to our database. Perform the following operations to do this connection.

1) In the NetBeans IDE with our project opened, open the **Services** window.
2) Right-click on the **Databases** folder and select the **New Connection** item.
3) In the opened New Connection Wizard, click the dropdown arrow in the **Driver** combo box, and select the **Oracle Thin** item, since we installed this kind of driver.
4) Click on the **Add** button and browse to our JDBC driver, **ojdbc8.jar**, which is located in the folder **C:\Temp**. Refer to Appendix H to get more details about this location. Select this driver and click on the **Open** button to return to the New JDBC Driver wizard. Click on the **Next** button to continue.

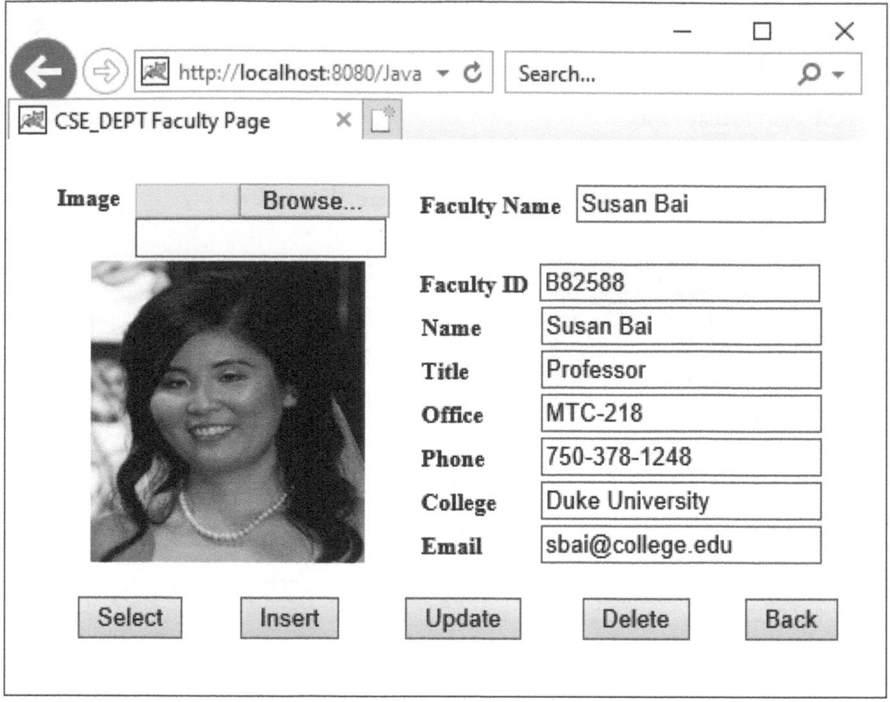

FIGURE 8.85 The retrieved new faculty record.

5) In the opened New Connection Wizard, all other connection parameters, including the **`Host`**, **`Port`** and **`Service ID`**, have been setup by the system, and the only parameters you need to enter are username and password. Enter them into the related boxes as shown:

   a. User Name: `CSE _ DEPT`
   b. Password: `oracle _ 18c`

Your finished New Connection Wizard should match the one shown in Figure 8.86.

Pay special attention to the content in the **`JDBC URL`** box, which is our completed connection URL, and click on the **`Test Connection`** button to make and check this connection. A **`Connection Succeeded`** message is displayed if this connection is successful.

Click on the **`Next`** button to select the database schema. Keep the default schema, **`CSE _ DEPT`**, as the schema, and click on the **`Next`** button.

Modify the connection name by cutting off the attached **`[CSE _ DEPT on Default schema]`** to get our final Input connection name as: **`jdbc:oracle:thin:@localhost:1521:XE`**, and click on the **`Finish`** button to complete the database connection.

Now that our database is connected, we can open it to check our data insertion. In the opened **`Services`** window, expand each of the following folders:

1) Our database connection URL
2) Our database, **`CSE _ DEPT`**
3) The **`Tables`** folder

Now right-click on our **`Faculty`** Table and select the **`View Data`** item to open this Table. The opened **`Faculty`** Table is shown in Figure 8.87.

New Connection Wizard

Customize Connection

Driver Name: Oracle Thin (Service ID (SID))

Host: localhost Port: 1521

Service ID (SID): XE

User Name: CSE_DEPT

Password: ••••••••••

Remember password

Connection Properties Test Connection

JDBC URL: jdbc:oracle:thin:@localhost:1521:XE

Connection Succeeded.

< Back Next > Finish Cancel Help

FIGURE 8.86 The finished New Connection Wizard.

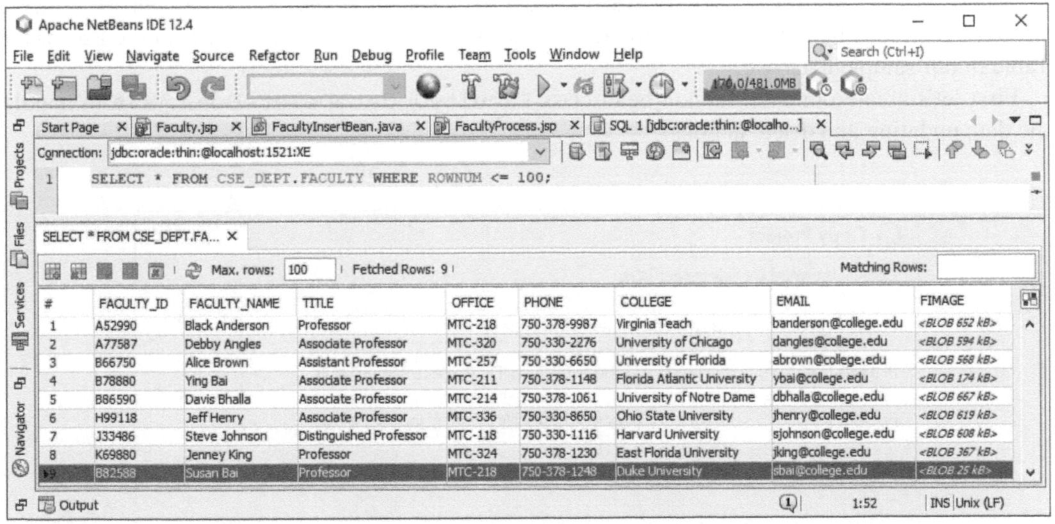

FIGURE 8.87 The opened Faculty Table with the new inserted faculty record.

The new inserted faculty member, `Susan Bai`, has been inserted at the bottom of this Table, and this record is highlighted in Figure 8.87. Our data insertion using JavaServer Pages and Java beans is successful! To keep our database clean and neat, it is generally recommended to delete this new faculty member from the **Faculty** Table. However, we will to keep it right now since we can test the data delete action by using this record in the next section.

A complete Web application project, **JavaWebOracleInsert**, which contains the LogIn.jsp, Selection.jsp, Faculty.jsp, FacultyProcess.jsp, FacultyQuery.jsp and FacultyInsertBean.java files, can be found in the folder **Class DB Projects\Chapter 8** in the **Students** folder on the CRC Press ftp site (refer to Figure 1.2 in Chapter 1).

8.5.3 Update and Delete Data from the Faculty Table Using JSP and Java Beans Techniques

To use the JavaServer Pages and Java bean techniques to perform data updating and delete actions against the **Faculty** Table, we need to perform the following operations:

1) Create a new Java Session bean class, **FacultyUpdateDeleteBean.java**, to handle the data updating and delete actions.
2) Modify the model controller page, **FacultyProcess.jsp**, to handle the faculty data collection and manipulation.

Now let's create a new project, **JavaWebOracleUpdateDelete**, based on our existing project, **JavaWebOracleInsert**. Perform the following operations to complete this creation:

1) In the **Projects** window, right-click on the project **JavaWebOracleInsert** and select the **Copy** item from the popup menu to open the **Copy Project** wizard, as shown in Figure 8.88.
2) Enter our new project name, **JavaWebOracleUpdateDelete**, into the **Project Name** box; browse to the default project folder, **C:\Class DB Projects\Chapter 8**, as the **Project Location**, which is shown in Figure 8.88; and click on the **Copy** button.

A new project, **JavaWebOracleUpdateDelete**, is generated and added into our **Projects** window. Next let's build the code for the related pages to update or delete records in the **Faculty** Table in our sample database.

First let's create our Java session bean class **FacultyUpdateDeleteBean.java** to handle the data updating and delete actions.

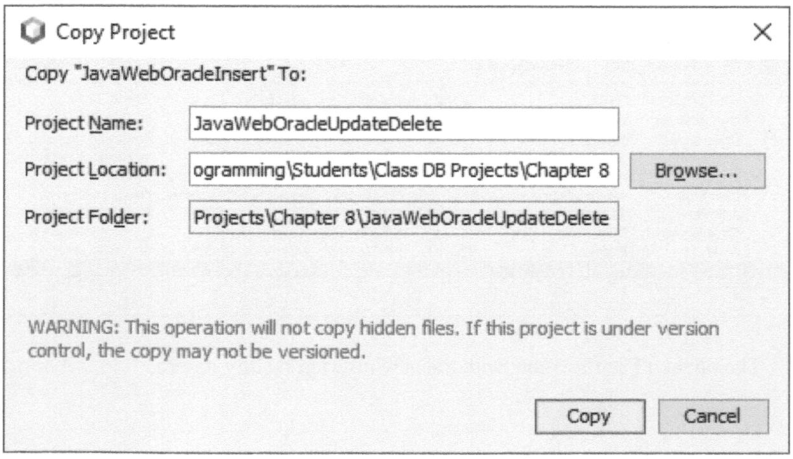

FIGURE 8.88 The copied project JavaWebOracleUpdateDelete.

8.5.3.1 Create a New Java Session Bean Class

Perform the following operations to create a new Java session bean class:

1) Right-click on our new project, **JavaWebOracleUpdateDelete**, in the **Projects** window and select the **New > Java Class** item from the popup menu to open the **New Java Class** wizard.
2) Enter **FacultyUpdateDeleteBean** into the **Class Name** field and select **JavaWebOracleSelect Package** from the **Package** combo box.
3) Keep all other default settings and click on the **Finish** button.

In the created **FacultyUpdateDeleteBean.java** class, we need to create two new methods, **UpdateFaculty()** and **DeleteFaculty()**. These two methods are used to perform the data updating and deleting operations against our sample database. Figure 8.89 shows the first part of the code used to perform the data update actions.

Let's have a closer look at the code for these two methods to see how it works.

A. Some useful packages are imported first, since all Oracle database-related classes and other components are defined in those packages.
B. Seven class properties related to the associated columns in the **Faculty** Table are declared first. These properties are very important, since they are directly mapped to the associated columns in the **Faculty** Table. All of these properties can be accessed by using the associated **getter()** method defined in the second code part of this class. A class-level database connection object, **con**, is also created.
C. In the constructor of this class, a **try-catch** block is used to load the Oracle JDBC driver. The **catch** block is used to track and collect any possible exception during this database driver loading process.
D. The database connection URL is defined. Refer to Section 6.3.3.2 in Chapter 6 to get more detailed information about this URL definition.
E. Another **try-catch** block is used to connect to our sample Oracle database with the desired username and password. The **catch** block is used to track and collect any possible exception during the database connection process.
F. The main data updating method, **UpdateFaculty()**, is defined with the selected faculty update information as the argument. This argument is a String array that contains all seven pieces of updated faculty information without **faculty _ id**. A local integer variable, **numUpdated**, and the update statement are first created, with the faculty ID as the positional dynamic parameter.
G. A FileInputStream object, **fis**, is created and works as a handler of the InputStream for the updated faculty image later.
H. A new File object, **fimage**, is also generated to convert the updated faculty image that is stored in a string variable, **upFaculty[6]**, to a file object, and it will be further converted to an InputStream object later to be written into the **Faculty** Table.
I. The updated query string is generated with eight positional parameters to make this update action ready.
J. Starting from a **try** block, the **prepareStatement()** method is called to create a PreparedStatement object, **pstmt**.
K. Six setter methods are used to set the positional parameters in the update statement with the positional order. This order must be identical to that defined in the input argument **upFaculty[]**, which is a String array.
L. With another **try-catch** block, a new FileInputStream object, **fis**, is generated with the File **fimage** as the argument to convert that File to a FileInputStream object and assign

```
   package JavaWebOracleSelectPackage;
A  import java.sql.*;
   import java.io.File;
   import java.io.FileInputStream;
   import java.io.FileNotFoundException;
   import java.io.InputStream;
   import java.util.logging.Level;
   import java.util.logging.Logger;

   public class FacultyUpdateDeleteBean {
B    private String facultyID;
     private String facultyName;
     private String office;
     private String title;
     private String phone;
     private String college;
     private String email;
     static Connection con;

     public FacultyUpdateDeleteBean() {
C      try {
            Class.forName("oracle.jdbc.OracleDriver");
        }
        catch (Exception e) {
           System.out.println("Class not found exception!" + e.getMessage());
        }
D       String url = " jdbc:oracle:thin:@localhost:1521:XE";
E       try {
           con = DriverManager.getConnection(url,"CSE_DEPT","oracle_18c");
        }
        catch (SQLException e) {
           System.out.println ("Could not connect!" + e.getMessage());
           e.printStackTrace();
        }
     }
F    public int UpdateFaculty(String[] upFaculty) {
       int  numUpdated = 0;
G      FileInputStream fis = null;
H      File fimage= new File(upFaculty[6]);

I      String query = "UPDATE  Faculty SET faculty_name=?, title=?, office=?, phone=?, college=?," +
                     "email=?, fimage=? " + "WHERE faculty_id= ?";
J    try {
        PreparedStatement pstmt = con.prepareStatement(query);
K       pstmt.setString(1, upFaculty[0]);          // FacultyNameField
        pstmt.setString(2, upFaculty[1]);          // TitleField
        pstmt.setString(3, upFaculty[2]);          // OfficeField
        pstmt.setString(4, upFaculty[3]);          // PhoneField
        pstmt.setString(5, upFaculty[4]);          // CollegeField
        pstmt.setString(6, upFaculty[5]);          // EmailField
L       try {
            fis = new FileInputStream(fimage);
        } catch (FileNotFoundException ex) {
          Logger.getLogger(FacultyInsertBean.class.getName()).log(Level.SEVERE, null, ex);
        }
M         pstmt.setBinaryStream(7, (InputStream)fis, (int)(fimage.length()));
N         pstmt.setString(8, upFaculty[7]);          // FacultyIDField
O         numUpdated = pstmt.executeUpdate();
       }
P    catch (SQLException e) {
          System.out.println("Error in Statement!" + e.getMessage());
       }
Q      return numUpdated;
     }
     .........
```

FIGURE 8.89 The first part of the code of the Java bean class file.

```
A   public String getFacultyID() {
      return this.facultyID;
    }
B   public String getFacultyName() {
      return this.facultyName;
    }
C   public String getOffice() {
      return this.office;
    }
D   public String getTitle() {
      return this.title;
    }
E   public String getPhone() {
      return this.phone;
    }
F   public String getCollege() {
      return this.college;
    }
G   public String getEmail() {
      return this.email;
    }
  }
```

FIGURE 8.90 The second part of the code of the Java bean class file.

it to that new created object. The **catch** block is used to check and inspect any possible exception for this file if it cannot be found.

M. Then a system method, **setBinaryStream()**, is executed to assign the faculty image file as a binary stream sequence to the seventh input position parameter, **fimage**, to the Update query statement.
N. The **setString()** method is executed again to setup the eighth input positional parameter, **faculty_id**, to the query **WHERE** clause in the Update query statement.
O. The **executeUpdate()** method is executed to perform this data update action, and the returned result, which is the number of the rows that have been successfully updated in the **Faculty** Table, is assigned to the local integer variable, **numUpdated**.
P. The **catch** block is used to track and collect any possible exceptions during this data update operation.
Q. The data update result is returned to the calling method.

The second part of the code for this Java bean class is shown in Figure 8.90. Let's have a closer look at this piece of code to see how it works.

A. Starting from step A, including steps C through G, seven getter methods are defined, and they are used to pick up all seven properties defined at the beginning of this class.

In fact, the code for this Java bean class is similar to that we built in our Java help class file, which includes loading the JDBC driver, defining the database connection URL, connecting to database and executing the appropriate method to perform related data actions to our database.

Let's modify the **FacultyProcess.jsp** page to do the faculty data collection and manipulation.

8.5.3.2 Modify the FacultyProcess Page to Handle Faculty Data Updating

Double-click on the **FacultyProcess.jsp** page in the **Projects** window and perform the following modifications to this page to use the Java bean **FacultyUpdateDeleteBean.java** to perform the faculty record update actions:

1) Move the cursor to just under the line **`else if (request.getParameter("Up date")!= null)`**, then open the **`Palette`** window by going to **`Window > IDE Tools > Palette`**. In the opened **`Palette`** window, browse to the **`JSP`** tab, drag the **`Use Bean`** icon and place it at the cursor location that is just under the **`else if`** code line, as mentioned previously.
2) In the opened **`Insert Use Bean`** dialog, enter **`UpdateFaculty`** in the **`ID`** field and **`JavaWebOrcleSelectPackage.FacultyUpdateDeleteBean`** in the **`Class`** filed. Select **`session`** from the **`Scope`** combo box, and then click on the **`OK`** button. A JSP directive that contains the bean id, bean scope and class is added to this block.
3) Add a JSP directive to the Java bean class **`FacultyUpdateDeleteBean.java`**:

   <jsp:setProperty name="UpdateFaculty" property="*" />

4) Add the opening and ending JSP directives **`<%`** to enclose those two JSP directives we added previously.

The code related to steps 1~4 is shown in the top on Figure 8.91. Add the code shown in steps A~G in Figure 8.91 into this block. Let's have a closer look at this code to see how it works.

A. A local integer variable, **`update`**, is created and used to hold the run result of executing the **`UpdateFaculty()`** method in the Java bean class **`FacultyUpdateDeleteBean`** with the bean id of **`UpdateFaculty`**.
B. Eight **`getParameter()`** methods are used to pick up eight pieces of updated faculty information stored in the eight fields in the **`Faculty.jsp`** page. The eight collected pieces of new faculty information are assigned to eight local String variables.

```
    else if (request.getParameter("Update")!= null) {
    //process the faculty record updating
1    %>
2    <jsp:useBean id="UpdateFaculty" scope="session" class="JavaWebOracleSelectPackage.FacultyUpdateDeleteBean" />
3    <jsp:setProperty name="UpdateFaculty" property="*" />
4    <%
A         int update = 0;
B         String fname = request.getParameter("NameField");
          String office = request.getParameter("OfficeField");
          String phone = request.getParameter("PhoneField");
          String college = request.getParameter("CollegeField");
          String title = request.getParameter("TitleField");
          String email = request.getParameter("EmailField");
          String f_id = request.getParameter("FacultyIDField");
          String fImage = request.getParameter("Faculty_Image");
C         if (fImage.isEmpty())
            response.sendRedirect("Faculty.jsp");
          else {
D           String[] upf = {fname, title, office, phone, college, email, fImage, f_id };
E           update = UpdateFaculty.UpdateFaculty(upf);
F           if (update == 0)
              response.sendRedirect("Faculty.jsp");
G           else {
                for (int index = 1; index < 8; index++)
                    session.setAttribute(F_Field[index], null);
H               response.sendRedirect("Faculty.jsp");
            }
          }
     }
    .........
```

FIGURE 8.91 The modified code for the Update block.

C. If the user forgot to select an updated faculty image with this data update, the program is directed to return to the **Faculty.jsp** page to enable the user to do that selection without any update action being performed. The function of this data update action is that the user must select an updated faculty image to continue the data update. The same faculty image should be selected if the user does not want to update that faculty image.
D. A new String array, **upf[]**, is created, and it is used to hold eight pieces of updated faculty information stored in the eight local String variables.
E. The **UpdateFaculty()** method in our Java bean is executed to update a faculty record with these eight pieces of faculty information in the **Faculty** Table. The eight pieces of updated faculty information are stored in the String array **upf[]** that works as the argument for this method. The run result of this method is returned and assigned to the local integer variable **update**.
F. If the run result is 0, it means that no record has been updated in the **Faculty** Table, and this data update action fails. In that case, we need to re-display the **Faculty.jsp** page to enable users to re-update that faculty record.
G. Otherwise, if the run result is non-zero, it means that at least one faculty record has been updated in the **Faculty** Table. We can clean up all seven fields that contain seven pieces of updated faculty information in the **Faculty.jsp** page to enable users to either to test the update or update another faculty record.
H. We need to re-display the **Faculty.jsp** page to enable users to perform the next action.

Prior to building and running this Web application, make sure that the faculty image to be selected and updated, in this case, **David.jpg**, has been stored in a desired default project folder, in this case **C:\Class DB Projects\Chapter 8\JavaWebOracleUpdateDelete\web\FImages**. Of course, you can select any other folder you like to store these faculty images.

Now we can build and run our project to test this faculty record update function. Click on the **Clean and Build Main Project** button to clean up and build our project. Then click on the **Run** button to run our project. Enter the appropriate username and password, such as **jhenry** and **test**, to finish the login process, and select the **Faculty Information** item from the **Selection.jsp** page to open the **Faculty.jsp** page.

To update a faculty record, first let's perform a query operation to retrieve and display that faculty record. Enter a faculty name, such as **Ying Bai**, into the **Faculty Name** field and click on the **Select** button. All seven pieces of information related to that faculty member are retrieved and displayed on this page. Now enter six pieces of updated information into the associated six fields without the **Faculty ID** field, as shown in Figure 8.92, and click on the **Browse** button in the File Selector box to browse and select the updated faculty image, **David.jpg**, as our updated faculty image. The finished update record for the faculty member named **David Bell** is shown in Figure 8.92.

Click on the **Update** button to try to update this faculty record in the **Faculty** Table in our sample database. Immediately you can see that all TextFields become blank with the null value, which means that this data update is successful.

To confirm this data update action, two methods could be used. The first is to use the **Select** button on the **Faculty.jsp** page to retrieve the updated faculty record from the **Faculty** Table. To do that, enter **David Bell** in the **Faculty Name** field, and then click on the **Select** button. You can see that the updated record is retrieved and displayed in the seven fields with the updated faculty image, as shown in Figure 8.93.

Our data update action using the JavaServer Pages and Java bean is successful! Now just click on the **Back** and **Exit** buttons to terminate our project.

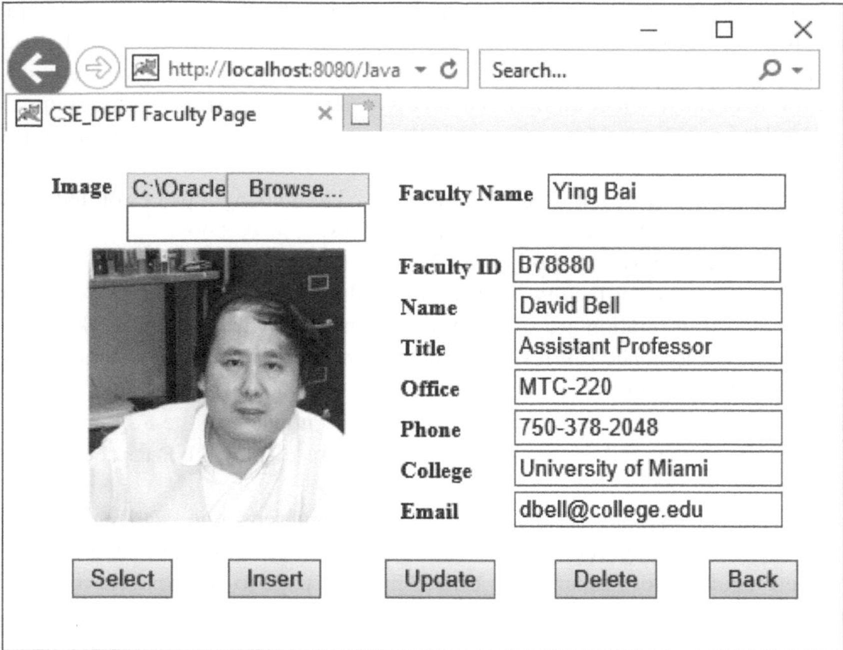

FIGURE 8.92 The updated faculty information.

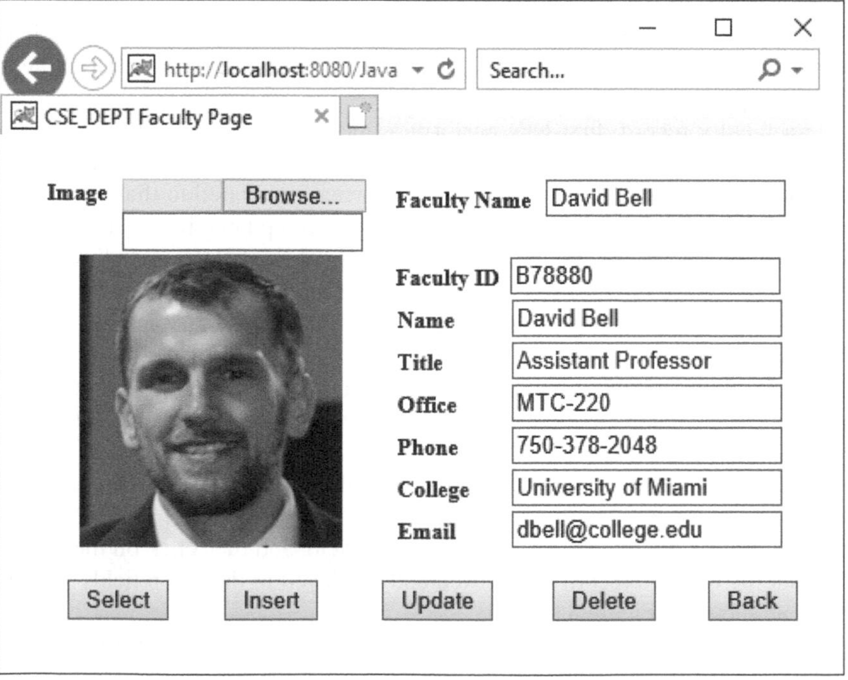

FIGURE 8.93 The run result of confirming the data update action.

The second way to confirm this data updateis to open the **Faculty** Table. Perform the following operations to open the **Faculty** Table to check this update action:

1) In the NetBeans IDE 12.4, open the **Services** window by clicking on it at the top and expand the **Databases** node to find the URL folder, **jdbc:oracle:thin:@localhost:1521:XE**.
2) Right-click on the URL, select the **Connect** item and enter the password, **oracle _ 18c**, to connect to our sample database.
3) Then expand our database, **CSE _ DEPT**, and **Tables**. Right-click on the **Faculty** Table and select the **View Data** item to open this Table.

You can see that the faculty record with the original **faculty _ id** of B78880 has been updated.

It is highly recommended to recover the updated faculty record back to the original one. Run the project again and refer to Table 8.3 to perform another data update to do the recovery.

When doing this recovery or update action, the original faculty image file, **Bai.jpg**, can be found in the folder **Images\Faculty** in the **Students** folder on the CRC Press site (refer to Figure 1.2 in Chapter 1). One can copy and paste it into any local folder to use it.

8.5.3.3 Add a Method to the Java Bean to Perform Faculty Data Deleting

To perform a faculty record delete action, we need to perform the following operations:

1) Add a new method to the Java session bean **FacultyUpdateDeleteBean** to handle the faculty record delete action.
2) Modify the **FacultyProcess.jsp** page to do the faculty data collection and delete action.

TABLE 8.3
The Original Data for Faculty Member Ying Bai

faculty_id	faculty_name	office	phone	college	title	email	fimage
B78880	Ying Bai	MTC-211	750–378–1148	Florida Atlantic University	Associate Professor	ybai@college.edu	Bai.jpg

```
  .........
  public int DeleteFaculty(String fname) {
A      int numDeleted = 0;
B      String query = "DELETE FROM Faculty WHERE faculty_name = ?";
       try {
C         PreparedStatement pstmt = con.prepareStatement(query);
D         pstmt.setString(1, fname);
E         numDeleted = pstmt.executeUpdate();
       }
F      catch (SQLException e) {
          System.out.println("Error in Statement!" + e.getMessage());
       }
G      return numDeleted;
  }
  .........
```

FIGURE 8.94 The code for the DeleteFaculty() method.

Let's first add a new method, **DeleteFaculty()**, into our Java session bean class file, **FacultyUpdateDeleteBean**, to handle the faculty record delete action. Create a new method, **DeleteFaculty()**, and enter the code shown in Figure 8.94 into this Java Bean class file.

Let's have a closer look at this piece of code to see how it works.

A. A local integer variable, **numDeleted**, is created, and it is used to hold the run result of executing the **DeleteFaculty()** method in the Java bean class **FacultyUpdateDeleteBean.java** with the bean id **DeleteFaculty**.
B. The delete statement is created with the **faculty _ name** as the positional dynamic parameter.
C. A **try-catch** block is used to perform the data delete action. The **prepareStatement()** method is called to create a PreparedStatement object, **pstmt**.
D. The setter method is used to setup the positional dynamic parameter **faculty _ name**.
E. The **executeUpdate()** method is executed to perform the data delete action, and the run result, which is the number of the rows that have been successfully deleted from the **Faculty** Table, is assigned to the local integer variable **numDeleted**.
F. The **catch** block is used to track and collect any exceptions during the data delete operation.
G. The data delete result is returned to the calling method.

Let's modify the **FacultyProcess.jsp** page to do the faculty data collection and delete actions.

8.5.3.4 Modify the FacultyProcess Page to Handle Faculty Data Deleting

Double-click on the **FacultyProcess.jsp** page in the **Projects** window to open this page, and perform the following modifications to this page to use the Java bean **FacultyUpdateDeleteBean.java** to perform the faculty record delete action:

1) Move the cursor to the **else if (request.getParameter("Delete")!= null)** block, just under that code line, then open the **Palette** window by going to **Window > IDE Tools > Palette**. In the opened **Palette** window, browse to the **JSP** tab, drag the **Use Bean** icon and place it inside the **else if** block.
2) In the opened **Insert Use Bean** dialog, enter **DeleteFaculty** in the **ID** field and **JavaWebOracleSelectPackage.FacultyUpdateDeleteBean** in the **Class** field. Select **session** from the **Scope** combo box. Click on the **OK** button to close that dialog. A JSP directive that contains the bean id, bean scope and class is added to that block.
3) Add a JSP directive to the Java bean class **FacultyUpdateDeleteBean.java** as shown:

   <jsp:setProperty name="DeleteFaculty" property="*" />

4) Add opening and ending JSP directives to enclose two JSP directives we added in steps 1 and 4 in Figure 8.95.

The code related to steps 1~4 is shown in the top on Figure 8.95. Add the code shown in steps A~D in Figure 8.95 into this block.

Let's have a closer look at this code to see how it works.

A. A local integer variable, **delete**, is created and it is used to hold the run result of executing the **DeleteFaculty()** method in the Java bean class **FacultyUpdateDeleteBean** with the bean id of **DeleteFaculty**.
B. The **getParameter()** method is used to pick up the name of the faculty to be deleted from the **Faculty** Table. The retrieved faculty name is assigned to the local variable **fname**.
C. The **DeleteFaculty()** method in our Java bean is executed to delete a faculty record based on the selected faculty name from the **Faculty** Table. The run result of this method is returned and assigned to the local integer variable **delete**.
D. We need to re-display the **Faculty.jsp** page to enable users to perform the next action.

```
   ........
   else if (request.getParameter("Delete")!= null) {
    //process the faculty record deleting
1   %>
2     <jsp:useBean id="DeleteFaculty" scope="session" class="JavaWebOracleSelectPackage.FacultyUpdateDeleteBean" />
3     <jsp:setProperty name="DeleteFaculty" property="*" />
4    <%
A      int delete = 0;
B      String fname = request.getParameter("FacultyNameField");
C      delete = DeleteFaculty.DeleteFaculty(fname);
D      response.sendRedirect("Faculty.jsp");
    }
   else if (request.getParameter("Back") != null) {
          fQuery.CloseDBConnection();
          response.sendRedirect("Selection.jsp");
         }
      %>
    </body>
   </html>
```

FIGURE 8.95 The modified code for the Delete block.

Now we can build and run our project to test this faculty record delete function. Click on the **Clean and Build Main Project** button to perform cleaning up and building our project. Then click on the **Run** button to run our project. Enter the appropriate username and password, such as **jhenry** and **test**, to finish the login process, and select the **Faculty Information** item from the **Selection.jsp** page to open the **Faculty.jsp** page.

To delete a faculty record, first let's perform a query operation to retrieve and display that faculty record. Recall that in Section 8.5.2.2, when we inserted a new faculty member named **Susan Bai** into the **Faculty** Table in our sample database, we did not remove it from our database. Now we can test the delete action by deleting that faculty member from our database.

Enter a faculty name, **Susan Bai**, into the **Faculty Name** field and click on the **Select** button. All seven pieces of information related to that faculty member are retrieved and displayed on this page. Now click on the **Delete** button to try to delete this record from our **Faculty** Table. Immediately you can see that all TextFields become blank with null values, which means that our data delete action is successful.

To confirm this data delete action, two methods could be used. The first is to use the **Select** button in the **Faculty.jsp** page to try to retrieve this deleted record from the **Faculty** Table. To do that, enter the deleted faculty name, **Susan Bai**, in the **Faculty Name** field and click on the **Select** button. You can see that all seven fields are displayed with nulls, as shown in Figure 8.96, which means that the faculty member **Susan Bai** has been deleted from the **Faculty** Table permanently. Now click on the **Back** and **Exit** buttons to terminate our project.

The second way to confirm this data delete action is to open the **Faculty** Table. Perform the following operations to open the **Faculty** Table to check this data delete action:

1) In the NetBeans IDE 12.4, open the **Services** window by clicking on it from the top and expand the **Databases** node to find the URL folder, **jdbc:oracle:thin:@localhost:1521:XE**.
2) Right-click on that URL; select the **Connect** item; and enter the password, **oracle _ 18c**, to connect to our sample database.
3) Then expand our database, **CSE _ DEPT**, and **Tables**. Right-click on the **Faculty** Table and select the **View Data** item to open this Table.

You can see that the faculty record with the name of **Susan Bai** has been deleted. Our data delete action using the JavaServer Pages and Java bean is successful!

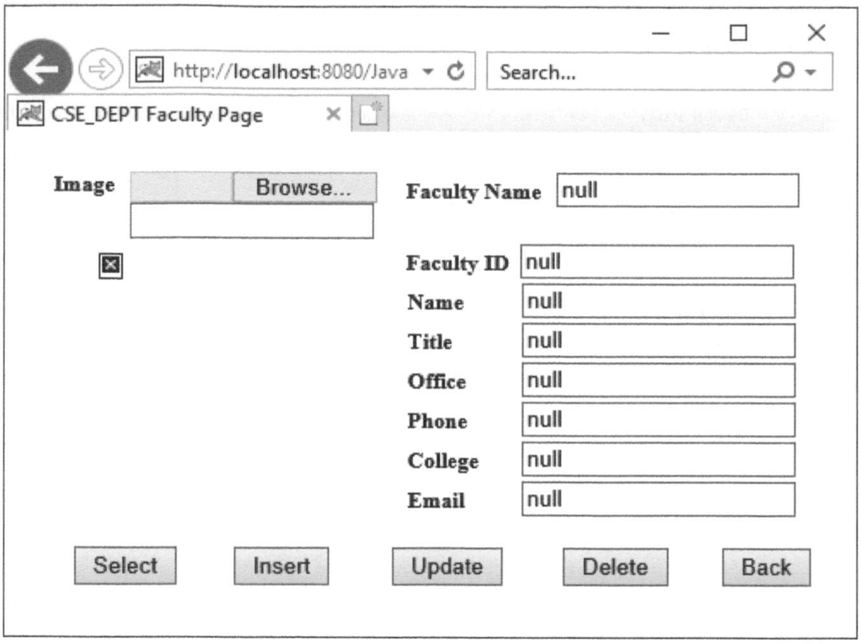

FIGURE 8.96 The confirmation of the faculty data deletion action.

But the story is not complete. The delete process would become very complicated and many more records both in the parent and the child Tables would be deleted if the deleted faculty member were an original one who was in the database when the database is generated, not one inserted into our database later.

The reason for that is when we delete an original faculty member, such as **`Ying Bai`**, from the **`Faculty`** Table that is a parent Table, not only is that faculty record in the **`Faculty`** Table deleted, but all records related to that faculty member in all child Tables, such as **`LogIn`**, **`Course`** and **`StudentCourse`**, are also deleted. Because a cascading delete relationship was setup between the parent and child Tables when we built this database in Chapter 2, the faculty login record in the **`LogIn`** Table and all courses taught by that faculty member in the **`Course`** Table will be deleted when the faculty member is deleted from the **`Faculty`** Table. Also, because the **`Course`** Table is a parent Table relative to the **`StudentCourse`** Table, all courses taken by students and taught by the deleted faculty member will also be deleted from the **`StudentCourse`** Table.

To recover these deleted records, one needs to recover all of the deleted records related to the deleted faculty member in those four Tables. An easy way to do this recovery is to use Oracle SQL Developer combined with our current project. For your convenience, we show these original records in Tables 8.4~8.7 again, and you can add them back to those four Tables to complete the data recovery.

To do this recovery, perform the following operations in the following order:

1) Run our current project again and refer to Table 8.4 to perform a data insert action by using the **`Insert`** button to insert the faculty member **`Ying Bai`** to recover the faculty record in the **`Faculty`** Table first, since it is a parent Table.
2) Open the Oracle SQL Developer and three Tables, **`Course`**, **`LogIn`** and **`StudentCourse`**, and refer to Tables 8.5~8.7 to add those records back to those Tables to recover the related faculty information in those Tables.

TABLE 8.4
The Deleted Faculty Record in the Faculty Table

faculty_id	faculty_name	title	office	phone	college	email	fimage
B78880	Ying Bai	Associate Professor	MTC-211	750–378–1148	Florida Atlantic University	ybai@college.edu	Bai.jpg

TABLE 8.5
The Deleted Course Records in the Course Table

course_id	course	credit	classroom	schedule	enrollment	faculty_id
CSC-132B	Introduction to Programming	3	TC-302	T-H: 1:00–2:25 PM	21	B78880
CSC-234A	Data Structure & Algorithms	3	TC-302	M-W-F: 9:00–9:55 AM	25	B78880
CSE-434	Advanced Electronics Systems	3	TC-213	M-W-F: 1:00–1:55 PM	26	B78880
CSE-438	Advd Logic & Microprocessor	3	TC-213	M-W-F: 11:00–11:55 AM	35	B78880

TABLE 8.6
The Deleted Login Records in the LogIn Table

user_name	pass_word	faculty_id	student_id
ybai	come	B78880	NULL

TABLE 8.7
The Deleted Student Course Records in the StudentCourse Table

s_course_id	student_id	course_id	credit	major
1005	T77896	CSC-234A	3	CS/IS
1009	A78835	CSE-434	3	CE
1014	A78835	CSE-438	3	CE
1016	A97850	CSC-132B	3	ISE
1017	A97850	CSC-234A	3	ISE

When doing the first recovery job, the original faculty image file, **Bai.jpg**, can be found in the folder **Images\Faculty** in the **Students** folder on the CRC Press site (refer to Figure 1.2 in Chapter 1). One can copy and paste it into any local folder to use it.

Another point is that you must recover the **Faculty** Table first, and then you can recover other records in other Tables, since the **faculty _ id** is a primary key in the **Faculty** Table. An easy way to do this recovery is to use the **Insert** button with its method in this project to insert the deleted faculty record based on data in Table 8.4. Then you can exit our project and use Oracle SQL Developer to add all other data items for other Tables by hand based on the data in Tables 8.5~8.7.

A complete Web application project, **JavaWebOracleUpdateDelete**, which contains LogIn, Selection, Faculty.jsp, FacultyProcess.jsp, FacultyQuery.jsp and FacultyUpdateDeleteBean.java files, can be found in the folder **Class DB Projects\Chapter 8** in the **Students** folder on the CRC Press ftp site (refer to Figure 1.2 in Chapter 1).

8.6 QUERY THE COURSE TABLE USING JAVASERVER PAGES AND JSP IMPLICIT SESSION OBJECT

In this section, we discuss how to perform a data query from the **Course** Table in our sample Oracle database, **CSE _ DEPT**, via the **Course.jsp** page we built in Section 8.4.1.4.

Basically the function of this page is to enable users to retrieve all courses, that is, all **course _ id** values, taught by the selected faculty member and display them in the CourseList box. Also, the course details related to a selected **course _ id** from that CourseList box will be retrieved and displayed in six TextFields in that page.

To save time and space, we can copy and modify the project **JavaWebOracleSelect** to make it our new Web application project, **JavaWebOracleCourse**. Perform the following steps to create this new project:

1) In the **Projects** window, right-click on the project **JavaWebOracleSelect** and select the **Copy** item from the popup menu to open the **Copy Project** wizard, as shown in Figure 8.97.
2) Enter our new project name, **JavaWebOracleCourse**, into the **Project Name** box; browse to the default project folder, **C:\Class DB Projects\Chapter 8**, as the **Project Location**, which is shown in Figure 8.97; and click on the **Copy** button.

A new project, **JavaWebOracleCourse**, is generated and added into our **Projects** window. Next let's add some JSP pages and build the code for the related pages to perform the data query from the **Course** Table in our sample database.

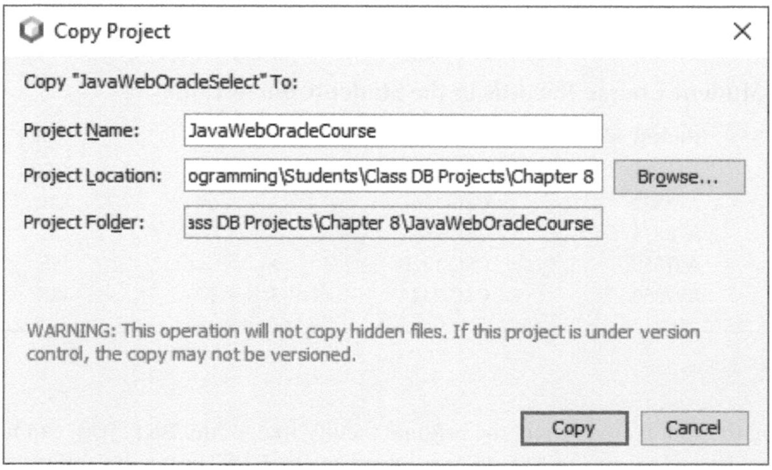

FIGURE 8.97 The opened Copy Project wizard.

8.6.1 Modify the Course.jsp Page

The **Course.jsp** page works as a client or a view to provide the display function for all user input and query results. We need to modify this page to enable it to forward the user's inputs to the controller page, **CourseProcess.jsp**, and furthermore to call the Java Model or Java Bean **CourseQuery.java** to process our data query. Also this client page needs to return to the **Selection.jsp** page if the user clicks on the **Back** button.

First let's do some modifications on this page to add two functions:

1) Add a **Details** button under the CourseList box, since we need this button to trigger an event on the **CourseProcess.jsp** page and Java Bean to retrieve the course details related to a **course _ id** if it is selected from the CourseList box by the user.
2) Add a piece of JSTL code to collect all **course _ id** values retrieved from the database and display them in the CourseList box.

Two methods can be used to add the **Details** button; one is to use a piece of JSP code and add it directly into the **Course.jsp** file, and the other is to use Microsoft Office Publisher 2007 to graphically add the button to the **Course.html** page and then save it as a JSP page. Here we try to use the first way to add this button, since it is easier.

Open this page by double-clicking on it in the **Projects** window, and perform the modifications shown in Figure 8.98 to this page. All modified code is in bold. Let's have a closer look at this piece of modified code to see how it works.

A. Since we need to use the JSTL core with embedded C tags in this page to dynamically populate the CourseList box, we need to include that library first.
B. Use this piece of code to replace the original code for this **<select></select>** tag (around line 321). The purpose of this piece of code is to populate all fetched **course _ id** values in the CourseList box for a selected faculty member by the user. All **course _ id** values will be retrieved and collected from our database and stored in a HashMap list object later in our Java Bean class. The name of that HashMap object is **c _ course**, which contains two columns, **key** and **value**. The former represents a key for a **course _ id**, and the latter is the **course _ id** value. The syntax ${} is used to store a value for a variable in JSTL C tags. A **<c:forEach>** tag is used for **course _ id** population purposes.
C. Copy this piece of code and add it directly under the **</select>** tag. The purpose of this piece of code is to add a **Details** button just under the CourseList box in the **Course.jsp** page to enable users to click it to trigger an event to get details for a selected **course _ id** from the CourseList box by the user.
D. From step D through step I, we use the embedded JSP code to assign the selected and queried course columns from our **Course** Table to the **value** tags of the associated text field in **Course.jsp** using the **getAttribute()** method of the session class. In this way, if a queried course row has any change, it will be immediately reflected in each text field in our **Course.jsp** page. Thus, a direct binding between the text fields in our **Course.jsp** page and the queried course columns in our Java Bean class is established.
J. In steps J to N, a **name** attribute is added to each **Submit** button tag. This attribute is very important, since we need to use it to identify each submit button on the next page, our controller page, **CourseProcess.jsp**, using the **getParameter()** method of the **request** object to direct control to the different pages to handle different data query and data manipulation actions in the **Course** Table in our sample Oracle database, **CSE _ DEPT**.

```
A  <%@ taglib uri = "http://java.sun.com/jsp/jstl/core" prefix = "c" %>
   .........
   <form method=post action=".\CourseProcess.jsp">
   .........
   <v:imagedata src="" o:title="&lt;EMPTY&gt;"/><v:shadow color="#ccc [4]"/>
   .........
B  <select name="c_course" size=7 v:shapes="_x0000_s1027">
    <c:forEach items="${c_course}" var="c_course">
      <option value="${c_course.key}">${c_course.value}</option>
   </c:forEach>
   </select>
C  <input type=submit value="Details" name="Details" v:shapes="_x0000_s1040">
   <![if !pub]></span><![endif]><!--[if gte vml 1]><v:shape id="_x0000_s1039"
    type="#_x0000_t201" style='position:absolute;left:75pt;top:150pt;width:39.75pt;
    height:17.25pt;z-index:14' stroked="f" insetpen="t" o:cliptowrap="t"> <v:path insetpenok="f"/>
    <o:lock v:ext="edit" rotation="t" text="t"/></v:shape><![endif]--><![if !pub]><span
   style='position:absolute;top:170.0pt; left:75.0pt;z-index:14'><![endif]>
   .........
D  <input name=CourseIDField maxlength=255 size=22
    value="<%=session.getAttribute("courseID") %>" type=text v:shapes="_x0000_s1029">
   .........
E  <input name=CourseNameField maxlength=255 size=22
    value="<%=session.getAttribute("courseName") %>" type=text v:shapes="_x0000_s1033">
   .........
F  <input name=ScheduleField maxlength=255 size=22
    value="<%=session.getAttribute("schedule") %>" type=text v:shapes="_x0000_s1035">
   .........
G  <input name=ClassroomField maxlength=255 size=22
    value="<%=session.getAttribute("classroom") %>" type=text v:shapes="_x0000_s1037">
   .........
H  <input name=CreditField maxlength=255 size=22
    value="<%=session.getAttribute("credit") %>" type=text v:shapes="_x0000_s1039">
   .........
I  <input name=EnrollmentField maxlength=255 size=22
    value="<%=session.getAttribute("enrollment") %>" type=text v:shapes="_x0000_s1041">
   .........
J  <input type=submit value=Select name="Select" v:shapes="_x0000_s1044">
   .........
K  <input type=submit value=Insert name="Insert" v:shapes="_x0000_s1045">
   .........
L  <input type=submit value=Update name="Update" v:shapes="_x0000_s1046">
   .........
M  <input type=submit value=Delete name="Delete" v:shapes="_x0000_s1047">
   .........
N  <input type=submit value=Back name="Back" v:shapes="_x0000_s1048">
   .........
O  <input name=FacultyNameField maxlength=255 size=22 value=" <%=session.getAttribute("facultyName")%>"
    type=text v:shapes="_x0000_s1045">
   .........
```

FIGURE 8.98 The modified code for the Course.jsp page.

O. Similar to steps D through I, the `facultyName` variable in our Java Bean class is bound to this `FacultyNameField` in this page to set a connection between that variable and the TextField on this page.

A view of the modified `Course.jsp` page is shown in Figure 8.99. Now let's take a look at our controller page, `CourseProcess.jsp`.

8.6.2 Create the CourseProcess.jsp Page

The purpose of this page is to direct control to the different help class files based on the button clicked by the user on the `Course.jsp` page. The following Java Bean class files will be triggered and executed based on the button clicked by the user on the `Course.jsp` page:

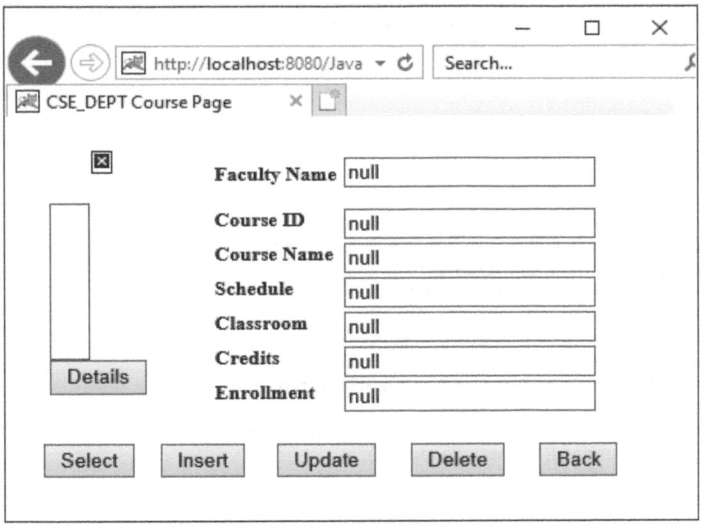

FIGURE 8.99 The modified Course.jsp page.

1) If the user clicked the **Select** button, control will be directed to the course data query Java Bean class file **CourseQuery.java** to perform the course record query function.
2) If the user clicked the **Insert** button, control will be directed to the course data insertion Java Bean class file **CourseInsertBean.java** to do the course record insertion.
3) If the user clicked the **Update** or **Delete** button, control will be directed to the course record update and delete Java Bean class file **CourseUpdateDeleteBean.java** to perform the associated data manipulation.
4) If the user clicked the **Back** button, control will be returned to the **Selection.jsp** page to enable users to perform other information query operations.

Now let's create the **CourseProcess.jsp** page.

Right-click on our **JavaWebOracleCourse** project in the **Projects** window and select the **New > JSP** item from the popup menu to open the **New JSP File** wizard. Enter **CourseProcess** in the **File Name** field and click on the **Finish** button.

Double-click on our new created **CourseProcess.jsp** page in the **Projects** window, under the **Web Pages** folder, to open this page. Enter the code shown in Figure 8.100 into this page. The new entered code is in bold.

Now let's have a closer look at this code to see how it works.

A. You can embed any import directory using the JSP directive in a HTML or a JSP file. The format is **<%@ page import="java package" %>**. In this page, we embed one package, **JavaWebOracleSelectPackage.***, since we will build our Java Bean class file **CourseQuery.java** under that package in the next section. We also embed a Java library, **java.util.HashMap**, since we need it to build our HashMap object list, **c _ course**.
B. Here a String array, **C _ Field[]**, is generated, and its purpose is to map to six fields in the **Course.jsp** page. In fact, we can use this array to clean up all those fields when users forget to input a faculty name for the course data query.
C. A new instance of our Java Bean class, **CourseQuery**, that will be created in the next section, **cQuery**, is created since we need to use properties and methods defined in that class to perform course data query functions.

```
A  <%@ page import="JavaWebOracleSelectPackage.*" %>
   <%@ page import="java.util.HashMap" %>
   <%@ page contentType="text/html" pageEncoding="UTF-8"%>
   <html>
     <head>
       <meta http-equiv="Content-Type" content="text/html; charset=UTF-8">
       <title>Course Process Page</title>
     </head>
     <body>
      <%
B     String[] C_Field = {"courseID","courseName","schedule","classroom","credit","enrollment"};
C     CourseQuery cQuery = new CourseQuery();
D     if (request.getParameter("Select")!= null) {
        //process the faculty record query
E       String fname = request.getParameter("FacultyNameField");
F       cQuery.getCourse(fname);
G       session.setAttribute("facultyName", cQuery.getFacultyName());
        session.setAttribute("c_course", cQuery.c_course);
H       RequestDispatcher requestDispatcher = request.getRequestDispatcher("/Course.jsp");
        requestDispatcher.forward(request, response);
      }
I     else if (request.getParameter("Details")!= null) {
J       String key = request.getParameter("c_course");
K       HashMap selCourse = (HashMap)session.getAttribute("c_course");
L       String cid = (String)selCourse.get(key);
        if (cid != null) {
M         boolean res = cQuery.QueryCourse(cid);
N         if (!res) {
            for (int index = 1; index < 7; index++)
              session.setAttribute(C_Field[index], null);
          }
O         else {
            session.setAttribute("courseID", cQuery.getCourseID());
            session.setAttribute("courseName", cQuery.getCourseName());
            session.setAttribute("credit", cQuery.getCredit());
            session.setAttribute("classroom", cQuery.getClassroom());
            session.setAttribute("schedule", cQuery.getSchedule());
            session.setAttribute("enrollment", cQuery.getEnrollment());
          }
P         response.sendRedirect("Course.jsp");
        }
Q     } else if (request.getParameter("Insert")!= null) {
          //process the course record insertion
          }
R       else if (request.getParameter("Update")!= null) {
          //process the course record updating
          }
S       else if (request.getParameter("Delete")!= null) {
          //process the course record deleting
          }
T       else if (request.getParameter("Back") != null) {
          cQuery.CloseDBConnection();
          response.sendRedirect("Selection.jsp");
          }
      %>
    </body>
    </html>
```

FIGURE 8.100 The code for the CourseProcess.jsp page.

D. The **`getParameter()`** method defined in the session class is executed to identify which submit button has been clicked by the user in the **`Course.jsp`** page. As you know, in all, we have five buttons on the **`Course.jsp`** page. All form data, including all text fields, list boxes and submit buttons, will be submitted to the **`CourseProcess.jsp`** page when any of five buttons is clicked. If a button is clicked, the **`getParameter()`** method with the name of that clicked button as the argument will return a non-null value. In this way, we can identify which button has been clicked. We use a sequence of **if-else if** selection structures to check all five buttons to identify the clicked button.

E. If the **Select** button is clicked by the user, the **getParameter()** method with the button's name as argument will return a non-null value. This means that the user wants to perform a course record query from the **Course** Table in our sample database. Again, the **getParameter()** method with the name of the faculty name field, **FacultyNameField**, is used to pick up a desired faculty name that is entered by the user from the **Course.jsp** page. The picked-up faculty name is assigned to a local String variable, **fname**.

F. Then the method **getCourse()** defined in the Java Bean class file **CourseQuery.java** is called to query all courses, that is, all **course_id** values, based on the selected faculty name, **fname**, obtained from step E.

G. If the **getCourse()** method is executed successfully, which means that all matching **course_id** values have been retrieved and stored in our HashMap object list, **c_course**, a session method, **setAttribute()**, is used to pass the HashMap list from the server side to the client page, **Course.jsp**, to enable the latter to recognize and use it later. The **facultyName** variable is also passed to the client page to make sure that it is displayed correctly in that client page after a new refreshed page is sent back from the server.

H. A system method, **getRequestDispatcher()**, and the **forward()** method are used to pass the variables or objects to the client page, **Course.jsp**. The forward slash indicates that the page is located in the current folder.

I. If the **Details** button is clicked by the user, it means that all course (**course_id**) for the selected faculty member have been retrieved and displayed in the CourseList box in our **Course.jsp** page. When users click a **course_id** from that CourseList box, we need to generate code to query details for that selected **course_id** and display them in six TextFields in our client page.

J. First we need to pick up the key for the selected **course_id** since all **course_id** values are stored in a HashMap list, **c_course**, with an associated key that is an integer sequence number represented as a string, such as "1", "2" and so on. Here the system method **getParameter()** is used for that purpose. A point is that this method can only return a String. But the **c_course** is a HashMap object list. The result of executing this method is to return a key value, since it is the first variable in that list.

K. An instance of our HashMap class, **selCourse**, is generated and assigned with our HashMap object list, **c_course**. A session method, **getAttribute()**, is used to transfer the HashMap object from our Java Bean class to this controller page. The class HashMap must be prefixed to this method to convert the object to the HashMap list. This system method is a popular way to transfer objects among JSP pages as long as they are in the same session.

L. The **get(key)** method of the HashMap class is executed to obtain the selected **course_id** value related to the key obtained in step J. The obtained **course_id** is assigned to a local String variable, **cid**, to be used in the next step.

M. If the **cid** variable contains a valid value, the **QueryCourse()** method that will be built in our Java Bean class later is called to get all the details for the obtained **course_id**.

N. If the execution of the method **QueryCourse()** fails, a **false** is returned to indicate this. In that case, we need to cleanup all six TextFields by setting them to **null** with a **for()** loop. The system method **setAttribute()** and the string array **C_Field[]** are used for that purpose.

O. Otherwise, the query is successful. The **setAttribute()** method is used to set up all properties defined in the Java Bean class file with database query results by using the associated getter methods in that class.

P. The system method **sendRedirect()** is issued by the server to direct control back to our client page, **Course.jsp**, to reflect and display all of the query results on that page.

Q. From step Q to step S, a sequence of **getParameter()** methods are used to identify which button on the client page has been clicked. A non-null value will be returned if a button, such as Insert, Update or Delete, has been clicked by the user. We will build a related Java bean class to handle these related queries later.

T. If the **getParameter("Back")** method returns a non-null value, it means that the **Back** button has been clicked by the user in the **Course.jsp** page and the user wants to return to the **Selection.jsp** page to perform other data query operations. The **CloseDBConnection()** method is first executed to close the connection to our sample database, and then the **sendRedirect()** method is called to do this return function.

Now let's build our Java Bean class or Java model file, **CourseQuery.java**, to handle all course data query actions, getter methods, class properties and related business logic.

8.6.3 Create the Java Bean or Java Model File, CourseQuery.java

To create our Java help class file, **CourseQuery.java**, to handle the course record query, right-click on our project, **JavaWebOracleCourse**, in the **Projects** window and select the **New > Java Class** item from the popup menu to open the **New Java Class** wizard. Enter **CourseQuery** in the **Class Name** field and select **JavaWebOracleSelectPackage** from the **Package** combo box. Click on the **Finish** button to create the new Java help class file.

Now let's develop the code for the new Java Bean class file. Double-click on our new created Java Bean class file, **CourseQuery.java**, in the **Projects** window to open this file, and enter the code shown in Figure 8.101 into this file. Because of the large size of this piece of code, we divide this coding process into two parts. The first part is shown in Figure 8.101, and the second part is shown in Figure 8.102. The new entered code is in bold.

Let's have a close look at the new added code in Figure 8.101 to see how it works.

A. A group of libraries and a package are imported first, since all Oracle database-related classes and data operation methods are defined in those libraries and packages. A java.util.HashMap library is also imported here, since we need some classes defined in that library to build our HashMap object list, **c_course**.

B. Seven local properties related to the associated columns in the **Course** and **Faculty** Tables in our sample database are declared first. These properties are very important, since they are directly mapped to the associated columns in those Tables. All of these properties can be accessed by using the associated **getter()** method defined at the bottom of this class.

C. A **public** HashMap object, **c_course**, is declared and initialized to null, and we will build this object by filling in all queried **course_id** values to this list later. In fact, this object can be defined as a **private** object and can be accessed by calling a **getter()** method, **get_CourseID()**, defined in the second part of the code for this class. Here we just define it as **public** to make it easy to access.

D. A static or a class level connection object, **con**, is defined here to let it be accessed by all methods defined in this class file.

E. Inside the constructor of this class, a database connection process is executed to connect to our sample database, and the connection object is stored in the class-level object, **con**.

F. A user-defined method, **CloseDBConnection()**, is defined, and it is used to close the database connection if all data queries are completed.

G. Another user-defined method, **getCourse()**, is defined here with a faculty name as the input argument. The function of this method is to perform a database query to retrieve all matching **course_id** values based on a selected faculty member and fill those **course_id** values into our HashMap object list, **c_course**, which will be used by our Controller **CourseProcess.jsp** to display them in the CourseList box located at our client **Course.jsp** later.

```
A  package JavaWebOracleSelectPackage;
   import java.sql.*;
   import java.util.HashMap;
   public class CourseQuery {
B    private String courseID;
     private String courseName;
     private String credit;
     private String classroom;
     private String schedule;
     private String enrollment;
     private String facultyName;
C    public HashMap c_course = null;
D    static Connection con;
E    public CourseQuery() {
       try {
            Class.forName("oracle.jdbc.OracleDriver");
         }
         catch (Exception e) {
            System.out.println("Class not found exception!" + e.getMessage());
         }
         String url = "jdbc:oracle:thin:@localhost:1521:XE";
         try {
            con = DriverManager.getConnection(url,"CSE_DEPT","oracle_18c");
         }
        catch (SQLException e) {
            System.out.println("Could not connect!" + e.getMessage());
            e.printStackTrace();
       }
     }
F    public void CloseDBConnection()
     {
       try{
         if (con != null)
           con.close();
       }catch (SQLException e)  {
         System.out.println("Error in close the DB! " + e.getMessage());
       }
     }
G    public void getCourse(String fname) {
H      int index = 0;
       HashMap<String, String> sCourse = new HashMap<String, String>();
I      String query = "SELECT Course.course_id FROM Course JOIN Faculty " +
                      "ON (Course.faculty_id = Faculty.faculty_id) AND (Faculty.faculty_name = ?)";
J      if (fname.isEmpty()) setCourse(null);
K      try{
           PreparedStatement pstmt = con.prepareStatement(query);
           pstmt.setString(1, fname);
           ResultSet rs = pstmt.executeQuery();
L          while (rs.next()){
             sCourse.put(String.valueOf(index), rs.getString(1));
             index++;
           }
M          setCourse(sCourse);
N          setFacultyName(fname);
       }
O      catch (SQLException e) {
         System.out.println("Error in Statement! " + e.getMessage());
         setCourse(null);
       }
     }
```

FIGURE 8.101 The first part of the code for the Java Bean class CourseQuery.java.

H. First a local integer variable, **index**, is declared and initialized to zero, and it works as a key number to be inserted into our HashMap object list later to build our HashMap object. Also, an acting HashMap object, **sCourse**, is generated with a key and a value format; both are String variables.

I. A joint query method is used for the **course _ id** query operation. As you know, there is no **faculty _ name** column available in the **Course** Table, and the only available column in the **Course** Table is **faculty _ id**. Therefore for a given faculty name, one needs to perform two queries, one to the **Faculty** Table and the other to the **Course** Table, to get all desired **course _ id** values. The first query is used to get a matching **faculty _ id** based on the selected faculty name, and the second query gets all matching **course _ id** values based on the **faculty _ id**. It is more efficient to use this joint query to perform these queries.

J. To make sure of the correctness of this query, first we need to check whether the input faculty name argument is an empty or blank string. If it is, we will not build our HashMap object.

K. Then a **try-catch** block is used to perform the joint query to get all **course _ id** values.

L. To pick up all queried **course _ id** values, a **while()** loop is used with the **next()** method as the loop condition to collect all **course _ id** values. Because only one column is returned for this query, the method **getString(1)** is used to get that column. The **put()** method is used to build our HashMap object by filling each **course _ id** that is obtained from the **getString(1)** method as a value and each **index** that is converted to a String as the key.

M. This step is very important in building our real HashMap object, **c _ course**. A user-defined **setter()** method, **setCourse()**, which will be built in the second part of the code, is executed to assign our acting HashMap **sCourse** object to our real HashMap object, **c _ course**. The argument of this method is our acting HashMap object, **sCourse**.

N. Another user-defined **setter()** method, **setFacultyName()**, is also executed to make sure to display the selected faculty name in the FacultyNameField on our client **Course.jsp** page even if that page may be updated due to a refreshed page sent to the server.

O. The **catch** block is used to monitor and check any possible exception during the query and data operations. If any error happens, we will not build our HashMap object.

Now let's take care of the second part of the code for this Java Bean class, which is shown in Figure 8.102.

A. The user-defined method, **QueryCourse()**, is defined starting from here. The function of this method is to collect the details for each course (**course _ id**) selected by the user from the CourseList box in our client page and return and display them on our client page **Course.jsp**. The selected **course _ id** works as an input argument with this method.

B. The Oracle query statement is generated first to collect all details related to the selected or input **course _ id** that works as the query criterion.

C. A **try-catch** block is used to perform the course detail query with a **PreparedStatement**, and the collected result is assigned to a ResultSet object, **rs**.

D. A **while()** loop is used with the **rs.next()** method as the loop condition to repeatedly collect all course details and assign each of them to the associated property defined in our JavaBean class by using a sequence of **getString()** methods. A **true** is returned to the controller **CourseProcess.jsp** page to indicate the success of running this method.

E. The **catch** block is used to monitor and detect any possible exception when this query process is executed. A **false** will be returned if any error is encountered.

F. In steps **F** to **M**, a sequence of **getter()** methods are defined, and they are used to obtain and return each related property defined in this Java Bean class. These **getter()** methods include collecting all course details and our HashMap object, **c _ course**.

```
   .........
A  public boolean QueryCourse(String cid) {
B      String query = "SELECT course_id, course, credit, classroom, schedule, enrollment FROM Course " +
                      "WHERE course_id = ?";
C      try{
          PreparedStatement pstmt = con.prepareStatement(query);
          pstmt.setString(1, cid);
          ResultSet rs = pstmt.executeQuery();
D         while (rs.next()){
             courseID = rs.getString(1);
             courseName = rs.getString(2);
             credit = rs.getString(3);
             classroom = rs.getString(4);
             schedule = rs.getString(5);
             enrollment = rs.getString(6);
          }
          return true;
       }
E      catch (SQLException e) {
          System.out.println("Error in Statement! " + e.getMessage());
          setCourse(null);
          return false;
       }
    }
F   public String getCourseID() {
       return courseID;
    }
G   public String getCourseName() {
       return  courseName;
    }
H   public String getCredit() {
       return  credit;
    }
I   public String getClassroom() {
       return  classroom;
    }
J   public String getSchedule() {
       return  schedule;
    }
K   public String getEnrollment() {
       return  enrollment;
    }
L   public String getFacultyName() {
       return this.facultyName;
    }
M   public HashMap get_CourseID() {
       return c_course;
    }
N   public void setFacultyName(String f_name) {
       this.facultyName = f_name;
    }
O   public void setCourse(HashMap sCourse) {
       this.c_course = sCourse;
    }
  }
```

FIGURE 8.102 The second part of the code for the Java Bean class CourseQuery.java.

N. Steps N and O define two `setter()` methods used to set FacultyName and our HashMap object, `c _ course`, to the property in this class.

At this point, we have completed all code building and development for our Web application project. Now let's build and run our project to test the desired functions of the project.

Click on the `Clean and Build Main Project` button on the top to build the project, and then click on the `Run` button (green arrow button on the top) to run the project.

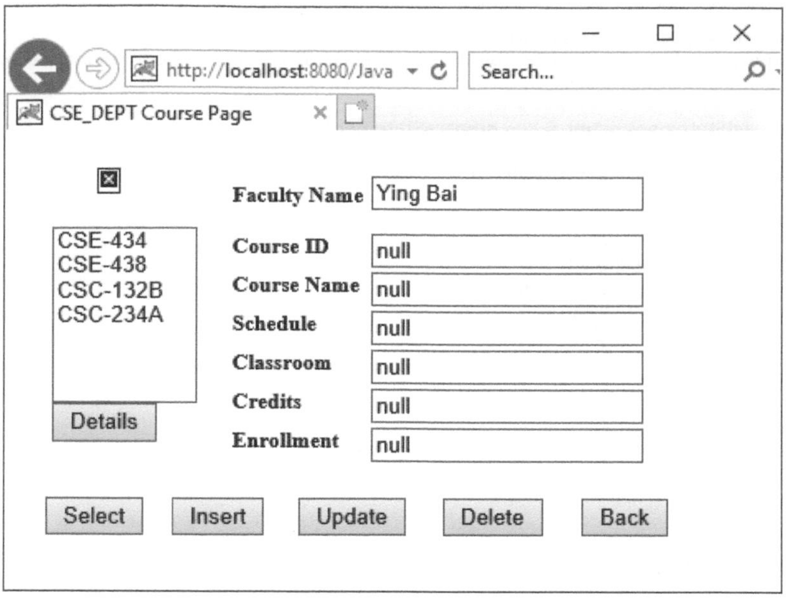

FIGURE 8.103 The run status of the Course.jsp page.

After the project is built and deployed, the LogIn page is displayed. Enter the appropriate username and password, such as **jhenry** and **test**, to complete the login process. Select the **Course Information** item from the Selection page and click on the **OK** button to open the **Course.jsp** page. Enter a desired faculty name, such as **Ying Bai**, into the Faculty Name box, and click on the **Select** button to select all courses (**course_id**) taught by this faculty member. All courses (**course_id**) taught by this faculty member are collected and displayed in the CourseList box, as shown in Figure 8.103.

Now select a desired **course_id**, such as CSC-132B, from the CourseList box by clicking on it, and click on the **Details** button to get all details about this course. All course details related to the course CSC-132B are collected and displayed in six TextFields on the right, as shown in Figure 8.104.

Our Web application project used to query the **Course** Table in our sample database is successful.

One can try to get course details for any other course to confirm the function of this project. Now click on the **Back** button to return to the Selection page, and click on the **Exit** button to terminate our project.

A complete Web application project, **JavaWebOracleCourse**, can be found in the folder **Class DB Projects\Chapter 8** in the **Students** folder on the CRC Press ftp site (refer to Figure 1.2 in Chapter 1).

8.7 CHAPTER SUMMARY

Most key techniques and knowledge in Java Web database programming are fully discussed and analyzed in this chapter with real project examples. The most popular and important techniques in Java Web database programming, such as JavaServer Pages (JSP), JavaServer Faces (JSF) and Enterprise Java Beans (EJB), are introduced and discussed in detail in different sections in this chapter.

Starting from an introduction to the fundamental Java Web server Servlets and HTML Web pages, a comprehensive historical review of Java Web application development and implementation

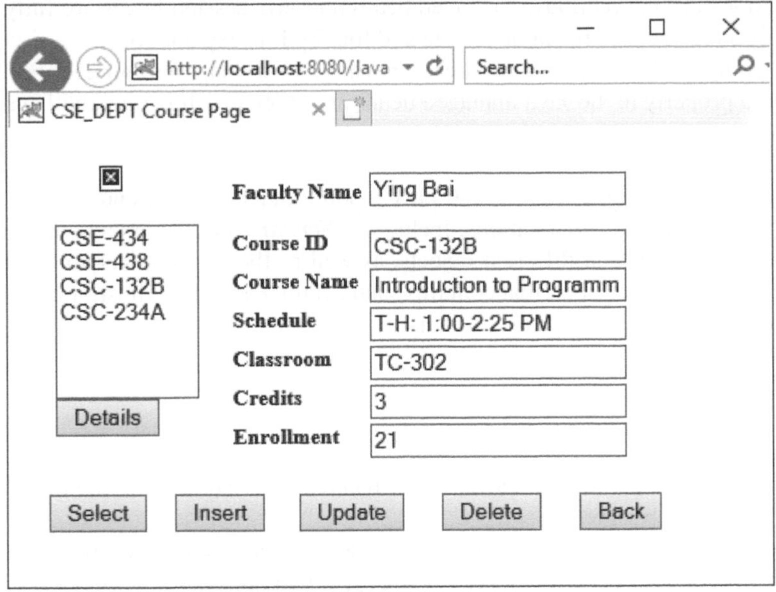

FIGURE 8.104 The run result of getting all course details.

is provided with example code. Then an introduction to the development of JavaServer Pages and Java help classes to improve Java Web database applications is given with some code examples.

To effectively improve and enhance the efficiency and quality of Java Web database applications, the Java core techniques, Java beans and Java enterprise edition (Java EE 7), are discussed and analyzed in detail with a few code examples.

Following a quick introduction to the Java EE Web application models, three actual Java Web database projects are introduced and discussed in detail.

The first project, **`JavaWebOracleSelect`**, which is built based on some key techniques listed previously, is used to access an Oracle 18c XE database with the runtime object method. Five popular Web pages, **`LogInPage.jsp`**, **`SelectionPage.jsp`**, **`FacultyPage.jsp`**, **`CoursePage.jsp`** and **`Student.jsp`**, which work as Web views, are built and developed with JSP techniques. The Tomcat server that works as a Web server and the Java help classes and Java beans that work as models are developed and implemented to provide users both a global and detailed picture of the process of Java Web database application building and development.

The second project, **`JavaWebOracleInsert`**, which is built based on the JSP and Java Bean techniques, is used to insert new records into the Oracle database with the help of Java Beans techniques. The binding relationships between each attribute of the tags in JSP pages and the associated property in the Java bean class are built and illustrated in detail with actual example code and step-by-step explanations in the coding process.

The third project, **`JavaWebOracleUpdateDelete`**, which is built based on JSP pages and Java Bean techniques, is used to manipulate the Oracle database.

Some important techniques and points in developing and building a successful Web database application are emphasized and highlighted as follows:

- Different data actions are performed and illustrated using the coding process and line-by-line explanations, including data query, data insertion and data update and delete actions.
- The Web project structure and navigation process are developed with the help of the Web configuration file, **`faces-config.xml`**, with actual examples and step-by-step illustrations.

- The relationships between Java managed beans and Java session beans are fully discussed and analyzed using actual example code and line-by-line explanations.
- The mapping relationships between each attribute in the tags on our JSP pages and the associated property in the Java managed beans are explicitly illustrated with a real coding process.

After finishing this chapter, readers will have a solid understanding and a clear and complete picture of Java Web database applications, including Web structures, components, navigation and mapping relationships between different objects, as well as the connections among those components. It hard to find a similar book that contains such detailed and clear illustrations on these topics about Java Web applications in the current market.

HOMEWORK

I. True/False Selections

_______1. When a Servlet is created, the **init**() method is called to do the initialization for the Web server.

_______2. When a request is received by the Servlet, it creates two objects; request and response. Then the Servlet sends these two objects to the **service**() method, in which these two objects are further processed.

_______3. Conventional Web applications are built with a Servlet as a Web container and JSF pages as Web clients.

_______4. Unlike a common gateway interface (CGI), a Servlet can be used to create dynamic Web pages during the server-client communication process.

_______5. To interface to the client to get user data, most of the time, the Web server calls the **getParameter**() method that belongs to the **request** object.

_______6. The so-called implicit objects in JSP are objects that are automatically available in JSP because they are automatically instantiated as the project runs.

_______7. Among those implicit objects, **request**, **response** and **session** are most popular objects and are often used in the interface between clients and servers.

_______8. To use a Java bean, the JSP provides three basic tags: <jsp:useBean id="**bean name**" class="**bean class**" scope = "page|request|session|application"/>

_______9. To embed any Java code into a HTML page, the JSP directive <%@ page /> must be used.

______10. Navigation from one page to another can be done in two ways. One is directly to use code by writing a JSP tag such as <jsp:forward /> or an HTML hyperlink in the JSF file. Another way that is provided by JSF is to use the application configuration resource file `faces-config.xml` to build navigation rules.

II. Multiple Choice

1. The <from-view-id> tag is used to define a navigation ____________.
   a. Source
   b. Terminal
   c. Destination
   d. None of these

2. To bind a Java bean's property to an associated attribute of a tag in the JSF page, one needs to use the ____________.
   a. Expression language (EL) with the syntax #(managedbean.property)
   b. Expression language (EL) with the syntax #{managedbean.property}

c. Expression language (EL) with the syntax #[managedbean.property]
d. Expression language (EL) with the syntax ${managedbean.property}

3. A typical Java bean class should contain ____________.
   a. All properties
   b. All properties, setter methods
   c. All properties, setter and getter methods
   d. All properties, setter and getter methods as well as user-defined methods
4. Java beans need to be conFigured in the Web configuration file **faces-config.xml** so that the implementation can automatically create a new ____________ of the beans as needed.
   a. Statement
   b. Method
   c. Instance
   d. Project
5. Before you can use a Servlet such as FacesServlet on the server side from a Web browser, you need to map the FacesServlet to a path in your deployment descriptor file ____________.
   a. Web pages
   b. WEB INF file
   c. Web configuration file
   d. web.xml
6. To separate presentation and business logic, we can use ____________ pages to present our GUI and the ____________ to store our data to perform business-related logic.
   a. HTML, Java help class
   b. XML, JSF pages
   c. JSP, Java beans
   d. JSF, JSP pages
7. All JSF tag components are represented by a tree of components whose root is UIViewRoot, which is represented by the ____________ tag. All JSF component tags must be enclosed in this ____________ tag.
   a. UIComponent
   b. UITree
   c. <h:form>
   d. <f:view>
8. A JSP form, which is submitted to the Web server when a button is clicked, is represented by the ____________ tag. The tags representing the form components, such as textfields and buttons, must be nested inside this tag.
   a. <f:form>
   b. <h:form>
   c. <h:view>
   d. <f:view>
9. If the required attribute is set to true, this means that the inputText ____________.
   a. Cannot be empty
   b. Must be filled with something by the user
   c. Both of these
   d. Neither of these

10. A Web application is a dynamic extension of a web or application server. There are two types of Web applications: __________ and __________.
    a. Dynamic, static
    b. Single-tier, multi-tier
    c. Web server, web client
    d. Presentation-oriented, service-oriented

III. Exercises

1. Provide a brief description of a Java EE three-tier Web application with EJB.
2. What is the difference between a Java EE with EJB and a Java EE without EJB?
3. What are popular Java EE components?
4. Provide a brief description to illustrate the interaction between a Web client and a Web application.
5. Provide a brief description of Java EE containers.
6. Refer to Section 8.4.5 to develop a Java Web application, **`JavaWebOracleStudent`**, to query the **`Student`** Table in our sample Oracle database, **`CSE _ DEPT`**, using JavaServer pages and the JSP implicit session object.

Hint 1: Copy the project **JavaWebOracleSelect** that is located in the folder **Class DB Projects\Chapter 8**, which is in the **Students** folder on the CRC Press ftp site (Refer to Figure 1.2 in Chapter 1). Modify that project and make it your new project.

Hint 2:Usean existing **Student.jsp** page located in the folder **HTML and JSP Pages** in the **Students** folder on the CRC Press ftp site (Refer to Figure 1.2 in Chapter 1). Modify that page based on Section 8.4.5.2 to make the desired **Student.jsp** page.

Hint 3: Create a **StudentProcess.jsp** page based on Section 8.4.5.3.

Hint 4: Create a Help or Java Bean class **StudentQuery.java** based on Section 8.4.5.4.

Hint 5: Create a new folder, **SImages**, in the project folder, **JavaWebOracleStudent\web**. Go to the CRC Press ftp site and copy all student images from the folder **Images\Students** in the **Students** folder and paste them into our created folder, **SImages**.

Hint6: Go to the site jstl-1.2.jar to download the**JSTL-1.2.jar** file and add it to the **Libraries** folder in your project, since we need to use the JSTL library for the JSTL **<c:>** tab in the **Student.jsp** page to display all courses taken by the student in the CourseList box.

Hint 7: Add the tab**<%@ taglib uri = "http://java.sun.com/jsp/jstl/core" prefix = "c" %>** to the top of the **Student.jsp** page to use the JSTL **<c:>** tab.

Hint 8: Add a public **HashMap** object, **s_course**, to the **StudentQuery.java** file. It is used to store all courses taken by the selected student.

Hint 9: Build a new method, **getStudentCourse**(), in the **StudentQuery.java** file to collect all courses (**course_id**) taken by the student and assign them to the HashMap **s_course** by building a setter, **setStudent_Course**(), in the same file.

Hint 10: Put the following code in the **StudentProcess.jsp** file, just under the sequence of **session.setAttribute()** methods to setup the connection between the Java Bean **StudentQuery.java** and the client page **Student.jsp** file:

```
sQuery.getStudentCourse(sQuery.getStudentID());
request.setAttribute("StudentQuery", sQuery);
request.setAttribute("s_course", sQuery.s_course);
RequestDispatcher requestDispatcher = request.getRequestDispatcher("/Student.jsp");
requestDispatcher.forward(request, response);
```

Hint 11: Put the following code on the Student.jsp page to replace the original code in the <select></select> tag:

```
<select name="s_course" multiple size=4 v:shapes="_x0000_s1029">
<c:forEach items="${s_course}" var="s_course">
<option value="${s_course.key}">${s_course.value}</option>
</c:forEach>
</select>
```

9 Develop Java Web Services to Access Databases

We provided a very detailed discussion of Java Web applications in the last chapter. In this chapter, we will concentrate on another Java Web-related topic—Java Web Services.

Unlike Java Web applications, in which the user needs to access the Web server through the client browser by sending requests to the server to obtain the desired information, Java Web Services provide an automatic way to search, identify and return the information required by the user through a set of methods installed in the Web server, and those methods can be accessed by a computer program, not the user, via the Internet. Another important difference between Java Web applications and Java Web services is that the latter do not provide any graphic user interfaces, and users need to create GUIs themselves to access Web services via the Internet.

After finishing this chapter, you will be able to

- Understand the basic popular Java Web services models
- Understand the structure and components of SOAP/WSDL-based Java Web services, such as simple object access protocol (SOAP); web services description language (WSDL); and universal description, discovery and integration (UDDI)
- Create correct SOAP namespaces for Web Services to make usernames and identifiers unique in the user's document
- Create suiTable security components to protect Web methods
- Build professional Java Web Service projects to access our sample database to obtain required information
- Build client applications to provide GUIs to consume a Web Service
- Build professional Java Web Service projects to access our sample database to insert new information into the database
- Build professional Java Web Service projects to access our sample database to update and delete information against the database

In order to help readers successfully complete this chapter, first we need to provide a detailed discussion of Java Web Services and their components.

9.1 INTRODUCTION TO JAVA WEB SERVICES

Web services are distributed application components that are externally useful and available. You can use them to integrate computer applications that are written in different languages and run on different platforms. Web services are language and platform independent because vendors have agreed on common Web service standards.

Essentially, Web Services can be considered a set of methods installed on a Web server that can be called by computer programs installed on clients through the Internet. Those methods can be used to locate and return the target information required by computer programs. Web Services do not require the use of browsers or HTML, and therefore Web Services are sometimes called *application services*.

A complete Web services stack, Metro, developed by Sun Microsystems, covers all of a developer's needs from simple Java Web services demonstrations to reliable, secure and transacted web services. Metro includes Web Services Interoperability Technologies (WSIT). WSIT supports

DOI: 10.1201/9781003304029-11

enterprise features such as security, reliability and message optimization. WSIT ensures that Metro services with these features are interoperable with Microsoft. NET services. Within Metro, Project Tango develops and evolves the codebase for WSIT.

Several programming models are available to Web service developers. These models can be categorized into two groups, and both are supported by the NetBeans IDE:

- **REST-based:RE** presentational **S**tate **T**ransfer is a new way to create and communicate with Web services. In REST, resources have uniform resource identifiers (URIs) and are manipulated through HTTP header operations.
- **SOAP/WSDL-based:** In traditional Web service models, Web service interfaces are exposed through WSDL documents (a type of XML), which have URLs. Subsequent message exchange is in SOAP, another type of XML document.

Let's have a little more discussion of these two kinds of Web services.

9.1.1 REST-Based Web Services

REST-based or RESTful Web services are collections of Web resources identified by URIs. Every document and process is modeled as a Web resource with a unique URI. These Web resources are manipulated by the actions that can be specified in an HTTP header. Neither SOAP, WSDL nor WS-* standards are used. Instead, message exchange can be conducted in any format—XML, JavaScript Object Notation (JSON), HTML and so on. In many cases, a Web browser can serve as the client.

HTTP is the protocol in REST. Only four methods are available: GET, PUT, POST and DELETE. Requests can be bookmarked and responses can be cached. A network administrator can easily follow what is going on with a RESTful service just by looking at the HTTP headers.

REST is a suiTable technology for applications that do not require security beyond what is available in the HTTP infrastructure and where HTTP is the appropriate protocol. REST services can still deliver sophisticated functionality. NetBeans IDE Software as a Service (SaaS) functionality lets you use Facebook, Zillow and other third-party-provided services in your own applications.

Project Jersey is the open-source reference implementation for building RESTful Web services. The Jersey APIs are available as the **RESTful Web Services** plug-in for NetBeans IDE.

RESTful Web services are services built using the RESTful architectural style. Building Web services using the RESTful approach is emerging as a popular alternative to using SOAP-based technologies for deploying services on the internet, due to its lightweight nature and the ability to transmit data directly over HTTP.

The NetBeans IDE supports rapid development of RESTful Web services using Java Specification Requests (JSR 311), a Java API for RESTful Web Services (JAX-RS) and Jersey, the reference implementation for JAX-RS.

In addition to building RESTful Web services, the NetBeans IDE also supports testing, building client applications that access RESTful Web services and generating code for invoking Web services (both RESTful and SOAP-based.)

Here is the list of RESTful features provided by the NetBeans IDE:

1) Rapid creation of RESTful Web services from JPA entity classes and patterns.
2) Rapid code generation for invoking Web services such as Google Map, Yahoo News Search and StrikeIron Web services by dragging and dropping components from the RESTful component palette.
3) Generation of JavaScript client stubs from RESTful Web services for building RESTful client applications.
4) Test client generation for testing RESTful Web services.

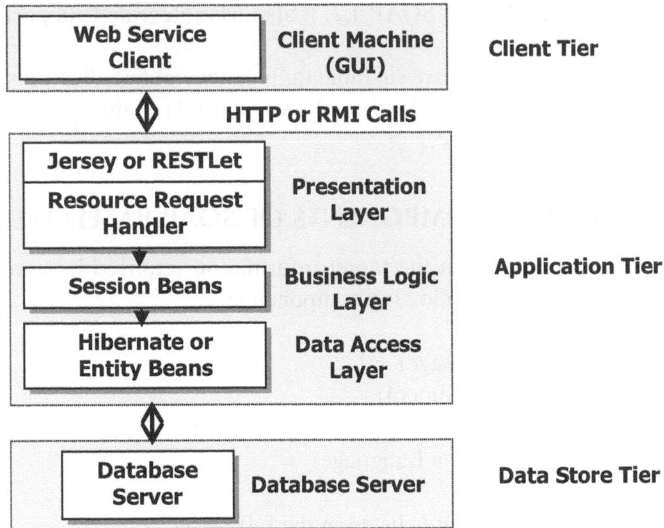

FIGURE 9.1 The architecture of multi-tier Web services.

5) Logical view for easy navigation of RESTful Web service implementation classes in the project.
6) Fully integrated Spring framework, providing Spring transaction handling.

A structure and architecture of using a RESTful model to build a Web service is shown in Figure 9.1.

Next let's take a look at SOAP-based Web services.

9.1.2 SOAP-Based Web Services

In SOAP-based Web services, Java utilities create a WSDL file based on the Java code in the Web service. The WSDL is exposed on the net. Parties interested in using the Web service create a Java client based on the WSDL. Messages are exchanged in SOAP format. The range of operations that can be passed in SOAP is much broader than what is available in REST, especially in security.

SOAP-based Web services are suitable for heavyweight applications using complicated operations and for applications requiring sophisticated security, reliability or other WS-* standards-supported features. They are also suiTable when a transport protocol other than HTTP has to be used. Many of Amazon's Web services, particularly those involving commercial transactions, and the Web services used by banks and government agencies are SOAP based.

The Java API for XML Web Services is the current model for SOAP-based Web services in Metro. JAX-WS is built on the earlier Java API for XML Remote Procedure Call (JAX-RPC) model but uses specific Java EE 7 features, such as annotations, to simplify the task of developing Web services. Because it uses SOAP for messaging, JAX-WS is transport neutral. It also supports a wide range of modular WS-* specifications, such as WS-Security and WS-ReliableMessaging.

When you create a Web service client, you have the option of using either the JAX-WS or JAX-RPC model. This is because some older JAX-RPC services use a binding style that is not supported by JAX-WS. These services can only be consumed by JAX-RPC clients.

Metro Web services are interoperable with Apache Axis2 Web services. Apache Axis2 is an open-source implementation of the SOAP submission to the W3C. Two popular implementations of the Apache Axis2 Web services engine are Apache Axis2/Java and Apache Axis2/C. In addition,

Axis2 not only supports SOAP 1.1 and SOAP 1.2, it also has integrated support for RESTful Web services.

Because SOAP-based Web services are suiTable for heavyweight applications using complicated operations and applications requiring sophisticated security and reliability, in this chapter, we will concentrate on this kind of Web service.

9.2 THE STRUCTURE AND COMPONENTS OF SOAP-BASED WEB SERVICES

To effectively find, identify and return the target information required by computer programs, a SOAP-based Web Service needs the following components:

1) XML (Extensible Markup Language)
2) SOAP (Simple Object Access Protocol)
3) UDDI (Universal Description, Discovery and Integration)
4) WSDL (Web Services Description Language)

The functionality of each component is listed in the following.

XML is a text-based data storage language and uses a series of tags to define and store data. That is, tags are used to mark up data to be exchanged between applications. The marked-up data then can be recognized and used by different applications without any problem. As you know, the Web Services platform is XML + HTTP, and the HTTP protocol is the most popular Internet protocol. However, XML provides a kind of language that can be used between different platforms and programming languages to express complex messages and functions. In order to make the code used in Web Services be recognized by applications developed in different platforms and programming languages, XML is used for coding in Web Services.

SOAP is a communication protocol used for communications between applications. Essentially, SOAP is a simple XML-based protocol to help applications developed in different platforms and languages exchange information over HTTP. Therefore, SOAP is a platform-independent and language-independent protocol, which means that it can be run on any operating system with any programming language. That is, SOAP works as a carrier to transfer data or requests between applications. Whenever a request is made to the Web server to request a Web Service, that request is first wrapped in a SOAP message and sent over the Internet to the Web server. Similarly, when the Web Service returns the target information to the client, the returned information is also wrapped in a SOAP message and sent over the Internet to the client browser.

WSDL is an XML-based language for describing Web Services and how to access them. In WSDL terminology, each Web Service is defined as an abstract endpoint or port, and each Web method is defined as an abstract operation. Each operation or method can contain SOAP messages to be transferred between applications. Each message is constructed by using the SOAP protocol when a request is made from the client. WSDL defines two styles for how a Web Service method can be formatted in a SOAP message: a remote procedure call (RPC) and document. Both RPC- and document-style messages can be used to communicate with a Web Service using a RPC.

A single endpoint can contain a group of Web methods, and that group of methods can be defined as an abstract set of operations called a port type. Therefore, WSDL is an XML format for describing network services as a set of endpoints operating on SOAP messages containing either document-oriented or procedure-oriented information. The operations and messages are described abstractly and then bound to a concrete network protocol and message format to define an endpoint.

UDDI is an XML-based directory for businesses to list themselves on the Internet, and the goal of this directory is to enable companies to find one another on the Web and make their systems interoperable for e-commerce. UDDI is often likened to a telephone book's yellow or white pages. By using those pages, it allows businesses to list themselves by name, product, location or the Web services they offer.

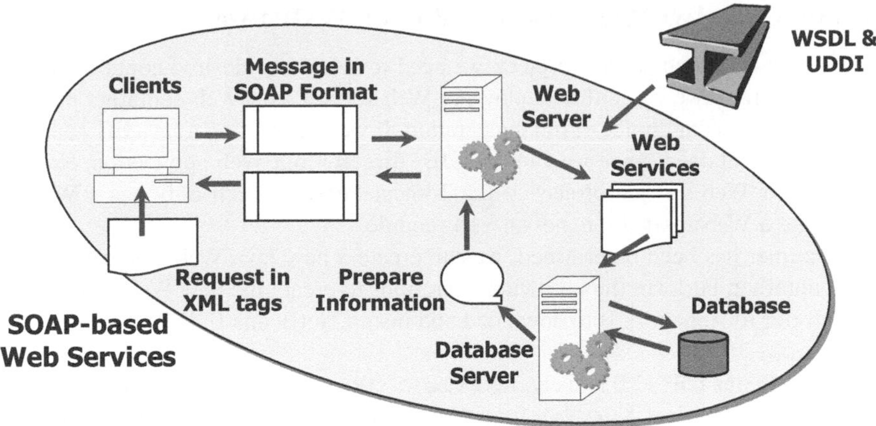

FIGURE 9.2 A typical process of a SOAP-based Web Service.

In summary, based on these components and their roles, we can conclude:

- XML is used to tag data to be transferred between applications
- SOAP is used to wrap data tagged in XML format in messages represented by the SOAP protocol
- WSDL is used to map a concrete network protocol and message format to an abstract endpoint and describe the Web services available in WSDL document format
- UDDI is used to list all Web Services that are available to users and businesses.
- Figure 9.2 illustrates these components and their roles in a Java Web Service process.

Now we have fundamental knowledge about SOAP-based Web Services and their components. Next let's see how to build a Web Service project.

9.3 THE PROCEDURE OF BUILDING A TYPICAL SOAP-BASED WEB SERVICE PROJECT

Different methods and languages can be used to develop various Web Services, such as C# Web Services, Java Web Services and Perl Web Services. In this section, we concentrate on developing Java Web Services using the NetBeans IDE. Prior to building a real Web Service project, let's first take a closer look at the procedure of building a Java Web Service project.

Unlike ASP.NET Web service applications, a Java SOAP-based Web service project is included in a Java Web application project in which the Web service can be deployed based on an appropriate container. Once a Java Web application project has been created with a desired container, you can create a new Java Web service project in the Web application project.

Usually, to build and implement a Java SOAP-based Web service project, you need to follow these steps:

1) Create a new Java Web application project with an appropriate container.
2) Create a new Java SOAP-based Web service project.
3) Add desired operations (methods) to the Web service to build desired functions for the Web service.
4) Deploy and test the Web service in the selected container.
5) Create Web service clients to consume the developed Java Web service.

Next let's use a simple Web service example, **`WSTestApp`**, to illustrate these steps.

9.3.1 Create a New Java Web Application Project, WSTestApp

Prior to creating a new Web service project, we need to select our desired container to deploy our Web service. Generally we can either deploy our Web service in a Web container or an EJB container. This depends on our choice of implementation. If we are creating a Java EE 7 application, we should use a Web container, since we can put EJBs directly in a Web application. However, if we plan to deploy our Web service project to the Tomcat Server, which only has a Web container, we need to create a Web application, not an EJB module.

After a container has been determined, we can create a new Java Web application project with the selected container. Perform the following operations to create the new Web application project, **WSTestApp** (refer to Appendix B to download and install NetBeans IDE 12.0):

1) Launch NetBeans IDE 12.0 and choose **File > New Project**. Then expand the **Java with Ant** folder, select **JavaWeb** from the Categories list and select **Web Application** from the **Projects** list. Then click on the **Next** button. You may need to download and activate the Java Web and EE libraries when you open this IDE the first time. Just click on the **Download and Activate** button and follow the instructions to complete the process.
2) Name the project **WSTestApp** and click on the **Browse** button to select a desired location for the project. In this application, we used **C:\Class DB Projects\Chapter 9** as our project location. Click on the **Next** button to continue.
3) In the opened Server and Settings wizard, Click on the **Add** button on the right of the Server combo box, select the **GlassFish Server** item from the list as our Web container and click on the **Next** button to open the Server Location wizard, as shown in Figure 9.3.
4) Keep the default given location to save our GlassFish Server, as shown in Figure 9.3. But you can select another location to save this server if you like.
5) Check the **license agreement** checkbox, select the **GlassFish Server 5.1.0** from the combo box and click on the **Download Now** button to download GlassFish Server 5.1.0. Your finished Server Location wizard should match the one shown in Figure 9.4. Click on the **Next** button to continue.
6) In the next wizard, Domain Location, just keep all default settings with no change and click on the **Finish** button to register our Web Server.

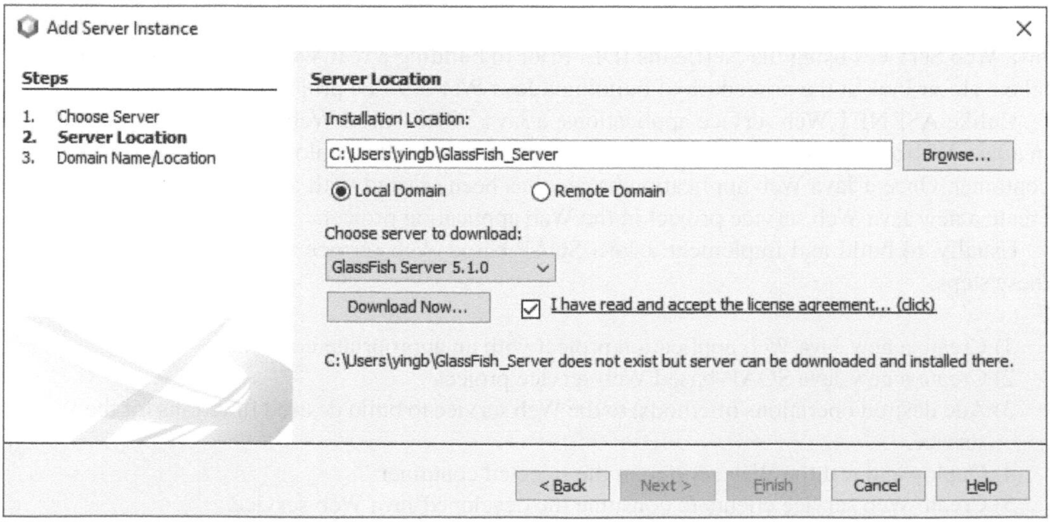

FIGURE 9.3 The opened Server Location wizard.

Add Server Instance

Steps

1. Choose Server
2. **Server Location**
3. Domain Name/Location

Server Location

Installation Location:

C:\Users\yingb\GlassFish_Server | Browse...

Local Domain | Remote Domain

Choose server to download:

GlassFish Server 5.1.0

Download Complete | I have read and accept the license agreement... (click)

Download & Install completed in 5 minutes, 10 seconds.

Detected a GlassFish Server 5.1.0 install. Click Next to register remote or custom local domains.

< Back | Next > | Finish | Cancel | Help

FIGURE 9.4 The finished Server Location wizard.

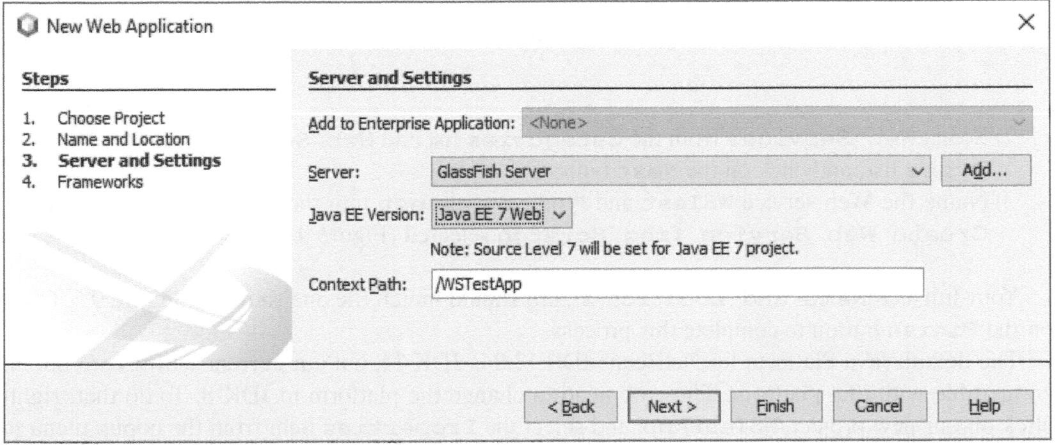

FIGURE 9.5 The opened Server and Settings wizard.

7) In the next wizard, Server and Settings, select the **`Java EE 7 Web`** from the **`Java EE Version`** combo box, as shown in Figure 9.5, and click on the **`Next`** button to continue.
8) In the next wizard, Frameworks, just keep all default settings with no change and click on the **`Finish`** button to complete the Web project creation process.

Now that a Web application has been created with a selected Web container, next we can create our new Web service project, **`WSTest`**.

9.3.2 Create a New Java SOAP-Based Web Service Project WSTest

The function of this Web service is to add two integers together and return the result. Perform the following operations to create this new Web service project **`WSTest`**:

1) In the opened **`Projects`** window, right-click on our new created project, **`WSTestApp`**, and select the **`New > Other`** menu item to open the **`New File`** wizard.

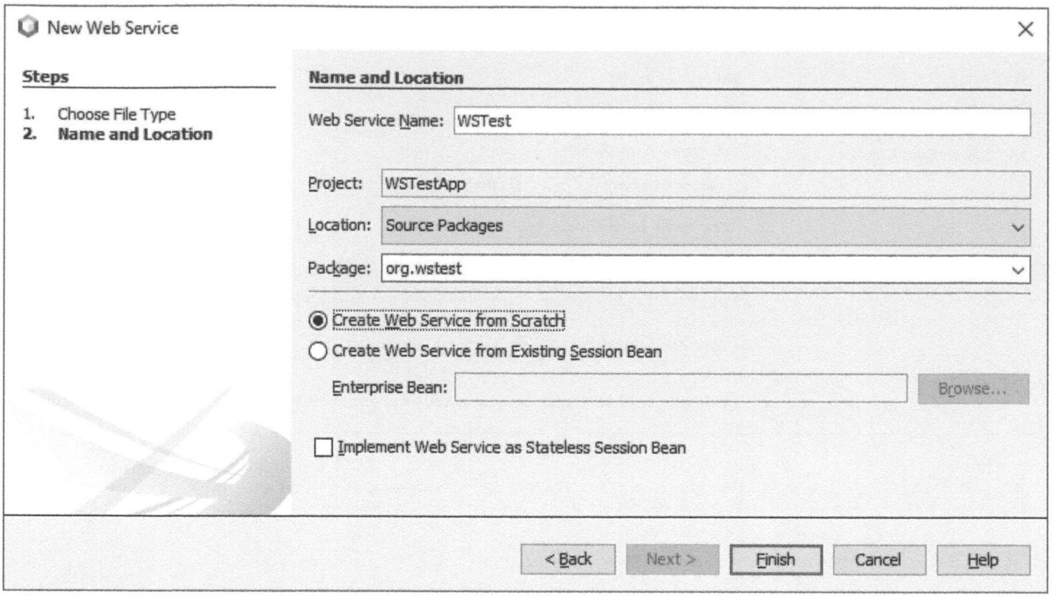

FIGURE 9.6 The finished Name and Location wizard.

2) Select **Web Services** from the **Categories** list and **Web Service** from the **File Types** list, and click on the **Next** button.
3) Name the Web service **WSTest** and type **org.wstest** into the **Package** field. Leave **Create Web Service from Scratch** selected (Figure 9.6).

Your finished **Name and Location** wizard should match the one shown in Figure 9.6. Click on the **Finish** button to complete this process.

The default Java Platform for NetBeans IDE 12.0 is JDK 14, but our current settings are not all compatible with that platform. Thus, we need to change the platform to JDK 8. To do that, right-click on our new project, **WSTestApp**, and select the **Properties** item from the popup menu to open the Project Properties wizard for this project.

In the opened Project Properties wizard, click on the **Libraries** node under the **Categories** list, click on the drop-down arrow in the **Java Platform** box and select **JDK 1.8** from the box. Your finished Project Properties wizard is shown in Figure 9.7.

If you cannot find the JDK 1.8 platform, click on the **Manage Platforms** button on the right of the Java Platform box to open the Java Platform Manager wizard. Perform the following steps to add the JDK 1.8 Platform to our project:

1) Click on the **Add Platform** button located at the lower-left corner to open the Select platform type wizard.
2) Keep the default type, **Java Standard Edition**, and click on the **Next** button.
3) Browse to the location where the JDK 1.8 was installed; in our case, **C:\Program Files\Java\jdk1.8.0_271**. Click on this item to select it and click on the **Next** button.
4) In the next wizard, Platform Name, just keep all default settings and click on the **Finish** button to complete this process. Click on the **Close** button to close the Manager wizard.

Now click on the drop-down arrow in the **Java Platform** box, select **JDK 1.8** from the box to change the platform and click on the **OK** button to confirm the change.

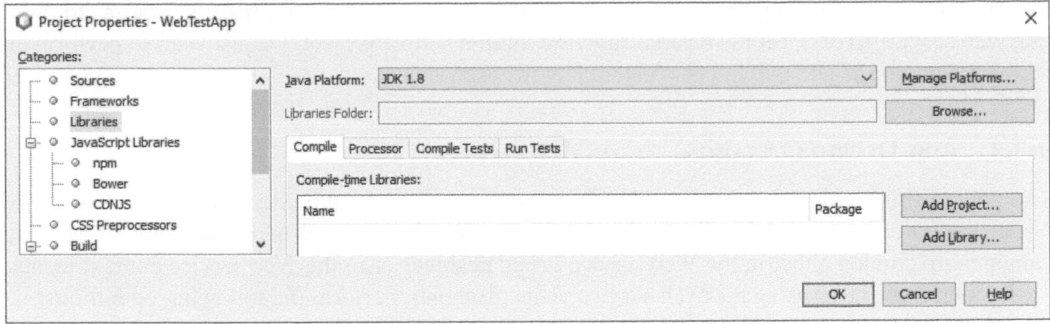

FIGURE 9.7 The finished Project Properties wizard.

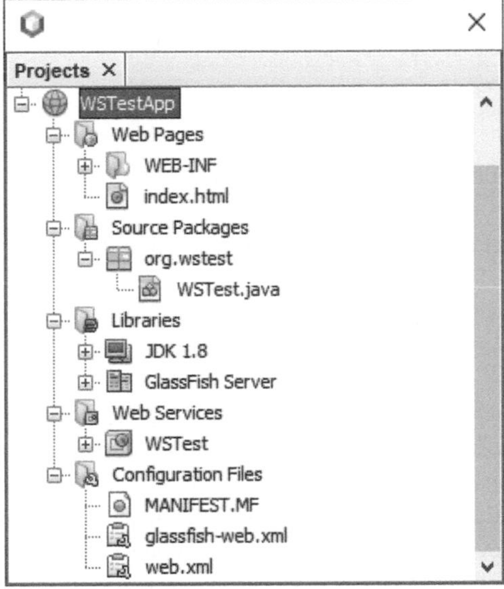

FIGURE 9.8 New added components for our new Web service project.

After a new Web service project, **`WSTest`**, is created with the changed platform, the following components are added into our Web application, **`WSTestApp`**:

1) A new node named **`org.wstest`** with a new Java class, **`WSTest.java`**, has been added to the **`Source Packages`** node in our application. The Java class file **`WSTest.java`** is the main body of this Web service, and all functions of this Web service should be performed by adding operations or methods into this class.
2) A new node named **`Web Services`** with a new icon, **`WSTest`**, has been added into our Web application. This **`WSTest`** icon is our target Web service output file that can be tested later when it is built.
3) A new file named **`web.xml`** has been added into the **`Configuration Files`** node in our project. This file is called the Web deployment descriptor file, and it is used to define how to deploy our Web service on a server.
4) Some Metro Web service libraries have also been added into the **`Libraries`** node in our project to provide support to our Web service development.
5) All of these new added components are shown in Figure 9.8.

Now we can add new operations or methods into our main body class, **WSTest.java**, to build our Web service to perform the desired function. In this simple project, we just want to perform an addition function to add two integers entered by the user via a client.

9.3.3 Add Desired Operations to the Web Service

The goal of this service project is to add two integers received from a client via an operation. The NetBeans IDE 12.0 provides a dialog for adding an operation or a method to a Web service. You can open this dialog either in the Web service visual designer or in the Web service context menu.

To open this dialog using the Web service visual designer, perform the following operations:

- Open our Web service main file, **WSTest.java**, by double-clicking on it in the **Projects** window.
- Click on the **Design** button at the top of this window.

To open this dialog using the Web service context menu:

- Find our target Web service output file, **WSTest**, from the **Web Services** node in the **Projects** window.
- Right-click on that node to open the context menu.

In the opened service designer, right-click on the default operation, **hello**, and select the **Remove Operation** item from the popup menu to remove this default operation, since we do not need it. Then click on **Add Operation**, and a dialog box appears to enable us to add and define a new operation. Perform these steps to add a new addition operation or method:

1) In the upper part of the **Add Operation** dialog box, type **Add** in the **Name** field and **int** in the **Return Type** drop-down list. In the lower part of the **Add Operation** dialog box, click on the **Add** button and create a parameter with a type **int** named **Input1**. Then click on the **Add** button again and create the second parameter with a type **int** called **Input2**. Your finished **Add Operation** dialog should match the one shown in Figure 9.9.
2) Click on the **OK** button to close this dialog. The new added operation is displayed in the visual designer, as shown in Figure 9.10.
3) Click on the **Source** button at the top of this window to open the code window of the Web service main body file, and you can see that our new Web operation or method **Add()** has been added into this class, as shown in Figure 9.11.
4) In the opened WebMethod **Add()**, enter this code into the method:

```
int result = Input1 + Input2;
return result;
```

At this point, we have finished developing our Web service project, and next we need to deploy it to the selected Web container and test it with some consuming projects.

9.3.4 Deploy and Test the Web Service on the Selected Container

The NetBeans IDE provides a server test client to help us test our Web service after it has been successfully deployed. Perform the following operations to deploy our Web service to our Web container, GlassFish:

1) Click on the **Clean and Build Main Project** button on the top to build our project. Then right-click on our project, **WSTestApp**, in the **Projects** window and choose

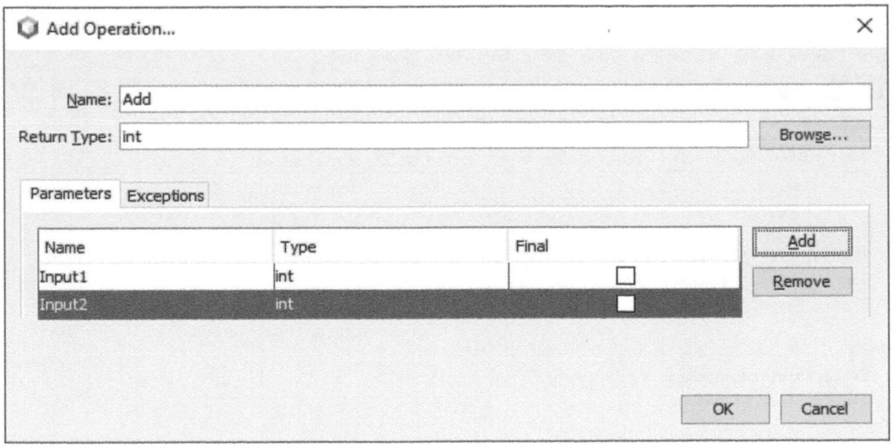

FIGURE 9.9 The finished Add Operation dialog.

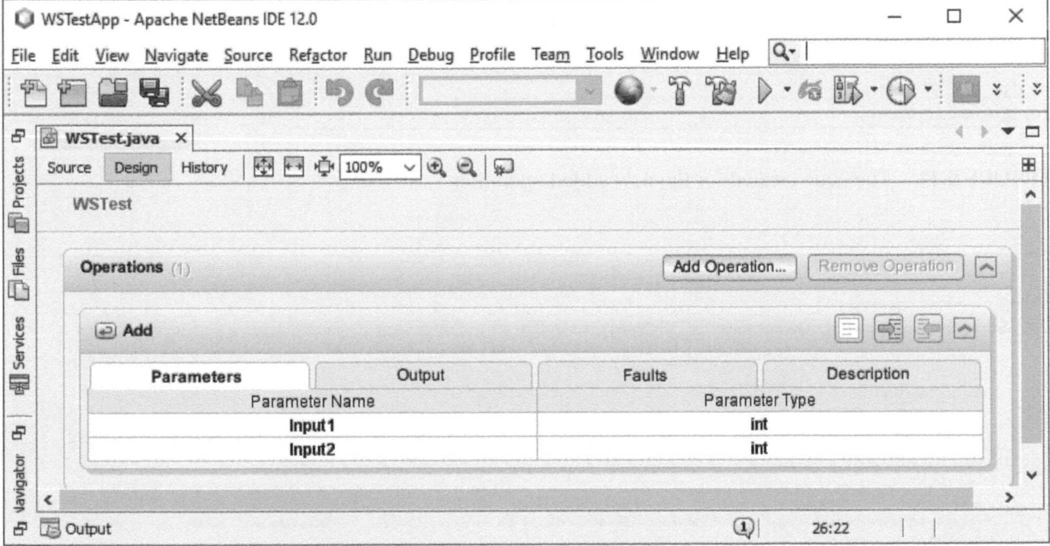

FIGURE 9.10 The opened visual designer.

the **Deploy** item. The NetBeans IDE will start the application server, build the application and deploy the application to the server. You can follow the progress of these operations in the **WSTestApp** (run-deploy) and the GlassFish server in the **Output** window.

2) If everything is fine, a successful deploy result should be obtained and displayed in the Output window, as shown in Figure 9.12.

We can use the GlassFish Test Service client to test our service to confirm its function. To test our Web service, perform the following operations:

1) In the opened **Projects** window, expand the **Web Services** node under our project; right-click on our target Web service output file, **WSTest**; and choose the **Test Web Service** item.

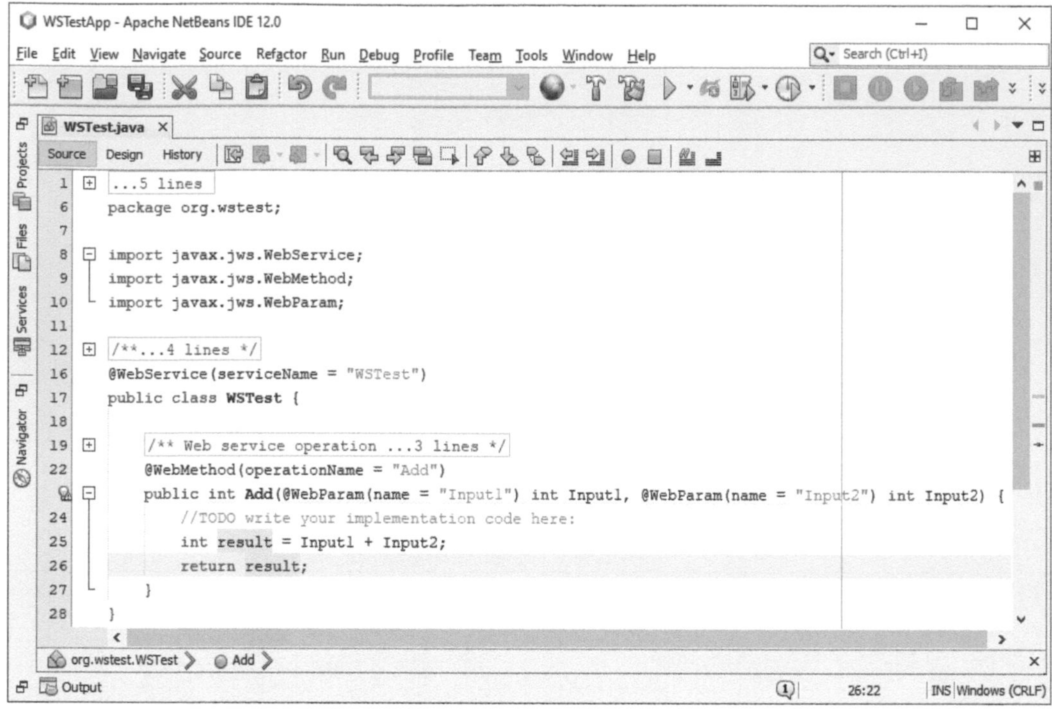

FIGURE 9.11 The code created for the new added operation.

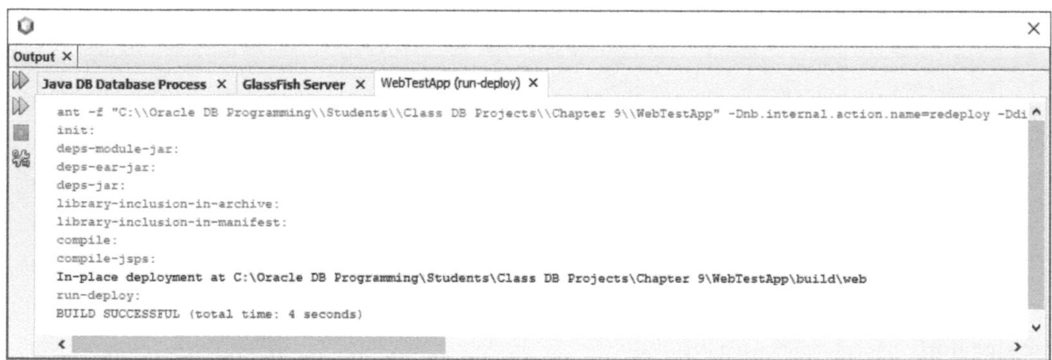

FIGURE 9.12 The deployment result.

2) The NetBeans IDE will display a test page in your browser, which is shown in Figure 9.13, if everything is fine.

To test our Web service project, enter `6` and `3` in the two input boxes, and click on the `add` button. You can see that a successful run result of our Web service is displayed with an addition result of `9`, which is shown in Figure 9.14.

If you encounter a `WS00041 Service Exception`, refer to Appendix K to solve it.

One point to be noted is that if you are using the Tomcat Web server as your application server, you will not find this tester page; only a testing successful page is displayed without any page test

FIGURE 9.13 The Web Service testing page.

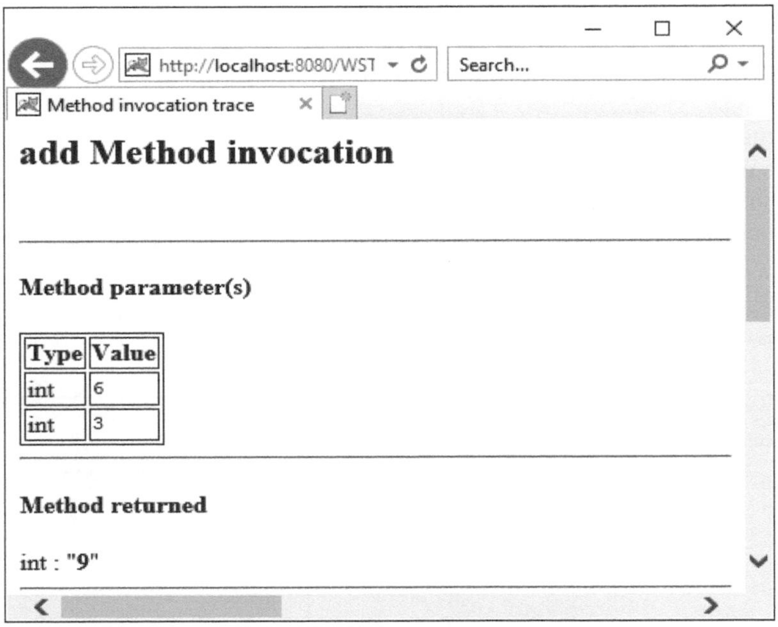

FIGURE 9.14 The Web Service test result.

function available. Also, if you are deploying a Web service built with the EJB module, you cannot find a test page either, since the NetBeans IDE 12.0 does not support a test function for any EJB module.

Next let's build a Web service-consuming project to consume our Web service.

9.3.5 Create Web Service Clients to Consume the Web Service

In fact, you can develop any kind of Java application as a project to consume a Web service, such as desktop Java with an Ant project, a Java Web application.

To make this client project simple, we prefer to build a simple Java desktop application project, **WSTestClient**, to consume the Web service.

Perform the following operations to create our client project:

1) Choose **File > New Project** to open the **New Project** wizard. Select **Java with Ant** from the **Categories** list and **Java Application** from the **Projects** list, and click on the **Next** button to continue.
2) Name the project **WSTestClient** and select an appropriate location for this client project. Leave the **Create Main Class** checkbox checked and accept all other default settings. Your finished **Name and Location** wizard should match the one shown in Figure 9.15. Click on the **Finish** button to create the new project.
3) Right-click on our new client project's **WSTestClient** node in the **Projects** window and choose **New > Web Service Client** to open the **New Web Service Client** wizard.
4) Click on the **Browse** button next to the **Project** radio button to browse to our Web service project, **WSTest**, as shown in Figure 9.16. Click on our Web service, **WSTest**, and click on the **OK** button.
5) In the next wizard, **New Web Service Client**, just click on the **Finish** button to complete this consuming project creation process.
6) A new node named **Web Service References** with the following components has been added into our client project, **WSTestClient**, as shown in Figure 9.17:

   a. Our target Web service output file, **WSTest**
   b. Our Web service class file, **WSTestService**
   c. Our Web service port file, **WSTestPort**
   d. Our operation **Add()** method

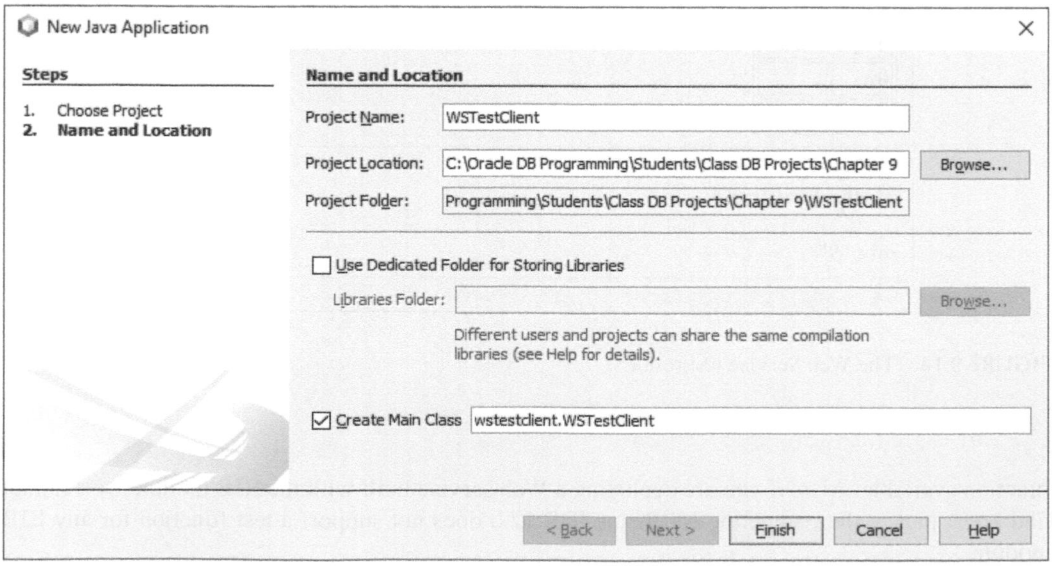

FIGURE 9.15 The finished Name and Location wizard.

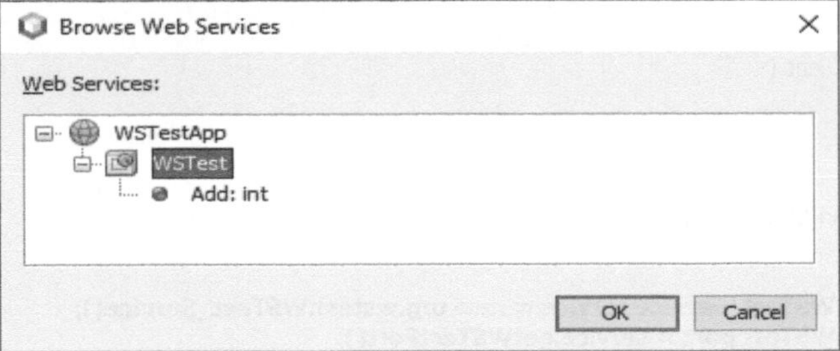

FIGURE 9.16 The Web service browse wizard.

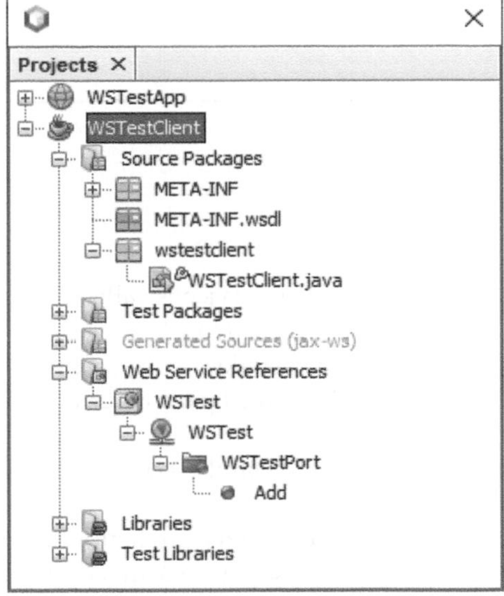

FIGURE 9.17 The new added Web Service References node and components.

Now let's build the code for this consuming project to consume our Web service. Perform the following operations to build the code for this consuming project:

1) Double-click on our main class file, **`WSTestClient.java`**, located at the **`Source Packages\wstestclient`** node to open the code window of this file.
2) Enter the code shown in Figure 9.18 into the **`main()`** method on this file.

Let's have a closer look at this piece of code to see how it works.

1) A **`try-catch`** block is used to call our Web service to perform a two-integer addition operation.
2) A new Web service instance, **`service`**, is created based on our Web service class, **`WSTestService`**. The syntax of creating this new service has been changed since NetBeans 8, and the service class must be presented with **`WSTest _ Service`**.
3) The **`getWSTestPort()`** method is executed to get the current port used by our Web service. This port is returned and assigned to a new port instance, **`port`**.
4) Two testing integers are created and initialized as 8 and 7, respectively.

```
  package wstestclient;
  public class WSTestClient {
      /**
       * @param args the command line arguments
       */
  public static void main(String[] args) {
      // TODO code application logic here
A     try {
B        org.wstest.WSTest_Service service = new org.wstest.WSTest_Service();
C        org.wstest.WSTest port = service.getWSTestPort();
D        int a = 8, b = 7;
E        int result = port.add(a, b);
F        System.out.println("Result = " + result);
      }
G     catch (Exception ex){
         System.out.println("exception" + ex);
      }
    }
  }
```

FIGURE 9.18 The code for the main() method.

5) The operation method **Add()** in our Web service is called to perform the addition operation. The run result of this method is assigned to a local variable named **result**.
6) The result is displayed in the **Output** window. Any exception during this Web service calling process will be tracked and displayed by the **catch** block in step G.

Now let's build and run our client project to call the **Add()** method built in our Web service to perform the two-integer addition operation.

Click on the **Clean and Build Main Project** button to build our client project. Then right-click on our project **WSTestClient** and select the **Run** menu item from the popup menu. The run result is shown in Figure 9.19.

It can be seen that calling our Web service is successful, and the addition result of **15** has been returned. Our first Web service project is successful.

At this point, we have learned some fundamental knowledge and have a basic understanding about Java Web services. Now let's start building some real Java Web services projects to perform database query and manipulation operations against our sample database.

9.4 GETTING STARTED WITH JAVA WEB SERVICES USING NETBEANS IDE

In the following sections, we will develop and build different Java Web services projects based on our Oracle Database XE 18c database system with different consuming projects to perform desired database operations.

By adding different operations or methods to our Web service projects to access and manipulate data in Tables, such as the **Faculty** and **Course** Tables, in our sample Oracle database, we can perform the following data queries and manipulations:

1) Query data from the **Faculty** Table in our Oracle database with **QueryFaculty()**.
2) Insert data into the **Faculty** Table in our Oracle database with **InsertFaculty()**.
3) Update and delete data against the **Faculty** Table in our Oracle database with the **UpdateFaculty()** and **DeleteFaculty()** operations.
4) Query data from the **Course** Table in our Oracle database with **QueryCourse()**.

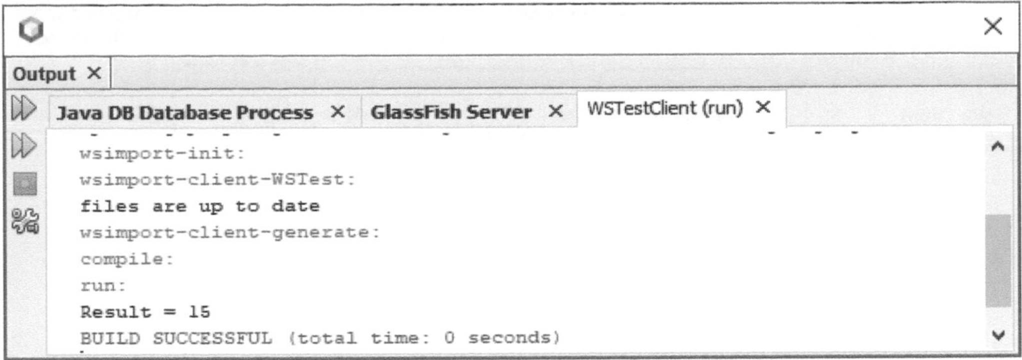

FIGURE 9.19 The run result of calling our Web service.

5) Query detailed course information from the Course Table in our Oracle database with **`DetailCourse()`**.
6) Update and delete data against the Course Table in our Oracle database with the **`UpdateCourse()`** and **`DeleteCourse()`** operations.

For each Web services project, we need to build an associated client project to consume the Web services project to test its function. The following client projects will be built:

1) Window-based client project to consume the Web service to access the **`Faculty`** and **`Course`** Tables in our Oracle database.
2) Window-based client project to consume the Web service to insert data into the **`Faculty`** and **`Course`** Tables in our Oracle database.
3) Window-based client project to consume the Web service to update and delete data against the **`Faculty`** and **`Course`** Tables in our Oracle database.
4) Web-based-based client project to consume the Web service to access the **`Faculty`** and **`Course`** Tables in our Oracle database.
5) Web-based-based client project to consume the Web service to insert data into the **`Faculty`** and **`Course`** Tables in our Oracle database.
6) Web-based-based client project to consume the Web service to update and delete data against the **`Faculty`** and **`Course`** Tables in our Oracle database.

In fact, we can develop any kind of client project to consume a Web service, either a standard Java desktop application, which is called a Window-based consume project, or a JSP page, which is called a Web-based consume project. We will develop and build different client projects to consume our Web services to enable our projects to meet real-world needs.

Let's start with the query of the **`Faculty`** Table in our Oracle database.

9.5 BUILD JAVA WEB SERVICE PROJECTS TO ACCESS AND MANIPULATE THE FACULTY TABLE

In this section, we will discuss how to query and manipulate the **`Faculty`** Table against our Oracle database using Java Web services. To make our Web Services project simple, we will use the following components to fulfill the query and manipulation actions:

- Build different operations or methods in our Web services as interfaces to communicate with Web clients that will be built in the future to perform desired data actions.

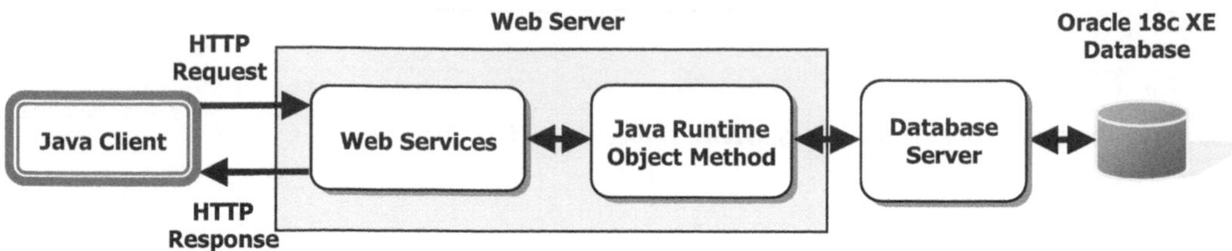

FIGURE 9.20 The structure and components used in our Web services.

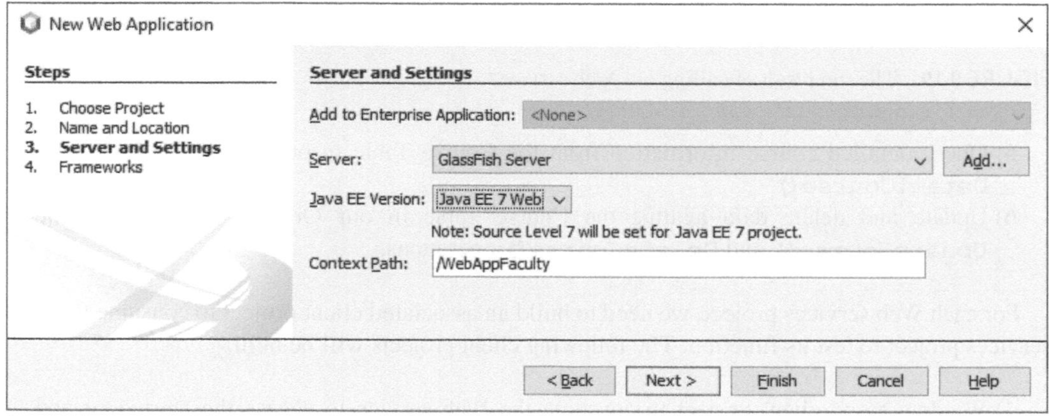

FIGURE 9.21 The finished Server and Settings wizard.

- Use the runtime object method to actually access and query our sample Oracle database.
- The structure and components used in our Web services are shown in Figure 9.20.
- Now let's create our first Web service project to perform data query and manipulation against our sample database.

9.5.1 Create a New Java Web Application Project, WebAppFaculty

When creating a new Web service application project, we need to select a desired container to deploy our Web service. Generally we can either deploy our Web service in a Web container or an EJB container. In this application, we prefer to use a Web container, since we are creating a Java EE 7 application.

Perform the following operations to create our Web application project, **`WebAppFaculty`**:

1) Launch NetBeans IDE 12.0 and choose **`File > New Project`** (Ctrl-Shift-N). Expand the **`Java with Ant`** folder, select **`Java Web`** under the **`Categories`** list and **`Web Application`** from the **`Projects`** list. Click on the **`Next`** button to continue.
2) Name the project **`WebAppFaculty`** and click on the **`Browse`** button to select a desired location for the project. In this application, we used **`C:\Class DB Projects\Chapter 9`** as our project location. Click on the **`Next`** button to continue.
3) Select **`GlassFish Server`** as our Web container and **`Java EE 7 Web`** as the Java EE version. Your finished **`Server and Settings`** wizard should match the one shown in Figure 9.21. Click on the **`Finish`** button to complete the new application creation process.

Now that a Web application has been created with a selected Web container, next we can create our new Web service project, **WebServiceFaculty**.

9.5.2 Create a New Java SOAP-Based Web Service Project WebServiceFaculty

The function of this Web service is to perform data queries and manipulations to our sample Oracle 18c XE database and return the result. Perform the following operations to create this new Web service project, **WebServiceFaculty**:

1) In the opened **Projects** window, right-click on our new created project, **WebApp Faculty**, and select the **New > Other** menu item to open the **New File** wizard.
2) Select **Web Services** from the **Categories** list and **Web Service** from the **File Types** list, and click on the **Next** button.
3) Name the Web service **WebServiceFaculty** and type **org.ws.oracle** into the **Package** field. Leave **Create Web Service from Scratch** selected.

Your finished **Name and Location** wizard should match the one shown in Figure 9.22. Click on the **Finish** button to complete this process.

Next let's handle adding new operations and code for the operations or methods in our Web service.

9.5.3 Add the First Web Operation to Our Web Services to Perform a Data Query

The main purpose of using the Web service in this section is to query data from the **Faculty** Table in our sample database; thus, we need to add a new operation, **QueryFaculty()**. Perform the following steps to add **QueryFaculty()** into our Web service project:

1) Click on the **Design** button at the top of the window to open the Design View of our Web service project, **WebServiceFaculty.java**.
2) First let's remove the default **hello** operation by right-clicking on it, and select **Remove Operation** item from the popup menu.

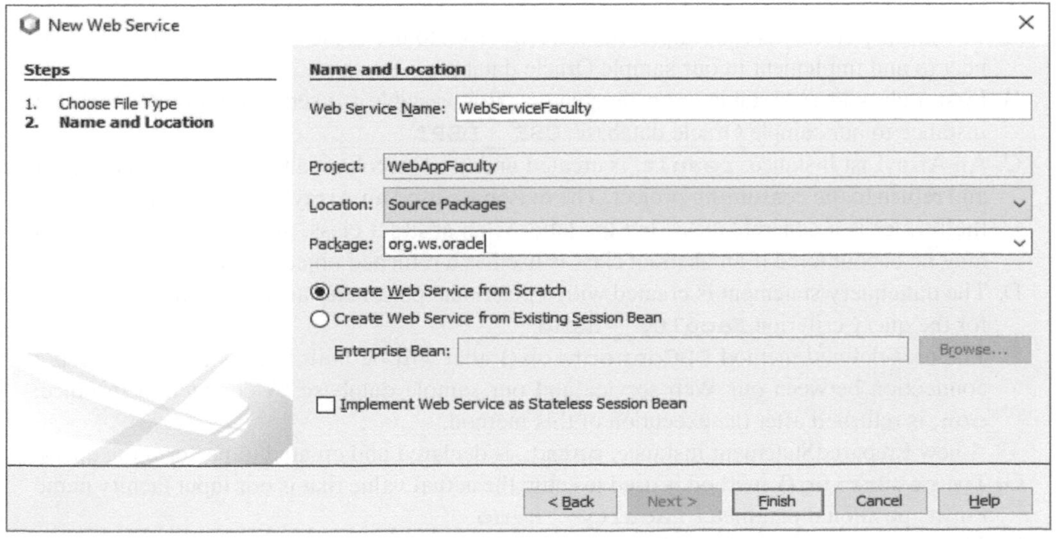

FIGURE 9.22 The finished Name and Location wizard.

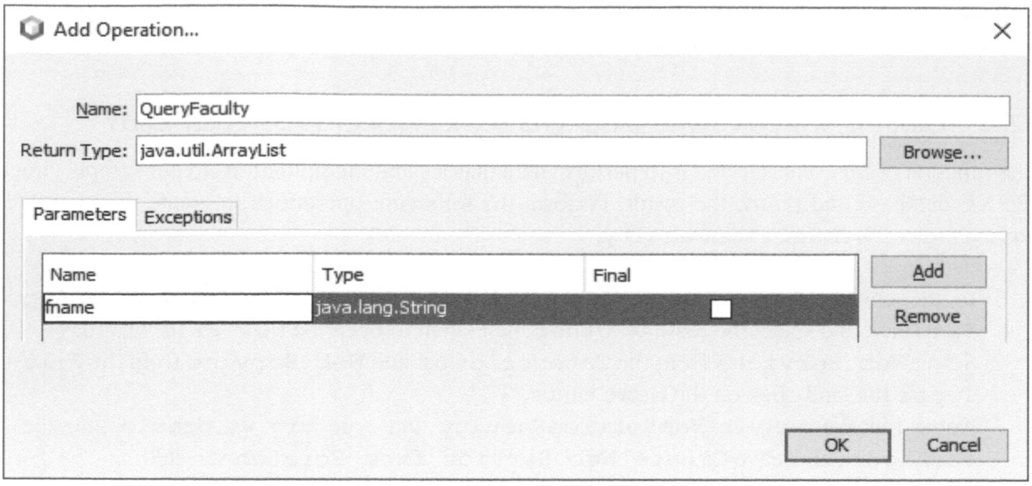

FIGURE 9.23 The finished Add Operation wizard.

3) Click on the **Add Operation** button to open the **Add Operation** wizard.
4) Enter **QueryFaculty** into the **Name** field and click on the **Browse** button next to the **Return Type** combo box. Type **ArrayList** into the **Type Name** field, select the item **ArrayList (java.util)** from the list and click on the **OK** button.
5) Click on the **Add** button and enter **fname** into the **Name** parameter field. Keep the default type **java.lang.String** unchanged and click on the **OK** button to complete the new operation creation process.

Your finished **Add Operation** wizard should match the one shown in Figure 9.23.

Click on the **Source** button at the top of this window to open the code window of our Web service project. Let's develop the code for this new operation.

In the opened code window, enter the code shown in Figure 9.24 into the new operation. Let's have a closer look at this piece of code to see how it works.

A. The java.sql library is first imported, since we need to use some of its components to connect to and implement in our sample Oracle database.
B. First a class-level variable, **con**, is created. This variable is used to hold the connection instance to our sample Oracle database, **CSE _ DEPT**.
C. An ArrayList instance, **result**, is created and used to collect and store our query result and return to the consuming project. The reason we used an ArrayList and not a List is that the former is a concrete class, but the latter is an abstract class, and a runtime exception may be encountered if an abstract class is used as a returned object to the calling method.
D. The data query statement is created with a positional parameter as the dynamic parameter for the query criterion **faculty _ name**.
E. The user-defined method **DBConnection()** that will be built later is called to setup a connection between our Web service and our sample database. A connection instance, **con**, is returned after the execution of this method.
F. A new PreparedStatement instance, **pstmt**, is declared and created to perform the query.
G. The **setString()** method is used to setup the actual value that is our input faculty name for the positional parameter **faculty _ name**.
H. The query is performed by calling the **executeQuery()** method, and the query result is returned and stored in a ResultSet object, **rs**.

```
  package org.ws.oracle;
A import java.sql.*;
  import java.util.ArrayList;
  import javax.jws.WebService;
  import javax.jws.WebMethod;
  import javax.jws.WebParam;

  @WebService(serviceName = "WebServiceFaculty")
  public class WebServiceFaculty {
B   Connection con = null;
    @WebMethod(operationName = "QueryFaculty")
    public ArrayList QueryFaculty(@WebParam(name = "fname") String fname) {
      //TODO write your implementation code here:
C     ArrayList<String> result = new ArrayList<String>();
D     String query = "SELECT * FROM Faculty WHERE faculty_name = ?";
      try {
E         con = DBConnection(con);
F         PreparedStatement pstmt =con.prepareStatement(query);
G         pstmt.setString(1, fname);
H         ResultSet rs = pstmt.executeQuery();
I         ResultSetMetaData rsmd = rs.getMetaData();
J         while (rs.next()){
            for (int colNum = 1; colNum <= rsmd.getColumnCount() - 1; colNum++)
              result.add(rs.getString(colNum));
          }
K         con.close();
L         return result;
      }
M     catch (Exception ex) {
        System.out.println("exception is: " + ex);
        return null;
      }
  }
```

FIGURE 9.24 The code for the new operation, QueryFaculty().

I. To get more related information about the queried database, the `getMetaData()` method is executed, and the result is stored in a ResultSetMetaData instance, `rsmd`.
J. `while()` and `for()` loops are used to pick up each column from the queried result that is stored in the ResultSet object `rs`. In fact, the `while`() loop only runs one time since only one matching faculty row will be returned. The `getColumnCount()` method is used as the upperbound of the `for()` loop, but this upper bound must be decreased by 1 since totally there are eight (8) columns in the `Faculty` Table, but we only need to query and pick up the first seven (7) columns. The last column is the faculty image object, but it cannot be added into the ArrayList as a String object. Thus, this query only returns the first seven columns in a matching faculty row.
K. The `close()` method is executed to disconnect from our sample database.
L. The queried result is returned to the calling method.
M. The `catch` block is used to track and display any exception during the data query process, and a `null` will be returned if one occurs.

During the coding process, you may encounter some runtime compiling errors. The main reason for those errors is that some packages are missing. To fix these errors, just right-click on any space inside this code window, and select the `Fix Imports` item to add those missing packages.

Now let's build our user-defined method, `DBConnection()`, to setup a connection to our sample database from our Web service project.

```
  private Connection DBConnection(Connection conn) {
A     try {
            Class.forName("oracle.jdbc.OracleDriver");
        }
B       catch (Exception e) {
            System.out.println("Class not found exception!" + e.getMessage());
        }
C       String url = "jdbc:oracle:thin:@localhost:1521:XE";
D     try {
            conn = DriverManager.getConnection(url,"CSE_DEPT","oracle_18c");
        }
E       catch (SQLException e) {
            System.out.println("Could not connect!" + e.getMessage());
            e.printStackTrace();
        }
F     return conn;
  }
```

FIGURE 9.25 The code for the user-defined method DBConnection().

9.5.4 Build the User-Defined Method DBConnection()

To make our Web service project simple, we will use the Java runtime object method to perform the database connection function. In the opened code window of our Web service project, **WebServiceFaculty.java**, enter the code shown in Figure 9.25 to create and define the connection method **DBConnection()**.

Let's have a closer look at this piece of code to see how it works.

A. A **try-catch** block is used to perform the database connection function. First the Oracle JDBC driver is loaded using the **forName()** method.
B. The **catch** block is used to track and detect any possible exception for the JDBC driver loading process. The debug information will be displayed using the **System.out.println()** method if an exception occurs.
C. Our sample Oracle database connection URL is defined and used to set up a connection to our sample database. Refer to Section 6.3.3.2 in Chapter 6 to get more details about the connection URL.
D. Another **try-catch** block is used to set up a connection to our sample database using the **getConnection()** method that belongs to the DriverManager class with the username and password as arguments.
E. The **catch** block is used to detect and display any possible exception during this connection process.
F. The established connection object is returned to the calling method.

Next let's add the second Web operation to our Web Service project to query and get a matching faculty image for the selected faculty member.

9.5.5 Add the Second Operation to Our Web Service to Query the Faculty Image

Perform the following operations to add a new operation, **QueryImage()**, into our Web service:

1) Click on the **Design** button at the top of the window to open the **Design View** of our Web service project file, **WebServiceFaculty.java**.
2) Click on the **Add Operation** button to open the **Add Operation** wizard.

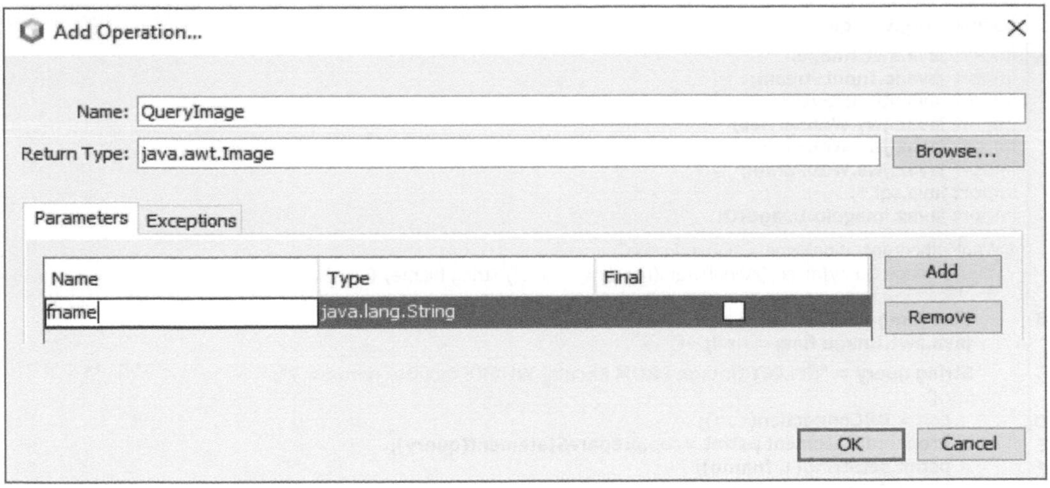

FIGURE 9.26 The finished Add Operation wizard.

3) Enter **QueryImage** into the **Name** field and click on the **Browse** button next to the **Return Type** combo box. Type **Image** into the **Type Name** field, select the item **Image (java.awt)** from the list and click on the **OK** button.
4) Click on the **Add** button and enter **fname** in the **Name** parameter field. Keep the default type **java.lang.String** unchanged and click on the **OK** button.

Your finished **Add Operation** wizard should match the one shown in Figure 9.26. Click on the **OK** button again to complete the second add operation process.

Click on the **Source** button at the top of this window to open the code window of our Web service project. In the opened code window, enter the code shown in Figure 9.27 into the new added operation.

Let's have a closer look at this piece of code to see how it works.

A. Some useful packages are first imported into the source window for this operation. You can right-click on the code window and select **Fix Imports** from the popup menu if you do not want to declare these packages yourself when this piece of code is done.
B. Some local objects and variables are declared here; the **bimg** is a **Blob** object since we need to retrieve a desired faculty image from the **Faculty** Table and the image is a Blob format in our database column. **fimg** is a type of **Image** object since this type of object can be used as a returned object from the Web Service project. Since this object belongs to the **java.awt.Image** class, a full package name is used.
C. The query string is declared with **faculty _ name** as an input position parameter.
D. A **try-catch** block is used to perform the image query operation. First a connection method, **DBConnection()**, which will be built in the next section, is executed to connect to our sample database, **CSE _ DEPT**.
E. A new PreparedStatement instance, **pstmt**, is declared and created to perform the query.
F. The **setString()** method is used to set up the actual value that is our input faculty name for the positional parameter **faculty _ name**.
G. The image query is performed by calling the **executeQuery()** method, and the query result is returned and stored in a ResultSet object, **rs**.
H. To get more detailed information about the queried database, the **getMetaData()** method is executed, and the result is stored in a ResultSetMetaData instance **rsmd**.

```
  package org.ws.sql;
A import java.awt.Image;
  import java.io.InputStream;
  import java.util.ArrayList;
  import javax.jws.WebService;
  import javax.jws.WebMethod;
  import javax.jws.WebParam;
  import java.sql.*;
  import javax.imageio.ImageIO;
  @WebMethod(operationName = "QueryImage")
     public Image QueryImage(@WebParam(name = "fname") String fname) {
        //TODO write your implementation code here:
B       Blob bimg = null;
        java.awt.Image fimg = null;
C       String query = "SELECT fimage FROM Faculty WHERE faculty_name = ?";
        try {
D          con = DBConnection(con);
E          PreparedStatement pstmt =con.prepareStatement(query);
F          pstmt.setString(1, fname);
G          ResultSet rs = pstmt.executeQuery();
H          ResultSetMetaData rsmd = rs.getMetaData();
I          while (rs.next()){
              for (int i = 1; i <=rsmd.getColumnCount(); i++) {
J                if (i == rsmd.getColumnCount()){
                    bimg = rs.getBlob("fimage");
K                   InputStream in = bimg.getBinaryStream();
                    fimg = ImageIO.read(in);
L                   break;
                 }
              }
           }
M          con.close();
           rs.close();
           pstmt.close();
           return fimg;
        }
N       catch (Exception ex) {
           System.out.println("exception is: " + ex);
           return null;
        }
     }
  }
```

FIGURE 9.27 The code for the second operation QueryImage().

I. `while()` and `for()` loops are used to pick up the queried faculty image stored in the ResultSet object `rs`. In fact, the `while()` loop only runs one time since only one matching faculty row will be returned. The `getColumnCount()` method is used as the upper-bound of the for loop, and it should be equal to 8, since the eighth column in the `Faculty` Table stores the desired faculty image.

J. An `if` selection structure is used to check if the eighth column has been retrieved. If it is, the `getBlob()` method is executed to pick up the image in that column and assign it to the local object `bimg`, which is a Blob-type object.

K. The system method `getBinaryStream()` is used to convert the Blob object to an `Image` object, `fimg`, with another system method, `read()`, that belongs to the `ImageIO` class.

L. Then a `break` instruction skips out and terminates this `for` loop.

M. A sequence of cleaning jobs is performed to close all used objects, and the queried faculty image is returned.

N. The `catch` block is used to catch and display any possible error during the image query.

At this point, we have finished all code development for our Web service used to perform queries to our **Faculty** Table. Prior to building and running our project to test its functions, we need first to set up the Oracle JDBC driver and our correct Java platform.

9.5.6 Setup the Correct JDBC Driver and Java Platform for Our Web Service

Perform the following steps to complete the JDBC Driver setup process:

1) Right-click on our project, **WebAppFaculty**, in the **Projects** window and select the **Properties** item to open the project properties wizard.
2) Click on the **Libraries** node and click on the **Add JAR/Folder** button to open the Windows Explorer to locate our installed JDBC Driver for Oracle 18c XE, **ojdbc8.jar**.
3) Browse to the location where the JDBC Driver is installed (refer to Appendix H to download this driver). In our case, it is **C:\Temp**. Click the file **ojdbc8.jar** to select it and click on the **Open** and **OK** buttons to add it into our project.
4) Click on the drop-down arrow on the right of the **Java Platform** box, select **JDK 1.8** and click on the **Change Platform** button in the popup menu to make this change valid.

Your finished **Project Properties** wizard should match the one shown in Figure 9.28. Click on the **OK** button to complete the JDBC driver addition operation.

9.5.7 Deploy the Web Service Project and Test the Data Query Function

Perform the following operations to build and deploy our Web service project:

1) Click on the **Clean and Build Main Project** button to build our Web service.
2) Right-click on our Web application, **WebAppFaculty**, and select the **Deploy** item to deploy our Web service. If everything is fine, a successful deployment result should be displayed, as shown in Figure 9.29.
3) To test this Web service, right-click on our target service output file, **WebServiceFaculty**, under the **Web Services** node in our project, and select the **Test Web Service** item.
4) The tested page is opened and displayed. Then enter a desired faculty name such as **Ying Bai** into the text field and click on the **queryFaculty** button to call our Web service. The run result is shown in Figure 9.30.

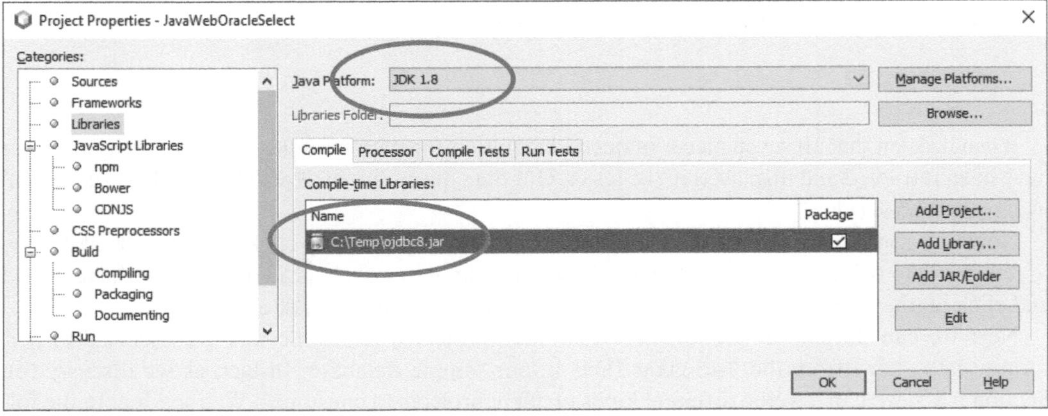

FIGURE 9.28 The finished Project Properties wizard.

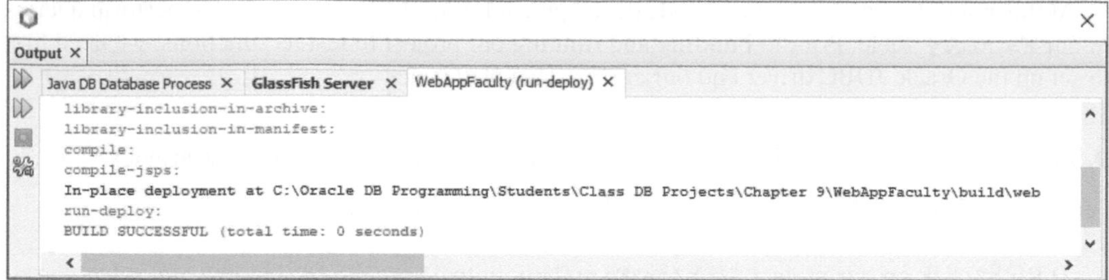

FIGURE 9.29 The deployment result of our Web service project.

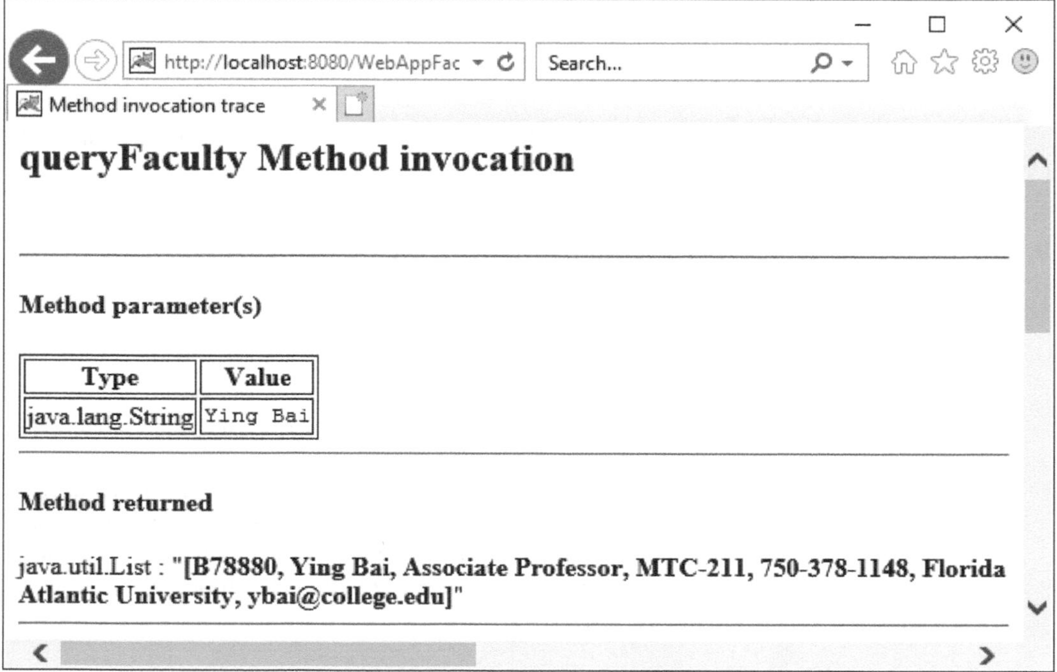

FIGURE 9.30 The test result of our Web service project.

It can be seen that all seven pieces of queried faculty information for the selected faculty member have been retrieved and displayed in the tester. Our data query for our **`Faculty`** Table is successful using our Web service.

Now let's continue to test the second operation, **`QueryImage()`**, by clicking on the **`Back`** button to return to the original test page. Enter a desired faculty name such as **`Ying Bai`** in the text field and click on the **`queryImage`** button. The selected faculty image is **`[B@66c557e1`**.

Next we can develop a Windows or Web client project to consume this Web service to perform a data query from the **`Faculty`** Table in our sample database. In fact, as we discussed in Section 9.3.5, we can develop different kinds of client projects to consume a Web service. In the following sections, we will discuss two popular client projects, Window-based and Web-based clients, to consume our Web service to perform queries to our **`Faculty`** Table.

If you encountered an ORA-12505 error during Web testing, open the Services wizard by typing Services.msc into the Start box. Then stop and start both files, OracleOraDB18Home1TNSListener and OracleServiceXE, to reset/restart the listener.

First let's discuss how to build a Window-based client project to consume our Web service.

9.6 BUILD A WINDOW-BASED CLIENT PROJECT TO CONSUME THE WEB SERVICE

To save time and space, we can use the Window-based project **OracleSelectFaculty** we developed in Section 6.3 in Chapter 6 to build our new client project, **WinClientFaculty _ Select**. That project can be found in the folder **Class DB Projects\Chapter 6**, which is located in the **Students** folder on the CRC Press ftp site (refer to Figure 1.2 in Chapter 1).

9.6.1 Copy the FacultyFrame and MsgDialog Components as GUIs

Perform the following operations to create a GUI for our Window-based client project, **WinClientFaculty _ Select**, to consume our Web service:

1) Launch NetBeans IDE 12.0 and choose **File > New Project**.
2) Select **Java with Ant** and **Java Application** from the **Categories** and **Projects** lists, respectively. Click on the **Next** button.
3) Name the project **WinClientFaculty _ Select** and select a desired folder to save this project. Uncheck the **Create Main Class** checkbox. Your finished **Name and Location** wizard should match the one shown in Figure 9.31. Click on the **Finish** button to create this project.

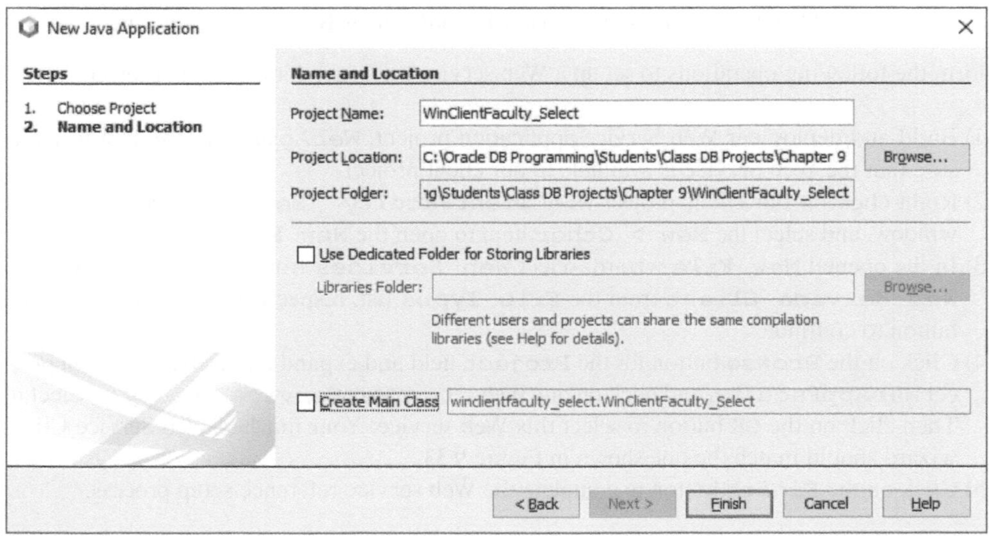

FIGURE 9.31 The finished Name and Location wizard.

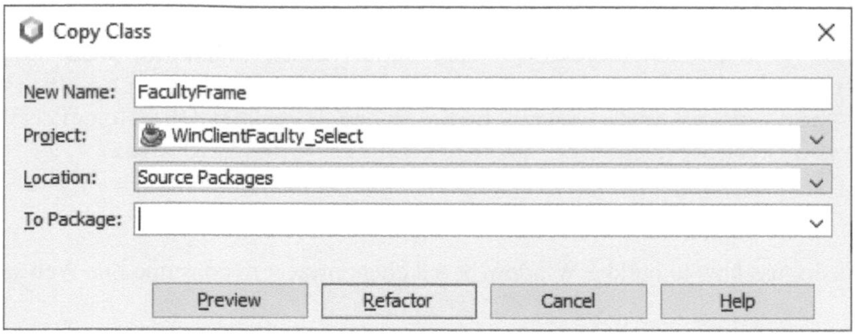

FIGURE 9.32 The finished Copy Class wizard.

4) Go to the **Students** folder on the CRC Press ftp site and load and open the project **OracleSelectFaculty** from the folder **Class DB Projects\Chapter 6**.
5) In the opened project, right-click on the Faculty Frame file **FacultyFrame.java** under the project package node, and select the **Refactor > Copy** item to copy this form file.
6) In the opened **Copy Class–FacultyFrame** wizard, select our new project, **WinClientFaculty _ Select**, from the **Project** combo box and remove the **1** after the **FacultyFrame** from the **New Name** field. Your finished **Copy Class** wizard is shown in Figure 9.32.
7) Click on the **Refactor** button to make a refactored copy of the frame file.
8) Return to our new project, **WinClientFaculty _ Select**, and you can see that a copied **FacultyFrame.java** file has been pasted in the default package in our project.

Perform a similar **Refactor** operation to copy the **MsgDialog.java** file and paste it into our new client project. Next let's develop the code to call our Web service to perform the faculty data query. However, before we can begin the coding process, we must first setup or create a Web service reference for our **WinClientFaculty _ Select** project to enable our project to recognize the Web service and call it when it is instructed to do so.

9.6.2 Create a Web Service Reference for Our Window-Based Client Project

Perform the following operations to set up a Web service reference for our client project:

1) Build and deploy our Web Service application project, **WebAppFaculty**, first to make sure that the Web Service is available to our client project.
2) Right-click on our client project **WinClientFaculty _ Select** in the **Projects** window, and select the **New > Other** item to open the **New File** wizard.
3) In the opened **New File** wizard, select **Web Services** from the **Categories** and **Web Service Client** from the **File Types** list, respectively. Click on the **Next** button to continue.
4) Click on the **Browse** button for the **Project** field and expand our Web application project **WebAppFaculty**, and click on our Web service **WebServiceFaculty** to select it. Then click on the **OK** button to select this Web service. Your finished Web Service Client wizard should match the one shown in Figure 9.33.
5) Click on the **Finish** button to complete the Web service reference setup process.

Immediately, you can see a new node named **Web Service References** has been created and added to our client project. Expand this node, and you can see the associated Web service port and our Web service operations, such as **QueryFaculty()** and **QueryImage()**, under that node.

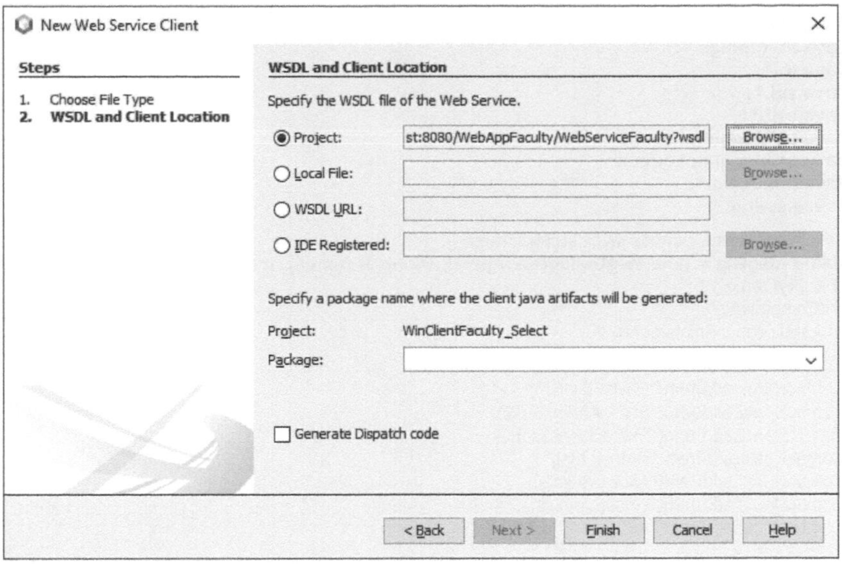

FIGURE 9.33 The finished New Web Service Client wizard.

Now let's develop the code to call the Web service to perform the data query from the **Faculty** Table in our sample database.

9.6.3 Develop the Code to Call Our Web Service Project

The coding process is divided into two parts: the modification to the original code and creation of new code. First let's do some modifications to the original code in the FacultyFrame class. Perform the following code modifications to make this project our Web consuming project:

1) Double-click on our new copied **FacultyFrame.java** file from our project to open it.
2) Click on the **Source** button at the top to open the code window.
3) Go to the constructor of this class, and remove all three query methods from the ComboMethod object.
4) Open the **SelectButtonActionPerformed()** event handler and remove all code inside this event handler.

Now let's develop some new code to perform the faculty data query by calling our Web service operations.

In the **Design** view of the FacultyFrame form window, double-click on the **Select** button to open its event method, **SelectButtonActionPerformed()**. Then enter the code shown in Figure 9.34 into this method. The new added and modified code is in bold.

Let's have a closer look at this piece of code to see how it works.

A. Some useful packages and classes related to Java development, such as **image**, **imageio**, **swing** and **File**, are imported first since we need to use some related classes defined in those packages to perform data and image queries and display in this Form.
B. A new ArrayList instance, **al**, is created to receive and hold the query result.
C. A **try-catch** block is used to call our Web service to perform the faculty data query operation. First a new Web service instance, **service**, is created based on our Web service class, **WebServiceFaculty _ Service**. Starting with NetBeans IDE 7, the

```
A  import java.awt.*;
   import java.awt.image.*;
   import java.io.*;
   import java.sql.*;
   import java.util.*;
   import java.util.logging.Level;
   import java.util.logging.Logger;
   import javax.imageio.*;
   import javax.swing.*;

   public class FacultyFrame extends javax.swing.JFrame {
     MsgDialog msgDlg = new MsgDialog(new javax.swing.JFrame(), true);
     public FacultyFrame() {
          initComponents();
          this.setLocationRelativeTo(null);  // set the faculty Form at the center

          ComboName.addItem("Ying Bai");
          ComboName.addItem("Davis Bhalla");
          ComboName.addItem("Black Anderson");
          ComboName.addItem("Steve Johnson");
          ComboName.addItem("Jenney King");
          ComboName.addItem("Alice Brown");
          ComboName.addItem("Debby Angles");
          ComboName.addItem("Jeff Henry");
     }
     private void SelectButtonActionPerformed(java.awt.event.ActionEvent evt) {
      // TODO add your handling code here:
      JTextField[] f_field = {FacultyIDField,FacultyNameField,TitleField,OfficeField,PhoneField,CollegeField,EmailField};
B     ArrayList al = new ArrayList();

      try {
C       org.ws.oracle.WebServiceFaculty_Service  service = new org.ws.oracle.WebServiceFaculty_Service();
        org.ws.oracle.WebServiceFaculty  port = service.getWebServiceFacultyPort();
D       al.clear();
E       al = (ArrayList)port.queryFaculty(ComboName.getSelectedItem().toString());
F       for (int col = 0; col < al.size(); col++)
            f_field[col].setText(al.get(col).toString());
        }
G       catch (Exception ex){
            System.out.println("exception: " + ex);
        }
H       try {
I            if (!ShowFaculty()){
                msgDlg.setMessage("No matched faculty image found!");
                msgDlg.setVisible(true);
             }
          } catch (SQLException | IOException ex) {
            Logger.getLogger(FacultyFrame.class.getName()).log(Level.SEVERE, null, ex);
          }
     }
```

FIGURE 9.34 The modified code for the SelectButtonActionPerformed() method.

syntax to create a new service has changed, and an underscore is used between the service class name and the Service keyword to represent the service class. Similarly, a service port is also generated by calling a system method, **`getWebServiceFacultyPort()`**, to get the current port used by our Web service. This port is returned and assigned to a new port instance, **`port`**.

D. Before we can call our Web service, make sure that our ArrayList object **`al`** is empty by executing the **`clear()`** method.

E. The **`queryFaculty()`** method defined in our Web service is called to perform this faculty data query. Two points to be noted are: 1) the argument of this method is a selected faculty name obtained from the **`getSelectedItem()`** method from the Faculty Name combo box **`ComboName`**. Since this method returns an object, a **`toString()`** method must be attached to convert it to a string. 2) An ArrayList cast must be used to make sure that the returned query result is an ArrayList type since an ArrayList<String> type is used in our Web service project. The query result is assigned to our ArrayList instance, **al**.

F. A **for()** loop is used to pick up each column from the query result using the **get()** method. Two points to be noted are: 1) the argument of the **get()** method indicates the index of each column in the returned query result is a single row, and the data type of this method is an object. Therefore, a **toString()** method must be attached to convert it to a string. 2) To assign each column to each item in the **f _ field** array, the **setText()** method must be used.

G. The **catch** block is used to track and display any possible exception during the Web service calling process.

H. Another **try-catch** block is used to call a user-defined method, **ShowFaculty()**, that will be built later to call our Web method to query and display a selected faculty image.

I. The user-defined method **ShowFaculty()** is modified by removing its argument. The code for this method will be built later.

Now let's build the code for our user-defined method **ShowFaculty()** to get and display a selected faculty image by calling another operation, **QueryImage()**, built in our Web Service.

In the opened **FacultyFrame.java** file, browse to the **ShowFaculty()** method and replace all original code with the code shown in Figure 9.35.

```
    private boolean ShowFaculty() throws SQLException, IOException{
A     byte[] bimg = null;
      Image img = null;
      int imgId = 1, timeout = 1000;
      MediaTracker tracker = new MediaTracker(this);
      try {
B       org.ws.oracle.WebServiceFaculty_Service service = new org.ws.oracle.WebServiceFaculty_Service();
C       org.ws.oracle.WebServiceFaculty port = service.getWebServiceFacultyPort();
D       bimg = port.queryImage(ComboName.getSelectedItem().toString());
E       ByteArrayInputStream binput = new ByteArrayInputStream(bimg);
        img = ImageIO.read(binput);
      }
F     catch (Exception ex){
         System.out.println("exception: " + ex);
      }
G       String imgPath = System.getProperty("user.dir");
H       String fimgName = ComboName.getSelectedItem().toString() + ".jpg";
I       File outfile = new File(imgPath + "/" + fimgName);
        ImageIO.write((RenderedImage) img, "jpg", outfile);
J       img = this.getToolkit().getImage(fimgName);
        Graphics g = ImageCanvas.getGraphics();
K       tracker.addImage(img, imgId);
L       try{
          if(!tracker.waitForID(imgId, timeout)){
             msgDlg.setMessage("Failed to load image");
             msgDlg.setVisible(true);
             return false;
          }
M         }catch(InterruptedException e){
            msgDlg.setMessage(e.toString());
            msgDlg.setVisible(true);
            return false;
          }
N         g.drawImage(img, 0, 0, ImageCanvas.getWidth(), ImageCanvas.getHeight(), this);
          return true;
    }
```

FIGURE 9.35 The modified code for the ShowFaculty() method.

Let's have a closer look at the modified code to see how it works.

A. Some local objects are declared first, which include a byte[] array object, **bimg**, and an Image object, **img**, and both objects are used to hold the created **byte[]** image array and converted Image object. Both integer variables, **imgId** and **timeout**, are used to keep the image ID and timeout value when displaying this image in the Canvas object in our client.
B. A **try-catch** block is used to call our Web service to perform the faculty data query operation. First a new Web service instance, **service**, is created based on our Web service class **WebServiceFaculty _ Service**. Starting with NetBeans IDE 7, a keyword **_ Service** must be appended after the Web Service name to create a new service object.
C. The **getWebServiceFacultyPort()** method is executed to get the current port used by our Web service. This port is returned and assigned to a new port instance, **port**.
D. Now our Web Service operation, **QueryImage()**, is called with the selected faculty name as the argument to retrieve the selected faculty image from our sample database and assign it to our local variable **bimg**. One issue is that this returned object is an Image type when it is defined in our Web Service, but now we are using a **byte[]** array data type to hold this image. The reason for that is the default conversion by NetBeans IDE.
E. Two code lines in this section are used to convert the data type of this returned image from **byte[]** to Image. A **ByteArrayInputStream** object and **ImageIO.read()** method must be used for this conversion.
F. A **catch** block is used to detect and report any error for the conversion process.
G. In order to store our retrieved faculty image in our current project folder, the system method **getProperty()** with our current directory (**user.dir**) is used, and the current folder is assigned to a local string variable, **imgPath**.
H. To get the selected faculty image, we need to get the current selected or queried faculty name from the Faculty Name combo box, convert this item to a string and attach "**.jpg**" to the image file name. We need to use the name of this faculty image later to store and display this selected faculty image in the Canvas.
I. To save this converted faculty image in our current project folder, a new File object is generated with the image path and name. A system method, **ImageIO.write()**, is used to complete this image-saving job.
J. To display the selected faculty image, the **getImage()** method that belongs to the abstract class **Toolkit** is executed to load the selected image. Since the Toolkit class is an abstract class, we use the **getToolkit()** method to create it instead of generating it by invoking its constructor. The **getGraphics()** method is called to get a Graphics context, and our **ImageCanvas** works as an image holder for this faculty image.
K. The **addImage()** method that belongs to the MediaTracker class is called to add our image with its ID into the tracking system.
L. A **try-catch** block is used to begin a tracking process, and the **waitForID()** method is called to execute the tracking. If a timeout occurs for the tracking process, which means that the selected faculty image has not been loaded into the project, a warning message is displayed using our **MsgDialog** object, and a **False** is returned to indicate this error.
M. Any other possible exception or error will be caught by the **catch** block and be displayed in our **msgDlg** dialog.
N. If no timeout error happens, which means that the selected faculty image has been loaded into our project and is ready to be displayed, the **drawImage()** method is executed to display it in the **FacultyFrame** Form window. We want to display this image starting from the origin of the Canvas object, which is the upper-left corner of the canvas (0, 0), with a width and height that are identical to those of the canvas. Therefore, the **getWidth()** and **getHeight()** methods are called to get both of them from the canvas object. A **true** is returned to the main program to indicate that the execution of this method is successful.

Before we can build and run our client project to test this faculty query, add one more code line, **`System.exit(0);`** to the bottom of the **`BackButtonActionPerformed()`** handler or method in the Source window of the **`FacultyFrame`** class to terminate our project if the **`Back`** button is clicked.

Now we are ready to build and run our client project to test its function to call our Web service to perform the faculty data query.

9.6.4 Build and Run Our Client Project to Query Faculty Data via Web Service

Prior to building and running our client project, make sure that our Web Service application project, **`WebAppFaculty`**, has been built and deployed. Click on the **`Clean and Build Main Project`** button to build our client project. If everything is fine, click on the **`Run Main Project`** button to run our client project.

A message box may pop up to request the main starting class. Just select our FacultyFrame class as the starting class, and click on the **`OK`** button to run the project. The FacultyFrame form window is displayed, as shown in Figure 9.36.

Select a desired faculty member, such as **`Debby Angles`**, from the Faculty Name combo box, and click on the **`Select`** button to query the detailed information for this faculty member via our Web service **`WebServiceFaculty`**. The queried result is displayed in the form, as shown in Figure 9.36. You can try to select any other faculty member to test the faculty data query function to confirm the correctness of our client and service projects.

Next let's build a Web-based client project to consume our Web service **`WebServiceFaculty`** to perform a faculty data query action.

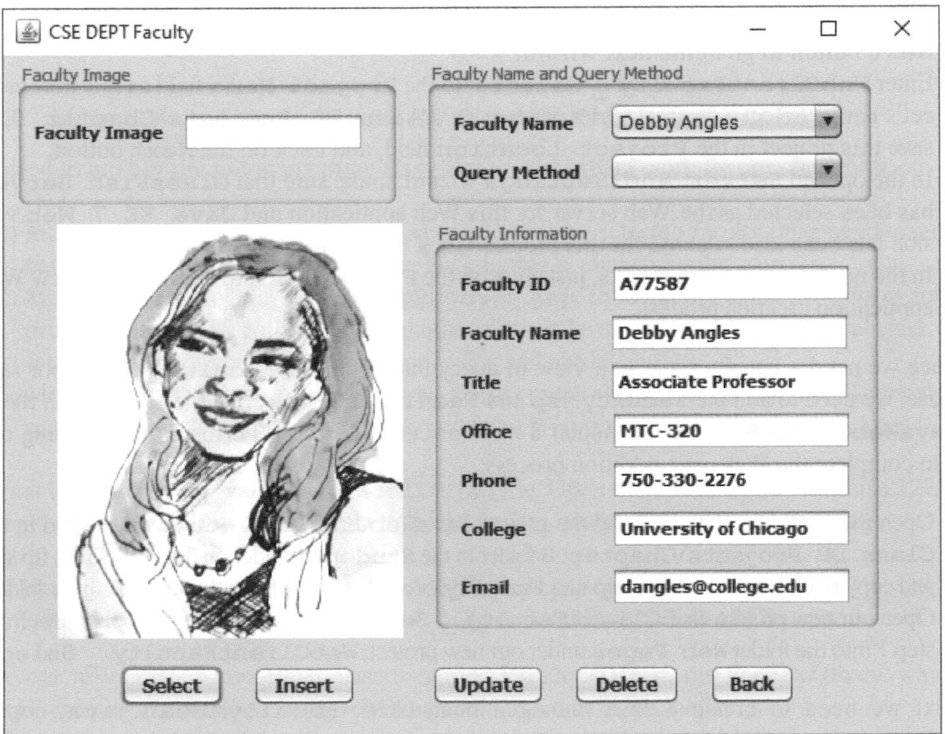

FIGURE 9.36 The run result of our client project.

```
<input type=submit value=Back name="Back" v:shapes="_x0000_s1048">
```

← with the following line:

```
<input type=button value=Back onclick="self.close()" v:shapes="_x0000_s1048">
```

The reason for this change is because the **Faculty.jsp** page in our previous projects will be returned to the **Selection.jsp** page if this **Back** button is clicked by the user, but in this Web Client project, **WebClientFaculty_Select**, we only rebuild the **Faculty.jsp** page without using any other pages; thus, we need to modify the code in the **Back** button event handler to terminate this project.

Now let's modify the **FacultyProcess.jsp** file to make it our new control class:

1) Replace the import package name **<%@ page import="JavaWebDBJSPSQLPackage.*" %>** with our new package **<%@ page import="webclient.*" %>** in codeline 10.
2) Replace the original constructor line (line 20), **FacultyQuery fQuery = new FacultyQuery();** with our new Java Bean class **FacultyMBean fQuery = new FacultyMBean();**.
3) Go to code line 40 and change the **FacultyQuery** to **FacultyMBean**, and the result of that code line should be:

   request.setAttribute("FacultyMBean", fQuery);

4) Remove the entire block **else if (request.getParameter("Back")!= null) {}** located at the bottom, at lines 122–125, since we do not want to use the **Back** button to return to any other page.

Finally, let's modify our model class **FacultyMBean.java**. First let's concentrate on the **QueryFaculty()** method. The function of this method is to:

1) Call our Web service operation **QueryFaculty()** to pick up a matching faculty record from the **Faculty** Table in our sample database.
2) Assign each queried column to the associated property defined in our Java managed bean class **FacultyMBean.java**.

Open the file **FacultyMBean.java** and perform the modifications as shown in Figure 9.38. The modified lines are in bold. This is the first part of the code of this class file. The second part's code will be shown later. Let's have a closer look at this piece of code to see how it works.

A. The class name is changed from **FacultyQuery** to **FacultyMBean**.
B. The type of the faculty image object is changed from the **Blob** to the byte[[] array.
C. A new instance of our Web Service class is generated with a new Web Service port.
D. Our second operation in our Web Service project, **QueryImage()**, is executed to get the selected faculty image and assign it to the image byte array **fbimg**, which is used later.

Also, delete the whole body for the method **CloseDBConnection()** from this Java Bean class.

Now let's take a look at our second part of code for this model class file, which is shown in Figure 9.39. The modified parts are in bold. In fact, only the contents of one method, **getFacultyImage()**, are modified. The function of this method is to convert the faculty image file from the byte[] array to a specified image format, **base64Image**, to enable it to be displayed in the Faculty Image box in our view class **Faculty.jsp** page. The **setBase64Image()** method is to set this converted image to the property **base64Image** defined in this class, which can be used by the image source tag in our view class later.

```
  package webclient;
  import java.sql.*;
  import java.util.ArrayList;
  import java.util.Base64;
A public class FacultyMBean {
     private String facultyID;
     private String facultyName;
     private String office;
     private String title;
     private String phone;
     private String college;
     private String email;
     private String base64Image;
B    byte[] fbimg = null;
     public FacultyMBean() {
     }
     public boolean QueryFaculty(String  fname) {
     ArrayList al = new ArrayList();
     try {
C          org.ws.oracle.WebServiceFaculty_Service service = new org.ws.oracle.WebServiceFaculty_Service();
           org.ws.oracle.WebServiceFaculty port = service.getWebServiceFacultyPort();
           al = (ArrayList)port.queryFaculty(fname);
           facultyID = al.get(0).toString();
           facultyName = al.get(1).toString();
           title = al.get(2).toString();
           office = al.get(3).toString();
           phone = al.get(4).toString();
           college = al.get(5).toString();
           email = al.get(6).toString();
D          fbimg = port.queryImage(fname);
       } catch (Exception ex) {
           System.out.println("Exception in Query Faculty Table: " + ex);
           return false;
       }
       return true;
     }
```

FIGURE 9.38 The completed code for the QueryFaculty() method.

At this point, we have completed all modifications for our three files. Before we can continue to build our project to call our Web Service, that is, to call related operations in our Web Service project to perform faculty data query from our sample database, we need to add our Web Service as a reference to our client project to enable the latter to recognize the former.

Now let's add a Web reference to our current Web-based client project to enable our client to know our Web service and its operations.

9.7.4 Add a Web Service Reference to Our Web-Based Client Project

Perform the following operations to set up a Web service reference for our client project:

1) Build and deploy our Web Service application project **WebAppFaculty** built in section 9.5.
2) Right-click on our client project **WebClientFaculty _ Select** in the **Projects** window, and select the **New > Other** item to open the **New File** wizard.
3) In the opened **New File** wizard, select **Web Services** from the **Categories** and **Web Service Client** from the **File Types** list. Click on the **Next** button to continue.
4) Click on the **Browse** button for the **Project** field and expand our Web application project **WebAppFaculty**, and click on our Web service project **WebServiceFaculty** to select it. Then click on the **OK** button to select this Web service. Your finished Web Service Client wizard is shown in Figure 9.40. Click on the **Finish** button to complete this process.

```
    public String getFacultyID() {
        return  this.facultyID;
    }
    public String getFacultyName() {
        return  facultyName;
    }
    public String getOffice() {
        return  office;
    }
    public String getTitle() {
        return  title;
    }
    public String getPhone() {
        return  phone;
    }
    public String getCollege() {
        return  college;
    }
    public String getEmail() {
        return  email;
    }
    public String getBase64Image() {
        return base64Image;
    }
    public void setBase64Image(String base64Image) {
        this.base64Image = base64Image;
    }

    public void getFacultyImage() throws SQLException{
A       if (fbimg != null)
        {
          base64Image = Base64.getEncoder().encodeToString(fbimg);
          setBase64Image(base64Image);
        }
    }
}
```

FIGURE 9.39 The second part of the code for the Java Bean class file.

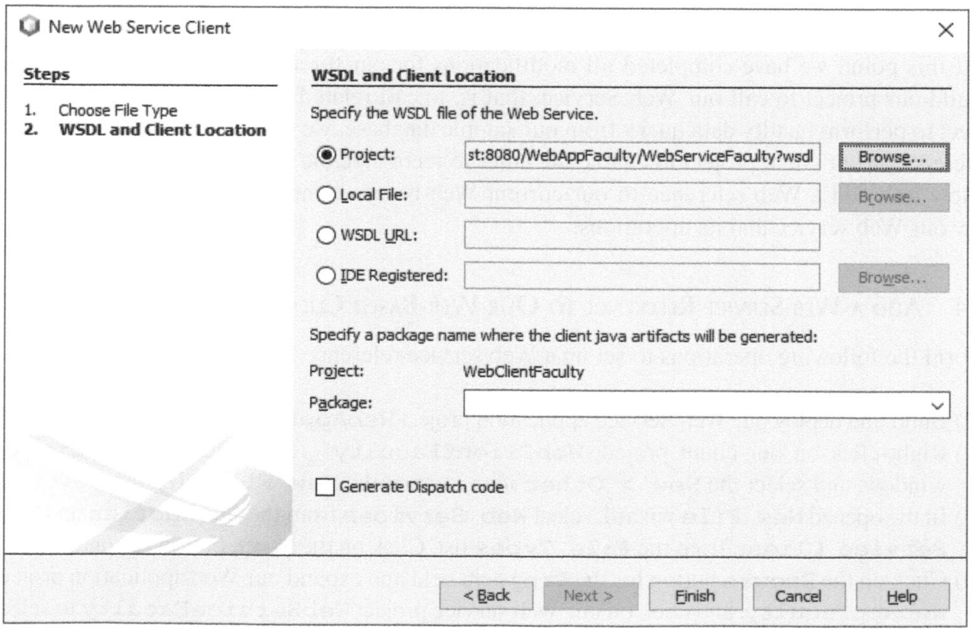

New Web Service Client

Steps

1. Choose File Type
2. **WSDL and Client Location**

WSDL and Client Location

Specify the WSDL file of the Web Service.

Project: st:8080/WebAppFaculty/WebServiceFaculty?wsdl Browse...

Local File: Browse...

WSDL URL:

IDE Registered: Browse...

Specify a package name where the client java artifacts will be generated:

Project: WebClientFaculty

Package:

Generate Dispatch code

< Back Next > Finish Cancel Help

FIGURE 9.40 The finished New Web Service Client wizard.

Immediately you can see a new node named **Web Service References** has been created and added into our client project. Expand this node, and you can see the associated Web service port and our Web service operations, **QueryFaculty()** and **QueryImage()**, under that node.

If you encounter a java.lang.ClassNotFoundException (com/sun/org/apache/xml/internal/resolver/CatalogManager) **error when adding this Web Service Reference, try to relocate the default Java JDK 14 folder. Generally it is located in** C:\Program Files\Java\jdk-14.0.1. **Move that** jdk-14.0.1 **folder to other folder, such as** C:\Temp, **on your machine. You need to select the default JDK for a popup MessageBox when you start the Apache NetBeans IDE 12.0 next time.**

Before we can build and run our Web client project to consume our Web Service, the last job we need to do is to set up the startup page, **Faculty.jsp**, to enable the Java Runner to know the starting point. Perform the following operations to complete this job:

1) Right-click on our client project, **WebClientFaculty _ Select**, in the **Projects** window, and select the **Properties** item at the bottom line from the popup menu to open that wizard.
2) In the opened wizard, click on the **Run** node.
3) Enter **./Faculty.jsp** into the **Relative URL** box on the right to make it our start page.
4) Click on the **OK** button to complete this process.

Now we are ready to build and run our client project to test its function. However before we can do that, make sure that our Web Service project **WebAppFaculty** has been built and deployed successfully.

9.7.5 Build and Run Our Client Project to Query Faculty Data via Web Service

Click on the **Clean and Build Main Project** button to build our client project. If everything is fine, click on the **Run Project** button on the top (green arrow) to run our client project.

On the opened Web page, which is shown in Figure 9.41, enter a desired faculty name such as **Ying Bai** into the **Faculty Name** field. Then click the **Select** button to perform a query for this selected faculty member. The query result is returned and displayed in this page, as shown in Figure 9.41. Click on the **Back** button to terminate this project if you like.

Our Web client project used to consume our Web service **WebServiceFaculty** is successful! A complete Web client project, **WebClientFaculty _ Select**, can be found in the project folder **Class DB Projects\Chapter 9** in the **Students** folder on the CRC Press ftp site (refer to Figure 1.2 in Chapter 1).

Next, let's discuss how to build a Web service to perform data insertion into our sample Oracle database.

9.8 BUILD JAVA WEB SERVICES TO INSERT DATA INTO THE ORACLE DATABASE

To perform a faculty record insertion to our sample database using our Web service, we need to add another operation called **InsertFaculty()** into our Web service project, **WebServiceFaculty**.

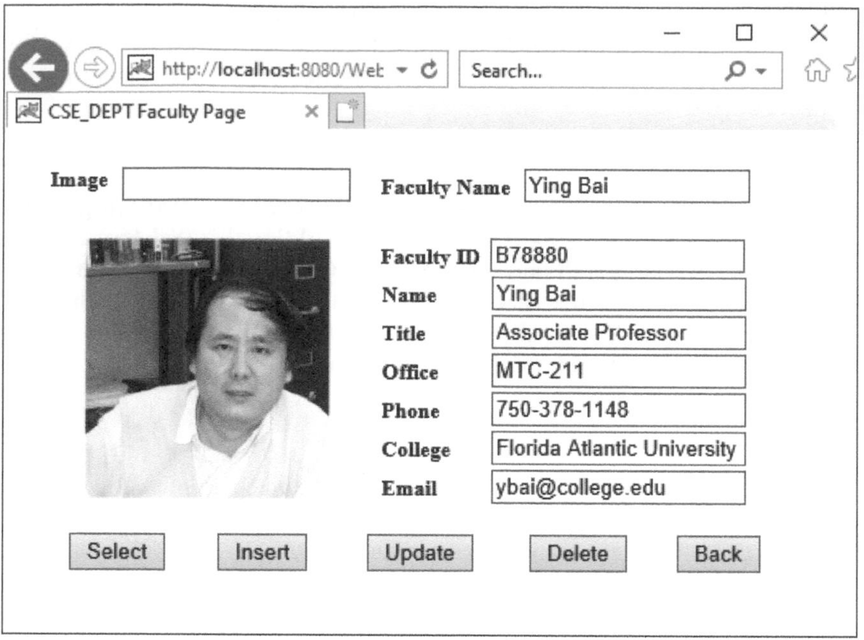

FIGURE 9.41 The test result for our Web client project.

9.8.1 Add a New Operation InsertFaculty() into Our Web Service Project

Perform the following operations to add this operation into our Web service:

1) Launch NetBeans IDE 12.0 and open our Web application project, **WebAppFaculty**, and open our Web service main class file, **WebServiceFaculty.java**in the **Projects** window.
2) Click on the **Design** button at the top of the window to open the Design View of our Web service class file **WebServiceFaculty.java**.
3) Click on the **Add Operation** button to open the **Add Operation** wizard.
4) Enter **InsertFaculty** into the **Name** field and click on the **Browse** button that is next to the **Return Type** combo box. Type **boolean** into the **Type Name** field, select the item **Boolean (java.lang)** from the list and click on the **OK** button.
5) Click on the **Add** button and enter **fdata** into the **Name** parameter field. Then click on the dropdown arrow of the **Type** combo box and select the **Choose** item to open the **Find Type** wizard. Type **Arraylist** into the top field and select the **ArrayList (java.util)** data type, and click on the **OK** button to select an ArrayList as the data type for the input parameter.

Your finished **Add Operation** wizard should match the one shown in Figure 9.42. Click on the **OK** button to complete the new operation creation process.

Click on the **Source** button on the top of this window to open the code window of our Web service class file. Let's build the code for this new added operation.

In the opened code window, enter the code shown in Figure 9.43 into this new added operation, **InsertFaculty()**.

Let's have a closer look at this piece of code to see how it works.

A. First a local integer variable, **numInsert**, is created, and it is used to hold the run result of inserting a new faculty record into our sample database.

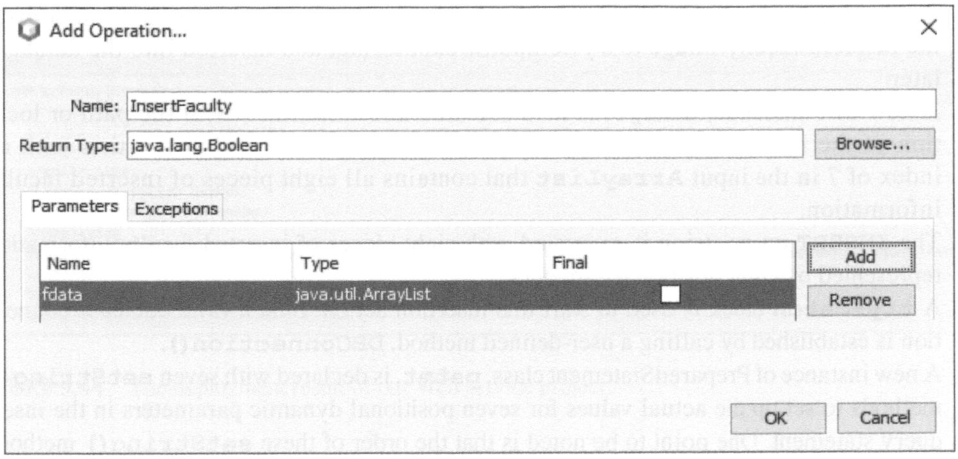

Add Operation...

Name: InsertFaculty

Return Type: java.lang.Boolean Browse...

Parameters Exceptions

Name	Type	Final
fdata	java.util.ArrayList	

Add Remove

OK Cancel

FIGURE 9.42 The complete Add Operation wizard.

```
  @WebMethod(operationName = "InsertFaculty")
    public Boolean InsertFaculty(@WebParam(name = "fdata") ArrayList fdata) {
      //TODO write your implementation code here:
A     int numInsert = 0;
B     FileInputStream fis = null;
C     File fimage= new File(fdata.get(7).toString());
D     String query = "INSERT INTO Faculty (faculty_id, faculty_name, title, office, phone, " +
                        "college, email, fimage) VALUES (?, ?, ?, ?, ?, ?, ?, ?)";
      try {
E       con = DBConnection(con);
F       PreparedStatement pstmt =con.prepareStatement(query);
        pstmt.setString(1, fdata.get(0).toString());
        pstmt.setString(2, fdata.get(1).toString());
        pstmt.setString(3, fdata.get(2).toString());
        pstmt.setString(4, fdata.get(3).toString());
        pstmt.setString(5, fdata.get(4).toString());
        pstmt.setString(6, fdata.get(5).toString());
        pstmt.setString(7, fdata.get(6).toString());
G       try {
            fis = new FileInputStream(fimage);
H       } catch (FileNotFoundException ex) {
I         Logger.getLogger(WebServiceFaculty.class.getName()).log(Level.SEVERE, null, ex);
        }
J       pstmt.setBinaryStream(8, (InputStream)fis, (int)(fimage.length()));
K       numInsert = pstmt.executeUpdate();
L       pstmt.close();
        con.close();
M       if (numInsert != 0)
          return true;
N       else
          return false;
      }
O     catch (Exception ex) {
        System.out.println("exception is: " + ex);
        return false;
      }
    }
  }
```

FIGURE 9.43 The code for the new operation, InsertFaculty().

Now you may find that our copied project contained some errors with red error indicators. The reason for that is because of our Web Service, since we need to update our Web Service Reference for the new project **WinClientFaculty _ Insert**.

9.9.1 Refresh the Web Service Reference for Our Window-Based Client Project

In order to call the **InsertFaculty()** operation in our Web service project, **WebService Faculty**, we need to refresh the Web reference in our Window-based client project to use the updated Web service project. Perform the following operations to refresh the Web service reference:

1) Build and deploy our Web Service application, **WebAppFaculty**, to make it available.
2) Open our Window-based client project, **WinClientFaculty _ Insert**, and expand the **Web Service References** node.
3) Right-click on our Web service, **WebServiceFaculty**, and choose the **Delete** item to remove this old Web reference.
4) Right-click on our Window-based client project, **WinClientFaculty _ Insert**, and select the **New > Web Service Client** item to open the **New Web Service Client** wizard.
5) In the opened wizard, click on the **Browse** button next to the **Project** field and expand our Web application, **WebAppFaculty**. Then choose our Web service, **WebServiceFaculty**, by clicking on it, and click on the **OK** button.
6) Click on the **Finish** button to complete the Web service reference refresh process.

Now that we have refreshed or updated the Web service reference for our Window-based client project **WinClientFaculty _ Insert**, next let's develop the code in our client project to call the Web service operation **InsertFaculty()** to perform faculty data insertion.

9.9.2 Develop the Code to Call Our Web Service Project

Open the Window-based client project **WinClientFaculty _ Insert** and double-click on our main class, **FacultyFrame.java**, to open it. Click on the **Design** button to open the graphic user interface. In this client project, we want to use the **Insert** button in this form as a trigger to start the faculty data insertion action. Therefore, double-click on the **Insert** button to open its event method, **InsertButtonActionPerformed()**, and enter the code shown in Figure 9.45 into this method.

Let's have a closer look at this piece of code to see how it works.

A. Some local objects are first declared, which include a File object, **imgFile**, which is used to hold the selected image file, and a new ArrayList instance, **al**, which is used to pick up and reserve the input new faculty data array.
B. A Java File Chooser instance, **imgChooser**, is generated, and it provides a file interface GUI to allow users to select a desired faculty image to be inserted into our database later.
C. The current directory, which is the folder of our current project, is selected, and this location will work as a default folder to store all selected faculty image files later.
D. The system method, **showOpenDialog()**, is executed to display the Chooser GUI to enable users to browse and select a desired faculty image to be inserted into our database later.
E. By checking one property, **APPROVE _ OPTION**, one can confirm whether the GUI operation is successful. If it is opened and an image has been selected, a **true** is returned. Then the selected image can be retrieved by calling a method, **getSelectedFile()**.
F. These two code lines are used to display the path and directory for the selected faculty image, and they are used for debugging purposes.
G. The **clear()** method is executed to make sure that the ArrayList instance is clean and empty before a new faculty record can be assigned to it.

```
  private void InsertButtonActionPerformed(java.awt.event.ActionEvent evt) {
     // TODO add your handling code here:
A    File imgFile = null;
     ArrayList al = new ArrayList();
B    JFileChooser imgChooser = new JFileChooser();
C    imgChooser.setCurrentDirectory(new File(System.getProperty("user.home")));
D    int result = imgChooser.showOpenDialog(this);
E    if (result == JFileChooser.APPROVE_OPTION) {
        imgFile = imgChooser.getSelectedFile();
F       System.out.println("Selected path: " + imgFile.getAbsolutePath());
        System.out.println("Selected file: " + imgFile.toString());
     }
G    al.clear();
H    al.add(0, FacultyIDField.getText().toString());
     al.add(1, FacultyNameField.getText().toString());
     al.add(2, TitleField.getText().toString());
     al.add(3, OfficeField.getText().toString());
     al.add(4, PhoneField.getText().toString());
     al.add(5, CollegeField.getText().toString());
     al.add(6, EmailField.getText().toString());
     al.add(7, imgFile.toString());
I    try {
        org.ws.oracle.WebServiceFaculty_Service service = new org.ws.oracle.WebServiceFaculty_Service();
        org.ws.oracle.WebServiceFaculty port = service.getWebServiceFacultyPort();
J       Boolean insert = port.insertFaculty(al);
K       if (!insert) {
           msgDlg.setMessage("The data insertion is failed!");
           msgDlg.setVisible(true);
        }
L       else
           ComboName.addItem(FacultyNameField.getText());
        }
M       catch (Exception ex){
          System.out.println("exception: " + ex);
        }
  }
```

FIGURE 9.45 The code for the Insert button event handler.

H. The **`add()`** method is used to pick up and add eight pieces of new faculty information into this new ArrayList instance, **`al`**. These eight pieces of new faculty information are entered by the user and stored in seven text fields and a File Chooser in the FacultyFrame window form. The **`toString()`** method is used to convert each piece of new faculty information obtained using the **`getText()`** method that returns an object data type to a String. The index is necessary since it is used to indicate the position of each parameter in this ArrayList. One point to be noted is the order of adding these text fields, which must be identical to the order of data columns in our **`Faculty`** Table.

I. A **`try-catch`** block is used to call our Web service operation, **`InsertFaculty()`**, to perform the faculty data insert action. First a new Web service instance, **`service`**, is created based on our Web service class, **`WebServiceFaculty _ Service`**. Then the **`getWebServiceFacultyPort()`** method is executed to get the current port used by our Web service. This port is returned and assigned to a new port instance, **`port`**.

J. The Web service operation **`InsertFaculty()`** is executed with the ArrayList instance **`al`** that has been filled with eight pieces of new faculty information as the argument of this method. The run result of that operation is returned and assigned to a Boolean variable, **`insert`**.

K. If the value of the variable **`insert`** is **`false`**, which means that no row has been inserted into our **`Faculty`** Table and this insertion has failed, the **`msgDlg`** instance is used to show this situation.

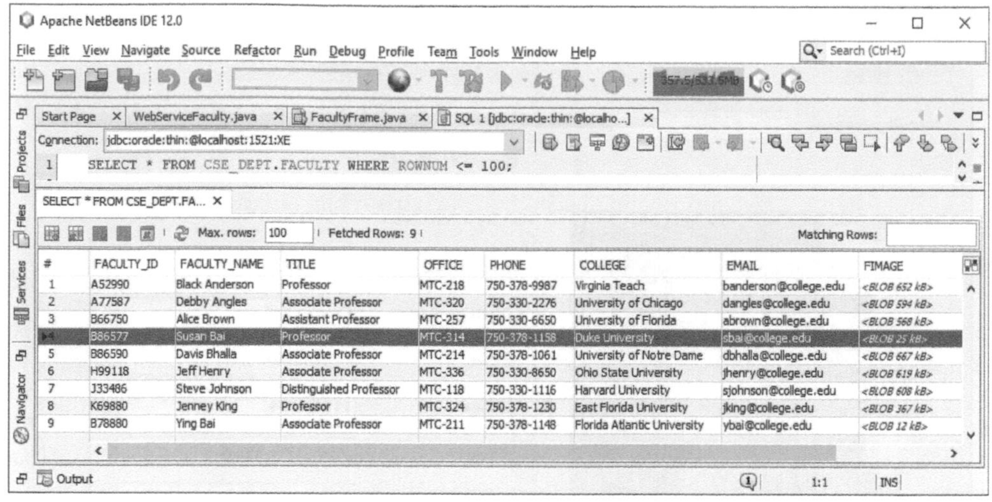

FIGURE 9.48 The opened Faculty Table in the NetBeans IDE.

Your opened **Faculty** Table is shown in Figure 9.48. It can be seen that the new faculty record, **Susan Bai**, with the **faculty _ id** of **B86577**, which is located in the fourth row, indicated by the dark color in this Table, has been successfully inserted into our database.

Next let's build a Web-based client project to consume our Web service to insert a new faculty record into the **Faculty** Table in our sample database.

9.10 BUILD A WEB-BASED CLIENT PROJECT TO CONSUME THE WEB SERVICE

We can still use the Web-based client project we built in Section 9.7, **WebClientFaculty _ Select**, to consume our Web service to perform the faculty data insertion action. But we prefer to modify that project and make it our new Web-based client project **WebClientFaculty _ Insert**. Let's copy that project and make it our new project. Perform the following steps to create our new project, **WebClientFaculty _ Insert**:

1) In the **Projects** window, right-click on the project **WebClientFaculty _ Select** and select the **Copy** item from the popup menu to open the **Copy Project** wizard.
2) Enter our new project name, **WebClientFaculty _ Insert**, into the **Project Name** box; browse to the default project folder, **C:\Class DB Projects\Chapter 9**, as the **Project Location**; and click on the **Copy** button.

A new project, **WebClientFaculty _ Insert**, is generated and added into our **Projects** window.

First let's add a Web service reference to our Web-based client project to allow it to use our Web service operations.

9.10.1 Refresh the Web Service Reference for Our Web-Based Client Project

In order to call the **InsertFaculty()** operation in our Web service project, **WebAppFaculty**, we need to refresh the Web reference in our Web-based client project, **WebClientFaculty _ Insert**, to use the updated Web service project. Perform the following operations to refresh the Web service reference:

1) Build and deploy our Web Service application project, **WebAppFaculty**, first.
2) Open our Web-based client project, **WebClientFaculty _ Insert**, and expand the **Web Service References** node.
3) Right-click on our Web service, **WebServiceFaculty**, and choose the **Delete** item to remove this old Web reference.
4) Right-click on our Web-based client project, **WebClientFaculty _ Insert**, and select the **New > Web Service Client** item to open the **New Web Service Client** wizard.
5) In the opened wizard, click on the **Browse** button next to the **Project** field and expand our Web application, **WebAppFaculty**. Then choose our Web service project, **WebServiceFaculty**, by clicking on it, and click on the **OK** button.
6) Click on the **Finish** button to complete the Web service reference refreshing process.

Now that we have refreshed or updated the Web service reference for our Web-based client project, **WebClientFaculty _ Insert**, next let's develop the code in our client project to call the Web service operation **InsertFaculty()** to perform faculty data insertion.

9.10.2 Develop the Code to Call Our Web Service Project

To call our Web Service project to insert a new faculty record into the Faculty Table in our sample database, we need to perform the following code modification and development:

1) Modify the view class **Faculty.jsp** file to add a File Selection function to enable users to select a new faculty image to be inserted into the database.
2) Modify the control class **FacultyProcess.jsp** page to direct the insert query to the related operational method defined in the Java Bean class **FacultyMBean.java** file.
3) Create and add code into the model class **FacultyMBean.java** to call the related operation, **InsertFaculty()**, defined in our Web Service to perform data insertion actions.

Let's handle these tasks one by one in the following section. First let's modify the view class **Faculty.jsp** by adding a File Selection function. Refer to Section 8.5.1 in Chapter 8 to perform this modification. For your convenience, we highlight the related modifications for that page in this part again. Perform the following steps to add this function:

1) Open the **Faculty.jsp** page and scroll down this file to find one of the input tags, which should be around line 381:

   <input name=FacultyImageField maxlength=255 size=18 value=""type=text v:shapes=" _ x0000 _ s1026">

2) Enter the following tag and locate it just above the tag shown previously.

   <input name=Faculty_Image maxlength=50 size=4 value=""type=file v:shapes=" _ x0000 _ s1026">

Your modified **Faculty.jsp** page should match the one shown in Figure 9.49. The new added tag part is in bold.

Next let's modify the controller class **FacultyProcess.jsp** file to direct the insert query to the related method defined in that class.

Open the controller class file, **FacultyProcess.jsp**, and perform the following modifications, as shown in Figure 9.50, to that file.

```
  public int InsertFaculty(String[] newFaculty) {
A     int numInsert = 1;
      ArrayList al = new ArrayList();
B     al.clear();
C     al.add(0, newFaculty[0]);
      al.add(1, newFaculty[1]);
      al.add(2, newFaculty[2]);
      al.add(3, newFaculty[3]);
      al.add(4, newFaculty[4]);
      al.add(5, newFaculty[5]);
      al.add(6, newFaculty[6]);
      al.add(7, newFaculty[7]);
      try{
D       org.ws.oracle.WebServiceFaculty_Service service = new org.ws.oracle.WebServiceFaculty_Service();
        org.ws.oracle.WebServiceFaculty port = service.getWebServiceFacultyPort();
E       Boolean insert = port.insertFaculty(al);
F       if (!insert) {
          System.out.println("The data insertion is failed!");
          return 0;
        }
      }
G     catch (Exception e) {
        System.out.println("Error in Insert Statement! " + e.getMessage());
        return 0;
      }
H     return numInsert;
  }
```

FIGURE 9.51 The modified code for the Insert() method.

9.10.3 Build and Run Our Client Project to Insert Faculty Data via Web Service

Prior to building and running this Web application, make sure that the new faculty image to be inserted into our database has been stored in your local folder, such as **`C:\Faculty Images`**. All faculty images can be found in the folder **`Images\Faculty`** in the **`Students`** folder on the CRC Press ftp site. One can copy and paste them to your local folder. Also make sure that our Web Service application project, **`WebAppFaculty`**, has been built and deployed.

Now click on the **`Clean and Build Main Project`** button to build our client project. If everything is fine, click on the **`Run Project`** button (green arrow) to run our client project.

On the opened view class **`Faculty.jsp`** page, enter the following data as a new faculty record into the seven related TextFields and select the desired faculty image.

- Faculty ID: `D58996`
- Name: **`Charley David`**
- Title: **`Professor`**
- Office: `MTC-114`
- Phone: `750-378-1500`
- College: **`University of Miami`**
- Email: **`cdavid@college.edu`**
- Fimage **`David.jpg`**

Then click on the **`Browse`** button in the File Selection box (right on the **`Image`** label) to select a desired faculty image, **`David.jpg`**, from your local image folder. The finished new faculty record is shown in Figure 9.52.

Click on the **`Insert`** button to try to call our Web service operation, **`InsertFaculty()`**, to insert this new faculty record into the **`Faculty`** Table in our sample database.

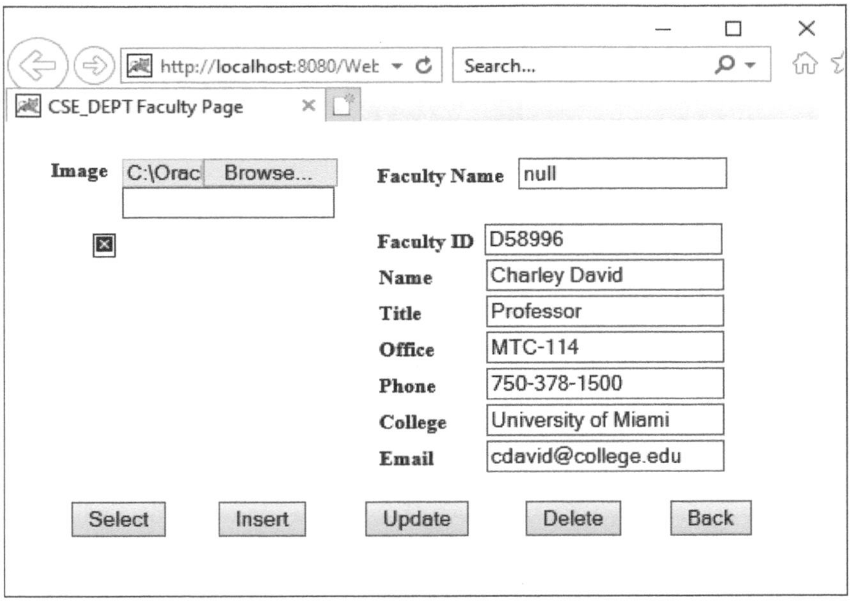

http://localhost:8080/Wet
Search...
CSE_DEPT Faculty Page
Image
C:\Orac
Browse...
Faculty Name
null
Faculty ID
D58996
Name
Charley David
Title
Professor
Office
MTC-114
Phone
750-378-1500
College
University of Miami
Email
cdavid@college.edu
Select
Insert
Update
Delete
Back

FIGURE 9.52 Seven pieces of new inserted faculty information.

http://localhost:8080/Wet
Search...
CSE_DEPT Faculty Page
Image
Browse...
Faculty Name
Charley David
Faculty ID
D58996
Name
Charley David
Title
Professor
Office
MTC-114
Phone
750-378-1500
College
University of Miami
Email
cdavid@college.edu
Select
Insert
Update
Delete
Back

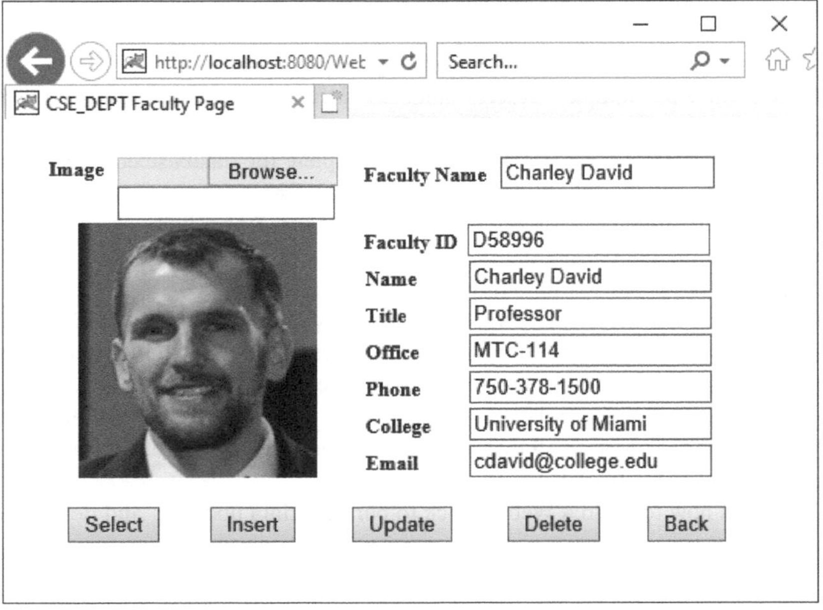

FIGURE 9.53 The confirmation of a new faculty record insertion.

To confirm this data insert, two methods can be used. The first way is to perform another query for the selected faculty `Charley David` by typing this name into the Faculty Name box and clicking on the `Select` button. Now you can find that seven pieces of new inserted faculty information have been retrieved and displayed in this page with the selected faculty image, as shown in Figure 9.53. Click on the `Back` button to terminate our project.

```
  @WebMethod(operationName = "UpdateFaculty")
    public Boolean UpdateFaculty(@WebParam(name = "fdata") ArrayList fdata) {
    //TODO write your implementation code here:
A   int numUpdated = 0;
B   FileInputStream fis = null;
C   File fimage= new File(fdata.get(6).toString());
D   String query = "UPDATE Faculty SET faculty_name=?, title=?, office=?, phone=?, college=?," +
                   "email=?, fimage=? " + "WHERE faculty_id= ?";
    try {
E       con = DBConnection(con);
F       PreparedStatement pstmt =con.prepareStatement(query);
G       pstmt.setString(1, fdata.get(0).toString());
        pstmt.setString(2, fdata.get(1).toString());
        pstmt.setString(3, fdata.get(2).toString());
        pstmt.setString(4, fdata.get(3).toString());
        pstmt.setString(5, fdata.get(4).toString());
        pstmt.setString(6, fdata.get(5).toString());
        pstmt.setString(8, fdata.get(7).toString());      // faculty_id
        try {
H           fis = new FileInputStream(fimage);
I       } catch (FileNotFoundException ex) {
          Logger.getLogger(WebServiceFaculty.class.getName()).log(Level.SEVERE, null, ex);
        }
J       pstmt.setBinaryStream(7, (InputStream)fis, (int)(fimage.length()));
K       numUpdated = pstmt.executeUpdate();
L       con.close();
M       if (numUpdated != 0)
          return true;
N       else
          return false;
    }
O   catch (Exception ex) {
        System.out.println("exception is: " + ex);
        return false;
    }
  }
}
```

FIGURE 9.56 The code for the new operation, UpdateFaculty().

Let's have a closer look at this piece of code to see how it works.

A. A local integer variable, **numUpdated**, is created first, and this variable is used to hold the run result of execution of the data update operation.
B. An instance of the FileInputStream class, **fis**, is generated and it is used to convert the updated faculty image to a FileInputStream format, and the converted image file can be updated to the database later.
C. A new File instance, **fimage**, is also declared and initialized with the path or location of the updated faculty image, which is located at the sixth position with an index of 6 on the input **ArrayList** that contains all eight pieces of updated faculty information. A point to be noted is that the variable in the seventh position (7) in the input ArrayList is the **faculty _ id** parameter.
D. The update query string is created with eight positional parameters. The query criterion is the **faculty _ id** that is the eighth positional parameter and placed after the **WHERE** clause.
E. A **try-catch** block is used to perform this data update action. First a user-defined method, **DBConnection()**, is called to set up a connection between our Web service and our sample database. A connection instance, **con**, is returned after the execution of this method.
F. A new PreparedStatement instance, **pstmt**, is created to perform this update query.

G. Seven **setString()** methods are used to set up the actual values for the seven positional dynamic updated parameters in the update query statement. One point to be noted is that the order of these **setString()** methods is not continuous from 1 to 8 because the seventh positional parameter is the updated faculty image, which will be processed separately, and the eighth positional parameter is the **faculty _ id**.
H. Another **try-catch** block is used to convert the updated faculty image to the FileInputStream format and make it ready to be written into the database.
I. The **catch** block is used to check any possible exception for this conversion. The exception information will be recorded into a system log file if it occurs.
J. The converted faculty image is written into the seventh positional dynamic parameter via a **setBinaryStream()** system method.
K. The update action is performed by calling the **executeUpdate()** method, and the update result is returned and stored in the local integer variable **numUpdated**.
L. The database connection is closed by executing the **close()** method since we have completed our data update action and need to disconnect our database.
M. The **executeUpdate()** method will return an integer to indicate whether this data update is successful or not. If a non-zero value is returned, which means that at least one row has been updated in our **Faculty** Table and this data update action is successful, a **true** is returned to the client project.
N. Otherwise, if a zero is returned, it means that no row has been updated in our sample database and this data update fails. A **false** is returned for this situation.
O. The **catch** block is used to track and display any exception during this data update process, and a **false** will be returned if one occurs.

Before we can build a Window-Based or Web-Based project to consume this Web Service project to test the data update function, let's take care of the code for the data delete action against our sample database using the Web service operation **DeleteFaculty()**.

9.11.2 Add a New Operation DeleteFaculty() to Perform Faculty Data Delete

Perform the following operations to add a new operation, **DeleteFaculty()**, into our Web service project, **WebServiceFaculty**:

1) Launch NetBeans IDE 12.0 and open our Web application project, **WebAppFaculty**, and our Web service main class file, **WebServiceFaculty.java**, in the **Projects** window.
2) Click on the **Design** button at the top of the window to open the Design View of our Web service class file **WebServiceFaculty.java**.
3) Click on the **Add Operation** button to open the **Add Operation** wizard.
4) Enter **DeleteFaculty** into the **Name** field and click on the **Browse** button that is next to the **Return Type** combo box. Type **boolean** into the **Type Name** field and select the item **Boolean (java.lang)** from the list, and click on the **OK** button.
5) Click on the **Add** button and enter **fname** into the **Name** parameter field to add a new parameter for this operation. Keep the default data type **java.lang.String** unchanged for this new added parameter **fname**.

Your finished **Add Operation** wizard should match the one shown in Figure 9.57. Click on the **OK** button to complete the new operation creation process.

Click on the **Source** button at the top of this window to open the code window of our Web service project. Let's build the code for this new added operation.

In the opened code window, enter the code shown in Figure 9.58 into the new operation.

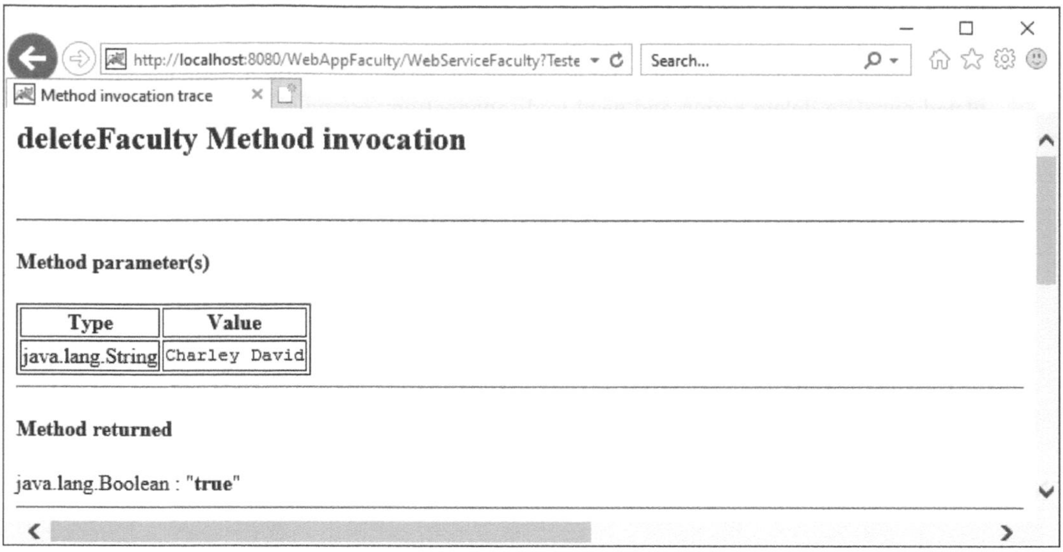

FIGURE 9.59 The test result of the delete operation.

Recall that when we built our sample Oracle database, **CSE _ DEPT**, in Chapter 2, we created all original columns in different Tables for an original faculty record. For example, for an original faculty member, **Ying Bai**, we setup a **faculty _ id** related to that member in the **LogIn** Table and detailed information with eight columns in the **Faculty** Table, some columns in the **Course** Table and some courses in the **StudentCourse** Table. These columns made some relationships via primary or foreign keys. If this kind of faculty record were deleted from the **Faculty** Table, all other related columns in other Tables would also be deleted.

Recalled that a cascaded update and delete relationship among our five Tables was established when we built our sample database in Chapter 2. Therefore, if an original faculty record, such as **Ying Bai**, were deleted from the **Faculty** Table, not only would that single faculty record be deleted from the **Faculty** Table but all columns related to that faculty member in other Tables, such as the **LogIn**, **Course** and **StudentCourse**, would also be deleted because of this cascade relationship.

If that kind of delete action is performed, it is highly recommended to recover the deleted faculty and related records in our **Faculty**, **LogIn**, **Course** and **StudentCourse** Tables. An easy way to do this recovery is to use records shown in Tables 9.1–9.4 and follow these steps:

1) First run either the **WinClientFaculty _ Insert** or **WebClientFaculty _ Insert** project to insert the deleted faculty record shown in Table 9.1.
2) Use the Oracle SQL Developer to add the related records shown in Tables 9.2~9.4 one by one manually.

The order of these operations is very important when doing the recovery, since the **Faculty** Table is a parent Table and the **faculty _ id** of the deleted faculty record is a primary key in the Faculty Table. Thus, the faculty record must be recovered prior to recovering any other records in any other Tables.

Next we can develop a client project to consume this Web service to perform data update and delete actions to the **Faculty** Table in our sample database. First let's discuss how to build a Window-based client project to consume our Web service.

TABLE 9.1
The Deleted Record in the Faculty Table

faculty_id	faculty_name	office	phone	college	title	email	fimage
B78880	Ying Bai	MTC-211	750–378–1148	Florida Atlantic University	Associate Professor	ybai@college.edu	Bai.jpg

TABLE 9.2
The Deleted Records in the Course Table

course_id	course	credit	classroom	schedule	enrollment	faculty_id
CSC-132B	Introduction to Programming	3	TC-302	T-H: 1:00–2:25 PM	21	B78880
CSC-234A	Data Structure & Algorithms	3	TC-302	M-W-F: 9:00–9:55 AM	25	B78880
CSE-434	Advanced Electronics Systems	3	TC-213	M-W-F: 1:00–1:55 PM	26	B78880
CSE-438	Advd Logic & Microprocessor	3	TC-213	M-W-F: 11:00–11:55 AM	35	B78880

TABLE 9.3
The Deleted Records in the LogIn Table

user_name	pass_word	faculty_id	student_id
ybai	come	B78880	NULL

TABLE 9.4
The Deleted Records in the StudentCourse Table

s_course_id	student_id	course_id	credit	major
1005	T77896	CSC-234A	3	CS/IS
1009	A78835	CSE-434	3	CE
1014	A78835	CSE-438	3	CE
1016	A97850	CSC-132B	3	ISE
1017	A97850	CSC-234A	3	ISE

9.12 BUILD A WINDOW-BASED CLIENT PROJECT TO CONSUME THE WEB SERVICE

We can still use the Window-based client project **`WinClientFaculty _ Insert`** we built in Section 9.9 to consume the Web service to perform faculty data update and delete actions. One point to be noted is that although a Web reference to our Web service was established in Section 9.9, we

H. A sequence of **add()** methods is used to pick up and add eight pieces of updated faculty information into this new ArrayList instance, **al**. These eight pieces of updated faculty information are entered by the user and stored in seven text fields and the File Chooser in this FacultyFrame window form. The **toString()** method is used to convert the pieces of faculty information obtained using the **getText()** method that returns an object data type to a String. The index is necessary since it is used to indicate the position of each parameter in this ArrayList. One point to be noted is the order of adding these text fields, which must be identical to the order of columns in our **Faculty** Table.

I. A **try catch** block is used to perform the calling of our Web service operation, **UpdateFaculty()**, to perform this faculty data update action. First a new Web service instance, **service**, is created based on our Web service class, **WebServiceFaculty _ Service**. Then the **getWebServiceFacultyPort()** method is executed to get the current port used by our Web service. This port is returned and assigned to a new port instance, **port**.

J. The Web service operation **updateFaculty()** is executed with the ArrayList instance **al** that has been filled with eight pieces of updated faculty information as the argument of this method. The run result of that operation is returned and assigned to a Boolean variable, **update**.

K. If the value of the variable **update** is **false**, which means that no row has been updated in our **Faculty** Table and this update action has failed, the **msgDlg** instance is used to show this situation.

L. Otherwise, if the value of the **update** variable is **true**, which means that the data update action is successful, the new updated faculty name will be added into the Faculty Name combo box **ComboName** using the **addItem()** method.

M. The **catch** block is used to track and display any possible exception during this Web service operation execution.

Next let's build the code to perform the faculty data delete action.

9.12.3 Build the Code to Call the DeleteFaculty() Operation

Open our Window-based client project, **WinClientFaculty _ UpdtDelt**, and double-click on our main class, **FacultyFrame.java**, to open it. Click on the **Design** button to open the graphic user interface. In this client project, we need to use the **Delete** button in this form as a trigger to start the faculty data delete action. Therefore double-click on the **Delete** button to open its event method, **DeleteButtonActionPerformed()**.

Enter the code shown in Figure 9.61 into this **DeleteButtonActionPerformed()** event handler. Let's have a closer look at this piece of code to see how it works.

A. A **try catch** block is used to call our Web service operation **DeleteFaculty()** to perform the faculty data delete action. First a new Web service instance **service** is created based on our Web service class, **WebServiceFaculty _ Service**. Then the **getWebServiceFacultyPort()** method is executed to get the current port used by our Web service. This port is returned and assigned to a new port instance, **port**.

B. The Web service operation **DeleteFaculty()** is executed with the selected faculty name as the argument of this method. The run result of that operation is returned and assigned to a Boolean variable, **delete**.

C. If the value of the returned variable **delete** is **false**, which means that no row has been deleted from our **Faculty** Table and the data delete action has failed, the **msgDlg** instance is used to show this situation. Otherwise, the data delete action is successful.

D. The **catch** block is used to track and display any possible exception during this Web service operation execution.

```
  private void DeleteButtonActionPerformed(java.awt.event.ActionEvent evt) {
   // TODO add your handling code here:
   try {
A      org.ws.oracle.WebServiceFaculty_Service service = new org.ws.oracle.WebServiceFaculty_Service();
       org.ws.oracle.WebServiceFaculty port = service.getWebServiceFacultyPort();
B      Boolean delete = port.deleteFaculty(ComboName.getSelectedItem().toString());
C      if (!delete) {
          msgDlg.setMessage("The data deleting is failed!");
          msgDlg.setVisible(true);
       }
     }
D    catch (Exception ex){
        System.out.println("exception: " + ex);
     }
  }
```

FIGURE 9.61 The complete code for the DeleteButtonActionPerformed() method.

At this point, we have completed all code development for our Window-based client project for the data update and delete actions. Now let's build and run our client project to call and test our Web service to perform faculty data update and delete actions.

9.12.4 Build and Run Our Client Project to Update and Delete Faculty Record via Web Service

Prior to building and running our client project to consume our Web Service project, make sure that our Web Service application project, **`WebAppFaculty`**, has been successfully built and deployed to make it ready to be called by the client project.

Click on the **`Clean and Build Main Project`** button to build our client project. If everything is fine, click on the **`Run Main Project`** button to run our client project.

The FacultyFrame form window is displayed. First let's perform a faculty query action. Select a desired faculty member, such as **`Ying Bai`**, from the Faculty Name combo box and click on the **`Select`** button to query the detailed information for this faculty via our Web service **`WebServiceFaculty`**. The queried result is displayed in seven text fields and the PictureBox with the selected faculty image.

Now enter a updated faculty record with the following six pieces of updated faculty information into six text fields, shown in Figure 9.62.

- Name: **`Michael Bai`**
- Title: **`Assistant Professor`**
- Office: **`MTC-200`**
- Phone: **`750-378-2000`**
- College: **`Stanford University`**
- Email: **`mbai@college.edu`**

Click on the **`Update`** button to browse and select the desired updated faculty image; in this case, it is **`Michael.jpg`**, and then try to call our Web service operation, **`UpdateFaculty()`**, to update this faculty record in our sample database. Keep our project running and do not terminate it.

To confirm the data update action, two methods can be used. First we can use the **`Select`** button to retrieve the updated faculty record from our sample database to confirm the update action. To do that, go to the **`Faculty Name`** combo box, and you can see that the updated faculty name, **`Michael Bai`**, has been added into this box. Click this name to select it and click on the **`Select`** button. You can find that six pieces of updated faculty information have been retrieved and displayed in this form window, as shown in Figure 9.63. Our data update is successful!

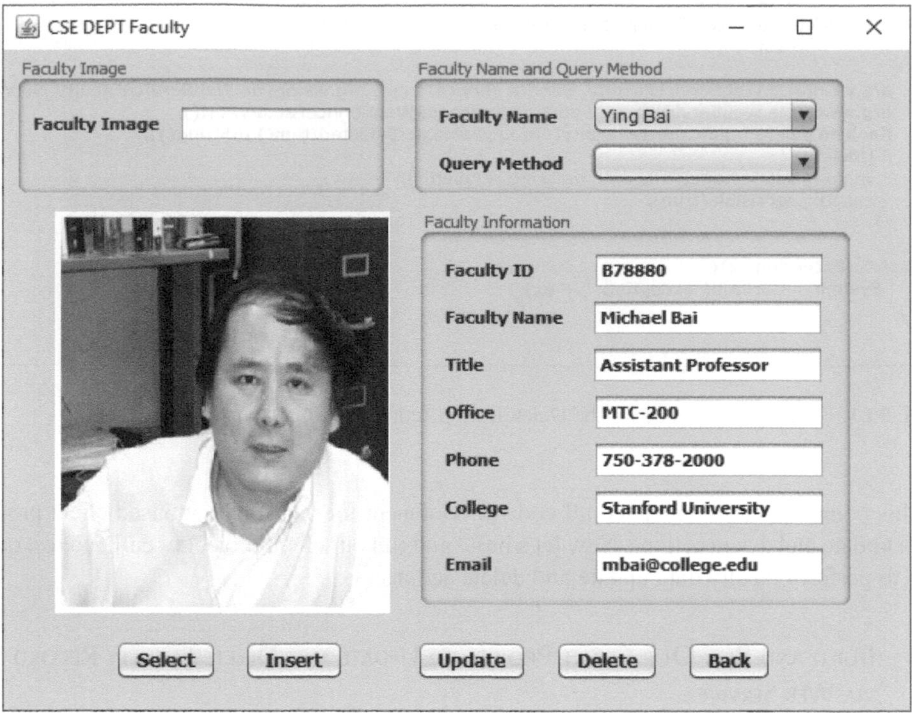

FIGURE 9.62 Six pieces of updated faculty information.

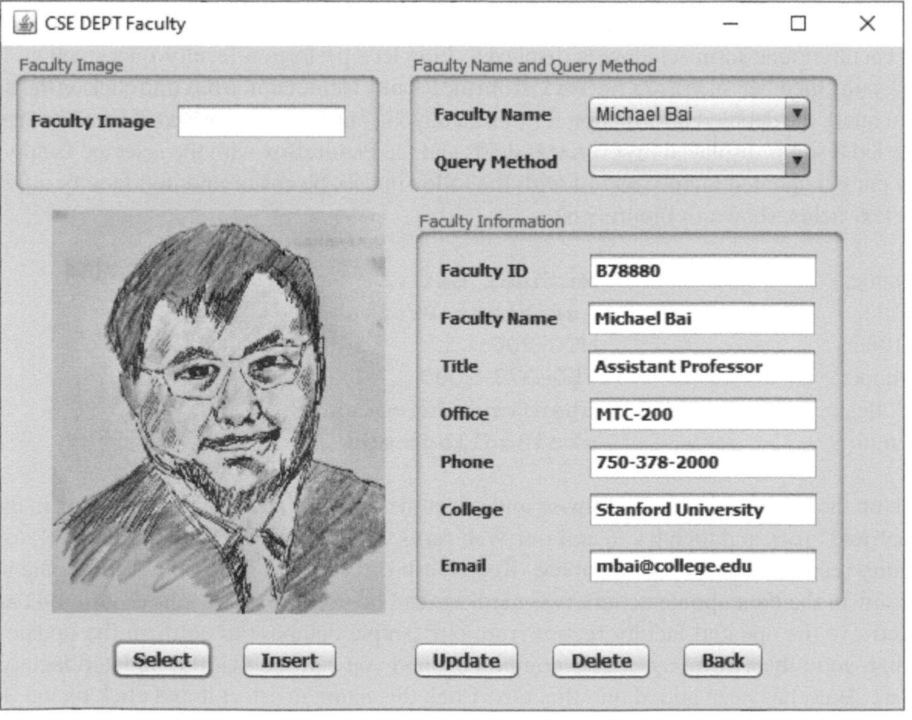

FIGURE 9.63 The updated faculty information.

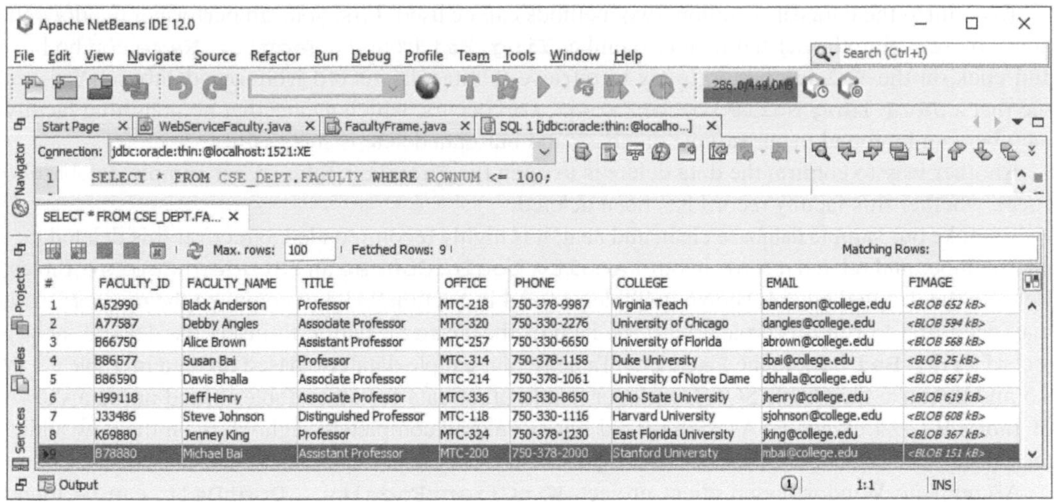

FIGURE 9.64 The opened Faculty Table in the NetBeans IDE.

TABLE 9.5
The Original Faculty Record in the Faculty Table

faculty_id	faculty_name	office	phone	college	title	email	fimage
B78880	Ying Bai	MTC-211	750–378–1148	Florida Atlantic University	Associate Professor	ybai@college.edu	Bai.jpg

The second way to confirm the data update action is to open our **Faculty** Table using either the **Services** window in the NetBeans IDE or the Oracle SQL Developer to check whether the faculty record has been updated. To do that using the **Services** window in the NetBeans IDE 12.0, perform the following operations:

1) Open the **Services** window and expand the **Databases** node.
2) Right-click on our Oracle database URL: **jdbc:oracle:thin:@localhost:1521:XE;**, and select the **Connect** item to try to connect to our database. Enter **oracle _ 18c** into the Password box and click on the **OK** button.
3) Expand our sample database, **CSE _ DEPT**, and **Tables**.
4) Right-click on the **Faculty** Table and select the **View Data** item.

Your opened **Faculty** Table is shown in Figure 9.64. It can be seen that the faculty record with the **faculty _ id** of **B78880**, which is located at row 9 and had been highlighted, has been successfully updated.

However, it is highly recommended to recover this updated faculty record to the original one to keep our database clean. Refer to Table 9.5 to perform another data update action by using the **Update** button on this FacultyFrame Form to recover this faculty record to the original one with the faculty name as **Ying Bai**. Now click on the **Back** button to terminate our project.

Next let's test the faculty record delete action via our Web service operation **DeleteFaculty()**. Keep the faculty member **Ying Bai** selected in the Faculty Name combo box, and click on the **Delete** button to try to call our Web service operation **DeleteFaculty()** to delete this faculty record from our sample database.

To confirm the data delete action, two methods can be used. First you can perform a faculty data query by selecting the deleted faculty member **Ying Bai** from the **Faculty Name** combo box, and click on the **Select** button to try to retrieve this faculty record from our database. You can see that a **Java.lang.NullPointerException** occurs, which means that no matching faculty member can be found in our sample database and our data delete is successful.

Another way to confirm the data delete is to open the **Faculty** Table in our sample database to check whether this faculty record has been deleted.

To make our sample database clean and neat, it is highly recommended to recover this deleted faculty member and related records in our **Faculty**, **LogIn**, **Course** and **StudentCourse** Tables. Refer to the original records shown in Tables 9.1~9.4 in Section 9.11.3 to complete the recovery. You may need first to run this project with the help of the **Insert** button to insert the deleted faculty record **Ying Bai** back to the **Faculty** Table in our sample database based on data in Table 9.1 or 9.5 and then use the Oracle SQL Developer to add other data for other Tables based on data shown in Tables 9.2~9.4 manually. As each record line is entered completely, right-click on the new added record line and select the **Commit Changes** item from the popup menu to add that record.

A complete Window-based client project, **WinClientFaculty _ DpdtDelt**, can be found in the folder **Class DB Projects\Chapter 9** that is located in the **Students** folder at the CRC Press ftp site.

Next let's build a Web-based client project to consume our Web service to insert a new faculty record into the Faculty Table in our sample database.

9.13 BUILD A WEB-BASED CLIENT PROJECT TO CONSUME THE WEB SERVICE

We can still use the Web-based client project **WebClientFaculty _ Insert** we built in Section 9.10 to consume our Web service to perform the faculty data updating and delete action. But we prefer to modify that project and make it our new Web-based client project, **WebClientFaculty _ UpdtDelt**. Let's copy that project and change it to our new project. Perform the following steps to create our new project, **WebClientFaculty _ UpdtDelt**:

1) In the **Projects** window, right-click on the project **WebClientFaculty _ Insert** and select the **Copy** item from the popup menu to open the **Copy Project** wizard.
2) Enter our new project name, **WebClientFaculty _ UpdtDelt**, into the **Project Name** box; browse to the default project folder, **C:\Class DB Projects\Chapter 9**, as the **Project Location**; and click on the **Copy** button.

A new project, **WebClientFaculty _ UpdtDelt**, is generated and added into our **Projects** window. Some errors may be involved in our Java Bean class, **FacultyMBean.java**, and this is due to the updated Web Service we built by adding two new operations, **UpdateFaculty()** and **DeleteFaculty()**. To solve this error, we need to update or refresh our Web Reference in our new project.

Now let's modify the Web service reference to our Web-based client project to allow it to use our updated Web service operations.

9.13.1 Refresh the Web Service Reference for Our Web-Based Client Project

Perform the following operations to refresh the Web service reference:

1) Build and deploy our Web Service project, **WebAppFaculty**, first to make it ready.
2) Expand the folder **Web Service References** under our new project, right-click on the **WebServiceFaculty** and select the **Delete** item to remove this old reference.

3) Right-click on our Web-based client project, **WebClientFaculty _ UpdtDelt**, and select the **New > Web Service Client** item to open the **New Web Service Client** wizard.
4) In the opened wizard, click on the **Browse** button next to the **Project** field and expand our Web application, **WebAppFaculty**. Then choose our Web service class, **WebServiceFaculty**, by clicking on it, and click on the **OK** button.
5) Click on the **Finish** button to complete the adding Web service reference process.

Now build our new project, and the related error should have disappeared.

At this point, we have refreshed our Web service reference to our Web-based client project, **WebClientFaculty _ UpdtDelt**. Next let's develop the code in our client project to call the Web service operations **UpdateFaculty()** and **DeleteFaculty()** to perform faculty data update and delete actions. The main code is inside the Java Bean class file, **FacultyMBean.java**.

First let's take care of the data update operation **UpdateFaculty()**.

9.13.2 Develop the Code to Call Our Web Service Operation UpdateFaculty()

The main coding process includes two parts: generate code in the Java managed bean class **FacultyMBean.java** and add code into the Control class **FacultyProcess.jsp** page.

A binding relationship between the **action** attribute of the **Update** command Button in our JSP page **Faculty.jsp** and the **Update _ Faculty()** method that will be built in our Java managed bean **FacultyMBean.java** has been established. Therefore we can concentrate on the code developments for the **Update _ Faculty()** method in our Java managed bean class.

Open our Web-based client project, **WebClientFaculty _ UpdtDelt**, and double-click on the **FacultyMBean.java** in the **Projects** window to open this managed bean class file. Add the code shown in Figure 9.65 as a new method, **Update _ Faculty()**, into this class file; locate it just under the **InsertFaculty()** method.

```
A  public int Update_Faculty(String[] upFaculty) {
B    int numUpdated = 1;
     ArrayList al = new ArrayList();
C    al.clear();
D    al.add(0, upFaculty[0]);     // faculty_name
     al.add(1, upFaculty[1]);     // title
     al.add(2, upFaculty[2]);     // office
     al.add(3, upFaculty[3]);     // phone
     al.add(4, upFaculty[4]);     // college
     al.add(5, upFaculty[5]);     // email
     al.add(6, upFaculty[6]);     // fimage
     al.add(7, upFaculty[7]);     // faculty_id
E    try{
        org.ws.oracle.WebServiceFaculty_Service service = new org.ws.oracle.WebServiceFaculty_Service();
        org.ws.oracle.WebServiceFaculty port = service.getWebServiceFacultyPort();
F       Boolean update = port.updateFaculty(al);
G       if (!update) {
           System.out.println("The data updating is failed!");
           return 0;
        }
     }
H    catch (Exception e) {
        System.out.println("Error in Update Statement! " + e.getMessage());
        return 0;
     }
I    return numUpdated;
   }
```

FIGURE 9.65 The new generated code for the Update_Faculty() method.

```
   .........
   else if (request.getParameter("Update")!= null) {
           //process the faculty record updating
A          %>
B          <jsp:useBean id="UpdateFaculty" scope="session" class="webclient.FacultyMBean" />
C          <jsp:setProperty name="UpdateFaculty" property="*" />
D          <%
E          if (request.getParameter("Faculty_Image")== null)
              out.println("Select a valid faculty image!");
F          else {
              int update = 0;
G             String fname = request.getParameter("NameField");
              String office = request.getParameter("OfficeField");
              String phone = request.getParameter("PhoneField");
              String college = request.getParameter("CollegeField");
              String title = request.getParameter("TitleField");
              String email = request.getParameter("EmailField");
              String fImage = request.getParameter("Faculty_Image");
              String f_id = request.getParameter("FacultyIDField");
H             String[] upf = {fname, title, office, phone, college, email, fImage, f_id };
I             update = UpdateFaculty.Update_Faculty(upf);
J             if (update == 0)
                 response.sendRedirect("Faculty.jsp");
K             else {
                 for (int index = 1; index < 8; index++)
                   session.setAttribute(F_Field[index], null);
                 response.sendRedirect("Faculty.jsp");
              }
           }
       }
   else if (request.getParameter("Delete")!= null) {
           //process the faculty record deleting
L          %>
M          <jsp:useBean id="DeleteFaculty" scope="session" class="webclient.FacultyMBean" />
N          <jsp:setProperty name="DeleteFaculty" property="*" />
O          <%

P          int delete = 0;
Q          String fname = request.getParameter("FacultyNameField");
R          delete = DeleteFaculty.Delete_Faculty(fname);
           response.sendRedirect("Faculty.jsp");
           }
S          %>
     </body>
   </html>
```

FIGURE 9.67 The completed code for two methods.

D. A JSP opening tag, `<%`, is used to begin our Java code development process.

E. First we need to check whether the user has selected a desired faculty image for the data update. If no faculty image has been selected, the system method **`getParameter()`** will return a **`null`**; then another system method **`out.println()`** is used to indicate this case, and the program returns to the Control class **`FacultyProcess.jsp`** without any further operations.

F. Otherwise, it means that a valid faculty image has been selected and the data update action can be executed. First a local integer variable, **`update`**, is declared and initialized to 0. This variable will be used to hold the data update result later.

G. Eight system methods, **`getParameter()`**, are used to pick up eight pieces of updated faculty information from the related TextFields in our View class **`Faculty.jsp`** page, which are entered by the user, and assign each of them to the related String variable.

H. All eight pieces of updated faculty information are collected into a String array, **`upf`**, that will work as an argument to be passed with the user-defined method **`Update_Faculty()`** defined in our Java Bean class to perform data update action in the next line.

I. The data update action is performed by calling our method, **Update _ Faculty()**, that is prefixed with our active Bean class ID, **UpdateFaculty**, which is defined by using the **jsp:useBean** action tag in step B.
J. The run result of calling **Update _ Faculty()** method is returned and assigned to our local integer variable, **update**. If the returned value is 0, it means that no faculty record has been updated and this data update action fails. The **Faculty.jsp** page is resent or redisplayed to indicate this situation.
K. Otherwise, if the returned value is nonzero, it means that at least one faculty record has been updated, and all seven TextFields are cleaned up to enable users to test or check this data update action. The original **Faculty.jsp** page is redisplayed.
L. As we did before, move the cursor to the **else if (request.getParameter("De lete")!= null)** block, then type a JSP ending tag, **%>**, under the **else if** statement, and click on the **Enter** key from the keyboard to get a new line under the **else if** block.
M. Following steps B, C and D, use **jsp:useBean** and **jsp:setProperty** action tags to create our active Bean with ID of **DeleteFaculty** and setup all properties for that Bean to allow all JSP pages to access them in the scope of the session with steps N and O.
P. A local variable, **delete**, is created, and it is used to hold the data delete result later.
Q. The system method **getParameter()** is used to get the faculty name as a criterion and whose record will be deleted from the **Faculty** Table in our sample database.
R. The data delete action is performed by calling our method, **Delete _ Faculty()**, that is prefixed with our active Bean class ID, **DeleteFaculty**, which is defined in step M.
S. Finally, a JSP ending tag **%>** is used to terminate our Java code.

Now let's build and run our Web client project to call our Web service operations to perform the faculty data update and delete actions.

9.13.5 Build and Run Our Client Project to Update and Delete Faculty Record via Web Service

Prior to building and running our Web client project, build and deploy our Web Service project to make it ready. Click on the **Clean and Build Main Project** button to build our client project. If everything is fine, click on the **Run Main Project** button (greenarrow) to run our client project.

The **Faculty.jsp** page is displayed. First let's perform a faculty query action. Select a desired faculty member, such as **Ying Bai**, from the Faculty Name combo box and click on the **Select** button to query the detailed information for this faculty. The queried result is displayed in seven TextFields and the Image Box with the selected faculty image.

Now enter an updated faculty record with these six pieces of updated faculty information into six TextFields (keep the Faculty ID with no change), which is shown in Figure 9.68.

- Name: **Michael Bai**
- Title: **Assistant Professor**
- Office: **MTC-200**
- Phone: **750-378-2000**
- College: **Stanford University**
- Email: **mbai@college.edu**

Then click on the **Browse** button located on the right of the **Image** label on the top to select a desired image for this updated faculty member, such as **Michael.jpg**. All faculty image files are located in the folder **Images\Faculty**, which is in the **Students** folder at the CRC Press ftp site. You can copy all of image files and store them to one of your local folders to use them.

9.14 BUILD JAVA WEB SERVICE PROJECT TO ACCESS COURSE TABLE IN OUR SAMPLE DATABASE

We have provided very detailed discussions and analyses on accessing and manipulating the **Faculty** Table in our sample database. Starting from this section, we will concentrate on accessing and manipulating data in the **Course** Table in our sample database.

9.14.1 Create a New Java Web Application Project, WebAppCourse

First let's create a new Java Web Application project as a container. Perform the following operations to create our new Web application, **WebAppCourse**:

1) Launch NetBeans IDE 12.0 and choose **File > New Project**. Expand the **Java with Ant** folder and select **JavaWeb** from the **Categories** list and **Web Application** from the **Projects** list, then click on the **Next** button.
2) Name the project **WebAppCourse** and click on the **Browse** button to select a desired location for the project. In this application, we used the **C:\Class DB Projects\Chapter 9** as our project location. Click on the **Next** button to continue.
3) Select **GlassFish Server** as our Web Server and **Java EE 7 Web** as the Java EE version, your finished **Server and Settings** wizard should match the one shown in Figure 9.71. Click on the **Next** button to go to the next wizard.
4) In the opened Frameworks wizard, click on the **Finish** button to complete the new application creation process.

Now that a Web application has been created with a selected Web container, next we can create our new Web service project **WebServiceCourse**.

9.14.2 Create a New Java SOAP-Based Web Service Project WebServiceCourse

The function of this Web service is to execute related operations in this Web service and furthermore to call the associated methods defined in our Java session beans to perform data queries and manipulations to the **Course** Table in our sample database.

Perform the following operations to create this new Web service project, **WebServiceCourse**:

1) In the **Projects** window, right-click on our new created project, **WebAppCourse**, and select the **New > Other** menu item to open the **New File** wizard.

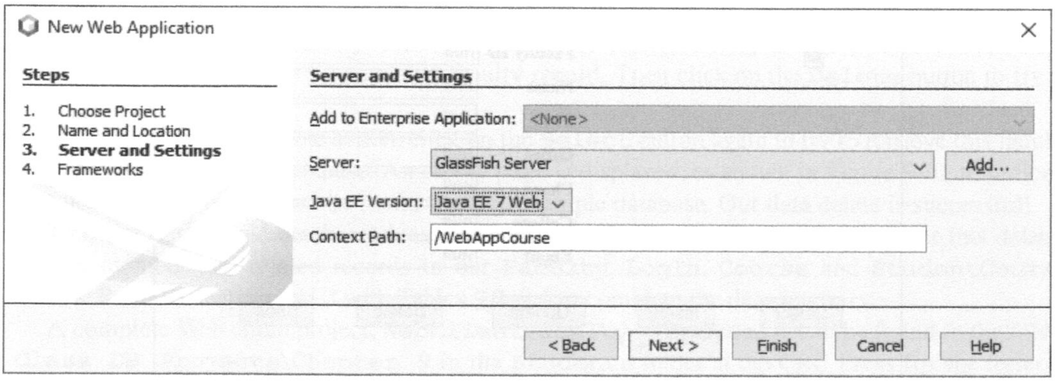

FIGURE 9.71 The finished Server and Settings wizard.

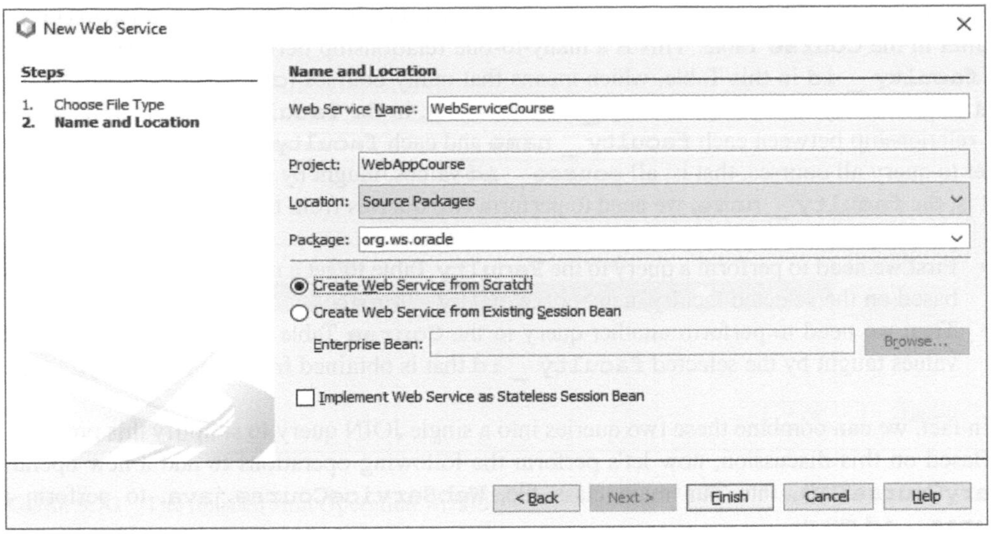

FIGURE 9.72 The finished Name and Location wizard.

2) Select **Web Services** from the **Categories** list and **Web Service** from the **File Types** list, and click on the **Next** button.
3) Name the Web service **WebServiceCourse** and type **org.ws.oracle** into the **Package** field. Leave **Create Web Service from Scratch** selected.

Your finished **Name and Location** wizard should match the one shown in Figure 9.72. Click on the **Finish** button to complete this process.

9.14.3 The Organization of Web Service Operations

The main purpose of using our Web service is to query and manipulate data from the **Course** Table in our sample database. Therefore, we need to add some new operations to the Web service project. We will add five new operations based on the sequence of five operational tasks on the **Course** Table. This means that we will add the following five operations into this Web service project to perform related course information query and manipulation actions:

QueryCourseID():	Query all **course_id** taught by the selected faculty member.
QueryCourse():	Query detailed information for the selected **course_id**.
InsertCourse():	Insert a new course record into the **Course** Table.
UpdateCourse():	Update an existing course record in the **Course** Table.
DeleteCourse():	Delete a course record from the **Course** Table.

Next let's start to build these five Web operations in our Web Service project one by one. We can combine all operations in one Web Service class file, **WebServiceCourse.java**.

9.14.4 Create and Build Web Service Operations

Let's create each Web operation one by one starting from **QueryCourseID()**.

Recall that when we built our sample database in Chapter 2, especially when we built the **Course** Table, there was no **faculty _ name** column available in the **Course** Table, and the

```
  package org.ws.oracle;
A import java.sql.*;
  import java.sql.SQLException;
  import java.util.ArrayList;
  import javax.jws.WebService;
  import javax.jws.WebMethod;
  import javax.jws.WebParam;
  @WebService(serviceName = "WebServiceCourse")
    public class WebServiceCourse {
B    Connection con = null;
C    private Connection DBConnection(Connection conn) {
        try
        {
           //Load and register Oracle database driver
D          Class.forName("oracle.jdbc.OracleDriver");
        }
E       catch (Exception e) {
           System.out.println("Class not found exception!" + e.getMessage());
        }
F       String url = "jdbc:oracle:thin:@localhost:1521:XE";
G       try {
           conn = DriverManager.getConnection(url,"CSE_DEPT","oracle_18c");
        }
H       catch (SQLException e) {
           System.out.println("Could not connect! " + e.getMessage());
           e.printStackTrace();
        }
I       return conn;
     }
  @WebMethod(operationName = "QueryCourseID")
J    public ArrayList QueryCourseID(@WebParam(name = "fname") String fname) {
        //TODO write your implementation code here:
K       ArrayList<String> result = new ArrayList<String>();
L       String query = "SELECT Course.course_id FROM Course JOIN Faculty " +
                       "ON (Course.faculty_id = Faculty.faculty_id) AND (Faculty.faculty_name = ?)";
M    try {
           con = DBConnection(con);
N          PreparedStatement pstmt =con.prepareStatement(query);
O          pstmt.setString(1, fname);
P          ResultSet rs = pstmt.executeQuery();
Q          ResultSetMetaData rsmd = rs.getMetaData();
R          while (rs.next()){
              for (int colNum = 1; colNum <= rsmd.getColumnCount(); colNum++)
                 result.add(rs.getString(colNum));
           }
S          con.close();
           rs.close();
           pstmt.close();
T          return result;
        }
U       catch (Exception ex) {
           System.out.println("exception is: " + ex);
           return null;
        }
     }
  }
```

FIGURE 9.74 The code for the Web service operation QueryCourseID().

S. A sequence of cleaning jobs is performed to close all used objects.
T. The queried result stored in the local variable `result` is returned to the calling method.
U. The `catch` block is used to catch and display any possible error during this query.

http://localhost:8080/WebAppCourse/WebServiceCourse?Tester

WebServiceCourse Web Ser...

WebServiceCourse Web Service Tester

This form will allow you to test your web service implementation (WSDL File)

To invoke an operation, fill the method parameter(s) input boxes and click on the button labeled with the method name.

Methods :

public abstract java.util.List org.ws.oracle.WebServiceCourse.queryCourseID(java.lang.String)

queryCourseID ( )

FIGURE 9.75 The testing status of our Web Service project.

During the coding process, you may encounter some runtime compiling errors. The main reason for those errors is that some packages are missing. To fix these errors, just right-click on any space inside this code window, and select the **`Fix Imports`** item to add those missingpackages.

At this point, we have finished all code for the **`course_id`** query. Now let's build and test our Web service to test the **`course_id`** query function.

9.14.4.2 Build and Run the Web Service to Test the CourseID Query Function

Prior to building and running our Web Service to test its function, we need to add our Java JDBC Driver, `ojdbc8.jar`, that is located in the folder `C:\Temp`. Refer to Appendix H to get more details about downloading and installing this driver. Perform the following operations to add this JDBC driver into our Web Service project:

1) Right-click on our Web application, **`WebAppCourse`**, in the **`Projects`** window and select the **`Properties`** item to open its Properties wizard.
2) Click on the **`Libraries`** node on the left under the **`Categories`** list.
3) Click on the **`Add JAR/Folder`** button on the right and browse to the location where our JDBC driver is stored, which is `C:\Temp` in our case.
4) Select the JDBC driver `ojdbc8.jar` and click on the **`Open`** button to add it into our project.

Now click on the **`Clean and Build Main Project`** button at the top of the window to build our Web service project. Then right-click on our Web service application project **`WebAppCourse`** and choose the **`Deploy`** item to deploy our Web service.

If everything is fine, expand the **`Web Services`** node under our Web service project, right-click on our Web service target file **`WebServiceCourse`** and choose the **`Test Web Service`** item to run our Web service project. The run status of our Web service is shown in Figure 9.75.

Enter a desired faculty name, such as **`Jenney King`**, into the text field and click on the **`queryCourseID`** button to test the query function. The test result is shown in Figure 9.76.

It can be seen from Figure 9.76 that all **`course_id`** taught by the selected faculty member **`Jenney King`** have been retrieved and displayed at the bottom of this page, and our **`course_id`** query via Web service is successful!

Next let's handle the creating and coding process for the second Web service operation, **`QueryCourse()`**, to query and get course details for the selected **`course_id`**.

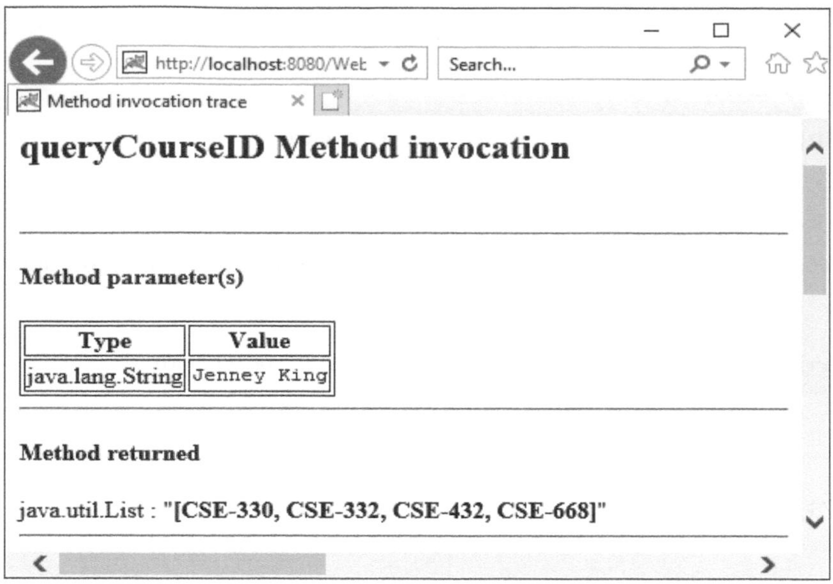

FIGURE 9.76 The test results of our Web Service project.

9.14.4.3 Create and Build the Web Operation QueryCourse()

Perform the following operations to add a new operation, `QueryCourse()`, into our Web service project to perform the course details query:

1) Double-click on our Web service main class file, `WebServiceCourse.java`, from the `Projects` window to open it.
2) Click the `Design` button at the top of the window to open the Design View of that class.
3) Click on the `Add Operation` button to open the `Add Operation` wizard.
4) Enter `QueryCourse` into the `Name` field and click on the `Browse` button that is next to the `Return Type` combo box. Type `Arraylist` into the `Type Name` field and select the item `ArrayList (java.util)` from the list, and click on the `OK` button.
5) Click on the `Add` button and enter `CourseID` into the `Name` parameter field. Keep the default type `java.lang.String` unchanged.

Your finished `Add Operation` wizard should match the one shown in Figure 9.77. Click on the `OK` button to complete the new operation creation process

Now click on the `Source` button on the top of this window to open the code window of our Web service project. Let's build the code for this new added operation.

In the opened code window, enter the code shown in Figure 9.78 into this new added operation. Let's have a closer look at this piece of code to see how it works.

A. An ArrayList instance `result` is created, and this variable is an array list instance used to collect and store our query result, and return to the consuming project.
B. A single query statement is declared with one dynamic position parameter, `course _ id`. This statement is used to query all course details related to the selected `course _ id`.
C. A `try-catch` block is used to perform the query job. First our user-defined method, `DBConnection()`, is called to set up a valid database connection to our sample database.
D. A new PreparedStatement instance, `pstmt`, is created to perform this query.

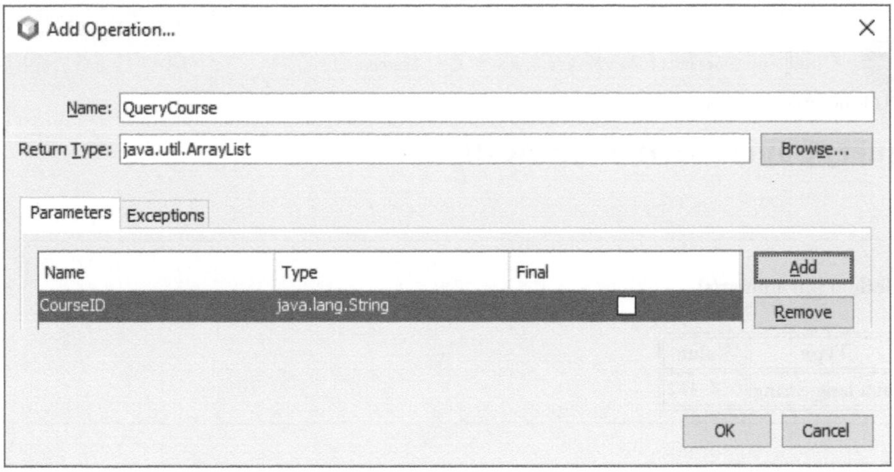

FIGURE 9.77 The completed Add Operation wizard.

```
  @WebMethod(operationName = "QueryCourse")
    public ArrayList QueryCourse(@WebParam(name = "CourseID") String CourseID) {
      //TODO write your implementation code here:
A     ArrayList<String> result = new ArrayList<String>();
B     String query = "SELECT * FROM Course WHERE course_id = ?";
      try {
C       con = DBConnection(con);
D       PreparedStatement pstmt =con.prepareStatement(query);
E       pstmt.setString(1, CourseID);
F       ResultSet rs = pstmt.executeQuery();
G       ResultSetMetaData rsmd = rs.getMetaData();
H       while (rs.next()){
          for (int colNum = 1; colNum <= rsmd.getColumnCount() - 1; colNum++)
            result.add(rs.getString(colNum));
        }
I       con.close();
        rs.close();
        pstmt.close();
J       return result;
      }
K     catch (Exception ex) {
        System.out.println("exception is: " + ex);
        return null;
      }
  }
```

FIGURE 9.78 The code for the Web service operation QueryCourse().

E. The **`setString()`** method is used to set up the actual value for the positional dynamic parameter in the query statement.
F. The query is performed by calling the **`executeQuery()`** method and the query result is returned and stored in a ResultSet object, **`rs`**.
G. To get more detailed information about the queried database, the **`getMetaData()`** method is executed, and the result is stored in a ResultSetMetaData instance, **`rsmd`**.
H. A **`while()`** and **`for()`** loop are used to pick up all pieces of queried course information stored in the ResultSet object **`rs`**. The **`for()`** loop is used to pick up each piece of detailed course information and add it into the ArrayList instance **`result`**. One issue to

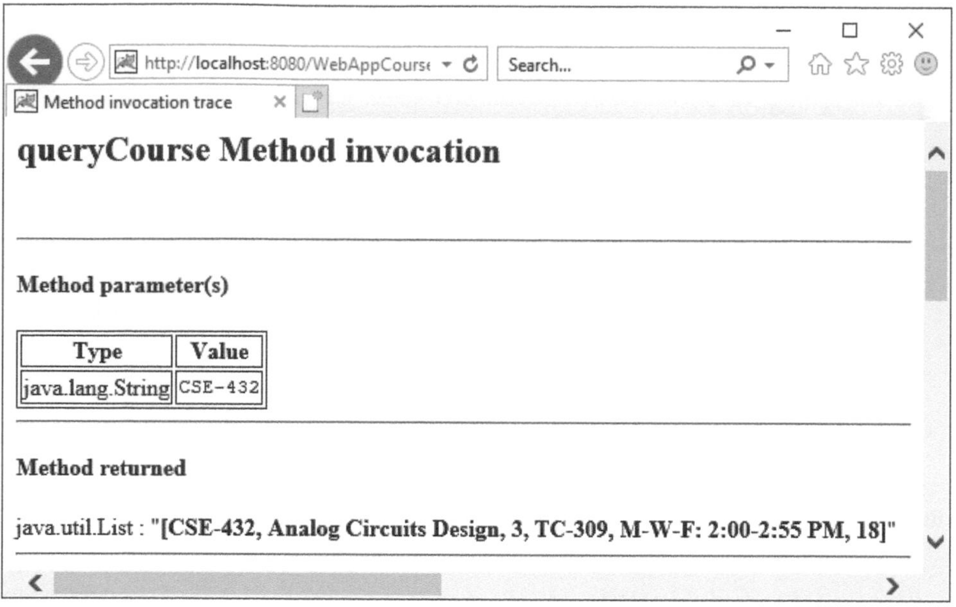

FIGURE 9.79 The test result for our Web Service operation, QueryCourse().

be noted is the upper bound of the loop count for this `for()` loop. Here we did not collect all pieces of detailed course information, since the last column in the `Course` Table is the `faculty _ id`, and we do not need this piece of information to be displayed in our Course Form when we consume this service later. Thus, the count for the last column is `getColumnCount()–1`.

I. A sequence of cleaning jobs is performed to close all used objects.
J. The queried result stored in the local variable `result` is returned to the calling method.
K. The `catch` block is used to catch and display any possible error during this query, and a `null` is returned to indicate this situation if any of errors really occurs.

Now let's build and test this Web Service operation by using the Web Service Tester.

Click on the `Clean and Build Main Project` button at the top of the window to build our Web service project. Then right-click on our Web service application project `WebAppCourse` and choose the `Deploy` item to deploy our Web service.

If everything is fine, expand the `Web Services` node under our Web service project and right-click on our Web service target file, `WebServiceCourse`, and choose the `Test Web Service` item to run our Web service project. Enter a desired `course _ id`, such as `CSE-432`, into the text field and click on the `queryCourse` button to test the query function. The test result is shown in Figure 9.79.

It can be seen from Figure 9.79 that all six pieces of detailed course information related to the selected `course _ id`, except the `faculty _ id`, have been retrieved and displayed at the bottom of this page, and our course query via Web service is successful! Close our Web page now.

Next let's handle creating and building our third Web service operation, `InsertCourse()`, to insert a new course record into the `Course` Table in our sample database.

9.14.4.4 Create and Build the Web Operation InsertCourse()

One issue to be noted to perform the new course insert action against our sample database is that we need to perform two queries for this operation, 1) query the `Faculty` Table to get the desired `faculty _ id` based on the input `faculty _ name`, and 2) insert a new course record based on the

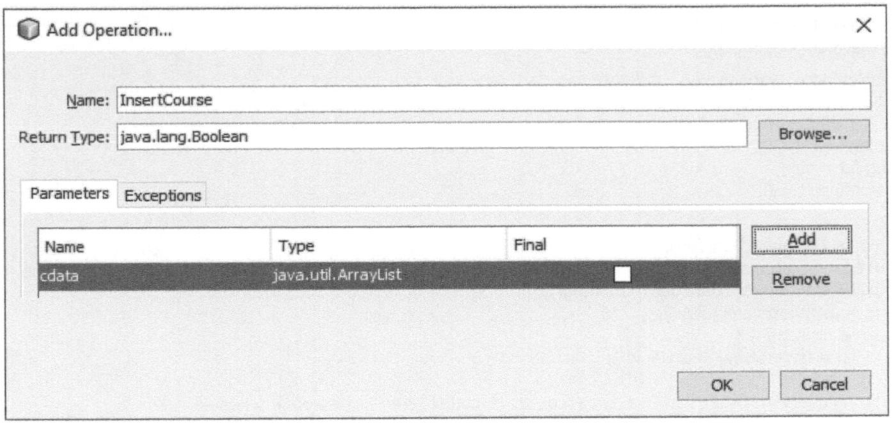

FIGURE 9.80 The completed Add Operation wizard.

queried **faculty _ id** from 1). The reason for that is because there is no **faculty _ name** column available in the **Course** Table, and the only connection between the **Faculty** and the **Course** Table in our sample database is a foreign key, **faculty _ id**, defined in the **Course** Table

Keep this fact in mind, and let's start to build this operation. First perform the following operations to add a new operation, **InsertCourse()**, into our Web service project:

1) Double-click on our Web service main class file, **WebServiceCourse.java**, from the **Projects** window to open it.
2) Click the **Design** button at the top of the window to open the Design View of that class.
3) Click on the **Add Operation** button to open the **Add Operation** wizard.
4) Enter **InsertCourse** into the **Name** field and click on the **Browse** button that is next to the **Return Type** combo box. Type **boolean** into the **Type Name** field and select the item **Boolean (java.lang)** from the list, and click on the **OK** button.
5) Click on the **Add** button and enter **cdata** into the **Name** parameter field. Then click on the dropdown arrow of the **Type** combo box and select the **Choose** item to open the **Find Type** wizard. Type **ArrayList** into the top field and select the **ArrayList (java.util)** data type, and click on the **OK** button to select an ArrayList as the data type for the input parameter.

Your finished **Add Operation** wizard should match the one shown in Figure 9.80. Click on the **OK** button to save this operation. Next let's build the code for this operation.

Click on the **Source** button on the top of this window to open the code window of our Web service class file, and enter the code shown in Figure 9.81 into this new added operation **InsertCourse()**. Let's have a closer look at this piece of new added code to see how it works.

A. One Java package with two classes, **java.util.logging.Level** and **java.util.logging.Logger**, is imported first at the top of this code window since we need them to find or create our logger file if any exception occurs later.
B. Some local variables, such as an instance of ResultSet, **rs**; a blank **faculty _ id** string, **fid**; and an integer variable, **numInsert**, are declared since we need to use them to hold some of our query results.
C. A **try-catch** block is used to do our first query for the **Faculty** Table to get a desired **faculty _ id** based on the selected **faculty _ name**. First a valid database connection is established by calling our user-defined method, **DBConnection()**.

```
A  import java.util.logging.Level;
   import java.util.logging.Logger;

   @WebMethod(operationName = "InsertCourse")
    public Boolean InsertCourse(@WebParam(name = "cdata") ArrayList cdata) {
B   //TODO write your implementation code here:
    ResultSet rs;
    String fid = null;
    int numInsert = 0;

    try {
C      con = DBConnection(con);
D      PreparedStatement pstfid =con.prepareStatement("SELECT faculty_id FROM Faculty WHERE faculty_name = ?");
E      pstfid.setString(1, cdata.get(0).toString());       // set faculty_name; cdata(0) = faculty_name
F      rs = pstfid.executeQuery();
G      while (rs.next()) {
          fid = rs.getString("faculty_id");
        }
H      String query = "INSERT INTO Course (course_id, course, credit, classroom, schedule, " +
                    "enrollment, faculty_id) VALUES (?, ?, ?, ?, ?, ?, ?)";

I      PreparedStatement pstmt =con.prepareStatement(query);  // cdata(0) = faculty_name
J      pstmt.setString(1, cdata.get(1).toString());            // cdata(1) = course_id
       pstmt.setString(2, cdata.get(2).toString());            // cdata(2) = course
       pstmt.setString(3, cdata.get(3).toString());            // cdata(3) = credit
       pstmt.setString(4, cdata.get(4).toString());            // cdata(4) = classroom
       pstmt.setString(5, cdata.get(5).toString());            // cdata(5) = schedule
       pstmt.setString(6, cdata.get(6).toString());            // cdata(6) = enrollment
K      pstmt.setString(7, fid);
L      numInsert = pstmt.executeUpdate();
M      con.close();
       rs.close();
N      if (numInsert != 0)
          return true;
O      else
          return false;
P      } catch (SQLException ex) {
          Logger.getLogger(WebServiceCourse.class.getName()).log(Level.SEVERE, null, ex);
          return false;
       }
   }
```

FIGURE 9.81 The detailed code for the operation InsertCourse().

D. A PreparedStatement object, **pstfid**, is generated with a connection object, **con**, and query statement to get the desired **faculty _ id** based on the selected **faculty _ name**, and the latter is a positional dynamic input parameter.
E. A system method, **setString()**, is executed to set up the input positional dynamic parameter that is stored in the input ArrayList instance, **cdata**; that is, it is located at the first position on that list, thus another system method **get(0).toString()** is used to pick it up.
F. The first query is executed by calling the system method **executeQuery()**, and the returned query result is stored in the instance of ResultSet class, **rs**.
G. A **while()** loop with its condition, **rs.next()**, is executed to pick up the selected **faculty _ id** by calling another system method, **getString()**. The argument of that method is the column name of the **faculty _ id** column in the **Faculty** Table.
H. The second query statement is created with seven input positional dynamic parameters. One point to be noted is that the order of those input positional parameters must be predefined with the input **faculty _ name** as the first one, followed by six pieces of new inserted course information.
I. Another PreparedStatement object, **pstmt**, is declared with the second query statement.
J. A sequence of **setString()** methods is executed to set up and initialize all seven input positional parameters, which include a new inserted course record and the selected **faculty _ name**.

K. The seventh positional dynamic parameter in the second query is the **faculty _ id**, which is obtained from the first query, not from the input ArrayList variable **cdata**.
L. The second query is executed by calling another **executeUpdate()** method, and the run result is returned and assigned to the integer variable **numInsert**.
M. A sequence of cleaning jobs is performed to close all objects we used for these queries.
N. If this data insertion is successful, a non-zero integer value would be returned, and a **true** is also returned to the consume project to indicate this situation.
O. Otherwise, if a zero is returned, which means that this data insertion fails and no record has been inserted into our database, a **false** is returned to indicate this error.
P. The **catch** block is used to monitor and track these query operations. A **false** would be returned if any exception occurs.

Now one can click on the **Clean and Build Project** button to build our Web Service project to compile and update this new operation. Next let's build our Web operation, **UpdateCourse()**.

9.14.4.5 Create and Build the Web Operation UpdateCourse()

Perform the following operations to add a new operation, **UpdateCourse()**, into our Web service project to perform a course update query:

1) Double-click on our Web service main class file, **WebServiceCourse.java**, from the **Projects** window to open it.
2) Click on the **Design** button at the top of the window to open the Design View of our Web service class file, **WebServiceCourse.java**.
3) Click on the **Add Operation** button to open the **Add Operation** wizard.
4) Enter **UpdateCourse** into the **Name** field and click on the **Browse** button that is next to the **Return Type** combo box. Type **boolean** into the **Type Name** field and select the item **Boolean (java.lang)** from the list, and click on the **OK** button.
5) Click on the **Add** button and enter **cdata** into the **Name** parameter field. Then click on the dropdown arrow of the **Type** combo box, select the **Choose** item to open the **Find Type** wizard. Type **ArrayList** into the top field and select the **ArrayList (java.util)** data type, and click on the **OK** button to select an ArrayList as the data type for the input parameter.

Your finished **Add Operation** wizard should match the one shown in Figure 9.82. Click on the **OK** button to create this operation. Next let's build the code for this operation.

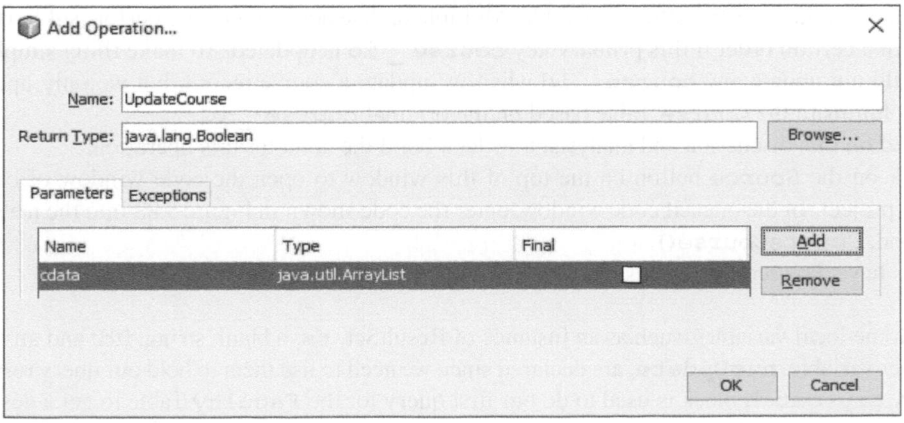

FIGURE 9.82 The completed Add Operation wizard.

```
  @WebMethod(operationName = "UpdateCourse")
    public Boolean UpdateCourse(@WebParam(name = "cdata") ArrayList cdata) {
    //TODO write your implementation code here:
A   ResultSet rs;
    String fid = null;
    int  numUpdate = 0;
    try {
B       con = DBConnection(con);
C       PreparedStatement pstfid =con.prepareStatement("SELECT faculty_id FROM Faculty WHERE faculty_name = ?");
D       pstfid.setString(1, cdata.get(0).toString());        // set faculty_name; cdata(0) = faculty_name
E       rs = pstfid.executeQuery();
F       while (rs.next()) {
          fid = rs.getString("faculty_id");
        }
G       String query = "UPDATE Course SET course = ?, credit = ?, classroom = ?, schedule = ?, " +
                       "enrollment = ?, faculty_id = ? WHERE course_id = ?";
H        PreparedStatement pstmt =con.prepareStatement(query);  // cdata(0) = faculty_name
I        pstmt.setString(1, cdata.get(1).toString());            // cdata(1) = course
         pstmt.setString(2, cdata.get(2).toString());            // cdata(2) = creit
         pstmt.setString(3, cdata.get(3).toString());            // cdata(3) = classroom
         pstmt.setString(4, cdata.get(4).toString());            // cdata(4) = schedule
         pstmt.setString(5, cdata.get(5).toString());            // cdata(5) = enrollment
         pstmt.setString(7, cdata.get(6).toString());            // cdata(6) = course_id
         pstmt.setString(6, fid);
J        numUpdate = pstmt.executeUpdate();
K        con.close();
         rs.close();
L        if (numUpdate != 0)
           return true;
M        else
           return false;
N     } catch (SQLException ex) {
         Logger.getLogger(WebServiceCourse.class.getName()).log(Level.SEVERE, null, ex);
         return false;
      }
  }
```

FIGURE 9.83 Detailed code for the operation UpdateCourse().

As we discussed in the previous chapters, to update a record in the **Course** Table, usually one does not need to update the primary key, **course _ id**; instead, one can insert a new course record with a new **course _ id** into the **Course** Table to simplify the update. The reason for that is because of cascaded update actions. **course _ id** is a primary key in the **Course** Table but a foreign key in the **StudentCourse** Table. Multiple update actions must be performed in multiple Tables in a certain order if this primary key **course _ id** is updated. To make thing simple, here we would not update any **course _ id** when we update a course record, but we only update all other columns in the **Course** Table based on the original **course _ id**.

Based on this discussion and analysis, now let's build the code for this operation.

Click on the **Source** button on the top of this window to open the code window of our Web service project. In the opened code window, enter the code shown in Figure 9.83 into the new added operation, **UpdateCourse()**.

Let's have a closer look at this piece of new added code to see how it works.

A. Some local variables, such as an instance of ResultSet, **rs**; a blank string, **fid**; and an integer variable, **numUpdate**, are declared since we need to use them to hold our query results.
B. A **try-catch** block is used to do our first query for the **Faculty** Table to get a desired **faculty _ id** based on the selected **faculty _ name**. First a valid database connection is established by calling our user-defined method, **DBConnection()**.

C. A PreparedStatement object, **pstfid**, is generated with a connection object, **con**, and query statement to get the desired **faculty_id** based on the selected **faculty_name**, and the latter is a positional dynamic input parameter.
D. A system method, **setString()**, is executed to set up the input positional dynamic parameter that is stored in the input ArrayList instance, **cdata**; that is, it is located at the first position on that list, so another system method, **get(0).toString()**, is used to pick it up.
E. The first query is executed by calling the system method **executeQuery()**, and the returned query result is stored in the instance of ResultSet class, **rs**.
F. A **while()** loop with its condition, **rs.next()**, is executed to pick up the selected **faculty_id** by calling a system method, **getString()**. The argument of that method is the column name of the **faculty_id**.
G. The second query statement is created with a standard Update query statement format with seven input positional dynamic parameters. One point to be noted is that the order of those input positional parameters must be defined with the input **faculty_name** as the first one, followed by six pieces of updated course information.
H. Another PreparedStatement object, **pstmt**, is declared with the second query statement.
I. A sequence of **setString()** methods is executed to set up and initialize all seven input positional parameters, which include an updated course record and the selected **faculty_name**.
J. The second query is executed by calling a system method, **executeUpdate()**, and the run result is returned and assigned to the integer variable **numUpdate**.
K. A sequence of cleaning jobs is performed to close all objects we used for these queries.
L. If this course updating is successful, a non-zero integer value would be returned, and a **true** is also returned to the consuming project to indicate that situation.
M. Otherwise, if a zero is returned, which means that the data update fails and no record has been updated in our database, a **false** is returned to indicate this error.
N. The **catch** block is used to monitor and track those query operations. A **false** would be returned if any exception occurred.

Now one can click on the **Clean and Build Project** button to build our Web Service project to compile and update this new operation. Finally let's build our Web operation, **DeleteCourse()**.

9.14.4.6 Create and Build the Web Operation DeleteCourse()

Perform the following operations to add a new operation, **DeleteCourse()**, into our Web service project to perform the course delete query:

1) Double-click on our Web service main class file, **WebServiceCourse.java**, from the **Projects** window to open it.
2) Click on the **Design** button at the top of the window to open the Design View of our Web service class, **WebServiceCourse.java**.
3) Click on the **Add Operation** button to open the **Add Operation** wizard.
4) Enter **DeleteCourse** into the **Name** field and click on the **Browse** button that is next to the **Return Type** combo box. Type **boolean** into the **Type Name** field and select the item **Boolean (java.lang)** from the list, and click on the **OK** button.
5) Click on the **Add** button and enter **cid** into the **Name** parameter field. Keep the default Type, **java.lang.String**, as the data type for this input parameter. Your finished **Add Operation** wizard should match the one shown in Figure 9.84.
6) Click on the **OK** button to create this new operation.

Next let's build the code for this operation.

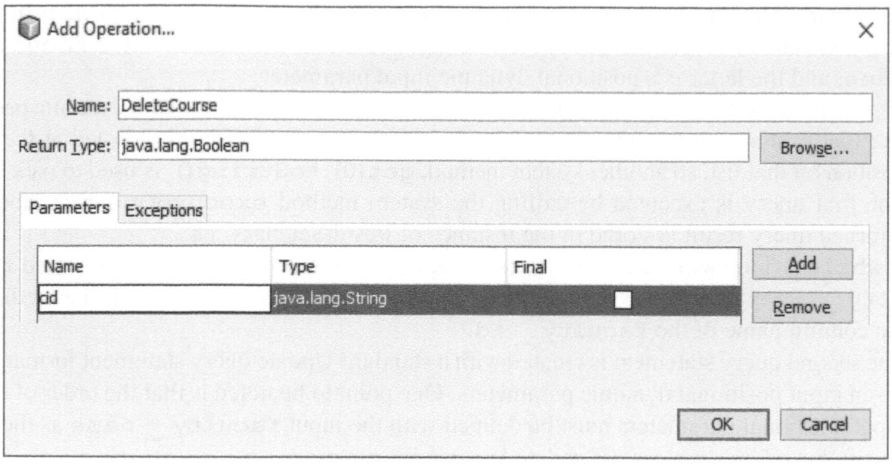

FIGURE 9.84 The completed Add Operation wizard.

```
  @WebMethod(operationName = "DeleteCourse")
  public Boolean DeleteCourse(@WebParam(name = "cid") String cid) {
     //TODO write your implementation code here:
A    int numDelete = 0;
     try {
B        con = DBConnection(con);
C        PreparedStatement pstmt =con.prepareStatement("DELETE FROM Course WHERE course_id = ?");
D        pstmt.setString(1, cid);                    // set course_id
E        numDelete = pstmt.executeUpdate();
F        con.close();
G        if (numDelete != 0)
           return true;
H        else
           return false;
I    } catch (SQLException ex) {
         Logger.getLogger(WebServiceCourse.class.getName()).log(Level.SEVERE, null, ex);
         return false;
     }
  }
```

FIGURE 9.85 Detailed code for the operation DeleteCourse().

Click on the **Source** button at the top of this window to open the code window of our Web service class file. In the opened code window, enter the code shown in Figure 9.85 into the new added operation, **UpdateCourse()**.

Let's have a closer look at this piece of new added code to see how it works.

A. A local integer variable, **numDelete**, is declared, and it is used to hold our query result.
B. A **try-catch** block is used to do our delete query for the **Course** Table to remove the target course record based on the selected **course _ id**. First a valid database connection is established by calling our user-defined method, **DBConnection()**.
C. A PreparedStatement object, **pstmt**, is generated with a connection object, **con**, and the delete statement with a selected **course _ id** as a positional dynamic input parameter.
D. A system method, **setString()**, is executed to set up the input positional dynamic parameter **cid**, which is the desired **course _ id** and works as a query criterion for this delete action.

E. The delete action is then executed by calling a system method, **executeUpdate()**, and the run result of this action is returned and assigned to our local variable, **intDelete**.
F. A cleaning job is performed to close the connection object we used for this query.
G. If this course delete is successful, a non-zero integer value would be returned, and a **true** is also returned to the consuming project to indicate success.
H. Otherwise, if a zero is returned, which means that the data delete fails and no record has been deleted from our database, a **false** is returned to indicate this error.
I. The **catch** block is used to monitor and track this query operation. A **false** would be returned if any exception occurred.

One can click on the **Clean and Build Project** button to build our Web Service project to update this new operation. Now we have completed all developments for our Web Service project. A complete Web Service application project, **WebAppCourse**, can be found in the folder **Class BD Projects\Chapter 9** in the **Students** folder at the CRC Press ftp site.

Next we can build some Windows-based or Web-based projects to consume these operations to perform related database actions to query, insert, and update and delete records from the **Course** Table in our sample database. First let's start with a Windows-based project.

9.15 BUILD WINDOWS-BASED PROJECT TO CONSUME THE WEB SERVICE PROJECT

To consume our Web Service project, we need to build some Windows-based projects to call different operations to perform related actions to our database.

To save time and space, we can use two of our projects, **WinClientFaculty _ Select**, which was built in Section 9.6, and **OracleSelectCourse**, developed in Section 6.3.8 in Chapter 6, to make them our new project. Perform the following steps to build our new Windows-based project, **WinClientCourse _ Select**, to call the related Web operations in our Web Service to perform the appropriate queries to the **Course** Table in our sample database.

1) Open the NetBeans IDE 12.0, and browse to our project, **WinClientFaculty _ Select**, which can be found in the folder **Class DB Projects\Chapter 9** in the **Students** folder on the CRC Press ftp site (refer to Figure 1.2 in Chapter 1), and copy and then save it to any local folder in your machine.
2) Right-click the project **WinClientFaculty _ Select** from your local folder and select the **Copy** item from the popup menu.
3) In the opened **Copy Project** wizard, change the project name to **WinClientCourse _ Select** in the **Project Name** box, select your desired location from the **Project Location** box and click on the **Copy** button.
4) Browse to the project **OracleSelectCourse**, which can be found in the folder **Class DB Projects\Chapter 6** in the **Students** folder on the CRC Press ftp site (refer to Figure 1.2 in Chapter 1), and copy and then save it to any local folder in your machine.
5) Open the project and expand the folder **Source Packages\OracleSelect FacultyPackage**, right-click on the Course Frame file **CourseFrame.java** under the project package node and select the **Refactor > Copy** item to copy this form file.
6) In the opened **Copy Class–CourseFrame** wizard, select our new project, **WinClient Course _ Select**, from the **Project** combo box and remove the **1** after the **Course Frame** from the **New Name** field. Your finished **Copy Class** wizard is shown in Figure 9.86.
7) Click on the **Refactor** button to make a refactored copy for this frame file.
8) Return to our new project, **WinClientCourse _ Select**, and you can find that a copied **CourseFrame.java** file has been pasted in the default package in our project.

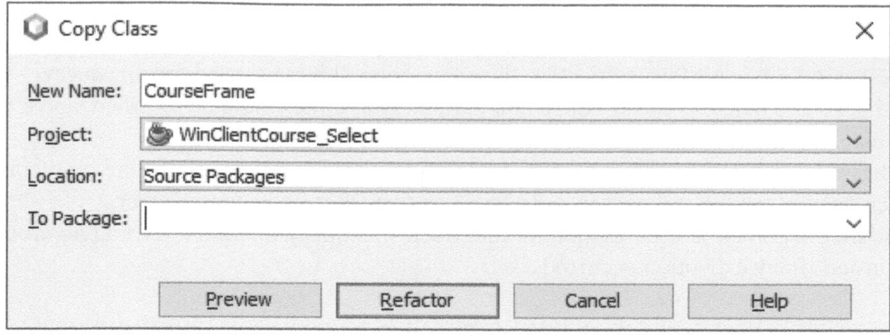

FIGURE 9.86 The completed Copy Class wizard.

9) Now expand our new project, **WinClientCourse _ Select**, from the **Projects** window in the NetBeans, which is **WinClientCourse _ Select→Source Packages→<default package>**; right-click on the file **FacultyFrame.java**; and select **Delete** item to remove this file, since we do not need this file in this project. Make sure to check the **Safely delete** checkbox and click on the **Refactor** button.
10) Double-click on our pasted **CourseFrame.java** to open it, and perform the following operations in the code window to make it our new class file:

   a. Remove the top code line: **ComboMethod.addItem("Java Callable Method");** from the constructor of this class.
   b. Remove all code from the **SelectButtonActionPerformed**() event handler.
   c. Remove all code from the **CourseListValueChanged()** event handler.

9.15.1 Update the Web Service Reference for Our Window-Based Client Project

Prior to any code development, we need first to update our Web Service Reference to enable our client project to use the correct Web Service. Perform the following operations to set up a Web service reference for our client project:

1) Build and deploy our Web Service application project, **WebAppCourse**, first to make sure that the Web Service is available to our client project.
2) Expand our **Web Service References** folder and right-click on the existing service file, **WebServiceFaculty**, and select the **Delete** item to remove this reference.
3) Right-click on our client project, **WinClientCourse _ Select**, from the **Projects** window, and select the **New > Other** item to open the **New File** wizard.
4) In the opened **New File** wizard, select **Web Services** from the **Categories** and **Web Service Client** from the **File Types** list. Click on the **Next** button to continue.
5) Click on the **Browse** button for the **Project** field and expand our Web application project, **WebAppCourse**, and click on our Web service, **WebServiceCourse**, to select it. Then click on the **OK** button to select this Web service.
6) Click on the **Finish** button to complete the Web service reference setup process.

Immediately you can find a new node named **Web Service References** has been created and added into our client project. Expand this node, and you can find the associated Web service port and our five Web service operations, such as **QueryCourse()** and **QueryCourseID()**, under that node.

Now build our new project by clicking on the **Clean and Built Project** button on the top. Next let's develop the code for these event handlers to access our Web operations to perform related queries to the **Course** Table in our sample database.

9.15.2 Develop the Code to Query Course Information from Our Web Service

In our Web service class file, **`WebServiceCourse`**, we built five operations with five different data actions against the **`Course`** Table in our database. Now we need to develop the code in our client project to call those five operations to access and query the **`Course`** Table in our sample database via five buttons in our client project, **`WinClientCouse _ Select`**, that is, in the **`CourseFrame.java`** class file. Each button has a one-to-one relationship with the related operation, as shown in Table 9.7.

Let's start our coding process from the **`Select`** button, that is, with its event handler or method **`SelectButtonActionPerformed()`**, in our client project.

9.15.3 Build Code for the Select Button Event Handler to Query CourseIDs

The function of this method is to query all **`course _ id`** taught by the selected faculty member when the **`Select`** button is clicked by the user. The queried result will be added and displayed in the Course ID List box in this CourseFrame Form window.

In the opened **`Design`** view of the CourseFrame Form window, double-click on the **`Select`** button to open this method or event handler. Enter the code shown in Figure 9.87 into this event handler. Let's have a closer look at this piece of new added code to see how it works.

A. A local variable, **`al`**, is created first, and it is an ArrayList instance, and it can be used to hold the query result in which all selected **`course _ id`** values are stored.

TABLE 9.7
The Relationship between Each Button's Method and Each Operation

Client Button and Method	Web Service Operation	Function
Select SelectButtonActionPerformed()	QueryCourseID()	Query all **course_id** taught by the selected faculty
CourseListValueChanged()	QueryCourse()	Query detailed information for selected **course_id**
Insert InsertButtonActionPerformed()	InsertCourse()	Insert a new course record into the **Course** Table
Update UpdateButtonActionPerformed()	UpdateCourse()	Update an existing course record in the **Course** Table
Delete DeleteButtonActionPerformed()	DeleteCourse()	Delete a course record from the **Course** Table

```
  private void SelectButtonActionPerformed(java.awt.event.ActionEvent evt) {
      // TODO add your handling code here:
A     ArrayList<String> al = new ArrayList();
      try {
B     org.ws.oracle.WebServiceCourse_Service service = new org.ws.oracle.WebServiceCourse_Service();
      org.ws.oracle.WebServiceCourse port = service.getWebServiceCoursePort();
C     al.clear();
D     al = (ArrayList)port.queryCourseID(ComboName.getSelectedItem().toString());
E     String[] alArray = al.toArray(new String[al.size()]);
F     CourseList.setListData(alArray);
G     }catch (Exception ex) {
        System.out.println("exception: " + ex);
      }
  }
```

FIGURE 9.87 The complete code for the SelectButtonActionPerformed() event handler.

B. A **try-catch** block is used to call our Web service operation, **QueryCourseID()**, to perform the query action. First a new Web service instance, **service**, is created based on our Web service class, **WebServiceCourse _ Service**. Then the **getWebServiceCoursePort()** method is executed to get the current port used by our Web service. This port is returned and assigned to a new port instance, **port**.
C. The ArrayList instance **al** is first cleaned to make it ready to store all queried **course _ id**.
D. The Web service operation **QueryCourseID()** is called to perform the course data query to collect all **course _ id** taught by the selected faculty member that is obtained from the **ComboName** combo box. The query result is returned and assigned to the local ArrayList instance **al**.
E. A conversion between an ArrayList object and a standard String array object is performed since we need to add this query result into the **CourseList**, but the latter can only accept a String array, not an ArrayList, as an argument to be added into this list.
F. The converted query results are sent to the Course ID List variable, **CourseList**, to have them displayed there using the **setListData()** method.
G. The **catch** block is used to track and display any possible exception during this **course _ id** query process.

Now we have finished all coding process for calling one of our Web service operations, **QueryCourseID()**, to query all **course _ id** based on the selected faculty member. Click on the **Clean and Build Project** button to build our project.

Before we can run and test our client project, two more issues must be solved: 1) make sure that our Web Service application project, **WebAppCourse**, has been built and deployed successfully. 2) Ensure the **CourseFrame.java** has been selected as the main class file.

Perform the following operations to set up**CourseFrame.java** as a main class file:

1) Right-click on our client project **WinClientCourse _ Select** from the **Projects** window, and select the **Properties** item at the bottom to open the Project Properties wizard.
2) In the opened wizard, click on the **Run** node on the left.
3) Enter or select the **CourseFrame** item in the **Main Class** box on the right by clicking the **Browse** button if you want to select it.
4) Click on the **OK** button to complete the main class setup process.

Click on the **Run Main Project** button to run our client project to test the **course _ id** query function. Select the **CourseFrame** as our main class and click on the **OK** button to the **Run Project** dialog if it is displayed to run our project.

In the opened client project, keep the default faculty member **Ying Bai** unchanged and click on the **Select** button to query all **course _ id** taught by this selected faculty. Immediately you can see that all four courses or four **course _ id** taught by this faculty member have been returned and displayed in the Course ID List box, as shown in Figure 9.88.

You can also try to query **course _ id** for other faculty members by selecting other faculty members from the Faculty Name combo box. Our client project in querying **course _ id** is very successful.

Next let's take care of the code for the **CourseListValueChanged()** method to query the detailed course information for a selected **course _ id** from the Course ID List.

9.15.4 Build Code for the CourseListValueChanged() Method to Get Course Details

The function of this method is that when users click a **course _ id** from the Course ID List box, the detailed course information, including the course title, credit, classroom, schedule and enrollment for the selected **course _ id**, will be retrieved and displayed in six text fields in this CourseFrame Form window.

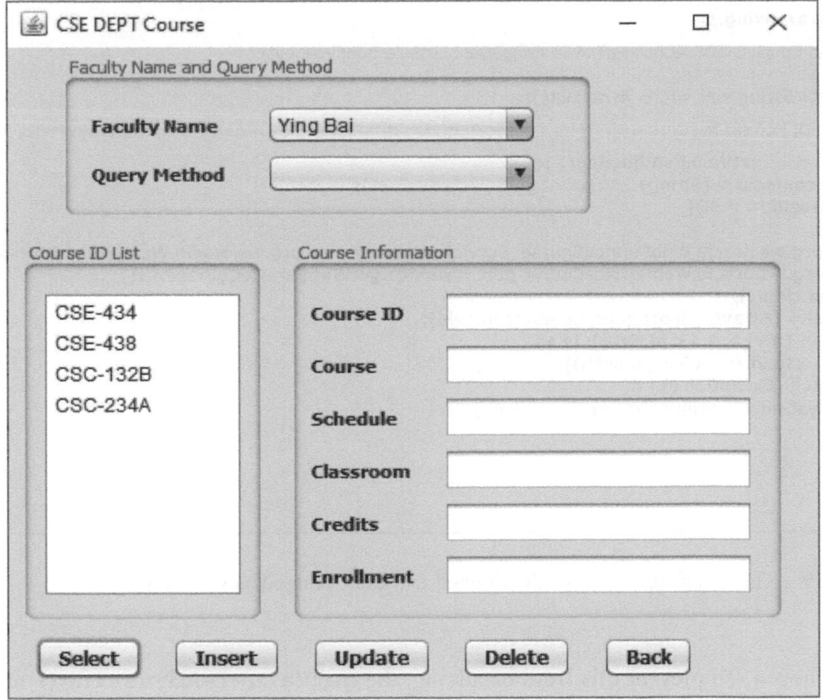

FIGURE 9.88 The run result of calling the Web operation QueryCourseID().

Perform the following operations to build the code for this method to perform that function:

1) Open our client project, **`WinClientCourse _ Select`**, if it has not been opened and open our main GUI, **`CourseFrame.java`**, by double-clicking on it.
2) Click on the **`Design`** button at the top of the window to open the GUI window, and right-click on our **`Course ID List`** Listbox and select **`Events > ListSelection > valueChanged`** item to open this method or event handler.
3) Enter the code shown in Figure 9.89 into this event handler.

Let's have a closer look at this piece of new added code to see how it works.

A. The **`JTextField[]`** is a component defined in the **`javax.swing`** package; thus, it should be imported first to enable us to use that component to generate our field array later. The advantage of using a JTextField[] that contains all our six TextFields is to simplify our assignment coding process and make these assignments shorter in code.
B. An ArrayList instance, **`al`**, is created first, and it is used to collect the queried course details stored in an ArrayList object that will be returned from the execution of the Web service operation **`QueryCourse()`**.
C. A JTextField array, **`cField[]`**, is created and initialized with six text fields in the CourseFrame Form. The purpose of this array is to store queried course details and display them in these six TextFields.
D. Since the JList component belongs to the **`javax.swing`** package, not the **`java.awt`** package, clicking on an entry in the CourseList box causes the **`itemStateChanged()`** method to fire twice. The first time is when the mouse button is depressed, and the second time is when it is released. Therefore, the selected **`course _ id`** will appear twice when

```
A  import javax.swing.*;
   private void CourseListValueChanged(javax.swing.event.ListSelectionEvent evt) {
     // TODO add your handling code here:
B    ArrayList<String> al = new ArrayList();
C    JTextField[] cfield = {CourseIDField, CourseField, CreditsField, ClassRoomField, ScheduleField, EnrollField};
D    if(!CourseList.getValueIsAdjusting() ){
       String courseid = (String)CourseList.getSelectedValue();
E      if (courseid != null){
         try {
F            org.ws.oracle.WebServiceCourse_Service service = new org.ws.oracle.WebServiceCourse_Service();
             org.ws.oracle.WebServiceCourse port = service.getWebServiceCoursePort();
G            al.clear();
H            al = (ArrayList)port.queryCourse(courseid);
I            for (int i = 0; i < al.size(); i++)
               cfield[i].setText(al.get(i));
J        }catch (Exception ex) {
           System.out.println("exception: " + ex);
         }
       }
     }
   }
```

FIGURE 9.89 The completed code for the CourseListValueChanged() event handler.

it is chosen. To prevent this from occurring, the **getValueIsAdjusting()** method is used to make sure that no item has been adjusted to be displayed twice. Then the selected **course_id** is assigned to a local String variable, **courseid**, by calling the **getSelectedValue()** method of the CourseList Box class.

E. Before we can proceed to the course query operation, first we need to confirm that the selected **courseid** is not a null value. A null value would be returned if the user did not select any **course_id** from the CourseList box but just clicked on the **Select** button to try to find all courses taught by a faculty member. Even if the user only clicked on the **Select** button without touching any **course_id** in the CourseList box, the system still acts as if a null **course_id** has been selected, and thus a null value will be returned. To avoid that situation, an **if** selection structure is used to make sure that no null value has been returned from the CourseList box.
F. A **try-catch** block is used to perform the call to our Web service operation **QueryCourse()** to get detailed course information. First a new Web service instance, **service**, is created based on our Web service class **WebServiceCourse_Service**. Then the **getWebServiceCoursePort()** method is executed to get the current port used by our Web service. This port is returned and assigned to a new port instance, **port**.
G. The ArrayList instance **al** is first cleaned up to make it ready to hold the retrieved course details in the next step.
H. The Web service operation **QueryCourse()** is called to perform this course data query to collect detailed course information for the selected **course_id**. The query result is returned and assigned to the local ArrayList instance **al**. A cast (ArrayList) is necessary for this assignment since the data type of **al** is an ArrayList<String> in this method.
I. A **for()** loop is used to pick up each piece of detailed course information and assign it to each text field in the **cField[]** array using the **setText()** method.
J. The **catch** block is used to track and display any possible exception during the course details query process.

At this point, we have finished all code for calling our Web service operation, **QueryCourse()**, to query detailed information for a selected **course_id**. Click on the **Clean and Build Project** button to build our project.

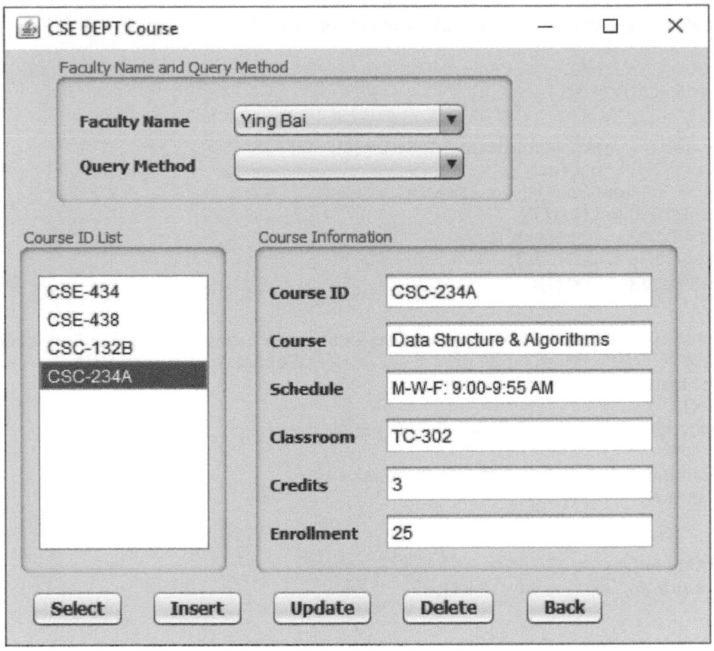

FIGURE 9.90 The run result of calling the Web operation QueryCourse().

Before we can run and test our client project, make sure that our Web Service application project **WebAppCourse** has been built and deployed successfully. Click on the **Run Main Project** button to run our client project to test the course details query function.

In the opened client project, keep the default faculty member **Ying Bai** unchanged and click on the **Select** button to query all **course_id** taught by this selected faculty member. Immediately you can see that all four courses or four **course_id** taught by this faculty have been returned and displayed in the Course ID List box. Then click on any **course_id** for which you want to get detailed information from the CourseList Listbox. The detailed course information for the selected **course_id** is retrieved and displayed in six TextFields, as shown in Figure 9.90. An example of course details for **course_id CSC-234A** is shown in the Figure.

A complete Window-based consuming project, **WinClientCourse_Select**, can be found in the folder **Class BD Projects\Chapter 9** in the **Students** folder at the CRC Press ftp site.

Next let's take care of the code for the **InsertButtonActionPerformed()** method to call our Web Service to insert a new course record into the **Course** Table in our sample database.

9.15.5 Build Code for the Insert Button Event Handler to Insert a New Course

The function of this method is to insert a new course record into the **Course** Table in our sample database when the **Insert** button is clicked by the user. A new course record will be inserted into our sample database when this method is complete.

To make thing simple, let's modify our project **WinClientCourse_Select** to make it our new project, **WinClientCourse_Insert**. Perform the following steps to build our new Windows-based project, **WinClientCourse_Insert**:

1) Browse to our project **WinClientCourse_Select**, which can be found in the folder **Class DB Projects\Chapter 9** in the **Students** folder on the CRC Press ftp site (refer to Figure 1.2 in Chapter 1), and copy and then save it to any local folder in your machine.

```
  private void InsertButtonActionPerformed(java.awt.event.ActionEvent evt) {
    // TODO add your handling code here:
A   JTextField[] cf = {CourseIDField, CourseField, CreditsField, ClassRoomField, ScheduleField, EnrollField};
    ArrayList al = new ArrayList();
B   al.clear();
C   al.add(0, ComboName.getSelectedItem().toString());    // faculty_name
    al.add(1, CourseIDField.getText());
    al.add(2, CourseField.getText());
    al.add(3, CreditsField.getText());
    al.add(4, ClassRoomField.getText());
    al.add(5, ScheduleField.getText());
    al.add(6, EnrollField.getText());
D   try {
        org.ws.oracle.WebServiceCourse_Service service = new org.ws.oracle.WebServiceCourse_Service();
        org.ws.oracle.WebServiceCourse port = service.getWebServiceCoursePort();
E       Boolean insert = port.insertCourse(al);
F       if (!insert)
          System.out.println("The data insertion is failed!");
G       else {
           for (int index = 0; index < cf.length; index++)
             cf[index].setText("");
        }
    }
H   catch (Exception ex){
       System.out.println("exception: " + ex);
    }
  }
```

FIGURE 9.91 The completed code for the InsertButtonActionPerformed() event handler.

2) Open NetBeans IDE 12.0 and right-click **WinClientCourse _ Select** in your local folder and select the **Copy** item from the popup menu.
3) In the opened **Copy Project** wizard, change the project name to **WinClientCourse _ Insert** in the **Project Name** box, select your desired location from the **Project Location** box and click on the **Copy** button.

The main source file, **CourseFrame.java**, under our **Source Packages** folder may generate some errors when this new project is created. The reason for that is due to a Web Reference issue. To fix this error, build and deploy our Web Service application project, **WebAppCourse**, and then rebuild our new project, **WinClientCourse _ Insert**.

Now let's develop the code for the **Insert** button's event handler to perform data insertions to the **Course** Table in our sample database. Open the **Insert** button's event handler by double-clicking the button from **Design** view, and enter the code shown in Figure 9.91 into the handler.

Let's have a closer look at this piece of code to see how it works.

A. A local Java TextField[] array, **cf**, and a variable, **al**, are created first. The former is used to hold all TextFields, and the latter is an instance of ArrayList class used to hold a new course record to be inserted into our database by calling our Web service operation **InsertCourse()** later.
B. The ArrayList instance **al** is cleaned up by using the **clear()** method to make sure that **al** is empty before it can be used to store any data.
C. A group of **add()** methods are used to add seven pieces of new course information into the ArrayList instance. One point is that the order in which to add these course parameters must be identical to the order of the columns in the **Course** Table in our sample database.
D. A **try-catch** block is used to perform the call to our Web service operation, **InsertCourse()**, to insert this new course record into our database. First a

new Web service instance, **service**, is created based on our Web service class, **WebServiceCourse _ Service**. Then the **getWebServiceCoursePort()** method is executed to get the current port used by our Webservice. This port is returned and assigned to a new port instance, **port**.

E. The Web operation **InsertCourse()** is called to insert this new course record stored in the argument **al** into the **Course** Table via our Web service. The execution result is returned and assigned to the local Boolean variable **insert**.
F. If a **false** is returned, which means that this data insertion fails, the system **println()** method is used to indicate this situation.
G. Otherwise, our data insertion action is successful if a **true** is returned. Then a **for()** loop is used to clean up all six TextFields to indicate that the data insertion is completed.
H. The **catch** block is used to track any possible exception during the data insertion process.

Now we have finished the coding process for our client project. Click on the **Clean and Build Main Project** button to build our project. Before running and testing our client project, make sure that our Web Service application project, **WebAppCourse**, has been built and deployed successfully. Click on the **Run Main Project** button to run our client project to perform the data insertion action.

In the opened client project, keep the default faculty member **Ying Bai** unchanged and click on the **Select** button to query all **course _ id** taught by this selected faculty member. Immediately you can see that all four courses (**course _ id**) taught by this faculty member have been returned and displayed in the Course ID List box. To insert a new course, enter these six pieces of new course information into the six TextFields on the right.

- Course ID: **CSE-549**
- Course: **AdvancedFuzzy Systems**
- Schedule: **T-H: 1:30-2:45 PM**
- Classroom: **TC-302**
- Credit: **3**
- Enrollment: **25**

Your finished CourseFrame window should match the one shown in Figure 9.92. Click on the **Insert** button to insert this new course record into the **Course** Table in our sample database. Immediately all six TextFields containing six pieces of information for a new course record are cleaned up to enable users to confirm the data insertion action.

To confirm the new course insertion action, two method scan be used. The easiest way is to use the **Select** button, that is, the code inside the event handler of that button, to try to retrieve all courses, that is, all **course _ id**, taught by the selected faculty member, **Ying Bai**. To do this, just click on the **Select** button to perform a query to get all **course _ id** taught by that faculty member. The run result is shown in Figure 9.93.

As shown in Figure 9.93, one can find that the new inserted course, **CSE-549**, has been retrieved and displayed in the Course ListBox. Click on that new **course _ id** in the CourseListBox, and the details about that course are displayed in six TextFields, as shown in Figure 9.93. Click on the **Back** button to terminate our client project.

The second way is to open the **Course** Table in our sample database to do this check. One can use the **Databases** icon inside the **Services** window in the NetBeans IDE 12.0 to connect to our sample database, **CSE _ DEPT**.

To do that, open the **Services** window and expand the **Databases** icon, then right-click on our database connection URL, **jdbc:oracle:thin:@localhost: 1251:XE;**, and select the **Connect** item. One may need to enter **oracle _ 18c** into the Password box to do this connection. Then expand our database and Tables in the sequence of **CSE _ DEPT** → **Tables** → **COURSE**. Then right-click on the **COURSE** Table and select the **View Data** item to open the **Course** Table. Browse to line 32 on

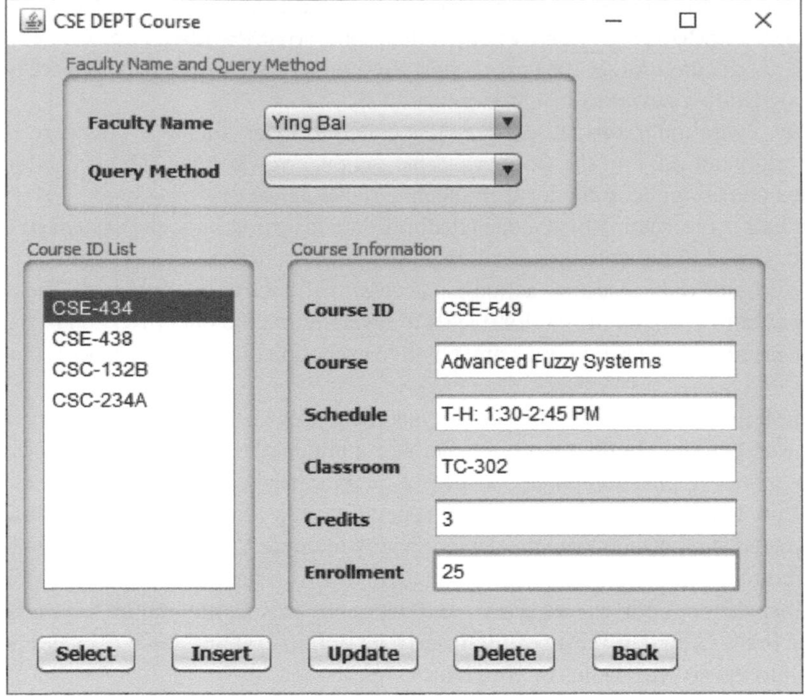

FIGURE 9.92 The new course record to be inserted into our database.

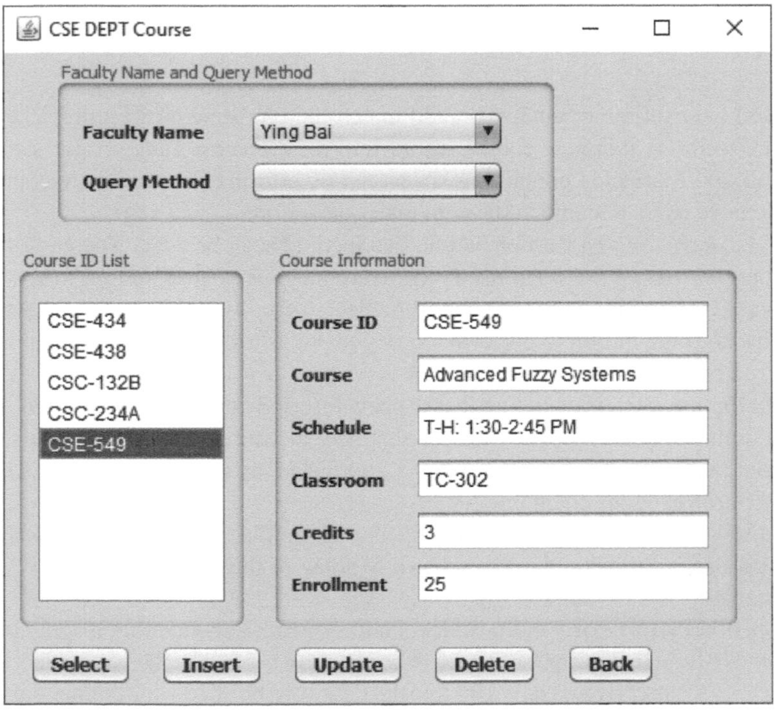

FIGURE 9.93 The check result for our new inserted course record.

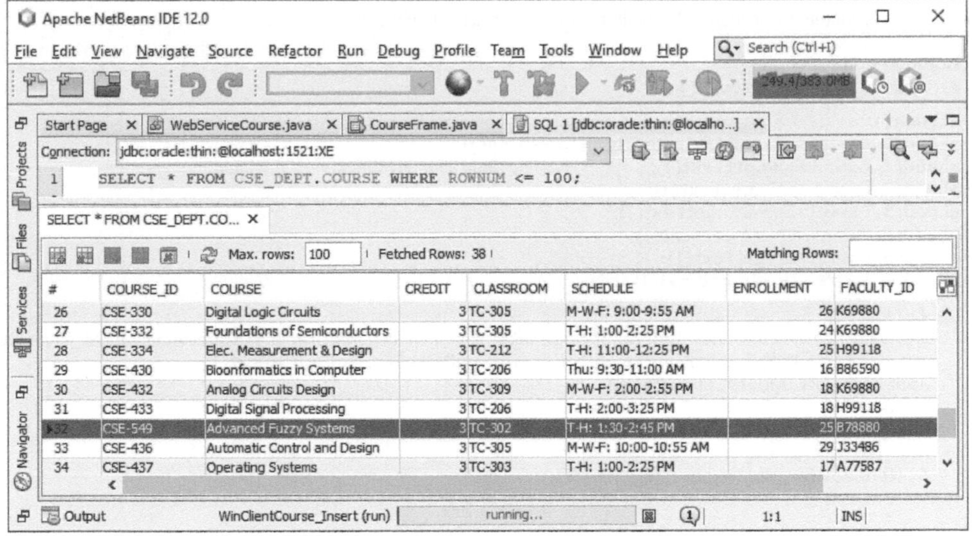

FIGURE 9.94 The new inserted course record in our sample database.

this Table, and you can see that our new inserted course, **CSE-549**, has been added there, as shown in Figure 9.94.

A complete Window-based consuming project, **WinClientCourse _ Insert**, can be found in the folder **Class BD Projects\Chapter 9** in the **Students** folder at the CRC Press ftp site (refer to Figure 1.2 in Chapter 1).

Next let's discuss how to perform a course update action to update an existing course in our sample database via Web service.

9.15.6 Build Code for the Update Button Method to Update Course Records

The function of this method is to update an existing course record when the **Update** button is clicked by the user. The existing course record will be updated on the **Course** Table in our sample Oracle database when this method is complete.

As we discussed in previous sections, all columns for the selected course record will be updated except the **course _ id** column, since it is a primary key and a cascaded update setup has been selected when we built this database. A very complicated update operational sequence would be executed if that primary key were updated. A much easier way to do that update is to insert a new course record with a new **course _ id**.

To make thing simple, let's modify our project **WinClientCourse _ Insert** to make it our new project, **WinClientCourse _ UpdtDelt**. Perform the following steps to build our new Windows-based project, **WinClientCourse _ UpdtDelt**:

1) Browse to our project **WinClientCourse _ Insert**, which can be found in the folder **Class DB Projects\Chapter 9** in the **Students** folder on the CRC Press ftp site (refer to Figure 1.2 in Chapter 1), and copy and then save it to any local folder in your machine.
2) Open NetBeans IDE 12.0 and right-click **WinClientCourse _ Insert** from your local folder and select the **Copy** item from the popup menu.
3) On the opened **Copy Project** wizard, change the project name to **WinClientCourse _ UpdtDelt** in the **Project Name** box, select your desired location from the **Project Location** box, and click on the **Copy** button.

```
  private void UpdateButtonActionPerformed(java.awt.event.ActionEvent evt) {
    // TODO add your handling code here:
A   Boolean update = false;
    ArrayList al = new ArrayList();
B   al.clear();
C   al.add(0, ComboName.getSelectedItem().toString());
    al.add(1, CourseField.getText());
    al.add(2, CreditsField.getText());
    al.add(3, ClassRoomField.getText());
    al.add(4, ScheduleField.getText());
    al.add(5, EnrollField.getText());
    al.add(6, CourseIDField.getText());
    try { // Call Web Service Operation
D      org.ws.oracle.WebServiceCourse_Service service = new org.ws.oracle.WebServiceCourse_Service();
       org.ws.oracle.WebServiceCourse port = service.getWebServiceCoursePort();
E      update = port.updateCourse(al);
F      if (!update)
          System.out.println("Error in course updating...");
G   } catch (Exception ex) {
       System.out.println("exception is: " + ex);
    }
  }
```

FIGURE 9.95 The completed code for the UpdateButtonActionPerformed() event handler.

The main source file, **CourseFrame.java**, in our **Source Packages** folder may generate some errors when this new project is created. The reason for that is due to a Web Reference issue. To fix this error, build and deploy our Web Service application project, **WebAppCourse**, and then rebuild our new project, **WinClientCourse _ UpdtDelt**.

Now let's first build the code for the **Update** button's event handler. In the opened **Design** view of the CourseFrame form window, double-click on the **Update** button to open its event handler. Enter the code shown in Figure 9.95 into this event handler. Let's have a closer look at this piece of code to see how it works.

A. Two local variables, **update** and **al**, are created first. The first is a Boolean variable used to hold the run result of execution of the Web service operation **UpdateCourse()**, and the second is an ArrayList instance used to store an updating course record to be updated in the **Course** Table in our sample database later.
B. The ArrayList instance **al** is cleaned up by using the **clear()** method to make sure that the **al** is empty before it can store any data.
C. A group of **add()** methods is used to add six pieces of updated course information into the ArrayList instance. The first parameter is a **faculty _ name** for whom a course record will be updated, and the seventh parameter is a **course _ id** that will work as a query criterion and will not be changed. One point is that the order of the course data must be identical to the order of the data in the ArrayList object **cdata** in our Web service operation, **UpdateCourse()**. Refer to that operation to make sure that both orders are identical.
D. A **try-catch** block is used to call our Web operation **UpdateCourse()** to update an existing course record via our Web service. First a new Web service instance, **service**, is created based on our Web service class, **WebServiceCourse _ Service**. Then a system method, **getWebServiceCoursePort()**, is executed to get the current port used by our Web service. This port is returned and assigned to a new port instance, **port**.
E. Our Web Service operation, **UpdateCourse()**, is executed to try to update the selected course record based on six pieces of updated information. The execution result is a Boolean variable, and it is returned and assigned to the local variable **update**.

F. If a **false** is returned, which means that this course data update has failed, the system **println()** method is used to indicate this situation.
G. The **catch** block is used to track and display any possible exception during the data update process.

Now we have finished the coding process for our client project to call our Web operation, **UpdateCourse()**, to update an existing course record in the **Course** Table based on the selected faculty member. Click on the **Clean and Build Main Project** button to build our project. Make sure that our Web Service application project, **WebAppCourse**, has been built and deployed successfully. Then click the **Run Main Project** button to run our client project to test the data update function.

In the opened client project, keep the default faculty member **Ying Bai** unchanged and click on the **Select** button to query all **course _ id** taught by this selected faculty member. Immediately you can see that all five courses or **course _ id** taught by this faculty member have been returned and displayed in the Course ID List box. To update an existing course, **CSE-549**, enter these six pieces of updated course information into the six TextFields:

- Course ID: **CSE-549**
- Course: **Modern Controls**
- Schedule: **M-W-F: 11:00-11:50 AM**
- Classroom: **TC-206**
- Credit: **3**
- Enrollment: **18**

Your finished CourseFrame window is shown in Figure 9.96. Click on the **Update** button to update this course record on the **Course** Table in our sample database.

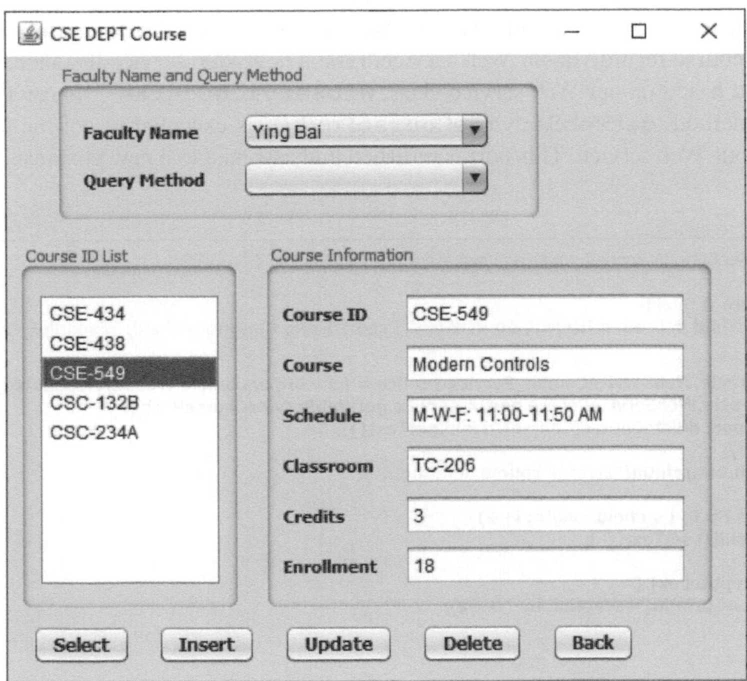

FIGURE 9.96 The updated course information for the course CSE-549.

To test the course record update action, there is more than one way to go. The first way is to retrieve that course, that is, the **course _ id**, and click on that **course _ id** from the Course ListBox to get details to confirm the data update action. To do that, just click the **Select** button again to get all courses (**course _ id**) taught by the faculty member **Ying Bai**, then click any other **course _ id**, such as **CSC-132B**, from the Course ID ListBox. Now click on **CSE-549** to retrieve its details. It can be seen that this course is really updated based on the update information shown in Figure 9.96. Our course data update using our Web Service is successful.

The second way to test the data update action is to connect to our sample database, **CSE _ DEPT**, and open the **Course** Table by using the **Databases** icon in the **Services** window inside the NetBeans IDE to confirm the data update action.

Generally it is recommended to recover this updated course on the **Course** Table in our sample database to keep our database neat and clean. However, we will keep this course right now since we need to use this record to perform the course delete action in the following section.

9.15.7 Build Code for the Delete Button Method to Delete Course Records

The function of this method is to delete an existing course record from our **Course** Table when the **Delete** button is clicked by the user. The existing course record will be permanently deleted from the **Course** Table in our sample Oracle database when this method is complete.

Open the **Delete** button's event handler and enter the code shown in Figure 9.97 into the event handler. Let's have a closer look at this piece of code to see how it works.

A. Two local variables, **delete** and **cfield[]**, are created first. The former is a Boolean variable used to hold the run result of execution of the Web service operation **DeleteCourse()**, and the latter is a JTextField array used to hold all TextFields in our CourseFrame Form. The purpose of using this JTextField array is to make it easier to clear all TextFields when this delete action is executed.
B. A **try-catch** block is used to call our Web operation **DeleteCourse()** to delete an existing course record via our Web service. First a new Web service instance, **service**, is created based on our Web service class, **WebServiceCourse _ Service**. Then a system method, **getWebServiceCoursePort()**, is executed to get the current port used by our Web service. This port is returned and assigned to a new port instance, **port**.

```
  private void DeleteButtonActionPerformed(java.awt.event.ActionEvent evt) {
    // TODO add your handling code here:
A   Boolean delete = false;
    JTextField[] cfield = {CourseIDField, CourseField, CreditsField, ClassRoomField, ScheduleField, EnrollField};
    try { // Call Web Service Operation
B       org.ws.oracle.WebServiceCourse_Service service = new org.ws.oracle.WebServiceCourse_Service();
        org.ws.oracle.WebServiceCourse port = service.getWebServiceCoursePort();
C       delete = port.deleteCourse(CourseIDField.getText());
D       if (!delete)
           System.out.println("Error in course deleting...");
E       else {
           for (int i = 0; i < cfield.length; i++)
              cfield[i].setText("");
        }
F   } catch (Exception ex) {
       System.out.println("exception is: " + ex);
    }
  }
```

FIGURE 9.97 The completed code for the DeleteButtonActionPerformed() event handler.

C. The Web service operation DeleteCourse() is called to delete an existing course record from our Course Table based on the selected course _ id. The run result is returned and assigned to the local variable delete.
D. If a false is returned, which means that this course data delete has failed, the system println() method is used to indicate this.
E. Otherwise, the data delete is successful. A for() loop is used to clean up all six TextFields to indicate this situation, too.
F. The catch block is used to track any possible exception during the data delete process.

Now we have finished the coding process for calling and executing our last Web service operation, DeleteCourse(), to delete an existing course record from the Course Table based on the selected course _ id. Click on the Clean and Build Main Project button to build our project. Click on the Run Main Project button to run our client project to test the course data delete function.

In the opened client project, keep the default faculty member Ying Bai unchanged and click on the Select button to query all course _ id taught by this selected faculty member. Immediately you can see that all five courses (course _ id) taught by this faculty member have been returned and displayed in the Course ID ListBox. To delete an existing course, CSE-549, just click on the course _ id from the Course ID Listbox and click on the Delete button.

To confirm the course delete action, two methods can be utilized. First, one can use the Select button to retrieve the deleted course from our database. To do that, just keep the selected faculty member Ying Bai in the Faculty Name combo box unchanged and click on the Select button. It can be seen that all returned courses (course _ id) taught by the selected faculty member are displayed, but without CSE-549. Another way is to open our Course Table in our sample database in the Services window inside the NetBeans IDE 12.0 to check whether this course has been deleted.

At this point, we have finished building and developing a Windows-based project to consume our Web Service project for the Course Table in our sample database. A complete Window-based client project, WinClientCourse _ UpdtDelt, can be seen in the folder Class DB Projects\Chapter 9 that is in the Students folder at the CRC Press ftp site (refer to Figure 1.2 in Chapter 1).

Next let's build a Web-based client project to consume this Web service.

9.16 BUILD A WEB-BASED CLIENT PROJECT TO CONSUME OUR WEB SERVICE PROJECT

To consume our Web Service project, we can also build some Web-based client projects to call different operations to perform related actions to our database. The structure of this Web-based client project is shown in Figure 9.98.

The Java Managed bean works as an interface to talk to Web Service to perform physical query operations to our Course Table in our sample database.

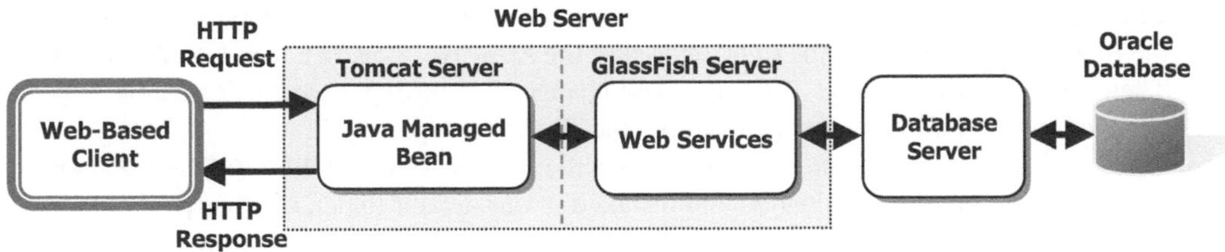

FIGURE 9.98 The architecture of our Web-based client project.

9.16.1 Create a Web-Based Client Project, WebClientCourse _ Select

To save time and space, we can modify one of our projects, **JavaWebOracleCourse**, we built in Chapter 8 and make it our new project. You can find this project on the CRC Press ftp site (refer to Figure 1.2 in Chapter 1), in the **Students\Class DB Projects\Chapter 8** folder. You can copy and paste that project to your local folder. Before we can modify that project to make it our new client project, the following conditions are required:

1) Another popular Web server, Tomcat server, was used as a container for that project, so we need to install and add the Tomcat server to our new project before we can do modifications to that project and make it our new client project.
2) Some JSTL cores with related embedded C tags were used for that project, that is, used for the view class **Course.jsp** file, so an associated JSTL library file should be installed and added into our new client project.

Now perform the following steps to build our new Web-based client project, **WebClient Course _ Select**.

1) Open NetBeans IDE 12.0 and the **Services** window, and expand the **Servers** folder. Currently only the **GlassFish Server** is displayed.
2) Right-click on the **Servers** folder and select **Add Server** item to open the Add Server Instance wizard.
3) Select the **apache Tomcat or TomEE** item from the Server list and click on the **Next** button.
4) In the next wizard, click on the **Browse** button located on the right of Server Location box to locate our downloaded Tomcat 8.0.27 Web server from Section 8.4.2.1 in Chapter 8, which is **C:\Program Files\Apache Software Foundation**, select our Web server folder **Apache Tomcat 8.0.27** by clicking on it and click on the **Open** button to select this server.
5) You can enter any desired username and password into the **Username** and **Password** box if you'd like to get more protection for this server. In our case, just enter **tomcat** and **oracle _ 18c** into those two boxes as the username and password for this server.
6) Keep the **Create user** checkbox checked to generate the new user for this server. Your finished **Installation and Login Details** wizard is shown in Figure 9.99.
7) Click on the **Finish** button to complete the adding Tomcat Web server process.
8) Now open NetBeans IDE 12.0 and the **Projects** window, and browse to your local folder where the copied project **JavaWebOracleCourse** is located. Then right-click on that project and select the **Copy** item from the popup menu to open the **Copy Project** wizard.
9) Enter our new project name, **WebClientCourse _ Select**, into the **Project Name** box, browse to your local project folder as the **Project Location** and click on the **Copy** button. A new project, **WebClientCourse _ Select**, is generated and added into our **Projects** window.
10) Right-click on our new project, **WebClientCourse _ Select**, in the **Projects** window and select the **Properties** item to open the Project Properties wizard.
11) Click on the **Run** node under the **Categories** list, then click on the dropdown arrow on the **Server** combo box on the right, and select the **Apache Tomcat or TomEE** server.
12) Then go to the **Relative URL** box and change the starting page to **/Course.jsp**. Click on the **OK** button to complete adding the Tomcat server.
13) Finally we need to check and confirm that whether the JSTL library file, **JSTL-1.2.jar**, has been successfully downloaded and installed in our default folder, **C:\Temp**. If not, go to the site **jstl-1.2.jar** to download **JSTL-1.2.jar** file and add it to the **C:\Temp** folder. You do not need to add this library into our new project, since it was done by the original project.

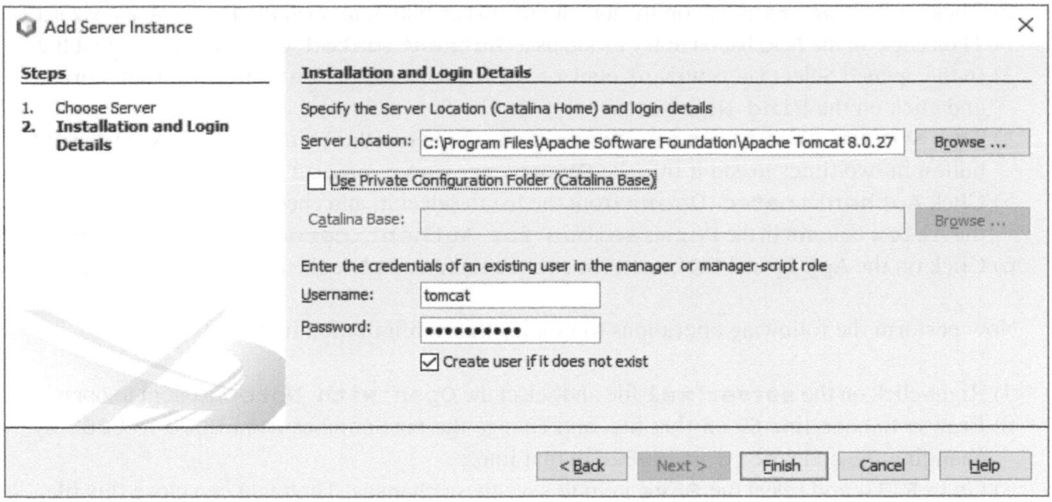

FIGURE 9.99 The finished Installation and Login Details wizard.

Now let's add a Web Service reference to our Web-based client project to allow it to use our Web service operations.

9.16.2 Add a Web Service Reference to Our Web-Based Project and Change the Ports

In order to call an operation in our Web service application project, **`WebAppCourse`**, we need to add the Web reference in our Web-based client project, **`WebClientCourse_Select`**, to direct all calls to our Web service project. Perform the following operations to add the Web service reference:

1) Build and deploy our Web Service project, **`WebAppCourse`**, to make it ready.
2) Right-click on our Web-based client project, **`WebClientCourse_Select`**, and select the **`New > Web Service Client`** item to open the **`New Web Service Client`** wizard.
3) In the opened wizard, click on the **`Browse`** button that is next to the **`Project`** field and expand our Web application, **`WebAppCourse`**. Then choose our Web service class file, **`WebServiceCourse`**, by clicking on it, and click on the **`OK`** button.
4) Click on the **`Finish`** button to complete the Web service reference addition process.

Prior to building the code for our pages and Java Bean class file, we need first to modify the related Web server HTTP port numbers since currently two Web Servers are utilized for our client projects: GlassFish and Tomcat, and both of them may use the same port to start the service. To avoid any conflict from a duplicated port number, we need to change some of them to avoid this duplication error.

We prefer to keep the HTTP port for the GlassFish server, so we can modify the Tomcat server's starting HTTP port number. We need to access the default server configuration file of the Tomcat server, **`server.xml`**, to do any modifications for those ports. Perform the following operations to enable us to access that configuration file:

1) Open the Windows Explorer and browse to the default location for that configuration file, which is **`C:\Program Files\Apache Software Foundation\Apache Tomcat 8.0.27\conf`**. Then right-click on the configuration file **`server.xml`**, and select the **`Properties`** item to open its Properties wizard.

2) Click on the **Security** tab on the top and the **Edit** button to open the Permissions wizard. Then click on the **Add** button to try to add us as **Authenticated Users** to access that file.
3) In the opened Select Users wizard, click on the **Advanced** button on the lower-left corner, and click on the **Find Now** button.
4) Then select **Authenticated Users** from the list at the bottom and click on the **OK** button in two times to add it into the **Group or user names** list.
5) Click **Authenticated Users** from the list to select it, and check all checkboxes under the **Allow** column in the **Permissions for Authenticated Users** at the bottom.
6) Click on the **Apply** and **OK** button (in two times) to complete the authentication process.

Now perform the following operations to modify this configuration file:

1) Right-click on the **server.xml** file and select the **Open with Notepad** item to open it.
2) Browse to code line **69** on that file, and change the port number from **8080** to **8082** by changing the code: **port = "8082"** in that line.
3) Go to **File** and select the **Save** item to save these changes. Then you can close this file.

One point to be noted is that you must stop and exit the NetBeans IDE 12.0 prior to doing those modifications to the configuration file to make it effective. Those modifications may not be effective or available if the NetBeans IDE is open.

Now that we have added a Web service reference to our Web-based client project, **WebClientCourse _ Select**, next let's develop the code in our client project to call Web service operations to perform related course data query actions. The main code concentrates on building the transaction JSP file, **CourseProcess.jsp**, and Java Managed Bean class file, **CourseQuery.java**.

We can still use the original code on the course query part in the **CourseProcess.jsp** page and add code to the **Insert**, **Update** and **Delete** course parts on that page later, solet's start from our Java Bean class file, **CourseQuery.java**.

9.16.3 Modify the Java Bean CourseQuery.java and the Control File CourseProcess.jsp

Open the NetBeans IDE 12.0 in Administrator mode by right-clicking on the NetBeans IDE icon on the desktop and select **Run as administrator** item. Launching the NetBeans IDE 12.0 in this way is very important to enable us to build and run our client projects correctly. Otherwise you may encounter runtime errors when you run our client project. Double-click on our Java Bean class file **CourseQuery.java** from the **Projects** window to open this file, and perform the following modifications to the code inside two methods, **getCourse()** and **QueryCourse()**:

1) Remove all original code from the constructor of this Java Bean class file, since we do not need any code to connect to our sample database; this connection job is handled by operations in our Web Service project.
2) Remove the entire method **CloseDBConnection()** with all code for that method, since closing can be handled by operations in our Web Service.
3) Modify the first part of code inside the methods **getCourse()** and **QueryCourse()** as shown in Figure 9.100. The modified parts are indicated with bold.

Let's have a close look at the modified code in Figure 9.100 to see how it works.

A. A Java package, **java.util.***, that included the **ArrayList** and **HashMap** classes is imported into this file, since we need to use those components to store collected course details later.
B. Remove all original code from the constructor of this class and keep it empty, since we do not need to use it in this project.

```
  package JavaWebOracleSelectPackage;
  import java.sql.*;
A import java.util.*;
  public class CourseQuery {
    private String CourseID;
    private String CourseName;
    private String Credit;
    private String ClassRoom;
    private String Schedule;
    private String Enrollment;
    private String facultyName;
    public HashMap c_course = null;
B  public CourseQuery() { }
C  public void getCourse(String fname) {
D    int index;
     ArrayList<String> al = new ArrayList();
     HashMap<String, String> sCourse = new HashMap<String, String>();
E    if (fname.isEmpty()) setCourse(null);
F    try{
        org.ws.oracle.WebServiceCourse_Service service = new org.ws.oracle.WebServiceCourse_Service();
        org.ws.oracle.WebServiceCourse port = service.getWebServiceCoursePort();
G       al.clear();
H       al = (ArrayList)port.queryCourseID(fname);
I       for (index = 0; index < al.size(); index++) {
           sCourse.put(String.valueOf(index), al.get(index));
        }
J       setCourse(sCourse);
        setFacultyName(fname);
      }
K     catch (Exception e) {
        System.out.println("Error in Statement! " + e.getMessage());
        setCourse(null);
      }
  }
L public boolean QueryCourse(String cid) {
     ArrayList<String> al = new ArrayList();
M    try{
        org.ws.oracle.WebServiceCourse_Service service = new org.ws.oracle.WebServiceCourse_Service();
        org.ws.oracle.WebServiceCourse port = service.getWebServiceCoursePort();
N       al.clear();
O       al = (ArrayList)port.queryCourse(cid);
P       courseID = al.get(0);
        courseName = al.get(1);
        credit = al.get(2);
        classroom = al.get(3);
        schedule = al.get(4);
        enrollment = al.get(5);
Q       return true;
R    }catch (Exception ex) {
        System.out.println("exception: " + ex);
        return false;
     }
  }
```

FIGURE 9.100 The first part of the modified code for the Java bean CourseQuery.java.

C. The first course query method, **getCourse()**, is declared with a selected faculty name as the argument. This method is used to call one of our Web Service operations, **QueryCourseID()**, based on the selected faculty name to get all **course _ id** taught by that faculty member and display them in the Course ID ListBox in the **Course.jsp** page.

D. Some local variables, including an ArrayList instance, **al**; an integer variable, **index**; and a HashMap object, **sCourse**, are declared, and they are used to store the queried **course _ id** and work as a loop counter to build a HashMap object to save the queried **course _ id**.

E. A pre-checking action is performed to make sure that the input argument to this method is not empty, in other words, that a valid faculty name is included.
F. A **try-catch** block is used to call our Web operation **QueryCourseID()** to get all **course _ id** via our Web service. First a new Web service instance, **service**, is created based on our Web service class, **WebServiceCourse _ Service**. Then a system method, **getWebServiceCoursePort()**, is executed to get the current port used by our Web service. This port is returned and assigned to a new port instance, **port**.
G. The ArrayList instance **al** is cleaned up by using the **clear()** method to make sure that **al** is empty before it can be used to store any data.
H. Our Web Service operation **QueryCourseID()** is executed with a selected faculty name as the argument, and the query results are assigned to our ArrayList object, **al**.
I. A **for()** loop is used to collect all queried **course _ id** from the ArrayList instance **al** and add each of them into our HashMap instance **sCourse** with a pair of an index and a value; both are the String data type.
J. A user-defined method, **setCourse()**, is executed to assign the **sCourse** result to our class member **c _ course**, which is a HashMap object defined in our **CourseQuery** class. Another user-defined method, **setFacultyName()**, is used to set the selected faculty name during the Web page refresh process.
K. A **catch** block is used to track and detect any possible exception during this query process, and the resulting HashMap instance will be set to **null** if any error occurs.
L. Another user-defined method, **QueryCourse()**, which is used to query the details for a selected CourseID, is declared with the argument **cid**, which is an input **course _ id**. Also an ArrayList instance, **al**, is generated, and it is used to store the queried course details later.
M. A **try-catch** block is used to call our Web operation **QueryCourse()** to get all details for a selected course via our Web service. First a new Web service instance, **service**, is created based on our Web service class **WebServiceCourse _ Service**. Then the system method **getWebServiceCoursePort()** is executed to get the current port used by our Web service. This port is returned and assigned to a new port instance, **port**.
N. The ArrayList instance **al** is cleaned up by using the **clear()** method to make sure that **al** is empty before it can be used to store any data.
O. Our Web Service operation, **QueryCourse()**, is executed with a selected **course _ id** as the argument, and the query results are assigned to our ArrayList object, **al**.
P. A sequence of system methods, **get()**, is used to pick up each item of the queried course details in **al** and assign each of them to the related class variable. One point to be noted is the order of these assignments, and it must be identical to the column order in our **Course** Table in our sample database, **CSE _ DEPT**.
Q. A **true** is returned to indicate that this query is successful.
R. The **catch** block is used to track and detect any possible exception during this query process, and a **false** would be returned if any error occurs.

Now let's do some modifications to the second part of the code for our Java Bean class. Just add three user-defined methods, as shown in Figure 9.101, into our **CourseQuery** class. No explanations need to be given due to the simplicity of these methods.

Next let's modify the control class **CourseProcess.jsp** page. Open the code window for that page, and the only modification to that page is to remove the code **cQuery.CloseDBConnection();**, which is located at line 59 on that page, since we removed that method from our Java Bean class file in the previous operations.

Now we have completed all code development for our client project. Next let's build and run our project to consume our Web Service to query the **Course** Table in our sample database.

```
public class CourseQuery {
.........
  public void setFacultyName(String f_name) {
    this.facultyName = f_name;
  }
  public void setCourse(HashMap sCourse) {
    this.c_course = sCourse;
  }
  public HashMap get_CourseID() {
    return c_course;
  }
}
```

FIGURE 9.101 The second part of the modified code for the Java bean CourseQuery.java.

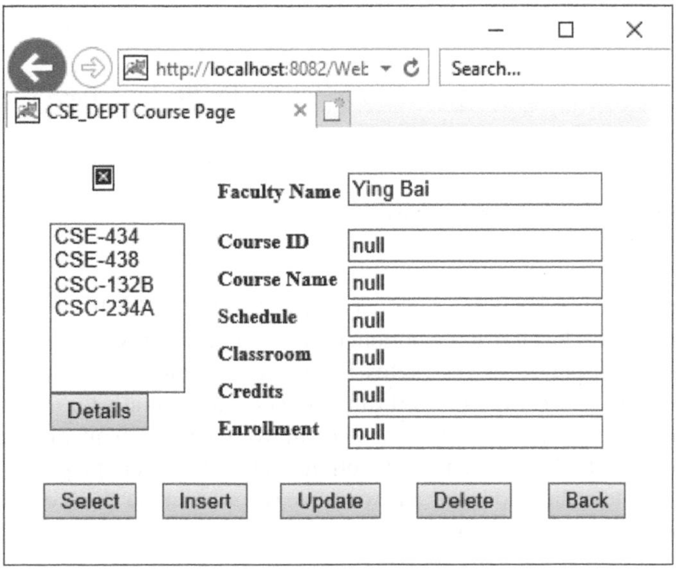

FIGURE 9.102 The run status of our client project.

9.16.4 Build and Run Our Client Project to Query Course Record via Our Web Service

Prior to building and running our client project, make sure that our Web Service application project, **WebAppCourse**, has been built and deployed successfully.

Perform the following operations to build and run our client project, **WebClient Course _ Select**:

1) Click on the **Clean and Build Main Project** button to build our project, that is, build our **CourseProcess.jsp** page and our Java bean class file **CourseQuery.java**.
2) Click on the **RunProject** button on the top (green arrow) to run our client project.

Enter a valid faculty name, such as **Ying Bai**, into the Faculty Name box, and then click on the **Select** button to query all courses (**course _ id**) taught by this faculty member. All four courses (**course _ id**) are retrieved from our database and displayed in the CourseList box, as shown in Figure 9.102.

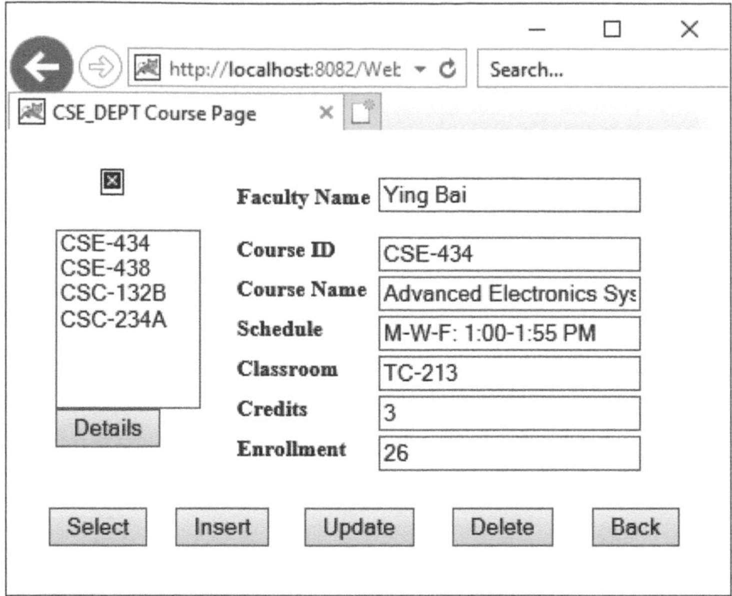

FIGURE 9.103 The query result for the course details.

Now select a **course _ id** in the CourseList box, such as **CSE-434**, by clicking it, and then click the **Details** button that is located at the bottom of the CourseList box. All course details related to this **course _ id** are displayed in the six TextFields on the right, as shown in Figure 9.103.

One can try to check other **course _ id** values to get course details for the selected **course _ id**. Our Web-based client project used to consume our Web Service to query course information is successful. Click on the **Back** and then **Exit** button to close our client project.

Next let's concentrate on how to insert a new course record into the **Course** Table in our sample database via our Web-based client project.

9.16.5 Build a Web Client Project to Insert New Course Records via Our Web Service

To save time and space, we can modify one of our projects, **WebClientCourse _ Select**, we built in the last section and make it our new project. Perform the following operations to make our new project, **WebClientCourse _ Insert**:

1) Open NetBeans IDE 12.0 in the Administrator mode and right-click on the project **WebClientCourse _ Select** from the **Projects** window. Then select the **Copy** item from the popup menu to open the **Copy Project** wizard.
2) Enter our new project name, **WebClientCourse _ Insert**, into the **Project Name** box, and browse to your local project folder as the **Project Location**, and click on the **Copy** button. A new project, **WebClientCourse _ Insert**, is generated and added into our **Projects** window.

After this new project is generated, a few errors may occur in our Java Bean class file **CourseQuery.java**. To fix those errors, just build our new project by clicking on the **Clean and Build Project** button on the top to update the Web Service reference.

Now let's develop the code for this new project. The main code for inserting a new course record is concentrated on our transaction JSP page, **CourseProcess.jsp**, and Java bean class

```
   .........
   else if (request.getParameter("Insert")!= null) {
     //process the course record insertion
     %>
A    <jsp:useBean id="Insert_Course" scope="session" class=" JavaWebOracleSelectPackage.CourseQuery" />
     <jsp:setProperty name="Insert_Course" property="*" />
     <%
B    boolean res = false;
C    String cid = request.getParameter("CourseIDField");
     String cname = request.getParameter("CourseNameField");
     String credit = request.getParameter("CreditField");
     String classroom = request.getParameter("ClassroomField");
     String schedule = request.getParameter("ScheduleField");
     String enroll = request.getParameter("EnrollmentField");
     String fname = request.getParameter("FacultyNameField");
D    String[] cnew = {fname, cid, cname, credit, classroom, schedule, enroll};
E    res = cQuery.Insert_Course(cnew);
F    if (!res)
         response.sendRedirect("Course.jsp");
G    else {
           for (int index = 0; index < C_Field.length; index++)
             session.setAttribute(C_Field[index], null);
H          response.sendRedirect("Course.jsp");          }
     }
   else if (request.getParameter("Update")!= null) {
       //process the course record updating
     }
   .........
```

FIGURE 9.104 The code for the Insert Course block in the CourseProcess.jsp page.

file, **`CourseQuery.java`**. Let's first take care of the code development for the transaction page, **`CourseProcess.jsp`**.

Double-click on the page from the **`Projects`** window to open it and enter the code shown in Figure 9.104 into the **`else if (request.getParameter("Insert")!= null)`** block.

Let's have a closer look at this piece of code to see how it works.

A. Two JSP directives are declared first, and they are used to set up the Java bean, session, class and property used on this JSP page. The **`Insert _ Course()`** method will be built in our Java bean class later, and the underscore between the **`Insert`** and the **`Course`** is to distinguish this method from a similar operation, **`InsertCourse()`**, in our Web Service. These two directives must not be enclosed by a pair of **`<% . . . %>`** symbols.
B. Starting from step B, the following code will be Java code to be embedded into this page, so an opening symbol, **`<%`**, is used to start this part. Since the Web operation **`InsertCourse()`** in our Service returns a Boolean result, to hold it, a Boolean variable, **`res`**, is created first.
C. To set up a new course record that contains seven pieces of new course information, seven system methods, **`getParameter()`**, are used to pick up each piece of new course information from the related TextField in our client page, **`Course.jsp`**, and assign each of them to a related local String variable.
D. Then a String[] array is created and initialized with those seven local variables to make a new course record ready to be sent to the Java bean class.
E. The **`Insert _ Course()`** method that will be defined in our Java bean class is executed with the initialized String[] as the argument. The run result of this method is returned and assigned to our local Boolean variable, **`res`**.
F. If a **`false`** is returned, which means that the execution of this method fails, then the client page, **`Course.jsp`**, is refreshed to make it ready for the next operation.

```
  ........
  public boolean Insert_Course(String[] newCourse){
A     boolean insert = false;
      ArrayList al = new ArrayList();
B     al.clear();
C     al.add(0, newCourse[0]);
      al.add(1, newCourse[1]);
      al.add(2, newCourse[2]);
      al.add(3, newCourse[3]);
      al.add(4, newCourse[4]);
      al.add(5, newCourse[5]);
      al.add(6, newCourse[6]);
D     try{
        org.ws.oracle.WebServiceCourse_Service service = new org.ws.oracle.WebServiceCourse_Service();
        org.ws.oracle.WebServiceCourse port = service.getWebServiceCoursePort();
E       insert = port.insertCourse(al);
F       if (!insert) {
          System.out.println("The data insertion is failed!");
        }
      }
G     catch (Exception e) {
        System.out.println("Error in Insert Statement! " + e.getMessage());
        return false;
      }
H     return insert;
    }
  }
```

FIGURE 9.105 The added code for the Insert_Course() method in the Java bean.

G. Otherwise, the running of the method is successful and a new course record has been inserted into the **Course** Table in our sample database, so all TextFields in the client page will be reset to null to allow users to check the insertion result.
H. The view page, **Course.jsp**, is also refreshed to indicate the success of the data insertion.

Next let's build the code for our Java bean class file, **CourseQuery.java**. Double-click on this file in the **Projects** window in the folder **Source Packages\JavaWebOracleSelectPackage** to open it and enter the code shown in Figure 9.105 into the bottom of this file. Let's have a closer look at this piece of code to see how it works.

A. Two local variables, **insert** and **al**, are generated first. The former is a Boolean variable used to hold the run result of execution of our Web Service operation, **InsertCourse()**, and the latter is an instance of the ArrayList class, which is used to store seven pieces of information for a new inserted course record.
B. The ArrayList instance **al** is cleaned up by using the **clear()** method to make sure that **al** is empty before it can be used to store any data.
C. A sequence of **add()** methods is used to add all seven pieces of new course information into the ArrayList instance **al**, which will be passed as an argument to our Web Service operation, **InsertCourse()**, later.
D. A **try-catch** block is used to call our Web operation **InsertCourse()** to insert a new course record into our sample database via our Web service. First a new Web service instance, **service**, is created based on our Web service class **WebServiceCourse _ Service**. Then the **getWebServiceCoursePort()** method is executed to get the current port used by our Web service. This port is returned and assigned to a new port instance, **port**.
E. The Web Service operation **InsertCourse()** is executed with an argument, **al**, that contains seven pieces of new course information, and the run result is returned and assigned to the local Boolean variable **insert**.

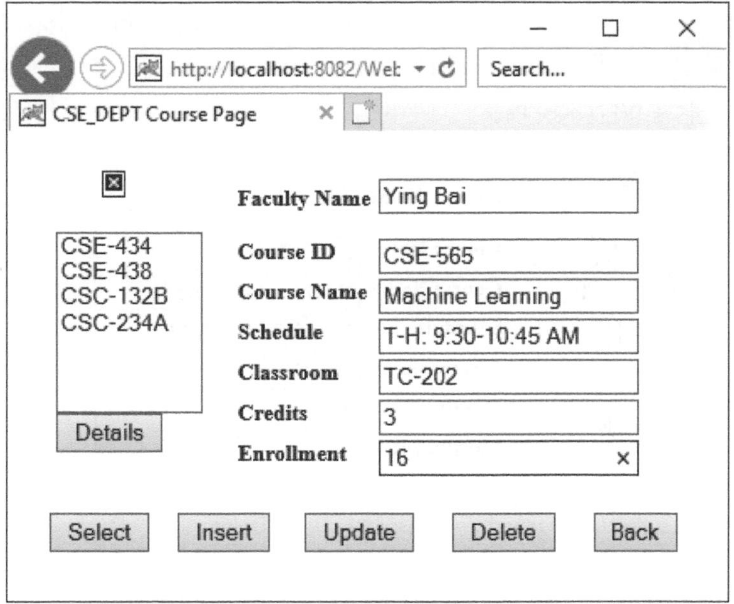

FIGURE 9.106 The run status and result of inserting a new course record.

F. If the returned Boolean value is **false**, which means that this data insertion action failed, a system method, **println()**, is used to indicate this. Otherwise, this data insertion is successful.
G. The **catch** block is used to monitor and check any possible exception during this insertion process. A **false** is returned to the calling program if any error occurs.
H. Otherwise, a **true** is returned to indicate the success of this data insertion action.

Now we have finished all code for the new course insertion action. Let's build and run our client project to consume our Web Service to insert a new course record into the **Course** Table in our sample database.

Prior to building and running our client project, make sure that our Web Service application project, **WebAppCourse**, has been built and deployed successfully.

Perform the following operations to build and run our client project, **WebClient Course _ Insert**:

1) Click on the **Clean and Build Main Project** button to build our project.
2) Then click on the **Run Project** button (green arrow) on the top to run our project.

When the project runs and the course page is opened, enter a valid faculty name, such as **Ying Bai**, into the Faculty Name box, and then click on the **Select** button to query all courses (**course _ id**) taught by this faculty member. All four courses (**course _ id**) should be retrieved from our database and displayed in the CourseList box, as shown in Figure 9.106.

Let's test inserting a new course record into the **Course** Table in our sample database. Keep the selected faculty member, **Ying Bai**, with no change and enter the following six pieces of information as a new course record into the six related TextFields in this course page:

- Course ID: **CSE-565**
- Course Name: **Machine Learning**
- Schedule: **T-H: 9:30-10:45 AM**

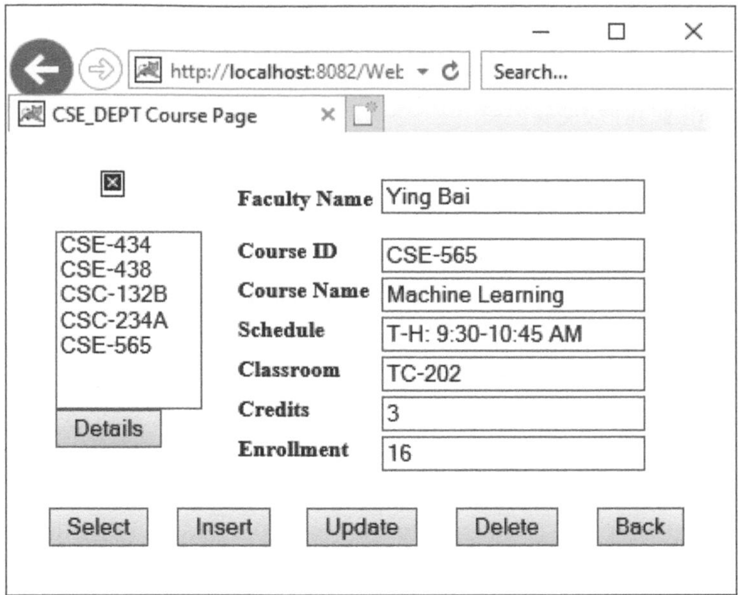

FIGURE 9.107 The confirmation result of the new inserted course record.

- Classroom: `TC-202`
- Credit: `3`
- Enrollment: `16`

Click on the **`Insert`** button to try to insert this new course record into the **`Course`** Table in our sample database, **`CSE _ DEPT`**. If this insertion action is successful, the client page **`Course.jsp`** is refreshed to clean all contents to null in each TextField.

To check the data insertion, just click on the **`Select`** button to retrieve all courses (**`course _ id`**) taught by the selected faculty member, **`Ying Bai`**. One can see that the new inserted course, **`CSE-565`**, is retrieved and displayed in the CourseList box, as shown in Figure 9.107.

Select this new inserted course from this CourseList box by clicking on it, and then click on the **`Details`** button to get details for this course record. The details about this new inserted course are displayed in six TextFields, as shown in Figure 9.107. Our data insertion with our Web client project is successful!

Click on the **`Back`** and the **`Exit`** buttons to close our project.

Another way to confirm the data insertion is to open the **`Course`** Table via the **`Services`** window in the NetBeans IDE. After opening the **`Services`** window, expand the **`Databases`** icon and connect to our sample database by right-clicking on our database URL. Select the **`Connect`** item and enter the password, **`oracle _ 18c`**, to connect to our sample database. Then expand our database, **`CSE _ DEPT`**, and **`Tables`** folders, right-click on the **`COURSE`** Table and select the **`View Data`** item to open this Table. One can see that the new course is really inserted into the **`Course`** Table; it is located on the bottom line that has been highlighted, as shown in Figure 9.108.

Next let's build and develop the code for our client project to access our Web Service to update a selected course in our **`Course`** Table.

9.16.6 Build Our Client Project to Update Course Records via Our Web Service

Generally there is no need to update a **`course _ id`** when updating a course record, since a better way to do that is to insert a new course record and delete the old one. The main reason for this is that a

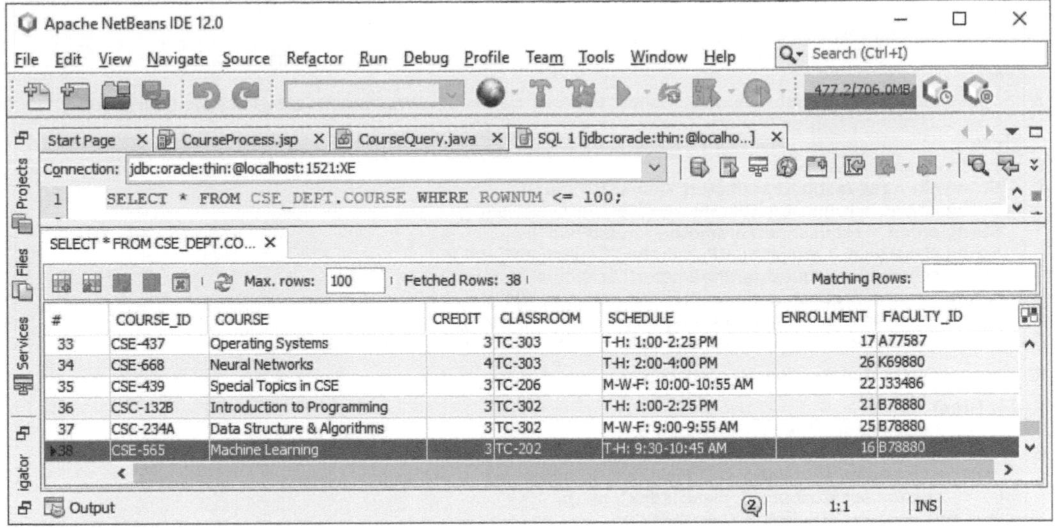

FIGURE 9.108 The opened Course Table in our sample database.

very complicated cascaded update process would be performed if a **course _ id** were updated, since it is a primary key in the **Course** Table but a foreign key in the **StudentCourse** Table. To update a primary key, one needs to update foreign keys first in the child Tables and then update the primary key in the parent Table. This will make our updateprocess very complicated. In order to avoid this confusion, in this section, we will update a course record by changing any column except the **course _ id**, and this is a popular way to update a Table and widely implemented in most database applications.

To save time and space, we can modify one of our projects, **WebClientCourse _ Insert**, we built in the last section and make it our new project. Perform the following operations to make our new project, **WebClientCourse _ Update**:

1) Open NetBeans IDE 12.0 in Administrator mode and right-click on the project **WebClientCourse _ Insert** in the **Projects** window. Then select the **Copy** item from the popup menu to open the **Copy Project** wizard.
2) Enter our new project name, **WebClientCourse _ Update**, into the **Project Name** box, and browse to your local project folder as the **Project Location**, and click on the **Copy** button. A new project, **WebClientCourse _ Update**, is generated and added into our **Projects** window.

After this new project is generated, a few errors may occur in our Java Bean class file **CourseQuery.java**. To fix those errors, just build our new project by clicking on the **Clean and Build Project** button on the top to update the Web Service reference.

Now let's develop the code for the **Update** button in our client project, that is, in the client page **Course.jsp**, to update a course record via our Web Service. The main code concentrates on two files, the transaction page, **CourseProcess.jsp**, and our Java bean class file, **CourseQuery.java**. Let's first take care of the code development for the transaction page, **CourseProcess.jsp**.

The main function of this piece of code is to coordinate the update query and provide a valid interface between the client page and the Java bean to make that query smoother.

Double-click on this page in the **Projects** window to open it and enter the code shown in Figure 9.109 into this page, that is, into the **else if (request.getParameter("Update")!= null)** block.

```
  .........
  else if (request.getParameter("Update")!= null) {
   //process the course record updating
   %>
A  <jsp:useBean id="Update_Course" scope="session" class="JavaWebOracleSelectPackage.CourseQuery" />
   <jsp:setProperty name="Update_Course" property="*" />
   <%
B  boolean res = false;
C  String cid = request.getParameter("CourseIDField");
   String cname = request.getParameter("CourseNameField");
   String credit = request.getParameter("CreditField");
   String classroom = request.getParameter("ClassroomField");
   String schedule = request.getParameter("ScheduleField");
   String enroll = request.getParameter("EnrollmentField");
   String fname = request.getParameter("FacultyNameField");
D  String[] cupdate = {fname, cname, credit, classroom, schedule, enroll, cid};
E  res = cQuery.Update_Course(cupdate);
F  if (!res)
      response.sendRedirect("Course.jsp");
G  else {
        for (int index = 0; index < C_Field.length; index++)
          session.setAttribute(C_Field[index], null);
        response.sendRedirect("Course.jsp");
     }
  }
  else if (request.getParameter("Delete")!= null) {
     //process the course record deleting
  }
  .........
```

FIGURE 9.109 The code for the Update Course block in the CourseProcess.jsp page.

Let's have a closer look at this piece of code to see how it works.

A. Two JSP directives are declared first, and they are used to set up the Java bean, session, class and property used on this JSP page. The **`Update _ Course()`** method is to be built in our Java bean class later, and the underscore between the **`Update`** and the **`Course`** is to distinguish this method from a similar operation, **`UpdateCourse()`**, in our Web Service. These two directives must not be enclosed by a pair of `<% . . . %>` symbols.
B. Starting from step B, the following code will be Java code to be embedded into this page, so an opening symbol, `<%`, is used to start this part. Since the Web operation **`UpdateCourse()`** in our Web Service returns a boolean result, to hold it, a local boolean variable, **`res`**, is created and initialized first.
C. To set up an updated course record that contains six pieces of updated course information, seven system methods, **`getParameter()`**, are used to pick up each piece of updated course information (including **`course _ id`**, but it will not be updated) from the related TextField in our client page, **`Course.jsp`**, and assign each of them to a local String variable.
D. Then a String[] array is created and initialized with those seven local variables (keep **`course _ id`** with no change) to make an updated course record ready to be sent to the Java bean class in the next step.
E. The **`Update _ Course()`** method that will be defined in our Java bean class is executed with the initialized String[] as the argument. The run result of this method is returned and assigned to our local boolean variable **`res`**.
F. If a **`false`** is returned, which means that the execution of this method fails, then the client page, **`Course.jsp`**, is refreshed to make it ready for the next operation.
G. Otherwise, the running of the method is successful, and the selected course record is updated in the **`Course`** Table in our sample database, so all TextFields in the client page will be reset to **`null`** to allow users to check the updateresult.

```
  ........
  public boolean Update_Course(String[] upCourse){
A     boolean update = false;
      ArrayList al = new ArrayList();
B     al.clear();
C     al.add(0, upCourse[0]);        // faculty_name
      al.add(1, upCourse[1]);        // course_name
      al.add(2, upCourse[2]);        // credit
      al.add(3, upCourse[3]);        // classroom
      al.add(4, upCourse[4]);        // schedule
      al.add(5, upCourse[5]);        // enrollment
      al.add(6, upCourse[6]);        // course_id
D     try{
        org.ws.oracle.WebServiceCourse_Service service = new org.ws.oracle.WebServiceCourse_Service();
        org.ws.oracle.WebServiceCourse port = service.getWebServiceCoursePort();
E       update = port.updateCourse(al);
F       if (!update)
          System.out.println("The data updating is failed!");
      }
G     catch (Exception e) {
        System.out.println("Error in Updating Statement! " + e.getMessage());
        return false;
      }
H     return update;
  }
```

FIGURE 9.110 The code for the Update_Course() method in the Java bean.

Next let's handle the coding process in our Java bean class file, `CourseQuery.java`. Double-click on this file in the `Projects` window in the folder, `Source Packages\JavaWebOracleSelectPackage`, to open it, and enter the code shown in Figure 9.110 into the bottom of this file. Let's have a closer look at this piece of code to see how it works.

A. Two local variables, `update` and `al`, are generated first. The former is a Boolean variable used to hold the run result of execution of our Web Service operation, `UpdateCourse()`, and the latter is an instance of the ArrayList class, which is used to store seven pieces of information for an updated course record.
B. The ArrayList instance `al` is cleaned up by using the `clear()` method to make sure that `al` is empty before it can be used to store any data.
C. A sequence of `add()` methods is used to add all six pieces of updated course information (including `course _ id`) into the ArrayList instance `al`, which will be passed as an argument to our Web Service operation `UpdateCourse()` later.
D. A `try-catch` block is used to call our Web operation, `UpdateCourse()`, to update a selected course record in our sample database via our Web service. First a new Web service instance, `service`, is created based on our Web service class `WebServiceCourse _ Service`. Then the `getWebServiceCoursePort()` method is executed to get the current port used by our Web service. This port is returned and assigned to a new port instance, `port`.
E. The Web Service operation `UpdateCourse()` is executed with an argument, `al`, that contains all pieces of updated course information, and the run result is returned and assigned to the local Boolean variable `update`.
F. If the returned Boolean value is `false`, which means that this data update action fails, a system method, `println()`, is used to indicate this situation. Otherwise, the data update is successful.
G. The `catch` block is used to monitor and check any possible exception during the data update process. A `false` is returned to the calling program if any error occurs.
H. Otherwise, a `true` is returned to indicate the success of this data update action.

Now we have finished all code for this course update action. Let's build and run our client project to consume our Web Service to update a selected course record on the **Course** Table in our sample database.

Prior to building and running our client project, make sure that our Web Service application project, **WebAppCourse**, has been built and deployed successfully.

Perform the following operations to build and run our client project, **WebClient Course _ Update**:

1) Click on the **Clean and Build Main Project** button to build our Web-based client project.
2) Then click on the **Run Project** button (green arrow) on the top to run our project.

When the course page opens, enter a valid faculty name, such as **Ying Bai**, into the Faculty Name box, and then click on the **Select** button to query all courses (**course _ id**) taught by this faculty member. All five courses (**course _ id**) should have been retrieved from our database and displayed in the CourseList box.

Now let's test updating an existing course record, **CSE-565**, from the **Course** Table in our sample database. Keep the selected faculty member, **Ying Bai**, with no change, click on the course **CSE-565** from the CourseList box to select it, then click on the **Details** button to get all details about this course. Then enter the following five pieces of information as an updated course record into the six related TextFields in this course page:

- Course Name: **Deep Learning**
- Schedule: **M-W-F: 2:00-2:50 PM**
- Classroom: **TC-314**
- Credit: **3**
- Enrollment: **22**

Now click on the **Update** button to try to update this course record from the **Course** Table in our sample database, **CSE _ DEPT**. If this update action is successful, the client page is refreshed to clean up all content in each TextField to null, as shown in Figure 9.111.

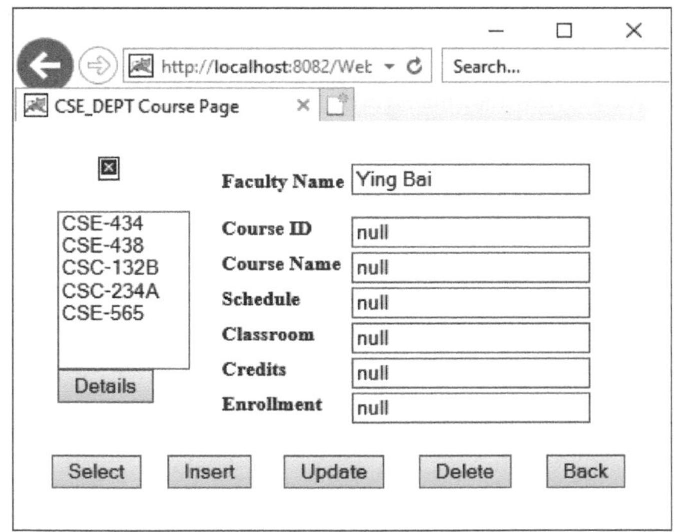

FIGURE 9.111 The run result for updating course CSE-565.

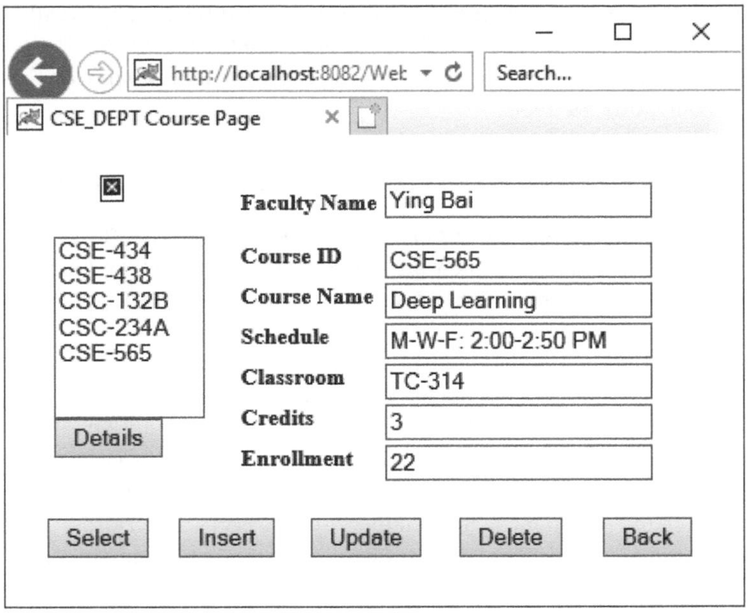

FIGURE 9.112 The confirmed course data update result.

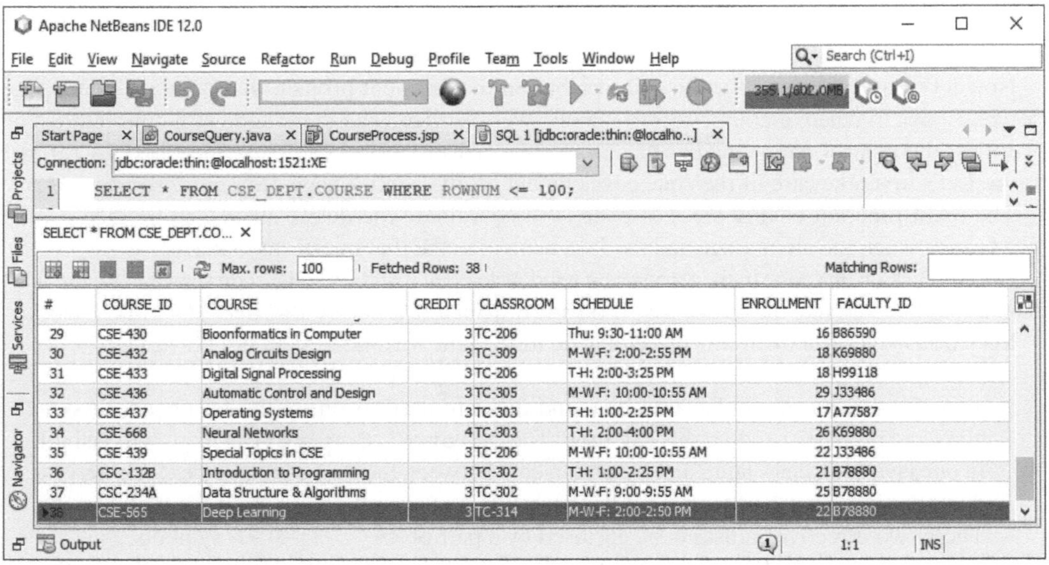

FIGURE 9.113 The updated course CSE-565 in the Course Table.

To confirm the data update, just click on the **Select** button to retrieve all courses (**course _ id**) taught by the selected faculty member **Ying Bai**. Then click on the item **CSE-565** from the CourseList box, and click on the **Details** button to get all details about this updated course. One can see that the course, **CSE-565**, has been updated in six TextFields, as shown in Figure 9.112.

Click on the **Back** and the **Exit** buttons to close our project.

Another way to confirm the data update is to open the **Course** Table via the **Services** window in the NetBeans IDE. The opened **Course** Table is shown in Figure 9.113.

One can see from the opened **Course** Table that the course **CSE-565** is really updated in this Table, and it is located at the bottom of the Table, as shown in Figure 9.113.

Next let's build and develop the code for our client project to access our Web Service to delete a selected course in our **Course** Table.

9.16.7 Build Our Client Project to Delete Course Records via Our Web Service

To save time and space, we can modify one of our projects, **WebClientCourse _ Update**, we built in the last section and make it our new project. Perform the following operations to make our new project, **WebClientCourse _ Delete**:

1) One can find the project **WebClientCourse _ Update** in the folder **Class DB Projects\Chapter 9** in the folder **Students** on the CRC Press ftp site (refer to Figure 1.2 in Chapter 1). Copy and store that project to one of your local folders.
2) Then open the NetBeans IDE 12.0 in the Administrator mode, browse and right-click on the project **WebClientCourse _ Update** in the **Projects** window. Then select the **Copy** item from the popup menu to open the **Copy Project** wizard.
3) Enter our new project name, **WebClientCourse _ Delete**, into the **Project Name** box, and browse to your local project folder as the **Project Location**, and click on the **Copy** button. A new project, **WebClientCourse _ Delete**, is generated and added into our **Projects** window.

After this new project is generated, a few errors may occur in our Java Bean class file, **CourseQuery.java**. To fix those errors, just build our new project by clicking on the **Clean and Build Project** button on the top to update the Web Service reference.

Now let's build the code for the **Delete** button in our client project, that is, in the client page **Course.jsp**, to delete a course record via our Web Service. The main code still concentrates on two files, the control page **CourseProcess.jsp** and our Java bean class file **CourseQuery.java**. Let's first take care of the code development for the control page, **CourseProcess.jsp**.

The main function of this piece of code is to coordinate the delete query and provide a valid interface between the client page and the Java bean to make that query smoother.

Double-click on that page in the **Projects** window to open it and enter the code shown in Figure 9.114 into this page, that is, into the **else if (request.getParameter("Delete")!= null)** block.

Let's have a closer look at this piece of code to see how it works.

A. Two JSP directives are declared first, and they are used to set up the Java bean, session, class and property used on this JSP page. The **Delete _ Course()** method will be built in our Java bean class later, and the underscore between the **Delete** and the **Course** is to distinguish this method from a similar operation, **DeleteCourse()**, in our Web Service. These two directives must not be enclosed by a pair of **<% . . . %>** symbols.
B. Starting from step B, the following code will be Java code to be embedded into this page, so an opening symbol,**<%**, is used to start this part. Since the Web operation **DeleteCourse()** in our Web Service returns a Boolean result, to hold it, a Boolean variable, **res**, is created and initialized first.
C. To set up a course record that will be deleted from the **Course** Table in our sample database, a system method, **getParameter()**, is used to pick up the selected **course _ id** that is related to a course record to be deleted from the related TextField in our client page, **Course.jsp**, and assign it to a local String variable **cid**.
D. The **Delete _ Course()** method that will be defined in our Java bean class is executed with the initialized **cid** as the argument. The run result of this method is returned and assigned to our local Boolean variable **res**.

```
  .........
  else if (request.getParameter("Delete")!= null) {
   //process the course record deleting
  %>
A <jsp:useBean id="Delete_Course" scope="session" class="JavaWebOracleSelectPackage.CourseQuery" />
  <jsp:setProperty name="Delete_Course" property="*" />
  <%
B boolean res = false;
C String cid = request.getParameter("CourseIDField");
D res = cQuery.Delete_Course(cid);
E    if (!res)
        response.sendRedirect("Course.jsp");
F    else {
          for (int index = 0; index < C_Field.length; index++)
            session.setAttribute(C_Field[index], null);
          response.sendRedirect("Course.jsp");
         }
  }
  else if (request.getParameter("Back")!= null) {
      //process the course record deleting
      response.sendRedirect("Selection.jsp");
  }
```

FIGURE 9.114 The code for the Delete Course block in the CourseProcess.jsp page.

E. If a **false** is returned, which means that the execution of this method fails, then the client view page, **Course.jsp**, is refreshed to make it ready for the next operation.
F. Otherwise, the running of that method is successful and the selected course record has been deleted from the **Course** Table in our sample database, so all TextFields in the client page will be reset to **null** to enable users to check the data delete action.

Next let's build the code for our Java bean class file, **CourseQuery.java**. Double-click on this file in the **Projects** window, under **Source Packages\JavaWebOracleSelect-Package**, to open it and enter the code shown in Figure 9.115 into the bottom of this file. Let's have a closer look at this piece of code to see how it works.

A. A local boolean variable, **delete**, is generated first and it is used to hold the run result of execution of our Web Service operation, **DeleteCourse()**, later.
B. A **try-catch** block is used to call our Web operation, **DeleteCourse()**, to delete a selected course record from our sample database via our Web service. First a new Web service instance, **service**, is created based on our Web service class, **WebServiceCourse _ Service**. Then the **getWebServiceCoursePort()** method is executed to get the current port used by our Web service. This port is returned and assigned to a new port instance, **port**.
C. The Web Service operation **DeleteCourse()** is executed with a String argument, **dCourse**, that is a valid **course _ id**, which is related to a course record to be deleted from our database.
D. If a **false** is returned, which means that this data delete action fails, a system method, **println()**, is used to indicate this. Otherwise, the data delete is successful.
E. The **catch** block is used to monitor and check any possible exception during the data delete process. A **false** is returned to the calling program if an error really occurs.
F. Otherwise, a **true** is returned to indicate the success of the data delete action.

Now we have finished all code for this course delete action. Let's build and run our client project to consume our Web Service to delete a selected course record from the **Course** Table in our sample database.

```
    .........
    public boolean Delete_Course(String dCourse){
A     boolean delete = false;
B     try{
          org.ws.oracle.WebServiceCourse_Service service = new org.ws.oracle.WebServiceCourse_Service();
          org.ws.oracle.WebServiceCourse port = service.getWebServiceCoursePort();
C         delete = port.deleteCourse(dCourse);
D         if (!delete)
            System.out.println("The data deleting is failed!");
      }
E     catch (Exception e) {
        System.out.println("Error in Deleting Statement! " + e.getMessage());
        return false;
      }
F       return delete;
    }
```

FIGURE 9.115 The code for the Delete_Course() method in the Java bean.

Prior to building and running our client project, make sure that our Web Service project, **WebAppCourse**, has been built and deployed successfully.

Perform the following operations to build and run our client project, **WebClientCourse_Delete**:

1) Click on the **Clean and Build Main Project** button to build our project.
2) Then click on the **Run Project** button (green arrow) on the top to run our project.

As the project is running, enter a valid faculty name, such as **Ying Bai**, into the Faculty Name box, and then click on the **Select** button to query all courses (**course_id**) taught by this faculty member. All courses (**course_id**) are retrieved and displayed in the CourseList box.

Now let's test deleting an existing course record, **CSE-565**, from the **Course** Table in our sample database. Keep the selected faculty member, **Ying Bai**, with no change, and click on the course **CSE-565** from the CourseList box to select it. Click on the **Details** button to get more details about this course, as shown in Figure 9.116. Then click on the **Delete** button to try to remove this course record from the **Course** Table in our sample database.

To confirm or test the data delete action, keep the selected faculty member **Ying Bai** with no change, and click on the **Select** button again to try to retrieve all courses (**course_id**) taught by this faculty member. Immediately one can see that four courses (**course_id**) are returned and displayed in the CourseList box without course **CSE-565**. This confirms that course **CSE-565** has been deleted successfully from the **Course** Table in our sample database.

Another way to confirm the course delete action is to open the **Course** Table in our sample database, **CSE_DEPT**, by using the **Services** window in the NetBeans IDE 12.0 environment. The course **CSE-565** cannot be found in our **Course** Table, which means that it has been deleted from the **Course** Table.

It is highly recommended to recover any deleted records to keep our database clean. An easy way to do this recovery is to perform another insert action via the **Insert** button on our client page to insert this course record in the **Course** Table. Refer to course details displayed in the six TextFields shown in Figure 9.116 to do this recovery.

Click on the **Back** and the **Exit** buttons to terminate our Web client project.

9.17 CHAPTER SUMMARY

A detailed discussion and analysis of the structure and components of Java Web services are provided in this chapter. Two popular Java Web services, REST-based and SOAP-based services, are

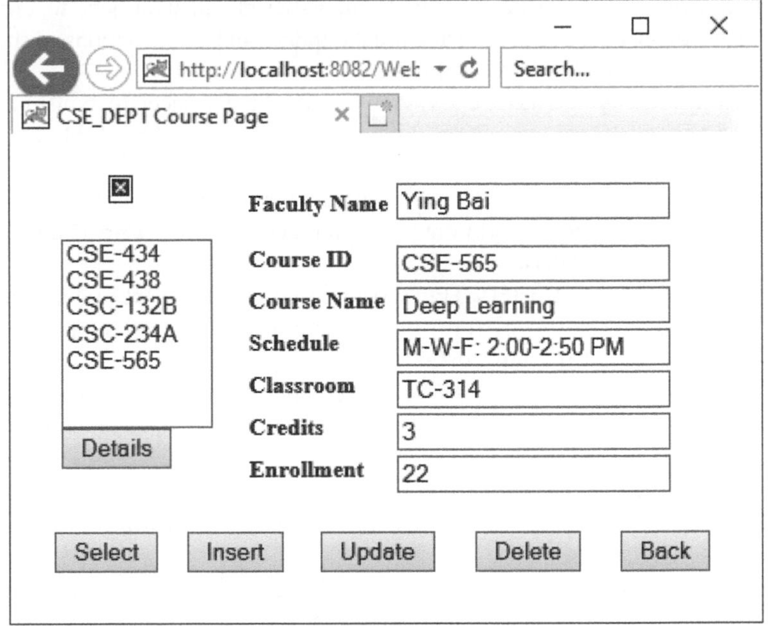

FIGURE 9.116 The run and test results of deleting a course record.

discussed in detail with real projects. The procedure of building a typical SOAP-based Web service project is introduced with a real project example.

In Section 9.3, an example test SOAP-based Web Service project, **WSTest**, is discussed and analyzed to provide users a complete picture with a detailed procedure to illustrate how to build, deploy and consume a Web Service project step by step.

Starting in Section 9.5, some typical SOAP-based Web service projects, such as **WebAppFaculty** and **WebAppCourse**, which can be used to access and manipulate data against an Oracle 18c XE database, are discussed and analyzed in detail with real project examples.

To consume these kinds of Web services, 13 real client projects are developed and built with detailed coding processes and illustrations:

- **WinClientFaculty _ Select**: A Window-based client project to consume the Web service **WebAppFaculty** to perform a data query to the **Faculty** Table in our sample Oracle 18c XE database.
- **WinClientFaculty _ Insert**: A Window-based client project to consume the Web service **WebAppFaculty** to perform data insertion actions to the **Faculty** Table in our Oracle 18c XE sample database.
- **WinClientFaculty _ UpdtDelt**: A Window-based client project to consume the Web service **WebAppFaculty** to perform data update and delete actions to the **Faculty** Table in our sample Oracle 18c XE database.
- **WinClientCourse _ Select**: A Window-based client project to consume the Web service **WebAppCourse** to perform data queries to the **Course** Table in our sample Oracle 18c XE database.
- **WinClientCourse _ Insert**: A Window-based client project to consume the Web service **WebAppCourse** to perform data insertion actions to the **Course** Table in our Oracle 18c XE sample database.

- **WinClientCourse _ UpdtDelt**: A Window-based client project to consume the Web service **WebAppCourse** to perform data update and delete actions to the **Course** Table in our sample Oracle 18c XE database.
- **WebClientFaculty _ Select**: A Web-based client project to consume the Web service **WebAppFaculty** to perform data query to the **Faculty** Table in our sample Oracle 18c XE database.
- **WebClientFaculty _ Insert**: A Web-based client project to consume the Web service **WebAppFaculty** to perform data insertion actions to the **Faculty** Table in our sample Oracle 18c XE database.
- **WebClientFaculty _ UpdtDelt**: A Web-based client project to consume the Web service **WebAppFaculty** to perform data update and delete actions to the **Faculty** Table in our Oracle 18c XE sample database.
- **WebClientCourse _ Select**: A Web-based client project to consume the Web service **WebAppCourse** to perform data queries to the **Course** Table in our Oracle 18c XE database.
- **WebClientCourse _ Insert**: A Web-based client project to consume the Web service **WebAppCourse** to perform data insertion actions to the **Course** Table in our sample Oracle 18c XE database.
- **WebClientCourse _ Update**: A Web-based client project to consume the Web service **WebAppCourse** to perform data update actions to the **Course** Table in our Oracle 18c XE sample database.
- **WebClientCourse _ Delete**: A Web-based client project to consume the Web service **WebAppCourse** to perform data delete actions to the **Course** Table in our Oracle 18c XE sample database.

All of these real example projects have been compiled, built, tested and debugged and can be used without modifications. To use these project examples, one needs to install

- Java JDK 8.0 (jdk1.8.0_271)
- Apache NetBeans IDE 12.0
- Java JDBC Driver for Oracle (ojdbc8.jar)
- GlassFish Web application server (v5.1)
- Tomcat Web application server (v8.0.27)
- Oracle 18c XE database

All of these software tools and drivers can be downloaded and installed on the users' computer free of charge. Refer to the related appendices for the download and installation processes.

HOMEWORK

I. True/False Selections

______1. Unlike Java Web applications, Java Web Services provide an automatic way to search, identify and return the desired information required by the user through a set of methods installed in the Web server.

______2. Java Web services provide graphic user interfaces (GUIs) to enable users to access Web services via the Internet.

______3. Web Services can be considered a set of methods installed in a Web server and can be called by computer programs installed on the clients through the Internet.

______4. Two popular Java Web services are: REST-based and SOAP-based services, and both are supported by NetBeans IDE.

_______5. Both Web service models, JAX-WS and JAX-RPC, are popular and updated models used in Web service development.

_______6. Compared with REST-based service, SOAP-based Web services are more suiTable for heavyweight applications using complicated operations and for applications requiring sophisticated security and reliability.

_______7. Unlike ASP.NET Web services, a Java SOAP-based Web service project is included in a Java Web application project in which the Web service can be deployed based on an appropriate container.

_______8. To access a Web service, one does not have to call any operation defined in the Web service.

_______9. Before one can call a Web service operation, a Web service reference must have been established for the client project.

______10. It is unnecessary to update a Web service each time when consuming it in a client project; however, one must deploy that Web service each time when starting it from the NetBeans IDE.

II. Multiple Choice

1. In a SOAP-based Java Web Service, the SOAP means ____________.
   a. Statement Object Access Protocol
   b. Simplified Object Access Protocol
   c. Simple Object Access Protocol
   d. Structure Object Access Protocol

2. In a REST-based Java Web Service, the REST means ____________.
   a. REpresentational State Transfer
   b. REpresentational State Transmitter
   c. REpresentational Status Transfer
   d. Rapid Essential State Transfer

3. When using a REST-based Web service, only four methods are available: ____________.
   a. INPUT, OUTPUT, POST, and DELETE
   b. SAVE, PUT, POST, and DELETE
   c. GET, EXECUTE, POST, and DELETE
   d. GET, PUT, POST, and DELETE

4. The protocol used in the REST-based Web services is ____________.
   a. FTP
   b. XML
   c. HTTP
   d. TCP/IP

5. To effectively find, identify and return the target information required by computer programs, a SOAP-based Web Service needs the following components, ____________.
   a. XML and WSDL
   b. SOAP, UDDI and WSDL
   c. UDDI, XML and SOAP
   d. WSDL, XML, UDDI and SOAP

6. SOAP is a simple ____________-based protocol to help applications developed in different platforms and languages exchange information over ____________.
   a. HTML, HTTP
   b. XML, HTTP
   c. FTP, TCP/IP
   d. XML, Internet

7. In WSDL terminology, each Web Service is defined as a ___________ and each Web method is defined as an abstract ___________.
   a. Method, function
   b. Service, operation
   c. Endpoint, function
   d. Port, operation
8. SOAP is used to wrap and pack the data tagged in the ___________ format into the messages represented in the ___________ protocol.
   a. XML, SOAP
   b. HTML, HTTP
   c. FTP, TCP/IP
   d. SOAP, XML
9. When building a Java Web service, a ___________ that contains Web container for the ___________ must be built first.
   a. Web service, Web application
   b. Web client, Web consuming project
   c. Web service, Web client project
   d. Web application, Web service
10. To consume a Web service, a ___________ must be established in the client project.
   a. Web service reference
   b. Web service operation
   c. Web service directory
   d. All of them

III. Exercises
1. Provide a brief description of the advantages of using a SOAP-based Web service.
2. Illustrate the structure and components of SOAP-based Web services.
3. Provide a brief description of the procedures of building a typical SOAP-based Web service project.
4. Provides a brief description of how to establish a Web service reference for a given client project to enable the latter to consume that Web service.
5. Explain the operational sequence of adding a Web service operation into a method in a client project to enable the latter to call that operation.
6. Using the structure shown in Figure 9.117, build a Web service project, **WebAppStudent**, and replace the Java runtime object with the Java managed bean to perform a data query against the **Student** Table in our sample Oracle 18c XE database, **CSE_DEPT**.

   Hint: Refer to a similar project, **WebAppFaculty**, built in this chapter.

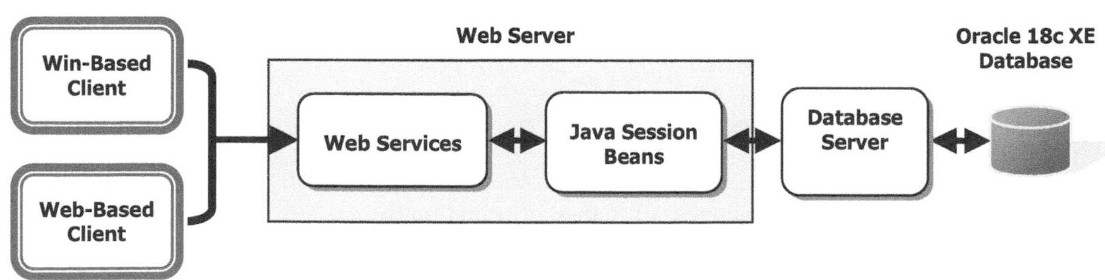

FIGURE 9.117 The structure of building a new Web service project.

7. Develop a Window-based client project, **WinClientStudent**, to consume the Web Service project **WebAppStudent** built in the last exercise to query the **Student** Table in our sample Oracle 18c XE database, **CSE_DEPT**.

   Hint: Refer to a similar project, **WinClientFaculty_Select**, built in this chapter.

8. Develop a Web-based client project, `WebClientStudent`, to consume the Web Service project `WebAppStudent` built in Exercise 6 to query the `Student` Table in our sample Oracle 18c XE database, `CSE _ DEPT`.

   Hint1: Refer to a similar project, `WebClientFaculty _ Select`, built in this chapter with `Student.jsp`.

Appendix A: Download and Install Oracle Database XE 18c

Similar to Oracle Database 11g XE, for most applications, you only need to download and install the Oracle Database 18c XE Server component if you want to use it as a standard product, since it provides both an Oracle database and tools for managing Oracle databases.

Oracle Database XE also provides a client component. However, usually you do not need to install it unless you want to perform remote database connections for remote clients located at different sites. For most applications, you only need to download and install the Oracle Database 18c XE server on your computer, which can connect to the database from the same computer on which you installed the server, and then administer the database and develop Java-based database applications.

I. Download Oracle Database 18c XE

Go to: https://www.oracle.com/database/technologies/xe-downloads.html to begin the download process. Perform the following operations to complete the download and installation process:

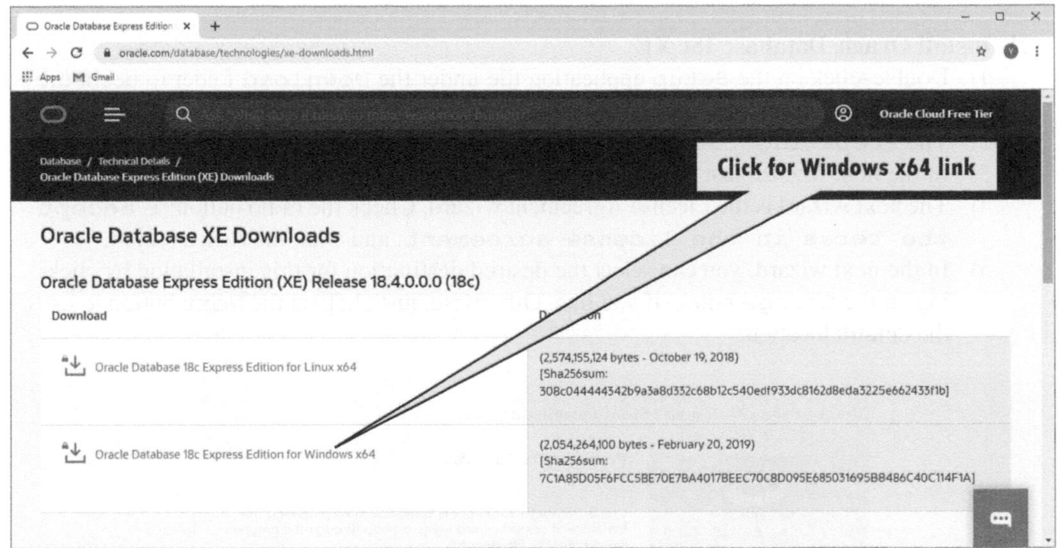

FIGURE A.1 The opened Download wizard (Copyrighted by Oracle and used with permission).

1) Click on the second link, Oracle Database 18c Express Edition for Windows x64, to begin this process, as shown in Figure A.1.
2) In the next widget, click on the checkbox: `I accept the Oracle License Agreement`, and click on the `Download OracleXE184 _ Win64.zip` button to download it.
3) On the next sign-in page, you need to create a new login account in the Oracle Technology Network (OTN). Enter your confirmed username and password, and click

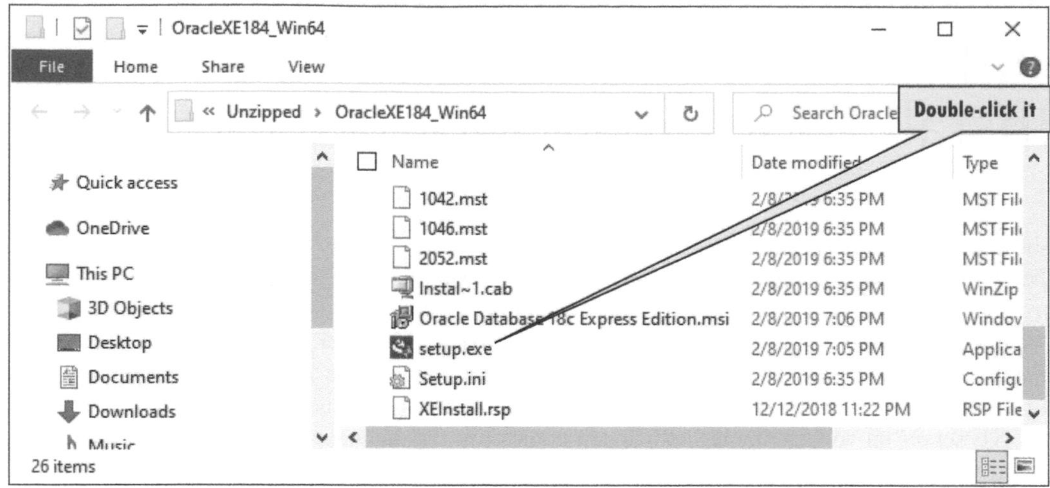

FIGURE A.2 The downloaded Oracle Database 18c Express Edition.

on the **`Sign in`** button to complete the sign-in process. The download process starts (be patient; it may take a while to complete the process).

4) Double-click on the downloaded zip file **`OracleXE184 _ Win64.zip`** located at the lower-left corner to unzip it when this download process is done.

II. Install Oracle Database 18c XE

1) Double-click on the **`Setup`** application file under the **`Download`** folder to begin the installation process, as shown in Figure A.2.
2) The **`Preparing to Install`** wizard is displayed, as shown in Figure A.3.
3) In the next wizard, just click on the **`Next`** button to continue.
4) The next wizard is the License Agreement wizard. Check the radio button: **`I accept the terms in the license agreement`**, and click the **`Next`** button.
5) In the next wizard, you can select the desired destination for this installation by clicking on the **`Change`** button if you like. Otherwise, just click on the **`Next`** button to use the default location,

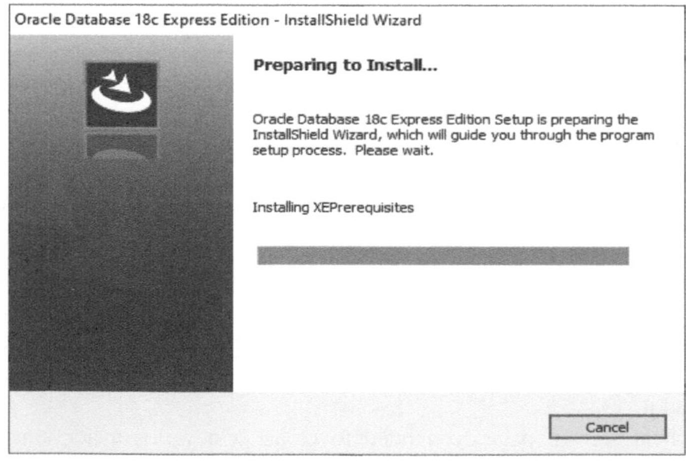

FIGURE A.3 Select the desired location for this installation (Copyrighted by Oracle and used with permission).

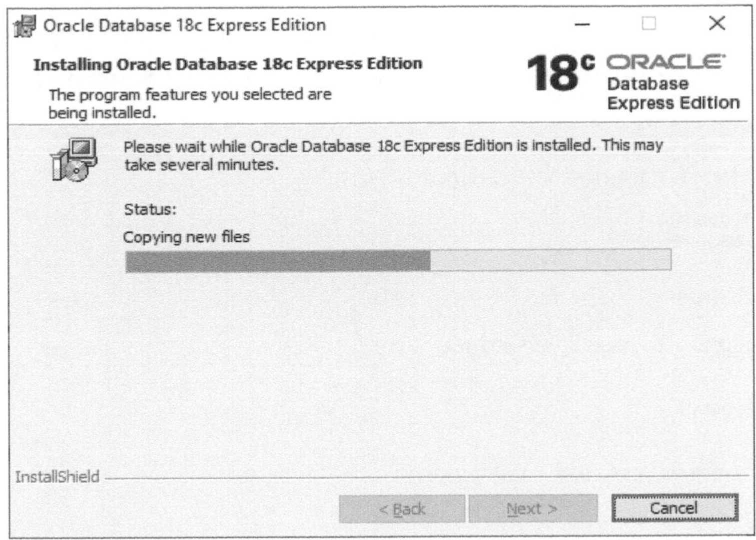

FIGURE A.4 The installation process starts (Copyrighted by Oracle and used with permission).

6) In the next wizard, one can enter a desired password, such as **`oracle _ 18c`**, and then click the **`Next`** button to continue.
7) Click on the **`Install`** button in the next wizard to begin the installation process, as shown in Figure A.4.
8) When the installation process completes, as shown in Figure A.5, click on the **`Finish`** button to close the process.

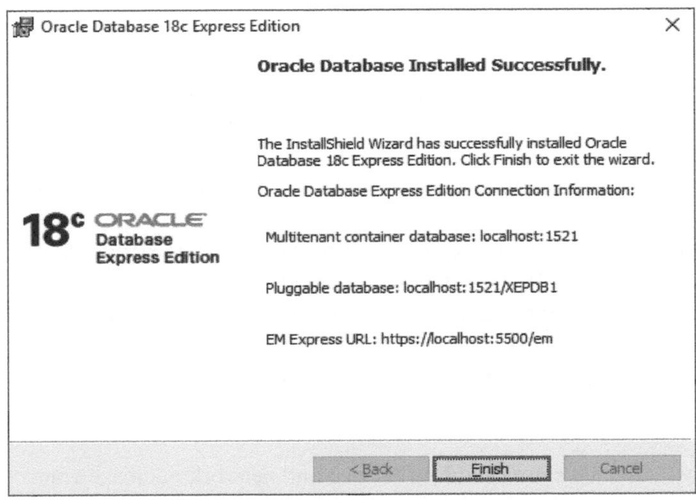

FIGURE A.5 The installation process completes (Copyrighted by Oracle and used with permission).

9) Now you can check some important documents related to this installation. One of the most important documents is the **`tnsnames.ora`** file, which is located at **`C:\app\yingb\product\18.0.0\dbhomeXE\NETWORK\ADMIN`** in my case. The path after **`C:\app`**, **`yingb`**, is the user name on the computer, and it should be replaced by your user name on your computer. Open this file using Notepad, and you can find some important parameters for Oracle Database 18c XE, as shown in Figure A.6.

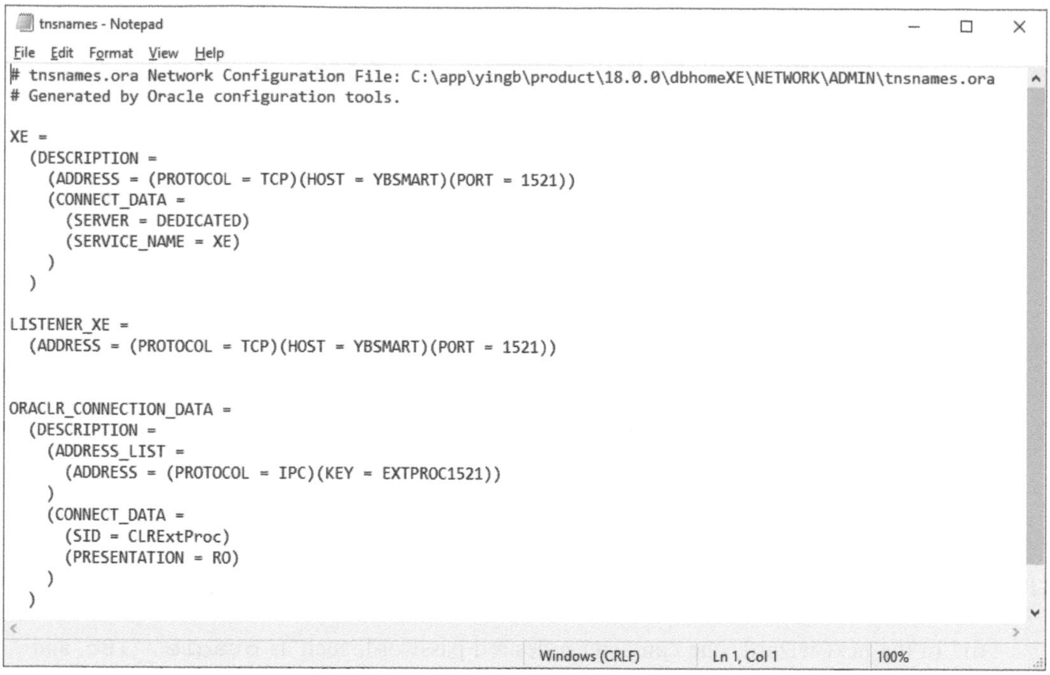

```
tnsnames - Notepad
File Edit Format View Help
# tnsnames.ora Network Configuration File: C:\app\yingb\product\18.0.0\dbhomeXE\NETWORK\ADMIN\tnsnames.ora
# Generated by Oracle configuration tools.

XE =
  (DESCRIPTION =
    (ADDRESS = (PROTOCOL = TCP)(HOST = YBSMART)(PORT = 1521))
    (CONNECT_DATA =
      (SERVER = DEDICATED)
      (SERVICE_NAME = XE)
    )
  )

LISTENER_XE =
  (ADDRESS = (PROTOCOL = TCP)(HOST = YBSMART)(PORT = 1521))


ORACLR_CONNECTION_DATA =
  (DESCRIPTION =
    (ADDRESS_LIST =
      (ADDRESS = (PROTOCOL = IPC)(KEY = EXTPROC1521))
    )
    (CONNECT_DATA =
      (SID = CLRExtProc)
      (PRESENTATION = RO)
    )
  )
Windows (CRLF)    Ln 1, Col 1    100%
```

FIGURE A.6 The opened tnsnames.ora file.

The following important parameters can be found in this file:

A. The full address of Oracle Database 18c XE on my computer, which is **TCP\YBSMART\1251**, represents the **protocol\host\port**. **YBSMART** is the author's computer's name, and it should be replaced by your computer's name.
B. The installed Oracle database server name, which is **XE**.

These parameters are important, since we need to use them to create and connect an Oracle data source to our applications later.

Now we can open the tool named **Oracle Database Configuration Assistant** to create a new Oracle Database 18c XE database or modify an existing one from our computer by going to **Start\All Programs\Oracle-OraDB18Home1\Database Configuration Assistant**. The opened assistant is shown in Figure A.7.

It looks totally different from Oracle Database 11g XE. Yes, starting with18c, a lot of new functions have been added into the Oracle database server and tools. Different tabs have different purposes.

Most of the new added tabs are used for the Web and network database controls and operations. You can go through entire workspace to get a full understanding of this new product by clicking and viewing each tab one by one. Click on the **Next** button to open the **Configuration** or **Creation Mode** page, as shown in Figure A.8.

This concludes our download and installation process for Oracle Database 18c XE. We will create and build our sample database, **CSE _ DEPT**, using a third-party tool called Oracle SQL Developer in Chapter 2.

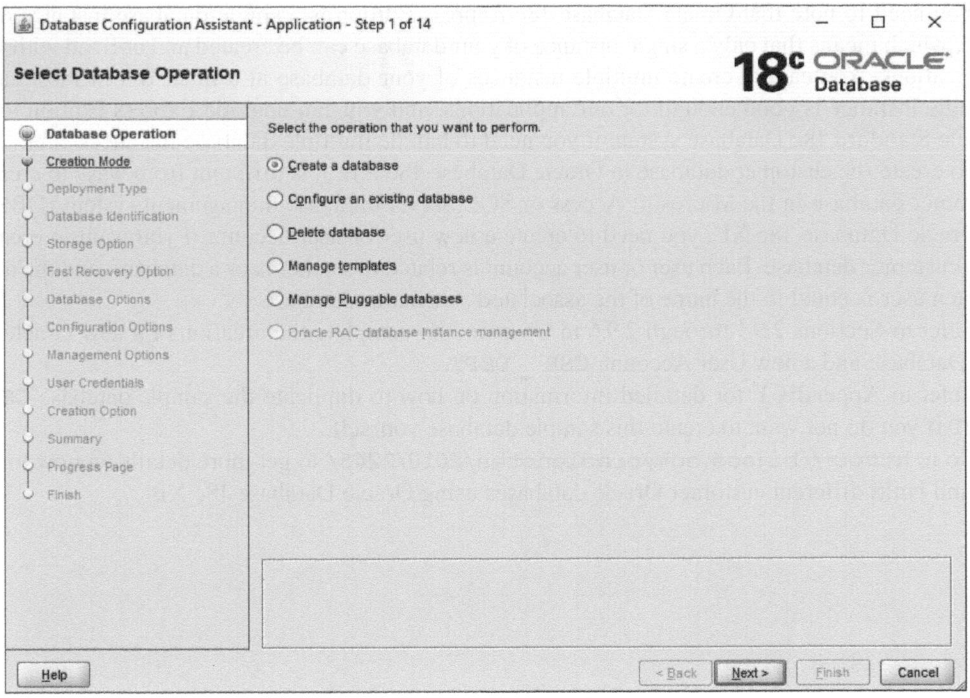

FIGURE A.7 The home page of Oracle Database 18c XE (Copyrighted by Oracle and used with permission).

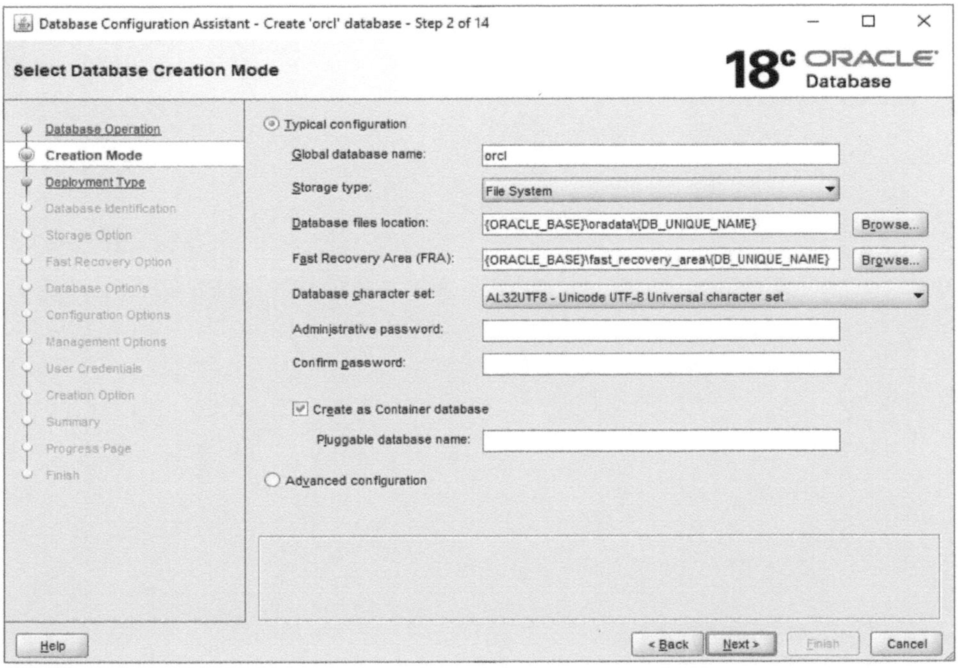

FIGURE A.8 The configuration page of Oracle Database 18c XE (Copyrighted by Oracle and used with permission).

You need to note that Oracle Database 18c Express Edition is a single-database instance database, which means that only a single instance of your database can be created and utilized with your applications. You cannot create multiple instances of your database at a time. But in most cases, a single instance is good enough for our applications, and you can upgrade Express Edition to the Oracle Standard 18c Database system if you need to handle multiple database instances later.

To create the customer database in Oracle Database 18c XE, it is different from ways to create a customer database in the Microsoft Access or SQL Server database management system (DBMS). In Oracle Database 18c XE, you need to create a new user or user account if you want to create a new customer database. Each user or user account is related to a schema or a database, and the name of each user is equal to the name of the associated schema or database.

Refer to Sections 2.9.1 through 2.9.6 in Chapter 2 to complete the creation of a new Oracle 18c XE Database and a new User Account, **CSE _ DEPT**.

Refer to Appendix E for detailed information on how to duplicate the sample database **CSE _ DEPT** if you do not want to create this sample database yourself.

Go to **https://bijoos.com/oraclenotes/2018/2246/** to get more details on how to create and build different customer Oracle databases using Oracle Database 18c XE.

Appendix B: Download and Install Apache NetBeans 12.0

Prior to installing Apache NetBeans 12.0, a Java Development Kit (JDK) must be installed. Refer to Appendix N to install JDK 14, since that JDK is compatible with IDE 12.0.

Perform the following operations to download and install Apache NetBeans IDE 12.0.

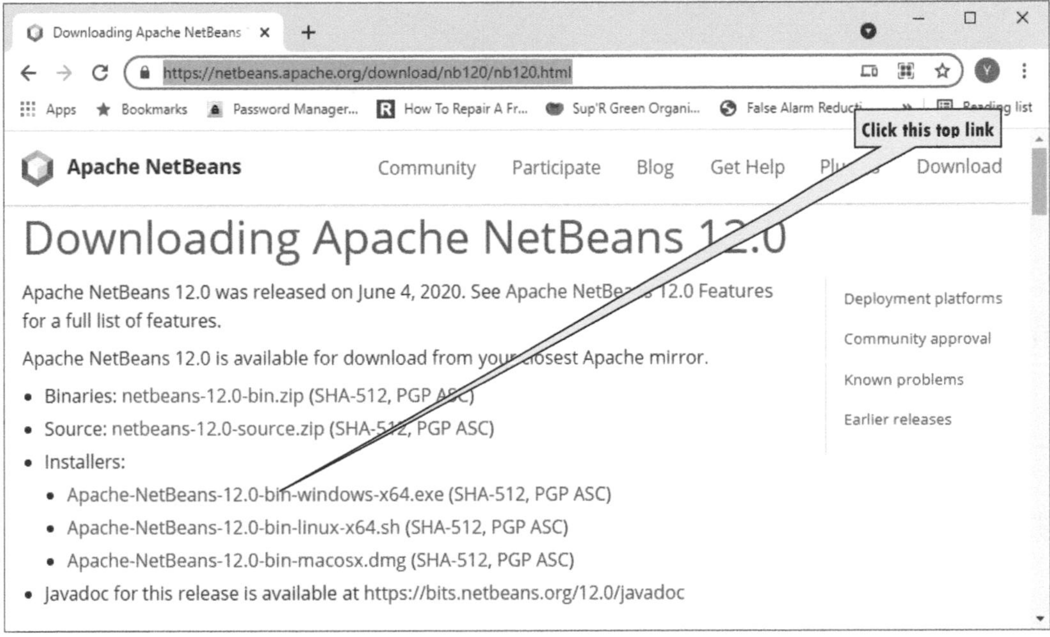

FIGURE B.1 The opened wizard for downloading Apache NetBeans 12.0.

1) Go to: **`https://netbeans.apache.org/download/nb120/nb120.html`** to open the download and installation page, as shown in Figure B.1.
2) Click on the link: **`Apache-NetBeans-12.0-bin-windows-x64.exe (SHA-512, PGP ASC)`** to begin the downloading process (Figure B.1).
3) Click on the top link, **`https://dlcdn.apache.org/netbeans/netbeans/12.0/Apache-NetBeans-12.0-bin-windows-x64.exe`**, which is under the **`HTTP`** tag, to start the download and installation process (Figure B.2). It may take a while to complete the download due to the large size of the file (358 MB).
4) When the download process is done, double-click the **`Apache-NetBeans-12.0-bin-windows-x64.exe`** file in the **`Download`** folder on your computer to open the Configuring the Installer wizard (Figure B.3). Click on the **`Next`** button to continue when this process is done.

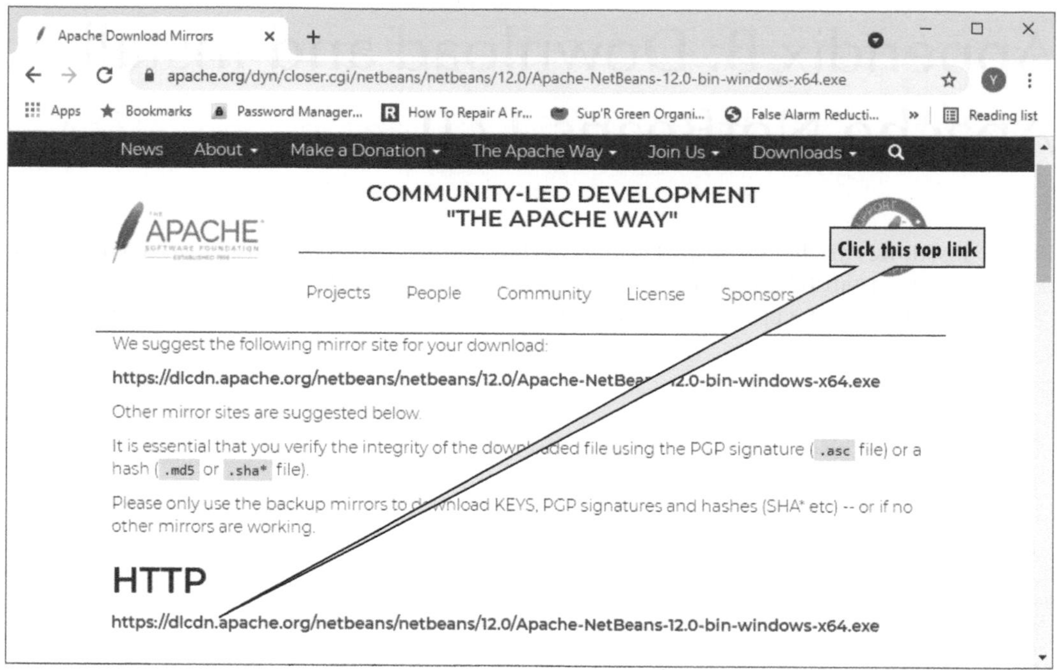

FIGURE B.2 The opened downloading page.

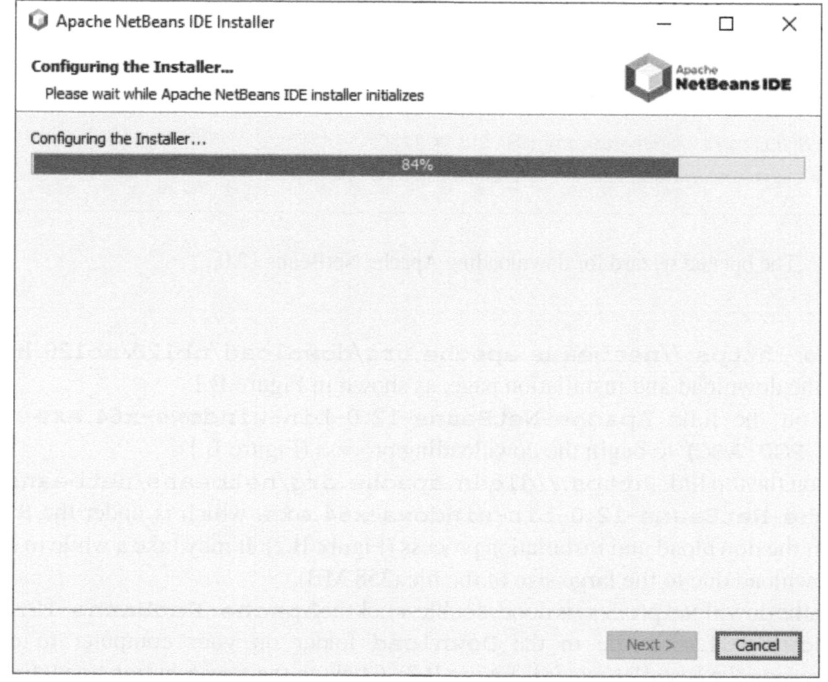

FIGURE B.3 The opened configuring the installer wizard.

5) The next wizard, the License Agreement wizard, is opened as shown in Figure B.4. Check the `License Agreement` checkbox and click on the `Next` button to continue.

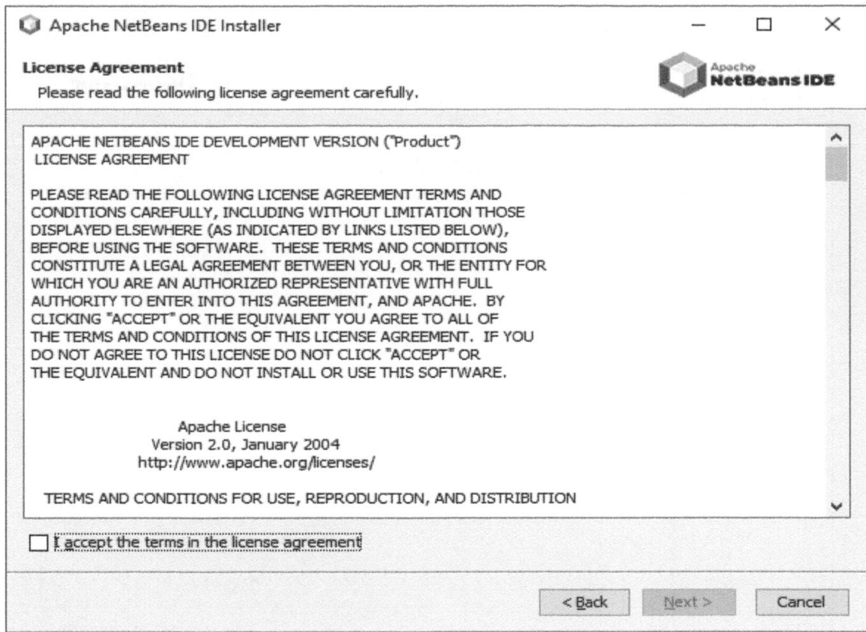

FIGURE B.4 The opened license agreement wizard.

6) The next wizard, Installation Destination, is opened, as shown in Figure B.5. Keep all default settings and click on the `Next` button to continue the installation process.
7) Click the `Install` button in the next wizard to start the installation process (Figure B.6).

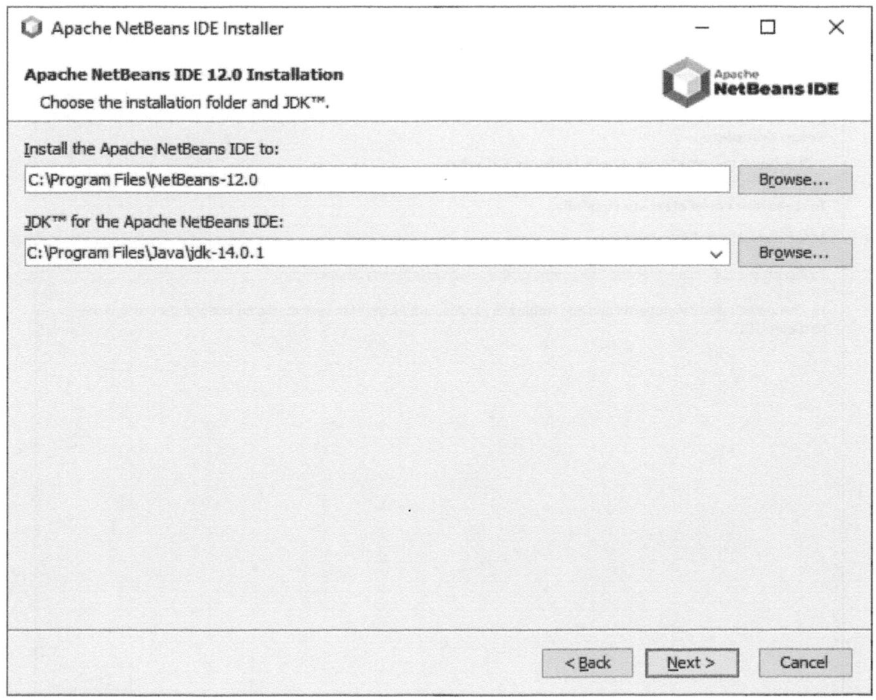

FIGURE B.5 The opened installation destination wizard.

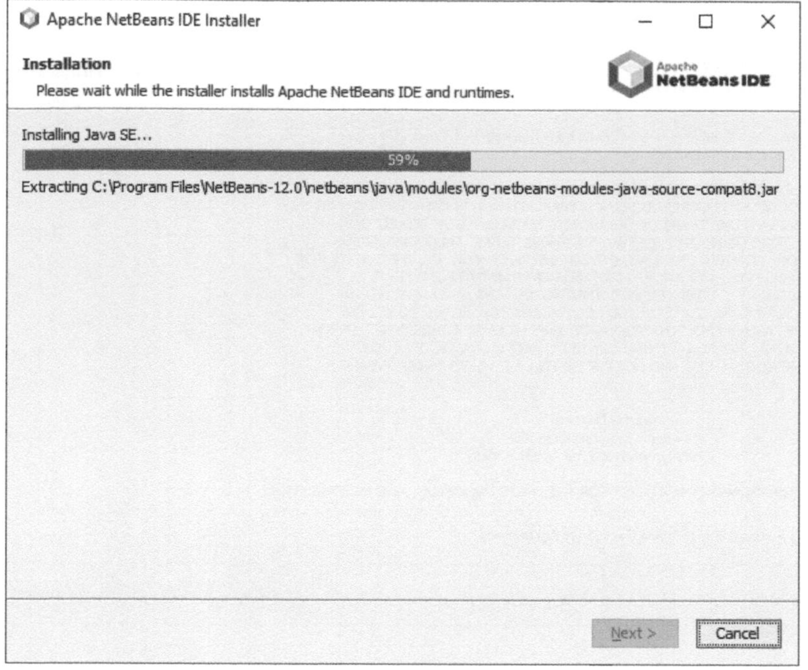

FIGURE B.6 The installation process starts.

8) When the installation process is done, as shown in Figure B.7, click on the `Finish` button to complete the process.

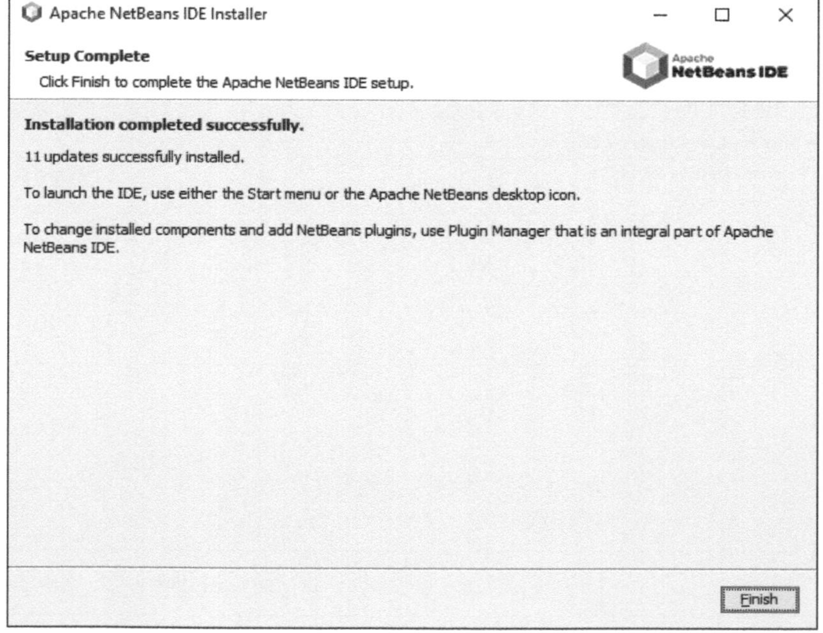

FIGURE B.7 The finished installation process.

Appendix C: Download and Install Oracle SQL Developer

1) Go to **https://www.oracle.com/tools/downloads/sqldev-downloads.html**.
2) Select and click on the **Download** link located at the right of the platform **Windows 64-bit with JDK 8 included**, as shown in Figure C.1, to begin the download process.

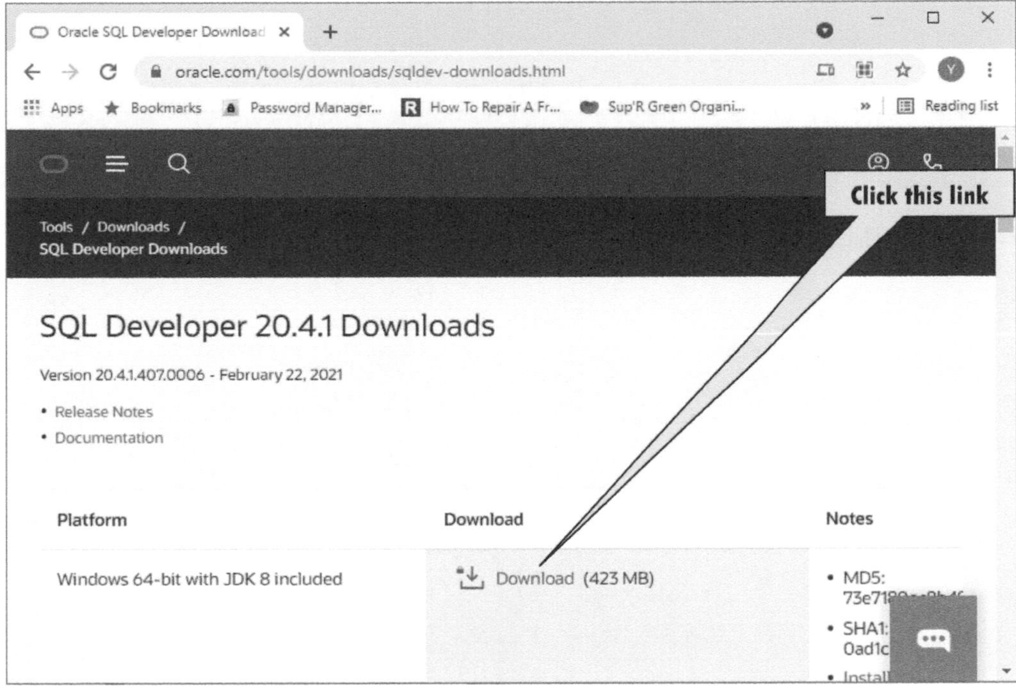

FIGURE C.1 The opened download page for Oracle SQL Developer (Copyrighted by Oracle and used with permission).

3) You may need to create a new Oracle account and login with your username and password to start the download process.
4) Click on the downloaded zip file, **sqldeveloper-20.4.1.407.0006-x64.zip**, on the lower-left corner when the download process is done to unzip this file. The attached sequence number, which is the latest version number of Oracle SQL Developer, maybe different; it depends on the current version of the tool.
5) Double-click on the **sqldeveloper.exe** file from the unzipped folder to start the installation process.
6) When the unzip process is done, double-click on the **sqldeveloper.exe** file to begin the installation process, as shown in Figure C.2.
7) Click on the **OK** button to automatically report issues to Oracle.
8) When the installation process is completed, you can right-click on **sqldeveloper.exe** and select **Pin to taskbar** to save it to the task bar for further use.

9) Next time, you just need to double-click on the pinned icon to start using this tool.

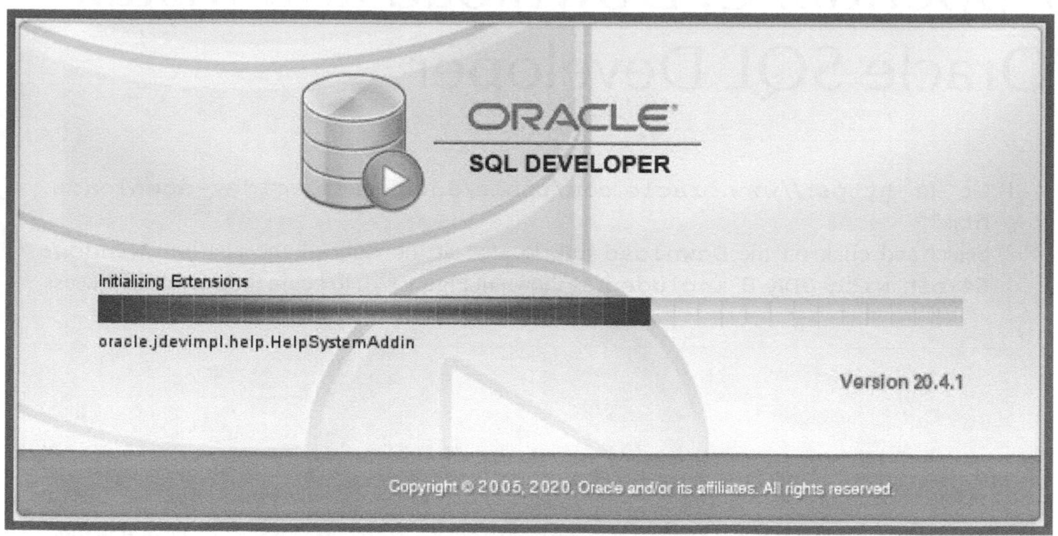

FIGURE C.2 The installation process (Copyrighted by Oracle and used with permission).

Appendix D: Download and Install DevExpress WinForms

When we built the **Faculty** and **Student** Tables, we need to store faculty and student images into Oracle 18c XE database directly. Due to the updated properties of the Oracle 18c XE database, an image can be directly stored into the database column as an image object; in fact, it is a binary large object (**BLOB**) data type.

With the help of a product developed by Developer Express Incorporated, that is, a user interface component, DevExpress WinForms, we can directly insert an image into an Oracle 18c XE database column via the Microsoft Visual Studio. NET platform without any coding process.

In order to use this component, one needs to download DevExpress WinForms. Perform the following steps to complete the download and installation process.

1) Go to the **https://www.devexpress.com/#ui site**.
2) Click on the **WinForms** icon, as shown in Figure D.1, to open the 30-day free trial dialog.

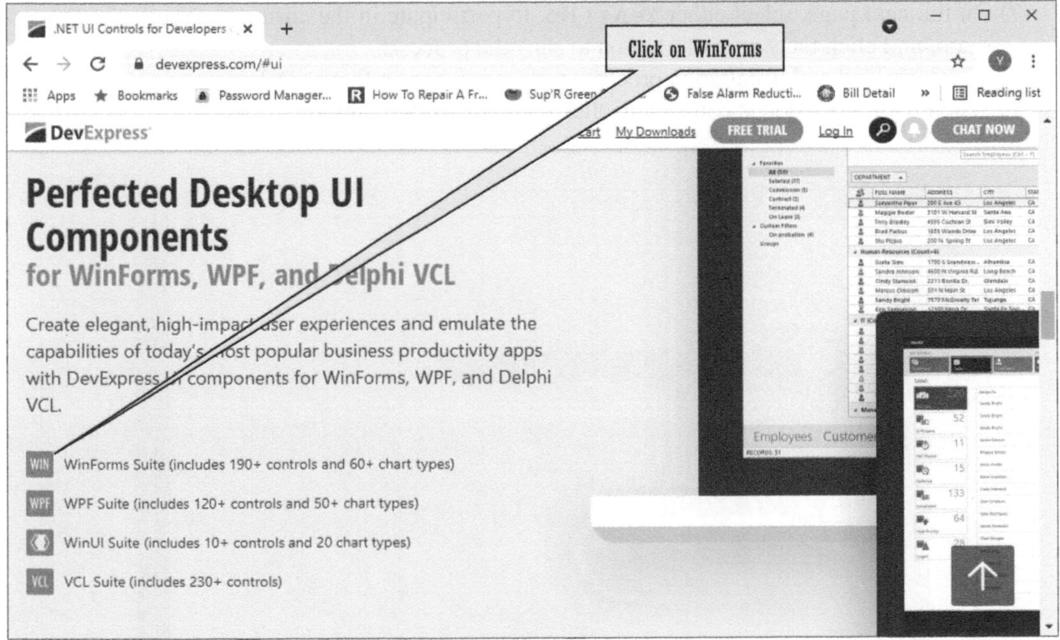

FIGURE D.1 The opened site for the DevExpress WinForms component.

3) Click on **FREE 30-DAY TRIAL** button to begin the download process. An execuTable file, **DevExpressUniversalTrialSetup-20210624.exe***, is downloaded. Click on the **.exe** file to run it.
4) Click on the **Trial Installation** button to start the installation process.
5) Click all other icons to deselect them except the **WinForms Controls** icon (Figure D.2), and click on the **Next** button to install this component only.

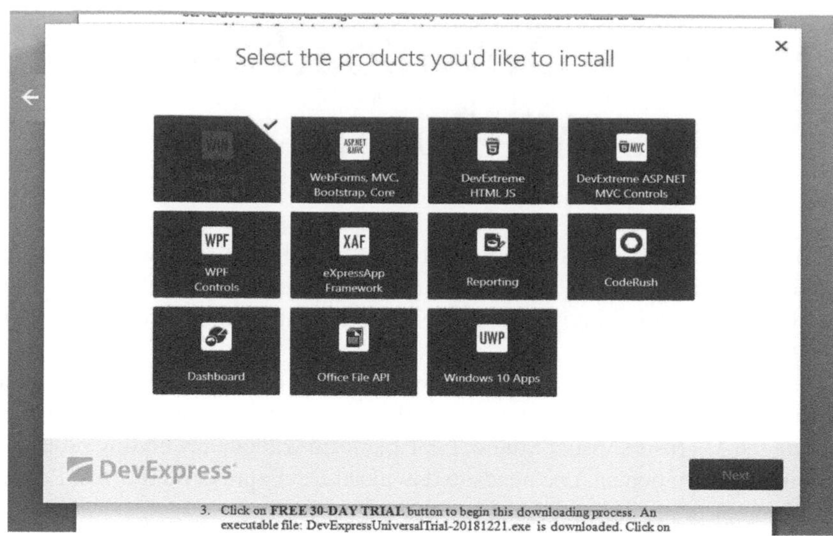

FIGURE D.2 Select WinForms Controls to install the DevExpress WinForms component.

6) Click on the **`Accept & Continue`** button for the next page to continue.
7) On the next page, select either **`Yes`** or **`No`**, to participate in the customer experience program, and click the **`Install`** button to start the process.
8) The download and installation process starts, as shown in Figure D.3.
9) When the installation is completed, click on the **`Finish`** button.

FIGURE D.3 The download and installation process starts.

Appendix E: How to Use the Sample Database

An exported Oracle sample database, **CSE _ DEPT**, which is used in this book, has been stored in the **Sample Database** folder in the **Students** folder at the CRC Press ftp site (refer to Figure 1.2 in Chapter 1). The purpose of exporting this sample database is to make the database development process easier for readers to save their time and energy and to enable them to copy and duplicate it in their Oracle database environment.

To duplicate the sample database, readers can copy the exported database, **CSE _ DEPT.sql**, from the **Sample Database** folder in the **Students** folder at the CRC Press ftp site and save it in any desired folder on the reader's local machine, such as the **Document** folder. Then follow the steps to complete the database duplication process. It is assumed that **CSE _ DEPT.sql** is in the **Document** folder on the user's local computer, as **Document\CSE _ DEPT.sql**.

1) Refer to Appendix A to complete the download and installation of Oracle Database 18c XE.
2) Refer to Appendix C to complete the download and installation of Oracle SQL Developer.
3) Refer to Section 2.9 in Chapter 2, that is, from Sections 2.9.1 to 2.9.2, to complete the creation of a new Oracle 18c XE Database and a new User Account, **CSE _ DEPT**.
4) Expand the new created User Account, **CSE _ DEPT**, under the **Other Users** folder in Oracle SQL Developer, and click on the **Tables** folder to select it.
5) Then go to **File|Open** to open the **Open** wizard, as shown in Figure E.1.

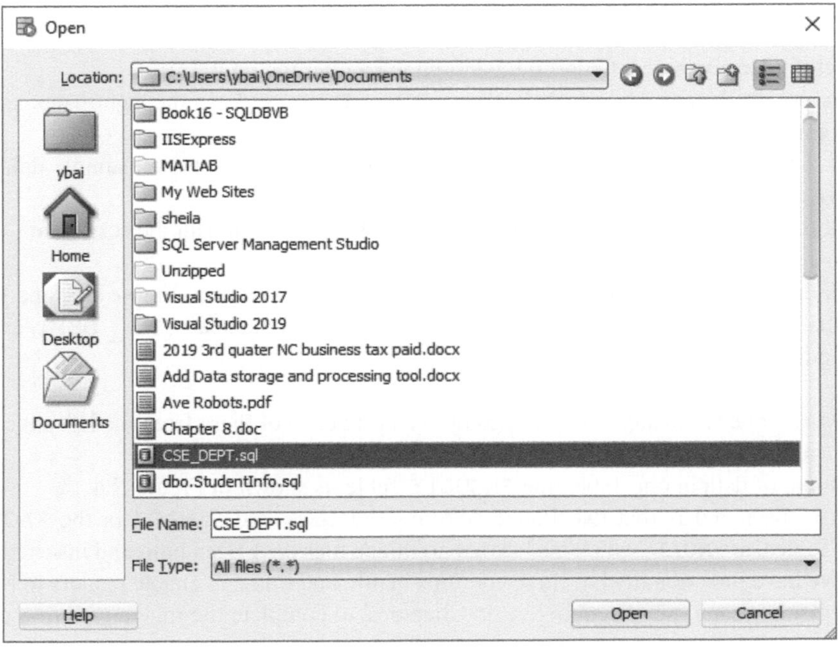

FIGURE E.1 The opened Open wizard.

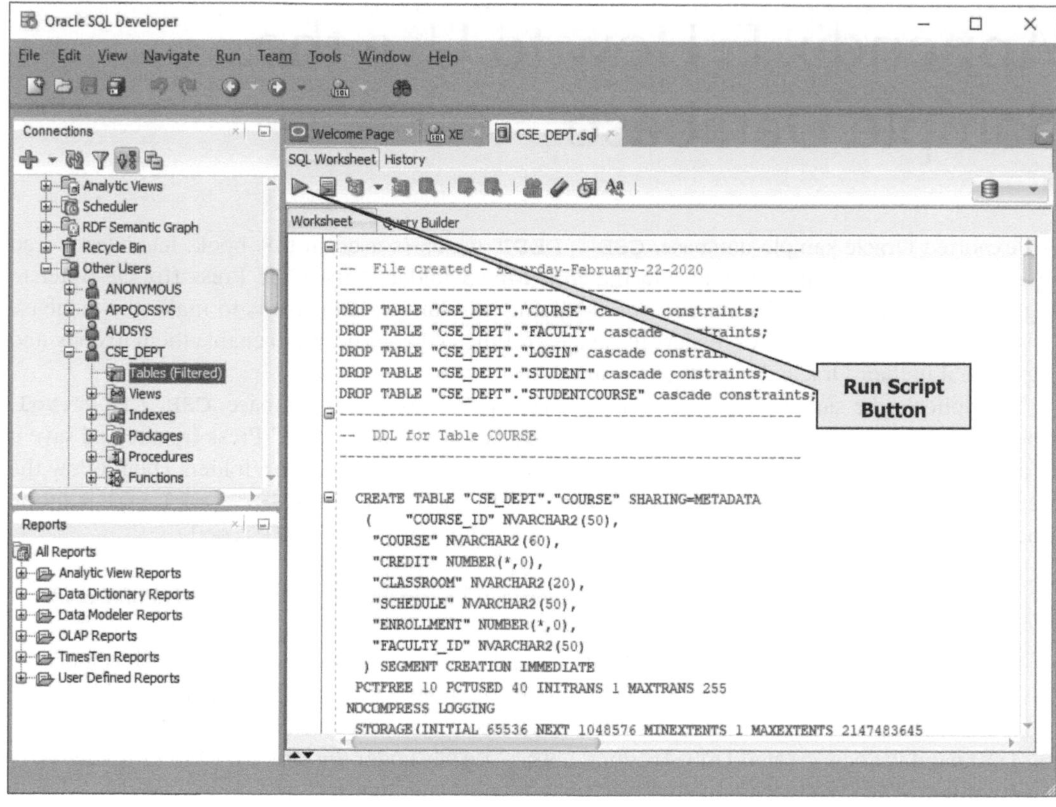

FIGURE E.2 The opened sample database, **CSE _ DEPT.sql** (Copyrighted by Oracle and used with permission).

6) Select the **Documents** folder in the left pane by clicking on it.
7) Then choose the pasted sample database, **CSE _ DEPT.sql**, in the right pane, as shown in Figure E.1.
8) Click on the **Open** button to open the sample database. The opened sample database is shown in Figure E.2.
9) Click on the **Run Script** button, as shown in Figure E.2, to run the script file.
10) The run result is shown in Figure E.3.
11) Click on the **Refresh** button on the upper-left pane, as shown in Figure E.3, and you can see that all five Tables have been added into our sample database, **CSE _ DEPT**, as shown in Figure E.3.

Now you can check the duplicated Tables by selecting each of them from the left pane and clicking on the **Data** tab on the top of the right pane one by one.

An example of data in one Table, the **FACULTY** Table, is shown in Figure E.4.

A point to be noted is that two image columns, **FIMAGE** and **SIMAGE** in the **FACULTY** and **STUDENT** Tables, are **NULL**, which means that no image files have been built and inserted into these columns. We have intentionally left these columns blank, and this will enable readers to insert those images themselves later. See Section 2.9.7 in Chapter 2 to complete the image insertion process.

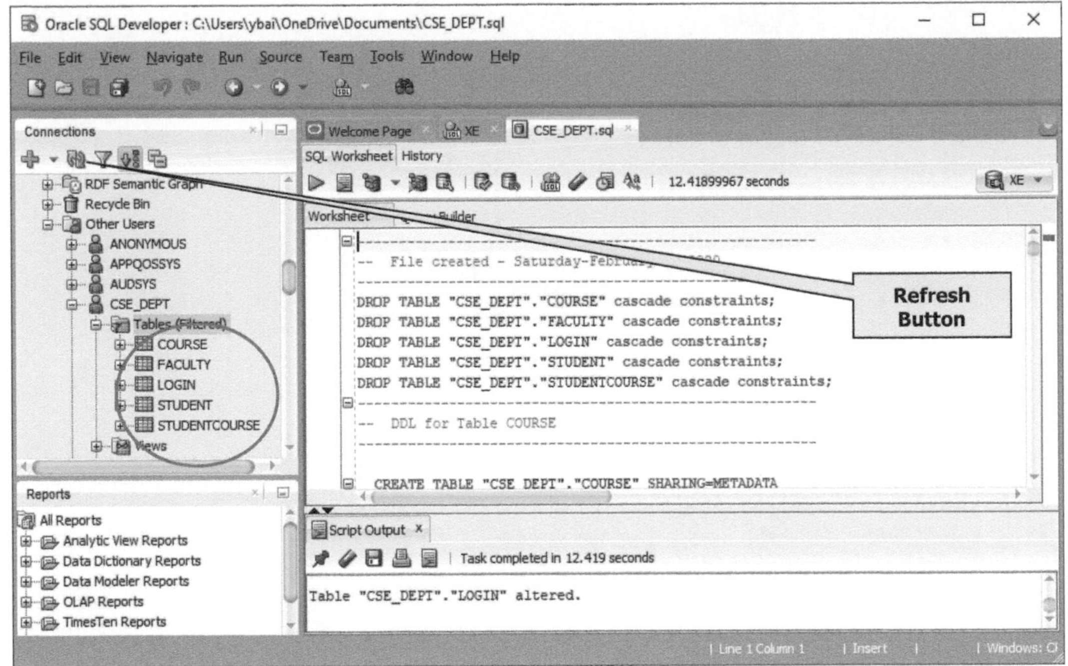

FIGURE E.3 The run result (Copyrighted by Oracle and used with permission).

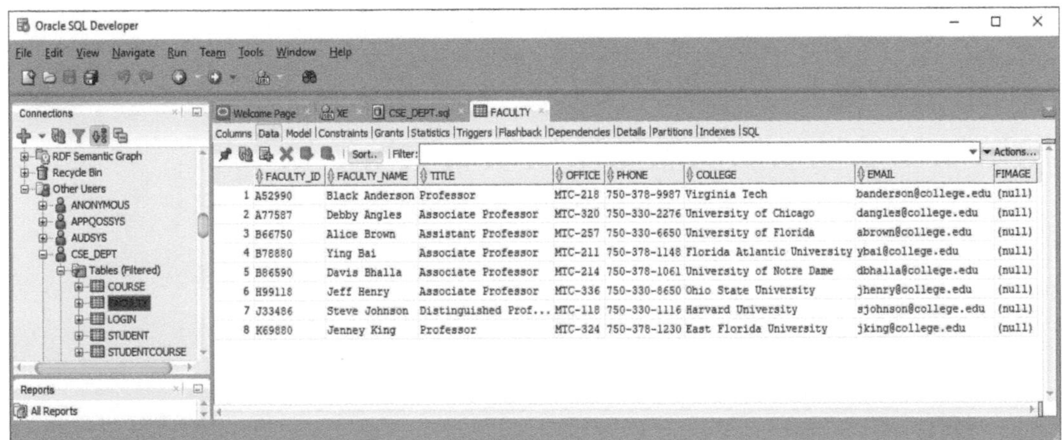

FIGURE E.4 Example data in the FACULTY Table (Copyrighted by Oracle and used with permission).

Appendix F: How to Export the Sample Database

In Appendix E, we introduced how to use our Oracle sample database, **CSE _ DEPT**, which was built in Chapter 2 by using the Import method in Oracle SQL Developer.

In this section, we will discuss how to export our sample database, **CSE _ DEPT**, to enable other users to import it into their blank database to simplify the database building process.

Assume that we export the sample database into a desired folder, such as the **Documents** folder on the user's local machine. Perform the following steps to complete the export process:

1) Open Oracle SQL Developer and connect to our database by clicking on **XE** under the **Recent** list and entering the password **oracle _ 18c** in the **Password** box to complete the login process.
2) Expand **Other Users**, and our user account, **CSE _ DEPT**, folder and the **Tables** folder.
3) Select our five Tables, **COURSE**, **LOGIN**, **FACULTY**, **STUDENT** and **STUDENTCOURSE**, by pressing and holding the **Ctrl** key and clicking on each of these Tables.
4) Then right-click on the selected Tables and select the **Export** item from the popup menu to open the Export wizard, as shown in Figure F.1.

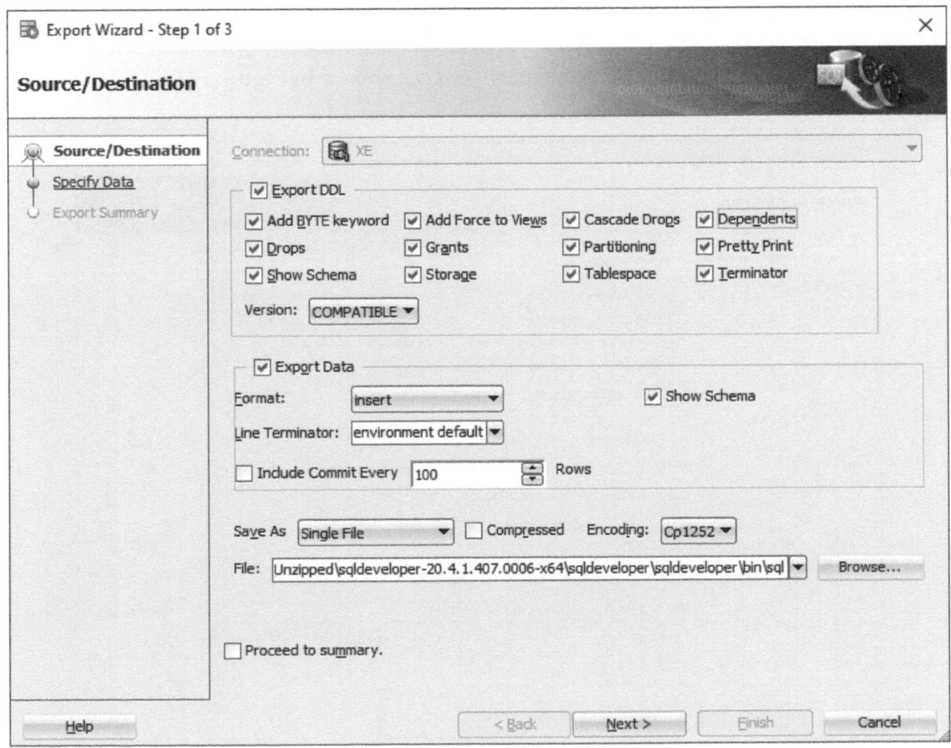

FIGURE F.1 The opened Export wizard (Copyrighted by Oracle and used with permission).

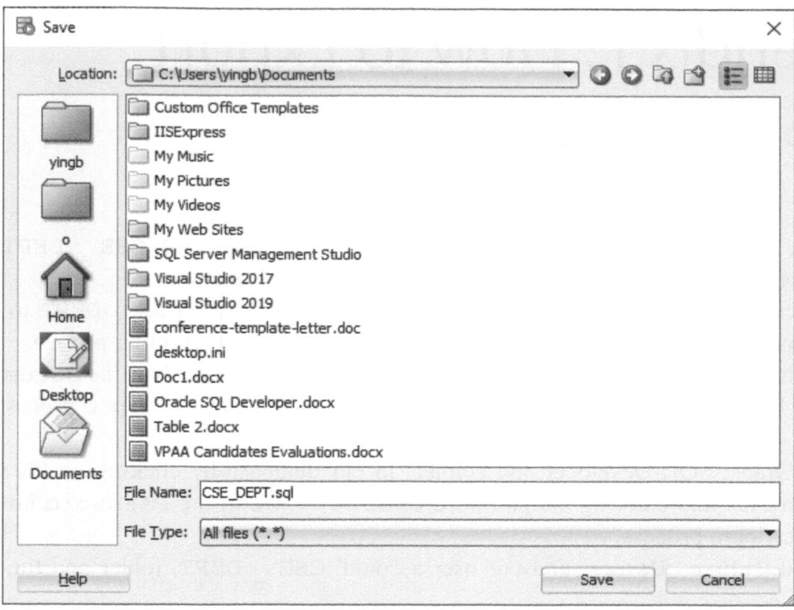

FIGURE F.2 The opened Save wizard.

5) Select all checkboxes under the **`Export DDL`** group by checking each of them, as shown in Figure F.1.
6) Click on the **`Browse`** button to open the **`Save`** wizard to select the location to save our exported database file, as shown in Figure F.2.
7) Click on the **`Documents`** icon on the left pane and enter the exported database file's name as **`CSE _ DEPT.sql`** in the **`File Name:`** box, as shown in Figure F.2.

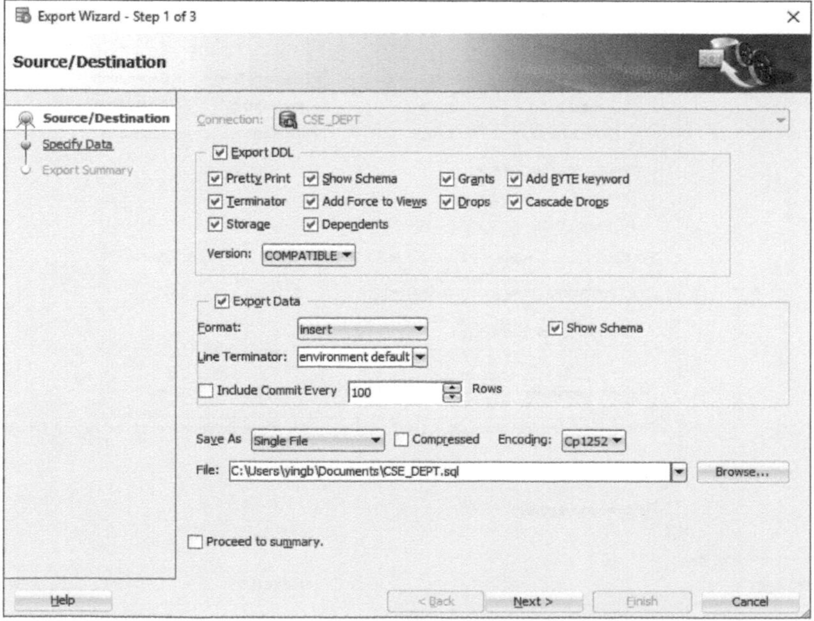

FIGURE F.3 The finished Export wizard (Copyrighted by Oracle and used with permission).

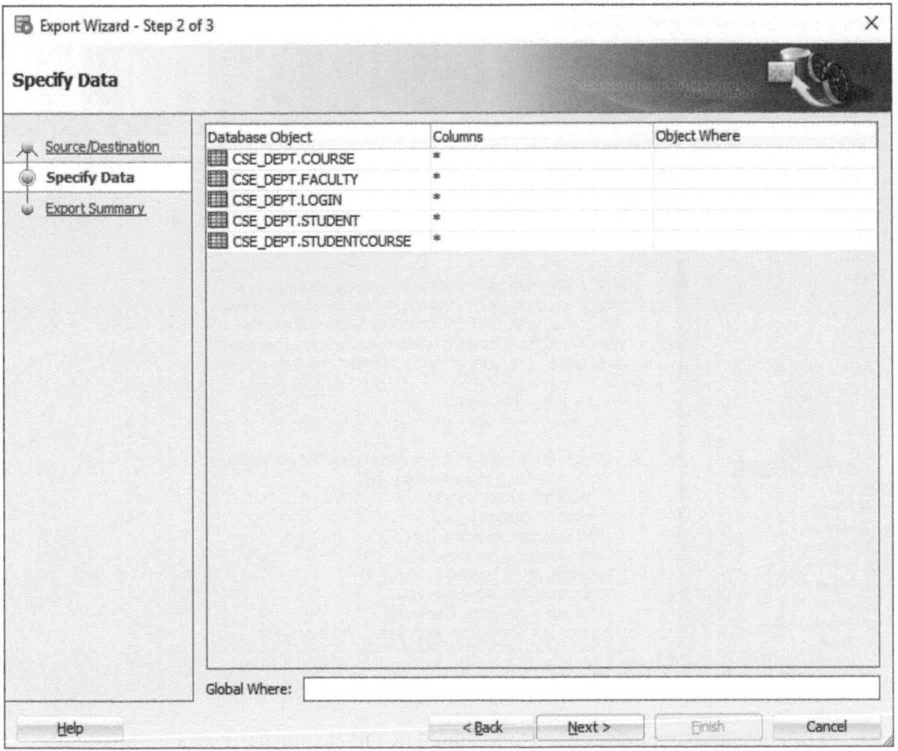

FIGURE F.4 The second step of the Export wizard (Copyrighted by Oracle and used with permission).

8) Then click on the **Save** button to close the **Save** wizard.
9) Your finished Export wizard should match the one shown in Figure F.3.
10) Click on the **Next** button to open the second step of the Export wizard, as shown in Figure F.4.
11) Click on the **Next** button again to go to the next step, since we do not want to make any modifications to the location for this file.
12) On the next step of the Export wizard, click on the **Finish** button to complete the export operation.
13) The export process starts, as shown in Figure F.5.
14) The final export results are shown in Figure F.6.
15) Now if you open the **Documents** folder on your local machine, you can find the exported file **CSE _ DEPT.sql**.
16) You can save the exported database file to any location for future import usage.

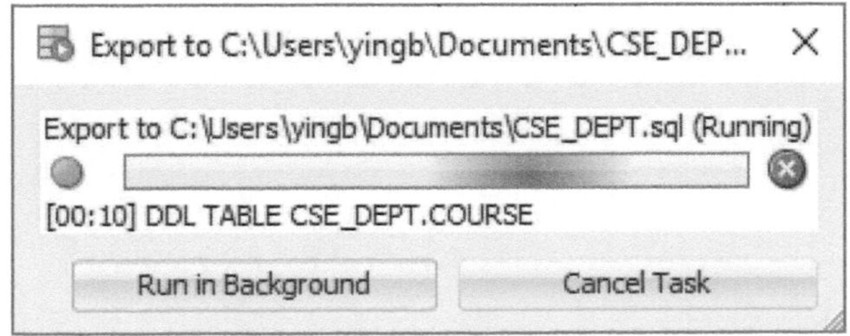

FIGURE F.5 The export build process (Copyrighted by Oracle and used with permission).

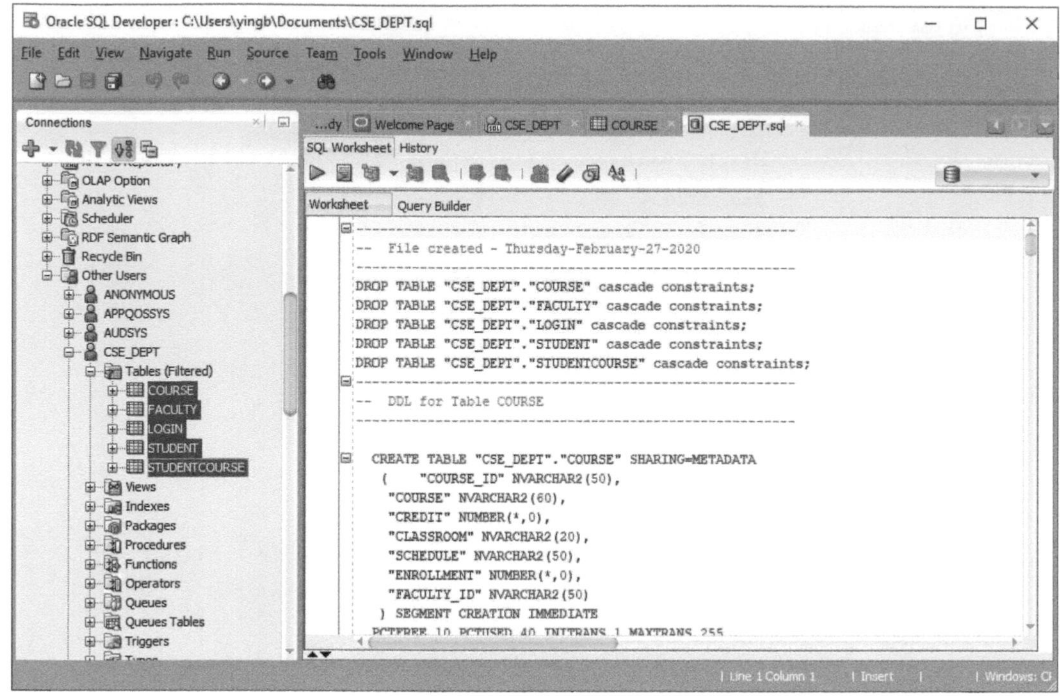

FIGURE F.6 The completed export results (Copyrighted by Oracle and used with permission).

Now you can close Oracle SQL Developer after the sample database has been exported.

Appendix G: Download and Install dotConnect Express

Go to the site https://www.devart.com/dotconnect/oracle/compatibility.html to download **dotConnect for Oracle 9.14 Express**, since this tool is free. The opened window is shown Figure G.1.

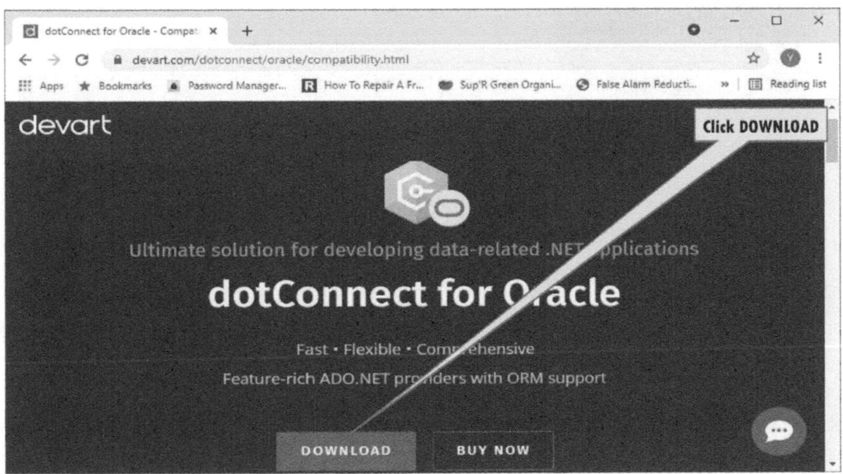

FIGURE G.1 The download start page.

1) On the opened page, click on the **DOWNLOAD** button to continue this process.
2) You may need to create an account and login to this site to continue.
3) Click on the **DOWNLOAD** button on the right of **dotConnect for Oracle 9.14 Express** item to begin the download process (Figure G.2).

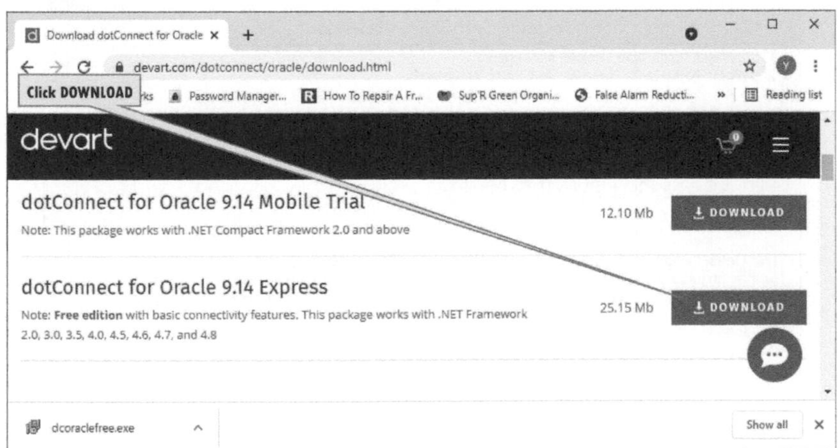

FIGURE G.2 The download starting wizard.

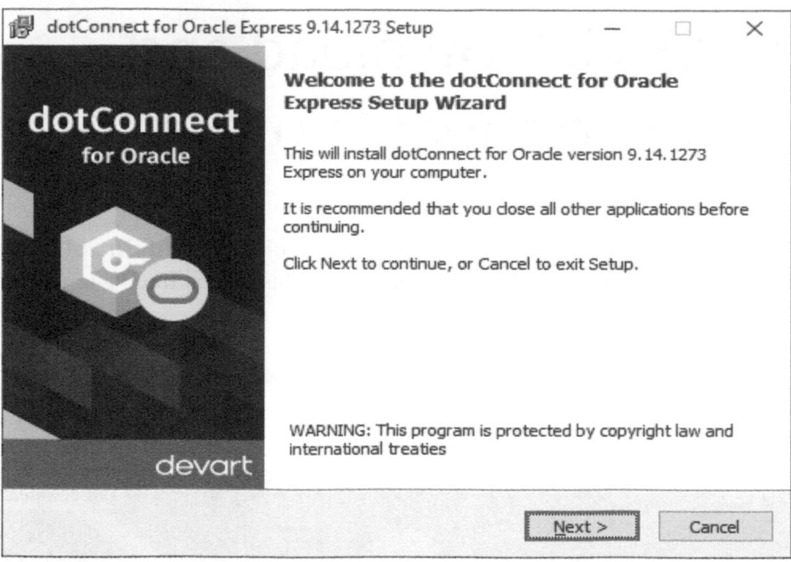

FIGURE G.3 The initial installation wizard.

4) When the download is done, double-click the downloaded file, **`dcoraclefree.exe`**, to start the installation. The installation wizard is shown in Figure G.3. Click on the **`Next`** button.
5) In the next wizard, License Agreement wizard, check the **`I accept the agreement`** radio button, as shown in Figure G.4, and the **`Next`** button to continue.
6) The destination to install this software is shown in the next wizard, as shown in Figure G.5, to enable you to select the desired folder to install the tool. Keep the default location unchanged and click on the **`Next`** button to go to the next wizard.

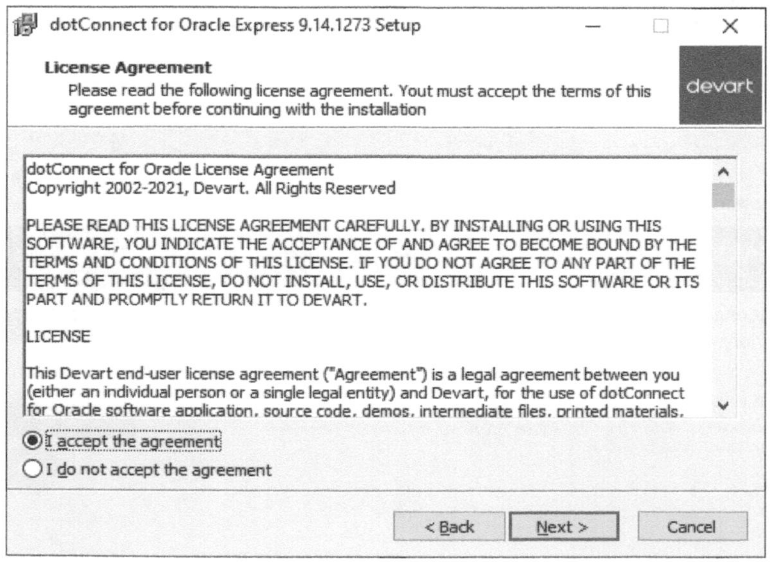

FIGURE G.4 The license agreement wizard.

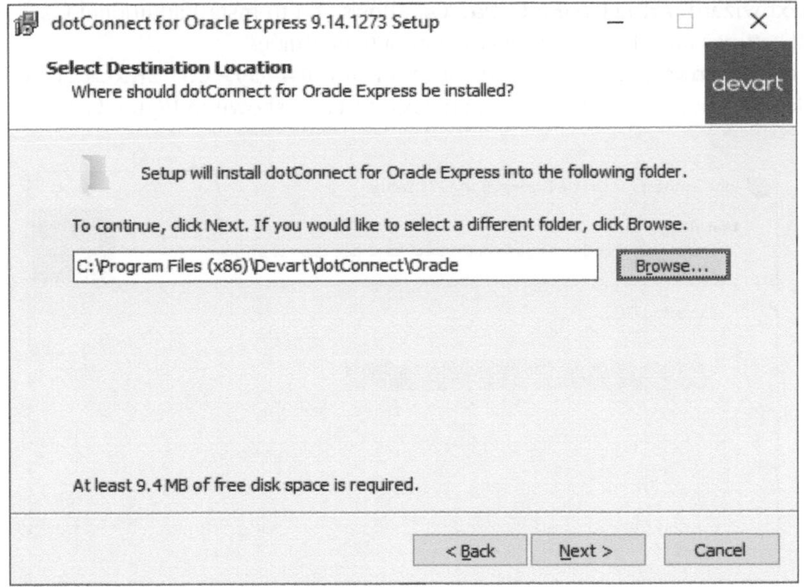

FIGURE G.5 The installation destination wizard.

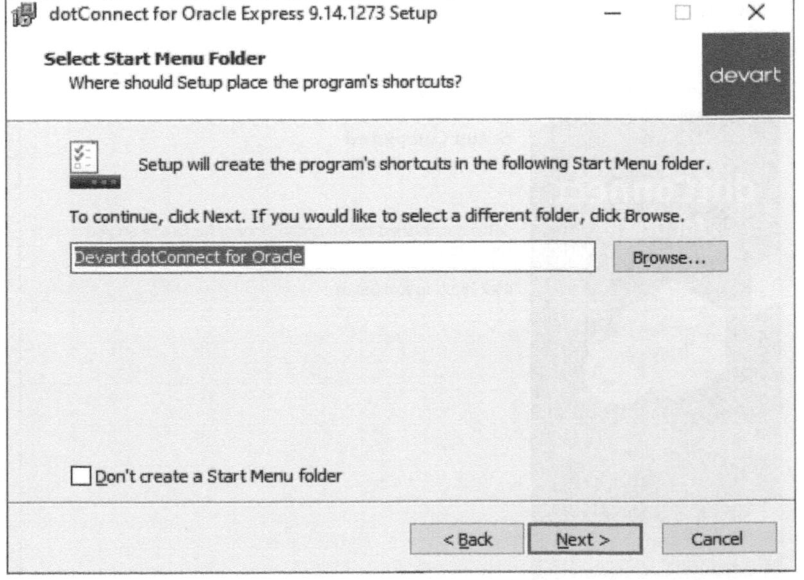

FIGURE G.6 The Select Start Menu Folder wizard.

7) The next wizard, the Select Components wizard, is used to enable you to select the desired elements to be installed. For our applications, we need to install all the components. Keep the default selection and click on the **`Next`** button to continue.
8) In the opened Select Start Menu Folder wizard, as shown in Figure G.6, keep the default folder to save the start menu and click on the **`Next`** button.

9) The next wizard, **`Additional Tasks`**, allows you to install additional tasks. Keep the default settings and click on the **`Next`** button to continue.
10) Click on the **`Install`** button on the next wizard, **`Ready to Install`**, to begin the installation process. The installation process starts, as shown in Figure G.7.

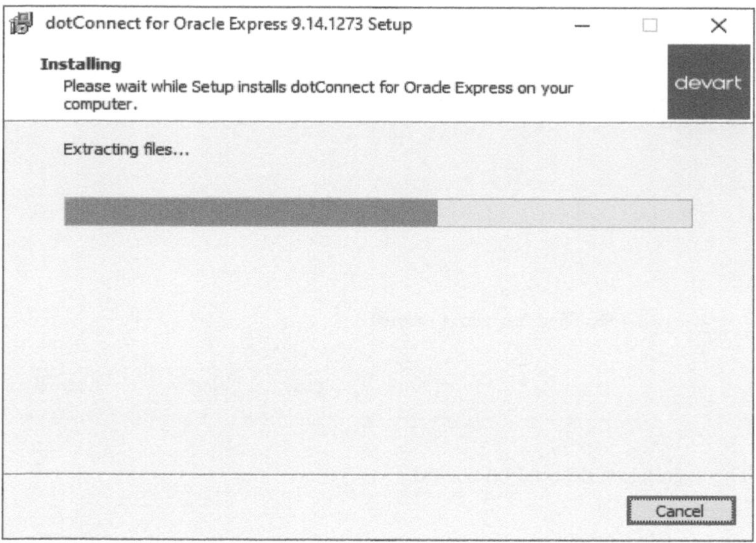

FIGURE G.7 The installation process starts.

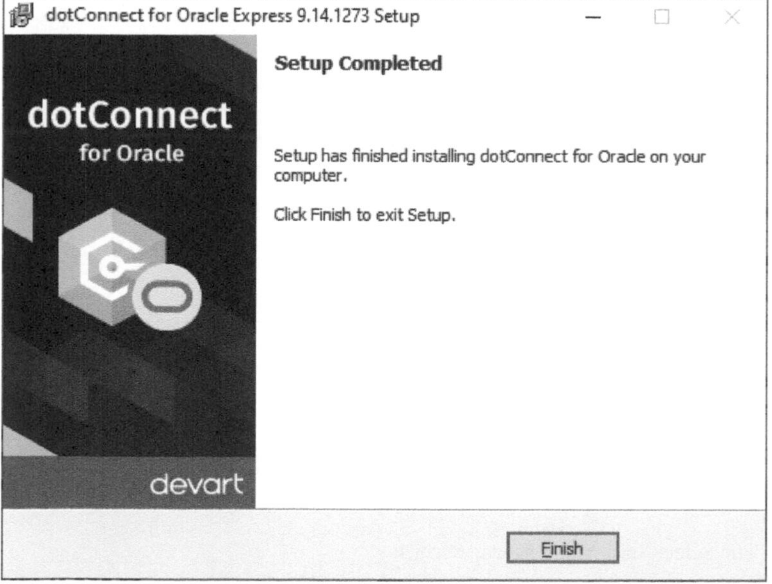

FIGURE G.8 The option to add the documentation wizard.

11) When the installation process is complete, as shown in Figure G.8, click on the **`Finish`** button to complete the process.

Now you can open Visual Studio. NET 2019 to confirm the installation as well as the components installed by this installation. Perform the following operations to check the components related to this installation:

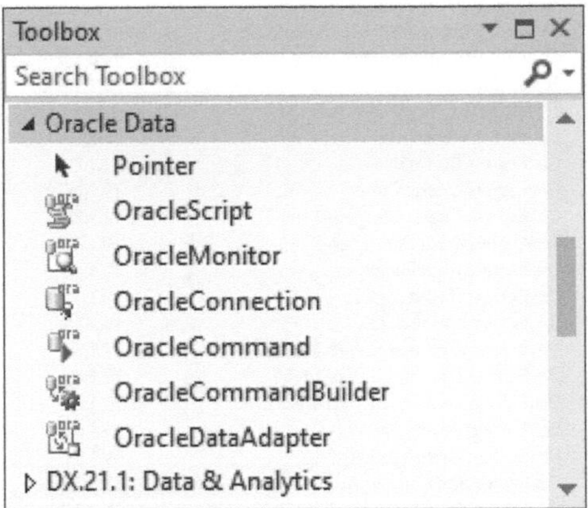

FIGURE G.9 Added Oracle data components.

1) First create a new Visual Basic.NET 2019 Windows Forms App (.NET Framework) project with any desired name, such as `DotConnect Test Project`.
2) Then open the `Design View` or the Form window of the new created project and the `Toolbox` window. Browse to the `OracleData` subfolder, which is shown in Figure G.9. You can see that some new components related to Oracle data access have been added to this folder; they are:

- OracleScript
- OracleMonitor
- OracleConnection
- OracleCommand
- OracleCommandBuilder
- OracleDataAdapter

3) Right-click on the new created project, `DotConnect Test Project`, in the Solution Explorer window, and select the `Add|Reference` item to open the Add Reference wizard, which is shown in Figure G.10.
4) Expand the `Assemblies` icon and select the `Extensions` item. Then scroll down in the. NET Framework 4.7.2 window, and you can see that two Oracle-related libraries, `Devart.Data` and `Devart.Data.Oracle`, have been added into the reference library under the. NET Framework 4.7.2 tab.
5) Select these two libraries by checking their related checkboxes on the left.
6) Click on the `OK` button to add these two libraries into our project, `DotConnect Test Project`.

To confirm that both libraries have been added into our project, expand the `References` item under our project, `DotConnect Test Project`, in the Solution Explorer, and you can see these two libraries, as shown in Figure G.11.

We need to add these two library references into all our projects later when we build our applications to access the Oracle database.

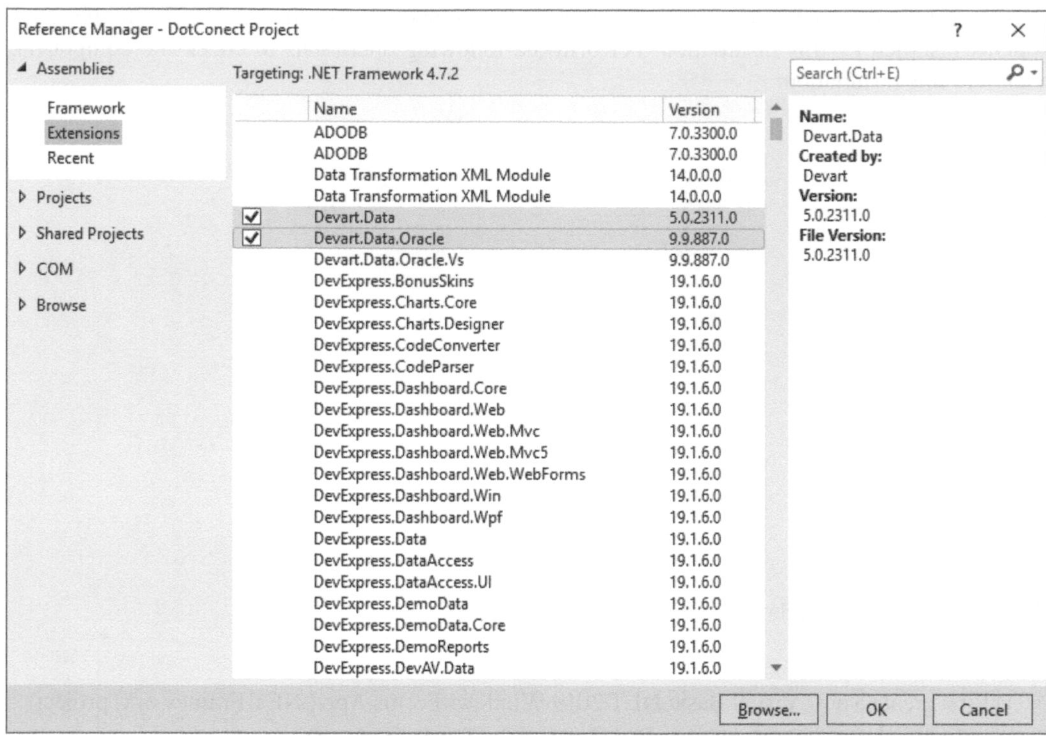

FIGURE G.10 Some added reference libraries.

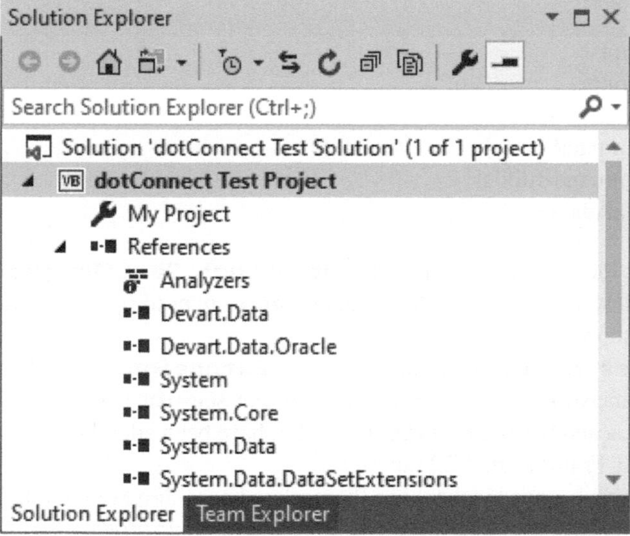

FIGURE G.11 Two new added libraries.

Appendix H: Download JDBC Driver for Oracle XE 18c

Perform the following operations to download the JDBC driver for Oracle 18c XE:

1) Go to link **`https://www.oracle.com/be/database/technologies/appdev/jdbc-downloads.html`** to open the download page, as shown in H.1.

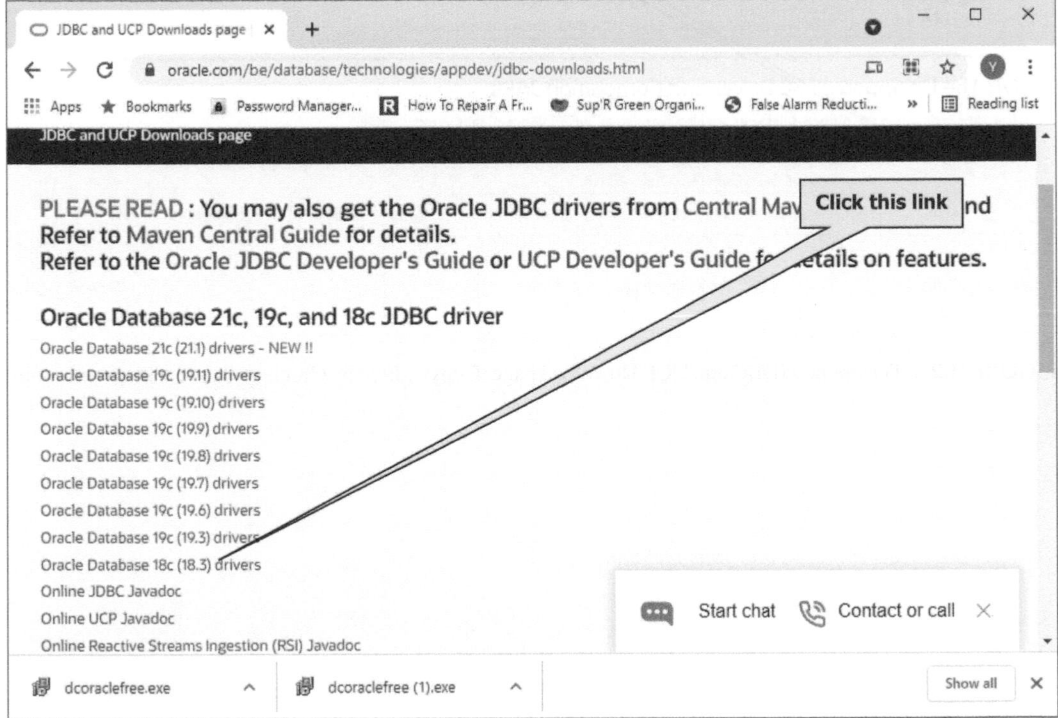

FIGURE H.1 The opened JDBC download page (Copyrighted by Oracle and used with permission).

2) On the opened download page, click on the **`Oracle Database 18c (18.3) drivers`** link to continue.
3) On the opened 18.3 JDBC and UCP Download page, as shown in Figure H.2, click on the **`ojdbc8.jar`** link.
4) Click on the **`Keep`** button in the popup dialog box to allow the driver to be downloaded to your machine.
5) When the download process is done, the driver file **`ojdbc8.jar`** is downloaded to your default **`Download`** folder on your machine.
6) Move the driver file to the **`C:\Temp`** folder if you like. Otherwise, you can save it to any folder you like.

Try to remember this folder, since later on when we connect to our Oracle 18c XE sample database, **`CSE _ DEPT`**, we need to use this driver with this folder.

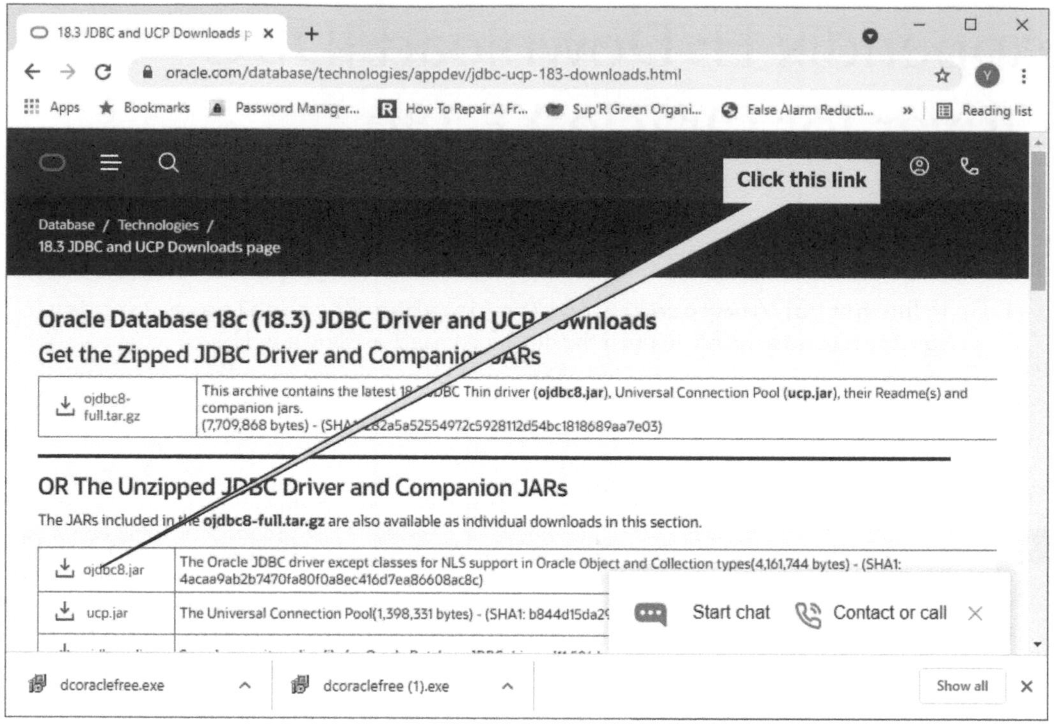

FIGURE H.2 The opened JDBC and UCP Download page (Copyrighted by Oracle and used with permission).

Appendix I: Download and Install Tomcat Server 8.0.27

1) Go to link **`https://archive.apache.org/dist/tomcat/tomcat-8/v8.0.27/bin/`** to open the download page, as shown in Figure I.1.

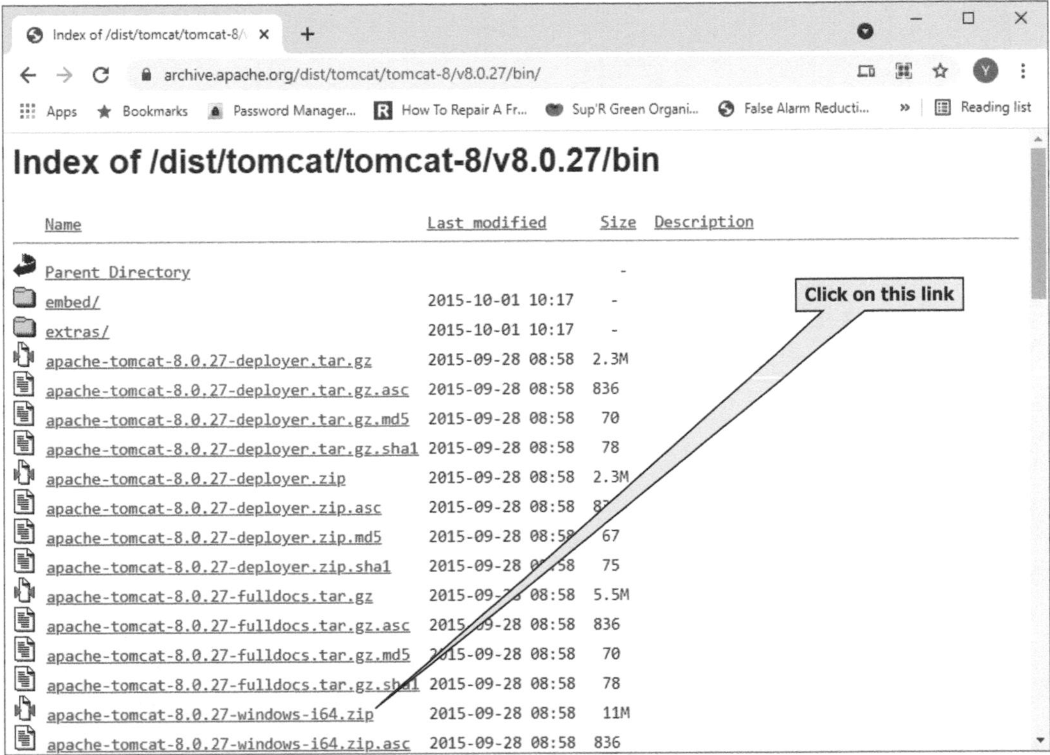

FIGURE I.1 The opened download page for Tomcat 8.0.27.

2) Click on the file **`apache-tomcat-8.0.27-windows-i64.zip`**to begin the download process for the Web server.
3) When the download process is done, double-click on the file in your **`Download`** folder in your computer to unzip the server file.
4) After the server file is unzipped, change the name of the unzipped folder to **`Apache Tomcat 8.0.27`**, and save it to a desired location on your local `C:\` drive. In our case, we saved it to a folder, **`C:\Program Files\Apache Software Foundation`**. Try to remember this location, since we need to add this Web server into our Web application projects later.

Appendix J: Download and Install Java JDK 8

1) Go to link **`https://www.oracle.com/java/technologies/javase/javase-jdk8-downloads.html`** to open the download page for JDK 8, as shown in Figure J.1.

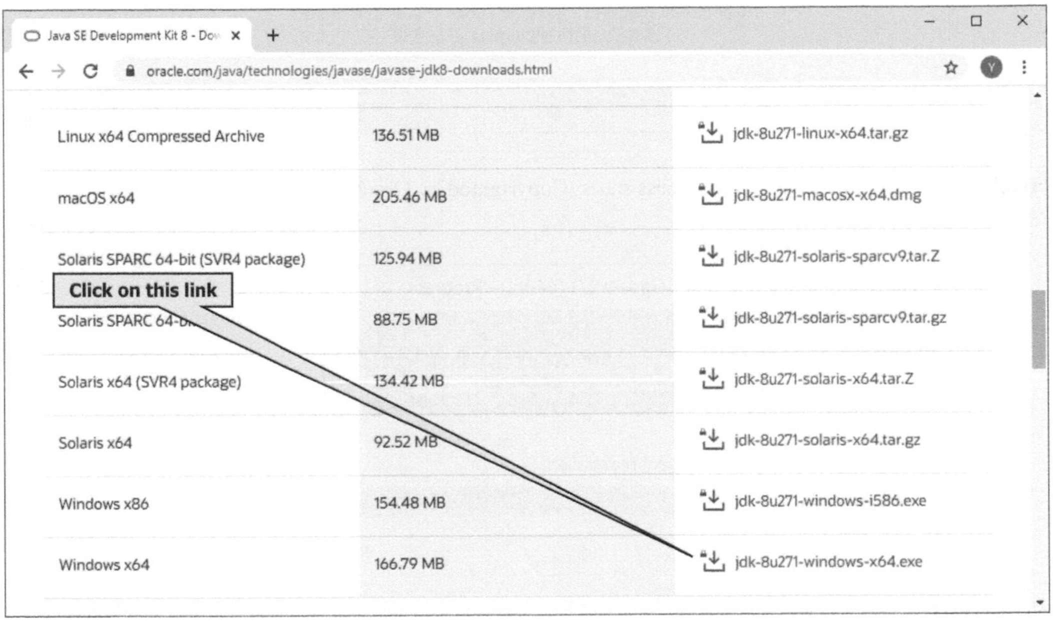

FIGURE J.1 The opened download page for JDK 8 (Copyrighted by Oracle and used with permission).

2) Click on the **`Accept License`** checkbox and the **`Download jdk-8u271-windows-x64.exe`** button to begin the download process. You may need to log into start the process.
3) When the download process is done, click on that downloaded file to run the installation. In the next wizard, as shown in Figure J.2, click on the **`Next`** button to start.

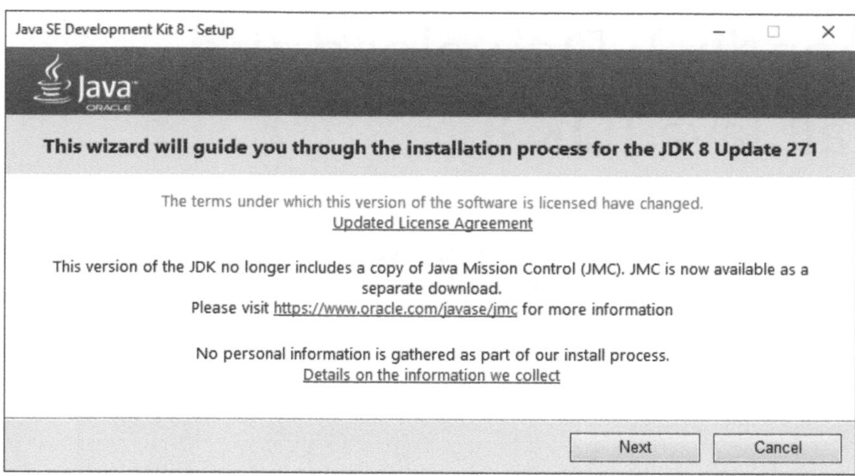

FIGURE J.2 The pre-installation process starts (Copyrighted by Oracle and used with permission).

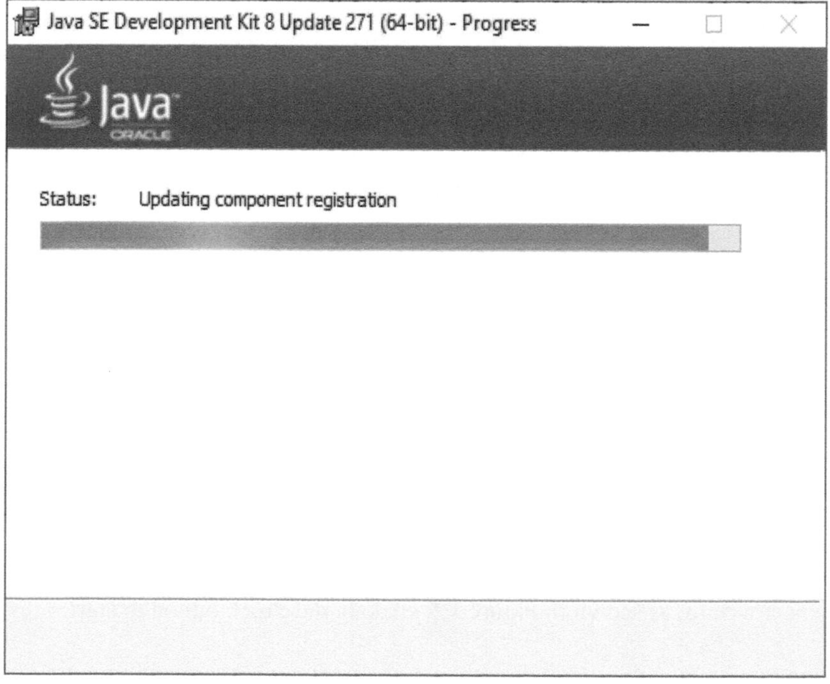

FIGURE J.3 The pre-installation process starts (Copyrighted by Oracle and used with permission).

4) Click on the **Next** button in the next wizard to select the default location, **C:\Program Files\Java/jdk1.8.0 _ 271**, to begin the pre-installation process, as shown in Figure J.3.
5) The pre-installation process starts.
6) Click on the **Next** button in the next wizard to confirm the installation target location. The installation process starts, as shown in Figure J.4.

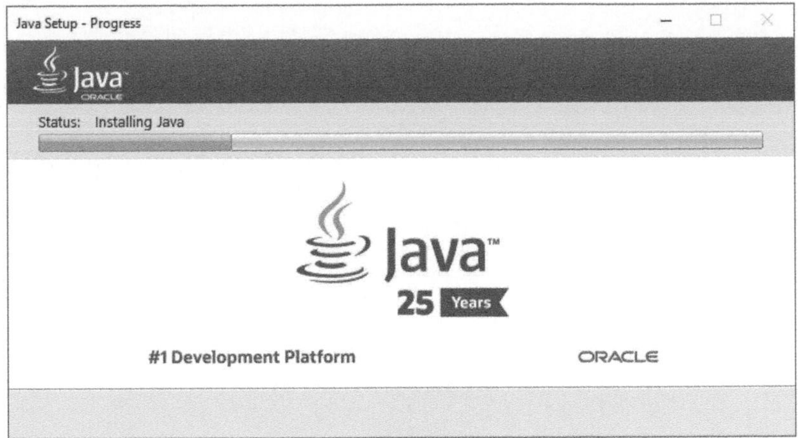

FIGURE J.4 The installation process starts (Copyrighted by Oracle and used with permission).

When the installation process is completed, as shown in Figure J.5, click on the `Close` button.

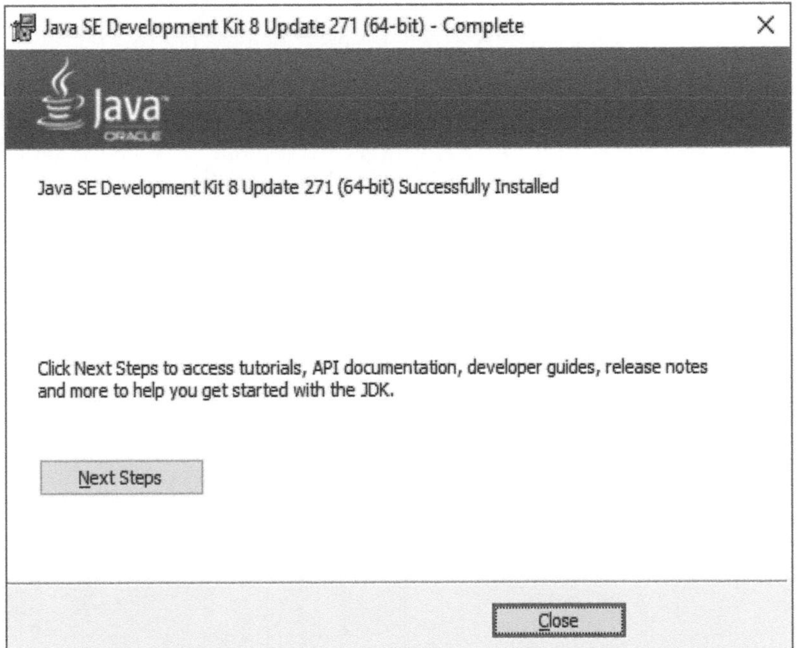

FIGURE J.5 The installation process is completed (Copyrighted by Oracle and used with permission).

Appendix K: Trouble Shooting for the WS00041 Service Exception

Usually this exception is not encountered when only a single NetBeans IDE, such as NetBeans IDE 12.0, is installed and used on your machine. However, if multiple NetBeans IDEs, such as NetBeans IDE 12.4 and 12.0, are installed on your computer, you may encounter this exception when you run the GlassFish Tester Page in NetBeans IDE 12.0.

To solve this issue, perform the following steps to make sure that only a single instance of NetBeans IDE 12.0 is installed in your computer:

1) Open the Control Panel and uninstall both NetBeans IDEs, including NetBeans IDE 12.4 and NetBeans IDE 12.0.
2) After both IDEs have been removed, reboot your computer to make the uninstallations take effect.
3) Then go to the folder where both NetBeans IDEs were installed; these folders depend on the installation process. Two possible folders the maybe used are: **`C:\Program Files\NetBeans-12.0`** and **`C:\Program Files \NetBeans-12.4`** and **`C:\Program Files (x86)\NetBeans-12.0`** and **`C:\Program Files (x86)\NetBeans-12.4`**.
4) Manually delete these two folders, **`NetBeans-12.0`** and **`NetBeans-12.4`**, and all sub-folders if they were not removed in the uninstallation process.
5) Also go to the folder, **`C:\Users\your _ name\AppData\Roaming \NetBeans`**, on your computer and delete the folders, **`12.0`** and **`12.4`**.
6) Reinstall NetBeans IDE 12.0 by using the downloaded. exe file stored in your local **`Download`** folder.

Now you can start NetBeans IDE 12.0 to create any new Web application or Web Service projects with no problem when using the GlassFish Tester Page.

Appendix L: Download and Install Apache NetBeans 12.4

Prior to installing Apache NetBeans 12.4, a Java Development Kit must be installed. Refer to Appendix N to install JDK 14, since that JDK is compatible with IDE 12.4.

Perform the following operations to download and install Apache NetBeans IDE 12.4.

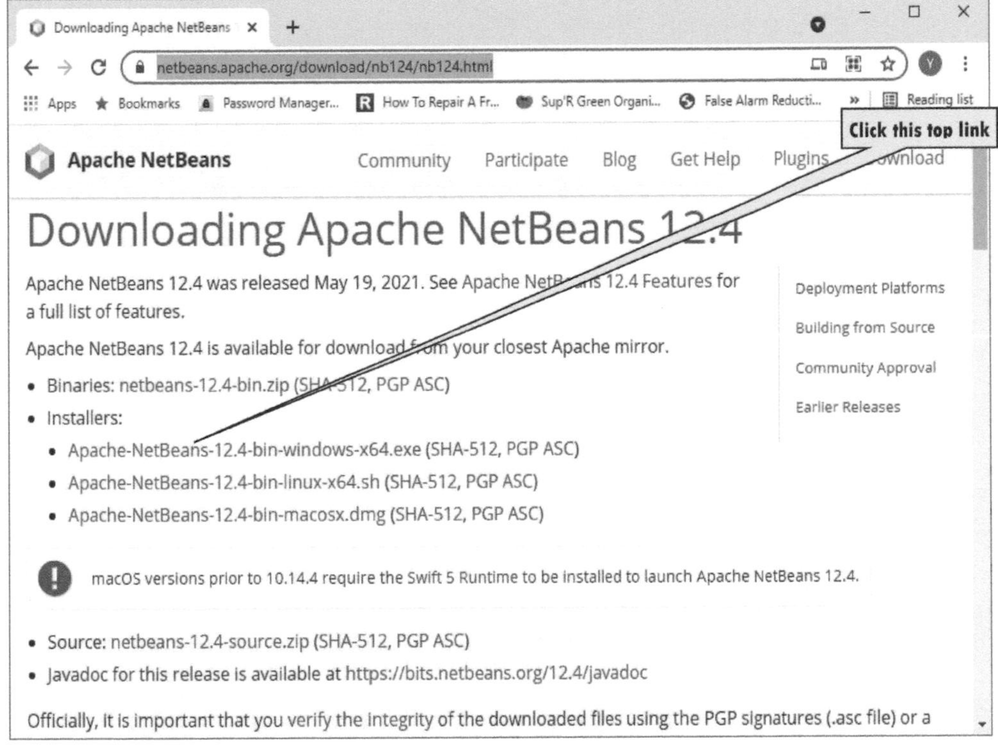

FIGURE L.1 The opened wizard for downloading Apache NetBeans 12.4.

1) Go to **`https://netbeans.apache.org/download/nb124/nb124.html`** to open the download and installation page, as shown in Figure L.1.
2) Click on the link: **`Apache-NetBeans-12.4-bin-windows-x64.exe (SHA-512, PGP ASC)`** to begin the download process (Figure L.1).
3) Click on the top link, **`https://apache.claz.org/netbeans/netbeans/12.4/Apache-NetBeans-12.4-bin-windows-x64.exe`**, which is under the **`HTTP`** tag, to start the download and installation process (Figure L.2). It may take a while to complete the download due to the large size of the file (409 MB).
4) When the download process is done, double-clicktheApache-NetBeans-12.4-bin-windows-x64.exe file in the **`Download`** folder at your computer to open the Configuring the Installer wizard (Figure L.3). Click on the **`Next`** button to continue when the process is done.

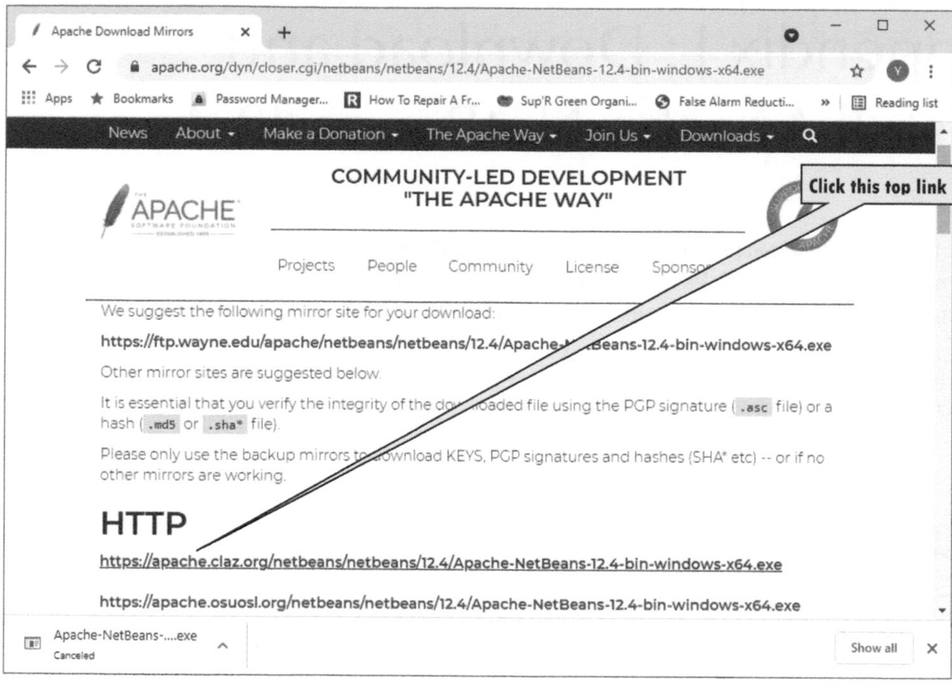

FIGURE L.2 The opened download page.

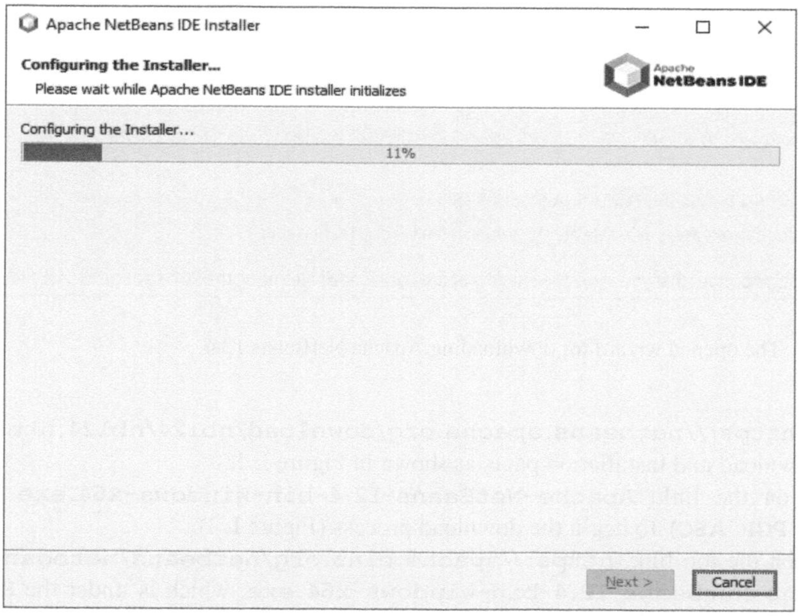

FIGURE L.3 The opened configuring the installer wizard.

5) The next wizard, the License Agreement wizard, is opened, as shown in Figure L.4. Check the **`License Agreement`** checkbox and click on the **`Next`** button to continue.

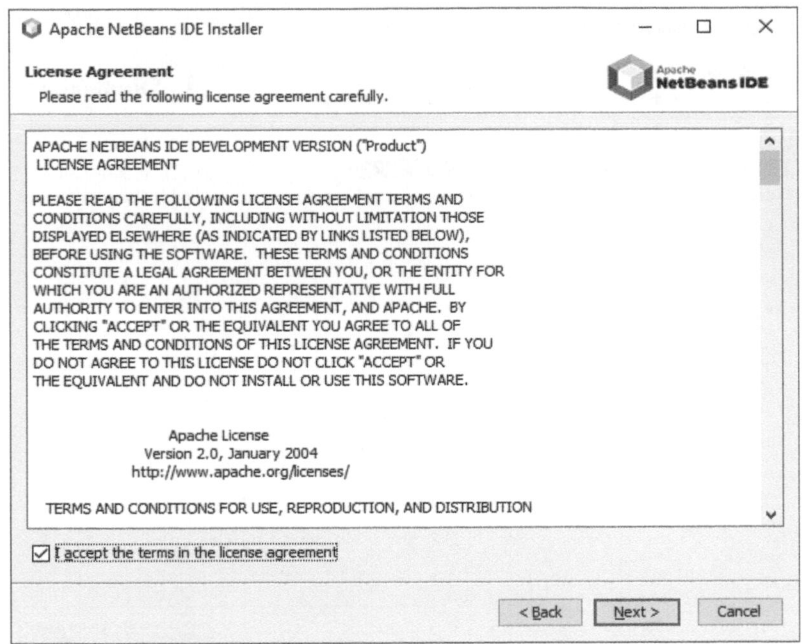

FIGURE L.4 The opened license agreement wizard.

6) The next wizard, the Installation Destination wizard, is opened, as shown in Figure L.5. Click on the `Next` button to keep the default location and continue the installation process.
7) Click on the `Install` button in the next wizard to start the installation process, as shown in Figure L.6.

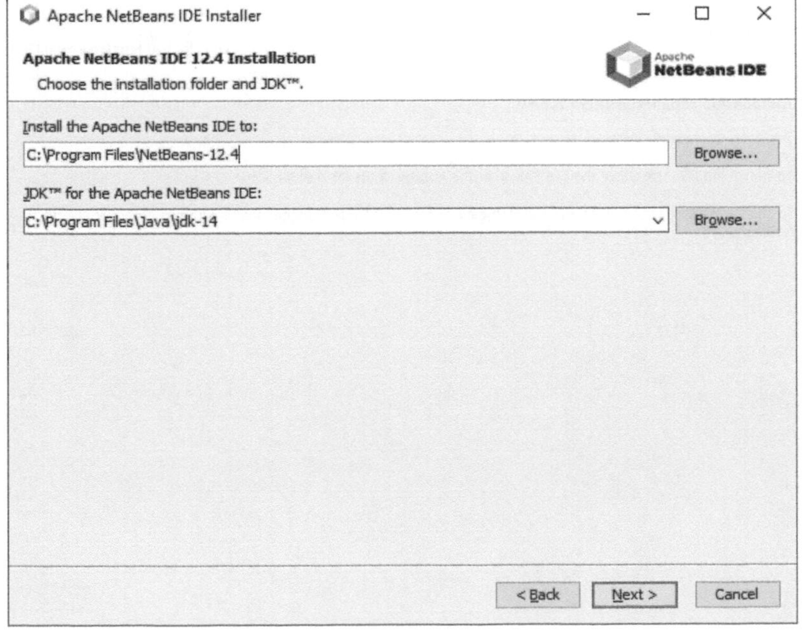

FIGURE L.5 The opened installation destination wizard.

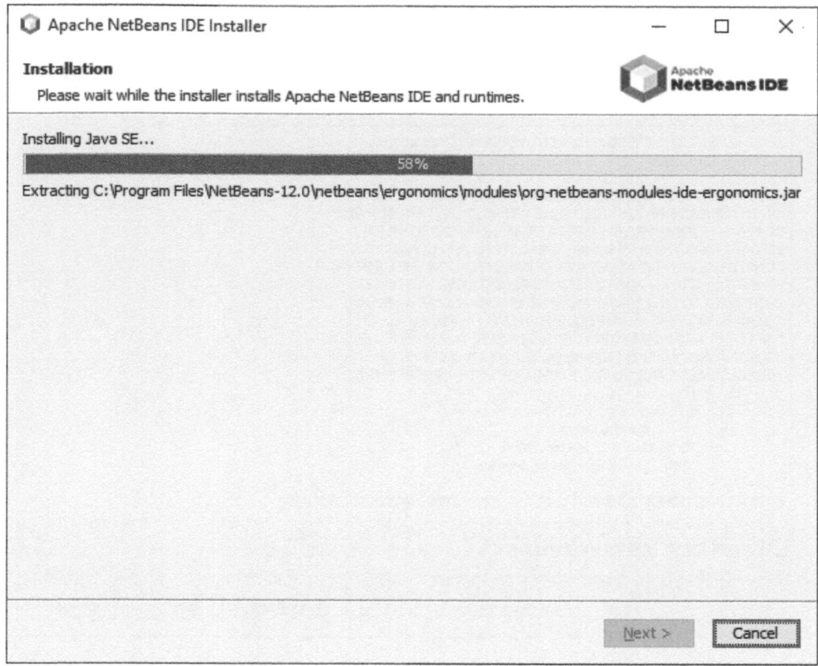

FIGURE L.6 The installation process starts.

8) When the installation process is done, as shown in Figure L.7, click on the **`Finish`** button to complete the process.

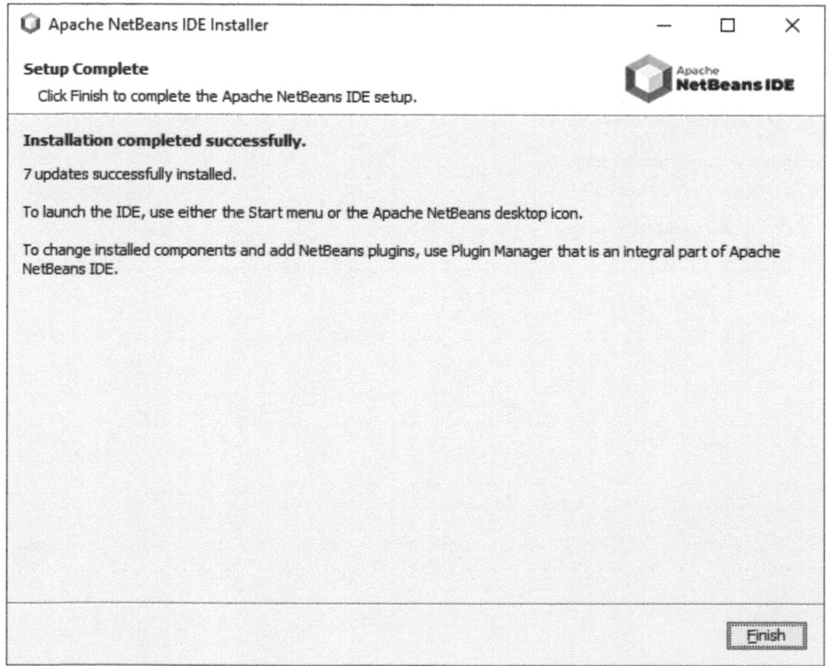

FIGURE L.7 The installation process finished.

Appendix M: ConFigure Apache NetBeans 12.0 for Initial Runs

When you run the Apache NetBeans IDE 12.0 in the first time and try to open a Web-related project, you may need to download and install some required packages and libraries. Perform the following operations to complete the configuration.

1) Double-click on the Apache NetBeans 12.0 icon on the desktop to run it.
2) When you open any Web-related project, such as **WebAppFaculty**, an Apache NetBeans IDE Installer is displayed, as shown in Figure M.1.
3) Click on the **Next** button to begin the installation process for the support library.

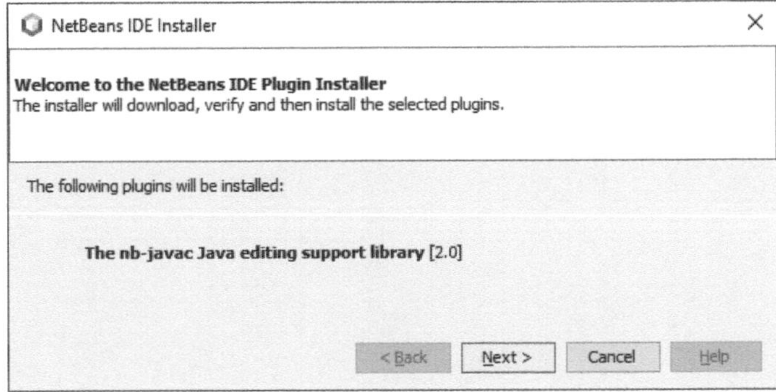

FIGURE M.1 The opened Apache NetBeans IDE Installer.

4) In the next wizard, as shown in Figure M.2, check the **License Agreement** checkbox and click on the **Install** button to continue.
5) Click on the **Finish** button when the installation is done.

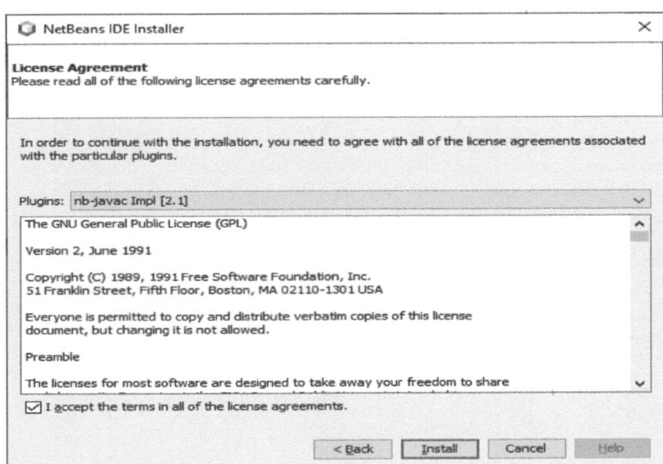

FIGURE M.2 The opened License Agreement wizard.

Appendix M: Configure Apache NetBeans 12.0 for Initial Runs

Appendix N: Download and Install Java JDK 14

Perform the following operations to download and install JDK 14.0.1:

1) Go to **`https://www.oracle.com/java/technologies/javase/jdk14-archive-downloads.html`** to open the download page, as shown in Figure N.1.

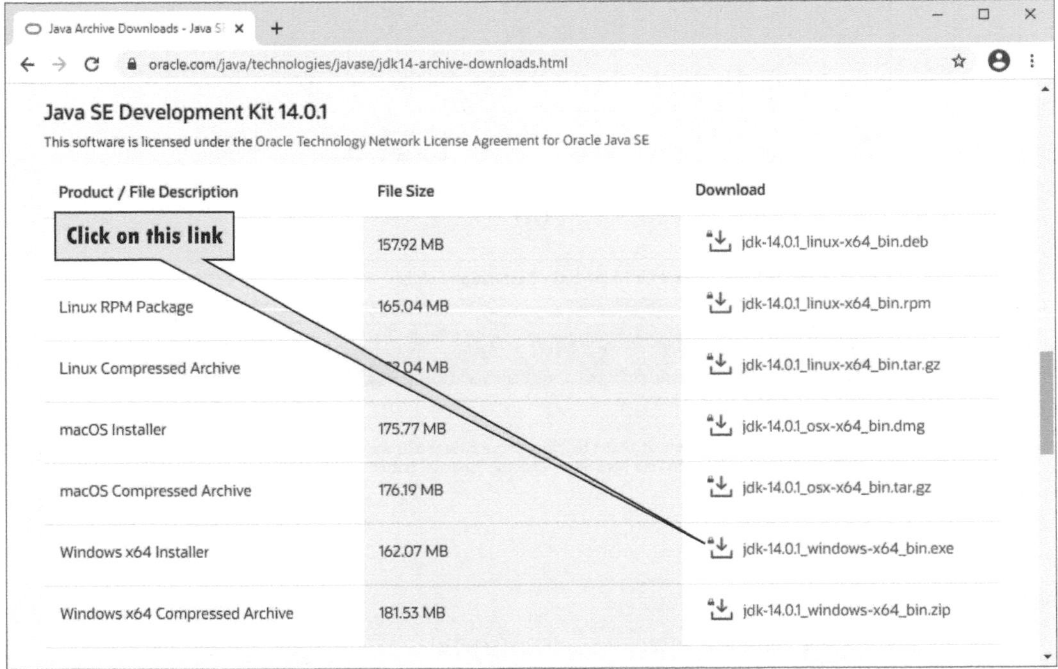

FIGURE N.1 The opened download page for JDK-14 (Copyrighted by Oracle and used with permission).

2) In the next wizard, as shown in Figure N.2, click on the **`Download jdk-14.0.1 _ windows-x64 _ bin.exe`** button to continue the process.

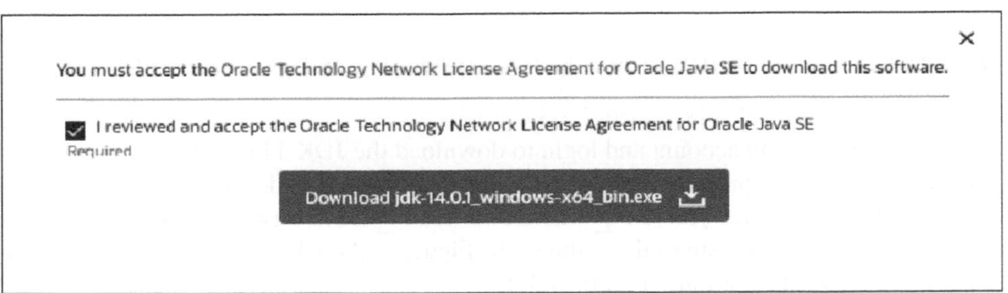

FIGURE N.2 The opened Oracle Technology Network License wizard (Copyrighted by Oracle and used with permission).

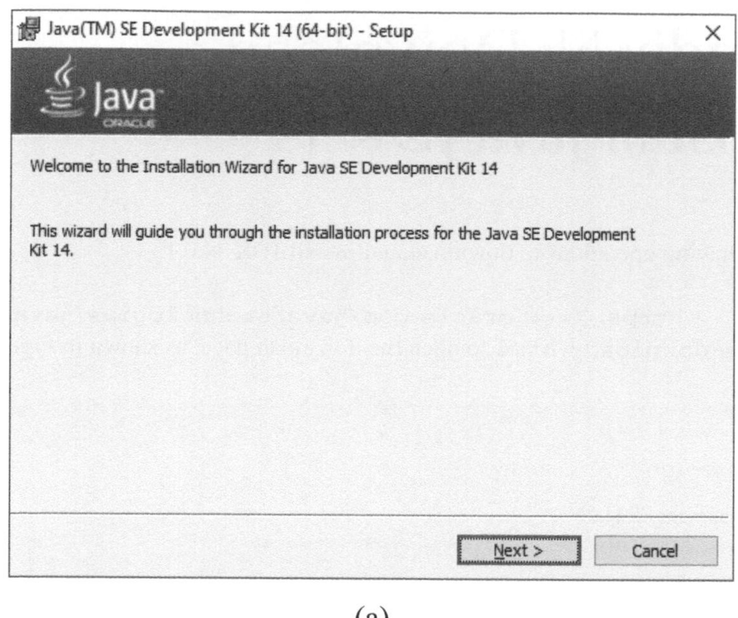

(a)

(b)

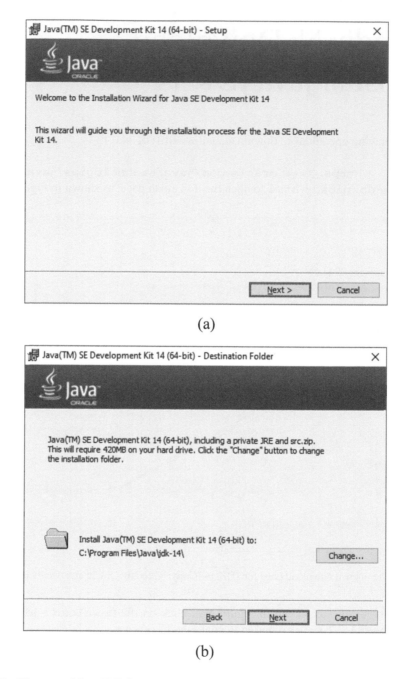

FIGURE N.3 The opened Java JDK Setup wizards (Copyrighted by Oracle and used with permission).

3) You need to create an account and login to download the JDK 14.0.1 file.
4) When the download process is done, go to the **`Download`** folder on your local machine and double-click on the **`jdk-14 _ windows-x64 _ bin.exe`** to install the JDK. The installation wizard is displayed, as shown in Figure N.3a. Click on the **`Next`** button for next two wizards to continue (Figure N.3b).

The installation process starts, as shown in Figure N.4.

When the installation process is completed, as shown in Figure N.5, click on the **Close** button to complete it.

Now you can find a new folder, **jdk-14**, in the **C:\Program Files\Java** folder in your computer.

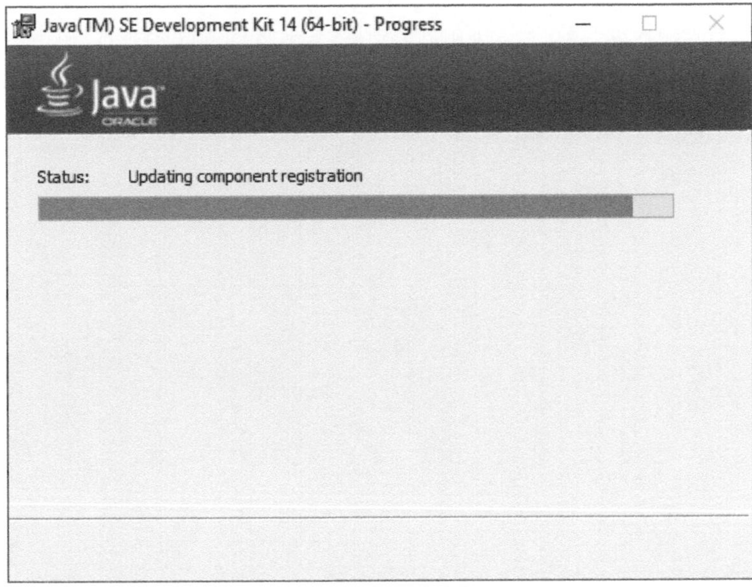

FIGURE N.4 The installation process starts (Copyrighted by Oracle and used with permission).

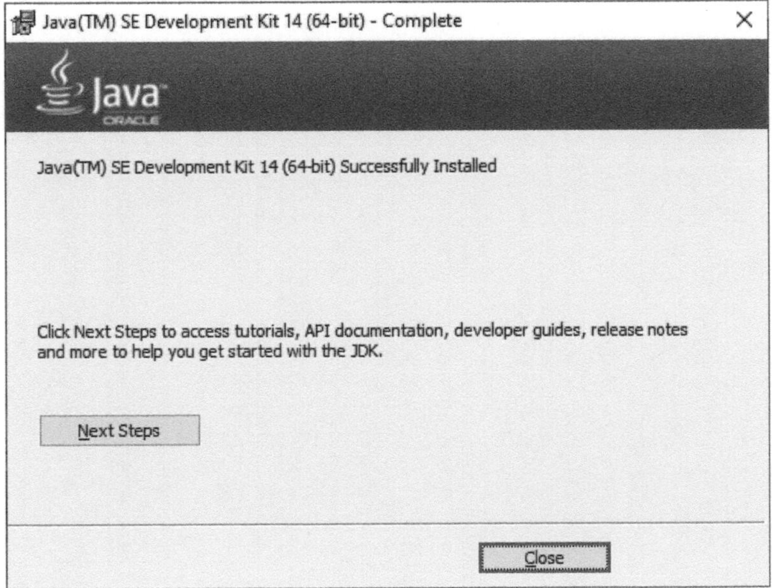

FIGURE N.5 The installation process is completed (Copyrighted by Oracle and used with permission).

Index

<c:forEach> tag, 379
<img> tag, 347–348
.\symbol, 284, 335

A

abstract class, 199, 212–213, 414, 426, 473
Abstract Windowing Toolkit (AWT), 123
acceptsURL() method, 92
action attribute, 283–284, 287, 299, 301, 304, 307–308, 335, 344, 348, 463
ActionListener, 137, 139
actionPerformed() event, 138, 152
Add() method(s), 408, 410, 439, 445
addImage() method, 198–199, 426
addItem() method, 176, 180, 440, 458
Ant script, 131, 148
Ant targets, 131
Apache Ant, 131, 147
Apache Axis2/C, 397
Apache Axis2/Java, 397
Apache Axis2 Web services, 397
Apache Tomcat, 126, 331, 333, 500–501
application client modules, 310
application scope, 293
application server layer, 88
application tier, 397
ArrayList (java.util), 414, 434, 449, 472, 476, 479, 481
ArrayList class, 492, 508, 513
ArrayList instance, 487–490, 492, 496, 503–504, 508, 513
ArrayList<String> type, 425
ArrayList type, 425
attributes, 16

B

backing beans, 297–298, 315
Base64 format, 347
Base64 string format, 347
BaseRowSet abstract class, 212–213
beginTransaction() method, 290
bgcolor attribute, 300
bitmap indexes, 30
Blob (Binary Large Object) format, 347
BLOB, 39–40, 52, 60, 63–64, 115, 181, 271
body tag, 300
ByteArrayOutputStream class, 354

C

C# Web Services, 399
CachedRowSet class, 82, 85, 211
CachedRowSet component, 213
CachedRowSet interface, 212
CallableStatement interface, 97, 103, 105, 185–186, 188, 204, 208, 219
CallableStatement method, 98, 103, 183–185, 194, 207, 219, 222, 252, 255, 257–259, 262, 264–265, 267, 271
CallableStatement query string, 103–104, 185, 255, 257, 260, 262, 267
call level interface (CLI), 73
candidate key, 17
Canvas control, 162
Canvas object, 197, 200, 426
cardinality, 16, 21, 30
cascade delete, 17
cascade update, 17
CHAR, 109, 191
Class.forName() method, 70, 84, 90, 121, 166, 168, 220
classpath, 131, 143, 149, 166
clear() method, 424, 438, 445, 457, 464, 492, 496, 504, 508, 513
client layer, 88
client server database, 25
client-side classes, 317
client tier, 88, 309–310, 397
clustered index, 28
commandButton tag, 301, 308
commit(), 95
common gateway interface (CGI), 275, 390
composite primary key, 22
conceptual design, 12
Concurrency Type, 240, 268–269
Concurrent Versions System (CVS), 126
connect() method, 69, 72, 89, 91–92, 120–121, 168
connected RowSet, 85
Connection class, 71, 94–95, 104–105, 177, 181, 186, 240, 257, 262, 267
ConnectionPoolDataSource object, 78–79
Connection Pooling API, 78–80, 86
connection URL, 93
connectivity, 18, 67, 72, 84, 167
ContactEditorUI form, 134
Context interface, 76
control files, 30
createStatement() method, 99, 155, 223, 279, 281
cursorMoved event, 83, 213
CURSOR_TYPE, 191, 193, 205

D

data access methods, 303–304
database administrators (DBAs), 10
database connection URL, 158, 245, 251, 352, 364, 367, 369, 416, 473, 493
database engine, 25–26, 29, 116
database file, 25
database layer, 87–88
DatabaseMetaData interface, 115, 117–118, 179–181, 219
data consistency, 11, 65
data file, 27, 29
data independence, 11, 64
data integrity, 10–11, 64
data manipulation language (DML), 108
data model, 9, 11–12, 15
data object, 16

data sharing, 10
DataSource interface, 70, 75
data store tier, 397
DBMS related protocol, 87–88
DECIMAL, 98, 106, 119, 188–189
deleteRow() method, 241, 251, 268
deployable unit, 317
deployment descriptor, 275, 298, 302–303, 310, 315, 317, 391, 403
deployment descriptor file web.xml, 302
destroy() method, 313
disconnected RowSet, 72, 82, 85, 211, 213
dispose() method, 175, 177
distributed transaction, 80
document root, 317
domain indexes, 30
drawImage() method, 198, 200, 426
Driver class, 69–70, 72, 84, 89–92, 121, 168, 172
Driver.connect() Method, 91–92, 120–121
DriverManager class, 68–70, 72, 83, 89–91, 155, 168, 220, 223, 416, 473
DriverManager.getConnection() method, 92–94, 120–121
DriverManager.registerDriver() method, 69, 90, 168

E

EJB container, 400, 412
EJB modules, 310
embedded C tags, 379, 500
enforce referential integrity, 17, 28
Enterprise Information System (EIS), 309
Enterprise JavaBean (EJB), 1–2, 4, 124, 126, 151, 309–310, 312–313, 388, 392, 400, 407, 412
Enterprise Server, 318
entities, 12, 16, 18–21, 66, 124
entity class, 219
entity integrity, 16, 27, 64, 66
entity integrity rule, 16, 64
entity manager, 223
entity relationship model, 16
ER diagram, 16, 18, 66
ER notation, 21
executeQuery object, 155, 223
exit() method, 177

F

FacesServlet, 298, 302–305, 391
FacesServlet Web container, 298
fetching by column, 114, 171
fetching by row, 113, 171, 182
FileInputStream class, 436, 450
file processing system, 9–10
FilteredRowSet, 212
first normal form, 22
Fix Imports, 124, 415, 417, 436, 475
for attribute, 301
foreign keys, 9, 12, 17, 28, 43, 50, 65–66, 231, 454, 511
form data, 283–284, 335
form tag, 300, 307, 335
forName() method, 70, 84, 90, 121, 166, 168, 220, 416, 472
forward() method, 352, 383
free-form Java project, 148, 150
function based indexes, 30

G

GenericServlet class, 313
getAttribute() method, 287, 296, 301, 348, 379
getBinaryStream(), 355, 418
getBlob() method, 182, 418
getColumnCount() method, 115–117, 171, 415, 418
getConnection() method, 70, 75, 77, 90–94, 120–121, 172–173, 220, 279, 281, 339, 416, 473
getCurrentSession() method, 290
getDatabaseProductVersion() method, 117
getDriverVersion() method, 117
getGraphics() method, 199, 426
getHeight() method, 200, 426
getImage() method, 197–199, 426
getMetaData() method, 115–117, 171, 181–182, 196, 209, 415, 417, 473, 477
get() method, 425
GET method, 396, 488, 521
getMoreResults() method, 111
getObject() method, 189, 207, 217, 220
getParameterMetaData() method, 118–119, 181
getParameter() method, 276–279, 284, 288, 290, 295, 336, 345, 349, 351, 374, 379, 382–383, 390
getProperty() method, 301
getRequestDispatcher() method, 348, 351, 383
getResultSet() method, 95, 107, 111, 113, 121, 170, 183, 221
getSelectedFile(), 227, 438–439, 457
getSelectedItem() method, 182, 424
getSelectedValue() method, 209, 490
getString() method, 114, 171, 174, 189, 208, 216, 282, 340, 354
getter() methods, 288, 290, 295–296, 386
getText() method, 173, 439, 458
getToolkit() method, 197, 199, 426
getUpdateCount() method, 70–71, 107–108, 111, 170, 183, 221
getValueIsAdjusting() method, 209, 490
getWidth() method, 199, 426
getXXX() method, 72, 98, 103–105, 112–115, 170–171, 185–186, 188–189, 204, 220, 255
GlassFish server, 330, 405, 501
GlassFishWeb server, 149
global transaction, 79
Graphics context, 197–199, 426
Groovy and Grails, 123

H

HashMap object, 379, 381, 383–384, 386–387, 392, 503–504
Hibernate, 125, 290, 295, 319, 397
Hibernate session, 290
Hibernate session class, 290
Hibernate session object, 290
HTTP port, 501
HttpServlet class, 313

HTTPServletRequest object, 311
HTTPServletResponse object, 311

I

id attribute, 300, 308
imagedata tag, 348
ImageIO class, 418
ImageIO.write() method, 426
Image object, 58, 61, 198, 417–418, 426
Import Project, 148
indexes, 28, 30
init() method, 275, 313, 390
InitialContext object, 77
initialization parameter file, 30
IN parameter, 96–97, 101, 105, 186–188
inputSecret tags, 308
InputStream() method, 187–188
InputStream type, 187
inputText tag, 300–301, 307
insertRow() method, 241, 243
Inspector window, 135
Integer class, 257, 263
integrated databases, 9–10
IP Address, 93, 168–169
isClosed() method, 177, 341

J

Java Ant applications, 4, 149
Java API for XML Remote Procedure (JAXRPC), 397
Java API for XML Web Services (JAXWS), 397
java.awt.Image class, 417
Java Beans, 1–4, 151, 281, 309, 311, 313, 388–389
Java class library, 131, 140–141, 149–150
Java Database Connection Driver, 149
Java Database Connectivity API, 167
Java desktop application, 2, 150, 408, 411
Java Development Kits (JDK), 149
Java EE 7, 1, 333, 389, 397, 400–401, 412, 428, 470
Java EE containers, 311–312, 337, 392
Java EE module, 310, 312
Java EE platform, 275, 309, 311–312
Java EE server, 275, 312–313
Java File Chooser instance, 438, 457
Java frameworks, 319
Java free form project, 131
JavaFX, 123–126, 128–129, 131, 150–151
Java managed beans, 292, 297, 299, 390
JavaMessage Service (JMS) API, 316
JavaMessage Service (JMS) messages, 313
Java Messaging XML (JMX), 319
Java Mobile Edition (Java ME), 126
Java Naming and Directory Interface (JNDI), 67, 70, 76, 167
Java package, 141, 202–203, 214, 340, 360, 368, 479, 502
Java Persistence API (JPA), 150
Java Platform Manager, 402
Java project with existing sources, 148–149
JavaScript Object Notation (JSON), 396
Java Server Page (JSP), 279
JavaServer Pages Standard Tag Library (JSTL), 314
Java Servlet, 1, 88, 211, 285, 308–309, 311, 313–314, 317
Java Servlet API, 313
Java session bean, 366–367, 373
Java Standard Edition (Java SE), 126
Java Transaction API (JTA), 80, 316
Java Transaction Service (JTS), 67
java.util.HashMap library, 384
Java Virtual Machine (JVM), 123, 314
Java Web frameworks, 318
Java Web modules, 317
Java Web server Servlets, 388
JAX-RPC clients, 397
JAX-RPC model, 397
JAX-RPC services, 397
JBoss Application Server, 151
JButton, 136–137
JDBC 2.0 core API, 167
JDBC 2.0 Optional Package, 78
JDBC 2.0 Standard Extension API, 70, 75
JDBC 3.0, 167, 212
JDBC 4.0, 67, 84, 167, 211, 239
JDBC connection URL, 93
JDBC DataSource, 75
JDBC driver-based connection pooling, 77
JDBC escape syntax, 109–110
JDBC metadata interfaces, 115, 120, 180
JDBCODBC Bridge Driver, 73
JDBC Oracle URL, 339
JDBC RowSet, 3, 75, 81, 212
JDBCRowSet class, 82, 211
JDBC Standard Extension API, 75, 78, 83, 167
JDBC Uniform Resource Locators (URLs), 93–94, 121–122, 168, 279, 281, 364
JDialog class, 175, 203
JDialog Form, 134, 151, 163, 165
JEUS 7 application server, 151
JFluid, 127, 130
JFrame Form, 134, 139, 150–152, 159–160, 163, 172, 176
JLabel, 136
JNDI Context instance, 77
JNDI naming service, 70, 76–79, 81, 84
JNDI subcontext, 77
JoinRowSet, 212
Joint Engine Technology, 25
JPA entity classes, 396
JPanel Form, 134, 151
JPanel object, 136
JSF core library, 299
JSF custom tag library, 298
JSF engine, 304–305
JSF Form, 124
JSF HTML library, 299
JSF navigation handler, 305
JSF tag libraries, 299
JSF tags, 292, 297–300
JSP compiler, 314
JSP container, 278, 314
JSP directive <%@ page />, 295, 390
JSP directive tag, 284, 345
JSP form, 307, 351, 391
JSP forward directive, 285, 345
JSP implicit object, 286, 290, 301

JSP implicit session object, 290, 346, 378, 392
JSP layer, 319
JSP page import tag, 336
JSP syntax, 314
JSP tag <jsp:useBean />, 295
JSP tags, 279, 314
jsp:setProperty action tag, 465, 467
jsp:useBean action tag, 465, 467
JSTL-1.2.jar file, 500
JSTL core, 379–380, 392, 500
JSTL C tags, 379

L

list() method, 290
logical design, 11–12, 30, 64
lookup() method, 77

M

main() method, 142, 144–145, 409–410
many-to-many relationship, 19–20
MediaTracker class, 197–199, 426
message-driven bean, 151, 313
message tag, 301
Metro Web service libraries, 403
Microsoft Office Publisher 2007, 320
model view controller (MVC), 136, 220, 298–299, 319, 346
Modern Java frameworks, 319
moveToInsertRow() method, 241–242
multiple ResultSet objects, 97, 104, 185, 221

N

name attribute, 335, 348, 379
Named Query, 219
native-API-partly-Java driver, 73
Native-Protocol-All-Java Driver, 75
navigation destinations, 299
navigation rules, 298–299, 305–306, 315, 390
navigation source, 299
Navigator window, 130, 135
NetBeans Base IDE, 126
NetBeans module, 125, 150
NetBeans Platform, 3, 123, 125, 127, 150–152
NetBeans Profiler, 127
NetBeans Refactor, 130
NetBeans Source, 130
NetBeans Team, 130
NetBeans Visual Library, 126–127
network computer (NC), 82
non-clustered indexes, 28
NullPointer exception, 216
NUMERIC, 27, 98, 106, 188

O

OCI drivers, 169
onclick attribute, 284, 335, 344
open XA standard, 80
Oracle core JDBC implementation, 167
Oracle Cursor, 196, 221
Oracle Database 18c Express Edition, 155
Oracle database connection URL, 158, 245, 251, 416, 473
Oracle JDBC driver, 157, 168,, 367, 416, 419, 472
Oracle JDBC thin driver, 155
OracleJobSchedulerXE, 343
OracleOraDB18Home1TNSListener, 158, 343, 421
Oracle package, 192, 194–195, 205–207, 219–220
OracleServiceXE, 421
oracle.sql, 67, 167
Oracle stored procedures, 3, 69, 95, 97, 103, 185, 219, 252
Oracle syntax, 104, 185
out object, 276–277
OUT parameter, 97–98, 103–106, 185, 188–189, 220
outputStream.toByteArray() method, 348
outputText tag, 301
Output window, 146, 182, 234, 237, 405, 410

P

package body part, 190
package definition part, 190
Page scope, 292–293
paint() method, 198
Palette window, 135–136, 165, 338, 361, 370, 374, 444, 465
ParameterMetaData interface, 115, 118, 180, 219
ParameterMetaData object, 96, 118–119
parseInt() method, 142
password files, 31
Perl Web Services, 399
personal digital assistant (PDA), 82
physical design, 11–12, 64
PL/SQL statement, 192, 204
PooledConnection interface, 81
PooledConnection objects, 78
PostgreSQL JDBC driver, 78
posting page, 276
POST method, 283, 396, 521
prepareCall() method, 105, 186, 196, 257, 262, 267
PreparedStatement class, 71, 97, 173, 181, 436
PreparedStatement interface, 96, 100–103, 118, 122, 204
prepareStatement() method, 100, 183, 340, 354, 367, 374
presentation-oriented Web application, 311
primary keys, 9, 16–17, 23, 40, 64, 118
println() method, 276, 416, 429, 465, 472, 493, 497, 499
Properties window, 53, 61, 135–136, 145, 159
PUT method, 396, 521

Q

QueryCourseID() method, 471–473, 486–489, 503–504
QueryImage() method, 416, 420, 422, 425–426, 430, 433

R

RDBMSs, 80–81, 97, 103, 185
reading page, 276
redo log files, 31
Refactor button, 422, 485–486
referential integrity, 9, 17, 28, 66
referential integrity rules, 17
registerDriver() method, 69, 90, 168
registerOutParameter() method, 98, 105–106, 188, 196, 220
relational data model, 9, 15
Relative URL, 341–342, 433, 500

Remote Procedure Call (RPC), 398
removeRowSetListener() method, 82, 213
RequestDispatcher class, 348, 351
request object, 275–277, 311, 349, 379, 390
request scope, 293
required attribute, 307, 391
resource adapter modules, 310
RESTful client applications, 396
RESTful service, 396
RESTful Web services, 396, 398
REST services, 396
ResultSet class, 72, 115, 170–171, 173, 241, 268, 480, 483
ResultSet.CONCUR_UPDATABLE, 243, 247, 250, 270
ResultSet enhanced functionalities, 239
ResultSetMetaData interface, 115–117, 179–181, 219
ResultSet Type, 240, 269
ResultSet.TYPE_FORWARD_ONLY, 269–270
ResultSet.TYPE_SCROLL_INSENSITIVE, 269–270
ResultSet.TYPE_SCROLL_SENSITIVE, 247, 250, 270
rowChanged event, 83, 213
rowsetChanged event, 83, 213
RowSet Listeners, 82, 213
RowSet object, 4, 72, 81–83, 211–213, 219–220
runtime deployment descriptor, 318

S

secondary Ant script, 148
second normal form, 21–23
self.close() method, 284, 335, 344, 430
sendRedirect() method, 288, 295, 351–352, 384
Server Explorer, 63, 191
server-side utility classes, 317
service() method, 275, 390
service-oriented Web application, 311
Servlet class, 277–278, 298, 310, 313
Servlet interface, 313
session bean, 151, 294, 313, 366–367, 373
session.getAttribute() methods, 296, 348
session implicit object, 281
session scope, 293
setAttribute() method, 288, 351, 383, 392
setBinaryStream() method, 359, 369, 436, 451
setCommand() method, 216
setInt() method, 173
setListData() method, 488
setLocationRelativeTo() method, 172, 176
setMessage() method, 165–166, 338, 429
setObject() method, 101, 187
setProperty tag, 293–295
setText() method, 138–139, 338, 425, 490
setter() method, 354–355, 386–387
setVisible() method, 176
setXXX() method, 83, 100–101, 103–105, 185–188, 204, 213
showOpenDialog() method, 438, 457
sid, 169, 271
simple object access protocol (SOAP), 395
singleton session beans, 313
smallint, 40
SOAP-based Web services, 1, 397–398, 521–522
SOAP messages, 398
SOAP namespaces, 395
SOAP protocol, 398–399
SOAP web services, 395
Software Development Kits (SDK), 133
source code management, 130–131
Source Editor, 144, 147
split() method, 142
SQL92 syntax, 104, 185–186, 195, 207, 220
SQL Server Express, 213
statement class, 70–71, 83, 94, 169, 183
statement interface, 95–99, 102–104, 107, 111, 170, 204
static data, 99, 314
static HTML pages, 318
static resource files, 316
stored procedure DeleteCourse(), 265–266
stored procedures, 27, 29, 190
stored procedure UpdateCourse(), 259
submit button tag, 304, 348, 379
subname, 93–94, 168, 172, 220
subprotocol, 172
Sun Java Studio Creator, 126
Sun Java Studio Enterprise, 126
Sun Studio, 126
Swing API, 123
Swing Application Framework, 127
swing containers, 135
swing controls, 135
Swing Menus, 135
swing windows, 135, 198
Symfony Framework, 124–125

T

taglib directive, 298–300, 306
Tasks window, 130
thin client, 72, 82, 211
third normal form, 21, 23–24
Tomcat Web server, 149, 330–331, 333, 406, 500
Toolkit class, 197, 199, 426
toString() method, 173, 424–425, 439, 458
transaction log files, 28
two-phase commit protocol, 81
two-tier model, 87–88, 120
type attribute, 283, 335
Type class, 68
Type I driver, 73
Type II driver, 73–74
Type III driver, 74
Type IV driver, 75, 84
Type IV JDBC driver, 155

U

UIComponent class, 298–299
uniform resource locator (URL), 91
universal description, discovery and integration (UDDI), 395
Updatable ResultSet, 242–243, 247, 250
Updatable ResultSet object, 240–242, 245–246, 249–251, 268–269
updateRow() method, 241, 247, 268
UPDATE statement, 124, 261, 367, 463
updateString() methods, 242, 246
updateXXX() methods, 241–242, 246

V

validator attribute, 300
value attribute, 300–302, 304, 307
value-binding expressions, 301
ValueChanged() method, 488
VARCHAR, 105–106, 188–189, 219
vector, 112, 170
views, 27, 29
view tag, 299–300

W

waitForID() method, 199, 426
Web application deployment descriptor, 310, 317
Web application framework, 318
Web archive (WAR) file, 317
Web components, 297, 311–312, 316–318
Web deployment descriptor, 298, 302–303, 315, 403
Web frameworks, 319
Web modules, 310, 317–318
Web resources, 317, 396
WebRowSet class, 211
Web service endpoints, 311
Web service port, 408, 422, 433, 486
Web service references, 408–409, 422, 433, 438, 443, 456, 462, 486
web services description language (WSDL), 395
Web Services Interoperability Technologies (WSIT), 395
WS-Reliable Messaging, 397
WS-Security, 397

X

XA compliant JTA modules, 80
XAConnections, 80–81
XADataSource, 80–81
XA functionality, 80
XAResource, 80
XATransactionIDS, 81
XHTML pages, 317
XML deployment descriptors, 275
XML editor, 306
XML Remote Procedure Call (JAX-RPC) model, 397
X/Open standard, 80